THE LIFE OF JESUS

MARCELLO CRAVERI

THE LIFE OF JESUS

Translated by Charles Lam Markmann

THE ECCO PRESS

New York

First published in 1989 by The Ecco Press
26 West 17th Street, New York, NY 10011
Published simultaneously in Canada by
Penguin Books Canada Ltd., Ontario
Printed in the United States of America

Published by arrangement with Grove Press

Originally published as *La vita di Gesú,*
by Feltrinelli Editore, Milan, Italy
Copyright © 1966 by Giangiacomo Feltrinelli Editore

Library of Congress Cataloging-in-Publication Data

Craveri, Marcello, 1914-
    [Vita di Gesú. English]
    The life of Jesus / Marcello Craveri :
translated by Charles Lam Markmann. — 1st ed.
        p. cm.
    Translation of: La vita di Gesú.
    Reprint. Originally published:
    New York: Grove Press, 1967.
    Bibliography: p.
    Includes index.
    1. Jesus Christ—Biography.
    2. Christian biography—Palestine.
I. Title.
BT301.2C713   1989   232.9'01—dc20   [B]   89-35808

ISBN 0-88001-238-2

10 9 8 7 6 5 4 3 2 1

Preface

I have undertaken *The Life of Jesus*—that is to say, the history of his life, of his teaching, of the development of Christianity—with full consideration for all current and recent theories, but with the intention of remaining as impartial as possible toward the often contradictory approaches of the various schools. The aim that I have set myself is that of never losing sight of Jesus as an individual born into a clearly defined society at a clearly defined point in history, and hence of striving to understand his life, his ideas, his behavior as the product of a particular culture and unique historical circumstances.

As a result of numerous studies, some quite recent, of the history and customs of the Hebrew people in the period of the New Testament, and the lucky discovery a few years ago of several scrolls of a religious sect—a sect to which Jesus himself may have belonged—near the Dead Sea, it is possible to grasp the significance of the flowering of Christianity in the setting of contemporary religious fervor. The study of the religion of Christ in relation to the other beliefs of the time makes it possible also to assign to it a more precise historical position.

The basic sources for the life and the preaching of Jesus are still, of course, the Gospels: the four canonical ones, and also, with all due reservations, the apocryphal versions, including the two most lately discovered, attributed to Thomas and Philip. But the Gospels should not be taken as a point of departure; most certainly, they are rather a first point of arrival, inasmuch as they were written at least a half-century after the death of Jesus and commingle the misty personal recollections of the disciples, the earliest Christological speculations of the primitive Judeo-Christian community, and the often opposing ideas of Paul of Tarsus—and even later additions. In separating these various layers, the best guides are the writings of the Fathers and Doctors of the Church (beginning with the Epistles of Paul, which antedate the Gospels themselves, and the Acts of the Apostles), documents that testify through the centuries to a zealous labor of interpretation, adaptation, and correction of the message of Jesus in conformance with the changes that occurred as the organization of the Church progressed.

It is most difficult for me to accept the thesis of the rationalists that a great part of the Gospel narrative is a distortion of everyday, prosaic facts into miracles and supernatural events, either through the ingenuous credulity of the writers or, worse, through their deliberate desire to deceive. Nonetheless, I have frequently quoted these rationalistic explanations, if only as a matter of curiosity. The interesting results achieved by modern studies in New Testament philology, and especially the researches in the language of Palestine undertaken by the German school known as *Formgeschichte* ("form history") lead one to believe that, on the contrary, the authors of the Gospels frequently presented myths and doctrines in the form of realistic accounts (consonant with the modes of expression familiar to their society). I have often accepted the findings of the anti-myth school, which attempts to rephrase in modern language the religious concepts expressed by the Evangelists in terms of mythology.

Careful comparisons of the Latin text of the Vulgate with the Greek Gospels and the probable equivalent expressions in Hebrew and in Aramaic have also enabled me on occasion to discover errors in quotation, interpretation, and translation that nevertheless are the bases of beliefs taught by the Church and even of major points of doctrine.

As for the Gospels themselves, I should point out to the reader that on the basis of important studies made by German theologians, I consider the Gospel of Mark (or at least an Ur-Markus that has since been lost) to have been the model for all the others. Therefore, I rely primarily on Mark, and in my citations I give it priority over Matthew, even though Christian tradition accepts the latter as the oldest of the Gospels.

All this scholarly apparatus, however, has not prevented me—at least I hope it has not—from writing a book that will interest readers of every kind. I have endeavored to produce a volume which, without sacrificing a solid scientific foundation or considerable documentation, remains pleasurable reading. It has not always been possible to avoid specialized terminology, but I have tried in each case to clarify it, and Greek words are always followed not only by transliteration into Roman characters but also by translation.

I hope my work will not have been worthless and I risk the further hope that it may serve at least to arouse the interest of other students in the material I have treated, so that others who follow may be able to go further.

MARCELLO CRAVERI

Turin
January, 1967

TRANSLATOR'S NOTE

Wherever Dott. Craveri has quoted directly from the Bible, his quotations have been presented for English and American readers in the wording of the King James Bible, with the exception of a few cases in which other versions are used for purposes that are clear from the text.

C. L. M.

Contents

xii CONTENTS

List of Figures

THE LIFE OF JESUS

[1]

JOSEPH AND MARY

Nazareth

En Nasira, a little village in Galilee hidden in a narrow valley about twelve hundred feet above sea level, is today accepted by Christian tradition as the ancient Nazareth, the home of Jesus.

According to some scholars, however, Nazareth—or, rather, *Nātzrath*, or *Notzereth*—never existed.[1] They hold that the epithet of Nazarene, which is coupled with the name of Jesus in the writings of and on the New Testament, does not refer to his place of origin but should be traced to the Aramaic word *Nazirā'*,[2] which in those times was applied to those who had taken lifelong or temporary vows of chastity and abstinence and who wore their hair unshorn as long as their vows were in effect. Other students contend that the etymology derives from the Syriac word *nasayā'*, which means "protected by God."[3] But here the etymological connection is rather uncertain.[4]

Such arguments would have little legitimacy if in the days of Jesus there had ever been any definite reports of a place called Nazareth. But the locality had never been mentioned before it was cited by the authors of the Gospels, nor does the name appear in the writings of any of their contemporaries. Furthermore, the Gospel attributed to Matthew even raises the suspicion that the epithet of Nazarene for Jesus was artificially coined, for Matthew says[5] that the birth of Jesus fulfilled a prophecy of the Old Testament: "And there shall come forth a rod out of the stem of Jesse, and a branch shall

3

grow out of his roots."[6] In that case, the word would come from *nētser*, which means "branch," "shoot," "scion."

In this connection, it would be well to determine at once how much value can be ascribed to the Biblical prophecies that are so plentiful in the Gospels. Since for the ancient Hebrews every occurrence was the realization of a plan made by God *ab aeterno*, "historical" criticism amounted in fact to the search for utterances in the sacred texts that would seem in some way to have predicted and announced the advent of contemporary people and events. Hence, Biblical prophecy was a seal authenticating the manner in which such persons and events had been predetermined by divine providence. Frequently, however, in order to adapt the historical fact more certainly to the prophecy, a forced meaning was given to the Biblical passage or the fact itself was misrepresented.

But this is no reason to approach the Gospels with invariable suspicion as to their honesty. For the most part, their authors told of actual events, interpreting them according to the patterns of their culture, or—following the literary conventions of their society— rendered religious myths in the form of realistic narratives.[7] Our task, therefore, is not only to reconstruct the historical truth, divorcing it from myth, but also to understand how the myth itself could have come into being.

In any case, wherever Jesus might have come from, the place must not have been very different from En Nasira or any other Near Eastern village even today. The climate dictates an extremely simple kind of house, which has not changed in centuries: little cubes of stone and mud covered with very white plaster, devoid of windows, topped with a flat roof formed by strewing reeds and branches over crude beams and thickly covering the whole with clay or with a mixture of mud and stone that hardens in the sun.[8] This roof provides a kind of terrace, reached by an external stairway attached to a wall. There the men spend much of their time, especially at the end of the day, savoring the breezes and sitting idly or lying in the shade, while the women busy themselves with the drying of figs, grapes, carobs, and dates.[9] Palestinian houses are often bunched in twos or threes round a common courtyard, bounded on the open sides by low rock walls. In a corner of the courtyard there is a small

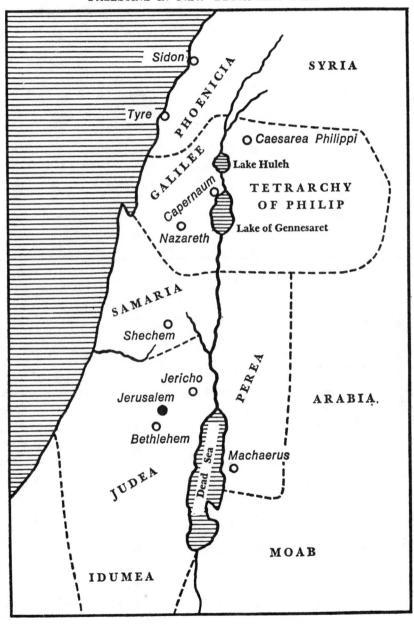

FIGURE I
PALESTINE IN NEW TESTAMENT TIMES

clay oven for baking bread, and a mill for grinding grain.[10] Almost always the house is shaded by a fig tree.

It was in such surroundings that Jesus spent his childhood.

Joseph and Mary

Nothing definite is known about the parents of Jesus. Only two of the four canonical Gospels speak of them, giving their names: Joseph and Mary.

Joseph is a genuine Hebrew name. Mary (Miriam), however, is of Egyptian origin. The first Jewish woman to bear this name was the legendary sister of Moses. But in the time of Jesus it was quite common in Palestine. Perhaps its pronunciation had already evolved from *Miryām* into *Maryām*,[11] unless this was a later change as a form of homage to the Madonna. Actually, the new pronunciation makes it possible to relate the name to the Aramaic word *mār(ā')*, which means "Lord," or to other roots, so that many other interpretations (more than seventy!) can be drawn, among them: Majestic, Sublime (*mārōm*), Beloved of God (*mir yām*), Bringer of Light (*māreh*), Affliction (*mārāh*), and Bitter Sea (*mār yām*).

But all these speculations on the name of Mary are of very late date. The New Testament itself is centered on Christ, and Mary holds a subordinate place except in two chapters in Luke, interpolated no one knows when, and a few verses in Matthew. Mark, without mentioning her name, tells us only that the mother of Jesus tried to dissuade her son from his work, because she was convinced that he was mad.[12] John alludes twice, also without mentioning her name, to the "mother of Jesus."[13] The Apostolic Epistles ignore her altogether. In the Acts of the Apostles she is mentioned only once, with the brothers and sisters of Jesus, as a member of the disciples' group.[14]

As for Joseph, even his occupation is not known with certainty. Tradition has him a carpenter, and in Arab legend, too, he is Yusef ben Yarakub, *en neggiār*—Joseph, son of Jacob, "carpenter."[15] But the text of the Gospels says only τέκτων (*tektōn*),[16] which can be read in the broad sense as "builder of houses"—that is, both woodworker and stoneworker.[17]

Only the necessity of making Jesus seem a national messiah who would establish a new kingdom for Israel could finally bring Joseph out of his obscurity and grow him a royal family tree to show the descent of Jesus from no less a personage than King David. In fact, by this time, the dynasty of David was extinct, and the groups that could properly have vied for the throne of Judea, had the country been liberated from Rome, were the Herodian and Hasmonean families and the sect of the Boethusians. But the laudatory prophecies that in David's time had foretold to him and his successors their eternal rule of the Hebrew people aroused the hope among the preservers of the tradition that now, in the days of servitude, an unknown descendant of the ancient king would rise to liberate the country and restore the ancestral glory.

We have not just one but two genealogies of Joseph, and hence of Jesus, which appear in the Gospel attributed to Matthew and in that ascribed to Luke.[18] The two genealogies, however, differ widely. Whereas the Gospel of Matthew traces the ancestry of Jesus back to Abraham, that of Luke professes to lead directly to Adam (and therefore to God) and rounds off the line with a total of seventy-five generations. In the latter part of the line, which should certainly have been the easiest to reconstruct—the portion, that is, from David to Jesus—not only are the names completely different in the two genealogies, but the number of them is also impossibly at variance. Luke, in fact, lists forty-one persons for that portion, while Matthew names only twenty-seven. Hence there is a discrepancy of fourteen generations, which, chronologically calculated, even if an average of only twenty-five or thirty years is assumed for each, amounts to a disparity of about four centuries![19] Moreover, both genealogies violate known historical truth: the names of some kings who actually belonged to the dynasty of David are omitted and the names of others are placed in the wrong order.[20]

Matthew's list—most remarkably—includes the names of four women in the line of descent, and from what we learn in the Old Testament none of these women was an exemplar of proper behavior: the incestuous Tamar;[21] Rahab, the harlot of Jericho;[22] the treacherous Ruth;[23] and David's mistress, Bath-sheba.[24] One authority has explained that these women were cited by Matthew to refute the accusations of those enemies of Christianity who attacked the reputation of Mary for having conceived her first child in an irregular fashion.[25]

Obviously, neither the errors of Matthew and Luke nor the dubious credibility of the two genealogies can diminish the importance of Jesus and his mission for the modern world. But for Jewry at that time it was most important to prove that Jesus sprang from the line of David.

After a while, it occurred to some of the Church Fathers that to provide Joseph with royal ancestry while Mary's origins remained humble was less than fitting. Therefore, they sought to maintain that in fact one of the two genealogies referred not to Joseph but to Mary:[26] hence Mary, too, came from the seed of David. Here was a really brilliant solution, it seemed, to the embarrassment of the two conflicting lists. Quite aside from the fact that the text of the Gospels absolutely rules out such a supposition, there remains the even more inexplicable problem of four centuries' difference between the genealogies of David to Joseph and David to Mary.

However, Mary's descent from the family of David was accepted, and it was then easy to concoct relationships between the two spouses. A curious theory, first offered by John of Damascus (d. ca. 754), declares that Joseph's grandfather and Mary's great-grandfather were brothers:[27]

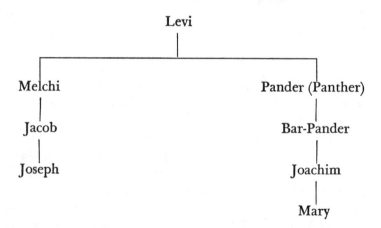

A bit more imagination brought the relationship of the two spouses even closer: Joseph was said to be the brother of Mary's mother. A native and resident of Bethlehem, he was supposed to have gone to Nazareth, at the invitation of his sister, to become engaged to his young niece.[28]

The Virgin

Almost as soon as Christianity had emerged from Palestine and begun to be preached in Hellenistic regions, the person of Jesus—as we shall see—was presented as a divine incarnation. This led to the necessity of erecting a new tradition around Mary as well, belittling her marriage to Joseph and attributing special prerogatives to her: God could not have chosen an ordinary mother to bear his child but required a pure virgin endowed with the moral and physical assets that would assure her being preferred above other women.

The imagination of the hagiographers had already invented an edifying and remarkable childhood for the mother of Jesus. Two of the apocryphal Gospels (rejected by the Church because they had not been "inspired"), the Protevangelium of James and the Gospel of Pseudo-Matthew, though written at least two hundred years after the death of Jesus, tell us that Mary was born to Anna and Joachim (no earlier document gives the names of her parents) when they were already old and had abandoned hope of children.[29] It is easy to see how this story is modeled on that of the birth of John the Baptist, contained in the Gospel of Luke.[30] The birthplace of Mary, according to some, was Nazareth itself or nearby Sepphoris; according to others, it was Jerusalem or neighboring Bethany.[31]

The birth of the child was so unexpected, the apocryphal narratives declare, that her parents decided to dedicate her to God. When she was three years old, they took her to the Temple of Jerusalem and entrusted her to the priests, that she might, under the vow of chastity, devote herself to worship. Here these Gospels doubly violate historical accuracy: among the Hebrews it was utterly impossible for a girl to be brought up in the Temple,[32] nor was there any custom of a vow of chastity for women. On the contrary, virginity was held to be a disgrace and a divine punishment, like that of sterility.[33] This is still the belief of the Arabs, who follow today the proverb that for a girl there can be only one procession: either to the marriage bed or to the grave.[34]

By this time, however (and this is confirmed by the canonical Gospels), the tradition of the marriage of Mary and Joseph had crystallized. Thus it became necessary to reconcile this marriage with the pretended requirement of the chastity of Mary. For this reason—again according to the apocryphal versions—Mary could remain in the Temple only until puberty: when the priests recognized that, at the age of twelve, she had passed out of childhood, they were concerned above all to prevent the contamination of the holy place by the unclean blood of her menstruation. To remove her from the Temple, they took it upon themselves to find her a husband, announcing to all the men of the district an unheard-of competition: each contestant was to be given a dry stick, and he whose stick first put forth buds and leaves would triumph. The victor was a carpenter from Bethlehem named Joseph; he married Mary and established himself with her in Nazareth, rather concerned about the delicate task entrusted to him. But, to bar Joseph categorically from any responsibility for the birth of Jesus, the imaginative apocryphal writers decided that he deserted Mary immediately after the wedding in order to resume his trade in some distant region.

Some time after the fourth century (the period when the deification of Mary began in earnest), the legend arose that Joseph was already aged and impotent when he married Mary, though until that time iconography had represented him as young and beardless. Thus, in violation of the canonical texts themselves, in which the earthly origin of Jesus is explicitly stated in several places and, repeatedly and without reservations, Joseph is considered his father,[35] now Joseph was to be relegated to the role of "putative" father, with all attention concentrated on Mary alone.

The Christian tradition delights in picturing the girl in her simple village life, occupied with her duties about the house or going to the fountain to fetch water. Even today there is only one fountain in En Nasira, and it is dedicated to Mary: Ain sitti Miryam.[36] The women file through the narrow alleys of the village as they did two thousand years ago, in the most stifling hours of the sultry days, bearing on their heads jars or pitchers filled with water, and moving slowly in the sun. Even now it is not unusual to find among these

Palestinian women that kind of beauty which is considered peculiar to the Madonna, as if by divine right: the eyes and hair are remarkably dark, the characteristic golden-bronze skin seems to diffuse a sweet scent of honey and cinnamon. The languid grace of their expressions and their movements is almost voluptuous.

So, indeed, does Luke portray Mary to us when he introduces her, calling her κεχαριτωμένη (kecharitōmenē),[37] "full of grace"—in other words, beautiful, comely, pleasing. Only later[38] was the word "grace" to acquire its theological connotation of "divine favor."[39]

Once it had become customary to portray Mary—not, however, before the fourth century—in icon and fresco, artists naturally felt impelled to make her as beautiful as possible. In the Renaissance, many, like Botticelli, assigned the same features to Mary and Venus; Filippo Lippi painted a number of Madonnas with his own mistress as model, bringing down on his head the outraged protests of Savonarola.

The Annunciation

It was just when Mary was approaching the fountain in Nazareth to fill her pitcher, according to the apocryphal Gospels, that the archangel Gabriel appeared to her, sent by God to announce to her that she had been chosen.[40] As transmitted by Luke, however, the legend portrays their meeting in the girl's own house.

The acceptance of angels as divine emissaries—both ἄγγελος (angelos) in Greek and mal'āk in Hebrew mean simply "messenger" —did not originate with the old Hebraic theology but derived from the star worship of the Assyrians and Babylonians and from Persian Mazdaism,[41] from which, indeed, the names of the angels were taken: Gabriel, Michael, Uriel, Jeremiel, Shealtiel, etc. Christianity inherited the angels from the Jewish religion, as "ministering spirits, sent forth to minister for them who shall be heirs of salvation,"[42] but it imagined them in strange ways. According to Origen (d. ca. 254), the angels guard the wholesomeness of air and water and protect the growth of vegetation; they guide souls into bodies and, after death, lead them to Paradise or to Hell.[43] According to Irenaeus (end of the second century) and others, the angels have tenuous, ethereal bodies "without flesh"; according to Origen, again, they are spherical; according to Tertullian (160–ca.220) and Augustine (354–430), they have bodies like men's; and so on.[44]

It is reasonable to believe that the ancient Hebrews thought of the angels as resembling handsome young men, since chapter 19 of Genesis relates that the inhabitants of Sodom tried to commit acts of pederasty with two angels who were staying with Lot and that Lot vainly offered instead his own two daughters, who were still virgins. Then, in the Middle Ages, the concept of the angel as a guardian and protector began to take shape. The idea was first expressed by Albertus Magnus and Thomas Aquinas.[45] The word "angel" thus came into the Latin language with a meaning different from its original one of "messenger."

At the time the Gospel story of the Annunciation was written, however, the word still held its primitive sense, and in just this guise did Gabriel present himself to Mary. When he came down to earth the girl was at home, according to what Luke tells us. This was surely not the luxurious residence rendered by Renaissance painters, out of artistic necessity as well as from a desire to pay homage to the Madonna, with spacious rooms, fine windows, and mosaic pillars and floors. Inside and out, the ordinary Palestinian's house was then, as it is today, almost squalid in its poverty.[46] A few straw mats that served as both seats and mattresses were spread over a floor of packed earth. Other amenities were few: an oil lamp with a wick, placed in the center of the room, which burned night and day; wineskins, pitchers, and baskets; a table; a wooden chest or cupboard for clothes and bedding. In one wall, a niche was usually hollowed out to serve as a closet.

Even a brief time after the death of Jesus, of course, it would have been impossible to identify the house, since none of his contemporaries thought of singling it out (the adoration of Mary did not yet exist). The devout of the Middle Ages settled on a cave in En Nasira and built a basilica on the site; it was several times destroyed by the Moslems and rebuilt by the Christians. After 1261, when Palestine seemed irremediably lost to Christians, there grew up a legend (which the Church, however, accepted as historical fact[47]) designed to save the faithful from the loss of so important an object of worship: the cave had been miraculously transported from Nazareth to Dalmatia and then, three years later, to Loreto, in Italy, just south of Ancona on the Adriatic coast. There is indeed, in the Cathedral of Loreto, a little house built on the model of those of Palestine. Once the Moslem persecutions had ended and Christian worship was again permitted in Palestine, the cave of En Nasira was reopened to the faithful. Today, consequently, there are two "authentic" homes of Mary—one in Loreto, one in En Nasira.

It was in the latter, obviously, that the angel appeared to the young woman and greeted her with the words that have become the opening of the well-known Catholic prayer: "Hail, thou that art highly favored, the Lord is with thee."[48] In Hebrew, the formula of greeting that is rendered in Latin as *Ave* ("Hail") would probably have been *Shalōm,* which not only means "peace"[49] but also expresses a wish for happiness, health, and security;[50] or else it might have been similar to *rōnni,* which means "exult," "rejoice." In order to compose the prayer Ave Maria, which appears for the first time in the *Antiphonary* of Gregory I (d. 604), the angel's greeting was rounded out with the Latin words *"benedicta tu in mulieribus"* ("blessed art thou among women") and with the tribute of Elisabeth: *"et benedictus fructus ventris tui"* ("and blessed is the fruit of thy womb"). The names of Mary and Jesus were added later: in the Eastern Church in the seventh century and in the Roman Church in the twelfth. The other words in the prayer, largely the creation of Bernardino of Siena (d. 1444), were not cast in their final form until the sixteenth century.[51] The approved wording of the prayer is now: "Hail, Mary, full of grace! the Lord is with thee; blessed art thou among women, and blessed is the fruit of thy womb, Jesus. Holy Mary, Mother of God! pray for us sinners, now, and at the hour of our death. Amen."

At the angel's greeting, Luke continues, Mary was troubled, and she tried to guess what such a salutation might mean. Then Gabriel said to her: "Fear not, Mary, for thou hast found favor with God. And, behold, thou shalt conceive in thy womb, and bring forth a son, and shalt call his name Jesus. He shall be great, and shall be called the Son of the Highest, and the Lord God shall give unto him the throne of his father David: And he shall reign over the house of Jacob forever; and of his kingdom there shall be no end."

"How shall this be," Mary replied, "seeing that I know not a man?"

"The Holy Ghost shall come upon thee, and the power of the Highest shall overshadow thee; therefore also that holy thing which shall be born of thee shall be called the Son of God. And, behold, thy cousin Elisabeth, she hath also conceived a son in her old age; and this is the sixth month with her who was called barren. For with God nothing shall be impossible."

"Behold the handmaid of the Lord; be it unto me according to thy word."[52]

Thereupon the angel vanished.

Blessed Among Women

Luke's narrative goes on to tell us that Mary, still perturbed for several days after Gabriel's visit and the revelation that he had made to her, decided to go and confide in her cousin Elisabeth,[53] who—as the angel had told her—was also pregnant.

If the account were authentic, one would have to conclude that it was not in Nazareth but in Bethlehem that Mary lived at that time. Although identification is difficult, Elisabeth's village, according to what is contained in Luke, must in fact have been in the hilly area of Judea, or more than ninety miles from Nazareth—in other words, an uncomfortable caravan journey of at least nine or ten days. At the same time, all three villages that boast of being the home of Elisabeth—that is, Hebron, Juttah, and Karem (now 'Ain Karim)—are quite close to Bethlehem and could have been reached in a few hours by a girl who set out quite alone. (See Figure II.)

But the story of Mary's visit to Elisabeth was originated simply to make it possible for Elisabeth herself to announce the subordination of her unborn son (who was to be John the Baptist) to Jesus.[54] This served the view of the first Christians, who, in opposition to John's disciples, wished to maintain the supremacy of the Nazarene.

Luke recounts that Elisabeth no sooner saw her cousin enter the house than the six-month-old foetus in her womb "leaped," and then, as if in response to a message, the older woman cried out: "Blessed art thou among women, and blessed is the fruit of thy

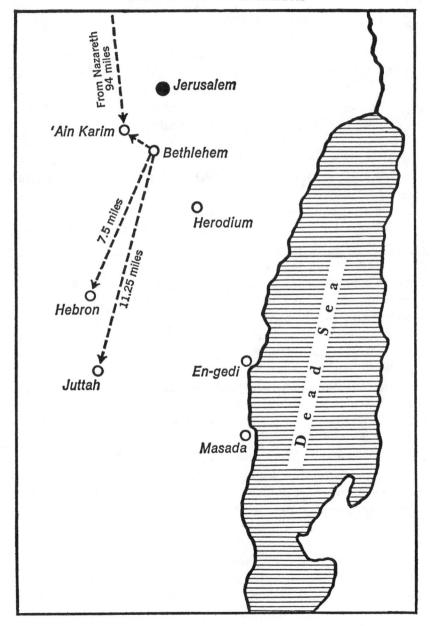

FIGURE II
MARY'S VISIT TO ELISABETH

womb. And whence is this to me, that the mother of my Lord should come to me? And lo, as soon as the voice of thy salutation sounded in mine ears, the babe leaped in my womb for joy." To wonder how Elisabeth could have known of Mary's pregnancy and of the destiny of her child would be too naïve.

After Elisabeth's greeting, Luke launches into a stream of genuine Biblical poetry, much of it an imitation of the Song of Hannah, in the Old Testament.[55] It is an inspired hymn of praise to the Madonna, called, because of its first word in the Latin version, the Magnificat. The passage stands by itself, as a mystical outburst by the Evangelist, and there is no ground for giving so much attention, as many exegetes have done, to the question whether it was spoken by Elisabeth in tribute to the Madonna or by Mary herself in her own honor. In the latter case, it would show, among other things, a certain lack of modesty in the young woman.

Mary, Luke's story adds, remained almost three months with Elisabeth, probably until after her cousin had given birth. At this point, the Gospel goes back to the story of John's birth, with which it had begun and which had been interrupted in order to insert the episode of the Annunciation. For the account of John's nativity, the author drew his inspiration from what the Old Testament had handed down about the births of Samson and Isaac to old and barren women, but he produced something much more imaginative and suggestive than the originals. He described the despair of Elisabeth and her aged husband, Zacharias, at their lack of children, her amazement when she found that she was pregnant, the consternation of Zacharias when he, a priest offering a sacrifice at the altar, beheld at his right hand the angel Gabriel not only announcing the unexpected birth of an heir but also prophesying that the son would be a great prophet and enjoining the parents to name him John. Then Luke relates that as a punishment for refusing to believe, Zacharias was stricken dumb until the day of John's birth—in fact, until the moment the prescribed name was given to the child, despite the violent objections of all his relatives.

It is a strange insistence that some scholars have shown in seeking some rationalistic explanation of this phenomenon of loss of speech, attributing it to a fainting fit brought on by the smoke of the incense, the monotonous rhythm of the prayers being recited by the congregation, and so forth,[56] or to a blood clot.[57] The purely legendary value of the story has utterly escaped them.

The Bitter Water That Causeth the Curse

From day to day, meanwhile, we are told by one of the apocryphal Gospels, Mary's womb was swelling, and, frightened, she returned to her home and hid herself from the sight of her neighbors.[58] Nonetheless, some explanation had to be made to her betrothed, Joseph. Among the Hebrews, betrothal (*qiddūshin* or *'ērūsīn*) was not, as it is today, a simple promise of marriage in the future that could be rescinded with ease, but a complete legal contract, so binding that if the future husband died before the marriage, the woman had the full status of a widow.[59] For some time—even as long as a year—the parties continued to live with their respective families while the marriage was being prepared, and any carnal connection during this time was strictly forbidden; in practice, however, as the rabbinical literature testifies, such relations occurred fairly frequently. In these cases, the bethrothal could not easily be broken; the law required a "bill of divorce" (*gēt*), signed by two witnesses, exactly as if the woman were a wife. If she was guilty of infidelity, she was punished as an adulteress, and the law for such cases was very harsh. By the time of Jesus, the penalty of death for adultery had been abolished in Palestine,[60] but there was no assurance of preventing such an outbreak of contempt among the culprit's kinsmen that they would stone her. Her act was what in some parts of the world today would be called an "insult to honor."

If there were no witnesses to testify to the woman's guilt, the suspected sinner had to submit to the ordeal of "the bitter water that causeth the curse," with a minutely detailed ritual.[61] The woman was led before the priest, who, having poured blessed water into a pottery vessel and mixed into it a handful of dust from the floor of the Tabernacle, addressed the mixture with incantations and terrible imprecations, then turned to the woman with these words: "If no man have lain with thee, and if thou hast not gone aside to uncleanness with another instead of thy husband, be thou free from this bitter water that causeth the curse: But if thou hast gone aside to another instead of thy husband, and if thou be defiled, and some man have lain with thee besides thy husband, the Lord make thee a curse and an oath among thy people, when the Lord doth make thy thigh to rot, and thy belly to swell; and this water that causeth the curse shall go into thy bowels, to make thy belly to swell, and thy thigh to rot." Then the priest wrote the same words on a parchment, immediately erasing them by plunging the parchment into the bitter water; thereupon the water was given to the woman to drink. If she was indeed an adulteress, the water was supposed to perform its penal function; if she suffered no ill effects, she was held guiltless.

Mary, since she had been formally betrothed to Joseph, should have been subjected to this ordeal if he questioned her innocence. And indeed, the first person to question the girl's purity was Joseph (on this point not only all the apocryphal but also all the canonical Gospels agree). When he saw that she was pregnant, two of the apocryphal Gospels say, he trembled all over and struck himself in the face; he threw himself back and forth on the floor, weeping bitterly and saying: "Lord God, take my soul, for now it is better for me to die than to live!" Rising, he addressed the girl: "My beloved, why hast thou done this thing?"

Tears streaming down her face, she sobbed: "I am pure. I have known no man."

Some women who were present sought to intervene, to ease Joseph's grief: "What art thou saying, Joseph? We know that no man has touched her. Every day an angel of the Lord speaketh with her, every day she is fed by the hand of the angel. If thou wouldst have our thought, it is none other than the angel of God that hath made her heavy with child."

But Joseph could not accept such an absurdity. "Why do ye make mock of me and seek to make me believe that an angel of God hath got her with child? Is it not that a man hath called himself an angel of the Lord and deceived her?"[62]

The wretched Joseph must have undergone days of frightful anguish. But a strange element is introduced by the apocryphal Evangelists: what disturbed him was not the offense done to him by Mary but the thought that he, an old man, might be accused of having taken advantage of a young girl. In the end he did turn to the ordeal of the bitter water that causeth the curse: but, instead of making his betrothed drink, he himself swallowed the water to prove his own innocence!

Arab legend has it that Joseph, tempted by Iblis, wanted to kill Mary.[63] But let us drop these ingenuous fantasies.

The canonical Gospel attributed to Matthew says only that Joseph was extremely concerned when he saw the condition in which Mary was "before they came together." The Greek text reads συνελθεῖν (sunelthein),[64] which in fact means that they had "come together"; but Catholic commentators, dedicated to preserving Mary's virginity, prefer to cling to the tradition of the Latin verb *convenire,* the ambiguity of which allows another interpretation: "before they went to live together."

Joseph, Matthew points out, was a "just" man, rigorous in his observance of the law.[65] Thus he would have been obliged to renounce his promised bride, but he was reluctant to expose her to public shame and decided to break with her in secret, turning her back to her family without gossip or scandal. Once again an angel stepped in to resolve the problem, explaining to Joseph that there was no ground for doubt because Mary actually was expecting a child of divine origin. With somewhat more credibility than Luke, Matthew contends that the angel appeared to Joseph in a dream. This might well have been an ordinary dream incident. In fact, when he awoke, Joseph did what the angel had advised—that is, what his own principles had suggested to him before he fled into his nightmare or warning dream. He took Mary to wife.

But he did not "know" her, the Evangelist says, until she had given birth to her first son.[66] In connection with this verb, it is to be remembered that both the Greek γιγνώσκω (*gignōskō*) and the Latin *cognoscere* have the connotation of sexual relations.

Who Was the Real Father of Jesus?

Why did Mary not tell Joseph at once of the remarkable experience of the Annunciation and thus spare him so much suffering? In the rationale of Christology, her silence makes no sense. On the contrary, it is hard to believe Mary capable of perpetrating such a deception, to the injury of her future husband. It can be justified only as a means for two Evangelists, Matthew and Luke, to confirm, through

Joseph's incredulity and a further angelic intervention, the miraculous truth of the divine origin of Jesus.

But their pious intention has also had a negative result. Suspicions of an act of adultery, artfully attributed by them to Joseph, have since been nurtured in the minds of many detractors of Christianity. Rather than recognize the simple fact that the whole tradition of the birth of Jesus is legend and that no shadow of marital infidelity ever troubled the peaceful union of Joseph and Mary, they accept adultery on her part and they titillate themselves in a search for the guilty man, often to the accompaniment of vulgarly tendentious allegations, insults, and slanderous nonsense.

The Talmud, the most important of post-Biblical sacred literature in Judaism, declares that Miriam, who was a hairdresser (*plicatricem capillorum mulierum*), was put aside by her carpenter husband, Pappos, for adultery, and that she gave birth in secret to Jesus, whose real father was a Roman soldier called Pander, or Panther.[67] Here it has been pointed out that a double error has been committed with respect to Mary's occupation: a confusion between Mary of Nazareth and Mary of Magdala, and another between the words *magdalāh* ("harlot") and *megaddeleh* ("hairdresser").[68]

The reference to a "son of Panther" has been interpreted by some as an error born of confusion with the Greek phrase "son of Parthenos [παρθένος]"—that is, son of a virgin.[69] However, it is not easy to explain how the word *parthenos* could migrate from Greek into Hebrew. Nonetheless, some students have taken the trouble to investigate the possible accuracy of the Talmudic tradition. There appears to be in Bingerbrück, Germany, the gravestone of a Roman soldier, born in Sidon in Phoenicia, whose name was Tiberius Julius Abdes Panther and who belonged to a cohort garrisoned in Palestine about A.D. 9.[70] The authority of the Talmud was such among the Fathers of the Church themselves that for a long time they found it necessary to explain the presence of this embarrassing fellow in the life of Jesus. Epiphanius made Panther the father of Joseph,[71] while John of Damascus called him a common ancestor of both Joseph and Mary.[72]

Aside from the Talmudic tradition, it appears that other rather slanderous theories on the paternity of Jesus were current in the early centuries. Tertullian reports that in the Roman pantomimes, which were a popular entertainment both licentious and satirical, there was an insulting joke directed at Jesus: *"Hic est ille fabri et quaestuariae filius"* ("This fellow is the notorious son of an artisan and a whore").[73] A nasty story of Alexandrine origin states without qualification that Jesus was begotten in an incestuous relation between Mary and her brother![74]

Even in modern times there has been no lack of overradical critics who have given credence to the theory of adultery. One of these, the German Heinrich Paulus, proposes the hypothesis that Mary, before her marriage to Joseph, was moved by sheer religious zeal to offer herself (with the cooperation of some man, of course) as the prospective mother of a messiah after she had been persuaded to this course by someone posing as an angel charged with a divine mission.[75] Another German rationalist, Karl E. Venturini, holds the view that the seducer was no less a personage than Joseph of Arimathea (who, according to the Gospels, appeared only after the Crucifixion, to place the body of Jesus in its own tomb).[76] Venturini supports his contention with reference to a similar case reported by Flavius Josephus, the most important Jewish historian of antiquity, who lived in the first century A.D. Josephus says that, about the time of Jesus, a Roman knight took advantage of the chaste wife of a nobleman, his compatriot, by causing her to be invited by the priest of Isis to the temple of the goddess, on the pretext that the jackal-god Anubis sought her love. Full of innocence and faith, Josephus adds, the lady consented; and she might thereafter have believed that she had conceived a divine being had not the knight's boastfulness induced him to tell her the truth.[77] According to another rationalist, Aurelio Turcotti, Elisabeth and Zacharias contrived a meeting between Mary and an Arab prince who was passing that way with his caravans![78]

More recently it has been argued by racists that, at least on his father's side, Jesus was "racially Aryan."[79] This theory, however, owes more to philosophical and political motivations than to historical considerations. It is true that Galilee was inhabited by many pagans (*Gālīl-ha-gōyīm*, in fact, means "land of the heathen"), and therefore it is not wholly impossible that Jesus might not have been completely Hebraic in origin; but these are speculations, and therefore historical criticism cannot take them into account.

[2]

THE INCARNATION

Favored of God

The attribution of a divine father to a human being is neither so remarkable nor so ingenious as to occasion surprise. Pagan mythology teems with such instances. The Greek hero Perseus was said to have been the son of the virgin Danaë, whom Zeus made pregnant by taking the form of a shower of gold. Hercules was the son of Alcmene, a mortal woman, and Zeus, who took advantage of her by assuming the shape of her husband, Amphitryon. Aeneas, on the other hand, was the son of a goddess, Aphrodite, and a man; Achilles was the son of a Nereid married to a mortal. Of Romulus it was told that Rhea Silvia had conceived him and his brother, Remus, when Mars was her lover. Even some historical figures were said to be of divine origin, such as Pythagoras, Plato, Aristotle, Alexander the Great, and Augustus himself, who was emperor when Jesus was born.

The Oriental religions, too, often employ the myths of incarnation and reincarnation of gods. Hence the comparativists (scholars who investigate the relations among religions) and the Orientalists see the influence of Egyptian and, in general, Oriental mythology in the Christian legend. In fact, the allusion made by the Gospel of Luke to divine intervention in the birth of Jesus ("the Holy Ghost shall come upon thee") readily brings to mind the Eastern myths in which incarnation is envisaged in terms of luminous radiations, gusts of wind, gathering clouds.[1] In India, the legend of Krishna the Redeemer is surprisingly similar to many of the details of the birth

22

of Jesus: the annunciation to the virgin Jasoda, the incarnation of the god Vishnu, the adoration of the shepherds, the persecution by the rajahs who ordered the killing of every male child born on the night of Krishna's nativity. In Egypt, on the walls of the Temple of Luxor, there is a bas-relief that goes back eighteen centuries before Christ and portrays the annunciation of the god Thoth to the virgin Isis, the conception of Horus, and the homage of the other gods. In the cult of Mithras, the god himself, in the form of light, enters the body of the virgin, and Mithras was born in a cave just after the winter solstice (December 25). In Buddhism, Buddha, the Enlightened, was begot by a god who appeared in the form of a cloud. Even today the Dalai Lama of Tibet is considered the incarnation of Buddha, and many Buddhists also view Jesus in this way.[2]

These and other close resemblances between Christianity and the Oriental faiths, however, are not enough to persuade one that the former was directly derived from the latter. There is only an obvious analogy, resulting from the proximity of the societies and the affinity of their cultural interests.[3] Furthermore, examples of the deification of heroes and of miraculous conceptions abound outside the Asian-African world, in cultures that could not have exerted any influence on Christianity or received any from it. Montezuma, the emperor of Mexico at the time of the Spanish conquest, was held to be the son of Tlaloc, the Aztec god of rain. In Australia, even in our time, the Arunta tribe believes that an ancestor of the clan may cause himself to be reborn by tossing a stick of wood (namatuna) to the woman he has chosen or by hanging it on a tree beneath which she will lie.

In the various attempts made during the early centuries of Christianity to explain the nature of the incarnation, concepts resembling those just outlined were common.[4] Tertullian, the second-century apologist, believed that a ray of light descended on Mary and became flesh, a hypothesis that is visibly analogous to the Egyptian legend (Tertullian was an African) of the cow that bore Apis, the bull, after having been impregnated by a ray of light. The Arab legend of the birth of Jesus says that the angel himself made Mary pregnant by breathing on her mezār, the colored kerchief every Oriental woman wore about her head.[5]

But, as we shall see in due course, the progress of the deification of Jesus more readily discloses a direct influence by the Greek mystery religions and by Hellenic philosophy.[6]

The difficulty for the Church in teaching clearly *how* the incarnation was accomplished, rather than leaving it wrapped in mystery, arose because the belief in the miraculous conception, which had taken shape when a tradition of the earthly origin of Jesus already existed, was superimposed on the belief that Jesus was the predicted descendant of David. The point at which the two beliefs join—with a manifest contradiction—is just that passage of Luke concerning the Annunciation: "He . . . shall be called *the Son of the Highest*: and the Lord God shall give unto him the throne of *his father David.*"

However, as is unanimously conceded by all the commentators, even the Catholics, this passage, like the entire story of the birth of Jesus, is written in a style that hardly harmonizes with Luke's characteristic sentence structure.[7] Plainly, the fragment was added later, and the insertion was made rather unskillfully.

"Virum Non Cognosco"

The myth of the divine origin of Jesus (which was not only an act of tribute and veneration on the part of the disciples but also essential to the concept of Jesus as redeemer) carried with it a motivation of asceticism and celibacy: since the Son of God could not have been begot naturally, it was necessary to postulate the absolute purity of his mother as well. In other words, she must have become pregnant without losing her virginity. To clarify so remarkable an event a number of suppositions were put forth,[8] all of them absurd and some downright amazing, like that of Ephraem Syrus (fourth century), according to whom the girl was impregnated auricularly: "[It] entered through the ear and hid itself in her womb."[9]

Only in the late Middle Ages was the question settled, by Thomas Aquinas, with one of those conclusions based on faith that every student boggles at: *"Miraculorum Dei quaedam sunt de quibus est fides sicut miraculum virginei partus . . . et ideo Dominus voluit ista occultiora esse, ut fides eorum magis meritoria esset"* ("Among the miracles of God, some are articles of faith, like the miracle of the Virgin Birth . . . and precisely because the Lord wished them to remain incomprehensible in order that faith in them be the more worthy").[10]

Indeed, such an event can be accepted only through faith. In nature parthenogenesis does not exist. If zoology admits the possibility in a few of the most primitive forms (aphids, phylloxera, crustaceans), it does so only because of the difficulty of clearly distinguishing between the ovum and the spermatozoon. Among human beings there have been rare cases of women who have become pregnant without an actual hymenal rupture, but this has invariably followed the introduction of some man's semen. Hence, all the efforts of the rationalists to find a scientific explanation of this phenomenon are useless. What escapes them is that the virginity of Mary is a religious belief, not a historical fact for which proofs must be adduced. Furthermore, it is a belief that does not go back to the time of Jesus, and therefore it can be disregarded by those who concern themselves with the historical, rather than the legendary, reconstruction of the life of Jesus himself.

The ancient Fathers, to justify their faith in the Virgin Birth, launched into a search for every passage in the Scriptures that could seem in any way to foretell the coming of a "son of God" to earth with the help of a virgin. The arbitrary nature of their efforts to give certain Biblical extracts the desired meaning can be seen from a single instance. The most important prophecy of the Virgin Birth of Jesus is supposed to be a saying of Isaiah: "Behold, a virgin shall conceive, and bear a son, and shall call his name Immanuel. Butter and honey shall he eat, that he may know to refuse the evil, and choose the good. For before the child shall know to refuse the evil, and choose the good, the land that thou abhorrest shall be forsaken of both her kings."[11]

But what is the meaning of Isaiah's prediction that the Savior (Immanuel) shall eat butter and honey? What need can there be for him, who is divine, to learn to distinguish between good and evil? What had the prophet in mind when he said that the land should be forsaken by its two kings?

These same Christian exegetes are constrained to admit that the prophecy is "difficult of interpretation."[12] Naturally, since the excerpt has nothing to do with the birth of Jesus. It is the ending of a discussion that Isaiah says he had with King Ahaz, in which the prophet reassured the king of the imminent destruction of his two enemies, the kings of Syria and Israel. The meaning of the passage is this: "Suppose[13] that a woman marries today and becomes pregnant: between now and the time when she gives birth [that is, within nine months], conditions should change. The times will be so much improved [butter and honey] that it will be possible to give the child a name of good omen [*Immānūēl*, in Hebrew, means 'God is with us,' or 'Savior']; and, before he reaches the age of reason—that is, of ability to distinguish between good and evil [four or five years]—your enemies will have been overcome."[14]

Moreover, the desired adaptation of the words of Isaiah could not have been made in a Hebraic environment.[15] Indeed, the original text speaks, not of a "virgin," but of a "young unmarried woman": this is the meaning of the word *'almāh.* The misunderstanding arose from the fact that the first translators of the Old Testament, the so-called Seventy, interpreted *'almāh* as the Greek word παρθένος (*parthenos*), which, like the Latin *virgo,* has both the generic connotation of a "woman yet to be married" and the explicit meaning of "virgin." The misunderstanding is impossible in Hebrew, in which *betūlāh* is the specific noun for "virgin." Even in the first centuries after Christ, some Fathers recognized the mistake,[16] but by then the prophecy of Isaiah had made it easy to corroborate the Virgin Birth.

Such a legend, in any case, was originated only to confer on Jesus a supernatural origin, "such as all founders of religions and heroes had," Jerome says,[17] and for at least three centuries the Church took no interest in what might have happened to Mary after her marvelous impregnation: whether she had normal relations with her husband and whether, as the Gospels testify, they had other children.

The Mother-Goddess

The glorification of Mary, which did not begin until the fourth century, owed its origin to special historical needs. After obtaining official recognition from the emperor Constantine I, Christianity, as the state religion, automatically included the whole mass of pagans who had never been converted. In order not to provoke too deep a rupture with the superstitions of the common people, Christianity had to absorb and adapt certain aspects—at least the most traditional —of pagan faith. Among other things there was the need to replace the concept of the mother-goddess, which, in Greek and Latin paganism and in the Oriental religions that had by then spread throughout the Roman Empire, always accompanied the idea of the father-god.

The most important goddess cult in Rome was that of the Great Mother of Phrygia, who in the West had taken the name Magna Mater Deum Idaea. It had been introduced in 204 B.C., when the Sibylline Books showed that only this goddess could save the city from the wrath of Hannibal, and her worship had thereafter been continued, with great festivals between March 15 and 27 of every year.[18]

About the second century before Christ, the cult of Isis had also begun to grow in the empire. At first she had symbolized the fertile properties of the Nile; then she had become the queen of sea and sky, governing the stars and therefore human destinies, and as such she was called Τύχη (*Tuchē*), or Fortune.[19] In A.D. 38, Caligula erected a magnificent temple in her honor. Later, Rome adopted the worship of the Phoenician Astarte, the siren-goddess of Ashkelon, and others.

Mary, too, was elevated to the level of these goddesses. Many statues of Isis were, in fact, transferred to the duty of representing the Madonna, to whom were also assigned such epithets of Isis as Redemptress, Star of the Sea, and Crown of Life.

But more was wanted; even more remarkable qualities were decreed for Mary, and chief among them was that of having preserved her own virginity not only in the act of impregnation but also in that of giving birth to Jesus. Curious discussions arose among the Fathers of the Church concerning the intimate details of her anatomy. Whereas, until then, it had been customary to speak of *vulva reserata*,[20] one now spoke of *uterus clausus*.[21]

About the end of the fourth century, John Chrysostom proposed the definition of Mary's "perpetual virginity": since her physical intactness had not been impaired by the birth of Jesus and she had maintained her virginity to the end of her life, she was to be called a virgin *ante partum, in partu, post partum*. This formula was to become dogma at the Lateran Council of 649 and was to be confirmed by the Tolentino Council of 675, because not everyone had freely accepted it.

Why then, the rationalists wonder, would Mary have married, if she wished and was obliged to remain virgin? The answers given to this obvious question were often frighteningly ingenuous: "to obey the wishes of her father";[22] "because marriage was a painful necessity imposed by local customs";[23] "because, if Mary had taken a vow and wanted to fulfil it, this was possible only under the protection of a lawful marriage";[24] "because there was an honorable man who would not take her by force but would instead protect her against violence, in pursuance of her previous vow."[25]

Enforced continence was thus imposed on Joseph also: "She loved him as a brother, in the manner of the angels, and he loved her with chaste reverence . . . : the virgin husband of a virgin bride."[26]

A further revision of the marital relations between Mary and Joseph, not only before but also after the birth of Jesus, was now required. There remained the embarrassing fact that the Gospels pointed clearly to brothers and sisters of Jesus. The obstacle was overcome, at first, by saying that these were really his stepbrothers and stepsisters, the children of Joseph by an earlier marriage; later, the argument that they were the "cousins" of Jesus was introduced. At the proper place we shall observe the inconsistency of these theories.

Hyperdulia

Meanwhile, the growth of hyperdulia (the ecclesiastical designation for the special veneration due the Madonna) enjoyed another major moment as the result of a new stage reached in the glorification of Jesus. First the son of an artisan, then the son of David, then the Son of God, after three centuries of impassioned debate Jesus became identified outright with God himself, in the first Ecumenical Council recorded in history—that of Nicaea, in 325.

Naturally, this step gave rise to a grave problem with respect to Mary: could she, as the mother of Jesus, that is, Χριστοτόκος (*Christotokos*), be considered also the mother of God, that is, Θεοτόκος (*Theotokos*)? The first to voice doubts was Nestorius, the patriarch of

Constantinople, in a vehement quarrel with Cyril, the archbishop of Alexandria. Some theologians today are still sorely bewildered on the subject: "How can God be begot?" Otto Hophan asked. "How can He, who springs from Himself, without a beginning, owe His origin to a woman?"[27] The same objections, in the fifth century, motivated the Nestorians. But Cyril's view prevailed, triumphing at the Council of Ephesus (431), and Mary was declared Deipara, Mother of God.

Until that time no cult of the Virgin had existed.[28] But after the Council of Ephesus the Mother of God began to be raised to a new pedestal. In the East, the faithful created the Feasts of Mary's Annunciation, of her Purification, of the Sleep of the Mother of God, and of the Nativity; in the West, they built churches in her name.[29] New attributes were ascribed to her, those, by this time, of Ceres, of Minerva, and of Venus; and even the temples belonging to these goddesses were rededicated to the adoration of Mary.

In short, Mary assumed the functions of divinity, with specific duties of redemption. As early as the second century, Justin Martyr, in his *Dialogue with Trypho*, had established a strange parallel between Mary and Eve: "Eve, paying heed to the words of the serpent, conceived disobedience and death; Mary, paying heed to the words of the angel, conceived him through whom God defeats the serpent and rescues from death those who do penance for their own sins."[30] Thus appeared, for the first time in patristic literature, the principle of recirculation, by which salvation comes to us in a manner similar to that in which damnation occurs: Eve wrought our downfall, Mary our redemption. Justin's thesis was restated in the fourth and fifth centuries, though even at that time there was no lack among the Church Fathers of those who doubted even the sanctity of Mary.[31]

In order to attribute to Mary the function of Eve in the opposite sense, a precise prophetic value was sought in the words with which Genesis speaks of the eternal conflict between man and the temptations of evil: "And I will put enmity between thee [the devil] and the woman, and between thy seed and her seed; it shall bruise thy head, and thou shalt bruise his heel" (Genesis 3:15). It is to be noted, however, that the Hebrew text refers the pronoun "it" to mankind (the seed of the woman), while the Church translation, in order to provide the desired prophetic sense, takes advantage of the feminine gender of "seed" in Latin (*stirps*) to make the pronoun feminine, referring to "woman" (Mary).

Similarly, every verse of the Old Testament that might allude however vaguely to the virtues and merits of Mary was exhumed. Thus she was declared to be the spiritual Eden,[32] ground for this being found in the Biblical passage: "And the Lord God planted a garden eastward in Eden; and there he put the man whom he had formed" (Genesis 2:8). What is described here is obviously the legendary earthly paradise and Adam, not Mary and Jesus. She was declared also to be Noah's ark,[33] because in giving birth to Jesus she saved humanity from eternal damnation; she was identified with Jacob's ladder,[34] because by means of it God descended to earth, and with the burning bush[35] that Moses saw on Mount Horeb in the desert, because it burned without being consumed, as Mary gave birth without impairing her virginal wholeness. She was likened to Aaron's rod,[36] which put forth shoots though it had neither roots nor soil, as she conceived without the seed of man; to Gideon's fleece,[37] which was miraculously covered with dew though the ground round it was dry; to Solomon's Temple,[38] which contained the Holy of Holies; and to the stopped fountain, the closed orchard, the cedar of Lebanon, the cypress of Zion, the rose of Jericho, the olive, the vine, cinnamon, balsam, incense . . . Prophecies referring to Mary and the nativity were described in such passages as these: "Then shall the earth yield her increase" (Psalms 67:6); "God hath wrought our salvation in the womb of the earth" (Psalms 74:12, in Catholic Bibles[39]); "In them [the night and the day] hath he set a tabernacle for the sun, which is as a bridegroom coming out of his chamber" (Psalms 19:4–5); "Wisdom hath builded her house" (Proverbs 9:1). But an end here, because the catalogue is infinite.

The assumption of Mary to the rank of divinity led naturally to the necessity of excluding any taint of sin in her. Augustine had early voiced the belief that Mary could not be confused with the rest of sinful mankind,[40] but only in 1546, at the Council of Trent, was an official proclamation issued that Mary had forever been spotless of all sin, even venial sin. This, the doctrine of the Immaculate Conception, had already been a subject of controversy. The first conflict over it occurred in the thirteenth century, between the Franciscans, who upheld it, and the Dominicans, who opposed it. In reality, the exclusion of Mary from original sin implied a divine conception on the part of Anna,[41] the presumed mother of the Madonna—something not anticipated in any evangelical testimony. Nevertheless, the Franciscan position pleased the papal court. Sixtus IV, in his bull *Cum praecelsa* of 1476, conceded this privilege of Mary, which was reiterated from time to time in the light of opposition from the Protestants and then from the Catholic modernists as well. Finally, in 1854, the doctrine was made an article of faith by Pius IX. Most opportunely, in February, 1858, the faithful received a resounding confirmation of the new dogma: the Madonna appeared to a fourteen-year-old shepherd girl, Bernadette Soubirous, with the words: "I am the Immaculate Conception," which contain, among other things, an error in language. Mary should have said, if anything: "I am the immaculately conceived."

The glorification of Mary has recently made further notable progress. In 1950, Pius XII declared as an article of faith the dogma that Mary, after her death, was assumed into heaven, body and soul.[42] In 1954, the Feast of Mary the Queen was proclaimed, though not without some dissent within the bosom of the Catholic clergy itself.

In addition to Mary's epithets of Virgin, Mother of God, Immaculate, Assumed, Queen, now there is talk from time to time of adding another: Mediator. The proposal was first set forth in 1902, at the Mariological Congress of Freiburg, in these terms:[43] In becoming, according to the flesh, the mother of Jesus, the redeemer and savior, Mary became at the same time, according to the spirit, the mother of all those whom Jesus came to redeem. Jesus wanted to associate his mother with himself as his "fellow redeemer of the human race." So, indeed, did Pius X describe the Madonna in an encyclical,[44] attributing to the Nazarene an intention that in actuality he had never evidenced.

The subject was reopened in September, 1958, at a Mariological Congress held in Lourdes. Some theologians dared to seek approval of the far more binding doctrine of "derivative universal mediation," under which no grace can be granted to man by God except through the mediation of Mary. To adopt scholastic terminology, Mary would advance from *causa strumentalis* to *causa efficiens* of redemption.

In September, 1964, the Polish cardinal Stefan Wyszynski overwhelmed everyone with his hyperdulia of the Madonna, urging

Vatican Council II to proclaim a new dogma that would establish Mary as the Mother of the Church. The proposal seemed inopportune to the great majority of the Council Fathers, the more so in view of the fact that the Council had been inaugurated with the proposition of seeking a more fraternal collaboration with the other Christian churches; a new Mariological dogma would certainly not have gratified the Protestant sects.[45] But only two months later, despite the contrary opinion of the Council, Pope Paul VI unexpectedly exercised his authority to proclaim Mary, on his own initiative, Mater Ecclesiae.[46]

So Mary was carried finally to the pinnacle of the Church, and, as Protestant theologians note, not without irony, the Christianity of Roman Catholicism today might well call itself Marianity.

[3]

THE GOSPEL OF THE NATIVITY

When Was Jesus Born?

Through the information offered by the Gospels concerning the birth of Jesus, we emerge at last from the legendary and begin to enter the historical. But the elements remain uncertain and debatable.

Luke tells us that in the year in which Jesus was born, an event of major importance occurred in Palestine: a census of the entire population, ordered by Cyrenius, the Roman governor of the province of Syria, of which Palestine was a dependency.[1] Matthew, however, reports that at this time Herod was king.[2] The two accounts are not difficult to check. The only census of Palestine known to history was ordered by Publius Sulpicius Quirinus (whom Luke calls Cyrenius), but it took place in A.D. 6 and 7—that is, six or seven years after the date generally accepted for the birth of Jesus.[3] Therefore, the Nativity would have to be redated as has been proposed by, among others, H. J. Holtzmann.[4] This creates serious problems, however, since the date of birth would no longer agree with the other dates that are supplied by the Gospels (baptism, death, etc.); or else the life of Jesus, which is traditionally considered to have covered at least thirty years, would be reduced to barely twenty-three or twenty-four.

The Christian exegetes, to avoid putting Luke in error, have been constrained to postulate another census, earlier than that of

33

Quirinus. But no historical evidence confirms this, and Luke himself says explicitly that the census to which he refers was the *first* in Palestine: "And this taxing was first made when Cyrenius was governor of Syria." Other translations—"this census was the first of those taken under Quirinus," or "this was the census that was taken before Quirinus became governor of Syria"—suggested by M. J. Lagrange and others, are tendentious and false.[5]

Without moving the date of the Nativity forward by six or seven years, it is better to assume an error on the part of the Evangelist, who, since he did not know the precise date of the birth of Jesus, having written almost a century after the event, based his account on an occurrence memorable to the Hebrew people that took place at approximately the same time.

As for Matthew's statement that Herod was king when Jesus was born, it is definitely known that Herod died in March of the year 4 B.C. Matthew's testimony, therefore, necessitates dating the birth of Jesus several years (at least four) earlier. Today, in general, scholars of all persuasions agree in accepting this procedure, which entails no inconvenience except that of adding a few years to the life of Jesus. The error in calculation, if any, was made not by Matthew but by Dionysius Exiguus, a Scythian monk living in Rome in the sixth century, who introduced the method of reckoning the Christian Era (B.C. and A.D.), which is still used.

But while many students are satisfied to fix the date of the birth of Jesus in precisely the year of Herod's death (4 B.C.), because it is closest to the traditional date, some others still find it necessary to go back a few years, preferring 7 B.C.[6] or 11 B.C.[7]

Bethlehem

On the subject of the birthplace of Jesus there are other controversies. While Matthew permits the hypothesis that Joseph and Mary, at the time of the Nativity, were living in Bethlehem and had not yet moved to Nazareth, Luke contends that they had to make the uncomfortable journey from the one city to the other in order to be counted in the census. This statement is rather debatable. It is unlikely that the Roman authorities would have imposed such ridiculous displacements on the Hebrew population. Besides, the order would have been extremely impracticable. Every Israelite would have been obliged to recall the residence of that paternal ancestor living when Joshua partitioned the land of Palestine among the twelve tribes (more than a thousand years before Christ), and then he would have had to seek out that place, if it still existed, to be inscribed in the census lists.[8] To the Romans what mattered was the number of residents of every inhabited place and their economic resources, not tribal affiliations.[9] Thus, the most efficient way to take the census was according to the place of residence, the method the Romans had always used.

It is all the more improbable, then, to imagine that Joseph would have dared to subject Mary, who had already come almost to term, to the exhaustion of such a journey (nine or ten days on camel- or donkey-back to cover the distance between Nazareth and Jerusalem). Preferable, therefore, is the assumption that Jesus was born in Nazareth itself[10] or, since it is not even certain that Nazareth existed, in some unidentified part of Galilee.[11] So much is true: the Evangelists always call Jesus "the Nazarene" or "the Galilean," and make no further reference to his birth in Bethlehem.

Further suspicion is aroused by Matthew's statement that Jesus was born "in Bethlehem of Judea: for thus it is written by the prophet," since Bethlehem was certainly the city of David.[12]

Bethlehem is a little village about eight miles from Jerusalem. Etymologically, its name means "the house of bread," but this appears to be a popular corruption of *Beth-Lahamu*—that is, "the house of the god Lah," who was a Babylonian divinity also venerated for a time by the Canaanites.[13] Near the village, pilgrims are still shown today the cave in which tradition has it that Jesus was born. A sacred building was constructed on the site in the fourth century, the Basilica of the Nativity, made possible by the generosity of Emperor Constantine and his mother, Helena, and subsequently destroyed, rebuilt, and embellished.

The belief that this is the exact spot on which the Messiah was born goes back to Justin Martyr, the second-century apologist,[14] and was endorsed, about a hundred years later, by the philosopher Origen.[15] The Church Father Jerome, who died in Bethlehem in 420, reports in addition that the holy cave was at one point consecrated by the heathen to the worship of Adonis, and a pleasant sacred grove planted before it, to wipe out the memory of Jesus.[16] Modern mythologists, however, reverse the supposition, insisting that the cult of Adonis-Tammuz originated the shrine and that it was the Christians who took it over, substituting the worship of their own god.[17]

According to the legend of the Gospels, Joseph and Mary had to take shelter in this cave, or, rather, in a kind of stable, equipped as it was with a manger, because, Luke says, they could find no room at "the inn."[18] This term should not make us picture a real tavern, but rather a caravansary (in Hebrew, *gerūth*), which was the equivalent of the present-day Arab *khān*: a large fenced enclosure surrounded by sheds, partitioned to make a number of small rooms.[19] Animals were left outdoors, within the fence, while the travelers rested in the sheds.

The tradition that places an ox and an ass in the cavern of the Nativity is assuredly no older than the third century. It arose from a mistaken reading of a passage in the prophet Habakkuk.[20] Instead of the text: "O Lord, revive thy work in the midst of the years, in the midst of the years make known," the version in the Septuagint and in the Latin translations based on it reads: ". . . in the midst of the beasts," because of the identity between the genitive plural of ζωή (*zoē*), which means "years," "ages," and that of ζῷον (*zōon*), which means "animals."[21]

The Nativity

To the sober narrative of the Nativity transmitted to us by Luke, the apocryphal Gospels have added other details. No sooner had Mary been seized by labor pains, they tell us, than Joseph hastened out in search of a midwife. The Protevangelium of James recounts Joseph's feelings:[22] in that sublime instant it seemed to him that everything round him had frozen, assuming the ecstatic immobility that, a few centuries later, was to inspire in St. Francis the concept of the Manger with its little images of the shepherds and the sheep.

The apocryphal Gospels take pleasure in describing at great length the amazement of the midwife (Salome or Zelomi) at the discovery that, even in the moment of giving birth, Mary preserved her virginity.

All this coming and going of people in the middle of the night, in a humble stable outside the village, and perhaps the moans and cries of Mary in her birth pangs, frightened some shepherds who were still awake, standing guard over their flocks. The moon had risen in brilliance, one of the apocryphal Gospels relates, and some of the shepherds were resting on the grass, telling stories, while another group, farther away, was singing.[23]

Luke says that the shepherds were informed by an angel, followed closely by a troop of the heavenly host who praised God, saying: "Glory to God in the highest, and on earth peace, good will toward men,"[24] or, as the most modern Biblical exegetes prefer to interpret it, ". . . and peace to men whom God loves,"[25] in which εὐδοκία (eudokia) means "benevolence," "protection," and is to be attributed to God, not to men.

The incident of the shepherds supports the supposition that the birth must have taken place in spring or autumn. During the winter, since the temperature falls well below freezing in Bethlehem and the rainy season lasts until March, animals cannot be left outdoors. In fact, until the fourth century, the dates most commonly accepted for the birth of Jesus were March 28, April 18, and May 29. Then a curious reckoning was made. Convinced that Jesus had lived exactly thirty years—counted, however, from the moment of the Incarnation rather than from that of his birth—the faithful calculated backward from the date of his death (accepted as April 6) and assigned him twenty-nine years and three months of actual life, the nine remaining months being those of his gestation. The date of the Nativity thus fell on January 6. In the Eastern Church, the day was marked for commemoration and given the name Epiphany (ἐπιφάνεια), in the etymological sense of "appearance," that is, the descent of the deity to earth.

But, in the West, special needs of adaptation to the environment caused the Church to set the date of the birth of Jesus as December 25. The fact is, it was necessary to replace the widespread pagan cult of Sol Invictus, which was based on an astronomical myth common to all the peoples of the Mediterranean basin.[26] The winter solstice falls between December 21 and 25, and winter, having reached its peak, is ready to give way to spring, when nature renews itself and is reborn; the sun begins to gain precisely on December 25, after the sign of the Virgin has reached the horizon. In Persia as in Phoenicia, in Egypt as in Syria, the powers of nature were honored in the myth of the virgin goddess who gives birth to the sun-god.[27] Horus, the Egyptian solar hero, was said to be the son of Isis, the immaculate virgin, queen of heaven. In Persian Magianism, the solar hero was Tammuz, the son of Mylitta or Ishtar, queen of the earth; and so on. In their exemplary tolerance in religious matters, the Romans had never opposed the growth of the sun festival in the empire, and December 25 was in fact known as Dies Natalis Solis Invicti. Indeed, under Emperors Heliogabalus (reigned 218–22), Gallienus (253–68), and Aurelian (270–75), the worship of Sol Invictus became the national cult of the empire.[28]

Ultimately, Constantine I (306–37) was able, through his skillful political manipulations, to join the Christian symbols to those of the sun cult. Thus the attributes of the sun-god passed to Jesus, and those of Isis and Astarte became the Madonna's. This fusion of the two faiths undoubtedly constituted a basic factor in the final triumph of Christianity. However, the mythologists, Arthur Drews in the forefront,[29] bluntly deduced from this that Jesus Christ had never existed historically, and they contended that his name was merely one of those given to the single sun-god who, under his various names, was worshiped by all Oriental peoples. There is no lack of other extravagant hypotheses, among them the argument that the story of the birth of Jesus is nothing but a transformation of the legend of Romulus (the son of Mars, brought up among shepherds, etc.).[30]

What is certainly disturbing is the total silence of early non-Christian writers on the subject of Jesus. His preaching, the sensational trial that led to his death under the auspices of Rome, the miracles ascribed to him, all should surely have evoked some reaction, however fleeting, in Greek or Roman or Jewish historians. Instead, we can at most assemble a few vague, general fragments on "the sect of the Christians." This remarkable fact is perhaps insufficient to corroborate the thesis of the many who deny the existence of Jesus, but it does lead one to believe at the least that, except to his followers, the contemporary importance of Jesus was minimal. It is also undeniable that only after its merger with paganism, and above all with the sun cult, was Christianity able to enrich its symbology and its liturgy.

In Rome, the feast day of Sol Invictus always marked the end of a festival even more ancient but equally dedicated to the celebration of the self-renewal of nature: the Saturnalia. Based on the mythical era of the god Saturn, supposed to have been an age of happiness, peace, and brotherhood among all men, the Saturnalia in those days was a time in which the Romans abandoned themselves to touching demonstrations of friendship and affection. Even slaves had the right to sit at table with their masters and be served by them during the festival. It was a simple matter for Christianity—which was based fundamentally on universal brotherhood—to replace the heathen belief in the age of Saturn without impairing the admirable customs of the Saturnalia.

Son of Israel

Hebrew law prescribed (Genesis 17:10–11, and Leviticus 12:3) that, eight days after birth, all male children were to be circumcised and that at that time they would receive their names. Even today, students of ethnology have not been able to explain clearly the origin and significance of circumcision. Perhaps it is a survival from an ancient rite of initiation into puberty, such as still exists among savage peoples, with analogous bloody rituals, like the placing of some ineradicable sign (tattoo, mutilation of a joint, extraction of incisor teeth, etc.) on the body of the boy growing out of his childhood.[31] In antiquity, religious circumcision was practiced not only by all the Semitic peoples but also, perhaps, by the Egyptians and the Ethiopians; today, it appears, it is practiced by some Australian tribes as well as by Jews and Mohammedans.

Circumcision probably has the symbolic value of a sacrifice to the god of fertility, and yet for the Jews and the Mohammedans it is a religious rite that attests the submission of each individual to the faith of his ancestors and "signifies" communion with God.[32] Philo of Alexandria, a philosopher of Jewish origin, asserts that it makes the body purer, enables one to avoid certain diseases, and facilitates procreation.[33] Some theologians, on the other hand, ascribe to circumcision the moral value of curbing lust.[34]

In any case, the Hebrew practice of circumcision was jeered at by the ancient Romans as shameful and grotesque. Many pagan writers assure us that in their baths and gymnasia the young Romans contemptuously addressed the Jews as *verpus* ("penis") or *recutitus* ("skinned"), and the physician Celsus declares that sometimes Jews had their foreskins sewed back on, in order to conceal their having been circumcised.[35]

The operation consists of an incision to remove the foreskin, and in ancient times it was performed by the child's own relatives. The son of Joseph and Mary too, like all Jewish boys, had to submit to the ritual eight days after his birth.[36] At that moment his parents gave him the name Jesus.

"Jesus" (the word is the same in Latin and comes from the Greek Iησοῦς) is the transliteration of the Aramaic *Yēshū*. Aramaic, the language then spoken in Palestine, belonged to the Semitic family. The older form corresponding to *Yēshū* was *Yēshuāh*, or *Jehosua*, which, etymologically, means "Jehovah is the savior" and which is given in the Old Testament as *Joshua*.

The mythologists, in their attempts to deny the historical existence of Jesus, seek in the symbolic meaning of his name a confirmation of their conviction that, through the name, the Christians sought to indicate nothing more or less than the sun-god, the savior of humanity.[37] But it has justly been called to their attention that faith in Jesus has made him a god, rather than the converse.[38] Hence, it makes little difference whether he be called by some other name and "Jesus" be merely an attribute. In addition, ample evidence may be cited from a variety of sources, not merely Biblical, that the name "Jesus" was not infrequent among the Jews.

The ritual observances that were supposed to accompany the entry of every son of Israel into life did not stop with circumcision and the selection of a name. The mother was considered unclean, just as in the period of her menstrual flow, for seven days if she had borne a son and for twice as long if the child was a girl. After that she had still to remain apart, not touching any holy thing and not being allowed to enter the Temple, for thirty-three days more if she had had a son and for sixty-six if the child was female. When this period had run its course, the woman was expected to undertake her own purification with the appropriate sacrifice: the offering of two pigeons or two young doves.[39]

Whether a boy or a girl, the child, if it was the first-born, belonged by law to Yahweh,[40] like the first-born of all domestic animals and the first fruits of the fields. Centuries before the birth of Jesus, an end had been put to the barbarous custom, common to all the primitive Semitic peoples, of sacrificing the first-born to idols in a ritual murder. The immolation had been supplanted by the symbolic offering of a yearling lamb to the priest. It was possible also, however, to redeem the first-born with a payment of five shekels.

The shekel (the word is the same in Hebrew), a silver coin of Phoenician origin, was the prescribed coin for all the sacred tributes to the Temple. It weighed somewhat less than half an ounce. A half-shekel corresponded roughly to two Greek drachmas or two Roman denarii, both of which were silver. The lesser Hebrew coin was the gerah (which means "grain" or "seed"), worth about one-twenty-fourth of a shekel, like the Roman as and the Greek obol; it represented the commercial value of a cluster of grapes or of four or five figs.

With much sacrifice, we can imagine, Joseph scraped together the necessary sum in order to take it to the Temple with Jesus and Mary when the ritual days of purification had been completed. Five shekels represented about as much as a humble artisan like Joseph could earn in twenty days of hard work.[41]

At the Temple

The Temple of Jerusalem, the religious and political focus of the Hebrew people, was, in the days of Jesus, being constructed for the third time. The most ancient structure, of Biblical memory, was the famous Temple of Solomon, built with cedars and spruces of Lebanon, which had been traded by Phoenicia in exchange for wheat and oil; its squared masses, which had required about two hundred thousand workmen,[42] had been destroyed by Nebuchadnezzar in 586 B.C. Seventy years later, on its ruins, the Hebrews returning from their Babylonian exile had built a more modest successor. Then Herod the Great, desiring to leave a monument to his own magnificence, had set about enlarging the building, by now some five hundred years old, and enhancing it with porticoes, terraces, walls, and ornaments in marble and gold.[43] The new additions, clumsy and ponderous (the Hebrews have left us no artistic achievements, whether in painting, in sculpture, or in architecture[44]), showed nonetheless some foreign influence, having been vaguely modeled on the pagan temples.

At the time when Joseph and Mary presented themselves for her purification, the work had not been completed and the labors were continuing. At the Nicanor Gate, which marked the boundary between that part of the Temple to which women were admitted and the section reserved for the men, the husband and wife stopped and offered the two young doves to a priest. Following the prescribed ritual, he placed one of the birds on the sacrificial altar, cut its throat, and, turning its head down, held the bird so that the blood flowed down the side of the altar. Then he removed the crop and the feathers, which he threw behind the altar on the side facing east; he broke the wings, without, however, cutting them or touching them with metal, and tossed the bird on a brazier, already burning, where it was completely consumed.[45] The other dove was also killed in the same manner, so that its blood was sprinkled on the altar, but the body was retained by the priest as his property.[46] The sacrifice having been completed, the priest approached Mary, who had stood with bowed head, and declared her cleansed. Then Joseph proffered the five shekels for the ransom of Jesus, and, with Mary and the new son of Israel, left the holy place.

Actually, before the purification, Luke injects a strange incident into his narrative. While Joseph was wandering in bewilderment among the porticoes of the Temple and Mary followed, tenderly cradling the baby in her arms, the obvious confusion of the rustic couple attracted the attention of an old man—"just and devout," Luke calls him—named Simeon.[47] He made haste to approach the family, and taking Jesus out of the arms of Mary, who flushed with anger, he spoke in prophecy, hailing the child as the expected Savior.

By a phenomenon rather frequent in the Gospels, this incident is duplicated, probably to emphasize the aura of lofty destiny that emanated from Jesus even as a child. Luke himself says that, immediately afterward, an eighty-four-year-old woman named Anna, who spent her days in fasting and prayer, never leaving the Temple and living on the charity of the faithful to whom she prophesied, hobbled up to the couple and, bent under her infirmities, looked on the child and acclaimed him as the Savior.[48]

This same Evangelist, Luke, had the good sense to temper the absurdity of such predictions by adding that Mary gave no credence to the praises lavished on her child.[49] The concentration with which she sought to dissuade Jesus from his religious activity almost as soon as he had begun it shows that she never believed he had been called. Besides, it is probable that Simeon and Anna had a thousand times heaped similar adulation on other infants brought to the Temple to be redeemed, in the hope of flattering the parents into greater alms.

The double prophecy, reported by Luke for purposes of homage, provides no basis, however, for believing that the expectation of a "savior" was in fact widespread among the populace or that his arrival was considered imminent. It is true that political and social conditions in Palestine in those days were so painful and intolerable that at least the poorest of the masses lived in constant agitation, wishing, even if with very little hope, for a complete upheaval. In no other people has pride of race taken such deep root as among the Hebrews, carried to the point of despising other peoples, and in no other people has th[...] a drive so capable of be[...] y form of oppression. T[...] rs from the day-to-day fa[...]

Living originally [...] e vast Semitic family, ha[...] l- dees about 1800 B.C., [...] s, and found refuge in the p[...] le Egyptians, who were much more advanced, brought about considerable change in their customs and religious beliefs. These Egyptian influences were already known to the ancients,[50] although many Catholics deny this today.[51] The Egyptian uprising of about 1300 B.C. that freed the land of the Nile from the oppression of the Hittites also rid it of the presence of the Hebrews.

This was a historic development for the Hebrew people. The second book of the Old Testament, Exodus, tells the epic of their flight to escape persecution by the Egyptians, through the treacherous marshes of the Nile Delta (the Biblical legend calls it a miraculous crossing of the Red Sea) and then across the desert. Moses, the man who, according to tradition, led the Hebrews and was able to prevent their dispersal, is celebrated as an exceptional being to whom miracles are ascribed, such as the universally known story of striking the rock and bringing forth water.[52] The Roman historian Tacitus was the first to offer a rationalistic explanation of this marvel: Moses had espied a herd of onagers (wild asses) running away behind some cliffs, and this had given the patriarch an intuitive certainty that somewhere near the cliffs there must be an oasis with a spring.[53] The discovery of water was a vast relief to the fugitives, who were thus enabled to carry on their trek for six days more and at last to reach the place where the desert ended and they could see the green plains of Moab in the land of Canaan. Their battles with the peoples already established in the region persisted for many years, and the Hebrews, who like all pastoral and nomadic peoples had lived divided into tribes, with a patriarchal, familial structure, recognized the need to unite under military leaders capable of organizing them for the conquest of the Promised Land. This was the period of the Judges, with its transition from the nomadic to the settled life, from the clan to the village.

Following the immediate precedent of the neighboring peoples, hostile or friendly, the Hebrews established their state in a monarchical form and developed their religion in a nationalistic direction. The priestly caste made certain of the absolute obedience of the people by spreading the legend of a "covenant" that God himself had entered into with Moses at the outset of the flight from Egypt. As the foundation of the Covenant, Yahweh promised the Hebrew people eternal protection and security in Palestine, *provided* they always observed his law and remained faithful to him. Yahweh was ready to make the Hebrews "a peculiar treasure to me above all people";[54] as multiplied as "the dust of the earth";[55] "as the stars of the heaven, and as the sand which is upon the sea shore."[56] They would become "a great nation,"[57] and they would occupy "this land, from the river of Egypt unto the great river, the river Euphrates."[58]

In exchange for these promised magnificences, the Hebrew people would be obligated to keep faith with the Law that the priests claimed to have discovered in the Temple of Jerusalem, written on scrolls going back to Moses himself. The commandments of the Law,

rigorously in force in the days of Jesus, were embodied in the Pentateuch—that is, the first five books of the Old Testament: Genesis,
Exodus, Leviticus, Numbers, and Deuteronomy.

The Expectation of the Messiah

After the Hebrews had finally conquered Palestine, their government continued to maintain its theocratic form. The power of
the priestly caste was unshakable, and the kings themselves had to
accept investiture through consecration with holy oil (olive oil perfumed with myrrh, cinnamon, calamus, and cassia).[59] Therefore, the
royal title was Messiah (in Hebrew, Māshīah; in Aramaic, Meshīhā),
which is the past participle of the verb māshah and means "a-
nointed." The Greek equivalent is Χριστός (Christos), which is also
the past participle of the verb "to anoint" (χρίω), phonetically transcribed into Latin as Christus.[60]

The country was definitively pacified under King David (d. ca.
973 B.C.); thus, by antonomasia, the realm was called the Kingdom of
David, and the Old Testament is full of prophecies that assure to the
king's dynasty perpetual possession of the throne. But the nation remained united only until 935 B.C., when, in reaction against administrative centralization and the fiscal exactions of King Solomon and
his son, Rehoboam, the old separatist tendencies took the ascendant
and the Hebrews split into two kingdoms, Israel and Judah. Between
721 and 586 B.C., both fell to Assyrian-Babylonian domination, and
their leaders were deported to Mesopotamia. In addition, many of
the artisans and merchants preferred to move to the conquerors'
country, where they could more easily amass money. Hence it is inaccurate to speak of the "Babylonian captivity." The only real victim
to suffer the consequences of the defeat was the common man, who
had no means of emigrating and remained where he was, abandoned
to his own resources and shamefully despoiled.

Even after the Babylonian dominance was terminated, the Hebrews never again regained their independence. At first they were
under the influence of the Persians, who had defeated the Babylonians, and then they were subjugated by Alexander the Great, the
conqueror of the Persians; ultimately—after having been the prize

for which the kings of Syria and Egypt contended in succession to Alexander—they came under Roman sovereignty.

The loss of liberty, the deterioration of social and economic conditions, and the decline of their religion were the causes that, from the period of the so-called Babylonian captivity on, gave rise among the Hebrews to the wave of seers (rō'hīm or hōzīm) and prophets (nebī'īm). Ever more numerous and more angry, they were the defenders of pure Yahwism against the introduction of foreign cults, mourning the vanished freedom of the nation as the consequence of the Jews' transgressions against the laws of God, but also arming the soul of the people with the promise of the return of divine protection if they would return to their ancient ways. The people consoled themselves for their misery and their subjection with the hope that, one day or another, some descendant of the house of David would appear to claim his rights to the throne and to restore the country to its past glory when he had been consecrated as the Messiah.

Flavius Josephus, the Jewish historian already cited who was virtually a contemporary of Jesus, says that what especially stimulated the Jews was "an ambiguous oracle," discovered in the text of the Holy Scriptures, according to which one of their compatriots in their own times would achieve domination over all the inhabited world.[61] With the passage of time, which made such an eventuality increasingly more improbable, the hope for such a champion tended, at least among the most miserable mass of the people, to magnify itself into the wish for a pacifying king who would bring about a period of justice and collective well-being.

The Slaughter of the Innocents

In the years immediately preceding the birth of Jesus, conditions in Palestine had grown even worse.[62] In 63 B.C., Pompey the Great had conquered the country and annexed it to Syria. His legate, Scaurus, in order to facilitate his occupation of Jerusalem, had insinuated himself into the rivalries of the last descendants of the Hasmoneans, Aristobulus II and Hyrcanus II. The latter, insensible in the face of the common danger and hoping only to assure himself the throne, assisted the Romans with his Idumean adviser, Antipater, besieging his brother, Aristobulus II, in the Holy City. Scaurus, having accomplished his purpose, dispensed summary justice, getting rid of Aristobulus II, conferring on Hyrcanus II the rank of high priest, with a certain political power over Judea, and appointing Antipater king of Idumea.

In 47 B.C., Julius Caesar, by now master of the Roman Empire, established Antipater as *epitropos* (procurator) of Judea as well, and granted him Roman citizenship. In 43, Antipater died, and his son Herod, who despite his extreme youth had already learned how to work his way into the good graces of the Romans, was appointed tetrarch of Judea by Mark Antony, who had ruled Asia as one of the triumvirate that included Octavian and Lepidus. A few years later, Herod managed to have himself named king of Judea by Emperor Augustus.

Endowed with exceptional talents of mind and body,[63] expert in the use of arms, a good leader, a first-class hunter, and prodigiously industrious, Herod the Great (73?–4 B.C.) possessed a marvelous intuition for politics, which clearly showed him, quite aside from all abstract ideology, where his own best interests lay.[64] Flattering those more powerful than himself, arrogant to those weaker, he was devoid completely of moral scruples. Furthermore, he was not a Jew: he was an Idumean, a barbarian, a usurper of power, and, what was worse, a friend of the Roman occupier. This was enough to explain the hate with which he was surrounded and the many plots that threatened his life. From the very beginning, therefore, he had to rule despotically and shrewdly in order to rid himself of his rivals. In fact, in order to legitimize his usurpation of the Judean throne, and in the hope of putting an end to the claims of the Hasmonean dynasty, he married the beautiful Mariamne of that family in 37 B.C., renouncing his first wife, the Arab Doris, with whom he had had a son named Antipater. But Mariamne, too, allowed herself to be persuaded by her mother, Alexandra, and her brother, Aristobulus III, to plot against Herod. Warned in time by his own sister, Salome, the tyrant exploded the intrigue and ordered the execution of all the participants, including his wife—Mariamne was barely twenty years old (she was twelve when she married him).

Herod then set out to gain the good opinion of his subjects and to demonstrate his might with grandiose building projects: the royal palace on the western hill of Jerusalem (although he preferred to spend his time in Jericho, in a delightful oasis only a few hours away from the capital) and the new Temple, on which work was still continuing when Jesus died. In addition, he rebuilt Sebaste, in Samaria, and Caesarea, on the coast.[65]

But in 7 B.C. his reign was plagued with another family plot. This time, the rebels were two of his own sons: Alexander and Aristobulus, whose mother was Mariamne the Hasmonean and whom he had sent to Rome for their schooling, in the home of the senator Asinius Pollio. Discovering the plot in time, perhaps through information from his eldest son, Antipater, Herod handed over to the mob of Jericho the three hundred accomplices of Alexander and Aristobulus: these two he caused to be strangled in Sebaste.

It is said that when Emperor Augustus learned of this crime, he summed it up in a skillful Greek pun: "It is better to be Herod's pig [ὗς, $h\bar{u}s$] than his son [υἱός, $hyos$]"[66]—an allusion to the Jews' well-known aversion to swine-flesh; Herod would not have killed a pig so lightly as he murdered his sons.

It was logical that to the population of Palestine those who had been killed in an unsuccessful attempt to rebel against the tyrant should seem victims. And this massacre· passed into contemporary memory as the Slaughter of the Innocents.

The Gospel story of a massacre of children less than two years old and born within the boundaries of Bethlehem, ordered by Herod on the occasion of the birth of Jesus,[67] gives ground for the belief that it was adapted from the historical fact just reported; it also offers analogies with the Biblical midrash (ancient Hebrew exegesis) of Moses, rescued from a slaughter of Hebrew children in Egypt,[68] and with similar legends in other Oriental religions.

The Comet and the Three Kings

If it is possible to concede that Matthew's account of the Slaughter of the Innocents is a modification of an authentic historical event that occurred in the period of the birth of Jesus, the year 7 B.C. becomes still more plausible as the date of the Nativity.

One must determine whether confirmation is to be found in the coincidence of the other important event also emphasized by Matthew: the appearance of a comet.[69] Since the Greek text of the Gospel speaks generically of an ἀστήρ (astēr)—that is, a "luminous heavenly body"—which the Latin Vulgate translates as *stella* ("star")—the researches of the astronomers have included, in addition to comets, the conjunctions of planets and other heavenly phenomena. Naturally, there is no lack of those who would deny the Gospel story any authenticity, and they recall that the births or the deaths of other famous persons were—according to legend—accompanied by similar manifestations. The Roman historian Justin relates that a comet appeared at the birth of Mithridates and at his accession to the throne; Suetonius records the appearance of a comet in the sky at the death of Julius Caesar;[70] and so on. Others argue that the comet was introduced by Matthew solely to fulfill a Biblical prophecy.[71]

The investigations of scientists into long-past celestial phenomena that might have had some relation with the one reported by Matthew have produced conflicting results. Edmund Halley, the astronomer who measured the parabolic movement of some twenty-four comets, succeeded in tracing one in particular, even in its most ancient appearances, but the nearest it came to the time of Jesus was A.D. 22, and hence it could not be accepted. According to the famous Kepler, a conjunction of Saturn and Jupiter in the constellation of Pisces, observed by him on December 17, 1603, should have been visible also, among other dates, in the year 7 B.C.[72] Kepler's finding seems to have been confirmed by the German P. Schnabel, who, in 1925, deciphering cuneiform texts in Babylonia, found reports of the same conjunction in the year 7 B.C. and who in fact was able to establish that in that year the phenomenon could be seen between the end of February and the first nights of December.[73]

And it is precisely Babylonia or Persia that must be considered the home of the Magi who, according to Matthew's narrative, reached Jerusalem under the guidance of the comet.[74] Matthew indicates their origin with the words ἀπὸ ἀνατολῶν (apo anatolōn), which mean, generically, "from the east." With respect to Palestine, such an expression can mean only Persia or Mesopotamia. The word "magician," which has the same Sanskrit root (*mahat*) as the Greek μέγας (mēgas) and the Latin *magnus,* was in fact employed for both the

Persian priest and the Chaldean soothsayer and astrologer. But it makes no sense to wonder, as for example Giuseppe Ricciotti does,[75] whether, in following that sign, the Magi expected to find their *Sanshyant*. The sacred writings of Persia, it is true, speak of a savior who shall be born of a virgin, but there is no mention of an astral phenomenon to announce his birth.

If it is unacceptable to admit that the episode of the Magi is a legend, one must believe that they were Persian or Chaldean astronomers, or disciples of Zoroaster,[76] who had gone to Jerusalem expressly to be present at the event that their calculations had foreseen.

How many were these Magi? Matthew does not say, and all the other Gospels, including the apocryphal ones, are silent on the subject. Oriental tradition puts their number at twelve. But the fifth-century Armenian Gospel of the Infancy limits them, for the first time, to three,[77] undoubtedly on the basis of the three gifts (gold, frankincense, and myrrh) that Matthew too says they presented to the infant. In this apocryphal Gospel, the three Magi are considered kings, and they are even identified by names: Melkon, or Melchior, king of the Persians; Gaspar, king of the Indians; and Balthasar, king of the Arabs. Later, popular imagination further embroidered the legend, transforming the Magi into representatives of the three races known to the ancient world: the white, the yellow, and the black, all paying tribute to Christianity. In modern times, they have been interpreted as "the old theologies that recognize the revelation; knowledge, which abases itself before innocence; riches, prostrating itself at the feet of poverty."[78]

According to Matthew, the arrival of the Magi in Jerusalem threw Herod into great apprehension;[79] perhaps in fear of a revolution,[80] he hastily summoned the chief priests and the learned men and ordered the massacre of all boys under two years of age in Bethlehem and its environs. We have already noted the historical event on which the story in all probability was based. Obviously, it was exploited to accentuate the special predestination of Jesus from the moment of his birth, without taking into consideration that it is a rather infelicitous invention to imagine God inaugurating the Savior's life on earth with so monstrous a deed and that, if Jesus were sent by God or if he were God himself, no human power could stop him before he had accomplished his mission.[81]

The flight into Egypt, in its turn, provides the apocryphal Gospels with subject matter for astounding tales and the stories of the newborn child's first miracles: serpents, lions, and leopards that prostrate themselves as he passes; wolves that amble peaceably among Joseph's sheep; palm trees that bow down spontaneously to offer their dates; heathen idols that in the presence of Jesus shatter in fragments to the ground . . .

The historical probability of the tribute of the Magi and the flight into Egypt is seriously compromised, too, by diverse chronological problems and contradictions. They defeat every effort of the harmonists—those exegetes who profess to be able to reconcile the stories of the canonical Evangelists and deny that any of the four might have slipped into inaccuracy. The most striking incongruity lies in the fact that Matthew puts the visit of the Magi immediately before the slaughter of the innocents and the flight into Egypt, while Luke, saying nothing of any of this, reports that Jesus was taken to the Temple forty days after his birth and that immediately afterward, Joseph, Mary, and the child went back to Nazareth.[82] If there had really been any danger for Jesus, Joseph would certainly not have dared to take him to Jerusalem and offer the child to the lion's jaws;[83] if, however, the visit of the Magi had followed the redemption in the Temple, the authorities would no longer have been able to find Jesus in Bethlehem. The harmonists are constrained to accept the fantasy that the visit of the Magi, the slaughter of the innocents, the flight into Egypt, and the return to Palestine were all compressed into the forty-day interval between the birth of Jesus and the ceremony in the Temple.[84] Not too much time for so many climaxes![85] The Gospel of Pseudo-Matthew resolves the problem (or complicates it) by setting the adoration of the Magi two years after the Nativity,[86] and this solution is also embraced by some modern students.[87]

The Roman liturgy has thus been the victim of a contamination of dates and names. As we have already noted, the Eastern tradition celebrates the birth of Jesus on January 6 under the name Epiphany, which means the "manifestation," or "appearance," of the deity on earth. The Western tradition, setting the date of the Nativity as December 25, in order to make it coincide with the feast of the sun-god, has assigned the visit of the Magi to January 6. In Italy, the word "Epiphany" has been corrupted into "Befana," and the religious anniversary has been overlaid with the myth of the Befana, the old witch who, the children believe, comes down the chimney with their presents.

From Herod to Antipas

If the story of the flight into Egypt has evolved, in the apocryphal Gospels, into a hodgepodge of unbelievable popular legends, the tales transmitted by the apocryphal Evangelists on the subsequent events of the childhood of Jesus are no less implausible. In the canonical Gospels, on the other hand, the only fact recounted is the removal of the holy family from Bethlehem to Nazareth. Matthew says that they stayed in Egypt until the death of Herod and then returned to Palestine, but, learning that Herod had been succeeded by his son Archelaus, they decided to abandon their home once more and live in Galilee.[88] The Evangelist apparently seeks to imply that Joseph feared in Archelaus a continuation of Herod's rages and persecutions.

No doubt these latest developments in Judea were such as to make a humble workman like Joseph, who wanted to savor in peace

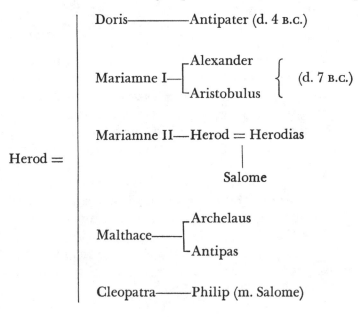

the simple joys of family life with a young wife and an infant son, look for a quieter residence. The last years of Herod's reign had been frightful. Always suspicious, he had finally had his heir, Antipater, imprisoned and, with another son, Herod, disinherited, dividing the kingdom among the three youngest sons: Archelaus and Antipas, the children of the Samaritan Malthace, and Philip, whose mother was Cleopatra of Jerusalem.

In 4 B.C., when he was in his seventies, Herod was stricken with a number of serious illnesses: intestinal infections, swellings of the legs, respiratory difficulties. He may have had ulcers or intestinal cancer.[89] At first he sought relief at the sulphur springs of Callirhoe (now Hamman er-Zārah) on the eastern shore of the Dead Sea, but seized with fainting fits at his first bath, he rushed back to his palace in Jericho.

Knowing that the tyrant's ailments were incurable and that he had little time to live, two Jerusalem teachers, Judas ben Sariphaeus and Mattathias ben Margalit, incited their disciples to revolt. Their first act was to tear down the golden eagle, a heathen symbol, that Herod had ordered affixed as an ornament on the main gate of the Temple. Though bedridden, Herod still had enough strength to put down the rebellion, ordering that the two instigators be burned alive, that forty of their accomplices be strangled, and that the high priest be deposed.[90] Flavius Josephus records an eclipse of the moon on the night the executions were carried out, and astronomical studies make it possible to establish the date as March 13 of the year 4 B.C.[91]

Well aware that discontent was widespread and that vengeance would be taken for the executions of Judas and Mattathias, Herod summoned many of the major notables of Judea to Jericho, under threat of death if they did not attend, and had them all herded into the hippodrome; then, weeping and pleading, he adjured his sister, Salome, to have them butchered by his troops as soon as he died.

Meanwhile, his diseases gave him no peace; the pain was at times so cruel that his cries and curses rang throughout the palace. In one of these spasms, while peeling an apple, he tried to kill himself with a knife, but was forcibly prevented by those in the room, as the horrified women ran shrieking through the building. Antipater

FIGURE III
GALILEE

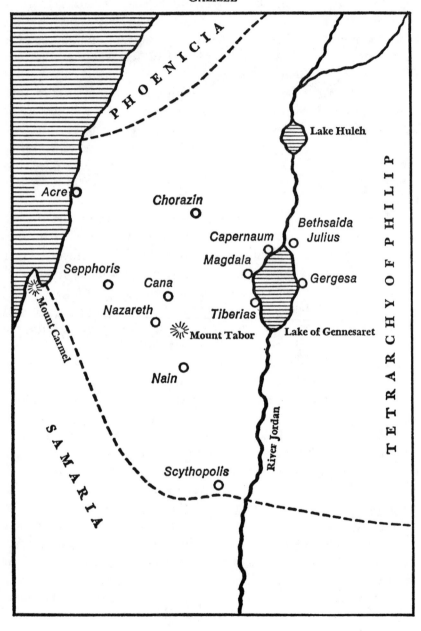

in his cell could hear the cries, and, hoping that what he was hearing was mourning at his father's death, prevailed on his jailer to set him free. Herod learned of this from the jailer. Though delirious, he mustered strength enough to raise himself on his elbows in his bed and to command his guards to find Antipater and kill him. Five days later, at the end of March of the year 4 B.C., Herod too was dead, after atrocious sufferings.

The tyrant's death set off a new rebellion, which broke out simultaneously in Judea, Perea, and Galilee.[92] But Herod's son Archelaus, heir to the royal title, made it clear that he was no less resolute and no less savage than his father. He had his troops at once surround the Temple, in the courtyards of which the rebels had gathered, and massacre everyone on the premises: three thousand persons, many of whom were harmless pilgrims who had come to Jerusalem for the feast of Passover.

It is not at all surprising that such a chain of bloody deeds should have induced Joseph to leave Judea and seek shelter in the opposite end of Palestine—in Galilee. (See Figure III.) Here the ruler was Antipas, the second in line of Herod's surviving sons. Actually, Augustus never fully accepted Herod's testament, and, abolishing the title of king, he divided the province of Palestine into four parts (tetrarchies). Archelaus, with the title of ethnarch, was given the region that included Judea, Idumea, and Samaria; Antipas, under the title of tetrarch, governed Galilee and Perea; and Philip, also called tetrarch, received the dry northern territories bordering on Syria—that is, Iturea, Gaulanitis, Trachonitis, Auranitis, and Batanea. The fourth tetrarchy, that of Abilene, which lay within Syria, adjoining Lebanon, remained in the hands of one Lysanias, a stranger to the family of Herod.

[4]

THE UNKNOWN YEARS

The Childhood of Jesus

How did Jesus spend his childhood in Nazareth?

The apocryphal Gospels contain a fantastic collection of strange incidents, intended to emphasize his power to perform miracles even in the earliest years of his life. Some of these tales are delightful in their naïveté and their picturesque realism; most are amazingly unseemly, for they portray a capricious, spiteful, and vindictive child, as omnipotent as a heathen god.[1] He beat two children to death because they had played some harmless trick on him; when their parents complained, he had them stricken blind. Similarly, he took revenge on the village schoolmaster, who tried in vain to make him learn the alphabet. Properly scolded by Joseph, who had seized him by the ear, Jesus retorted arrogantly: "Thou mayst look at me, but touch me not. Knowest thou not that I am not thy son? Let me alone!"

Aside from such absurd apocryphal stories, which are certainly later in origin than the fourth or fifth century A.D., there is no information on the boyhood of Jesus. Among the canonical Gospels, Luke alone refers to the period, and only briefly: "And the child grew, and waxed strong in spirit, filled with wisdom; and the grace of God was upon him."[2] Somewhat later, Luke makes a similar statement: "And Jesus increased in wisdom and stature."[3] This is the correct interpretation of Luke's text: ἡλικίᾳ καὶ χάριτι, rather than

56

with the meaning given by the Latin Vulgate: *"proficiebat aetate"* ("he grew in age"), which would be a tautology.

A historical reconstruction of the childhood of Jesus is therefore impossible. A curious book,[5] which attempts to establish an embarrassing parallelism between the life of Jesus and those of Napoleon I and Garibaldi, does however make one apt observation: the childhood of Jesus, like those of the two other great men, went its way without any remarkable occurrence that might have hinted at his destiny. We have to content ourselves with the idea of the normal existence of a little boy in the environment and circumstances of that time.

After the removal to Galilee, the family of Joseph and Mary increased, adding both sons and daughters. The canonical Gospels and some of the apocryphal Evangelists mention them often, and tell us the names of the sons: James (or Jacob), Joses (or Joseph), Judas, and Simon.[6] The Protevangelium of James adds the names of the daughters: Melkha and Eskha.

In connection with these brothers and sisters of Jesus, it is worth remarking that in the third and fourth centuries the Fathers of the Church began to engage in heated discussion of the subject. In his support of the perpetual virginity of Mary, Origen (d. ca. 254) was the first to suggest that the brothers of Jesus be considered his half-brothers, the children of an earlier marriage of Joseph.[7] Eusebius of Caesarea (d. 339), attributing the proposition to a nonextant history written by Hegesippus, fabricated the existence of a second Mary, sister to the Madonna, completely forgetting that, according to tradition, the Virgin had been an only child born almost miraculously to aged parents.[8] The second Mary was supposed to have been married to one Clopas (or Cleophas), Joseph's brother. The theory of Eusebius, or Hegesippus, was adopted by Jerome (d. 419), who, in a bitter battle with Helvidius, the monk Jovinian, and Bishop Bonosus of Illyria, declared explicitly that the so-called brothers of Jesus were in reality his "cousins."[9]

It would not be appropriate here to discuss the reasons of dogma that make it impossible for Christian theologians to accept the fact that Jesus really had siblings. Let us confine ourselves to a single remark on the weakness of the sole argument that might aid their thesis. They contend that since Hebrew lacked a word with the specific meaning of "cousin," the Evangelists must have been compelled to designate this relationship with the Hebrew word āḥ (in Aramaic, aḥā), which can mean "brother," "stepbrother," "cousin," "nephew," or, in general, any blood relative.[10] It is true that Hebrew lacks such a distinguishing term, but it must be pointed out that the Gospels of Mark, Luke, and John were written in Greek and that of Matthew was arrived at only through Greek tradition (if indeed it was not originally composed in that language). However, as for the Greek language, there is no question that it possesses separate nouns for "brother" and "cousin." Had the Evangelists been convinced that James, Joses, Judas, and Simon were not the brothers of Jesus, instead of ἀδελφοί (adelphoi) they would have used the word ἀνεψιοί (anepsioi). Moreover, in the Acts of the Apostles and in the Epistles of Paul, James at least is clearly identified as the brother of Jesus,[11] and the term cannot be interpreted to mean "brother *in* Jesus," as one student has suggested,[12] because for that concept both the Acts and the Epistles use a different formula. A modern Catholic investigator, Émile Le Camus, conceding the absurdity of the Madonna's having had a sister with the same name as her own, married to Clopas, has offered the suggestion that the Virgin herself, having been widowed, went to live with this Clopas or even was married to him: and then, in one way or another, the *cousins* of Jesus would have become his *brothers!*[13] Others believe that the two sisters—the two Marys—lived together after both had become widows.[14] Still others, accepting the existence of the second Mary, the wife of Clopas, inject a major complication by contending that the second, when she married Clopas, was already a widow with children (James and Joses), and that Clopas, too, was a widower with children (Judas and Simon).[15]

The Schooling of Jesus

Little fantasy is needed to suppose that Jesus, with his brothers/cousins, spent the days playing in the streets of Nazareth or wandering in the green countryside. Thus he learned by himself to recognize the various faces of nature, the people and places among which he lived, the fields, the plants, the animals.[16] Standing in the doorways of workshops, he watched how the skilled potters modeled jars and vases with light, caressing strokes of their deft hands; how sharp tools carved minute ornamentation into precious objects; he observed the tanners and the dyers; but above all he noted the patient drudgery of the men of the soil, the voices with which the shepherds called their flocks from the pen, the care with which the men sheared the sheep, led them to water, carried the smallest lambs in their arms . . .

On the Sabbath, a feast day for the Hebrews, he went with his father to the synagogue. This word, which comes from the Greek συναγωγή (sunagōgē), and which means "assemblage" or "community," has its Hebrew equivalent in knesset, which in Aramaic is kenīshtā'. It was an institution that had been born and developed during the Exile, as a makeshift place of worship for Jews too far away from the Temple of Jerusalem.[17] All the synagogues, built from the same design (a large hall between two colonnades or arcades),[18] were so oriented that the worshipers, once inside, always faced the Holy City. But there were no altars because no sacrifices were celebrated. The Jewish writer Robert Aron, who has published an interesting study of the society of Palestine in the days of Jesus, defines the synagogue as "a kind of club, which had no priesthood but where the faithful met to pray and to study."[19]

In the synagogue, the hazzan, aside from directing choirs, was also charged with teaching the elements of learning to the children. The Oriental didactic method (still employed today in many Asiatic countries) consisted of making all the students continually repeat in chorus, in a loud voice, the various verses and sentences they were to learn by heart. Consequently the verb shānāh ("to repeat") finally came to have the colloquial meaning of both "to teach" and "to learn." Besides, it would have been virtually impossible to learn directly by reading the scrolls. In Hebrew, words are (or were) all run together, and only their consonants were written. It was as if Dante, for example, composing the first line of his Divina Commedia ("Nel mezzo del cammin di nostra vita"), had written Nlmzzdlcmmn-dnstrvt. Yet once the passage had been learned by heart, it was easy to recognize the words in writing.

A fruitless debate has long been conducted on the question whether Jesus learned Greek as well.[20] One can in any case be absolutely certain that, in the Hebrew tradition, he received a thorough religious and patriotic indoctrination at home. This teaching governed, it is fair to say, every act and every moment of the day. The world in which the Israelite lived was wholly sacred, and in every circumstance, however commonplace or transient, he gave thanks to God, reciting a "blessing" (berākā): when he rose in the morning, when he dressed, when he laced his sandals, when he washed his hands, etc. There were blessings for meals, for sleep, even for the most intimate natural functions: "Blessed art thou, O Lord, who hast fashioned man with wisdom and hast created in him apertures and outlets. . . ."

The Christian tradition delights in imagining that on days when there was no school, Jesus loved to help his father in the carpenter shop—and it is not unlikely that this was so. Though it is barely credible, Justin Martyr, who lived more than a century later, insists that in Palestine he had often heard of ploughs fashioned in Joseph's shop and worked on by Jesus.[21]

Logically, Christian theology finds it vexing to have to admit that the Son of God, like all human beings, had to acquire knowledge through study.[22] Therefore, it was said that he possessed "the perfect knowledge of the blessed in heaven,"[23] but that he showed it only in stages, "otherwise he would not have been believed to be a real human being, if even in his childhood he had shown perfect maturity of knowledge and understanding."[24] Some have gone so far as to attempt to distinguish among the various kinds of knowledge available to Jesus:[25] (a) acquired knowledge, like all men; (b) inherent knowledge, through which, like God, he knew all the truths of the supernatural world; (c) beatific knowledge, the eternal enjoyment of the vision of God, a supernatural gift possible only for the blessed in heaven.

In the fourth and fifth centuries, however, the school of Agnoetism was strong. The name derived from the Greek ἄγνοια (agnoia), which means "ignorance," and the Agnoetae's theory was that Jesus, endowed with human characteristics as a real and concrete being, had shared in all the weaknesses of mankind, including ignorance. A similar view is held in modern days by the so-called kenotics, particularly the Anglican theologians—followers of the theory of kenosis (κένωσις), which means "dispossession" or "divestiture": God had given His son His own divine qualities (omniscience, omnipotence, omnipresence, etc.), but Jesus had made no use of them because he had stripped himself of them in order to limit himself.[26]

The esoterics, on the other hand, indulge themselves in the fantastic supposition that Jesus had prepared himself for his mission by traveling all during his youth—through India, Egypt, Persia— to the extent of becoming a disciple of the Lama of Tibet and the Himalayas, a follower of Buddha and Zoroaster![27]

In the Gospels, Jesus is shown as neither more nor less than other men of his time and class. Centuries earlier, Greek philosophy had laid the foundations for rationalism, but Jesus, in no way different from his contemporaries, still lived by superstition, believed in the devil and the angels, was convinced that disease was caused by demons in punishment for sin, saw the direct hand of God in all things human.

The First Passover

At the age of thirteen, when puberty began, the young Israelite left childhood behind and was invested as a Son of the Law (*bār mitzvāh*) in the Temple. This meant that he was now answerable for the performance of his religious and civic duties and that he had declared his submission to the commandments of the Law. Henceforth he was an adult and was obliged to go to Jerusalem each year to celebrate the Passover.

Actually, Luke reports that Jesus took part in this ceremony when he was only twelve.[28] The other Evangelists do not mention it. In any case, the rite was performed when Jesus went to Jerusalem for his first Passover.

To the Hebrews, Passover was one of the most important religious festivals. They converged on the Holy City not only from every part of Palestine but also from the most remote foreign lands in which they had settlements. In one year, Flavius Josephus says, three million persons went to Jerusalem for Passover.[29]

The festival was marked each year at the first full moon to follow the spring equinox. Since the Hebrew calendar divided the

months on a lunar basis—each began when the new moon appeared
—the first full moon of spring always fell on the fourteenth day of
Nisan, which was then reckoned as the first month of the year and
ran roughly from mid-March to mid-April.[30]

Passover was connected with the Hebrews' departure from
Egypt, as related in the Bible. The word (in Hebrew, *Pesaḥ*) does
not allude, however, as some believe, to "passing over" the Red Sea;
it derives from the legend that, in the tenth of the Egyptian plagues,
just prior to the Exodus, the angel of death "passed over" the houses
of the Jews and spared them. The Old Testament relates that Moses
ordered them, before they fled, to eat a quickly roasted lamb.[31] In
this immolation, students of comparative religion see the survival
of a ritual that goes back to prehistoric times: in many religions,
at a certain stage of development, the god is identified with a sacred
animal, which becomes the symbol (totem) and protector of a tribe
or of a group of blood relatives.[32] The immolation and the sacred
feast on the body of the animal thus assume the character of an
authentic theophagy: the victim, which represents the god, is consumed in order to renew the close tie between the faithful and their
deity and to obtain new strength.[33]

Other authorities offer a different explanation of the origin of
the totemic animal: it fulfills the unconscious need of the hunter to
spare some of his accustomed prey and thus to allay its anger and
turn aside its vengeance.[34]

Jesus, who was seeing this striking ceremony for the first time,
must certainly have been ineradicably impressed by it. His father
and the other men of the caravan that had traveled from Nazareth
had already seen to the purchase of the lamb, which was required
to be male, of unblemished fleece, and without physical defects, and
in the midst of a vast throng of pilgrims they all crowded into the
courtyard of the Temple. As the boy gazed in bewilderment on the
confusion of the noisy men and the thousands of bleating lambs,
he was suddenly transfixed by the high shrilling of trumpets. This
was the signal, given by a priest, that the number of worshipers in
the courtyard was now sufficient and the sacrifice could begin.[35] All
the rest of the faithful had to wait outside the Temple until their
turn arrived. Standing in two long rows, their hands and all their
robes already covered with blood, the priests dispatched the animals

with freshly whetted knives. Each priest caught the blood in a great cup, which, when it was full, he handed to a colleague. So, from hand to hand, the cups brimming with still-warm blood reached the altar, over which they were emptied.

All during the sacrifice, the worshipers were silent, while the priests chanted the Hallel, a selection from the Psalms that commemorated the miraculous flight of the Hebrews out of Egypt and that implored the blessing of God.

As soon as his lamb had been killed, the worshiper moved to one of the sides of the spacious courtyard, in the walls and columns of which hooks were embedded, to hang his animal and skin it. He had also to remove the entrails, including the liver and kidneys, and the tail, all of which were left in the Temple to be burned. The rest of the carcass, wrapped in the skin, was taken away. At sunset, the prescribed time, the animal was roasted, but its bones were not to be broken: it was impaled on two dried pomegranate branches in the form of a cross, the horizontal one intersecting the vertical at the level of the animal's shoulders.[36] Then the banquet, after prayers had been recited, proceeded according to a rigid program. The roast was seasoned with special salts and eaten with unleavened (ἄζυμος, *azumos*) bread—that is, bread not raised with yeast. This custom, too, has a special meaning, again recalling the flight from Egypt. Compelled to flee in haste, the Hebrews had had to snatch from the bins the dough that had been set to rise for making bread. But there had been no time for the leaven to work, and, when they made their first stop for rest and food, they could bake only unleavened bread.

Probably Jesus lay long awake that night. Since he was of a mystic turn, the events of the day and the solemn ritual of the banquet would have affected him profoundly. A thousand questions must have swirled in his mind, problems of basic religious meaning that neither his father nor the rustic hazzan of his village could have answered satisfactorily. His large, thoughtful eyes fixed on the arch of the night sky, the moon, and the infinite splendor of the stars, for the first time Jesus felt the mystery of divinity, of that God who had entered into a covenant with the patriarch Abraham, promising eternal protection to him and his posterity, that God who had watched over Isaac and Jacob and who had led Moses through the wilderness, but who now, angered by the lukewarm faith of the descendants of those patriarchs, seemed to have forgot his chosen people, and who, perhaps, was withdrawing his patronage until they should have repented and sued for forgiveness.

Jesus Among the Doctors

Since for the Jews the day began and ended with the sunset, the fifteenth day of Nisan immediately followed the sacrifice of the lambs. Commencing with the ritual feast, it was a day of "holy convocation."[37] Indeed, this was the most solemn period of the Passover. Under prohibitions even harsher than those governing the Sabbath, it was absolutely forbidden to engage in any activity.

But on the sixteenth of Nisan the streets of Jerusalem were again crowded with rejoicing pilgrims, on their way to the Temple to take part in another sacred ritual: the offering of a sheaf of wheat (matsāh) as the first fruit of the harvest. Actually, the harvest in Palestine began somewhat later, about the middle of April, but the observance had been established on this date, which was called matsōth (the plural of matsāh), in still another association with the deliverance from Egypt. When at last, after their heroic journey across the desert, the Israelites had crossed into the Promised Land, they could once more eat the fruits of the earth. They were in the valley of Jericho, which, lying near the Dead Sea in a depression more than sixteen hundred feet below sea level, enjoys a climate sufficiently warm and moist to allow grain to ripen earlier than in the other parts of Palestine.

The pilgrims were not obliged to spend the entire week of Passover in Jerusalem, but it is probable that in that year the group which included Joseph, Mary, and Jesus remained at least until the day of matsōth, because it was precisely on this day that a boy completing his twelfth or thirteenth year was to undergo the ritual of becoming bār mitzvāh. The Gospel of Luke, in fact, says that the holy family "fulfilled the days."[38]

What follows in Luke's account of the disappearance of Jesus is in no way unbelievable. There must have been wild confusion at the caravansary, where the camels and mules had been left, when the group decided to depart. It was a difficult task to lead out the animals, seat the women and the aged on them, and get under way without blocking the movement in the streets. Only at evening, when they made their first halt after about ten miles (because this was an ordinary day's march for a caravan), did Joseph and Mary become aware that their son was missing; they had assumed that he was farther back in the group, with some relative or friend.[39] Frightened, they went back at once to Jerusalem, allowing the caravan to go on without them. For one night and one day, they searched desperately through all the streets of the Holy City, in the caravansary, in every place they had stopped during their stay. At last, on the third day, they found the boy in the Temple, sitting among a group of "doctors," who were listening to him and questioning him.

These were the rabbis (teachers), who, following the traditional habit of the Jews, met regularly beneath the arcades of the Temple to discuss the problems of interpreting the Law. Anyone was free to join their discussions, but they were forbidden to ask payment. On other days, therefore, they worked at manual trades. Among the most famous rabbis of the time were Hillel and Shammai, each of whom had founded a school that had gathered a large following. Comparison of the doctrines handed down by these sages with certain passages of the Gospels seems to indicate that Jesus had known and followed the school of Hillel, which was less formal and more understanding and humane than that of his colleague.[40]

On this day, then, Jesus was there, sitting on the ground, a simple listener among other listeners.[41] Rabbinical custom dictated that only pupils, not rivals, might question the teachers, and Jesus hungered to know so many things concerning the faith of his fathers that his probing questions amazed everyone round him.[42] Yet there was nothing remarkable in the participation of a growing boy in such discussions. Flavius Josephus relates that he himself, at the age of fourteen, was accustomed to debate with the scholars of Jerusalem,[43] and we know from other records that the rabbis did not disdain to enter into argument with boys even younger. Hence, there is no need to suppose, as does the historian Maurice Goguel,[44] that the story of Jesus among the teachers was suggested by some confused tale of discord between Jesus and his family because of his plan to dedicate himself to religious preaching; nor to believe, with Bernhard Weiss,[45] that the incident points to a "revelation" of divinity on the part of Jesus—as if he, rather than the rabbis, had been conducting a school. In any case, it is certain that the author of this story, as contained in the Gospel of Luke, was not familiar with Palestinian customs and took no account of the fact that a Near Eastern boy of twelve or thirteen is already as mature in mind and body as Western youths are at eighteen or nineteen. The author thus saw at least an indication of precociousness in the behavior of Jesus.

When Mary had recovered her lost son after so much anguish, she could not restrain herself from angrily reproaching him for having, with typical boyish thoughtlessness, disappeared without a word to his parents: "Son, why hast thou thus dealt with us? behold, thy father and I have sought thee sorrowing." In the Greek text, it should be noted, Mary says, not "son" (which appears in a great many translations, including the King James), but, in obvious censure, "boy" (τέκνον, *teknon*),[46] rejecting the more affectionate term (υἱός, *hyos*). Jesus, excited by the arguments he had been having with the teachers, was not even aware of his impertinence in replying to his mother: "And why did ye seek me? Knew ye not that only here, in the house of God our Father, could I be found?"

Here I have made my own translation of the answer of Jesus, which in the text of the Gospels raises various problems.* First of all, not only the Greek but the Latin, literally translated, would read: "Knew ye not that I had to be *in these* [in Greek, ἐν τοῖς (*en tois*); in Latin, *in his*], that are of my Father?"[47] Therefore, the reply must be completed. Some consider it to mean "in this Temple,"[48] others "among these people."[49] In the second place, the play of words between Mary's phrase, "thy father," and that of Jesus, "my Father," would be impossible in Aramaic because that language lacks the possessive pronouns.[50] Finally, it is inconceivable that, at so early an age, Jesus would already have known of his divine paternity, if indeed he ever knew of it. The real meaning of his reply is obvious: he is declaring his determination to devote himself henceforth to religious activity. But, the Gospel passage concludes, his parents did not understand his meaning, and Jesus obediently returned with

* In the King James Bible, this passage reads: "How is it that ye sought me? wist ye not that I must be about my Father's business?"—TRANS.

them to Nazareth. His mother, nonetheless, "kept all these sayings in her heart,"[51] and a deep premonition made her weep in secret.

The Time Was Fulfilled

How did the vocation of Jesus begin? On the events of his life between the ages of twelve and thirty, the Gospels are inexplicably silent. Long ago Pascal complained: *"De trente-trois ans, il en vit trente sans paraître"* ("Out of thirty-three years, he lived thirty without making an appearance"). It is a long time, if we compare it to the three short years in which his public life was lived and ended. If we knew more, many of the questions relating to the origins of Christianity could be answered.

Was his vocation a sudden, unexpected summons, or did it grow out of prolonged, deliberate consideration? It is impossible to answer.

Socrates, the one man whose doctrines, whose dedication to the service of mankind, and whose unjust execution in the name of truth bring him closest to Jesus, was called to his mission by dreams and divine invitations, and finally by the words of the oracle Delphi to his friend Cherephon. Buddha grasped the nature of his duty at the moment of his first contact with the world, from which, until then, his father had kept him apart. St. Paul was suddenly illuminated on the road to Damascus. St. Augustine was called to conversion by a mysterious childish voice, which he ascribed to an angel. Of Jesus we have no knowledge in this respect. The greatest problem in attempting to present the history of his life is that of knowing how to distinguish the concept that he must have had of himself and of his mission from the concept of him that was entertained, after his death, by the first Christian community, by Paul and John, and, in the end, by the Fathers of the Church.[52]

Whatever the precise vocation of Jesus was, one may be sure that it became clarified step by step when he began to preach. Every man who has ever carried a great undertaking to completion and exerted a powerful influence on his time has always been helped by circumstances.[53] Genius, however great it be, is not enough for the innovator: it is necessary as well that the epoch in which the innovator's genius can demonstrate its full force be precisely that in which he is living. Born a hundred years earlier or later, Luther could never have accomplished his Reformation; today, Napoleon would be at most a run-of-the-mill general.

Jesus was no exception to this general rule. When he set about his mission, "the time," in the phrase of the Gospels, "was fulfilled." The political and social decadence of Palestine was reflected in increasingly intolerable social and moral ferment. The rich, and with them the priestly caste, lived in an attitude of extreme servility to their Roman conquerors. Their sole concern was the maintenance of their own privileges and their own wealth[54] and the preservation of reverence for the Temple, which entailed the obligation of offerings and the payment of tithes by the people at large. This party of collaborationist conservatives called themselves Sadducees (in Hebrew, *Saddukim*), perhaps after a putative founder called Zadok,[55] or more likely because the priestly class, which was a part of it, claimed descent from one Sadok, or Zadok, who had been the high priest in the days of David and Solomon.[56] The opposing party, to which the educated classes in particular adhered, rejected all compromise with the occupiers. It carried on the intransigent policy of the Hasideans (in Hebrew, *Hassidim*), who had been the great inspiration of resistance to erosive forces until the dynasty of the Maccabees allowed itself to be corrupted by foreign influences.[57] Therefore, they were called in the vernacular Pharisees (in Hebrew, *Perushim*, which means "separated"), although they preferred the name *Haberim*—that is, "equals," or fellow members. The masses, alienated from the economic interests of the Sadducees and indifferent to the intransigence of the Pharisees, yet compelled to suffer much more than these others from the weight of foreign oppression, were the more readily influenced by the words of the prophets and seers, who at one moment adjured them to be patient and at another sharpened their discontent in vehement tirades against the rich, the profiteers, and the enemies of God and country.

In A.D. 6, when Jesus was thirteen years old (if we accept the hypothesis that the date of his birth should be fixed in 7 B.C., the year of the so-called slaughter of the innocents and of the appearance of the comet), Palestine was the scene of important historic developments that heightened the unrest of the populace. In this year, a delegation of Jews went to Rome to protest against Archelaus, the ethnarch of Judea, Samaria, and Idumea. Augustus wished to mollify them, and, summoning Archelaus to Rome, exiled him to Gaul. But this made no improvement in the lives of the conquered Hebrews. In fact, the emperor decided to incorporate the three domains of Archelaus into Syria under the administration of a procurator directly responsible to the governor of Syria, who at that time was Sulpicius Quirinus. The first such procurator, known only as Coponius, established himself in Caesarea on the coast, with Greek and Syrian auxiliary troops (about three thousand men), and also posted an armed garrison in Jerusalem, in the Tower of Antonia, from which it was a simple matter to keep watch on the interior of the Temple and on the center of the city.[58] At the same time, Quirinus deposed the high priest then in office, replacing him with Annas, who was to retain the title until A.D. 15.[59]

The new territorial annexation naturally made a census necessary (the one mistakenly dated by Luke as the year in which Jesus was born). It was sharply inscribed in the memory of the Jews because it was accompanied by bloody events: a popular revolt in Jerusalem, which culminated in the siege on Sabinus, Roman procurator for taxes, in the Palace of Herod, and a simultaneous rising in Galilee, led by a certain Judas of Gamala, who was nevertheless called Judas the Galilean[60] because his headquarters were in the town of Sepphoris. This Judas was the son of another well-known rebel, Hezekiah, who had been executed at the order of Herod.[61]

Confronted by these grave affronts to the prestige of Rome, Quirinus was moved to invade Galilee, occupy Sepphoris, and put it to the torch, taking the entire population as slaves; then he marched to rescue Sabinus. His arrival loosed terror on Jerusalem. Thousands of persons were seized and some two thousand paid on crosses for their brave attempt at freedom.[62]

The forces of Judas the Galilean became known as Zealots, from the Greek ζῆλος (zēlos), which means "jealousy," "enmity," "opposition," or "rebellion," or as Cananaeans (κavavaîoι), from the Aramaic qan'ān (in Hebrew, qānnā'), which has the same meaning.[63] But the Romans called them sicarii, "dagger men," meaning "assassins." The Zealots were the extreme wing of the anti-Roman resistance party.[64]

Jesus could not have been unmoved by the events of his time:

Sepphoris was only two leagues from Nazareth, and the whole of Galilee had traditionally been a hotbed of fierce nationalism.[65] It is incredible that the young Jesus did not share the fears and the hopes of the people among whom he lived. But, even if later some Zealots were drawn to the ranks of his disciples, it is perhaps rash to suppose, as does Oscar Cullmann,[66] that Jesus himself was a member of this bloodthirsty sect. He was much more inclined to an attitude of hope for better times, based on his faith in divine providence. During his youth, he had probably subjected himself frequently, as a means of mortification, to the Nazirite oath, which, as we know, consisted of a vow of fasting, abstinence, and chastity.

Among the Essenes

Although his vocation had not yet become clearly defined in his own mind, we may suppose, Jesus often spent long periods in solitude and meditation, wandering through the Galilean countryside, sitting with taciturn shepherds who respected his silence, or resting on the shores of the Lake of Gennesaret (Sea of Galilee) to watch the fishermen laboriously hauling their nets to shore, while his heart was filled with hope and anxiety.

It is quite likely that during these long walks Jesus came into contact with some community of Essenes. They were a religious sect, organized about two centuries earlier, whose headquarters were in the vicinity of the Dead Sea, but a number of small branches were scattered throughout Palestine. The name of the sect may have been derived from the Aramaic *Hássîdîm* ("pious men," "saints"), or from *Hâsayim* ("physicians," "healers"), and hence the Essenes are often confused with the analogous Egyptian sect of the Therapeutae.[67] The Essenes were dissenters who had voluntarily adopted the monastic life, abandoning their families and renouncing their possessions in disgust at the conditions in the country. An extraordinary sect—such is the phrase of the learned Roman Pliny the Elder[68]— that never became extinct even though its members lived without women, because it constantly recruited new converts.

Almost daily the belief is gaining ground, despite the denials and the doubts of many students,[69] that Jesus was indeed a member of some Essene group. The first to suggest this was Karl F. Bahrdt

(1741–92), who was considered a dreamer;[70] offering more supporting evidence, the Jewish scholar Joseph Klausner (1874–1958) repeated the theory;[71] but it is only with the latest archaeological discoveries that we have confirmation of their hypothesis. These discoveries date only from 1947, when a Bedouin shepherd, having gone down into a ravine at 'Ain Feshkha near the ancient settlement of Khirbet Qumran (which may be derived from Gomorrah)[72] to look for one of his beasts, found himself at the entrance to some caves, under which there was a spacious room that was later recognized to be an Essene refectory. The room still contained utensils, vessels for rain water, and other implements. Some of the jars contained fascinating documents: the oldest Biblical manuscripts ever found, and the text of the Essenes' monastic rules, called the *Manual of Discipline*. These Dead Sea scrolls go back to the years immediately preceding the time of Jesus, as radioactive carbon-isotope tests have proved in experiments at the Institute of Nuclear Physics of the University of Chicago.[73]

The discovery of the Dead Sea manuscripts, not all of which have yet been examined and published, serve to enlighten us at last on the unknown period in the formation of the teachings of Jesus. If now we view Jesus in the perspective provided by these scrolls, we can anticipate a continuity and discern a direction in the drama that culminated in Christianity.[74]

Admission to the sect of the Essenes was determined by the result of a rigorous examination in which a master of the order sought to ascertain the earnestness of the candidate. Acceptance was followed by one year of probation as a neophyte and two years as a novice, during which the new Essene accompanied his older colleagues in their journeys through the surrounding countryside, where they performed works of charity for the poor and treated the ailing. Little by little, the novice learned the magic words that were to be pronounced in order to drive demons out of a body of which they had taken possession, the ritual gestures and empirical medical procedures to restore the sight of those afflicted with cataracts, mouth-to-mouth breathing techniques to revive the unconscious.

At the completion of his three preparatory years, the new Essene could take full part in the life of the community. The recent discoveries have made it possible for us to establish in detail the practices and the beliefs of the Essenes, which had previously been only vaguely deduced from the cursory descriptions given by Flavius Josephus.[75] At sunrise, all the monastics stood together at the edge of the desert, and, turning ecstatically toward the still-pale disk of the sun, they intoned impassioned prayers *quasi bacchantes furore divino.*[76] They devoted their mornings, aside from the agricultural and manual work required for their own subsistence, to copying and studying Biblical texts and to perfecting occult practices intended to enhance their mediumistic and hypnotic faculties. Each day at noon, the entire community went to a nearby river for the bath of purification. This was pure and simple baptism, in the efficacious form of total immersion, which had a deep symbolic meaning: it represented a spiritual purification from all the stains of sin.

For the Essenes, the flight from this world constituted also a flight from temptation coupled with an opportunity to live in absolute purity of body and soul, mortifying all earthly passions. But there is here only an apparent resemblance to the doctrines of Brahmanism and Buddhism: in these religions, the flight from the imperfect world consists in total inactivity, unconcern, and impassivity (nirvana),[77] whereas the Essenes did not practice a negative renunciation but a positive love of their fellow men, exemplifying humility, brotherhood, and rectitude.

Besides the baptismal purification (Rule VI:4–8), the *Manual of Discipline* also prescribed the confession of sins in the presence of the whole community (Rule I:24, and Rule II:1), the eucharistic meal with bread and wine (Rule VI:2–6), and so on. It now becomes obvious that the organization of the Essene communities is almost identical with that of the early Christian Church,[78] and this fact uncovers new avenues of investigation into the origins of Christianity itself, which no longer figures as a lone flower in a desert but instead shows strong links with the other beliefs of the time.

The most interesting of the similarities between Christianity and Essenism is that the sacred writings of the Essenes, too, tell of a Teacher of Righteousness who is yet to come, sent by God to punish the wicked and to reward "all those who follow the Law."[79] In some passages, indeed, these texts seem to treat of a Lord who has already appeared, who has suffered martyrdom, and who has reappeared to the faithful.[80]

[5]

THE INITIATION

The Forerunner

Jesus was initiated into his public life not by the Essenes but by a preacher, himself the leader of a community destined to outlive that of the Essenes: John the Baptist.[1] Nevertheless, many students believe that John himself had been a member of the Qumran community.[2]

The meeting of Jesus and John is clearly designated by the canonical Gospels as the inauguration of the work of Jesus. They also tell us the date. It was the fifteenth year of the reign of Tiberius, Luke says.[3] Tiberius Claudius Nero Caesar (42 B.C.–A.D. 37) had become emperor at the death of Augustus, on August 19, A.D. 14; the fifteenth year of the reign of Tiberius would thus fall between August 19, A.D. 28, and August 19, A.D. 29. Some authorities, however, admit the possibility that the Evangelist included the time in which Tiberius reigned in collaboration with Augustus—a period of two years.[4] In that case, the introduction of Jesus to his ministry would date from A.D. 26 or 27. But of course we cannot be sure even of this date. Perhaps Luke meant only to stress that both Jesus and John, having been born a few months apart, were now thirty years old, the age prescribed by Hebrew law for assuming the capacity of the priest.[5]

But it is plainly absurd to profess, as some do, to be able to calculate not only the month but the very day of their meeting.[6]

We can, rather, determine from an analysis of the historical conditions prevailing at this period whether circumstances provide

73

some sort of foundation for the sudden rebirth of the work of prophecy. As a matter of fact, in the year 26 Palestine had been once more upset and humiliated by political developments, and a resurgence of prophecy is not at all unlikely. These new developments might well have seemed a further unbearable triumph of the forces of evil—perhaps the final triumph that, as Biblical predictions had foretold, would prepare the ultimate catastrophe.

In that year, the new Roman procurator, Pontius Pilate, had taken over his post, under the protection of Lucius Aelius Sejanus,[7] but he had started out badly. His predecessors—Coponius (in office A.D. 6–9), M. Ambibulus (9–12), Annius Rufus (12–15), and Valerius Gratus (15–26)—out of a certain respect for the Jews' religious sensibilities, had refrained from placing images of the emperor in Jerusalem. Pilate, considering this tolerance on the part of the earlier procurators a mere sign of weakness unbecoming to Roman prestige, decided to replace the unadorned banners that marked the Roman garrison in the Holy City with standards topped by medallions portraying Tiberius. He elected to have the work done by night, assuming that the Jews would yield before the accomplished fact. But it did not happen so. The next day a massive deputation went from Jerusalem to Caesarea on the coast, where the procurator lived, to insist that he remove the standards.[8] Pilate stood firmly by his decision, and after five days of irritation at the Jews' persistence, he ordered them all to be herded into the hippodrome, where he threatened to have them beaten by soldiers with naked swords. Still the Jews refused to concede that they had been overcome. Even Herod's sons presented a petition to Tiberius, who bade Pilate remove the medallions from Jerusalem and place them in the Temple of Augustus in Caesarea.

To such a man as John, these events could easily seem portents of divine anger.

We already know from the Gospel of Luke the train of miraculous occurrences that surrounded the birth of this prophet, and we have pointed out how the entire New Testament is designed to make John appear as only the precursor of Jesus, always subordinate to him. The mythologists deny even the historical existence of John, whom they identify with the Babylonian solar deity Oannes.[9] But John (in Hebrew, *Yehōḥānnān,* or *Yōḥānān,* which means "God favored him") is mentioned also by a non-Christian author, Flavius Josephus, who confirms the basic facts given to us by the Gospels.[10]

John always wore a shirt of camel's hair, girded at the loins; he lived in the Judean desert, near the Dead Sea, eating locusts and wild honey, and he preached on the banks of the river Jordan. His garment and his diet were not mere personal eccentricities; these also were customs of the ascetic prophets, and were likewise derived from the Old Testament.[11] Locusts, in those days, were a common food in Palestine, as they were among all the Near Eastern peoples and among the Ethiopians. There were four edible species; they were ground and mixed with meal, salted, and smoked or roasted.[12] It is amusing to note that many of the apocryphal Gospels say nothing of the locusts as part of John's diet, on the theory that the prophet did not consume flesh in any form, even that of insects.[13]

It was not "in Bethany beyond Jordan" that he preached, as the Gospel of John tells us in the Vulgate,[14] because no town of that name existed on the farther bank of the river (the name was given much later to a village in this locale inhabited only by Christians; nor should the name be confused with the well-known Bethany near Jerusalem). Possibly the Vulgate meant Bethabara (the name used in the King James Bible), on the left bank of the river near the mouth, where a ford provided easy crossing for caravans coming from Moab. It is not impossible that the Vulgate translation was confused by *Bēth 'anīyā* and *Bēth 'aberā.*[15]

Spiritual Renewal

John's preaching was not too unlike that of all the prophets who had gone before him or that of his contemporaries, the Essenes.[16] He denounced the corruption of the times and warned of the imminence of the Day of Judgment: Yahweh would reward the "just" with an eternal life of bliss, but on the wicked his wrath would fall inexorably. "And now also the ax is laid unto the root of the trees," he thundered.[17] Nor was it any matter that all the children of Abraham would perish—God could create new men, possibly out of stones (in Hebrew there is a pun here on *'abānīm*, "stones," and *bānīm*, "sons"), to inhabit his new kingdom.[18]

The new kingdom is called "the kingdom of God"—in Greek, βασιλεία (basileia); in Aramaic, malkuthā—or else "the kingdom of the heavens," in which the word "heavens" (which in Hebrew has no singular) is synonymous with "God."[19]

In the apocalyptic and prophetic literature of the Old Testament, too, there are predictions that the time would be ripe for the inauguration of the new kingdom when evil had reached its peak: the world would be rent asunder by tremendous convulsions and God would rout the forces of evil.[20] But these ancient prophecies emphasized more than anything else the ominous vision of the destruction of the existing world. What was new in John's message (and what Jesus was to incorporate into his own preaching) was the promise that even sinners might enter into the kingdom, provided they repented and changed their way of living.

The Vulgate's phrase "facite poenitentiam" is not a wholly accurate translation of the call to μετάνοια (metanoia) that the Gospels attribute to John.[21] Metanoia does not really mean "repentance," but rather a mutatio mentis, a complete change of ideas and purposes. As metamorphosis is a physical transformation, a change of form, so metanoia is a spiritual transformation, the "renewal of the inner man."[22] Luther understood this fully when he wrote to Stampitz, his master and inspiration: "Metanoia in the New Testament does not carry the ecclesiastical meaning; rather, to do penance means to transform oneself in one's inmost soul. For the Christian, therefore, doing penance is not an act that is performed at a stated time: it is a mode of conduct to be observed throughout one's whole life."[23]

Baptism

As evidence of repentance, John demanded of the sinners who believed in him that they confess all their sins and be baptized in the Jordan: otherwise the emissary of God on the Day of Judgment (and John humbly acknowledged that he himself was unworthy even to unlace the sandals of the messenger)[24] would baptize them not with water but with fire that would consume them like worthless chaff.[25]

Confession and baptism—that is, "immersion in water," from the Indo-European root bath, through the Greek word βαπτίζω (*baptizō*)—are two ritual practices common to many religions.[26] Among primitive peoples of Africa, Asia, and North America, a belief still exists that public confession, accompanied by ablution, assists to a great degree in warding off evil. In Indian Brahmanism, evil, like disease, is a malefic force and substance that can be eliminated by bathing, and hundreds of the faithful gather every day to wash in the waters of the holy river Ganges.

In Judaism, too, there was and is a solemn ritual of public confession: on Yom Kippur, or the Day of Atonement (*Yōm ha-Kippurīm*), the high priest, in a loud voice, condemned the collective sins of the entire nation, asking God's pardon for them. Ablutions and sprinklings were employed not only in this ceremony but also by every priest before he performed any ritual whatever. In a similar fashion, the use of water as an element of the liturgy was taken over by the Church for purificatory benedictions and for consecrations. The custom of washing one's hands before prayer and that of using water in exorcism (*ad abigendos daemones morbosque pellendos*) led to the institution of the font of holy water in the churches.

But John's baptisms differed from these forms of ablution. They were much more like the purifying rite of the Essenes: a bath that symbolized a complete separation from the profane world and an introduction into a new state of purity.[27] Jesus, during his mission, imposed no baptism on his disciples, as the Gospel of John points out.[28]

The sacrament of baptism is of later origin. The Acts of the Apostles ascribe to Peter a commemorative sermon on the death of Jesus, which ends with this summons to the company of the faithful: "Repent [the *metanoia* of John], and be baptized every one of you in the name of Jesus Christ, for the remission of sins. . . . Save yourselves from this untoward generation." Afterward, to justify the ritual, additions were made to the Gospels of Mark and Matthew that credited its institution to Jesus himself during one of the reappearances that he made *after* his death.[29]

Paul, for his part, attributed to baptism a symbolic value that was quite different. For him, the immersion of baptism is a mystical burial, by means of which the believer is assimilated to Christ dead and buried—his sinful flesh dies and is entombed. But just as Christ rose from death, so the baptized man is a new man, who has "died unto sin"[30] and risen to new life. As in all Pauline theology, so in this interpretation of baptism one sees the clear influence of the rites of the Greco-Oriental mysteries and a great likeness to many of them, above all to the taurobolium, baptism with the blood of a bull, from which he who accepted it was believed to emerge *renatus in aeternum*.[31]

A modern theologian has offered this definition: "The water of baptism is to the believer what the womb of the mother is to the child."[32]

In the second century A.D., the apologist Tertullian propounded this strange explanation: "Since we are born in water and cannot save ourselves if we do not remain in it, we are little fish in Jesus Christ, our great fish."[33] The phrase was picked up, and also it suggested to the pictorial artists the idea of portraying Jesus in the symbolic form of a fish—all the more since the letters of the Greek word for "fish," ἰχθύς (*ichthus*), lend themselves to the formation of a curious acrostic in honor of Jesus: Ἰησοῦς Χριστὸς Θεοῦ Ὑιὸς Σωτήρ, or "Jesus Christ, Son of God, Savior."

In the course of the centuries, the Church has always vacillated between the two variant interpretations of baptism: a sacrament, following the view of Peter, that reconciles us with God and remits our sins; or a mystical rite, according to the view of Paul, that initiates the neophytes and introduces them into the bosom of the Church—hence, an act of faith.

Both interpretations have certain drawbacks. Accepting Peter's opinion that baptism has the power to cancel prior sins, the question has sometimes been raised whether the ceremony may not be repeated after a relapse into mortal sin. For some centuries, it was customary to postpone baptism until the last possible moment, even until the point of death.[34] Some went so far, when death had taken a Christian before he had been baptized, as to simulate his participation in a posthumous sacrament by hiding a living man under the bed of the corpse so that he could make the responses for the deceased to the officiating priest.[35]

Such abuses persuaded the Church to impose baptism on the newborn. At the same time, to eliminate the awkward possibility that the beneficiaries of the sacrament might nevertheless be lost as a consequence of later sins, the priests were authorized to remit sins committed *after* baptism provided the wrongdoers came to them and confessed.

From time to time the innovation aroused sharp protests, until the rise of the Anabaptists in Saxony at the beginning of the sixteenth century, in the heat of the Reformation. They argued that since baptism was an act of faith, it could be requested only for an adult capable of exercising his will and disposing of his own destiny.[36] Actually, the Church had already resolved this problem by separating from the baptismal rite all the elements that had originally had the quality of a seal of ratification and making them into another sacrament, that of confirmation, which was normally performed some years after baptism.

Others were angered by the fact that, if baptism is indispensable to the salvation of the Christian from the moment of his birth, those babies who by mischance die before they can be baptized are condemned, in spite of their innocence, to exclusion from salvation. The first to protest against this consequence were the Pelagians in the fourth century, fierce adversaries of Augustine, who contended that unbaptized children must suffer the penalty of damnation.[37]

Then some theologians condemned the prevailing practice in the West—justified though it was by considerations of climate—of baptizing not by immersion but by infusion (pouring a little water on the candidate) or by aspersion (sprinkling him).

Jesus as a Disciple of John

Why, if Jesus himself did not baptize, do the Evangelists attach so much importance to the fact that he was baptized by John? What need had Jesus, if he were the Son of God and therefore immune to human failings, of such a ceremony to purge him of sin? Such a doubt must already have entered the mind of the author of the apocryphal Gospel of the Nazarenes, who makes Jesus say: "What sin have I committed, that I should go to him and be baptized?"[38]

Obviously, even if it was to conflict with their subsequent later beliefs, the Evangelists were not able to suppress the fact that the Nazarene was a disciple of John. The incident of the baptism gives every indication of authenticity.[39] The followers of the Baptist survived for a long time side by side with the first Christians and often in conflict with them; it would have been easy to give the lie to any concealment by the authors of the Gospels.[40] If the beginnings of the public life of Jesus had been otherwise, there would have been no need for the early Christians to devise a Forerunner whom they would then have to relegate to a secondary rank.

Matthew's attempt to make John seem a mere instrument, who immediately recognized Jesus as the long-awaited Savior and even hesitated to baptize him, is not supported by the other writers (Luke's account of the meeting between Mary and Elisabeth is a later insertion). If John recognized that Jesus was the Messiah, why did he not become a Christian? Instead, he went on with his own preaching.

Unquestionably, Jesus was a follower of John, rather than the converse. In one way or another—as has only lately been shown—Christianity was born "as a splinter from the sect of John."[41] That sect, in fact, survived even after John's death and the spread of Christianity, the members being known as Mandeans, while the early Christians claimed for themselves the name Nazarenes, which, however, had already been used by John's followers to designate themselves in their writings.[42]

Indeed, it was the Baptist who first made Jesus aware of his own ministry:[43] Jesus listened to John and wanted to become his follower, drawn by an interest far greater than that of all John's other followers in that kingdom of justice which John preached was immediate.[44]

From the beginning, believers in Christ sought to find in his baptism a sign of divine consecration. The Ebionites, the Ophites, the Adoptianists, Cerinthus the heretic, Basilides, the first Apostles themselves, regarded that ceremony as the first moment of the Messiahship of Jesus: only then (and not, as came to be believed later, from the time of his birth) had God endowed him, like the Biblical prophets and seers, with his own illumination and adopted him as his son.[45]

The Gospels attribute to Jesus, in that instant, the sensation of supernatural communication (and perhaps this was the impression that Jesus later described to his disciples): the opening of the heavens as soon as he rose from the baptismal waters, the descent of the spirit of God on him in the tangible form (σωματικῷ εἴδει, *sōmatikō eidei*) of a dove, the sound of a voice in the clouds saying, "Thou art my chosen son, in whom I have shown myself." This is my correction of the Gospel text, ἐν ᾧ ἐδόκησα (*en hō edokēsa*) instead of εὐδόκησα (*eudokēsa*). This latter would make the sentence read: "in whom I have placed my love," or "with whom I am well pleased," which would be an unnecessary redundancy after the word "chosen" (ἀγαπητός, *agapētos*, in Hebrew, *bāḥîr*) had already been used. The second form seems to me an obvious corruption—and not a fortuitous one—of the original text, inspired by the desire to expunge the embarrassing declaration that only at that moment had God shown himself in Jesus, inspiring him to speak in his name. The version that I propose is no gratuitous inference because it is closer to the Biblical passage—"Thou art my son; this day have I begotten thee"[46]—that undoubtedly suggested the Evangelist's phraseology.

It is fruitless to wonder whether what seemed a sign from heaven to Jesus was really a commonplace flash of lightning followed by thunder,[47] or whether an unexpected burst of sunlight through clouds[48] was likened to the flight of a bird. What concerns us here is not the transformation of an atmospheric phenomenon into a divine manifestation but the objectivization of an impression. The word that means "spirit" in Hebrew (*rūaḥ*) is feminine in gender, and long before, in the Old Testament, the spirit of God, as a voice or an afflatus, had often materialized in the form of a dove: note, for example, the dove in Genesis that announces the end of the flood.[49] Given its feminine gender, there has been no dearth of heretics ready to accept it as "the spiritual mother" of Jesus.

In any case, whether one believes in an objective mark of benevolence given by God or in a subjective impression experienced by Jesus, the apparition remains to signal the recognition that his religious vocation had now been decided.

In the Wilderness

It is to the period of preparation by Jesus, or at least to its concluding phase, that one should also relate the "forty days" that he spent in solitude in the desert of Judea.[50] This desert, or wilderness, was the region that lies between the Dead Sea and the mountain chain that runs between Jerusalem and Hebron. It is a somewhat rolling country of chalky little hills of a grayish color that dazzle in the sunlight and are separated by narrow, sandy *widian* (the plural of *wadi*, "valley"). Little by little, as one goes farther into the desert, the vegetation becomes more sparse; but even the wispy trees and the dry grasses disappear entirely near the Dead Sea. This huge lake, lying some thirteen hundred feet below sea level, is extraordinarily salty (magnesium bromide and magnesium chloride are particularly abundant), with a densely bituminous basin. Its very waters seem dead because of their ponderous motionlessness and the desolation, out of which rise poisonous fumes that dry out virtually every form of life; no fish lives in these sterile waters, few plants or birds live near them.[51]

Nevertheless the first book of the Old Testament, Genesis, mentions some famous cities that rose on these once extremely fertile shores. Legend says that two of them, Sodom and Gomorrah, were destroyed by Yahweh with fire and brimstone because of the moral rot of their inhabitants. Archaeological investigations made in 1848 by an American scientific expedition verified that they were engulfed about two thousand years before Christ (the period of Abraham) in a frightful landslide, probably preceded by an earthquake[52] or some similar seismic disturbance that also uncovered the noxious saline and bituminous deposits of the subsoil.

Jesus spent forty days in this region, the Gospels say, walking pensively along the desolate, salt-encrusted sands, in an infinite silence broken only by the grating noise of his own steps, the distant howl of a jackal,[53] and, now and then, the splash of some huge block of asphalt that, tearing free of the sea bottom, surged to the surface.[54] Sometimes he would leave the barren waste to restore his strength in the shadow of a rare bush surrounded by a scanty growth of dried grass.

The writers of the Gospels relate that he fasted throughout the entire time. Forty is a symbolic number that occurs quite frequently in the Holy Scriptures to indicate a "very long" period: the deluge lasted forty days (Genesis 7:4), the Hebrews wandered forty years in the wilderness (Numbers 14:33), Moses fasted forty days on Mount Sinai (Deuteronomy 9:9), Elijah fasted forty days on Mount Horeb

(I Kings 19:8), forty were the years of desolation that Ezekiel fore-told to Egypt (Ezekiel 24:11), forty days were needed to embalm the body of Jacob (Genesis 50:3), and so on. Therefore, the Evangelists' statement that Jesus actually spent forty days in the wilderness—and more so the report that he fasted the whole time—are not to be taken literally. Even traditionalist exegetes admit today the absurdity of any such hypothesis, and concede that Jesus might have sustained himself on roots and wild honey.[55] Fasting was a venerable practice among the Semitic peoples,[56] but was never extended beyond one day. It was a kind of restriction and voluntary sacrifice that was believed to be pleasing to God,[57] and in certain cases it was also an ascetic custom in preparation for the religious life. It is in fact common knowledge that abstinence from meat in particular, com-bined with a moderate diet, predominantly vegetarian, causes physiological changes in the human body and makes it easier to curb aggressive and sexual drives. As an ascetic practice in memory of the fast of Jesus, the early Church enjoined on candidates for baptism an abstinence of forty days, and the period became known as Quadragesimal (from the Late Latin *quadragesima*). The practice degenerated, naturally, when baptism began to be performed on babies, but the Quadragesimal persisted, notably in the Middle Ages, as a period of penitence for all the faithful—with limitations on diet, abstinence from sexual relations, prohibitions against hunt-ing, amusements, weddings, etc. Today, in the Catholic Church, the Codex Juris Canonici (canon 1250 *et seq.*) is much less severe than the canonical law of the Middle Ages in its prescriptions of Lenten mortifications.

The Temptation

While Jesus was in the desert, the Evangelists say, he was tempted by Satan, who challenged him to transform stones into bread if he was really the favored Son of God. The Gospels, to be precise, say υἱὸς Θεοῦ (*hyos Theou*), "protected by God," and not ὁ υἱὸς Θεοῦ (*ho hyos Theou*), "the Son of God," as the Vulgate trans-lates it.[58] Then Satan led Jesus to "a pinnacle" of the Temple of Jerusalem and demanded that he throw himself off if he was convinced that the angels would hold him up. Finally, Satan took Jesus to a lofty mountain peak and "shewed unto him all the kingdoms of the world," promising to give him dominion over them if Jesus would worship him.[59]

Quite aside from the various inconsistencies of the tale (the Temple of Jerusalem had no pinnacles; nor was there any mountain high enough to enable one to see "all the kingdoms of the world," even if "the world" were taken to mean no more than Palestine or even one of its tetrarchies), a most serious question of doctrine remains to be resolved, a question that has troubled even the most credulous:[60] How could Satan hope to seduce Jesus, who was a superior being? Is not the dignity of the founder of Christianity compromised if the Devil is able to whisk him hither and thither by magic powers?[61] And, finally, who is Satan?

In the books of the Old Testament, the function of the Tempter is often ascribed to God himself or to one of his angels,[62] as a means of testing the faithful. Only very slowly did Biblical thought begin to draw a clear line of distinction, under the influence of the Parsees and the followers of Ormazd,[63] between the concept of God as infinite goodness and that of the Tempter, who, from the Hebrew root stn ("to block," "to attack," "to malign"), came to be called Sātān. The Greek translators used the equivalent word in their language, διάβολος (diabolos, meaning "malignant," "slanderous"), and from this the Latin diabolus was derived.

In the literature of the New Testament, Satan is generally defined as "the prince of this world," "the god of this age." So in this fashion a god of good is placed side by side with a god of evil, dangerously compromising the traditional Hebrew monotheistic conception that Christianity inherited. How is the existence of this second kind of supernatural power to be explained if God is one and all-powerful? In the second century, Justin Martyr forged the legend (suggested to him by Genesis 6:2) that Satan and his devils were once good angels, who had been deposed for having committed carnal sins with the daughters of men. Justin called them angeli fornicatores.[64] But how does this explain the existence of Satan early enough to have tempted Eve—that is, before there were any other "daughters of men" in the world? And why, if he is the absolute good, did God create beings of this nature, especially when he could foresee (since he is all-knowing) that through their works mankind would be afflicted with so much corruption and so much suffering?[65] And is this idea of a god who sacrifices his children not a kind of Saturnism?

As a result of the inadequacy of the theological explanations, the dualistic heresy has revived from time to time, openly espoused by Marcion, by the Manicheans (of whom Augustine as a youth was a follower), by the Cathari and Albigenses, by the Paulianists, etc. Even today the mass of the people continues to believe in the Devil, who may bewitch us at one moment with his seductive arts and at another terrify us with his most monstrous guises; and at night he joins the witches in their horrendous sabbaths.

But Jesus and his contemporaries took comfort from their confidence that, one day not too far off, the God of Goodness would finally and forever shatter the power of Satan.

Hence there is no occasion to wonder whether the story of the temptation in the wilderness was an invention of the Evangelists[66] or whether the name of Satan was employed to represent a human agent under orders to corrupt Jesus.[67] Temptations are virtually required in the lives of saints and prophets, in order to put the quality of their commitment to the test. From what we are told, Buddha fasted twenty-eight days and was tempted by Mara, the prince of the demons.[68] Zoroaster, who had withdrawn into a cave for meditation, was confronted by the god of evil, Ahriman, who promised him power and wealth. In the lives of the Christian saints, the temptations of St. Anthony, St. Francis, St. Theresa, and others are common knowledge.

Undoubtedly the temptation of Jesus also represents a spiritual conflict at the critical moment of renouncing forever the joys of this world in order to answer a religious vocation heavy with sacrifice. The only question that remains is whether the temptation took place in the form of a delirium, due to the weakness induced by his fast,[69] or of ecstatic suggestion,[70] or of hallucination.[71] Possibly, Jesus later described this inner drama in figurative terms that tradition has taken too literally.[72] If some allegorical significance is to be sought in it, one might say that it represents the endless struggle of the human will in its choice between the path of pleasure and that of duty. It is "the dualism of deciding,"[73] and in this sense, even if it in no way represents a historical event in the life of Jesus, it is equally capable of serving a definite educational purpose.

Russian thinkers and writers of the nineteenth century, impregnated with the poverty-worship of the Gospels as their compatriots of today have been indoctrinated with Marxist proletarianism, have given the story an interpretation harshly condemning the Church of Rome. The tempting demon, Feodor Dostoevsky says, showed Jesus the road that would lead to glory, to power, and to riches, but Jesus rejected it. The Church of Rome, on the other hand, has gone into the wilderness and embraced the counsel of the Tempter, seeking for itself the glory, the riches, and the temporal power.

"No Prophet is Accepted in His Own Country"

Having overcome his temptations, Jesus returned to John as the latter's disciple and followed him in his wanderings through Judea. It appears that they went also beyond its borders, as far into Samaritan territory as Aenon, near Salim.[74] But it was not very long before the master's preaching was abruptly silenced.

In his violent denunciations of the leaders responsible for the corruption of the times, John was rash enough to attack even Herod Antipas, who, as we know, was the tetrarch of Galilee and Perea. Antipas, who was congenitally ἀγαπῶν τὴν ἡσυχίαν (agapōn tēn ēsuchian) —"a lover of the quiet life," as he is called by Flavius Josephus[75]— had at that period all the more reason to be upset by seditious speeches with the danger of some popular uprising. He had installed himself, in fact, in his fortress of Machaerus (in Perea, not far from Bethabara, John's favorite place), to lead a war against his father-in-law, Aretas, king of the Nabateans. Antipas had married the latter's daughter a few years before and had now put her aside in order to live with Herodias, who, in her turn, had deserted her own husband, the brother of Antipas, in Rome and fled to Palestine with her lover, bringing her daughter, Salome.[76]

The adultery of Herodias and Antipas naturally provided matter for John's anger, and Antipas had him imprisoned in his fortress at Machaerus.[77] John's arrest scattered his disciples. Jesus, too, left the banks of the Jordan and went back to Nazareth. But he did not wish to let his master's message die out. The Gospels tell us that he decided to travel through Galilee repeating the words he had heard from John: "Repent, for the kingdom of heaven is at hand"; "The time is fulfilled: believe the gospel."[78]

The word "gospel" is the modern form of the Anglo-Saxon *god-spell*, a story from or about God. *God-spell*, however, has always been understood popularly to mean "good tidings," or "glad tidings," and was, because of that connotation, used as a translation of the Late Latin *evangelium*, from the Greek εὐαγγέλιον (*euangelion*), both of which mean "good tidings." The expression was derived from the passage in the Book of Isaiah that speaks of the return of the Hebrews from exile: "How beautiful upon the mountains are the feet of him that bringeth good tidings!"[79]

The good tidings that Jesus wanted to carry into Galilee were the imminence of the kingdom as John had preached it. But Jesus did not immediately find the same favor among his hearers that his master had enjoyed. Rather, his conduct aroused both suspicion and resentment among his countrymen.

The Gospels have preserved the humiliating episode in which Jesus figured on the occasion of his first preaching in the synagogue of Nazareth on a Sabbath.[80] He had gone there to take part in the religious observance. Until he spoke, the ceremony had gone smoothly along its customary precise course, which has remained virtually unchanged today, as the Jewish scholar Aron attests.[81] In the beginning, all the congregation, standing in the body of the sanctuary (a barrier separates the women from the men), chanted various psalms. Then an elder of the community, wrapped in his tallith, or prayer shawl, began the reading of the Ten Commandments (this was dropped, however, near the end of the first century) and then pronounced the Shema, the basic prayer of Hebrew monotheism, composed of passages from the Pentateuch. When the prayer was completed, the elder chanted the benedictions (*berakōth*), which are called today the Shemoneh Esreh (the Eighteen Benedictions) but which at that time numbered barely six. After each, the faithful, still standing, responded aloud: *'Āmēn*. The service ended with the Bareku, one of the oldest prayers. The elder recited the first part, "Blessed art Thou, O Lord, who deservest praise," and the congregation responded in chorus: "Blessed be the Eternal, deserving of praise, forever and ever."

At this point the *shammāsh*, a kind of sacristan of the synagogue, took from the wooden ark (*'arōn*) the parchment scrolls of the Pentateuch and the prophets, waiting for some member of the congregation to volunteer to read from them in Hebrew, in which they were written, and comment on them in Aramaic. In our times, the sacred texts are divided into fifty-two portions (*pārashōt*), one for each Saturday, so that the reading of the whole requires a year, but it appears that in the time of Jesus there were one hundred seventy-five *pārashōt*, the completion of which required almost three and a half years.

It was not necessary to know Hebrew perfectly: by now it was only the liturgical language, as Latin is for Catholics. The Holy Scriptures, as we have pointed out, were learned by rote: a glance was enough to enable one to recognize a passage and to start reciting it.

On this Saturday, Jesus volunteered to read and interpret. The Book of Isaiah was given to him, and he had barely opened the scroll when he saw the passage that I shall quote in its original form (Luke, apparently quoting from memory, varied it slightly): "The Spirit of the Lord God is upon me; because the Lord hath anointed me to preach good tidings unto the meek; he hath sent me to bind up the broken-hearted, to proclaim liberty to the captives, . . . to proclaim the acceptable year of the Lord, and the day of vengeance of our God. . . ."[82]

When he had finished reading out the passage of Isaiah, Jesus rolled up the scroll again, handed it back to the *shammāsh*, and sat down. Everyone was staring at him. After a long silence, Jesus solemnly spoke these prophetic words of commentary: "This day is this scripture fulfilled in your ears."[83]

The other worshipers eyed him questioningly; but there was more mistrust than amazement in their faces;[84] and they began to murmur to one another in shock:

"Is not this the carpenter, the son of Mary, the brother of James, and Joses, and of Juda [Judas], and Simon? And are not his sisters here with us?"[85]

Jesus caught the hostile sounds and cried: "Ye will surely say unto me this proverb, Physician, heal thyself. . . . Verily I say unto you, No prophet is accepted in his own country. [The apocryphal Gospel attributed to Thomas adds: 'And a doctor does not heal those who know him.'[86]] But I tell you of a truth: many widows were in Israel in the days of Elias [Elijah], when the heaven was shut up three years and six months, when great famine was throughout the land; but unto none of them was Elias sent, save unto Sarepta, a city of Sidon, unto a woman that was a widow. And many lepers were in Israel, in the time of Eliseus [Elisha] the prophet; and none of them was cleansed, saving Naaman the Syrian."[87]

The Nazarenes rose in anger against Jesus, shouting and threatening him. The word ran among them: he had dared to compare himself with Elijah and Elisha, and he scorned them all because they would not listen to him.[88] With difficulty Jesus forced a way through the crowd and left the synagogue. But they pursued him, and having caught up to him in the midst of the village, they very nearly threw him into a gorge behind the last houses. But, Luke relates, Jesus made his way through their midst and managed to escape.[89]

The three Synoptic Gospels—that is, those of Matthew, Mark, and Luke—all of which follow more or less the same narrative pattern, reveal a certain embarrassment at the fact, which was certainly no great tribute to their master, that Jesus was not listened to in Nazareth. But the Christian exegetes prefer to cling to the Gospel of John, which interprets this defeat as one *sought* by Jesus: he was forbidden to make converts in his own country because his message was to be carried to "all the peoples." It is too easy to emphasize the ingenuousness of such an explanation by pointing out that "all the peoples" must surely have included his own compatriots!

The Synoptic Gospels terminate the episode by informing us that Jesus, disillusioned at the unbelief of his own countrymen,[90] abandoned Nazareth and set out for the Lake of Gennesaret, which was not far away.

[6]

JESUS AS THAUMATURGE

At Capernaum

From Nazareth to the Valley of the Doves (Wadi el Hamam), where the plain of the Sea of Galilee begins, is a day's walk, which, to use the expression of the Gospel of John,[1] is only a descent (κατέβη, *katebē*) along the easy slopes of the hills. The Sea of Galilee, known in the days of Jesus as the Lake of Gennesaret (which means "the valley of flowers"), is the second basin through which the Jordan runs. Larger than Lake Huleh, it is, however, smaller than the Dead Sea; but, in contrast to the latter, with its appalling desolation, the Sea of Galilee is extremely rich in fish.

When Jesus reached its shores, a number of fishermen were busy casting their nets. These were of two kinds: the *ḥabāk* was thrown out after having been wound up round the fisherman's arm; the *mehatten*, with a rim like that of a birding net, was weighted at the bottom and opened in the water, where it was maintained by floats.

Disappointed but not discouraged by what had happened in Nazareth, Jesus looked for his first followers among these simple men. The Gospels of Mark and Matthew say that, having approached two of them, Simon and his brother, Andrew, and then two more, James and John, sons of Zebedee the fisherman, Jesus bade them join him as his disciples.[2] The curt sentence of the Gospels, Δεῦτε ὀπίσω μου (*Deute opisō mou*), "Come ye after me," was the traditional formal rabbinical invitation to become a master's pupil and to follow him wherever he went.[3]

Naturally we have to fill out the bare summary provided by the Evangelists. It is to be expected that Jesus conversed at length with the fishermen before he could persuade them to give up their accustomed ways and follow him in a venture full of uncertainties. It should be easy enough to ascertain whether the scholar Oscar Cullmann is correct in his supposition that all four, or at least Simon, belonged to the sect of the Zealots.[4] Simon was indeed called *bār-Jōna,* which ordinarily means "son of Jonah," but Cullmann points out that this form was not generally used in Palestine, whereas in Akkadian *barjona* was a synonym for "terrorist" and had acquired the same meaning in Hebrew.

Another hypothesis, suggested by the Gospel of John (which, however, describes the meeting between Jesus and his first disciples quite differently),[5] indicates that Simon and Andrew at least were already followers of John the Baptist and had known Jesus in that company.

Perhaps Jesus also had to give some evidence of his own powers. The Gospel of Luke ascribes the conversion of the four men to a miraculous catch that Jesus enabled them to make when, exhausted and dejected after a fruitless night of work, they had already brought their boats to shore. The improbability of Luke's story is obvious in a number of its details, well brought out by the modernist critic A. F. Loisy,[6] but there is no basis for the irony of those who pose the question whether Jesus had so low an opinion of Simon (who was later to be his successor) that he felt obliged to gain his respect by practicing magic.[7] The tale of the miraculous catch as inserted by Luke into his Gospel is explainable as a mythical elaboration suggested to him by the words of the two earlier biographers of Jesus: "Come ye after me, *and I will make you to become fishers of men.*"[8]

Jesus, who had by now made the difficult decision to leave both his birthplace and his family, established himself with these first disciples in their village, Capernaum,[9] or *Kephar-Naḥūm* (now called Khan Minyeh), northwest of the lake. It was then a fairly flourishing town, for it lay along the caravan route from the shores of the Mediterranean to Damascus. John, indeed, says that Simon and Andrew were born in Bethsaida, a village very near Capernaum,[10] but a little later he too tells us that Jesus and the disciples settled in Capernaum. (See Figure IV.)

Instead of the two brothers who were the sons of Zebedee, the Gospel of John identifies the third and fourth disciples as two men who were friends, Philip and Nathanael.[11] Philip became a disciple on the same simple bidding that Jesus had given to the first two: "Follow me." Nathanael's conversion, however, is reported by John in a curious incident which undoubtedly incorporates some obscure symbolic significance that escapes modern minds. He says it was Philip who, encountering his friend, ardently urged him to join the group. Nathanael's first reaction was rather skeptical: "Can there any good thing come out of Nazareth?"

But all his disbelief was vanquished by a cryptic conversation with Jesus, who, having barely caught sight of Nathanael, declared: "Behold an Israelite indeed, in whom is no guile!"

Stunned, Nathanael replied: "Whence knowest thou me?"

"Before that Philip called thee, when thou wast under the fig tree, I saw thee."

"Rabbi, thou art the Son of God; thou art the King of Israel."

But Jesus rebuked him gently: "Because I said unto thee, I saw thee under the fig tree, believest thou? thou shalt see greater things than these."

The Demoniac in the Synagogue

It was in the synagogue of Capernaum, when the Sabbath came, that Jesus tried again to launch the preaching that he had begun in Nazareth. The three Synoptic Gospels say that the people listened to him in astonishment, because Jesus spoke not as the Scribes but "as one having authority" (ὡς ἐξουσίαν ἔχων, *hōs exousian echōn*).[12] He did not confine himself to a pure and simple commentary on the text, in the manner laid down by the Scribes, who were the learned interpreters of the holy books; instead, he followed the inspiration that came from his own heart.[13]

Only narrowly, however, did Jesus avert an outbreak that would have had as disastrous an outcome as that in Nazareth. But this time he was able to turn the situation skillfully to his own advantage.

FIGURE IV
THE SEA OF GALILEE
(LAKE OF GENNESARET)

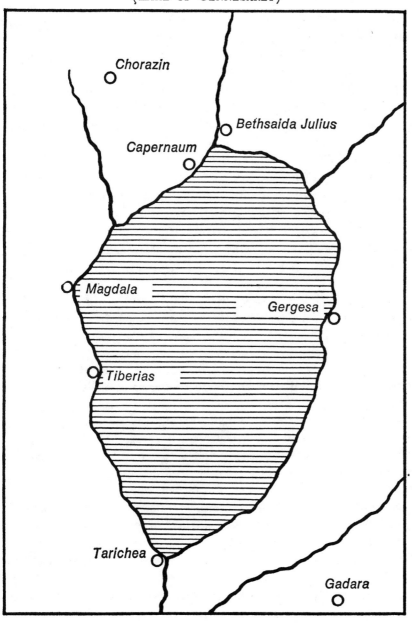

While he was speaking, two of the Evangelists tell us,[14] a man possessed by demons—in other words, a hysteric, though his illness could not have been too serious if he was allowed to take part in synagogue services[15]—who, like everyone else, was strongly moved but whose condition made him more excitable than the rest, cried out: "Let us alone; what have we to do with thee, thou Jesus of Nazareth? art thou come to destroy us?"

Annoyed by the unwarranted interruption, Jesus turned to the wretched man,[16] transfixing him with a fearful look, and, continuing to stare into his eyes as if he wished to hypnotize him, Jesus cried: "Hold thy peace, and come out of him."

Falling to the floor in convulsions, the man gasped and panted, and then he was suddenly quiet.

The universal amazement was infinite, the Gospels say. The general wonder evoked by so easy a resolution of a hysterical outburst is not at all remarkable if one understands the peculiar concept of such matters entertained by the Hebrews of the time. They were convinced that nervous diseases—hysteria, epilepsy—were caused by demonic possession, that they were the result of the entrance of evil spirits into the human body and that only some supernatural force could rout them. The "exorcists" who were able to cure such cases were therefore considered instruments of God.[17]

The attribution of such powers to Jesus, then, implies the Evangelists' intention to recognize in him at this stage the first sign of divine investiture. The termination of the crisis of hysteria, which we have described in the customary terms, is in fact recorded in the Gospels as an allegory—the hasty escape of the demon from the victim's body is caused by the words of Jesus. "And when the unclean spirit had torn him, and cried with a loud voice, he came out of him," Mark says; according to Luke, "when the devil had thrown him in the midst, he came out of him, and hurt him not."[18]

As a rule, there is some confusion between these demons and the diabolical powers governed by Satan. Actually, the Hebrew word *mazzīkīm*, by which the demons were known, has the generic meaning of "evil influences," "harmful forces"; correspondingly, Greek and Latin use πνεῦμα ἀκάθαρτον (*pneuma akatharton*) and *spiritus immundus*,[19] or else δαιμόνιον (*daimonion*) and *daemonium*.[20] The Hebrew word does not correspond precisely in meaning to those in

Greek and Latin, but as concepts they are all very close. The Greek *daimon* really refers to those bodiless and immortal beings, whether good or evil, that function as intermediaries between man and the gods. In similar fashion, the Roman religion had its genii of good and evil, and they existed in other religions, too, besides in Oriental and classical mythology: the trolls of Scandinavia, the elves of Germany, the pixies of the British Isles, the jinn of Islam, the onis of Japan, and so on.

Modern medical science has learned that the cure of hysterical and obsessive symptoms is possible in many cases through neuropsychiatric treatment, which ranges from the most sober scientific methods (narcosynthesis and psychoanalysis in American institutions) to the Indian practice of yoga (the Yoga Health Center in Bombay cures eighty per cent of its cases), and even to the empiric use of the peculiar hypnotic and suggestive powers of those individuals endowed with them—perhaps through the presence of a "magnetic essence," the existence of which was first proposed by Franz Mesmer and his followers at the end of the eighteenth century.

Despite all these scientific discoveries, the Catholic Church goes on believing in demonic possession, which it inherited from the early Hebrews, and even today it confers on its priests the power to exorcise, which ranks third in the lower sacred orders.[21]

Healings by Night

Ordinarily, in ancient Palestine, the power to cast out demons was not divorced from the more general capacity to cure other ailments as well. Jesus, who had acted forcefully in the case of the man possessed in the synagogue of Capernaum, was resoundingly acclaimed, and everyone was astounded at the discovery of his thaumaturgic qualities.

The first to profit by them, according to Mark and Luke, was Simon himself, who led the master to his own house and implored him to cure his mother-in-law, who was stricken with fevers. As before, Jesus used suggestion, pressing the old woman's hands and bidding her, by word and look, to rise from her pallet. Immediately, the two Gospels relate, the fevers vanished and the old woman was able to rise and welcome her guest with proper ceremony.

It was the Sabbath, a day of absolute rest for the Jews. But almost as soon as the sun had set,[22] marking the beginning of a new day, the residents of Capernaum began to throng before the house with all their sick, so that Jesus might heal them.

The most common diseases in Palestine were then (as they are still) those of the eyes, caused by the dust and the glaring sunlight. Even today, St. John's Hospital in Jerusalem alone treats thousands of victims of various eye maladies every year: cataracts, conjunctivitis, inflammation of the optic nerve, clouded vision, etc. Other infirmities too arise from the climatic conditions. The abrupt transitions from cold, rainy days to temperatures of a hundred and four degrees Fahrenheit in the shade, the humidity carried in from the sea by the west wind (so great that at night one finds one's garments soaked in a few hours), the unwholesomeness of certain regions—all are causes of dysentery, malarial fever, skin eruptions, smallpox, pruritus, and, finally and most fearfully, leprosy.

For all such diseases, too, the Hebrew people had a superstitious explanation: each one was really a kind of "uncleanness" incurred through the infraction of some ritual law.[23] The idea of illness was therefore closely linked to that of sin and punishment. Even death, according to the Holy Scriptures, was an extreme consequence of sin.[24] Analogous beliefs are found also in other religions, such as that of Isis.[25]

In Hebrew, the word *hēt'*, or *hattā'āh*, represented as much the guilt as its consequences, which for the most part were just such physical infirmities.[26] Cure, therefore, was held to be possible only if God granted his pardon and remitted the penalty, and it was to be sought only through special rites of purification and through offerings to the Temple. We have already seen (in the case of the purification of Mary after the fortieth day following her delivery) that normal physiological states, such as childbirth, were also considered diseases.

Generally, the rites of purification were to be accomplished not only through exorcism, sacrifices, and prayer, but also with the help of prescribed objects (such as water, oil, herbs, roots, and earth) to which some modest value was ascribed. Actually, unconscious empiric experience lay at the root of this superstition, since some of these elements did indeed have some medical properties. Even sputum was widely used, and it is known that saliva has a disinfectant value (as shown by the example of animals who always lick their wounds), which was recognized earlier, as the learned Pliny testifies, by the Greek and Roman physicians.[27] It was only that Hebrews used these natural products in conjunction with complicated procedures that obscured the direct efficacy of the instrument and transferred it to the accessory rituals. The rabbis taught, for example, that diseases of the eye should be treated with the sputum of the first-born son of a father rather than that of a mother's first son, and so on.

The Church inherited this "moral" concept of physical illness as a punishment or a proof to which God subjects us. Although the idea is scientifically untenable, it still has some practical value insofar as the fear of sin may sometimes deter man from excesses injurious to his health. Surely it would be preferable—as the scientist Julian Huxley hopes[28]—that through education man should learn to live properly without the need of being frightened by an illogical feeling of guilt.

The Church continues even to attribute, like the ancient Hebrews, certain limited powers to elements of nature and to ritualized prayers and supplications. Indeed, purification in the form of a water bath (baptism) and unction with olive oil have been raised to the dignity of sacraments. Even sputum serves still for the blessing at baptism: the priest moistens his finger with saliva to make the sign of the cross on the ears and the mouth of the child. Anointing with oil is based on the regulations contained in the Epistle imputed to James, the brother of Jesus: "Is any sick among you? let him call for the elders of the church; and let them pray over him, *anointing him with oil* in the name of the Lord; And the prayer of faith shall save the sick, and the Lord shall raise him up; and if he have committed sins they shall be forgiven him."[29]

Today, since in general even believers, when they are ill, send for the doctor rather than for the priest, this practice has fallen into desuetude, and unction is reserved for those *in extremis*. Nonetheless, the theologians do not rule out the possibility that it may also perform a physical cure.[30]

A Deaf-Mute and a Blind Man

In the various cures that he performed in Galilee, Jesus always worked in scrupulous accord with the rules that the rabbis had and have handed down, and which he had probably learned from the Essenes. But, perhaps fearing reprisals from the priests and officially licensed teachers, Jesus each time took his patient aside and urged him to tell no one who had healed him.[31] The Gospel of Mark describes with a fascinating wealth of detail (Matthew reports it more tersely) the cures of a deaf-mute and of a blind man.[32]

In the first case, Jesus, having sought privacy with a supplicant, ascertained the nature of his deafness, inserting a finger into each ear; then, having established that the trouble was a blockage that could be removed, he repeated the finger insertion after having first wet the finger tip with saliva. But he did not forget the magic word, to which he himself ascribed the greater part of the merit of the cure and which the Evangelist gives us in the original: *Ephphathā.* Mark translates this as "Be opened!" Then Jesus applied a kind of vigorous massage to the deaf-mute's tongue, "and the string [ὁ δεσμός, *ho desmos*] of his tongue was loosed," enabling him to speak.

With the blind man, too, Jesus worked in completely orthodox fashion. He took him by the hand and led him out of the village, and then repeatedly rubbing the man's eyes with a finger bathed in saliva, tried to detach the membranous film that had formed on the cornea. The Gospel of John says rather that Jesus spat on the ground, made mud with his saliva, and then applied the mixture to the man's eyes. After a while he asked: "Seest thou anything?"

"I see men," he replied, "as trees walking."

Then Jesus resumed rubbing, until the blind man could see clearly.[33]

The fact that the Gospels hesitate over this detail—the need to repeat the operation because it was not wholly successful at first—would seem to help authenticate the story. The Evangelists were trying to report not a "miracle"—which would have had to take place instantaneously—but a normal cure, and one that also offered a certain difficulty. On the other hand, Mark, in his earlier report of the first thaumaturgical attempts by Jesus in Capernaum on the night of the Sabbath, had said explicitly that Jesus had not been able to heal *all* the ailing who had gone to him.[84]

The Woman Who Bled

We know also today that in some kinds of illness the course of the malady is expedited if the patient cooperates through active, willed participation in the physician's work and complete faith in the physician himself.[35] Indeed, it is not unknown that pathological conditions against which medical science has admitted its impotence have been inexplicably cured through the work of some empiric "healer" enveloped in the notoriety of a wonder-worker or in the odor of sanctity. The mass of people makes no distinction between the saint who heals by moving his hands in a gesture of blessing and the quack who uses his for massage: intuitive common sense says that the one and the other alike must be endowed with extraordinary faculties, and it rallies blind supporters to both. Most often they claim to possess that mysterious "essence" on which science has not yet been able to make any pronouncements with certainty, but which indubitably exists in some individuals who feel it pulsing through their bodies and pressing to radiate and expand beyond.

The three Synoptic Gospels, in their references to the cures of Jesus, say repeatedly that Jesus "laid his hands on" the patient[36] or took the patient's hands between his own.[37] For that matter, the liturgical value of the laying on of hands is recognized also in modern theology.[38] That Jesus possessed this essence is shown most clearly by the incident of the woman who bled, reported by all three Synoptics.[39]

The woman, who was suffering from chronic loss of blood, had already consulted a number of physicians, who had attempted, in vain, all the remedies prescribed for the condition by the rabbis. She had been made to sit at the fork of two roads, holding a vessel full of wine, and they had come up stealthily behind her and cried out to the flow of blood to cease; she had been made to swallow a grain of barley from the stable of a white mule, and so forth.[40] Not only had the poor woman submitted to these bizarre remedies without improvement, but rather, Mark says, she had grown worse.

Having heard the reputation of Jesus, she hoped that the mere touch of his body would suffice to cure her, and so it happened. Going to him one day in the midst of a great throng, she stole close to him, and, without being noticed, she brushed her hand against the hem of his garment, or, as Luke[41] has it in the Greek text and the Vulgate, against one of the four fringes that, according to the Law, the Jews had to attach to their mantles.[42] As if by enchantment, she felt in her body that she had been healed of her illness.

Neither Jesus nor his disciples had seen the woman, but he felt that he had been touched, "knowing in himself that virtue had gone out of him" (ἐπιγνοὺς ἐν ἑαυτῷ τὴν ἐξ αὐτοῦ δύναμιν ἐξελθοῦσαν).[43] Surprised, then, he looked round and asked: "Who touched me?"

The disciples almost made fun of him: "Thou seest the multitude throng thee and press thee, and sayest thou, who touched me?"

But the woman, shaking with fear, threw herself at his feet and confessed the truth. Compassionately Jesus replied: "Daughter, thy faith hath made thee whole: go in peace."

The Daughter of Jairus

The Synoptic Gospels insert the story of the woman who bled into the account of another remarkable deed of Jesus.[44] As a matter of fact, the woman had intercepted Jesus while, followed by a large crowd, he was on his way to the home of an eminent man who had gone to beg Jesus to save his twelve-year-old daughter, who lay at the point of death. Mark and Luke say that the man was Jairus, one of the rulers of the synagogue (ἀρχισυναγώγος, archisunagōgos) of Capernaum.

Arriving at the house of Jairus, they found the child's mother already in the throes of despair, surrounded by relatives and neighbors who were condoling with her, weeping and lamenting aloud in the noisy manner of Near Eastern peoples.[45] Jesus sent away all the intruders and went into the child's room, accompanied only by her weeping parents and by three of his disciples: Simon, James, and John. As soon as he had looked at the girl, his face became calm and he sought at once to reassure her parents: "Weep not; she is not dead, but sleepeth." Taking her hand, in order to transmit his essence to her, he uttered the words: *"Talithā cūmi!"*

The girl's eyes opened and her breathing became more regular. Then Jesus bade farewell to her astounded parents, telling them also that they should give their daughter food. Once more he urged that nothing be said of the matter.[46]

The scholars of the liberal school[47] and the rationalists[48] speculate whether Jesus had not simply recognized an instance of apparent death, or a form of coma. In that case, the Evangelists would have been guilty of a blunder.

I do not believe that the authors of the Gospels intended—in good faith or in bad—to pass off such thaumaturgic acts as miracles, but rather only to point out in Jesus certain healing powers that are no longer common today and that in those times were thought to be somehow supernatural, perhaps the sign of a special divine protection.

The Leper

According to what the Gospels give us to understand, Jesus placed little importance on his thaumaturgic activities and undertook them with a certain reluctance. In fact, on the first occasion (the famous Sabbath night in Capernaum) he had even tried to evade the responsibility. Having gone there for the purpose of preaching repentance in preparation for the "kingdom of God," he was deeply grieved that instead he had been made into a healer.[49]

At that moment, however, he could not have refused without risking the immediate loss of his first followers, and he had been constrained to spend the better part of the night in healing the sick. But on the next day, he categorically refused to continue. Just after dawn, the Gospels say, he took advantage of a moment of repose to steal secretly out of Simon's house and went out into the countryside. His companions, concerned when they discovered his absence, overtook him when he stopped to pray: probably, carrying on the habit he had learned from the Essenes, he had looked for a place from which he could watch the sunrise.

Simon and the other disciples virtually reprimanded him, saying: "All men seek for thee."

But Jesus did not intend to let them persuade him to turn back and resume his cures. "Let us go into the next towns," he said, "that I may preach there also: for therefore came I away."

The Gospel of Luke and the Latin translation of that of Mark give this passage a theological interpretation: "for therefore I am sent" and "for therefore came I forth," respectively.[50] Hence some moderns have seen fit to modify the translation to: "for therefore I have gone out from the Father." But Mark's Greek text says ἐξῆλθον (exēlthon), which means only "I have gone out," with the particular sense of having left one's home or one's town.

But notwithstanding the declared purpose of Jesus to travel through Galilee and preach, it seems that outside Capernaum, as inside, the people were more concerned with the immediate gains to be had from his thaumaturgic skills than with the promise of a future kingdom of happiness. Mark says that the sick thronged to him from everywhere in the country and "they pressed upon him for to touch him," so that he had to rebuke them; and he asked that a boat be made ready for escape when the throng threatened to engulf him.[51]

In a village that the Gospels do not identify, there was an incident similar to that in Capernaum. This time an interruption by an ailing man while Jesus was preaching in the synagogue compelled him to break off his discourse and flee again, as he had had to do from Nazareth and Capernaum. However, Jesus was not asked in this case to work a cure in the narrow sense; rather, he was called on to perform an extremely delicate ritual act that by law was exclusively reserved to the priests: to certify that a cure had been accomplished in one of the most serious and most dangerous of contagious diseases, leprosy.

Leprosy was perhaps the worst disaster that could strike a Jew, and, since it was not easy to distinguish it from harmless eruptions or irritations of the skin, detailed rules had been drafted in the earliest times to guide the diagnoses by the priests to whom were entrusted the tasks of declaring the leper "unclean," ordering that he be utterly cast out of the community so that others not be contaminated, and, after having visited him periodically, determining whether he was cured.[52]

Now, the leper of whom the Gospels speak[53] was probably in this final stage: he had to undergo the final purification, and he turned to Jesus, mistaking him for a priest. Touched with pity at the leper's request and wishing not to disappoint those about him, Jesus violated the medico-legal rule—which was most strict in this respect—and assumed the responsibility of verifying that the leper had been "purified." The Gospels expressly employ the verb καθαίρειν (kathairein), which means "to purify,"[54] and never the verb θεραπεύειν (therapeuein), which means "to cure," "to heal," and which they use in all the other instances.

Jesus, indeed, stretched out his hand to the leper and said: "Be thou clean."

There are those who see in this gesture of the outstretched hand a sign of repulsion on the part of Jesus,[55] while others instead believe he sought to touch the leper's sores in order to determine whether scar tissue had yet formed;[56] but this might simply have been no more than a priest-like gesture, as of benediction.

A smile of joy lighted the face of the sufferer. But Jesus immediately regretted having assented to the leper's request too hurriedly, and, full of anger at the thought of the harsh punishment that might be imposed on him, he sent the leper away with a warning to tell no one of the occurrence[57] and an order to go to the chief priest for the ritual purification. In this way he sought, practically, to declare his own action null and void; but the story spread, and, to avert the danger of action against him by the priests, Jesus was compelled to flee from the village and to live hidden for some time in "desert places."[58]

The Paralytic

When he thought that the talk had subsided, Jesus ventured to leave his hiding place, but he did not return to that village; instead, he went back once more to Capernaum as the guest of Simon. Here, unfortunately, his reputation for miracles was still high and very soon he was again besieged by throngs whose demands were exhausting. The Synoptic Gospels are especially thorough in their accounts of the healing of a paralytic,[59] which is less interesting in itself than in some of the doctrinal questions connected with it.

According to the Gospels, the crowd round Simon's door was so dense that the paralytic could not be carried in. The man's family, therefore, broke through the roof of the house, carried him up on his bed and let him down outside so that the bed came to rest at the feet of Jesus. The rationalist critics enjoy pointing out the absurdity and the improbability of this undertaking—the lifting of a paralytic on a litter through the roof, the demolition work that threatened Jesus with a rain of mortar and stones, the lowering of the litter with some unimaginably complicated arrangement of ropes, etc.

But the Evangelists deliberately cite the difficulties of the task not only because the incident gives still another aspect of the thaumaturgic work of Jesus, already amply described, but also because they sought to show how success could reward unshakable faith prepared to surmount any obstacle whatsoever. In a rather artless manner, the Gospels' narrative lets it appear that the cure was arrived at, however, not through the faith of the paralytic but through that of his relatives! Indeed, "when Jesus saw *their* faith,"[60] he said to the patient: "Son, thy sins be forgiven thee."

A murmur ran through the crowd (to make the tale more effective, the Gospels say it contained some Scribes, the learned interpreters of the laws): "Why doth this man thus speak blasphemies?"

But Jesus cut them off sharply: "Why reason ye these things in your hearts? Whether it is easier to say to the sick of the palsy, Thy sins be forgiven thee; or to say, Arise, and take up thy bed, and walk? But that ye may know that the Son of man hath power on earth to forgive sins (he saith to the sick of the palsy), I say unto thee, Arise, and take up thy bed, and go thy way into thine house." And so the man did.

The Catholic exegetes, holding that the cure of the paralytic resulted only from these final words, see in the "forgiveness of sins" mentioned just before them a purely spiritual matter and a declaration by Jesus of his own divinity, which they find confirmed in the phrase "the Son of man"; this, according to them, is the equivalent of "the Son of God."

This is a tendentious interpretation that is based on two more or less deliberate equivocations. First of all, the statement "thy sins be forgiven thee" is (since disease was considered a divine punishment that could be canceled by repentance and prayer) the equivalent of "God hath pardoned thee." This was the formula ordinarily used by the priests in such circumstances, speaking as the interpreters of God. Hence it means, not that Jesus had arrogated a supernatural power to himself, but only that he had claimed priestly power. Even in the Old Testament there are instances of priests and prophets who made the same statement.[61] Jesus did not say: "I forgive thy sins," but he did say, in effect: "Thy sins be forgiven [and I will stand warranty for it]."[62] The outrage of the Scribes arose only from this pretension of Jesus to a priestly authority that they refused to recognize in him.

As for the phrase "the Son of man" (in Hebrew, *ben-ādām;* in Aramaic, *bar-nāshā*), used here for the first time by the Evangelists, it means literally "a man born to another man" and hence simply "a man," following the Eastern custom of patronymic identification.[63] It is extremely frequent in the Old Testament, both in the singular and in the plural. Ezekiel alone employed it ninety-four times, always with the meaning of "man," in contrast to God. Furthermore, the Hebrew language has quite a number of similar idioms formed with the word "son," generally to show a dependent relation. It is only in the New Testament that one finds "the sons of this world," "the children of light," "the sons of Satan," "the children of riches," "the children of lies," etc., instead of "the living," "the wicked," "the rich," "the liars," and so on.

Sometimes the formula "the Son of man" was also used impersonally, in the same way in which the Romans used *homo* and the modern French use *on*, which is simply a contraction of *homo*. Used by one who wishes to indicate himself, it amounts to the first person singular pronoun, in a manner similar to that of those writers who refer to themselves as "your reporter" or "the author."[64]

I do not understand why the phrase should mean "the Son of God" only when Jesus employs it, as the theologians,[65] with very few exceptions,[66] contend. What is more, the phrase is always spoken by Jesus in the Gospels; never does anyone apply it to him.

One cannot help wondering, too, how Jesus, especially at the outset of his ministry, could have given himself such a designation, which his audiences would not have understood. And one cannot help thinking that to call himself the Son of God, even later on, would have been an immodesty for which no other religious reformer, before or after Jesus, had the audacity, even Buddha or Mohammed, whose faiths have as many or more adherents. It is a definitive fact, demonstrated by a thorough reading of the Gospels, that the unequivocal phrase "the Son of God" was never used by Jesus when he was speaking of himself.[67]

In the specific case that concerns us here (the cure of the paralytic), the circumlocution employed by Jesus, "the Son of man," stands simply for "I" and serves an emphatic function. He had overcome the irresolution with which he had had to struggle on the occasion of the leper's purification—the hesitancy to assume priestly powers—and now he dared publicly to assert it as his right: "I, this man you see, have the power to forgive sins."

What gave Jesus so much confidence in so short a time? The Gospels, unfortunately, tell us nothing of the events of the interval; nor do they enlighten us at all on his inner crises or his secret decisions.

[7]

THE MIRACLES

The Centurion and the Widow of Nain

The entire first period of the work of Jesus in Capernaum and the surrounding area, to judge by the reports of the Evangelists, was almost exclusively restricted to the performance of cures and similar activities.

But little by little, as faith in him increased, progressively more significant acts were ascribed to him, to such a degree that a gradual evolution seems to be apparent: from ordinary healing (evidence of his supranormal thaumaturgic powers) to the purification of the leper and the remission of the paralytic's sins (testimony to his priestly authority), and then to the compelling deeds that prove the need for faith (already hinted at in the story of the paralytic), which alone can give assurance of salvation. At a certain point, indeed, it becomes difficult to differentiate between those episodes that are purely reports of cures and exorcisms, probably somewhat altered to satisfy the doctrine of the need for faith, and those that are actually myths invented to support this principle.

Such, for instance, is the case of the healing of the centurion's son in Capernaum,[1] a cure accomplished from a distance rather than as the result of direct treatment of the patient, without any aspect of telepathy (which in one way or another might still be susceptible of scientific explanation), but as a reward for faith. Furthermore, the fact that Matthew and Luke chose as their protagonist a centurion (ἑκατόνταρχος, *hekatontarchos*)[2]—that is, a Roman and hence a pagan

—is especially important, for it tends to show that the fable arose when Christianity had already gone beyond the stage of an ethnic religion restricted to the Hebrew people and considered itself accessible to the Gentiles as well. Luke is especially insistent on this point, recounting that the elders of the local synagogue begged Jesus to help the centurion, because, though an outlander, he had always been extremely well disposed to the citizenry of Capernaum.

Only the Gospel of John ignores this universalist aspect of the tale, and John speaks of a Jewish official (βασιλικός, *Basilikos*) instead of a Roman centurion.[3] What most concerns him is to emphasize the miracle of a cure accomplished from afar; and so, to make the affair even more remarkable, he pretends that while the patient was in his bed in Capernaum, Jesus healed him from several miles away, in Cana.

Otherwise, except for the minor detail that Matthew and John say the supplicant sought aid for his "son," while Luke says it was for his "servant," the evangelical accounts fill out the same skeleton. The centurion (or governmental official) approached Jesus most humbly; he dared not even hope that the Nazarene himself would go to his house, but he implored Jesus at least to command one of his disciples to attempt the cure:

"I am not worthy that thou shouldest come under my roof... but speak the word only [to one among thy disciples] and my servant [son] shall be healed. For I also am a man under authority, having soldiers under me: and I say to this man, Go, and he goeth; and to another, Come, and he cometh; and to my servant, Do this, and he doeth it."

Jesus was so favorably impressed by these words that he sent away the centurion with the assurance that at home he would find his son (servant) cured. Then Jesus exploited the incident to contrast the faith of this stranger to the unbelief of the Galileans, who always required tangible evidence and material proofs of his powers.

Luke alone recounts another miracle performed by Jesus immediately after this event: the resurrection of the only son of a widow living in Nain.[4] It is not hard to find the catechetical purpose of this story, nor to note its tenuous historical veracity, especially in that Luke, his imagination exhausted, put his story together out of snatches from the Bible: the miracle he attributes to Jesus exactly

duplicates the resurrection of the son of a widow in Zarephath by
the prophet Elijah in identical circumstances.[5]

Matthew furnishes an interesting detail at the end of the centurion episode: rebuking his unbelieving compatriots, Jesus threatens them with eternal darkness.[6] Regardless of the views of many
theologians, it seems impossible to recognize here the present concept of hell as a place of punishment for sins committed on earth.
Almost certainly, the word used by Jesus would have been *she'ōl*,
which in Hebrew means "a void," "a subterranean abyss," and which
by metonymy stood for the world of darkness and eternal silence
to which, according to the Hebrew religion, *all* the dead were con-
signed—they were in fact buried in the earth. Since, as we have
already seen, death itself was considered the extreme penalty for sin
and not a natural biological phenomenon, eternal life (on this earth,
of course) was promised to those who had faith and who lived
rigorously pure lives. But even the prophets and the psalmists of
the Old Testament had evinced a certain skepticism as to the
practical fulfillment of such a promise, given the natural tendency
of man to sin.

The Tempest Calmed

The Gospel tale that most dramatically tries to teach the necessity of faith is that of the calming of the storm on the Lake of
Gennesaret. Let us follow it in the Synoptic texts.[7]

One evening Jesus wanted to cross the lake by boat, and, during
the trip, lulled by the monotonous rhythm of the oars as they
whispered in the water, he fell asleep. Suddenly he was awakened by
his disciples, terrified by a storm that threatened to swamp the boat.
All were crying for his help:

"Master [Διδάσκαλε], carest thou not that we perish?"[8]

"Lord [Κύριε], save us: we perish."[9]

"Master, Master ['Επιστάτα, 'Επιστάτα], we perish."[10]

"Why are ye so fearful?" Jesus reprimanded them. "How is it
that ye have no faith?"

That he would reprove them and accuse them of lack of faith
because they took fright at a storm on the water is illogical if the

anecdote does not have the allegorical meaning mentioned above. The storm symbolizes the temptations of evil, the hardships of life, which only steadfast faith can overcome. In fact, the Gospel tale goes on, Jesus rose in the boat and with a commanding gesture of his hand bade the winds and the waters be calm, and they were calm. His action was not theatrical; he was commanding the demons of the storm exactly as he had commanded the demons that possessed men: both alike were hostile powers that troubled the peace of nature. But the value of the story lies in the calm and the serenity of Jesus even in the midst of the squall—a precept and an example of faith for the disciples.[11]

In the conviction that the Evangelists, dazzled by their admiration for Jesus, have always sought a miraculous, supernatural interpretation for his every act, the rationalists try to strip the calming of the tempest of all its miraculous content. Heinrich Paulus, for example, is of the opinion that in reality Jesus merely inveighed against the storm with some gesture arising from vexation at having been made to interrupt his sleep, and that he then tried to hearten his traveling companions because, from certain indications which they in their fear could not recognize, he could see that the storm was almost over.[12] Another scholar, D. F. Strauss, attempts to minimize the miracle of Jesus by comparing it with the much more remarkable inventions of modern science (the compass, the steamboat, etc.), which are directed toward the same end—that is, making navigation safe even in bad weather.[13]

Still others point out that identical miracles were reported to have been performed both before and after Jesus:[14] besides Moses, who is supposed to have parted the waters of the Red Sea, there was also Julius Caesar, who, according to tradition, encouraged his pilot during the dangerous crossing from Apollonia to Brindisi by telling him: "Have no fear, Caesar is with thee." In times much closer to our own, the miracle of calming a tempest was repeated, successfully, by Bishop Neophytos (d. 1731), of whom it is told that *"benedixit aquam eamque in mare proiecit, et continuo facta est tranquillitas."*[15] In any case, these other instances provide confirmation of what the Evangelists sought to show: the necessity of faith, which imparts confidence and courage. And it seems to me that in every instance it is a matter of faith unqualified, like faith in God and in his extraordinary powers, not merely—as the theologian Rudolf Bultmann contends—a specific "belief in miracles."[16]

The Man Possessed at Gergesa

Midway in their journey across the lake, after Jesus had calmed the troubled waters, they came to Gergesa (today's Gerga), which is almost in the center of the eastern shore. The terms Gerasenes[17] and Gadarenes,[18] given in the Gospels, are universally recognized as erroneous. Gergesa was the scene of another marvel,[19] which, however, reduced to its proper proportions, is only a case of exorcism again exploited to show the miraculous results of faith.

As soon as they had beached their boat, Jesus and the disciples encountered a strange being: a kind of raving lunatic, who had chosen to dwell in the burial caves on the sides of the mountain that sloped down to the lake. He had fled from the inhabitants of the region, who had tried several times to capture him and bind him with chains. Perhaps he was suffering from lycanthropy—the so-called werewolf affliction—because at night he roamed about, howling and beating himself with stones. At the sight of Jesus, the wretched lunatic ran toward him with threatening gestures and cried: "What have I to do with thee, Jesus, thou Son of God most high? I beseech thee, torment me not."

Unafraid, Jesus stood firm before the man, stared fixedly into his eyes, and began the ritual gestures of exorcism.

Anxious silent moments followed; the only sound was the madman's heavy breathing, which might prove only the prelude to a violent outburst. Anyone who has observed an attempt at exorcism or neuropsychiatric treatment in an institution knows how essential it is to allay the apprehensions of the patient. The ancient Palestinian healers knew this too, and, for just such a purpose, Jesus tried to lead the man to talk: "What is thy name?"

The reply was a madman's: "My name is Legion, for we are many." So the Evangelists give it, obviously alluding to the hundreds of demons by whom they believed he was possessed.

Suddenly he broke out in uncontainable rage. His howls, his agonizing moans, his convulsive gyrations frightened a herd of swine feeding nearby. Squealing shrilly, the animals fled from the spectacle and threw themselves into the lake.

When the swineherds, alarmed by all the noise, arrived, all was once more quiet, the poor madman, by now exhausted, lay almost asleep at the feet of Jesus and the disciples stood in silence round him. After a moment of shock, the swineherds demanded why these strangers had come to breach the peace of their countryside, and then they made Jesus and the disciples go back into their boat and cast off.

I took the liberty of revising the Gospels' account only where it relates that the swine (they numbered two thousand!) went mad and threw themselves into the lake because the demons, having obtained the permission of Jesus to do so, entered into their bodies after being forced to leave that of the man.

Quite logically, this passage is one of the most battered targets of liberal and rationalist criticism. The legend, they say, could not have originated in Palestine, where pigs had never been kept because the religious laws strictly prohibited the eating of their meat.[20] It might have been suggested by a tale popular some time after the period of Jesus: the story of the demon Legion, which, like the name, sprang from the presence of the Roman Tenth Legion in Palestine from A.D. 70 (the year of the destruction of the Temple) to A.D. 135. To be sure, the Tenth Legion did have the effigy of a wild boar on its standards.[21] It was the name and escutcheon of that legion, hated by the Jews as the symbol of foreign domination and of the devastation of their country, and hence as an emanation of evil, that gave the Evangelists the idea of the two thousand devils and the two thousand swine.[22]

But above all, the proof of the story's falsity lies for many critics in the supposition that Jesus should have allowed himself to be moved by the pleas of the devils, who were spirits of evil and his implacable adversaries, and that he should have allowed them to gain respite by quitting the body of the man and entering those of the beasts. Yet it is precisely in this improbability that the story's deepest expression of faith is to be found: to believe that Jesus was sent by God and to obey him blindly, the believer's faith in him must be so invincible that he would be thought capable of any act, however remarkable and incredible. *Credo quia absurdum* is the cry of the true Christian.

The Epileptic Boy

The need for faith is labored again in another story of healing, which, however, not all the Synoptic Gospels place chronologically in the same period of the life of Jesus.[23] Actually, it does not have precisely the same function as the other anecdotes we have examined thus far: it does not seek to bring out the need for faith on the part of those who believe, if they would obtain divine intervention to their advantage, but emphasizes rather the need for faith in God's ministers themselves, that they may be able to carry out such activities for the benefit of the faithful.

One day, the Gospels say, Jesus saw a number of people in heated argument with some of his disciples. Worried, he went up to them and asked: "What question ye with them?"

"Master," one of the crowd replied, falling to his knees before Jesus, "I have brought unto thee my son, which hath a dumb spirit [ἄλαλον, *alalon*]; and wheresoever he taketh him, he teareth him; and he foameth, and gnasheth with his teeth, and pineth away; and I spoke to thy disciples, that they should cast him out: and they could not."

The first reaction of Jesus to this story was an outburst of anger against his disciples: "O faithless and perverse generation! how long shall I be with you? how long shall I suffer you?" Then he asked that the boy be brought to him; and in that very moment the child was stricken with an attack that, on the basis of the symptoms described by his father, we should not hesitate to classify as epileptic. But in the days of Jesus, epilepsy, too, was attributed to the influence of demons.

While the unfortunate child lay writhing and foaming on the ground, Jesus asked the father: "How long is it ago since this came unto him?"

"Of a child: And ofttimes it hath cast him into the fire, and into the waters, to destroy him: but if thou canst do any thing, have compassion on us, and help us."

"What? *If thou canst do?* All things are possible to him that believeth."

The first part of this sentence, however, was erroneously given by the Vulgate and by almost all modern translators as: "If thou canst believe"; but the Gospel of Mark reads exactly: τὸ εἰ δύνῃ (*to ei dunē*), corresponding to my translation. Actually, Mark emphasizes the need for belief in God's ministers.

Here, in this sentence, is the central point of the story. And the Gospels make the point again, telling how, when they had returned home after Jesus had effected the cure, the disciples asked him: "Why could not we cast him out?"

"Because of your unbelief," Jesus said sharply. "For verily I say unto you, If ye have faith as a grain of mustard seed, ye shall say unto this mountain, Remove hence to yonder place, and it shall remove; and nothing shall be impossible unto you."

The passages in both Matthew and Mark conclude with a curious statement that has every appearance of repeating a rule for the clergy: "Howbeit, this kind goeth not out but by prayer and fasting."[24]

The Marriage at Cana

In the fertile Plain of Gennesaret, enclosed by the lake and the mountains, there were many towns, large and small, where Jesus could carry on his career as preacher and thaumaturge without going too far from Capernaum, which continued to be his headquarters. About three miles north of Capernaum was Chorazin (today called Khirbet Kerazeh), a small farming village; almost across from Capernaum, on the left bank of the Jordan where the river enters the lake, there were Bethsaida and the new town of Julias (which is now Khirbet et Tell), built by the tetrarch Herod Philip in honor of the daughter of Augustus; farther south, on the western shore of the lake, were Magdala (now Mejdel) and Tiberias, but Jesus did not visit Tiberias because it was too large and because it was inhabited predominantly by pagans.[25] To the west of the lake, however, about halfway between Tiberias and Nazareth, was Cana (now Kefr Kenna or, more probably, Khirbet Qana).

In this village of Cana, Jesus performed one of his most spectacular miracles, far different from the cures we have been discussing. This was the famous transformation of water into wine during a wedding feast.

Since the only account of the prodigy appears in the Gospel of John,[26] which is notorious for its utter lack of concern with veracity, as well as for its disregard of chronology in the life of Jesus, but which gives everything a theological and religious interpretation, the story must be carefully analyzed, with special attention to its symbolic meaning, which is undoubtedly what interested its author. Taken literally, the miracle of Cana lends itself (as it has lent itself since the earliest times) to remarkable suppositions and discussions. Even the most orthodox Doctors of the Church have castigated its inappropriateness and its untimeliness. Irenaeus criticizes Mary's excess of "importunateness" in demanding that her son perform a miracle;[27] John Chrysostom accuses her of too much "vanity" in showing herself off as the mother of the Messiah;[28] and so forth. Others take Jesus to task for what they consider a rude retort, a note of irritation—his answer to his mother's remark about the lack of wine: "Woman, what have I to do with thee?" For the Greek τί ἐμοὶ καὶ σοί (ti emoi kai soi), the corresponding idiomatic expression in Hebrew, which is not uncommon in the Bible, would have been mah-lī wālāk, which can also indicate plain surprise, as if one were to say: "Why do you come to me about these things?"[29]

More recent critics have directed attention to the embarrassing implications in John that Jesus was in the company of drinkers and was in truth abetting their indulgence by working a miracle.[30] A bizarre life of Jesus (written by a man who declares it was dictated to him by Jesus himself, in a vision) causes Jesus to say that he was most careful to refrain from such a miracle, that, had it been possible, he would gladly have changed the wine into water in order to prevent the horror of drunkenness![31]

According to others, the miracle was for Jesus a means of rectifying his own and his friends' negligence in forgetting to bring several jars of wine as a wedding gift, in consonance with custom.[32] Still others, no less imaginative, contend that Jesus wanted to play a joke: he had indeed brought jars of wine as a nuptial gift, but he had them put on the table only at the end of the dinner, pretending they contained water, in order to amuse the other guests.[33] And some students, finally, believe the disproportion between the amount of wine and the number of guests simply caused Jesus to water what there was.

Those who accept the miracle of Cana as authentic and search for some reason for an action so remarkable and of so little practical value (it was no recompense for faith, as the cures were) are as far off the track as the skeptics who suggest that John was trying to extract a miracle from a commonplace makeshift or, worse, from a joke by Jesus.[34]

John's story is valuable as a myth that is in perfect accord with the whole economics of his Gospel: timed right after the beginning of the ministry of Jesus, the transformation of the water into wine symbolizes the abundance of gifts that will be showered on those who believe in his word.[35] The Evangelist himself clearly signifies this meaning by employing an exaggeratedly large amount of water: six "waterpots," or jars, each containing two or three "measurers," which would amount to something between a hundred and twenty and a hundred and eighty gallons, since each "measurer" ($\mu\epsilon\tau\rho\eta\tau\acute{\eta}s$, metrētēs)—the King James Bible translates this as "firkin"—was the equivalent of about ten gallons. He finishes the story with a summation: "This beginning of miracles did Jesus in Cana of Galilee, and manifested forth his glory; and his disciples believed on him."

Allegorical meanings can also be sought in the individual details of John's account. As an instance, the statement by the governor of the feast to the bridegroom, "Thou hast kept the good wine until now," can mean that the salvation promised by Jesus will come in all its fullness and perfection only at the time he has set for it, after everything has been accomplished.[36]

It is not at all difficult to retrace the Biblical precedents that suggested the entire episode to the Evangelist, and such an investigation confirms its religious rather than historical character: Moses' striking water from the rock to save the chosen people in the drought of the desert,[37] the prophet Elijah's making it possible for the poor widow of Zarephath (the only person who believed in him) to draw from a tiny cruse an indefinite amount of oil, Elisha's helping of the widow in debt, by pouring from one pot enough oil to fill a number of jars, including those she had borrowed from her neighbors.[38]

These Old Testament miracles, then, quite as much as that of Jesus at the marriage feast in Cana, embody, in the imaginative language of Biblical literature, the concept of divine munificence in the protection of the faithful. The explanation of them as myths, created for the teachings and the reinforcement of the Church, rescues us from the dilemma of having either to refute them as absurdities or to accept them by faith alone and thus outrage our intelligence and our common sense.

Henceforth, the life of Jesus is conceived in Hellenistic manner as a revelation of God himself: the marvelous manifestation of divine action in the guise of earthly occurrences.[39]

What Is a Miracle?

According to the majority of theologians, belief in the miracles of Jesus is essential to Christianity. To deny that he performed them would mean to bleed him of divine essence, to look on him as no more than "the prototype of the believer," a mere man who preached a life of moral perfection and who furnished the first example of it. For others, however, his life as a redeemer and a teacher is of itself already too sublime to need prodigies.[40] We will come back again to this Christological controversy, which emphasizes, on the one hand, the material character of the person of Jesus as "the Son of God," and, on the other, the moral value of his teaching.

For the moment, it is of interest to us to examine scientifically the true nature of what is called a "miracle," its actual possibility and its credibility. First of all, what is a miracle? To start with Augustine's definition, a miracle is anything that happens *contra quam est nota natura*—that is, in defiance of the natural laws known to us.[41] Augustine's definition is undoubtedly satisfactory, and as a matter of convention, we can very well accept "miracle" to denote all that violates the normal laws of nature as we understand them or that occurs in a fashion different from what our experience tells us should be the case in the natural order of things. But our concept of the determining cause of such unusual events is quite different from that of the ancients. To the extent that they could not explain such things to themselves, they ascribed them to some mysterious supernatural intervention. Even as ultra-normal a phenomenon as the sprouting of seeds in the field, in the eyes of the ancient Hebrews, seemed a divine miracle whenever it recurred.[42]

Faced with an unusual occurrence, we of today limit ourselves to establishing that it has happened as the result of some modification of the laws of nature that is beyond our experience. To ascribe every unusual event to an unexpected and unhoped-for intervention of a divinity offends not only a materialistic conception of the universe but also spiritual idealism, which, even admitting that reality is not wholly embodied in the multiplicity of natural phenomena, nevertheless respects both their order and their causality, precisely because both are the creations of a superior intelligence that has anticipated everything and that has no occasion to make arbitrary changes in its own conduct.[43]

For the same reason, believers, who are more aware of the problem, should admit their perplexity when confronted with miracles.[44] To argue the possibility of a miracle as an event outside nature is to hoodwink the ignorance of the unlettered and to encourage their superstition. A miracle, in fact, according to Benedetto Croce's definition, is "the product of ignorance that projects itself into an inconceivable and absurd metaphysical reality."[45]

It is just such ignorance and fear of all events outside the normal course of things—even of atmospheric and seismic phenomena, such as lightning, thunder, and volcanic eruptions—that gave birth in antiquity to the conviction that they were the results of divine intervention. Once the acceptance of such intrusions on nature had entered into a system of ideas, it was easy to imagine that such forces might be capable of any caprice; and this, furthermore, accorded perfectly with the concept of divinity as an "all-powerful" being tyrannically disposing of the destinies of all things, and it contributed to the furtherance of respect and fear.[46] Even today, unfortunately, this is still the viewpoint of official theology, which finds it expedient to keep the faithful believing in miracles—as unexpected and extraordinary evidences of God's power—literally for the edification of faith, or, as Thomas Aquinas said, ad fidei comprobationem.[47]

Miracles in the New Testament

All the ancient religions, including those of the pagans, gave credence to extraordinary events imputed to various deities. Greek and Latin mythology is especially rich in stories of gods who raise or subdue storms, who inflict plagues or end them, who guide or deflect the arrows shot by heroes on battlefields, who make men fall in love, or go mad, or die, who assume human form or change men into gods, into animals, into rocks, into trees, into fountains. . . . The poetry of Homer and Virgil is filled with such fantasies. In his *Metamorphoses* alone, Ovid composed a remarkably long poem of fifteen books. To bring together all the miraculous events narrated in *The Annals of the Roman People* of Livy (otherwise a very sober scholar, who was writing in precisely those years Jesus was growing up) would make a vast volume.

Another historian, Tacitus, who flourished about fifty years after Jesus, reports miraculous cures effected by the Emperor Vespasian "by reason of a singular inclination of the gods in his favor" (*favor e coelis et inclinatio numinum*).[48] In the Asclepieion in Athens there were numerous inscriptions of thanks for miraculous cures performed by the god Asclepius (Aesculapius). The miracles attributed to Apollonius of Tyana, a philosopher who lived in the first century A.D., bear a remarkable resemblance to those of Jesus.

Origen, a Father of the Church, wrote a polemic work against the pagan Celsus, who maintained that Asclepius, too, had performed miracles and after his death (Zeus struck him with a thunderbolt) had appeared many times both to Greeks and to barbarians. In fact, the cult of Asclepius, as the Olympian god of medicine, was quite widespread some centuries before Christ, and there are great similarities between certain attributes of Jesus and those given to Asclepius, such as φιλανθρωπότατος (*philanthrōpotatos*), "the best friend of men," and Σωτήρ (*Sōter*), "Savior."[49] Many of the shrines of ancient Greece were near sacred springs to which the believers ascribed miraculous properties identical with those of Lourdes.[50]

Now, the credibility of Livy, Tacitus, and the other pagan writers is surely no less than that of the authors of the Gospels. Hence the miracles recounted by the latter have no probative value for the thesis of the superiority of Christianity to the other religions, and they are insufficient to demonstrate the divinity of Jesus.

We cannot subscribe to the argument of Christian theology—"the Gospels say that Jesus wrought miracles and therefore he was a divine being"[51]—but we do say, on the contrary, that the Evangelists were convinced Jesus was a divine being and therefore attributed miracles to him. What they did was the result of faith and adoration; thus, if we intend to conduct a serious historical investigation, we must necessarily examine in what circumstances and on what bases the tradition of each of the miracles recounted in the New Testament might have arisen, and we must study their meanings, notwithstanding the penalty of anathema with which the Church threatens all who do not believe in the reality of these miracles.[52]

Until now, the liberal and rationalist critics have made every effort to explain them away by viewing all of them as "inventions"[53] of the four Evangelists—either stupid bewilderment that led them to exaggerate ordinary things or efforts to report as acts performed by Jesus what were in fact only the subjects of his parables. The German scholar Adolf von Harnack, in particular, has classified them in detail.[54] We have already seen, however, how in most cases the rationalists reached ridiculous conclusions through the very method they employed to explain the New Testament miracles: for instance, the theory that the descent of the Holy Ghost was in reality a flash of lightning or a ray of sunlight piercing the clouds, or the hypothesis that Satan, the Tempter, was a man in the pay of the enemies of Jesus, or the supposition that Jesus played a trick at the wedding feast in Cana, etc., ranging as far as the extreme statement of L. A. Feuerbach that "the miracle is religion's sense of humor"![55] Nonetheless, they do not succeed even in this manner in "discovering" the real facts behind an account of a miracle. Harnack himself, concluding his analysis, is constrained to leave aside a certain number of extraordinary events which do not fall within any of the categories established by him and which he finds convenient to classify as "impossible of explanation."[56]

The fact is that not all the miracle stories of the New Testament are of the same kind. The latest advances in Christological studies have enlightened us on an area hitherto obscure. Above all, the German Protestant school of Formgeschichte ("form history," but generally known as "form criticism"), which studies the modes of thinking and language characteristic of Hebrew society and takes note of the propensity for imagery of expression, rich in metaphor and allegory, holds to the belief that most of the miracles should be viewed as so many "myths." Just as, for example, the journey of the Three Kings (the Magi) to the birthplace of Jesus symbolizes the homage of all races, the transformation of the water into wine at the marriage in Cana symbolizes the gifts of God to all who believe; and so on. The efforts of these theologians are therefore directed to the elimination of the myths in the accounts of the miracles, in order to discover what lies beneath them and to restate, in language appropriate to our modern mentality, their moral or dogmatic content.

This invalidates the charge made by the rationalists, who, attacking the good faith of the four writers on the life of Jesus, consider their texts to be reprehensible works of mystification. In reality, either the Evangelists have honestly set down cures and exorcisms actually performed by Jesus and ascribed by them, as contemporary beliefs dictated, to supernatural powers—that is, to "radiations of his divine character"[57]—or they have adopted the forms of expression familiar to them (derived from the literature of the Old Testament) to explain the fundamental myths of their religion. The latter is in truth the more frequent case: the Gospels are essentially catechetical works—that is, manuals for liturgical reading and for the instruction of the faithful.[58] The anti-myth thesis has begun to attract Catholic theologians, and, sometimes even more boldly than their Protestant colleagues, they attach a sacramental value to matters that are normally considered thaumaturgic acts: the restoration of sight to the blind, according to some of these scholars, symbolizes "the illumination of faith";[59] the cures and resuscitations of the paralyzed, the dying, and the dead represent "mankind fallen into sin and redeemed by faith"; and so on.

[8]

THE LAW AND THE PHARISEES

Levi (Matthew)

Since Capernaum lay at the frontier of the Tetrarchy of Herod Antipas, near the road that led from the Mediterranean coast to Damascus,[1] it served as a customs post for goods in transit, giving employment to numerous assessors in addition to the usual collectors of tithes on local production. One of these assessors, or publicans, as the Vulgate version of the New Testament calls them, became a disciple of Jesus. The Synoptic Gospels tell the story in their usual terse way: "[Jesus] said unto him, Follow me. And he arose and followed him."[2]

There is some debate as to the man's identity. Mark and Luke call him Levi, the son of Alphaeus (*Halphai*), whereas Matthew gives him his own name. Therefore, the Catholic exegetes, ruling out any possibility of discrepancies among the Gospels (it must be remembered that, for the Church, they were dictated by God), argue that Matthew was Levi's surname and consequently they like to assume that this Matthew is to be identified with the Evangelist himself. An ingenious solution may be that proposed by Klausner, who suggests that he was Matthew the son of Alphaeus the Levite.[3]

Whatever might have been the name of the new acolyte, we must believe that at least in the beginning the other disciples were not overly pleased at having him among them. The tax collector has never been a sympathetic character, and he was the less so to the

Hebrews, for the country was under foreign occupation and the tax collector was despised as a collaborationist. Besides, the fiscal system introduced by the Romans was of a kind that invited many abuses by collectors of tenuous scruple. Tax collection was let out by contract under the empire, and the contractor, acting as a personal guarantor of payment, was free to collect as much more than the amount due as he could exact for his own profit and to set up a contingency fund; this excess varied with the honesty of the individual. As soon as the harvest had been gathered, the publicans, or collectors recruited by the Roman contractors among the local populations, leveled the heaps of grain with shovels and then impressed each heap with a special wooden stamp; if anyone tried to remove some of the grain, the mark would disappear. The value of each heap was then reckoned and one-tenth was taken as the state's tax—or, if the collector was greedy, one-ninth or even one-eighth.[4]

For such reasons the publicans were hated by the people, who viewed them as bloodsuckers fattening on their fellows, and their calling was despised. They could not even testify in lawsuits, and no decent father would have allowed his daughter to marry one.

At Table with Publicans

It may be assumed that, when he joined the company of Jesus, Levi, or Matthew, feeling ashamed at having bled the poor of their money, gave up his hated post. But the fact that Jesus welcomed him among his followers and even accepted without hesitation the publican's invitation to dine in his house was a scandal such as had never been known in Capernaum.

The meal was shared, the Gospels report, by a number of other tax men, colleagues of Levi, and some "sinners."[5] This word is not to be read in its modern meaning. These were not real *abaryānīm*, who led depraved lives, but the individuals who were called in Hebrew *amē hā-'erets*, which means, literally, "men of the soil" but which in practice carried a strong pejorative connotation similar to "rabble" or "scum"—they led simple lives and paid little heed to the complicated rules that were supposed to govern the life of the ideal Jew.[6] The Sadducees and the Pharisees, who were the Jewish aristocracy, looked on them as a "crowd of good-for-nothings."[7] Even Rabbi Hillel, the kindliness of whose teachings gives them many resemblances to those of Jesus, declared that an *amē hā-'erets* had no conscience. Rabbi Jonathan asserted that because they disregarded the Law they deserved to be split in two, like fish.

This helps us to understand the anger of the strait-laced people of Capernaum when they heard that Jesus and his disciples had eaten with publicans and *amē hā-'erets*. The righteous, unable to restrain their comments, voiced their indignation to the followers of Jesus: "Why do ye eat and drink with publicans and sinners?"

Jesus answered for them with a forceful metaphor: "They that are whole have no need of the physician, but they that are sick. I came not to call the righteous, but sinners to repentance."

What Jesus meant is clear: he himself was the physician who had to treat those cast out by society, who had to educate and redeem the proletariat that hardly knew and barely practiced religion. But the nice people of Capernaum did not understand his thinking; they were convinced that "perfection" could never be achieved except through the meticulous observance of the prescribed rituals, combined with ablutions, fasts, and other forms of physical mortification. They went further and asked why Jesus and the disciples ate and drank with the publicans and sinners if they wanted them to repent, and Jesus, paraphrasing a well-known passage of the Old Testament,[8] replied that he wished them to know goodness, not to make sacrifices.

"Why," he was then asked, "do the disciples of John fast often, and make prayers, and likewise the disciples of the Pharisees; but thine eat and drink?"

"Can ye make the children of the bridechamber fast," he retorted, "while the bridegroom is with them? But the days will come, when the bridegroom shall be taken away from them, and then shall they fast in those days."

Jesus had apparently changed his views on fasting, which he had sometimes practiced in the desert of Judea either because of a vow taken as a Nazirite or as a form of spiritual purification. He had now conquered in himself the petty superstitions of his contemporaries (which were to reappear in the Middle Ages and which have continued into our day) and he had learned that it is non-sensical to view abstention from food as evidence of religious devotion. What counted was to do good, not to mortify the flesh in ridiculous sacrifices. Fasting is, if anything, a physiological need that one heeds when one is so borne down by cares and grief that they automatically eliminate any desire for food. Young men grieve when a close friend decides to marry and to abandon their careless pleasures; but there are certain occasions, such as a marriage feast, when one cannot impose on oneself the austerity of fasting.[9]

We should observe here that the phrase of the New Testament, οἱ υἱοὶ τοῦ νυμφῶνος (hoi hyoi tou nymphōnos), is given a wholly wrong Latin translation: filii sponsi, or "children of the bridegroom." Νυμφῶν (nymphōn) means "nuptial bed" or "bridal chamber," and Jesus was alluding to the young friends of the bridegroom who, by contemporary custom, attended on him and accompanied him all the way to the marriage bed. We cannot be sure whether it was the inaccurate Latin translation in the Vulgate that gave the exegetes the idea that Jesus sought here to prophesy about himself (he being the bridegroom who will one day depart and leave behind his sons)—a thought, however, that was foreign to the messianic expectation of his times[10]—or whether it was the theological interpretation itself (Jesus as God, of whom all men are children) that guided the hand of the Vulgate translator, Jerome. Such a prophecy concerning his own divine affiliation would be completely out of place in the passage in which it is inserted.

The indifference of Jesus to the practice of fasting, like his acceptance of an invitation to dine with publicans, shocked the people of Capernaum. Jesus remarked bitterly:[11] "No man putteth a piece of new cloth unto an old garment." New ideas never suit the stubborn mentality of the conservative, rooted in his traditional customs. Jesus knew how hard it was to eradicate prejudices—revolutionary ideas require wholly new men—and he phrased this conviction in a metaphor of the same kind as its predecessor: "Neither do men put new wine into old bottles: else the bottles break, and the wine runneth out, and the bottles perish; but they put new wine into new bottles, and both are preserved." Then he offered a further clarification: "No man also having drunk old wine straightway desireth new: for he saith, The old is better."

John's Doubts

The shock caused by Jesus also had a sequel somewhat later, when news of the arguments that had ensued with the inhabitants of Capernaum reached John the Baptist, who was still a prisoner of Herod Antipas in the fortress of Machaerus. The Baptist was particularly disturbed by the fact that his former disciple had dared to deny the importance of fasting, which he, on the contrary, had always practiced and which he had made the center of his own teaching. In addition, the behavior of Jesus in taking part in a profane feast with publicans and sinners was so far removed from the austere pattern of a prophet, as embodied in John the Baptist, that the precursor managed to communicate with Jesus through two old followers of his own. They carried John's reproof to Jesus: "Art thou he that should come, or do we look for another?"

It is hardly necessary to point out that these doubts in John contradict the hypothesis upheld by the Church that he had already recognized the Messiah in Jesus when he baptized him. The answer that Jesus gave to the two messengers shows that, out of respect for his precursor as well as out of modesty, he dared not even reply directly to what had been asked of him; instead, he submitted himself to John's judgment: "Go your way and tell John what things ye have seen and heard; how that the blind see, the lame walk, the lepers are cleansed, the deaf hear, the dead are raised, to the poor the gospel is preached."

These words, attributed to Jesus by two of the Evangelists, Matthew and Luke,[12] sound so much like a famous prophetic passage of the Old Testament[13] that sets forth the happy circumstances of the future "kingdom of God," and the expedient to which Luke himself resorts is so childish and artless (he has Jesus setting about at once to perform various miracles for the two emissaries in order to convince them of his powers), that they raise a justified suspicion as to their authenticity.

Both Gospels add that Jesus concluded his message to John by

saying: "And blessed is he, whosoever shall not be offended in me."
This extremely cryptic sentence has caused commentators of every
school to exhaust themselves searching for a logical interpretation
of it, but they err by giving it an allegorical meaning in reliance on
Latin (or even modern-language) translations, instead of going back
to the original Greek text. This reads: Μακάριός ἐστιν ὃς ἐὰν μὴ
σκανδαλισθῇ ἐν ἐμοί (*Makarios estin hos ean mē skandalisthē en emoi*),
and it should be noted that the pronoun *hos* is used demonstratively
("he") and not relatively ("whosoever"). Nor can one give the verb
skandalizein its modern meaning of "shock," "offend." Logically, it
was used in its original meaning, customary in classical Greek, of
"set up obstacles," "bewilder," "cause doubt." Hence the sentence of
the Gospels is in no way equivocal and means: "Blessed is he [John]
if he no longer doubts me." It is a respectful and quite delicate
utterance, by which Jesus hoped to reassure the prophet.

As soon as John's men had gone, Jesus gathered all his disciples
(among whom there were surely some old followers of the Baptist)
and launched into ardent praise of John:[14] "What went ye out into
the wilderness for to see? A reed shaken with the wind? But what
went ye out for to see? A man clothed in soft raiment? Behold, they
which are gloriously apparelled, and live delicately, are in kings'
courts. But what went ye out for to see? A prophet? Yea, I say unto
you, and much more than a prophet. For this is he, of whom it is
written, Behold, I send my messenger before thy face, which shall
prepare thy way before thee."

By quoting a Biblical passage,[15] Jesus sought to underline the
great significance of John in preparing men to receive the messianic
kingdom. But unforeseeably, immediately after these fine praises,
we find in the Gospels of Matthew and Luke[16] a strange statement
by Jesus that contradicts everything before it: "Verily I say unto
you, Among them that are born of women there hath not risen a
greater than John the Baptist: *notwithstanding, he that is least in
the kingdom of heaven is greater than he.*"

How is one to account for this sentence, so scant in respect for
John, coming as it does right after an impassioned panegyric? Can
one imagine, as E. L. Stapfer does, a petty feeling of vindictiveness
in Jesus:[17] "He refused to accept me as the Messiah; therefore he is
worth less than the least of my disciples"? Or perhaps a self-

aggrandizing but not too clear declaration, as Giuseppe Petrelli construes it:[18] "I [Jesus], who am less than God, am still greater than John"?

The historical interpretation of this strange speech may be this: Since the Gospel according to Matthew is known to have been the text of a Christian-Jewish community deeply opposed to the contemporary sect of the followers of John, the book neglected no opportunity to diminish the Baptist's importance, to the greater advantage of Jesus, and the addition to the speech of praise sprang from just this polemic necessity. The Gospel of Luke—which, as the reader can recognize by now, is built on Matthew's but does not always understand it or interpret it accurately—incautiously repeats the sentence derogatory of John but then quite coolly resumes the praises of the precursor: "And all the people that heard him, and the publicans, justified God, being baptized with the baptism of John. But the Pharisees and lawyers [Scribes] rejected the counsel of God against themselves, being not baptized of him."[19]

The apocryphal Gospel of Thomas also repeats Matthew's sentence denigrating John, but dilutes it, interpolating a baffling clause: "for fear that the eyes of such a one should be lost."[20] One student of this "Fifth Gospel," Jean Doresse, suggests therefore that the passage be revised to read: "It is only to avoid scandalizing and hurting some humble soul that I said: He who is smallest among you shall be higher than John!"[21]

But Luke manages to resolve even the conflict between Jesus and John over the fast, by putting a felicitously conciliatory speech into the mouth of Jesus: "Whereunto then shall I liken the men of this generation? and to what are they like? They are like unto children sitting in the market place, and calling one to another, and saying, We have piped unto you, and ye have not danced; we have mourned to you, and ye have not wept. For John the Baptist came neither eating bread nor drinking wine; and ye say, He hath a devil. The Son of man is come eating and drinking; and ye say, Behold a gluttonous man, and a winebibber, a friend of publicans and sinners! But wisdom is justified of all her children."[22]

The Jews, Jesus meant, were as capricious and fickle as children: if one spoke sorrowfully to them and bade them repent, they grew angry and refused to hear; if one gave them fine promises and words of hope, they did not believe and turned their backs.

The Woman Who Sinned

In further confirmation of the intention of Jesus to shatter the narrow-minded puritanism of his people, Luke tells the story of another scandalous dinner immediately after the first.[23] Jesus had been invited to dine at the house of a local Pharisee named Simon. While they were reclining on mats, in Near Eastern fashion, and eating their meal, a woman came stealthily into the room, walked unhesitatingly toward Jesus, threw herself at his feet, anointed them with myrrh, which she had brought with her in an alabaster box, bathed them with her tears, dried them with her flowing hair, kissed them ...

She was a public sinner, a woman whose custom it was to offer her voluptuous body for the satisfaction of the impure desires of men—one of those whom society contemptuously calls "fallen women." The master of the house, who had had no time or way to stop her, made no effort to hide his resentment, especially when he saw that Jesus did not even try to avoid the unclean contact and indeed welcomed her attentions. Smiling, Jesus explained his own behavior, beginning with a parable that really had little to do with the case (it dealt with a money-lender who forgave two debts of unequal amounts) and then going directly into the matter: "Seest thou this woman? I entered into thine house, thou gavest me no water for my feet: but she hath washed my feet with tears, and wiped them with the hairs of her head. Thou gavest me no kiss: but this woman, since the time [she] came in, hath not ceased to kiss my feet. My head with oil thou didst not anoint: but this woman hath anointed my feet with ointment. Wherefore I say unto thee, Her sins, which are many, are forgiven; for she loved much; but to whom little is forgiven, the same loveth little."

The traditional exegetes have sought to give the young woman a name: Mary. Some of them, beginning with Pope Gregory the Great in the sixth century, identify her (though there is nothing in the Gospels to support the hypothesis) with Mary of Magdala, others with Mary of Bethany (both of whom figure later in the life of Jesus), while still others make all three Marys a single person; this is the accepted belief in the Catholic liturgy.[24] In any case, in the rubrics of the faithful the episode is utilized to illustrate the reformation of sinners, and so the girl is generally identified as a "repentant sinner." In France, the word *madeleine* is used for prostitutes who seek to rehabilitate themselves in specially created religious institutions (*les hospices de la Madeleine*).

Such an interpretation is wholly alien to the spirit of the Gospel story and strips it of its truly new concept, which is genuinely Christian. Whether the episode is actually fact or whether, as is more likely, it was invented by the Evangelist to illustrate one facet of the doctrine of Jesus, its central theme is not repentance but love. The young woman is a sinner, and nothing gives us reason to believe that she repents, but her acts testify to a devotion and unselfish love so self-abasing and rare that they earn pardon for the most serious derelictions.

The Evangelist is seeking to oppose the rigidity of the moralists and their mean concept of rectitude—which they view as consisting in the scrupulous observance of rules within the bounds of a blind egotism devoid of compassion and of love for one's neighbor—with the positive value of love, even in those who have never been able to overcome the temptations of evil. Even more than a generous tribute to the young woman's kindness of heart, the words of Jesus are a harsh rebuke to the sterility of those who do not know love.

Paradoxically, the writer chose a form of sin that has aroused the greatest revulsion in the moralists of every age—the sin of the flesh—precisely because it affords so forceful a contrast between the kind of love that constitutes sin and the kind that represents redemption from sin—between ἔρως (*erōs*), sensual love, eroticism, lust, and ἀγάπη (*agapē*), love of one's neighbor, pity, compassion: what the Vulgate calls *caritas*. And this is a sentiment that one finds more easily in the slums, in prisons, and brothels, than among the most devoted church-goers. That is why Jesus had no hesitation in associating with humble fishermen, with publicans, with fallen women.

The bigot who vaunts her own chastity, her own zeal in the performance of religious duties, in the precise observance of fasts, and who is therefore convinced of her right to look down almost contemptuously on those who sin, is of less account than the prostitute who never goes to church and who does not know a prayer, but who is capable of weeping with those who weep, smiling on those who sorrow, saying a word of comfort to those who mourn, caressing the head of a child—of giving without demanding, of understanding the weaknesses of others without judging.

The Pharisees and the Torāh

The prominence so boldly given by Jesus to *caritas*, in contrast to ritualistic conduct and religious duties, outraged the more conforming of his co-religionists, who, by antonomasia, are described in the Gospels as "Scribes and Pharisees."

In effect, as an earlier chapter pointed out, the Pharisees (in Hebrew, *Perushīm*) were a kind of religious party that saw unforgivable sin in every neglect and imperfection in observance of the holy rules. The Scribes (in Hebrew, *Sopherīm*) were primarily the "doctors" whose commentaries on the sacred texts and whose learned discussions served to determine, for cases not explicitly covered by the holy writings or by tradition, the applicability of the precepts and prohibitions set forth by both.[25] The whole of the first five books of the Old Testament, the Pentateuch, was called the Law (in Hebrew, *Torāh*). But little by little, the Torah had been supplemented by oral tradition (*mishnāh*), which was later codified by the patriarch Judah ha-Nasi at the end of the first century A.D. (his written work is known as the Mishnah) and which finally developed into the Talmud, the sacred text par excellence of modern Jews. At the time of Jesus, the Pharisaic rabbis had already put together six hundred and thirteen precepts, both affirmative and negative, and in these they differentiated between major and minor precepts, according to the amount of effort demanded by obedience to them, and between great and small, according to their intrinsic importance.[26]

"The Pharisees," Flavius Josephus wrote, a few years after the death of Jesus, "are those who profess to have the most precise knowledge of our laws and our ceremonies."[27] This certitude, combined with their personal commitment to conform without fault to the laws themselves and to observe the prescribed ceremonials meticulously, persuaded the Pharisees that they represented authentic Jewish religiosity and that they could present themselves as models for their co-religionists. But their very meticulousness in fulfilling the law down to the most minute detail, their subtle exegeses and learned interpretations of the holy writings, to which they devoted themselves, often led them into excesses of pedantry and obstinacy.

This presumption and pettifogging were the targets of Jesus. For the Pharisees and the Scribes, divine protection had to be earned by presenting continual proofs of devoutness through fasts, prayers, offerings to the Temple, sacrifices, observance of the rites of purification, and the rest. Jesus believed that to this extent they had wandered from the true faith by becoming too formalistic, too attached to the letter rather than the spirit of the Torah.

The divergencies between Jesus and the Pharisees did not, however, arise out of doctrinal matters, as traditional Catholic exegesis would have us believe: it portrays the Pharisees in direct antithesis to the Christian ideal of life, as veritable "masters of error."[28] Even a cursory investigation is enough to demonstrate the surprising points of contact between the Pharisaic and the Christian religious conceptions. The views of Hillel and other rabbis recur more often than one might think in the preaching of Jesus, and many of the maxims later brought together in the Talmud are found in identical form in the Gospels. Pharisees, or, more accurately, Scribes, were the "doctors" of the Temple with whom Jesus disputed as a boy hearing and learning the Torah.

Jesus sought simply, in contrast to the Pharisees, to maintain the immunity from punishment and greater merit in the eyes of God that characterized the man who, faced with the choice between performing a good deed and at the same time violating some rule of law, did not hesitate to choose the good deed. But, even if we reduced it to its actual scope—criticism of the Pharisees' outward behavior—we could not, objectively, feel justified in declaring that the violent antagonism to the Pharisees that the Gospels ascribe to

Jesus was historically justifiable. The real motivation for the Pharisees' pedantry has not been understood and no one has been willing to accept it. They represented real Judaism, and not merely "extreme and sterile conservatism."[29] Deeply religious and sincerely patriotic, they considered the Temple the religious and national center of Israel, and their concern with total compliance with the precepts of the Torah as standards of day-to-day behavior was dictated by nothing but the desire to preserve their national customs and traditions unchanged. In racial and patriotic pride, they defended their ancestral religion with intransigent rigidity against the danger of foreign infiltration and contamination,[30] which was the greater then because of the Roman occupation of their country and the tendency of the Sadducean priestly caste and the Palestinian ethnarchs to collaborate with the occupier. The pious Pharisees locked themselves into isolation from daily contact with the pagans (the unclean gōyīm, as they were called in Hebrew). They turned their faces anxiously toward the holy place of the God of their fathers, fearful of its fall, as today the devout among the citizens of the modern state of Israel press their tearful eyes against the cracks in the great wall that divides Jerusalem so that they may look wistfully across Jordanian territory to Mount Moriah, where the Temple once soared.

No account has been taken of the honest intentions of the Pharisees at this period, or of their historical function. Only the repugnant immediate effects have been considered: pedantry, which mortified religion, and pride, which led them in the end to despise the populace, the amē hā-'erets, because these were not interested in putting the Pharisees' precepts into practice. The fact that these same Pharisees were sufficiently aware of their own faults to criticize themselves with biting irony[31] is disregarded (otherwise the invectives attributed to Jesus would seem less vehement and less offensive).

In truth, the hatred toward the Pharisees that emerges from the Gospels is imputable not to Jesus but to the first Christians (their preaching in Palestine had been crippled by the resistance of the Pharisees)[32] and above all to Paul, who, having decided to remove Christianity to the Greek and Latin world, expended all his strength to detach it once and for all from Judaism.

The Shabbāth

One observance in which the Jewish people admitted no exception, and which the Pharisees had exaggerated with their pettifoggery, was that of the weekly day of rest. The Sabbath (in Hebrew, *Shabbāth*) was almost certainly derived from the Babylonian *Shabattū*, the festival of the full moon,[33] but, all trace of any such origin having been lost, the Hebrews ascribed it to Biblical legend. The Sabbath recalled the seventh day of the creation, the day of rest imposed by God,[34] and it is first mentioned in Exodus, as a halt in the wandering through the wilderness: "This is that which the Lord hath said, To-morrow is the rest of the holy sabbath unto the Lord: bake that which ye will bake to-day, and seethe that ye will seethe; and that which remaineth over lay up for you, to be kept until the morning."[35] Immediately afterward, the counsel of Moses was translated into a specific legal command:[36] "The seventh day is the sabbath of the Lord thy God: in it thou shalt not do any work, thou, nor thy son, nor thy daughter, thy manservant, nor thy maidservant, nor thy cattle, nor thy stranger that is within thy gates."[37] Ultimately, the law went as far as to threaten the death penalty for violation of the order,[38] and this was confirmed by the incident of the man found gathering sticks on the Sabbath, who was stoned to death by order of Moses and Aaron.[39]

In the light of such precedents, it is not surprising that the Jews abstained from even the slightest work on the Sabbath. The Romans made fun of the custom as a mark of laziness,[40] but the Jews clung to it so rigidly that, in 63 B.C., during Pompey's siege of Jerusalem, they refused even to bear arms on the Sabbath and thus hastened the Roman victory.

The Talmudic evolution of the Sabbath law included some strange amendments. It was forbidden to put out fires, to mix feed for fowl, to sew even two stitches, to lift any weight, however light (such as a fan, or a ribbon that had not been attached to a garment), to write more than two letters of the alphabet, to kill a fly even when it was biting . . . A person might not walk more than a hundred paces at a time, and this rule was so rigid that it applied even to one who had become lost in a wood or who found himself in open country without refuge from wind or rain or the attacks of brigands. He who suffered from an aching tooth might rinse his mouth with vinegar, but he must not swallow any. The housewife must take care not to scatter too much seed before the fowl, lest the excess take root and seem to have been sown.

In modernized form, the Talmud catalogues other prohibitions that the religious Jew of today is supposed to observe: on the Sabbath he may not travel by train or automobile, he may not telephone, he may not be photographed, he may not handle money, etc. It is true that, then as now, a less devout Jew could easily find some loophole in order to evade the rules. It is forbidden to walk more than a hundred paces at a time? Very well then, carry a stool, stop and rest on it every hundred paces, and start again as on a new journey. It is forbidden to carry a packet of bank notes in one's pocket? What if the notes are in a roll instead of a packet?

But, in contrast with those who resorted to trickery to get around the Sabbath rules, there were others—and the Pharisees were the first among them—whose overscrupulous rigidity drove them to equivalent excesses in the opposite direction. The followers of two famous rabbis, Hillel and Shammai, for example, debated whether it was licit to eat an egg laid on the Sabbath, or one that was completed within the hen on that day and laid on the next![41]

It was precisely these excesses that Jesus combatted so hotly. The Gospels are full of instances in which he deliberately sought to violate the observance of the Sabbath, utilizing the action to explain to his disciples the uselessness of such blind obedience. The Sabbath habit was so solidly rooted in his compatriots, however, that Jesus did not succeed in eradicating it. After his death, two centuries passed before Christians of Jewish origin could persuade themselves to give up the festival of the Sabbath,[42] and even then this became possible only by replacing it with Sunday.

As a result, the division of the week into seven days, which was unknown in antiquity except among the Hebrews, has gained almost universal acceptance, and Sunday, in imitation of the Jewish Sabbath, has become a day of rest and of religious activity with specific prohibitions, although these are less severe than those of the Jews. Catholics, without doubt, are outdone in its observance by Protestants, who forbid not only working for money but even spectacles and sports on Sunday. So we have swung back to the Pharisaic mentality that Jesus condemned.

"The Sabbath Was Made for Man"

The first collision over the Sabbath between Jesus and the Pharisees[43] was also the clearest statement of his views on the matter. It happened on a Sabbath, perhaps in the month of Nisan. The Gospel of Luke calls it "*sabbato secundo primo*" ("the second first Sabbath"), which is meaningless, and all attempts at emendation, such as "on the second Sabbath after the first," are unsatisfactory. I think we may suppose the word *mense* ("month") has been lost from the original manuscript and the phrase should be read as "the second Sabbath of the first month of the year." Luke tells us that on such a day Jesus and his disciples were walking through a field of wheat, and, becoming hungry, they broke off a few stalks and ate the grains after they had ground them in their hands. If the story is true, we can assume that it was really the middle of the month of Nisan, the first ecclesiastical month of the year—in other words, April—because it is only then that raw grain can be eaten.

Reprimanded by some Pharisees, who witnessed this infringement on the repose of the Sabbath (harvesting and milling grain), Jesus retorted very much to the point by citing a far more serious case, though no one had ever condemned it, in which no less a person than King David had broken the religious law: he had entered the Temple in Nob, taking the showbread displayed on the altar of the sanctuary, and portioning it out for his companions to eat. The story is told in the Old Testament,[44] which also gives the name of the priest who connived at the sacrilege: Ahimelech, not, as the Gospel of Mark mistakenly has it, Abiathar. In the opinion of Jesus, David's offense was wholly justified: because "he was ahungered";[45] because "he had need."[46] Now the case of the disciples was the same. They, too, were hungry, and this need was sufficient to warrant the transgression of the prohibitions of the Law.

In their defense, Jesus explained to the Pharisees his concept of religion, which was based on charity and not on outward behavior:

"But if ye had known what this meaneth, I will have mercy, and not sacrifice, ye would not have condemned the guiltless." Then he became more specific: "The Sabbath was made for man, and not man for the Sabbath. Therefore the Son of man is Lord also of the Sabbath." As I have explained earlier, the words "the Son of man" are to be read simply "a man" and the thought of Jesus is clear. The weekly day of rest should be put to man's use, to refresh him after the six working days, not to impose penances and hardships on him. But traditional exegesis, prejudiced by the conviction that "the Son of man" should mean a declaration of his own divinity by Jesus, explains these words in a very different way, nullifying the very human and unselfish concern of Jesus with those who labor and are burdened: "I, the Son of man, am the Lord of the Sabbath," and hence: "The holy day should be dedicated to me alone"—not for rest but for worship!

On another Sabbath, Jesus was preaching in a synagogue where there was a man with a withered hand—ξηρά (xēra) means, literally, "dried out," "dry." The Aramaic Gospel of the Nazarenes (quoted by Jerome as the Gospel According to the Hebrews) states explicitly that the man was a mason, and that he himself asked Jesus to heal him.[47] The canonical Gospels allow the inference, however, that it was Jesus who wished to work the cure as an open defiance of those Pharisees who were present and who were on the watch to trap him in an infraction.[48] But Jesus "knew their thoughts," and he said to them: "I will ask you one thing: Is it lawful on the sabbath days to do good; or to do evil? to save life, or to destroy it?"

Actually, the Talmud specifies that the administration of medicine and the care of the ill are forbidden on the Sabbath except in cases of special urgency. The case of the arthritic mason certainly did not fall within this category. Nevertheless, Jesus massaged his hand[49] because to him this was a good act, the performance of which is always a duty, no matter the day. Again he was guided by the principle of pure charity unrestricted by laws. More to convince the worshipers in the synagogue than the Pharisees, he added an allegory:[50] "What man shall there be among you, that shall have one sheep, and if it fall into a pit on the sabbath day, will he not lay hold on it, and lift it out? How much then is a man better than a sheep?" The allegory, to be honest, has little pertinence: what the owner of the sheep does in order to prevent his own loss can hardly be deemed an act of charity.[51]

The Gospel of Luke also pursues the theme of the dispute between Jesus and the Pharisees over the performance of cures on the Sabbath, reporting two analogous incidents: the healing, through a laying on of hands, of a woman who had been forced by spinal troubles to walk bent for the preceding eighteen years,[52] and that of a sufferer from dropsy.[53] One must note the tendency to multiply cures of the same kind and to exaggerate them: the withered hand becomes a curved spine and finally a case of dropsy.

The derivation of Luke's two instances from Matthew's original model (the withered hand) is apparent not only in the punctual repetition of the same situations, almost with the same words, but especially in a bizarre slip: Luke, seeking to expand Matthew's metaphor of the endangered sheep, substituted "an ass or an ox," and through a clumsy copyist's mistake, the Greek text says "son" (υἱός, *hyos*) instead of "ass" (ὄνος, *onos*), with the following droll result: "Which of you shall have a son or an ox fallen into a pit, and will not straightway pull him out on the sabbath day?"[54] This error in the Greek text does not appear in the King James Bible, which was corrected to read "ass."

The Gospel of John, which as a rule does not follow the Synoptics, reports none of these tales but condenses the matter of Sabbath cures into a single episode laid in Jerusalem,[55] since John has Jesus constantly shuttling between Galilee and Jerusalem. In John's account, the miracle worked by Jesus is the Sabbath cure of a paralytic who was lying at the edge of a pool endowed with the same curative powers as Lourdes. This was the Pool of Bethesda, near the Sheep Gate, or sheep market. The man had never been able to immerse himself in the pool at the times when it was troubled by an angel who descended from heaven to give the pool its therapeutic power.

The anti-myth school—as well as the Jesuit Xavier Léon-Dufour[56]—sees in this a sacramental matter of doctrine: the paralytic who cannot enter the pool by his own efforts is the symbol of man who cannot be saved without the baptism of Jesus.

Unclean Hands

Another class of legal regulations of conduct that the Pharisees observed with an excess of zeal concerned "impurity"—that is, the danger of contagion and contamination.

Leviticus and Deuteronomy, first of all, devoted considerable space to listing the animals whose flesh it was lawful or forbidden to eat. With respect to mammals, they made it clear that only those who chewed the cud and had the cloven hoof were to be eaten; banned as "unclean," therefore, were the camel, the rabbit, and the hare (though ruminants, they lack the cloven hoof), and the pig (which has the cloven hoof but is not a ruminant). The forbidden birds included the eagle, the kite, the falcon, the crow, the ostrich, the seagull, the owl—and the bat. The grasshopper was considered the only edible insect. All the reptiles, the frogs, and the snails were unclean.

Other rules governed the use and cleanliness of household utensils. Even the size of the mouth of a terra-cotta or wooden jar was specified: at least the width of a pomegranate.

The laws intended to prevent the contagion of leprosy were especially detailed, as were the various forms of purification to be prescribed by the priest to meet the variations of the disease: isolated pustules or irruptions, scars or ulcers, etc.

The same degree of impurity was imputed to venereal diseases and to menstruation: whoever, even inadvertently, touched a man afflicted with gonorrhea or a woman during her menstrual period must immediately wash in clean water.

Other types of contamination required purification and also offerings to the Temple: contact with the body of a wild animal, a reptile, the bone of a dead man, a tomb, and so on. The aversions of the Jews extended even to simple contact with a foreigner, which was branded unclean; nor might they allow themselves to enter an alien's house.

Many of these prohibitions, obviously, were inspired, perhaps unconsciously, by motives of hygiene, but others were of exclusively religious origin, such as the prohibition against eating the sciatic nerve of a slaughtered animal, out of respect for Jacob, who, wres-

tling face to face with God, was injured in that part.[57] The reason
for the ban on eating pork is a matter of controversy. Here we are
probably confronted by some archaic recollection of a totemic
animal;[58] one can see nothing acceptable in the theory of those who
profess to find an economic purpose in the ban—an intention to
induce the Hebrews to cultivate the olive in order to replace swine
fat with olive oil.[59]

Jesus did not wish to alter these customs, which he himself
probably respected and which, indeed, were firmly implanted in the
first Apostles. The problem arose only when Christianity spread
among the Gentiles. The Acts of the Apostles tells us of the great
conflict that Peter suffered when he had to overcome his own resistance to entering the house of the pagan Cornelius, who had asked
him for baptism,[60] and the story goes on to explain how he later
sought to justify himself to the company of the faithful, insisting
that at any rate he had not eaten anything forbidden by the Law
as being unclean.[61] Paul was to be the first to ridicule these superstitions, mocking and rebuking Peter.[62]

Therefore, the Gospel incident we are about to look into is
not historically true, but dates back only to this conflict between
Paul and the Apostles.

Mark and Matthew relate that some of the Pharisees, seeing the
disciples of Jesus eating bread from unwashed hands, were outraged.[63] But Jesus looked scornfully at them and remarked ironically:
"Well hath Esaias [Isaiah] prophesied of you hypocrites, as it is
written, This people honoreth me with their lips, but their heart
is far from me. Howbeit in vain do they worship me, teaching for
doctrines the commandments of men." The quotation is actually
garbled, even if its meaning is only slightly altered. Isaiah said:
". . . their fear toward me is taught by the precept of men."[64]

Then Jesus summoned his disciples to him and taught them:
"Hearken unto me every one of you, and understand: There is
nothing from without a man that, entering into him, can defile him:
but the things which come out of him, those are they that defile the
man. If any man have ears to hear, let him hear."

The cleansing of hands before food, then, no longer mattered;
what was important was the choice between permitted and forbidden
food. And the disciples did not understand their master's teaching.

They were only bewildered by his sharp attack on the Pharisees, and they brought the matter to his attention: "Knowest thou that the Pharisees were offended, after they heard this saying?"

"Let them alone," he replied: "they be blind leaders of the blind. And if the blind lead the blind, both shall fall into the ditch."

Only later, when Jesus had gone into the house with the most intimate of his disciples, did Peter (acting as spokesman for the others) turn diffidently to his master: "Declare unto us this parable."

Jesus looked at them a moment in astonishment and then burst out: "Are ye also yet without understanding [ἀσύνετοι, asunetoi]? Do not ye yet understand, that whatsoever entereth in at the mouth goeth into the belly, and is cast out into the draught? But those things which proceed out of the mouth come forth from the heart; and they defile the man. For out of the heart proceed evil thoughts, murders, adulteries, fornications, thefts, false witness, blasphemies: These are the things which defile a man: but to eat with unwashen hands defileth not a man."

"Woe unto You, Scribes and Pharisees!"

The Pharisees, meanwhile, more stunned than angered by the words of Jesus, shook their heads somberly. "He is possessed of a devil," they said, amazed that a man possessed could nonetheless exorcise devils; and they concluded that Beelzebub had enabled him to rout the other evil spirits.

Beelzebub (in Hebrew, Ba'al zebūb), a Philistine deity worshiped in antiquity by the Israelites as well, was the god of the flies, whom it was necessary to propitiate in order to be safe from those dangerous carriers of infectious germs. The Greek text of the Gospels uses Βεεζεβούλ (Beezeboul), which is a transcription of Ba'al zebūl, the god of excrement. Whatever the attribute, he was a god of evil, an enemy of Yahweh, a "prince of devils," who may well be identified with Satan. Jesus uses both names in his answers to the Pharisees' insinuations: "Every kingdom divided against itself is brought to desolation; and a house divided against a house falleth. If Satan also be divided against himself, how shall his kingdom stand? . . . And if I by Beelzebub cast out devils, by whom do your sons cast them out? . . . No man can enter into a strong man's house, and spoil his goods, except he will first bind the strong man."[65]

Jesus meant that the forces of evil could be conquered only by antithetical powers—that is, Satan could be overcome only by the help of God. To declare that evil does battle against evil is a blasphemy, because it negates the need for God to intervene. Thus he concluded: "All sins shall be forgiven unto the sons of men, and blasphemies wherewith soever they blaspheme: But he that shall blaspheme against the Holy Ghost hath never forgiveness."

Ever since, theologians have sought to define these "blasphemies" against the Holy Ghost—or the spirit of God—as despair of one's own salvation, as the presumptuousness of seeking salvation without merit, as the denial of the truth of faith, as envy of the spiritual well-being of one's neighbor, as the flaunting of wickedness, as the decision not to repent.[66] But Jesus sought here only to combat the Pharisees' implications that his teaching did not conform to religious laws, and he seized the opportunity to rebut their accusations and warn his disciples against them. When he had cautioned against false prophets, who, coming in the guise of lambs, were yet voracious wolves, he added: "For a good tree bringeth not forth corrupt fruit; neither doth a corrupt tree bring forth good fruit. For every tree is known by his own fruit; for of thorns men do not gather figs, nor of a bramble bush gather they grapes. A good man out of the good treasure of his heart bringeth forth that which is good; and an evil man out of the evil treasure of his heart bringeth forth that which is evil; for of the abundance of the heart his mouth speaketh."

The conflicts between Jesus and the Pharisees become increasingly frequent and acute in the Gospels, but one can well say that the whole matter of the attack on the Pharisees' legalism and their hardness of heart (at least, so the Evangelists consider it) is summed up in a long speech reported in full only by Matthew.[67] It may be that here he has brought together various statements ascribed to Jesus on a number of occasions: in fact, fragments of this speech occur at divergent stages of the other Gospels.[68] According to Matthew, Jesus said of the Pharisees:

"All therefore whatsoever they bid you observe, that observe and do; but do not ye after their works: for they say, and do not. For they bind heavy burdens, and grievous to be borne, and lay them on men's shoulders; but they themselves will not move them with one of their fingers. But all their works they do for to be seen of men: they make broad their phylacteries, and enlarge the borders of their garments. And love the uppermost rooms at feasts, and the chief seats in the synagogues, and greetings in the markets, and to be called of men Rabbi, Rabbi."

The ironic allusion to the exaggerated dimensions of the "phylacteries" and the "borders" requires clarification. The phylacteries (in Hebrew, *tefillīn*) were leather boxes containing strips of parchment on which Biblical precepts were written; the boxes were strapped round the left arm and on the forehead. The borders mentioned by Jesus were fringes (in Hebrew, *shishiyōth*) of woollen thread, prescribed by the Mosaic law, at the corners of the prayer shawl, placed there to recall the Eternal's commandments.

Jesus pursued his indictment, leveling further accusations against the Pharisees: they demanded to be called *rabbi* ("teacher," "master") and *abba* ("father"), and they claimed omniscience, whereas only God was omniscient and the Father of all men. They placed more emphasis on the gold and the sacrifices brought to the Temple than on the Temple itself. They paid tithes of mint and anise and fennel, but they disregarded what was more important: the distinction between good and evil. Meticulously they cleansed their cups and their platters, lest the corpse of a gnat render the food unclean, and they were unaware that they swallowed whole camels —that is, that they were doing far worse things than eating a gnat. Nor did they remember that these vessels they kept so spotless were nevertheless stained with the fruit of their extortions and excesses. They demanded outrageous sums for the recitation of prayers and reduced widows to such misery that they had to sell their houses to pay for the prayers. They gave alms of such things as they had in their platters (τὰ ἐνόντα, *ta enonta,* meaning "what is over, on"), and so they thought they had obeyed their consciences.

It should be noted that this last particular, which is obviously a rebuke to the coldheartedness of the rich, can be changed arbitrarily into a command: "ye give" (indicative) into "give ye" (imperative) is a transposition as easily made in Greek and Latin and "what is over" can be interpreted as "the superfluity." So the sentence can become the mild exhortation: "Give of your surplus to the poor"

—that is, what is left when one is sated! But such an interpretation, which is belied by other commandments of Jesus to which we shall come in due course, has often been disposed of by commentators with common sense.

The apocryphal Gospel of Thomas contains a denunciation lacking in the Synoptics: "Cursed are they, the Pharisees, because they are like a dog which has lain in the cattle manger, but will neither eat the food there nor allow the oxen to eat it."[69] But this is apparently derived from a Greek proverb that stems in turn from one of Aesop's fables.[70]

Luke reports that a Scribe who had listened to the entire bill of particulars tried to protest,[71] but Jesus shut him off forcefully: "Ye are like unto whited sepulchers, which indeed appear beautiful outward, but are within full of dead men's bones . . . ye build the tombs of the prophets, and garnish the sepulchers of the righteous, . . . [but] ye are the children of them which killed the prophets. Fill ye up then the measure of your fathers. Ye serpents, ye generation of vipers. . . . That upon you may come all the righteous blood shed upon the earth, from the blood of the righteous Abel unto the blood of Zacharias [Zechariah] the son of Barachias [Berechiah], whom ye slew between the temple and the altar."[72] This final reference is incorrect: it was Zechariah, the son of Jehoida,[73] who died thus, and there is no connection with Zechariah, the son of Berechiah.

The whole catalogue of imprecation against the Pharisees is reminiscent of the Old Testament, and passages from the Psalms and the Proverbs are to be found in it.

If anything in this tirade can be imputed to Jesus, it was surely dictated by his determination to drive arid conformity out of men's hearts and to make them understand the importance of good works motivated by love. But, little by little, official Christianity has lapsed back again into Pharisaism. It has absorbed the whole exterior of Jewish worship with its diverse precepts for the observance of holy days, its fasts, its ablutions, the abstention from certain foods, and all the picturesque variety and extravagance of rites and ceremonials that in the Gospels were so harshly condemned.

[9]

JESUS AND THE APOSTLES

The Selection of the Twelve

The thaumaturgic activity with which Jesus had launched his work in Galilee and his firm opposition to the Pharisees had attracted a group of admirers who were prepared to follow him, confident of his authority and his powers. From then on, therefore, he could begin to think of teaching others, in order, with their help, to initiate his true kerygmatic mission:[1] the revelation (κήρυγμα, *kērygma*, means "message," "proclamation") of the good tidings, which he considered extremely urgent.

The Gospels of Mark and Matthew, indeed, tell us that one day, seeing the overwork and exhaustion of the peasants in the fields, like wretched animals left to themselves without anyone to care for them, he was utterly shocked.[2] The two Evangelists use the verb σπλαγχνίζεσθαί (*splangchnizesthai*), which means "to be shaken to the depths of the bowels." Then he recognized the need to carry some word of comfort to all. "The harvest truly is plenteous," he said, "but the laborers are few."[3] After spending a night in prayer, he called together his disciples and selected the twelve most trustworthy among them.

The choice of the Twelve Apostles is an event of the first importance in the history of Christianity. To reject its historical truth, taking the position that the first Apostles emerged only after the death of Jesus[4] as a "board of directors" of the initial Christian community, is to attack the legitimacy of the priesthood as not

145

having been instituted by Jesus himself. In fact, according to the Catholic Church, the rightful successors of the Apostles are the bishops and, subordinated to them, the entire clergy. As the Church developed, it naturally felt the need to erect a hierarchic organization and, of course, it sought to justify this prudent vision by the authority and the example of the selection of the Twelve by Jesus. The Protestant denominations, however, even though they cast no doubt on the authenticity of the evangelical narrative, do not recognize any intention by Jesus to establish a corps of priests, which, in their view, is repugnant to the principle of equality among all believers.

It would seem best to suggest that Jesus wanted to choose a band of loyal disciples who, according to rabbinical custom, would always follow him and assist him, rather than to create a priesthood, which at that of all periods had no reason for being. Apostleship was a temporary function, wholly *ad personam*. The onset of the farming season had drawn the peasants out of their villages and scattered them through the fields, and it was necessary to adopt what might be called a capillary procedure in preaching. The Apostles' task, in fact, was to travel through the countryside and propagandize in preparation for the arrival of Jesus. This mission justified the designation "apostle," which comes from a Greek word meaning "envoy," "messenger," "ambassador." It occurs rather infrequently in the Gospels: only once each in Matthew and Mark, six times in Luke. Jesus would have used the Hebrew word *shelīḥā* (plural, *shelīḥīm*), which means "one charged with a special mission";[5] this was a function long known among the Jews for maintaining contact with the various Jewish communities scattered abroad.[6] It is certain that even Paul considered apostleship a missionary duty.[7]

Only later did the word "apostle" become an honorable title, so much so that the Roman emperors, after their conversion to Christianity and following the example of Constantine, liked to be venerated by their subjects under the title of Thirteenth Apostle.

What were the names of the Twelve? The New Testament provides four different rosters (one in each of the Synoptic Gospels and the fourth in the Acts of the Apostles), and the Apostles are also frequently mentioned in the Gospel of John. However, there are substantial discrepancies among all five. If such holy books, on which the doctrine of the Church is founded, were written as tradition says by the Apostles themselves or by persons close to them, how much credence can we give them, as an angry German scholar wonders, when their authors cannot even learn the twelve correct names by heart as any child could do?[8]

The Gospels of Mark and Matthew list, though in different sequences, Simon (later called Peter) and his brother, Andrew; James and John, the sons of Zebedee; Philip; Bartholomew; Thomas; Matthew; James, the son of Alpheus; Thaddeus; Simon the Canaanite; and Judas Iscariot. The Gospel of Luke and Acts never mention Thaddeus, naming in his stead one Judas, the son (or brother) of James. The Gospel of John omits Bartholomew but includes Nathanael. Catholic exegetes think they can reduce the last four to two men: Thaddeus, they say, is the surname of Judas, the son of James, and Bartholomew is the patronymic of Nathanael (*bar-Talmai,* "son of Tholemaios"). But this does not resolve the doubts.

Who Were the Apostles?

The desire to know somewhat more than the names of the twelve collaborators of Jesus is legitimate, but data are few and dubious.

SIMON (*Shim'ōn*), as we know, was the fisherman of Capernaum (or, according to the Gospel of John, of Bethsaida) who, with his brother, Andrew, was the first to join Jesus, perhaps after having been a disciple of John the Baptist.[9] He lodged Jesus in his house and Jesus cured his mother-in-law of her fevers. The mention of the mother-in-law has seduced some commentators into idle speculation whether Simon was a widower or whether he deserted his wife for Jesus.[10] In a much discussed passage in Matthew, which we shall examine in time, it is said that Jesus gave Simon the surname of Peter (which in Greek and Latin means "stone," "rock," the meaning also of the Aramaic *Kēphas,* which is rendered in Greek as *Cephas*) and explicitly appointed him his successor.[11] Hence Catholicism traces the origin of the Papacy to him, and, in order to give the thesis greater authority, the legend has arisen that Simon Peter went to Rome to establish the first Christian community there and died a martyr under Nero. It is also said that the Gospel of Mark was written by a disciple of Simon Peter and repeats his preaching.[12] This is most unlikely, the more so since Mark does not even mention the investiture of Peter as head of the Church. The reading of the New Testament gives us the impression of Peter as a stout man, rough and simple in his ways,[13] rather slow of mind, sometimes a fearless missionary, sometimes weak and timid to the point of denying Jesus.

ANDREW (a Greek name), Simon's brother, was also a fisherman. Later biographers portray him without any historical basis as "great of stature, somewhat round-shouldered, with a large nose and heavy brows."[14]

JAMES, or Jacob (Ya'kob), the son of Zebedee, was among the first followers of Jesus, with Simon Peter and Andrew. He and his brother, John, were also fishermen at Capernaum. From the nickname that the Gospels say Jesus later gave to James and his brother ("Sons of Thunder"), it may be inferred that they were of impetuous and violent nature.[15] According to the Acts of the Apostles, James was ordered killed by Herod Agrippa I in A.D. 44.

JOHN (Yōḥānān) was the younger brother of James. Even though Acts explicitly says of him that, like Simon, he was "unlearned and ignorant,"[16] later apologists have tried to make him responsible for the Fourth Gospel, whose mystical and dogmatic content makes it precisely the least suitable to be ascribed to an unschooled Palestinian fisherman.[17] This Gospel presupposes in its author a knowledge of Greek philosophy that some students amateurishly imagine might have been acquired by John during his residence in Ephesus in the last years of his life.[18] The Gnostic interpretation of the life of Jesus contained in the Fourth Gospel compels the belief that it was written not many years before the second half of the second century. Perhaps there is some confusion of John the Apostle with John Presbyter.[19] To give John the Apostle time to learn Gnostic philosophy and write his Gospel, tradition kept him alive until A.D. 104, when he would have been old indeed.[20] The statement in Acts is much more probable: that he was executed with his brother, James, in A.D. 44.[21] In the accounts of the Gospels, as we shall see, he appears sometimes a rather mealymouthed and dreamy young man, sometimes a self-seeker who aspires to be the favorite of

Jesus and, to that end, does not hesitate to quarrel with his fellows, to be indiscreet and querulous, systematically striving to rank with Simon Peter and sometimes ahead of him in important matters.[22]

PHILIP (a Greek name) was that man of Bethsaida whom the Gospel of John names as the third disciple of Jesus, immediately after Simon Peter and Andrew.[23] In a letter written in A.D. 190 by Bishop Polycrates of Ephesus to Bishop Victor of Rome there is some mention of Philip, who married after the death of Jesus and had three daughters, one of whom, in fact, then lived in Ephesus. But it is quite possible that this is a confusion with another Philip. In 1945 some papyrus writings in Coptic were discovered at Nag Hammadi (Chenoboskion) in Upper Egypt, which contained an apocryphal Gospel attributed to Philip. But, as was pointed out at once by Robert Wilson, who was the first to examine the manuscripts,[24] their text was a sermon of Gnostic character, composed at the end of the second century.

BARTHOLOMEW (*bar-Talmai*) does not appear in the Gospel of John, but, since his name is always coupled with Philip's in the lists of Apostles handed down by the Synoptics and by Acts, it may be possible to identify him with that Nathanael who, in the Gospel of John, was introduced to Jesus by his friend Philip, and whom Jesus persuaded to be a disciple by saying that he had seen him "under a fig tree." A very late tradition has it that he attempted to proselytize in Arabia.[25] The apocryphal legend says of his physical appearance that he had "curling black hair, a ruddy complexion, large eyes, and a regular nose."[26]

MATTHEW (*Matthai*, a contraction of *Mattaniah*) is generally identified, as we already know, with Levi, the publican of Capernaum. It should be remarked, however, that Matthew is not an adapted name but is as authentically Hebraic as Levi. We have already discussed the various theories on the matter. The tradition according to which Matthew is the author of one of the Synoptic Gospels is based on statements by Bishop Papias of Hierapolis, in Asia Minor, toward the middle of the second century. But today even Catholic exegetes[27] are no longer so sure that this is the oldest of all the Gospels. This distinction, according to authoritative Protestant scholars, belongs to Mark or to some Ur-Markus, a model for all the others, that has been lost. To prove the identity of

Matthew the Apostle with the author of the Gospel and the publican Levi, it is customary to cite the exactness with which numbers and quantities are noted in the Gospel itself; this is taken to be an occupational habit of the former tax employee. Actually, he deals almost always with the number three or the number seven, a fact that leads one to infer, if anything, a predilection for cabalistic numbers. For that matter, the Gospel of John also indulges in the same odd play. Evidence to contradict the identification theory may lie in the fact that if Matthew was so good at calculations Jesus would have made him the treasurer of the band, but it was, rather, Judas Iscariot who held the post.

THOMAS (*Tōma*), who in Greek was called Didymos[28] inasmuch as both names mean "twin," became famous for his unbelief. Indeed, the Gospel of John says that Thomas did not believe in the resurrection of Jesus and that Jesus had to appear to him especially and bid him touch him with his hand.[29] This very privilege won remarkable prestige for Thomas among later generations. He is supposed to have preached in Persia and India; and since the third century an apocryphal Gospel has been ascribed to him, but it was regarded with suspicion by the official Church in that it was the text favored by the "perverse" Manicheans. In modern times, only a few passages of this Gospel, quoted by medieval writers, were known, but between 1945 and 1955 a complete version in Coptic was discovered.[30] Its content was immediately recognized to be of sufficient interest to warrant its being called the "Fifth Gospel." We have used it as a source here side by side with the other writings of the New Testament.

JAMES (*Ya'kob*), called "the Less" (though actually ὁ μικρός means "the Little") because of his stature, in order to distinguish him from the other Apostle of the same name, is difficult to identify. In some places the Gospels expressly call him "the brother of Jesus,"[31] and Flavius Josephus hints as much,[32] as does Bishop Eusebius of Caesarea in his *History of the Church* (fourth century).[33] But once the tradition that Jesus was an only child had gained strength, the rosters of Apostles in the Gospels of Mark and Luke were amended by adding "the son of Alpheus" to the name of James, but other passages were left uncorrected. Consequently, the reading of the sacred texts offers us both interpretations today, and

Catholic exegetes try in vain to reconcile them. The conviction of independent scholars that James the Less was the brother of Jesus is supported also by the major fact that after the death of Jesus he clearly emerges in Acts and the Epistles of Paul as one of the most authoritative figures in the Christian community of Jerusalem, of equal importance with Simon Peter, and sometimes above him. In a passage of his history, Eusebius has left us this portrait of James the Less: "He was holy even in his mother's womb. He never drank wine or fermented liquors, and throughout his life he ate only vegetables. He was never shorn or shaven and he never bathed. . . . He was the son of Joseph, father of Christ."

THADDEUS (*Taddai*), instead of whom the Gospel of Luke and the Book of Acts list Judas, the son (or brother) of James, is a man of whom nothing is known. Toward the second half of the third century a legend about him grew up: Abgar, king of Edessa, stricken with an incurable disease, had written to Jesus and asked him to come and heal him, and Jesus sent Thaddeus in his place.[34]

SIMON (*Shim'ōn*) was called "the Canaanite" to distinguish him from Simon Peter. As we have pointed out, the right name is "Cananaean" (from the Aramaic *qan'ān*), which means "zealot," the name given to the Galilean patriots of A.D. 6 who had attempted a revolt under Judah of Gamala.

JUDAS (*Yehūdā*), the twelfth Apostle, destined to betray Jesus, was called Iscariot, but it is not clearly known whether the epithet indicated his place of residence (Keryoth or Karioth or Sychar) or whether it was not rather the Semitic transcription of *sicarius* ("dagger man"), which was the Romans' name for the Zealots, and whether Judas might not, therefore, have belonged to the movement.[35] But the hypothesis is rather dubious.[36] Jesus appointed him treasurer, suspecting no treachery in him.[37]

The Apostles' Mission

With minor verbal differences, the three Synoptics report the instructions that Jesus gave the Apostles before he sent them forth on their propaganda travels.[38] Luke repeats and elaborates the same instructions a little later, adding the statement, unconfirmed by the other writers, that Jesus subsequently increased the number of the Apostles from twelve to seventy or seventy-two.[39] The Vulgate gives seventy-two, because it is equivalent to six times twelve, but the Greek text says seventy, which, however, is a symbolic number.

The instructions of Jesus were simple and exact. The Apostles were not to have bread, or wallets, or money, or staffs, or sandals—only the tunics in which they started out (Mark allows staffs and sandals). The poverty of their appearance had a precise purpose: it was the finest example for the humble among whom the Apostles were going to preach. It was the same spirit that, twelve centuries afterward, was to motivate Francis of Assisi in dictating the rules of his order.

The Apostles were not to stop along their way and waste time in exchanging greetings in the complicated formalities of Near Eastern etiquette.[40] In each village they were to find a house that would receive them, and, invoking peace (in Hebrew, shālōm) and blessings on it, they were to remain in it, refusing invitations from other persons. If any village was angered by their presence, Jesus warned wisely, they were not to provoke clashes but to leave, "shaking the dust from their feet." This was an allusion to the contemptuous ritual act prevalent among the Hebrews, and especially among the Pharisees, of ridding oneself of all dust on one's arrival from a pagan country before touching the holy soil of Palestine.

Matthew and, by imitation, Luke add a violent curse of Jesus on any place that would not hear the preaching of his Apostles: God would punish it more harshly than Sodom and Gomorrah.[41]

One particularly important instruction is to be found only in the Gospel of Matthew: the Apostles were not to go among the Gentiles and the Samaritans, but only among "the lost sheep of the house of Israel";[42] and Jesus said also: "Give not that which is holy unto the dogs, neither cast ye your pearls before swine."[43]

It was logical that Jesus should not contemplate making converts among the heathen but rather should consider his mission restricted to Jews who believed in their national religion. The very number of the Twelve Apostles has a close symbolic relation to the twelve tribes of Israel. Nor are the Gospels lacking in other harsh and scornful references to the heathen: they reflect that Semitic racialism to which even Jesus was not immune and which prevailed until

Christianity developed into a universal religion. The despised Gentiles also included the inhabitants of Samaria, most of whom were the descendants of colonists imported by the Assyrians during their occupation of Palestine and who rejected the veneration of the Temple in favor of their own rites.

Even after the death of Jesus, the Apostles clung tenaciously to their master's will. The Acts of the Apostles documents the Apostles' resistance to the tendency, especially among new converts, to make acceptance into Christianity available also to the pagans. The problem was bound inevitably to arise. As Christianity spread among the numerous groups of Jews scattered abroad—the so-called Diaspora (Διασπορά)—it could not help arousing interest among the non-Jewish residents of the host countries. But because of the strictly ethnic character of their religion, the Hebrews could not conceive the idea of religious conversion as we know it today—that is, unaccompanied by a change of nationality.[44]

Stephen and the Hellenists

Blocked by their mentality as men of the people and fanatical disciples of Jesus, the Apostles tended to remain too rigidly bound by their master's doctrine. It was undoubtedly profitable to the development of the Church that others began at this time to strive toward a more flexible interpretation of the message of Jesus. Such efforts were naturally led by new converts in the Diaspora: people who had never personally known Jesus, but whose thinking, even when it did not accord with the master's, was better adapted to the circumstances and the psychology of those to whom the message was to be carried.

It is impossible to elucidate the real thinking of Jesus without taking into consideration the contributions of these innovators. A common mistake is to discuss it *after* the examination of the Gospel accounts, without allowing for the fact that the Gospels were written during or after the height of the various conflicts and do not reproduce the authentic teaching of Jesus, but instead represent the conjuncture of the various interpretations, which, indeed, sometimes co-exist in a manner that can be rather confusing.

Not long after the death of Jesus, the first impetus was given to an important advance in Christianity by a group of "Hellenists," headed by Stephen. The Christians of the time lived much like any other Hebrew sect, continuing the veneration of the Temple, but they had already built their own administrative machinery and a credit fund for their brothers in need. Stephen is cited for the first time in Acts,[45] among those (the Seven Deacons) whom the Apostles had decided to elect in order to make certain of being able to meet the community's material needs. In fact, Stephen and the other Hellenists had complained "because their widows were neglected in the daily ministration."[46] Who these "Hellenists" or "Grecians" were is not too clear: perhaps the widows and orphans of former emigrants who had returned to Jerusalem from Greek cities,[47] or proselytes of Greek origin, converted to Judaism in some synagogue of the Diaspora.[48] Their protests resulted in making Stephen, until then unknown, one of the most important figures in the community as a deacon and giving him the opportunity to express his own views on the message of Jesus. Strange opinions they were, earning him the charge of blasphemy against the Temple. It was true, he said, that Jesus had declared a wish to destroy the Temple, and he had been quite right: the veneration of the Temple was another idolatry. The Most High, Stephen said, had never wished to dwell in temples made with hands: "The heaven is my throne and the earth is my footstool."[49] The priests were outraged and Stephen was immediately condemned to death by stoning.

The Church adores Stephen as her first martyr; but I truly believe the Apostles were quite convinced his sentence was just: the denial of the sanctity of the Temple could come only from the mind of someone who had lived too long abroad. Nevertheless, the so-called Hellenists, driven out of Jerusalem after Stephen's death, continued to expound his views in Phoenicia, on Cyprus, in Antioch.[50] Thus, at least in some localities of the Diaspora, the conviction developed that Jesus had preached a complete rupture with the traditional worship of the Jews. This does not mean that Christianity had begun to be viewed as a supranational, "catholic" religion. For Stephen and the Hellenists, the destruction of the Temple was to have resulted in a return to the ancient Tabernacle of the nomadic Hebrews, the plans of which God himself had given to Moses on

Mount Sinai.[51] Meanwhile, the new concept lent itself to misunder-standing and created the first breach in the rigid fealty that the early Christian community had thus far practiced toward the traditional religion.

The Apostle to the Gentiles

The evolution of Christianity from an ethnic to a universal religion was pushed farthest by Paul.

Paul (in Latin, *Paulus;* in Hebrew, *Shā'ūl*) is introduced to us by the Acts of the Apostles, with a coincidence that cannot be casual, as the young man at whose feet the garments of Stephen were laid by those who were preparing to stone the proto-martyr. At that time, Paul was far from joining the sect of Jesus. He had consented to the execution of Stephen, and was to go on for some years persecuting Christians.

Born in Tarsus in Cilicia to a family of Hebrew artisans that had emigrated there, he had, according to tradition, enjoyed a good rabbinical education. He himself boasted that in matters of the Law he was "an irreproachable Pharisee,"[52] a stupid boast,[53] for Paul had always shown himself remarkably removed from the Pharisaic mentality. The most extremely Jewish group of early Christendom, that of the Ebionites, was even to charge that he was not of pure Jewish blood.[54] He was imbued with Greek culture,[55] however confused in his assimilation of it, to the extent that it made of his writings a mixture of genuine philosophy and magic, expounded in tortuous and bewildering lines of argument, if it is assessed by the standards of Cartesian logic.[56]

From some indications of his appearance that he himself gives in his Epistles, from the Acts of Paul and Thecla, and from other apocryphal sources, we get the impression of a rather ugly man, quite short, heavy-set and round-shouldered, with a small bald head.[57] There is some debate—though the question is of no moment— whether he was married, celibate, or a widower.[58]

So proud of his Roman citizenship that he Latinized his own name, Paul was so little Jewish that he was the first to jeer at the finicky customs of his co-religionists and to call the perquisites of his race "dung" (σκύβαλα, *skubala*).[59] After his conversion, he preached abroad, as Apostle to the Gentiles and collaborator of God,[60] a Christianity notably different from that of the disciples of Jesus. On his own initiative and not without fierce struggles with them, whom he scornfully called "the posts" and "the super-Apostles," Paul not only often changed the master's message (as we shall see) but also drastically altered his very character.

From what we are told by Acts and the Pauline Epistles,[61] his conversion was sudden, apparently in A.D. 43 or 44, in consequence of a kind of vision in the desert along the road to Damascus—in actuality, a sunstroke that made him unconscious and kept him between life and death for three days. In short, he was converted by one Ananias, the head of the Christian community in Damascus, who, having helped him through his illness, lost no time in persuading him that he had been saved by the will of God. As soon as he was well, Paul began to preach a purely personal faith in the synagogue of Damascus itself and never once thought until three years later, as he himself asserts,[62] of returning to his own country and finally communicating with the Christian center in Jerusalem. But even then he stayed only a fortnight and saw no one but Peter and James, the brother of Jesus:[63] he did not have to account to anyone and he was not prepared to listen to advice even from the Apostles.

He did not return to Jerusalem for fourteen years, and then it was to settle the vital question whether non-Jews who embraced Christianity must be circumcised and hence obligated to obey the Mosaic law. Obviously, the critical issue was not the rite of circumcision in itself, but the acceptability of converts from paganism—that is, the extension of Christian theory to embrace all humanity rather than only the Chosen People. There was a violent dispute in Jerusalem, Paul and his friend Barnabas siding together against Peter and James. The Acts of the Apostles tries to minimize the conflict, making it appear that Peter quickly adopted Paul's view and that James recommended only that uncircumcised converts at least be forbidden to eat foods prohibited by the Law.[64] In other words, a compromise of a sort: no circumcision, but the legal inclusion of the aliens among the Chosen People. Paul tells a different version, however, declaring that the dispute in Jerusalem resulted in a decision to separate the two branches sharply:[65] one included circumcised

Jews who obeyed all the rules of the Law, the other embraced uncircumcised Gentiles to whom these rules meant nothing. With considerable impudence, Paul, who had never known Jesus, announced
that "the gospel of the uncircumcision was committed to me, as the
gospel of the circumcision was unto Peter (for he that wrought effec-
tually in Peter to the apostleship of the circumcision, the same was
mighty in me toward the Gentiles)."[66] He thereupon gave himself
the title of Apostle.

From then on, each of the two continued to preach his own religion in his own way. The first nucleus of Christians influenced by
Paul's thinking, which was to prevail, sprang up in Antioch. It was
clearly no longer the religion preached by Jesus but the cult of
"Christ" as a god.[67]

The Acts of the Apostles and the Epistles of Paul enable us to
follow the successive steps in Paul's life: his missionary journeys, his
inexhaustible activity, the alternation of success and failure. The
style of the Pauline Epistles—twisted, ungrammatical, full of repetitions, disjunctions, contradictions—reveals a disordered mind and a
chaotic culture, and a hardly sympathetic personality: while Paul
was angry and arrogant in his letters, when face to face with his
opponents he lacked the courage to state his own ideas.[68]

It was probably in A.D. 60 that he visited Jerusalem for the last
time. Here James implored him, in order to avoid trouble, to make a
show of loyalty to their ancestral faith by going to the Temple.[69] Paul
consented, but his mere appearance in the Temple sparked the anger
of the faithful: "Men of Israel, help: This is the man, that teacheth
all men everywhere against the people, and the law, and this place."
The providential appearance of a handful of Roman legionaries
narrowly averted a lynching, but they arrested Paul for disrupting
the peace. He tried to avoid a trial on the strength of his Roman
citizenship, by virtue of the exemption from corporal punishment
provided by the *jus civitatis*.[70] The legal technicality made it necessary to send him to Italy for a thorough study and adjudication of the
question.

The Book of Acts ends abruptly with the statement that Paul
spent two whole years in Rome without harm. We are left to hypothesis with regard to his ultimate trial and the circumstances and date of
his martyrdom, which tradition places in Rome itself. It is assuredly

not true that Peter was there at the same time and that the two old antagonists finished their lives together in the same martyrdom. But it is true that even the deaths of the two adversaries did not end the struggle between Petrinists and Paulinists. The dogmatic position of Judaicist Christian circles, that Paul was an apostate, persisted until the fifth century.[71]

Master and Disciples

After the harshly contentious texts of Acts and the Pauline Epistles, the reading of the Synoptic Gospels takes us back to the more peaceful atmosphere of the beginnings of the apostolate. They tell us nothing of the activities of the Twelve after their selection and during their propaganda tours, but they do say that, when these had been completed, the Apostles went back to Jesus and reported on their work. particularly proud that they had succeeded in exorcising and driving out demons.[72] Jesus was pleased with them.[73]

In addition to the Apostles, the Nazarene must have been surrounded by some other disciples. No names of any appear in the Gospels, but valuable evidence appears in Acts: after the death of Jesus, when it was necessary to replace the treacherous Judas, Peter suggested the selection of one of "these men which have companied with us all the time that the Lord Jesus went in and out among us."[74] Joseph bar-Sabas and Matthias were proposed, and the latter was chosen.

Luke informs us that there were also some women among the followers of Jesus; he had cured them of evil spirits or diseases.[75] They included Joanna, the wife of Chuza, Herod's steward; Susanna; and that "Mary called Magdalene" who began to be identified, after the sixth century, as the "repentant sinner" but who, on the other hand, was declared by a number of the apocryphal Gospels, including that attributed to Philip,[76] to be the *wife* of Jesus! Later, Luke also mentions Salome, the mother of the two Zebedees; and he gives us the further valuable fact that some of these women had means and "ministered to him of their substance."

The practice of material assistance by women to the companions of the faith was to become frequent in the Christian communities.

Both Acts and the Pauline Epistles record a number of such cases: Tabitha, or Dorcas,[77] who made tunics for the brethren in Joppa; Lydia, a shopkeeper in Thyatira; Phoebe, a deaconess in Cenchreae; Mary, for whom Paul exhorts his brethren to gratitude because she did so much for them; Priscilla (Prisca) of Corinth; Claudia; and others.

Citing the examples of the Apostles, Paul also defended, for himself and for his friend Barnabas, the right to be accompanied in their travels by "a sister [that is, a Christian], a wife, as well as other apostles, and as the brethren of the Lord, and Cephas."[78] Unfortunately, from the very beginning the presence of women in the Christian communities also gave rise to certain embarrassments, such that Paul himself had to step in on many occasions, warning: "Let your women keep silence in the churches; for it is not permitted unto them to speak. . . . And if they will learn any thing, let them ask their husbands at home: for it is a shame for women to speak in the church";[79] "But I suffer not a woman to teach, nor to usurp authority over the man, but to be in silence";[80] "But the younger widows, refuse; for when they have begun to wax wanton against Christ, they will marry; Having damnation, because they have cast off their first faith; And withal they learn to be idle";[81] "For if the woman be not covered, let her also be shorn: but if it be a shame for a woman to be shorn or shaven, let her be covered. For a man indeed ought not to cover his head, forasmuch as he is the image and glory of God: but the woman is the glory of the man. For the man is not of the woman; but the woman of the man; Neither was the man created for the woman; but the woman for the man."[82]

Contact with the Greek and Latin world, where women had for some time enjoyed wide freedom and great respect, and especially, later, the influence of the Germans, who had a chivalrous reverence toward women, somewhat softened Christianity's conception of woman as an inferior being. Nevertheless, the Church's contention that it has always promulgated the equality of the sexes is a lie. On the contrary, it is obvious, from Paul's days on, that the Church has always striven to compel the woman to submit to the man, and that centuries of ecclesiastical teaching have constantly striven to maintain this concept.

Perhaps it was only the disciples of Jesus' lifetime who really put into practice the exemplary brotherhood preached by their master, even if the vocatives "brethren" (ἀδελφοί, adelphoi) and "sisters" (ἀδελφαί, adelphai) recur frequently in almost a hundred and fifty years of New Testament writings.[83] After that, its decline can be followed step by step. The establishment of an ecclesiastical hierarchy superior to the community sealed its fate: the clerics continued to call one another "brother," but they never addressed the laity so except in their sermons, and by the beginning of the third century no layman would have dared to call a member of the clergy "brother."[84]

As for the term "Christians" (Χριστιανοί, Christianoi), a passage in Acts gives us reason to suppose that it was first adopted in Antioch when Paul was preaching, but many scholars give it a much later origin. The word, formed perhaps by pagans, "is a barbarism with a Greek root and a Latin suffix, which shows its vulgar source and an intention half scornful, half ironic; like the 'Caesarians' and the 'Pompeians,' these 'Christians' were viewed as members of the party of a 'Christ' no better qualified than themselves."[85] And it would seem that the Christians of the early period did not like their name.

Nor had the word "Christ," which means "the Anointed," become a proper name even in the Gospels, Acts, or the Pauline Epistles; Paul himself often used it before "Jesus," rather than after. The disciples addressed Jesus as "master," which in Aramaic is rabbi, and precedes the name, and they called him rabbōnī ("our master") when they spoke about him or addressed him without using his name.

To give his disciples unmistakable evidence of his affection for them, if we are to believe the Gospels, Jesus went so far as to renounce his family. While he was preaching one day in a synagogue, perhaps in the neighborhood of Nazareth,[86] or eating with his followers,[87] but in any case in the midst of a great throng, his relatives appeared at the door and asked permission to speak with him. Mary was so deeply concerned at the dangerous adventure on which Jesus had embarked that she questioned his sanity (quoniam in furorem versus est), and she had brought along her other sons, in the hope that they might be able to take him aside (κρατῆσαι αὐτόν, kratēsai auton) and persuade him to return home. Because of the great crowd around Jesus, they could not get near him; but someone told the master: "Behold, thy mother and thy brethren stand without, desiring to speak with thee."

Gesturing in vexation, Jesus replied: "Who is my mother? and who are my brethren?" Extending his hand to indicate all those who surrounded him, he added: "Behold my mother, and my brethren! For whosoever shall do the will of my Father which is in heaven, the same is my brother, and sister, and mother."

He imposed the same renunciation on those who wished to become his followers: "If any man come to me, and hate not his father, and mother, and wife, and children, and brethren, and sisters, yea, and his own life also, he cannot be my disciple."[88]

Of course, the immorality of such pronouncements (which were to be contradicted in other circumstances) is only apparent. Jesus renounced the traditional values of blood ties with a sophism solely to put greater emphasis on a bond that was even deeper and broader: the brotherhood of all who are joined in a single faith and a single mission. Undoubtedly the interpretation given to these words by a recent English sect, the Exclusive Brethren, is in error. The Exclusive Brethren expressly require the rejection of one's family in order to establish a single, absurd bond with one's brethren. The sect has been marked by instances of abandonment of children, divorce because of fanatical adherence to the sect by only one of the spouses, and so forth.

The Physical Appearance of Jesus

Ernest Renan, the author of a rather fictional life of Jesus which had wide success in the mid-nineteenth century and which we have already cited several times, believes that the fascination that Jesus had for men and especially for women was probably largely due to his physical appearance. Unfortunately we have no descriptions of him in the holy texts, which would allow us to confirm or refute Renan's romantic supposition. Even less could we expect to have inherited some pictorial or sculptural presentation of Jesus from his contemporaries. The second commandment of the Decalogue of Moses forbade the making of images of persons or things, in an attempt to combat the idolatry so widely prevalent in ancient times. Christians of Greek and Roman origin, however, felt no such scruples and sought to portray their god and their saints. In early Christian times, they assembled out of the flourishing classical art of their countries certain works to which they could ascribe symbolic meanings adapted to their new religion: the shepherd carrying the lamb on his shoulders, a praying figure, Orpheus enchanting the forces of nature, etc. They read Jesus into these works, but it was of course an allegorical portrait each time, with no pretense of reproducing the Nazarene's actual features.

At the same time, there was a great diversity of opinion between the Fathers of the Eastern and Western churches as to the physical person of Jesus. The East tended to the conviction that he was ugly, relying on a Biblical passage that was supposed to be a prophecy of the future Messiah: "He hath no form nor comeliness; and when we shall see him, there is no beauty that we should desire him. He is despised and rejected of men; a man of sorrows, and acquainted with grief: and we hid as it were our faces from him; he was despised."[89] Justin Martyr thus did not hesitate to describe Jesus: "Made ugly by the sufferings and the humiliations that he had endured";[90] Irenaeus said he was *"infirmus, ingloriosus et indecorus"*;[91] Clement of Alexandria, that he was αἰσχρός (*aischros*), or "base";[92] Origen, that he was "small, ungraceful, a mere zero";[93] Tertullian, that "he would not have been spat upon by the Roman soldiers if his face had not been so ugly as to inspire spitting";[94] and so on.[95]

The Byzantine missionaries taught that Jesus was lame in the right leg, and even today the Eastern crucifixes are characterized by the "Byzantine curve," which corresponds exactly to the position of a limp in the right leg when one tries to stand erect.

In the West, on the other hand, at least since the third century, the opinion prevailed among the Church Fathers that Jesus had been extremely handsome, and they justified their conviction with a Biblical psalm[96] that was actually a nuptial hymn (!): "Thou art fairer than the children of men; grace is poured into thy lips." John Chrysostom, Augustine, Jerome, and others also describe Jesus as a very handsome man. The monk Epiphanius, in the fourth century, specified that Jesus was six feet tall, that his complexion was like ripe wheat, that his nose was long, that his eyebrows were black, that his hair had a touch of red (ἐπιφοινισσομένη, *epiphoinissomenē*), and that he looked strikingly like his mother.[97]

In the Middle Ages, credence was given even to a letter that P. Lentulus (an unknown personage who called himself "governor of Jerusalem") was supposed to have written to the Roman Senate during the reign of Tiberius to provide information on Jesus. This is the letter's description of the founder of Christianity: "His hair is of a ripe hazel color, with a slight blue light; smooth as far back as his ears, but wavy and curled on the shoulders. His color is high, his nose and mouth have no defects. His beard is luxuriant, and parted at the chin; he is of average height and his body is well proportioned. . . ."[98]

Assuming absolute perfection even in the measurements of his body, the men of the Middle Ages decided that he was five feet five inches tall—exactly three times the Palestinian measure of length. Later, this was adapted, in Italy, to local standards of measurement: the Laurentian Code, which dates from the fourteenth century, puts his height at one and three-quarters meters (five feet eight inches), or three Florentine hands.[99]

As early as the eighth century, pictures and statues of Jesus, following contemporary models, were beginning to appear. To explain how after so many centuries it was possible to make an authentic portrait of the Savior, it was said that there had always been a traditional secret picture composed by none other than Luke. The first to tell of this legend was Andrew, metropolitan of Crete, in 710.[100] Backed up by such contentions, portraits of Jesus multiplied to such an extent that only a few years later Emperor Leo III the Isaurian had to order a harsh persecution against images, which led to passionate debates on the legitimacy of portraying Jesus and the danger of falling into heathen idolatry.

Nonetheless, images of Jesus continued to spread, with a certain freedom of inspiration, and portraits of other noble figures also came to be considered his. Such, for instance, was the case with a Byzantine icon, stolen in 730 from the patriarch of Constantinople and taken to Rome (it is still in the Church of St. John Lateran). It shows an emperor, clothed in purple and sitting on a golden throne richly ornamented with pearls and precious stones.[101]

Other images, even more remarkable, were created later. In the Basilica of St. Peter in Rome there is a cloth on which a face is imprinted. According to legend, it is the face of Jesus, who had to wipe his face as he was climbing the hill of Calvary, and the cloth was given to him by a pious woman named Veronica. In actuality, "Veronica" was not then a woman's name, but a corruption of *vera icona,* or "real image."

The famous winding sheet called the Holy Shroud, which is preserved in Turin, goes back only to 1453. It is a cloth about fourteen feet long and less than four feet wide, in which one can see brown stains that form a single shape, rather like two imprints of a human body, front and back, as if the sheet had been placed above and below a body and folded round the head. The shroud was presented in 1453 to Anna of Lusignano, the wife of Duke Ludovico I of Savoy, and it was said to be the winding sheet of Jesus, discovered in Jerusalem during the Crusades.

The authenticity of this relic (in various parts of the world there are some forty other Holy Shrouds, all of which are supposed to be genuine) has always been the subject of much debate. Thus far, however, the authenticity of the Holy Shroud of Turin has not been made an article of faith. Even some authoritative theologians permit themselves some doubt.[102] If only as a matter of scientific curiosity, however, it has continued to be studied. In 1898, the shroud was photographed for the first time, with unexpected results: the glass negatives, developed and retouched where they were clouded, showed an indubitable image of a human body, rather plainly visible. This aroused scientific interest, and as a result it was discovered that the impressions on the shroud had not been painted there (as had often been suspected) but had indeed been produced by contact with a body and its sweat, its blood, and the ointment of aloes and myrrh with which the body had been covered.

The analysis of the shroud has continued in the present century. In 1931, Professor Erie made better photographs, on the basis of which a Sindonological Congress, convoked in Turin in 1939, took various measurements, with these results, among others:[103]

Height	5 feet 5 inches
Arm length	24.5 inches
Leg length	33 inches
Head length	7.2 inches
Head width	5.76 inches

On the basis of the mesocephalic shape of the head, the man of the shroud might be classified, by ethnic type, as of a Mediterranean race; but the unusual height and other physical characteristics (broad shoulders, powerful thorax, very taut abdomen, solid musculature, etc.) would seem rather to classify him in Kretschmer's biotype.[104] The man who was selected to leave his image on the shroud of Jesus could not have been a Palestinian.

The Character of Jesus

Dr. Charles Binet-Sanglé, professor of psychology at the University of Paris, has written a weighty work in four volumes (altogether some two thousand pages)[105] in an attempt to classify the character of Jesus scientifically on the basis of the data available in the Gospels. We cannot wholly accept the conclusions of this study, which from the very outset appears to be neither objective nor dispassionate, but seems rather to proceed from a predetermination to force Jesus into existing patterns. However, we cite some of his findings as a curiosity.

According to Binet-Sanglé, the "theomania" of Jesus (as he calls his religious vocation) was noticeably determined by heredity: the excessive devoutness of his parents degenerated in him and in his brother, James, into a fixed idea.[106] The behavior of Jesus in this respect can be compared with the diagnoses of modern theomaniacs that have been made by authoritative students of mental illness. The theomaniacs studied by the director of the mental hospital of Charenton believe that they are inspired by God and called to launch religious reforms; they believe that they are invulnerable and immortal; they have frequent seizures of mysticism during which they claim to have seen divine apparitions, etc. J. Dagonet, a physician in Ste. Anne's Hospital in Paris, observes that for the most part theomaniacs are easily irritated, will not permit contradiction, and speak in tones of authority. B. Ball, professor of mental pathology in the Faculty of Medicine in Paris, asserts that the great religious innovators and reformers (as particular examples he cites Mohammed and Luther) have always been psychologically abnormal.

On the basis of the prolonged fast to which Jesus subjected

himself in the desert before he began his ministry, Binet-Sanglé states that the Nazarene suffered from a pathological fear of food or of eating.[107] His frequent journeys (from Nazareth to the banks of the Jordan, from there to the wilderness, then back to Nazareth, to Cana, to Capernaum and its environs, to Gergesa, again to Capernaum, to Phoenicia, to Caesarea, to Samaria and Judea, etc.) persuade the doctor that Jesus suffered also from dromomania (irrepressible wanderlust).[108] His chastity and his exhortations of his disciples to celibacy lead him to believe that Jesus was sexually impotent[109] and showed symptoms of homosexuality, in the light of his predilection for the young John.[110] The Gospels' reports that Jesus often spent nights in prayer are signs that he suffered from insomnia.[111] The temptation in the wilderness, the transfiguration, and other similar phenomena are used as a point of departure for a dissertation on the hallucinatory syndrome.[112] A detailed analysis of the sayings ascribed to Jesus by the Gospels leads to the conclusion that Jesus was egocentric, a maniac devoid of profundity of thought, incoherent and often amoral. In sum, Jesus was a "typical psychotic,"[113] a visionary, a paranoiac, a megalomaniac! Binet-Sanglé questions the diagnosis of J. Soury,[114] who found that Jesus suffered from syphilitic meningeal encephalitis, objecting on the grounds that Jesus manifested the first symptoms of derangement at the age of twelve and could not have contracted such a serious venereal disease so early in life! He is inclined to believe instead that the insanity of Jesus derived from inherited taints (perhaps alcoholism in his father), complicated by tuberculosis.[115]

In general, the rationalists, even without going to the extremes of Binet-Sanglé, agree in the conclusion that Jesus was a "visionary" and "presumptuous,"[116] that at times "his mind wavered," especially because "he was dizzied by the idea of the kingdom of heaven, forever dazzling his perceptions,"[117] or, at the very least, he was "a fanatic and a dreamer."[118]

Very different conclusions are reached by a curious study that recently appeared in Italy.[119] Its author, though he admits in advance that his method is specifically that of graphology, believes that he can apply it to what are really evidences of the character of Jesus—that is, to his speech and behavior as narrated by the Evangelists. He proceeds to a lengthy examination of the "qualities" of Jesus: creative initiative, rectitude, humility, the capacity to seize details, a degree of fastidiousness, eighty-five centigrade degrees (*sic*) of flexibility, cheerfulness with dignity, seventy-five centigrade degrees of evenness of temper and twenty-five of variability of mood, no vulgarity, no larcenous inclinations . . . One interesting observation made by the author, in my opinion, is that of the hypersensitivity shown by Jesus when, for instance, he sweated blood on the night of his arrest, and again when he inexplicably stood mute during his trial.[120] This was called an inheritance from the neuropsychological trauma suffered by his mother at his conception—not by reason of the uniqueness of the conception itself (miraculous, through the work of God) but because of her fear of being cast aside by her betrothed, Joseph.

None of these scholars takes into account that the conduct of Jesus, on the basis of which they profess to be able to reconstruct his character and his psyche, consists in fact only of *attributions* by the Evangelists, whose accuracy we can never establish. Certain pronouncements on his own divine origin, for example, or on the inevitability of his resurrection and return to earth, which in the mouth of Jesus can well seem the products of presumptuousness and fanaticism, are understandable attestations of faith on the part of the Evangelists. Certain baffling argumentations, which raise doubts about the mental capacity of Jesus, especially in the Fourth Gospel, are the products of mystical-philosophical divagations by the author of that book.

If we can separate the "Christ of faith," who is the creation of the fanaticism of his believers, from the "Jesus of history," who is obvious to us in the accounts of the Synoptic Gospels, the personality of Jesus emerges quite clearly: ultra-human, even in his sudden changes of mood, at one moment gentle and tender, almost feminine in his lassitude, at another sharp and vehement, quick to anger and scorn; often locked in deep sorrow, and above all moved by constant unrest, which is not a sign of madness—at least in my opinion—but the mark of a great soul, aware of an almost impossible mission that has become the ideal of his whole existence.

It was more or less in this fashion that the deeply religious Middle Ages understood him. In the apocryphal letter of the unknown Lentulus, quoted earlier, we find this portrait of the character of Jesus: "Terrible in his rebukes, gentle and friendly in his admonitions, cheerful yet maintaining his dignity. He has never been seen to laugh, but often to weep. . . . His speech is sober, rare, and modest."

[10]

THE GOOD TIDINGS

The Beatitudes

The good tidings that Jesus had been so eager to preach and that the outbreaks in Nazareth, in Capernaum, and in Gergesa had forced him to postpone are summarized in what is generally called the Sermon on the Mount. Matthew says specifically that for this preaching Jesus did in fact ascend a mountain. This could not possibly be Mount Tabor, as Christian tradition has it; Tabor is too far from Capernaum and it is ridiculous to believe that a crowd of Galileans would have made such a journey to hear the words of a prophet. The site might have been some modest rise, or more probably some cliff overlooking the Plain of Gennesaret, if the Evangelist did not after all improvise the detail to give a more impressive background to the first public oration of Jesus, on the order of the *mise-en-scène* provided by the Old Testament for Moses when he brought down the Law from Mount Sinai.[1]

Rather than a sermon, however, what Jesus delivered on this occasion was a series of maxims followed by explanatory illustrations. The comparison with Moses comes automatically to mind, but more as antithesis than as analogy. The famous Tables of the ancient patriarch set forth a catalogue of commandments, mostly in the form of prohibitions (e.g., "Thou shalt not steal"; "Thou shalt not kill"), which were supposed to have been inscribed by God in order to regulate community life in Israel, and it was assumed that transgressors would be subjected to the most stringent penalties. Jesus, on the other hand, offered a collection of "beatitudes," in which he, also acting as the interpreter of divine purpose, promised recompense to all who endured want, hunger and thirst, afflictions and persecutions, who were exploited because they were meek and mild, troubled in their quest for peace, ill rewarded for their generosity and faith, offended in the purity of their hearts.[2] Contrapuntally, he followed this with an array of interdicts against the rich, whose accumulation of wealth was often accomplished at the expense of the poor; against the greedy, who took no heed of the hunger of their neighbors; against the oppressor, the ingrate, the man of violence.[3]

The proclamation of the Beatitudes and the interdicts was no original contribution by Jesus. It brought together various utterances contained in the literature of the Old Testament, particularly in the Psalms and the Proverbs, which promised to the poor that their sufferings would end and that they would enjoy all the good things of the earth from which they had always been barred; here, too, the greed of the wealthy, injustice, and violence were rebuked.[4] Many exegeses of the Gospels, especially those by Jewish writers, have succeeded in making ever more prominent the close connection between the teachings of Jesus and the traditional Jewish religion. The Sermon on the Mount in particular has been adduced by some of these authors to show that these teachings already existed in the writings of Rabbis Ben Sirach, Levita, and others.[5]

Nonetheless, he took these expressions of faith in God out of their contexts and offered them with the certainty of their *imminent* realization, and in this lay the originality of Jesus and the secret of his magnetism. True, he still cozened his audiences with the mirage of illusory hopes, in the pattern of an old prophetic and apocalyptic tradition; but his words were deliberately chosen to gratify the thirst for justice among the *amē hā-'erets,* for he put aside grandiose portrayals of national prosperity and political resurgence and worked through the most humble and intuitive perceptions of social justice and personal happiness.[6] To those who had hitherto been excluded from them, he especially promised the enjoyment of worldly goods, and in the same breath he strewed maledictions and menaces on those who already had such goods.

This can well seem a demagogic approach. Why should a rich man be punished even when he has done no wrong? Why should the fearful, the vacillating, the incompetent enjoy the same gains as those who take risks, who work hard and willingly, who are persistent and intelligent? But demagogy was involuntary in Jesus. He was poor, and in the humble world in which he lived, he had certainly known all the bitterness and privation of the poor. He said what was in all their hearts, but it was there only in that inchoate, obscure shape that abstract concepts always take in untrained minds.[7]

Precisely because the Beatitudes represent an irrational, sentimental outcrop, one cannot profess to see Jesus as a social and political reformer.[8] His fond dream of an idyllic world in which all men would live in perfect brotherhood without any problems whatsoever, because God himself would see to the needs of each as he already provided for the flowers and the birds, is a utopia lacking any foundation in a logical program of reform.

The Kingdom of Heaven and This World

The disciples closest to Jesus had difficulty in following him in his conception of an anarchistic society. We can observe them as they try to create personal privileges, as they vie with one another for a place of honor beside the master, whose supremacy in the future kingdom they accept without discussion. And too, very often, they are content to dream of a world of earthly pleasures, as predicted in the vain promises of the Bible, rather than of a world made better through a spiritual renewal of mankind. Indications to this effect can be found especially in some of the apocryphal Gospels. That of Thomas, for instance, contains this prophecy: "For you have there, in Paradise, five trees which change not winter nor summer,"[9] which recurs unchanged in a Manichean psalm, while a Coptic treatise speaks of "the fragrant trees of Paradise," and of "the brooks that softly run, the palm trees and the dates that every tree bears," and so forth, recalling the fine Biblical fantasies of a world in which "the wheat shall grow as high as the cedars of Lebanon, and God shall cause grain to fall from heaven so that every man shall gather it in his hands. . . . Man shall no longer have to tread out the grapes: he need only carry a great cluster into his house, and leave it in a corner thereof, and he shall have wine in abundance for all the year."

The unexpected death of Jesus before the kingdom could become reality inevitably aroused disappointment and bewilderment. Then faith in Jesus surged up again and once more his followers embraced the hope of an imminent overthrow of the social order, merely postponing it for a little time until the Second Coming, or Parousia (παρουσία), of Jesus.[10]

Hence, real Christianity was born and has always lived, since the time of the first Christian community, in this tragic ambiguity. One might think that when the Second Coming did not materialize, the Nazarene's disciples would have finally recognized their error. And so the story of Jesus would have ended like that of any other prophet who had provided a momentary illusion for the poor, the weak, and the oppressed. But once again the message of Jesus was not allowed to vanish. Collating the Beatitudes with other major prophecies that the Gospels, as we shall see, were later to ascribe to the founder of Christianity, the theologians claimed the right to postpone the establishment of the kingdom to some indefinite future time. The proto-Christians' expectation of a "universal judgment" did not diminish, but, under the new conception, the Day of Judgment would put an end to this terrestrial world and establish another, supernatural and invisible, and situated geographically in some unspecified region of celestial space.

There can be no doubt that the Jews of that time—and hence Jesus and the Apostles—knew nothing of the idea of an Olympian world beyond the earth, which to them was the unique creation and the only possible world.[11] The Olympian concept derived from the influence of Greek philosophy. In fact, the first hint of it was given by Paul, who, speaking of the Second Coming, said that, at the moment when "the Lord himself shall descend from heaven with a shout, with the voice of the archangel, and with the trump of God, . . . the dead in Christ shall rise first: Then we which are alive and remain, shall be caught up together with them in the clouds, to meet the Lord in the air: and so shall we ever be with the Lord."[12] But the Synoptic Gospels do not yet allow us to imagine this establishment of the kingdom among the clouds. Credence for it was won among the faithful by playing on the Gospels' term "the kingdom of heaven," despite the fact that all the exegetes, including even the Catholics, agree that the expression is the exact equivalent of "the kingdom of God" and that the word "heaven" is used to indicate the idea of divinity rather than a geographical site.[13] Indeed, the phrase "kingdom of God" (in Hebrew, *malkūth 'elohīm;* in Aramaic, *malkūthā dī 'elāhā*) is never used in the Old Testament,[14] where, however, frequent use is made of the corresponding phrase, "kingdom of heaven."

We shall have to come back to this theological complication. For the moment, we are concerned rather with studying the serious social consequences created by the assignment of a more distant time and place to that kingdom that Jesus had prophesied was at hand in Palestine.

What he considered the intolerable injustices to which God would finally put an end (misery, hunger, persecution, the triumph of pride and violence) remain permanent conditions of life on earth. The religion of Jesus, which held out the joyous promise of a better life, has been imbued with passive resignation, and the belief has grown in the masses that suffering and abasement are the essential conditions of true merit, the only means of entering into eternal happiness.[15] Forgetting that Jesus never exalted wretchedness for its own sake, as a state of blessedness, but that he really offered the poor some hope of an early end to their suffering, some authors have produced such sentences as this, which has the bite of burning irony: "Did not Jesus Christ declare that the poor are blessed? Why then do they rebel at their poverty?"[16]

The fear that the unsatisfied aspirations to social justice to which Jesus had opened the hearts of the poor and the oppressed would break out in open revolt led the Church to cast deliberate doubt on the question whether Jesus had ever taken any interest in the problem of the poor, and to condemn those who contended that he had done so. As early as the end of the second century, those little groups of Christians who looked to the kingdom as the end of the misery of the humble (in Hebrew, *ebiōnīm*) were proclaimed heretics, and, in order to buttress the argument that the social content of their preaching could not be traced to Jesus, the Church invented a presumptive leader for them and called him Ebion.[17] Alterations were made in the Gospel of Matthew to weaken the two

Beatitudes that explicitly envisage the abolition of want and hunger. This Gospel does not read, as that of Luke does: "Blessed be ye poor," and "Blessed are ye that hunger now"; Matthew says: "Blessed are the poor *in spirit*," and "Blessed are they which do hunger and thirst *after righteousness*." Today, many people believe that such was the original form of what Jesus said,[18] without realizing there is then no point in the condemnations of the rich and the haughty or in any of the other harsh castigations of wealth strewn through the Gospels, nor in the categorical statement that "it is easier for a cord [κάμιλος, *kamilos,* and not καμήλος *kamēlos,* which means "camel"] to pass through the eye of a needle than for a rich man to enter the kingdom of heaven."

Jesus really meant that the poor were to inherit the kingdom without regard to their beliefs or to their religious practices.[19] At the very most, the later formula ("Blessed are the poor in spirit") is to be interpreted only as a corollary of the earlier, intended to exhort the rich: "Blessed are those who resolve to live spiritually as poor men even though they have wealth."[20]

Christian Brotherhood

Stripped of their polemic purpose, these declarations by Jesus were to be transformed, in his later teaching, into a call to combat social injustice with the principle of brotherly love. But one may argue that not even the earliest Christian communities succeeded in living altogether in accord with this spirit. One has only to recall the rivalries among the Apostles themselves, even while Jesus was still living, the betrayal by Judas, the conflicts—which were not merely ideological—among Peter, Paul, and James. Not even the much-acclaimed community of ownership was an accomplished fact. The complaints of the "Hellenists," which we have already mentioned, and the instance of Ananias and Sapphira, who were condemned to death for having held back some of their money from the community,[21] demonstrate the persistence of selfishness and egotism even in a society built on communistic foundations.

It would be unjust to disregard the works of charity and benevolence on the part of the Church in every period, but what is meant here is that such works, however widespread and munificent, can never assure the achievement of perfect social and economic equality. Men will never be equal as long as some are in a position to offer charity to others who are compelled to request it. Yet even when we condemn the inadequacy of the Church's social doctrine, we must recognize its merit in having at least temporarily contributed to the needs of so many people. One cannot suppress a certain emotion in reading the eloquent passage in which Tertullian proudly describes the eleemosynary organization of the Church of his times: "There exists among us a kind of common fund . . . in which each of us deposits a modest sum every month, or whenever he wishes to and can do so. No one is compelled to give; contributions are voluntary. This might be called the charity bank. One does not draw from it for feasts or wine or revelry, but to give help to the poor, to bury the dead, to assist orphans left without subsistence, to succor the helpless aged and the shipwrecked, and to help those who, for the sake of our faith, have been condemned to prison, to forced labor, or to deportation."[22]

The Christians' charitable system may have been established on the model of the old Greek ἔρανοι (eranoi), who were members of a mutual-assistance society, and the word "clergy" may be derived from the name of the κληρωτοί (klērōtoi), who were the administrative officers of the eranoi and who were chosen from among those who evinced the greatest honesty and earnestness.[23]

If economic equality was never achieved among these Christians (and it would have been impossible of achievement by such methods), it is permissible to doubt whether their renowned "social equality" ever existed, except perhaps in the apostolic age. The best evidence in its favor is the discovery of common burial places in Rome where members of the aristocracy were often interred with their servants but where the epitaphs never stressed the diversity of status. This was probably done, however, only because the aristocrats hoped to conceal their identities and thus to guard their relatives against persecution.[24] Contrary evidence may be drawn from the fact that even Monica, the mother of Augustine, forbade him to marry his mistress (who had borne his child) because the girl did not belong to their social class.

Similarly, it is utterly false for the Church to boast that it "abolished" slavery. Christians were not forbidden to own slaves: the Church limited itself to adjuring their masters to treat them humanely and to respect the virtue of the female chattels, but Paul's own Epistles are not sparing in their recommendations that slaves submit and obey. Slavery ended later, not through any influence of Christianity but through the changes that evolved in the economic system of production and the development of the more profitable and secure institution of the leased farm. True, Christianity has much to say by way of pity and consolation for the sufferings of slaves, the more so because, at least in the beginning, it recruited from among them the great mass of the faithful (it is estimated that, of the total population of sixty or seventy million in the Roman Empire at that time, not more than two million persons were really free[25]); but any practical program to reform the social order was wholly alien to Christianity. Nor was this ever to change. The Church has never contemplated an organization of society based on Christian principles, but has limited itself to helping, to the extent possible, those unfortunate individuals who live in a world already damned.[26] It is hardly necessary even to recall the vast inequality that prevailed in the Middle Ages between the feudal lords and the serfs attached to their lands, or the social disparities of our own day even in the bosom of the clergy itself.

Christianity as it is understood today assembles people of different social classes in brotherhood only in the sense that it requires all of them to believe in the same dogmas; it does not invite them to eliminate differences in caste. All the more, then, has the projection of the kingdom into a world both extra-terrestrial and extra-sensory brought Christians to a complete rejection of the brotherhood preached by the Nazarene. Imbued with the belief that they should conduct themselves on this earth as though they were not of it, the individuals who most sincerely seek to be Christians tend to evade mundane problems in order not to impair their hope of eternal salvation. Following this individualistic and antisocial pattern, in the best of cases the Christian is responsive only to a general principle of helping his neighbor, which, however, he views as an action that proves his devoutness and goes to his personal credit in the ledger of redemption.

The Church has strayed so far from the ideals of Jesus that every movement among the poor—who always rebel in periods of great economic depression—even if it draws its inspiration from the Gospels, has been condemned by the Church. In our own time, in fact, the Church strangled at birth a selfless program conceived within the rank and file of its own clergy, which of course proposed no revolutionary social reform but sought merely to testify to the solidarity of the Church with the working proletariat, the victim of modern capitalistic organization, and to bring apostates back to the faith. This was the movement of the "worker-priests." Founded in France in 1941 by Denis Cardinal Suhard, it strove to reconvert the masses to Christianity not only through vague and generalizing sermons from the pulpit but also by mingling among the unbelievers, living as they lived, sharing their pleasures and their griefs, their disappointments and their hopes, as Jesus had done.[27] The work of these daring, genuine apostles, trained in the Seminary of Lisieux, began in 1944. They wore overalls, they worked in mines, they climbed scaffoldings, they drove delivery trucks, they labored and drudged—and they tried through example, through precept, and through concrete help to teach the law of love that Jesus had preached. But, as might well have been expected, contact between these missionaries and a world in which, as a result of the indifference of the official Church, new ideologies, and especially Marxism, had meanwhile taken root, this contact had an osmotic result: some Communists became Christians, some worker-priests became convinced Communists. To eliminate such an embarrassment, which it viewed as far more important than the abandonment of a vast mass to its own devices, the Vatican intervened, first restricting and then altogether prohibiting the worker-priest movement.

The Social Encyclicals

Officially, in dealing with social problems, the Church has confined itself in modern times to abstract platonic pronouncements *ex cathedra,* to which it was forced to resort by the constant growth of socialist thought. The basic documents are three encyclicals— *Rerum novarum* of Pope Leo XIII (1891), *Quadragesimo anno* of Pope Pius XI (1931), and *Mater et magistra* of Pope John XXIII (1961)—which, in ever increasing degree (and one must recognize the fact), underline the responsibility of the rich to the poor. But that is all. Among Protestant observers,[28] too, the social doctrine of the Church is sympathetically viewed, particularly since it strives to erect a dam against the flood of Communism. But it should be noted at the outset that a mere appeal to the notion of Christian "charity" in the rich (who are neither always nor necessarily Christian) cannot be held forth as a means of definitively solving a problem of social and economic justice. In the second place, these encyclicals are far indeed from the spirit of the teachings of Jesus: they vigorously uphold the right of private property against the ideal of community ownership promulgated by Jesus; they maintain that it is impossible to have a world without social inequality, against the ideal of perfect brotherhood that Jesus preached; they declare that it is equally impossible to eliminate pain and anguish, again in contrast to the ideal of a world of total universal happiness as Jesus preached it; and they sing praises to poverty (which turns its back on corruption and vice)!

Undoubtedly, the caution of the Church can be justified by practical necessities. In the society in which we live, erected on the foundations of individual initiative, respect for property, cooperation —but not the abolition of class distinctions, etc.—a thoroughgoing activation of the Gospels' philosophy would lead to anarchy. So a contemporary French author, St.-Georges de Bouhélier, has paradoxically portrayed it in his play *La tragédie du nouveau Christ* (*The Tragedy of the New Christ*): Jesus returns among men of today and lives as a wanderer among failures, misfits, and prostitutes; he curses the world and denounces the rich, arousing suspicion and fear. But his disciples, stirred by his words, climax a day of religious celebrations by setting a city on fire. The law, the public-security forces, the clergy, and the mob join in anger against them and put them in prison. Jesus feels that the guilt is his and he suffers himself to be stoned.

The Kingdom and the Ancient Covenant

In its political and social aspects, the idea of the kingdom preached by Jesus came closer to the messianic anticipation of the masses, looking toward an economic upheaval, than to the official conception of the Messiah as king and captain that had been handed down by the prophetic books. In its religious sense, however, it fitted perfectly into the tradition. In other words, it was to represent the ultimate consummation or execution of an ancient "alliance," or "covenant," framed between Yahweh and the Hebrew people at the time of Abraham[29] and renewed with Moses.[30]

It is essential to remember that the word "alliance," or "covenant" (in Hebrew, *berīth*), is paralleled in the Gospels by διαθήκη (*diathēkē*), which has the same meaning, although Jerome unfortunately translated it into Latin as *testamentum*, which means something quite different. Hence, we speak of the "Old Testament" or the "New Testament" nowadays, often without knowing that these terms really mean "Old Covenant" and "New Covenant."

Under the Old Covenant, then, the Eternal undertook to consider the Hebrews his "chosen people," assuring them of power and prosperity on condition that they maintained unflagging obedience to his commandments. But the terms of the agreement were not always followed by the Hebrew people, and Yahweh in his turn, when he was angered by their derelictions, withheld his promised protection.[31] Obvious evidence of the reprisal lay in the misery of the masses, the subjection of Israel to foreign domination, the deportations, and the exiles.

But, since the Covenant did not entail a collective responsibility of the whole people, being a personal relation between God and each individual, it was not equitable that, because of the guilt of those who transgressed against divine law, the good as well should be deprived of a benefit to which they were entitled.[32] Therefore, from time to time the prophets refreshed the hopes of the good and sought to persuade the wicked to alter their ways, foretelling the time when Yahweh, resolving at last to carry out his obligation, would inaugurate a new order for the just, while all the unbelievers and the enemies of the people of Israel would be mercilessly wiped out. The Old Testament idea of a national resurgence was enriched, especially in post-Exilic Judaism under the influence of Parsee thought, by the notion of an even greater catastrophe: the destruction of this world and all its evils and the establishment of a new era of bliss.

Despite such utopianism and its consistent refutation by the immutable perdurability of the accustomed conditions of life, the prospect of a better world and the threat of a divine judgment operated to some degree to restrain the sinner and to exhort his brother to still greater obedience to the Law. John the Baptist, too, when he preached *metanoia,* meant by that a complete revision of one's way of life in order to ward off Yahweh's vengeance by adhering strictly to the observance of the Mosaic Law.

Jesus had no different concept of the kingdom, but for him, at least in the early period of his ministry, the mark of spiritual regeneration was not the vow of the believer to obey legal rules blindly, in a rigid conformism, but rather the decision to apply such rules intelligently to one's relations with one's fellows.[33] Rather than a preparation for the kingdom, respect for the Law was to Jesus the realization of the kingdom itself. Much has been said and written on this matter. Some have professed to see in the attitude of Jesus a revolutionary rejection of the traditional beliefs of his people: scorn for the sanctity of the Levites and for the rules of the Law in order to found a new concept of inner religion. It has been said that Jesus considered religion to be a natural tendency toward the good, requiring no man to be guided along the path of duty by external precepts and duties.[34]

Such enthusiasm must be reappraised, for it threatens to confuse Jesus with a modern freethinker. Jesus never went so far as to consider the idea of goodness an imperative of conscience. He always preached that man's behavior must be judged by an external standard (the will of God), which claims the right to influence one's free will by the promise of reward and the threat of punishment. His moral precepts, furthermore, were all derived from the Mosaic tradition and the holy books. Jesus did not create a "new" religion, nor did he formulate any doctrines on the nature of God, on his relations with his believers, on individual destinies, etc., that were not already well known to every Jew of his time.[35] Christianity is the product of an evolution that progressed particularly during the first four centuries of this era; it is not the work of one man.[36]

"Think Not That I Am Come to Destroy the Law"

The disputes over the validity of the Mosaic Law for the adherents of Christianity, as we have already pointed out, began *after* the death of Jesus, and they degenerated into open conflict between the

Judeo-Christians, headed by Peter and James, the brother of Jesus, who insisted that even non-Jewish converts must submit to circumcision, and Paul, who, since he wished to carry Christianity into Greco-Roman circles, naturally saw no utility in either circumcision or the observance of the Law. In fact, he tended to derogate the Torah altogether, arguing that, "when the Gentiles, which have not the law, do by nature the things contained in the law, [they] shew the work of the law written in their hearts."[37] Besides, he further objected, "the law is not made for a righteous man, but for the lawless and disobedient,"[38] because it serves only to give "the knowledge of sin"[39]—that is, it puts the wicked on notice and declares them sinners in the sight of God[40]—while the just live righteously of themselves and are saved because they "live by faith."[41]

But the Gospel of Matthew still preserves a declaration that flatly contradicts Paul's repudiation of the Law and that probably reflects the true belief of Jesus:[42] "Think not that I am come to destroy the law, or the prophets: I am not come to destroy, but to fulfill [πληρῶσαι, plērōsai]. For verily I say unto you, Till heaven and earth pass, one jot [the Hebrew letter yōdh, the smallest in the alphabet] or one tittle [we would say "one comma," because the Greek word, κεραία, keraia, means a tiny punctuation mark] shall in no wise pass from the law, till all be fulfilled."

Therefore, the Gospel continues, whoever transgresses against even the least of the commandments and teaches others to do likewise (an obvious thrust at Paul) shall be among the least in the kingdom of heaven, whereas he who carries out the commandments and teaches others to obey "shall be called great in the kingdom of heaven. For I say unto you, That except your righteousness shall exceed the righteousness of the scribes and the Pharisees, ye shall in no case enter into the kingdom of heaven."[43]

On the same subject, the Gospel attributed to Luke records instead (and out of place) an appraisal that Matthew had made on the role of John the Baptist: "The law and the prophets were until John: since that time the kingdom of God is preached, and every man presseth into it."[44] This is of course a declaration in favor of the Pauline thesis, but it cannot be invoked to attest to the real thinking of Jesus. Nor is this the only instance in which the Gospel of Luke—a purely synthetic work drawn from the other Synoptics[45]

—rearranges the Logia, or "Sayings," of Jesus at random and therefore changes their original meanings. Most clumsily, furthermore, the compiler lacked the forethought to strike out the next sentence, which, in downright contradiction of its predecessor, repeats almost word for word the anti-Pauline view of Matthew: "And it is easier for heaven and earth to pass, than one tittle of the law to fail."[46]

Later Christian theology, which ultimately embraced Paul's point of view (Christianity, in fact, spread widely in the Greco-Roman world but had little success among the Jews), not only considers Luke's interpretation correct but even endeavors to distort Matthew to fit the Pauline thesis, with a highly debatable commentary on his text. Indeed, Jesus' statement that he has come to *fulfill* the Law is translated as: "I am come to exceed the Law, to go beyond it, to make it superfluous," and thus this theology ascribes to the Greek word πληροῦν (*pleroun*) meanings that it has never had. In addition, "Till heaven and earth pass" is interpreted not as an affirmation of the eternal duration of the Law but as a prophecy of its imminent destruction: in other words, it is valid only until the end of this world—as Paul was to say later, it is only νόμος παιδαγωγός (*nomos paidagogos*), a "moment of preparation" for the inauguration of the kingdom.

But the word πληροῦν (*pleroun*) used by Matthew[47] has always meant "to accomplish," "to bring to a conclusion," like ποιεῖν (*poiein*), which Matthew uses immediately afterward.[48] The corresponding Hebrew word might have been *kiyyem* (in Aramaic, *kayyem*), which means "to confirm," "to ratify," "to validate."[49] Hence, in the passage in question, the only accurate interpretation is: *to establish and to defend the eternal validity of the Law.*

It is true that Jesus always had the realization of the kingdom in mind,[50] but he thought in terms not of an extra-terrestrial kingdom (this is the product of Pauline speculation) but rather of an earthly kingdom in which the precepts of "justice" would have more authority than ever. It is an undeniable fact that the Gospel of Matthew, to corroborate this avowed intention of Jesus to "confirm" the Law, cites some interpretations of the commandments in the Decalogue that are even more pedantic and punctilious than those offered by the Pharisees.[51]

The Decalogue

The Ten Commandments, attributed to Moses, are handed down by the Old Testament in two slightly different versions, which go back to the time between the seventh and the fourth centuries B.C.: the older is contained in Deuteronomy,[52] the later in Exodus.[53] Both are derived from the extremely ancient Code of Hammurabi, five centuries older than the presumed time of Moses. On the stele discovered in Susa by the French archaeologist Jacques de Morgan, King Hammurabi is shown in the act of receiving the Tables of the Law from the hands of the sun-god.[54] The Hebrew tradition, wanting in imagination, follows the same model with its legend of Moses on the peak of Mount Sinai in a blaze of sunlight.

The Mosaic Decalogue, in either version, was already more advanced than the earliest one, which goes back to the period of nomadic living and which Biblical criticism identifies in Exodus 34:14–26 (the priests' concern with making certain of generous offerings is worth noting):

1. "Thou shalt worship no other god: for the Lord, whose name is Jealous, is a jealous God . . ."
2. "Thou shalt make thee no molten gods."
3. "The feast of unleavened bread shalt thou keep. Seven days thou shalt eat unleavened bread . . ."
4. "All that openeth the matrix is mine; and every firstling among thy cattle, whether ox or sheep, that is male. . . . All the firstborn of thy sons thou shalt redeem."
5. "And none shall appear before me empty."
6. "Six days thou shalt work, but on the seventh day thou shalt rest."
7. "And thou shalt observe the feast of weeks, of the firstfruits of wheat harvest, and the feast of ingathering at the year's end."
8. "Thrice in the year shall all your men children appear before the Lord God . . ."
9. "Thou shalt not offer the blood of my sacrifice with leaven. . . . Thou shalt not seethe a kid in his mother's milk."
10. "The first of the firstfruits of thy land thou shalt bring unto the house of the Lord thy God."

Many of these regulations do not appear in the Mosaic Decalogue, for they were no longer suitable for a people that had given up wandering, and they were replaced by others on a higher moral level. Christianity has made still further changes in them. The Christian version was compiled by Augustine, at the beginning of the fifth century A.D., but it was again edited and shortened for the Catholic catechism at the time of the Council of Trent, in the sixteenth century.

A brief comparison will be valuable:

MOSAIC DECALOGUE

1. "Thou shalt have none other gods before me." (The importance of this is ritual, not theological: there shall be no adoration of strange gods.)
2. "Thou shalt not make thee any graven image, or any likeness of any thing that is in heaven above, or that is in the earth beneath, or that is in the waters beneath the earth: Thou shalt not bow down thyself to them."
3. "Thou shalt not take the name of the Lord thy God in vain." (The name of God has a magic power that only the priest may exercise.)
4. "Keep the sabbath day to sanctify it, . . . Six days thou shalt labor, and do all thy work: But the seventh day is the sabbath of the Lord thy God: in it thou shalt not do any work, thou, nor thy son, nor thy daughter, nor thy manservant, nor thy maidservant, nor thine ox, . . . that thy manservant and

CATHOLIC DECALOGUE

1. "You shall have no other gods besides me."

(No parallel; but even today the Church is not opposed to many forms of idolatry, such as the adoration of images, relics, etc.)

2. "You shall not take the name of the Lord your God in vain."

3. "Remember the holy days." (More vague than the Jewish commandment, this seems to allude also to other holy days besides Sunday. Besides, its aim is not rest for man but the fulfillment of worship.)

thy maidservant may rest as well as thou."

5. "Honor thy father and thy mother . . . that thy days may be prolonged."
6. "Thou shalt not kill."
7. "Neither shalt thou commit adultery."

8. "Neither shalt thou steal."
9. "Neither shalt thou bear false witness against thy neighbour."
10. "Neither shalt thou desire thy neighbor's wife, neither shalt thou covet thy neighbor's house, his field, or his manservant, or his maidservant, his ox, or his ass, or any thing that is thy neighbor's." (This is simply protection of private property.)

4. "Honor your father and your mother."

5. "You shall not kill."
6. "You shall not commit unclean acts." (More general than the Jewish commandment, this can embrace anything that offends modesty.)
7. "You shall not steal."
8. "You shall not bear dishonest witness."

9. "You shall not covet your neighbor's wife." (As it is currently interpreted, this is an unnecessary repetition of the Sixth Commandment.)

10. "You shall not covet your neighbor's goods." (An unnecessary duplication of the Seventh Commandment, it too, like the Jewish commandment, protects private property.)

The prime illustration of the method by which Jesus intended to "fulfill" the Law deals with the commandment that forbids murder: "Ye have heard that it was said by them of old time, Thou shalt not kill: and whosoever shall kill shall be in danger of the judgment: But I say unto you, That whosoever is angry with his brother without a cause, shall be in danger of the judgment: and whosoever shall say to his brother, Raca [that is, *Rākā,* the Hebrew for 'imbecile'], shall be in danger of the council: but whosoever shall say, Thou fool [μωρέ, *mōre*], shall be in danger of hell fire."[55]

Not only murder, then, according to Jesus, is to be punished, but even an ordinary angry outburst. Hence he is here broadening and perfecting the existing code. But the still more stringent moral conduct urged by Jesus is also always reinforced with the threat of punishment and is intended to establish a kind of personal ledger, as is shown by the words that come immediately afterward, in a kind of corollary: "If thou bring thy gift to the altar, and there rememberest that thy brother hath ought against thee, Leave there thy gift before the altar, and go thy way; first be reconciled to thy brother, and then come and offer thy gift. Agree with thine adversary quickly, whiles thou art in the way with him; lest at any time the adversary deliver thee to the judge, and the judge deliver thee to the officer, and thou be cast into prison."[56]

Jesus went on in the same fashion to clarify other commandments: "Ye have heard that it was said by them of old time, Thou shalt not commit adultery: But I say unto you, That whosoever looketh on a woman to lust after her hath committed adultery with her already in his heart."[57] Naturally, this meant a married woman, another's wife, in conformity with the Tenth Commandment, and not merely any woman at all.[58]

And again: "Ye have heard that it hath been said by them of old time, Thou shalt not forswear thyself, but shalt perform unto the Lord thine oaths: But I say unto you, Swear not at all: neither by heaven, for it is God's throne: nor by the earth: for it is his footstool: neither by Jerusalem: for it is the city of the great King. Neither shalt thou swear by thy head, because thou canst not make one hair white or black. But let your communication be, Yea, yea; Nay, nay: for whatsoever is more than these, cometh of evil."[59]

The Great Commandment

The Synoptic Gospels tell us that a Scribe who had heard Jesus discussing the Decalogue wanted to know which he considered the most important of the commandments. Jesus answered by quoting the Old Testament:[60] "Thou shalt love the Lord thy God with all thy heart, and with all thy soul, and with all thy mind. This is the first and great commandment. And the second is like unto it, Thou shalt love thy neighbor as thyself. On these two commandments hang all the law and the prophets."

Then the Scribe wanted to know who was his neighbor. Jesus replied with a question. Despoiled and beaten by robbers, a man lay near death in the middle of a road. A priest passed and drew aside from him; a Levite did likewise. Only a Samaritan halted, treated his hurts, found him a lodging, and gave him money to pay for healing. Which of the three, Jesus asked, was the beaten man's "neighbor"?

In cold fact, the question posed by Jesus had little pertinence to that of the Scribe: he did not say *who* is one's neighbor[61] (unless we are to infer that our "neighbor" is he who imposes a duty of help on us!), but rather he made it plain how one should behave toward one's fellow men. Not sterile religiosity, therefore, but acts of kindness establish true brotherhood among men.[62] Charity is not merely compassion for those who suffer, as the story of the good Samaritan would seem to indicate. "Though I bestow all my goods to feed the poor," Paul appropriately explains, "and though I give my body to be burned, and have not charity, it profiteth me nothing."[63] And Thomas Aquinas offers this theological definition: "Charity is not selfish love [*amor concupiscentiae*] but the love of pure friendship [*amor benevolentiae*], which seeks and rejoices in the good of the beloved rather than that of him who loves."[64]

In addition, the Gospels of Matthew and Luke had earlier put in the mouth of Jesus various sayings that further clarified the meaning of *caritas*: "Love your enemies, bless them that curse you"; "Lend, hoping for nothing again"; "As ye would that men should do unto you, do ye also to them likewise."[65]

All these maxims, in truth, are to be found strewn through the books of the Old Testament—further evidence of the strict orthodoxy with which, even in laying down rules of morality, Jesus clung to tradition. What Jesus really contributed was a purification of the old Law through the elimination of those precepts that still required hatred for one's enemies, contempt for strangers, and vengeance for personal offenses.

Truth compels one to recognize that other thinkers and religious reformers who preceded Jesus had already reached a similar—in some cases, a more advanced—moral conception. But they came from peoples who enjoyed a considerably higher degree of civilization than that of Palestine. Here is proof that the fundamentals of ethics always reflect the conditions of human society at any given stage of its history,[66] and that the value of the reformer lies above all in his proclaiming, ahead of others, the necessity of regeneration, and in his willingness to do battle for it. Buddha, for example, even though he lived six centuries before Jesus, was ready to extend to all living things in nature the precept of love that Jesus still restricted to human beings.[67]

Regrettably, Jesus lived in an environment so little developed that it allowed him to formulate only a moral law, which, however, was ultimately to impose itself and to triumph through a succession of favorable circumstances. In truth, it was rather inferior to that of the Greeks and Romans, which it was destined to eliminate. Pagan philosophy was rich in exhortations to love of one's fellows and to unselfishness, and these were founded on a rational logic that had no need to resort to the aleatory prospect of rewards and punishments. The ancient world is full of examples of renunciation, of purity of customs, of chastity, of honesty, of modesty (one can cite Orestes, Pylades, Cato, Lucrece, Virginia, Cincinnatus, Fabricius, etc.), without psychological complexes, fear of sin, or dread of hell fire.

Pagan philosophy sustained its ideals in the name of the universality of reason, directing its appeal to man's intelligence, his sensibilities, and his dignity, while Christianity projected these human endowments (reason as Logos) on to the will of God. Four hundred years before Jesus, Socrates taught, with perfect insight, that morality is inherent in man by reason of certain primordial values that form the principles of what we consider our duty, if not always of our actual behavior.[68] In their ideas on virtue, remarkable analogies exist between Jesus and Socrates—so remarkable that Erasmus, the great humanist, could pray: "*Sancte Socrate, ora pro nobis,*" and the Illuminati held the Greek in unlimited admiration, while for Voltaire Jesus became "the Socrates of Galilee"! But, unlike Socrates, Jesus did not consider the idea of justice synonymous with man's conscience, and he was constrained to make it the object of a divine commandment.[69]

Humility and Patience

The state of mind necessary to the realization of the kingdom—that is, the *metanoia* proposed by Jesus—required that good works be carried out not ostentatiously, in the sight of the world, but in secret.[70] The performance of an act of charity was not an occasion for the "sounding of trumpets" to command the admiration of one's fellows—the left hand was not to know what the right hand did. One was not to pray as the hypocrites did, striking exaggerated attitudes in the company of other believers in order to impress one's holy character on the world—it was better to pray in the solitude of one's own room. Fasting was not the occasion to go about with a face of sorrow and suffering, so that all might see one had not eaten—one should perfume the hair and wash the face as though going to a feast. Following the ideal program of justice according to the Gospels, these were methodical directives for the performance of the three principle functions of Jewish piety: charity, prayer, and fasting.

Jesus concluded his instructions by exhorting his disciples not only to be humble but also to be patient and to suffer injuries for the sake of peace. On this point, too, Socrates had anticipated Jesus, recognizing, according to his pupil Plato, the uselessness, not to mention the immorality, of opposing violence with violence and of resisting evil. Jesus, paradoxically, added that good must even submit to evil. Matthew and Luke ascribe this lesson to him: "Ye have heard that it hath been said, An eye for an eye, and a tooth for a tooth: But I say unto you, That ye resist not evil; but whosoever shall smite thee on thy right cheek, turn to him the other also. And if any man will sue thee at the law, and take away thy coat, let him have thy cloak also. And whosoever shall compel thee [the real meaning of ἀγγαρεύειν (*angareuein*) is "to requisition," a common practice in acquiring men and animals for public works] to go a mile, go with him twain."[71] And again: "Judge not, and ye shall not be judged"; "Condemn not, and ye shall not be condemned"; "Forgive, and ye shall be forgiven"; "Why beholdest thou the mote that is in thy brother's eye, but perceivest not the beam that is in thine own eye? . . . Thou hypocrite! cast out first the beam out of thine own eye, and then shalt thou see clearly to pull out the mote that is in thy brother's eye."[72]

It is obvious, as pointed out by the "consistent eschatology" school of theology headed by Johannes Weiss and Albert Schweitzer, that Jesus laid down these guidelines in view of the imminent advent of the kingdom. They thus constituted an interim ethic, a moral code intended solely as a temporary measure.

Nevertheless, when the kingdom did not come and it was transferred to a nonterrestrial world, these temporary guidelines became the moral law that must be obeyed by all who profess to be Christians, willing to embrace a universal love that includes even their enemies. The following passages show how Paul paraphrased the words of Jesus so as to make them a rule of Christian life: "Let love be without dissimulation. Abhor that which is evil; cleave to that which is good. Be kindly affectioned one to another with brotherly love; in honor preferring one another; . . . rejoicing in hope; patient in tribulation; continuing instant in prayer. . . . Bless them which persecute you. . . . Recompense to no man evil for evil . . . avenge not yourselves but rather give place unto wrath. . . . Therefore if thine enemy hunger, feed him; if he thirst, give him drink. . . . Be not overcome of evil, but overcome evil with good."[73]

In setting forth these rules Paul does not contradict himself, even though he affirmed in other passages in the same letter that "works" do not avail, that "faith" in Christ suffices. The Russian theologian Paul Evdokimov makes the astute observation that "the great and fundamental Pauline contrast is not between faith and works, but between works of the Law and works of faith."[74] I would add that tolerance and love of even one's enemies should not be regarded as works that will gain salvation, but as charismatic *effects* of faith, permanent inclinations of the mind and heart of the true Christian.

[11]

FAITH IN GOD

The Parables

The Pharisees' contempt for Jesus was motivated not only by his violent attacks on them but also by a certain resentment of his pretension to the right to discuss the Torah, to teach in public, and to assemble a band of disciples—in other words, to arrogate to himself the title of rabbi. The most learned of them had earned this rank through long, arduous, and deep study and had received it formally in a solemn ceremony of investiture by their own teachers. Furthermore, the rank of rabbi included the authority to act as a judge. The fringed mantles of which Jesus made light were the robes of office that the rabbis wore when they were performing their functions, a distinctive sign of dignity and high rank. With such status, they normally were supposed to travel mounted, even though their disciples had to follow them on foot.

Jesus refused these prerogatives (except on the occasion of his final entrance into Jerusalem, when he rode on an ass, to the great delight of the Apostles), but he did not forgo the right to follow the rabbinic methods in instructing his disciples, as in his discussion of the Decalogue.

Essentially, the didactic methods of the doctors of the Law consisted of stating to their pupils a halakah (a precept, a rule of the Law, etc.) and then explaining it through analogies with other Biblical passages, making inferences from a general case to various possible

individual cases, or generalizing from a particular instance.[1] This kind
of commentary was called haggadah. In such manner Jesus had explained the Fifth Commandment: "Ye have heard that it was said by
them of old time, Thou shalt not kill: and whosoever shall kill shall
be in danger of the judgment." This is the statement of the halakah.
Then: "But I say unto you, That whosoever shall be angry with his
brother without a cause . . . whosoever shall say to his brother, Raca,
. . . whosoever shall say, Thou fool . . ." These are the particulariza-
tions from the general statement. Jesus proceeded: "If thou bring
thy gift to the altar . . ." and here he generalized from a specific
instance.

On most occasions, for the sake of greater clarity, he resorted to
imaginative illustration. The master posed a rhetorical question:
"What is this like unto?" Then he answered with an instance that
explained the abstract concept in concrete terms.[2] The haggadah
thus developed into a mashal—that is, a special form of figurative
speech quite familiar to Oriental peoples generally, even in ordinary
conversation. One example of this may be seen in the story of the
Good Samaritan, by which Jesus sought to bring understanding to
the Scribe who had asked him to define love of one's neighbor.

The Gospel of John translates the Hebrew *māshāl* into the
Greek παροιμία (*paroimia*), which means "proverb," but such a translation is inexact. More frequently, the Synoptic Gospels use the word
παραβολή (*parabolē*), which means "comparison." But a mashal is often
something much more complex. Most often it is an apologue, that is,
a fictitious narrative that serves at once as comparison, metaphor, and
allegory. Or, to make matters clearer: Comparison is a confrontation
of two things, as when one says: "My baby is as beautiful as an angel."
A metaphor is an abbreviated comparison in which the *as* is eliminated and, sometimes, the order is reversed: "My baby is an angel,"
or: "That angel of a baby." An allegory substitutes the second object
for the first: "My angel . . ."

While we are generally accustomed to expressing our thoughts
in clear, orderly statements, the Orientals prefer to embroider theirs
in related series of parallel images, each of which adds something
new, preferably through simile or metaphor, even if these are im-
plicit rather than expressed, just as the Chinese resort to "allusions."
In order, for example, to voice the simple thought: "Come to me, all

of you who are wearied by life: I will show you how to endure it,"
Jesus said: "Come unto me, all ye that labor [like plowing animals]
and are heavy laden [like beasts of burden], and I will give you rest.
Take my yoke upon you [that is, as light a yoke as that borne by
Jesus], and learn of me [a parallel image]: for I am meek [like a
domestic animal] and lowly in heart [like an animal that obeys]."[3]

Allegory, then, is a rhetorical device through which a system of
ideas can be enunciated by means of another system of different ideas.
It is a sort of algebraic language in which certain conventionalized
symbols replace clearly defined ideas.[4] Thus, to offer another example, Dante's *selva oscura* ("dark forest") can be interpreted as "the
savage, brutish state [the forest] in which a man lives when he exists
without order or discipline and in vice and sin: he does not know
what is his own best interest or his duty—that is, he lives in darkness."

The parables of the Gospels frequently resort to similar methods, but the stories are not always interpreted allegorically in every
detail because some particulars may be mere flowery embellishment
or secondary description.[5]

The Parables of the Kingdom

The first parables that Jesus used in his preaching are called
the Parables of the Kingdom because through them he tried to make
his disciples understand exactly what characterized the realm of universal happiness that he had offered them and how it could be
brought into being only through the efforts of man himself and his
dedication to peace, harmony, and brotherhood, in accord with the
instructions that Jesus had given earlier when he "fulfilled" the Law.
The greater the number of those ready to live within this new bond
of love and to explain it to their fellows, the sooner would universal
happiness prevail. Whether Jesus meant a terrestrial kingdom, as his
contemporaries believed, or a heavenly one after death, as theologians
later came to believe, it was certain that its realization depended on
personal effort.

In the first of his parables, Jesus employed the example of the
sower: "When he sowed, some seeds fell by the wayside, and the fowls

came and devoured them up: Some fell upon stony places, where they had not much earth; and forthwith they sprung up, because they had no deepness of earth: And when the sun was up, they were scorched; and because they had no root, they withered away. And some fell among thorns; and the thorns sprung up, and choked them. But others fell into good ground, and brought forth fruit."[6]

The meaning of the parable is clear, but the disciples found it difficult to understand and their master had to elaborate: it was intended to illustrate the differences in men's willingness to receive the law of love and to put it into practice, whether because they allowed themselves to be seduced by the lures of evil (the birds), to be made sterile by selfish passions (the sun), or to be overwhelmed by everyday problems (the thorns).[7] It is curious how some heretical sects (the Priscillianists among them) have managed to find a quite different meaning in this parable. In their writings, they interpret Jesus' explanation as meaning "the sower represents the Prince of Evil, who recklessly casts about the souls of those of whom he has taken possession."[8]

Seven other parables in the Gospels (some of them retold by all the Evangelists, others appearing only once) deal with the establishment and the extension of the kingdom. Almost all appear immediately after the Parable of the Sower. The authors of the Gospels apparently found it worth while, for catechetical purposes, to bring together everything that Jesus said at any time on this subject, but it is ridiculous to speak of a specific "day of parables."[9] What is more, some of them, because of their conception of the kingdom, should not be ascribed to Jesus but were assuredly of later origin. A few emphasize the belief—held by Jesus and the first Christians—that the kingdom is an immediately attainable reality capable of progressive development. Others, however, in accord with later theological speculation, allude to a future kingdom that will be brought into being through some radical upheaval, accompanied by the violent separation of the unjust from the just; these parables exhort the faithful to await the Parousia—the Messiah's second descent to earth.

Let us turn to the parables of the first category.

"So is the kingdom of God, as if a man should cast seed into the ground, And should sleep, and should rise night and day, and the seed should spring and grow up, he knoweth not how. For the earth bringeth forth fruit of herself: first the blade, then the ear; after that, the full corn in the ear. But when the fruit is brought forth, immediately he putteth in the sickle, because the harvest is come."[10]

"Whereunto shall we liken the kingdom of God? or with what comparison shall we compare it? It is like a grain of mustard seed, which, when it is sown in the earth, is less than all the seeds that be in the earth: But when it is sown it groweth up, and becometh greater than all herbs, and shooteth out great branches; so that the fowls of the air may lodge under the shadow of it."[11]

Along the Jordan, an area that has all the qualities of sub-tropical flora, mustard seed (*Salvadora persica*) can produce a plant as large as a citrus tree, even though botanically it is classified as an arborescent plant. But there is a certain hyperbole in calling the mustard seed "less than all the seeds that be in the earth" and in considering its product "a tree."[12]

"The kingdom of heaven is like unto leaven, which a woman took, and hid in three measures of meal, until the whole was leavened."[13] The Greek "measure" used here was a σάτα (*sata*), which is a phonetic transliteration of the Aramaic *sāthāh* (in Hebrew, *seāh*), the equivalent of about a bushel.

The exegetes debate at length whether the Parable of the Mustard Seed was intended to allude to the potential breadth of the kingdom, while that of the leaven was meant to signify its potential depth—its extensive and intensive potentials[14]—or whether in both cases Jesus sought to contrast the small with the great.[15]

Certainly the interpretation given by traditional Catholic exegesis is extremely strange, to say the very least. Always resolved to find a hermetic content in every word of the parables, the Church often invests them with meanings alien to the mentality of Jesus and to the historical environment in which he carried out his mission. Hilary of Poitiers offers this commentary on the Parable of the Mustard Seed: "The branches of the tree are the Apostles, whose preaching goes out into the world; the birds that lodge in its shadow are the heathen, who seek safety under the tree." Paul, however, departing much less from the intention of Jesus, interprets the parable to mean that, however much or however little every Christian exerts himself to love his neighbor and to do acts of charity and gather alms, so much or so little shall he receive of divine grace.[16]

With comparisons similar to these, the Gospel of Thomas declares that the kingdom will come and grow in secret, in the same way in which a woman, without being aware of it, loses along the road the grain that she is carrying in a leaking vessel, and that the kingdom will be accomplished with the same certainty with which a murderer carries out his crime after many rehearsals.[17]

Two other parables, which are to be found only in Matthew and Thomas, differ from these in that they no longer insist on the power of the kingdom to expand, but instead they emphasize its worth. The kingdom, they say, is like a treasure buried in a field, or like a precious pearl: the man who knows the whereabouts of either will sell everything that he owns in order that he may buy the field or the pearl.[18]

And, finally, it is only in Matthew and Thomas that we find the two parables that were certainly composed after the death of Jesus, inspired by the new expectation of a future Second Coming that arose among the proto-Christians after the collapse of their hope for the immediate establishment of the kingdom. These predict a change by force. The first compares the change to the choice that fishermen make between the good and the worthless fish when they have drawn in their nets.[19] The other tells of a wicked man who, while his enemy slept, sowed the latter's wheat field with tares, or darnel (*Lolium temulentum*), in order to ruin his crop; but the victim waited until harvest time and then separated the tares from the wheat and burned them.[20] Matthew tells us that Jesus had to explain the meaning of this second parable to his unperceptive disciples: the sleeper is Jesus himself, the enemy is the devil, the harvest time is the end of the world, the reapers are the angels, the wheat is the righteous, and the tares are the wicked, who shall be punished with eternal fire.[21] Too many of these elements (the future Messiah, the angels, the penalty of hell fire) are historically later than the preachings of Jesus.

A Private Discipline?

A most important question is raised by a few obscure words inserted among the Parables of the Kingdom in the Synoptic Gospels—whether this method of teaching is suitable to its purpose. Mark and

Matthew report that the Twelve Apostles, troubled by his allegorical language, asked Jesus why he preached to the people in parables.[22]

"Unto you," their master responded, "it is given to know the mystery of the kingdom of God; but *unto them that are without,* all these things are done in parables: *That seeing they may see, and not perceive; and hearing they may hear, and not understand; lest at any time they should be converted, and their sins should be forgiven them."* And Matthew adds: "And in them is fulfilled the prophecy of Esaias [Isaiah], which saith, By hearing ye shall hear, and shall not understand; and seeing ye shall see, and shall not perceive: for this people's heart is waxed gross."[23] Similar thoughts are expressed by John.[24]

The perplexing problem may have its source in a passage from Paul: "But if our gospel be hid, it is hid to them that are lost: In whom the god of this world hath blinded the minds of them which believe not."[25] Thus it seems as if an attempt had been made to impute to Jesus the intention—which would be unbelievably absurd— of preaching to the people *in such a way that they could not understand* and could not be converted! And yet many Catholic scholars take this interpretation seriously: Giuseppe Ricciotti describes the words of Jesus as "an affectionate sarcasm";[26] Leopold Fonck declares that in this fashion Jesus sought to punish the Jews for their unbelief;[27] G. B. Alfano proffers the conclusion that the comment of Jesus is "a manifest allusion to the frightful state into which the Hebrew In general, however, unprejudiced exegesis refuses to impute to Jesus people had fallen by reason of its stiff-necked obstinacy";[28] and so on. so vengeful an attitude toward his own people.

In my own view, it is sufficient to recognize that Mark's "that" (ἵνα, *hina*) is, instead, "because" (ὅτι, *hoti*) in Matthew, and hence that Jesus intended to say: "I speak in parables because [not "in order that"] they would not understand." And it is hardly likely the Apostles would have been astounded at hearing Jesus preach in this traditional manner of the Hebrew masters, which had been developed expressly as a means of clarifying the more difficult concepts in terms acceptable to the Oriental mentality.

In my opinion, the misunderstanding results from the fact that on this subject the compiler of the Gospel of Mark exactly quoted the prophecy of Isaiah, including its "in order that" (ἵνα), without recognizing that in so doing he was imputing to Jesus a curse against the Hebrew people that was utterly foreign to his nature. Matthew suitably revised the quotation by simply replacing the conjunction.

Furthermore, all three Synoptic Gospels, as well as the apocryphal Gospel of Thomas, give the lie to all such inferences with their direct statements, among the Parables of the Kingdom, that it is the duty of every man who has learned the truth to make it clear, and that inevitably truth will sooner or later conquer: "Is a candle brought to be put under a bushel, or under a bed? and not to be set on a candlestick? For there is nothing hid, which shall not be manifested."[29] Matthew and Thomas contain another, similar figure: "A city that is set on an hill can not be hid."[30]

It is more logical that the Gospel excerpts in dispute should give rise to a suspicion that there was an underlying differentiation between a private system of ideas, reserved for the most trusted of the faithful,[31] and a public message for the masses.[32] That such a distinction should have been made by Jesus is unthinkable. His missionary work—the proclamation of the good tidings and the exhortation to live according to the principles of *caritas*—had absolutely nothing of a secret order. The success of the kingdom was based, rather, on the broadest possible audience that his teachings could reach. What is true, however, is that the need for some form of initiation and hence for some kind of inner doctrine arose only after the death of Jesus. This happened in the Christian community of the Diaspora and concerned the "mystery" of salvation, in conformity with the new Pauline conception of Jesus as a liberating god who had died after having assumed human form and who had risen again for our redemption. An initiation, in addition to giving the members of the sect a spiritual preparation, served also to exclude from the benefits of the mystical community those who were not yet ready to receive them.

The word μυστήριον (*mystērion*), which appears in the passages cited above, is borrowed from the Greek mystery cults, in which "mystery" meant "an occult truth that it is forbidden to reveal," while the corresponding word, *sōd*, means only "a secret," without any specific religious implication.

In medieval Christianity the catechumens—the candidates for baptism—were debarred from religious ceremonies for a long period;

and a *disciplina arcani,* which was incumbent on the faithful, is attested to especially by Tertullian, Lactantius, and Augustine, all of whom frequently used the expression *norunt qui initiati sunt* ("it is known to the initiate"), and often warned that the violation of religious secrecy was considered a sacrilege of the gravest sort.[33] In Latin, the initiatory rite corresponding to a "mystery" was called *sacramentum,* which to the Romans meant "an oath," "a solemn undertaking."

"Take No Thought for the Morrow"

Jesus was not concerned, then, with any esoteric doctrine; yet it is logical to suppose that privately he gave his disciples instructions that were more detailed than his pronouncements before random audiences. "With many such parables spake he the word unto them," Mark says, "and when they were alone, he expounded all things to his disciples."[34]

Sometimes, indeed, the ordinary folk embarrassed Jesus either through their ingenuousness or through their petty malice. Luke and Thomas report that one day a peasant who had heard Jesus promise economic equality and denounce the rich cried out to him: "Master, speak to my brother, that he divide the inheritance with me."[35]

For a moment, Jesus was at a loss in the face of the eternal conflict that dogs the advocates of the highest humanitarian principles when they are called on to put them into practice. If the rich man refused to share his substance with the poor man, what hope was there for the fulfillment of the wise lessons preached by Jesus? Against the specific question put to him by the peasant, the Nazarene could only defend himself by quibbling and telling a parable that condemned the lust for wealth in general terms without resolving the instant problem: "Man, who made me a judge or a divider over you? Take heed, and beware of covetousness: for a man's life consisteth not in the abundance of the things which he possesseth. . . . The ground of a certain rich man brought forth plentifully: And he thought within himself, saying, What shall I do, because I have no room where to bestow my fruits? And he said, This will I do: I will pull down my barns, and build greater; and there will I bestow all my fruits and my goods. And I will say to my soul, Soul, thou hast much goods, laid up for many years; take thine ease, eat, drink, and be merry. But God said unto him, Thou fool! this night thy soul shall be required of thee: then whose shall those things be, which thou hast provided?"

But how could Jesus have made himself believe that he would be seriously heard and obeyed when he invited an audience of peasants, as blindly convinced as their ancestors that only unremitting daily drudgery in the field could sustain such meager existence as they had, to lay down their tools and to concern themselves no longer with the problems of food, clothing, and shelter? And yet such was precisely the counsel that he gave his disciples privately: "Take no thought for your life, what ye shall eat, or what ye shall drink; nor yet for your body, what ye shall put on. . . . Behold the fowls of the air: for they sow not, neither do they reap, nor gather into barns; yet your heavenly Father feedeth them. Are ye not much better than they? Which of you by taking thought can add one cubit to his stature?"[36]

But it must be remarked here that ἡλικία (hēlikia) in this usage means "life" or "age," and not "stature," which is the accepted translation. If nothing else, it is laughable that anyone should try to add approximately twenty inches to his height by thinking about it! Similarly, it is equally inaccurate, in the continuation of his remarks, to refer to "the lilies of the field," for lilies do not grow in Palestine, which, however, has an abundance of red anemones. Hence, the rest of the passage should have read:

"Consider the anemones in the fields, how they grow; they toil not, neither do they spin: And yet I say unto you, That even Solomon in all his glory was not arrayed like one of these. Wherefore, if God so clothe the grass of the field, which today is, and tomorrow is cast into the oven, shall he not much more clothe you, O ye of little faith? Therefore take no thought, saying, What shall we eat, or, What shall we drink, or, Wherewithal shall we be clothed? For all these things do the Gentiles seek after: . . . But seek ye the kingdom of God; and all these things shall be added unto you. Fear not, little flock: for it is your Father's good pleasure to give you the kingdom. Think not of amassing treasure in this world, where moths and rust consume and thieves break in and steal; but think on the kingdom of heaven, where moths and rust consume not and no thieves break in and steal."

A belief in a world of happiness and well-being, untainted by cares or by the need to work, as in the mythical time of man's beginnings, is close to the hearts of all peoples. Greek and Latin literature, too, is full of longing for the age of Saturn, but always in terms of a formless utopia and of an era that can never be repeated. No pagan writer ever dared to promise seriously that the Golden Age would return, or, as a consequence, to propose that men adopt so disastrously idle a life.

Obviously, these exhortations of Jesus are conceivable only if one remembers that their advocate always believed in the imminent creation of a new world. And that little band of fishermen who made up the Galilean's following could put his counsels into practice, could be content to live on bits of grain stolen from other men's fields or on charity, because they believed that this was only a temporary state of affairs. Only a few years later, Paul was to be obliged to censure some of the more artless (or the overartful) Christians of Thessalonica who, while they waited for the Second Coming, lived up to the letter of what Jesus had said on the uselessness of labor and made themselves burdens on the community: "This we commanded you," he wrote, "that if any would not work, neither should he eat. For we hear that there are some which walk among you disorderly, working not at all. . . . Now them that are such we command and exhort, by our Lord Jesus Christ, that with quietness they work, and eat their own bread."[37]

The Lord's Prayer

Purged of its paradoxical impracticalities, the program laid down by Jesus remains in the Christian ethic as a summons to avoid overconcern with the problems of basic physical life—not, however, by persuading men of the necessity for a more reasonable use, and therefore a more equitable distribution, of material goods, but rather by deluding them that the goodness of God will not allow anyone to go without what he needs. Since this delusion is amply refuted by fact, Christians are reduced to the fantasy that in Paradise, after the death of the body, they will enjoy the physical and spiritual pleasures of which they can only dream in life.

The frequent references that Jesus made to God's providence led his disciples to ask him exactly how they should pray to God himself in order to be certain of receiving so much beneficence. On this subject, the Gospels of Matthew and Luke set forth the famous prayer that survives in the Catholic liturgy as the Pater Noster and in the Protestant rite as the Lord's Prayer, and they amplify it with various clarifying remarks and parables.[38] Its original form is probably the more schematic one contained in Luke, whose author must have purged it of the additions made in the text of the other Gospel.[39] Luke's version reads:

"Our Father, hallowed be thy name. Thy kingdom come. Thy will be done, as in heaven, so in earth. Give us day by day our daily bread [actually, ἐπιούσιον (epiousion) and the Hebrew māhār, which is found in the apocryphal Gospel According to the Hebrews, would make this read: 'Give us each day our bread for the next']. And forgive us our sins; for we also forgive every one that is indebted to us. And lead us not into temptation." The words "which art in heaven" (which appear in the King James Bible) are found in only a few manuscripts. I do not believe they can relate real words of Jesus, since, as stated above, the term "heaven" corresponded to "God," not to a geographical site. The ending, "but deliver us from evil," was added later.

The prayer is divided into two parts: a short adoration, in homage to the name of God, and then a more detailed request for the inauguration of the kingdom. A comparative study of the prayers of all epochs shows us that in every religion they serve primarily the purpose of placating the divine being and disposing him kindly toward the solution of a crisis of social or economic character, a concrete problem of daily existence (as in the case of the wretched Palestinians of the time of Jesus).[40] Seasonally stricken by drought, the Wakapomos of Lake Tana pray: "Give us rain. We are in agony. Send us clouds full of rain." The Denkas of the Nile, the Hottentot shepherds of southwest Africa, and other tribes have similar prayers.[41] On the other hand, the Bakongos dread windstorms, which cover their fields with sand, and they pray: "Father, temper the wind, for thy sons here are many!" The Masai ask for physical strength and an abundance of spoils.

Even the third-century apologist Cyprian of Carthage could analyze the Pater Noster, in his treatise *De dominica oratione*,[42] by noting that it was a public or general prayer: one says "our father," not "my father," and "our daily bread," not "my bread"; when one says "Thy kingdom come," this is not an aspiration on behalf of God, for he has always reigned and will reign forever, but one implores the kingdom "for us."

A more developed culture would later be capable of seeking in prayer an expression of mystical contact between God and man. Even so, modern Christianity demonstrates that naïve forms of supplication for temporal and material purposes (the end of a drought or a famine, the cure of a disease, etc.) have not entirely disappeared. A prayer of the patron saint Patrick, known as "the breastplate" because it "protects against the devil's arrows," is still said in Ireland: "Christ with me, Christ before me, Christ behind me, Christ within me, Christ under me, Christ above me, Christ at my right hand, Christ at my left hand,"[43] and so on.

A major psychological factor can also play a part in individual prayer: faith in unfailing divine protection becomes a nucleus of hope and strength that helps the believer to overcome the difficulties he encounters. There is something more. The solitude of the person who prays, mechanically repeating phrases that he has learned by heart, can augment the concentration of his thoughts and the flow of natural "magnetic fluids." Such was the case, for instance, in the experiments made by the Presbyterian minister Franklin Loehr and his followers. Having succeeded (as Loehr himself explains in one of his books[44]) in producing rapid progress or retardation in the cultivation of shrubs and in the germination of seeds while concentrating on them in their prayers, they were convinced that this was the result of the prayers. Perhaps they did not know that identical results had been obtained in the same kind of experiments, though without prayer, by the well-known magnetism expert Lafontaine, in 1841, by Professor Gravier at the end of that century, and by the Swiss professor Bertholet early in the present century, all with the same magnetic radiations, and then by Paul and Christiane Wasse through thought concentration in 1948 and by Dr. Riccardo de Silva in 1953.

Without going to Loehr's extreme, it is still apparent that Jesus attributed considerable influence to prayer because of his boundless faith in God: "What things soever ye desire when ye pray, believe that ye receive them, and ye shall have them";[45] "Ask, and it shall be given you; seek, and ye shall find; knock, and it shall be opened unto you."[46] In the Gospel of Thomas, too, there is a similar sentence, at the very beginning, but it develops differently: "Let him who seeks cease not to seek until he finds: when he finds he will be astonished; and when he is astonished he will wonder, and will reign over the universe!"[47] According to the word of Clement of Alexandria,[48] this passage recalls one of Plato in his *Theaetetus,* and is intended to denote the first step in knowledge, which consists of wonder at the contact with reality.[49] Other passages in Thomas adhere more closely to the concept expressed by the Synoptic Gospels (God readily grants whatever is asked of him in prayer).[50]

The Gospels contain other asseverations of faith in God: "What man is there of you, whom if his son ask bread, will he give him a stone? Or, if he ask a fish, will he give him a serpent? If ye then, being evil, know how to give good gifts unto your children, how much more shall your Father which is in heaven give good things to them that ask him?"[51] "Which of you shall have a friend, and shall go unto him at midnight, and say unto him, Friend, lend me three loaves; For a friend of mine in his journey is come to me, and I have nothing to set before him? And he from within shall answer and say, Trouble me not: the door is now shut, and my children are with me in bed; I cannot rise and give thee. I say unto you, Though he will not rise and give him because he is his friend, yet because of his importunity he will rise and give him as many as he needeth."[52]

Later, Luke clarifies this concept with a parable: a judge who neither feared God nor cared for man was besought by a widow who insisted that he enforce her rights, and ultimately he yielded to her in order to put an end to her calls on him.[53]

The parable cannot be allegorically interpreted (the judge being God and the widow being anyone who prays) to mean that God is to be nagged,[54] but it can well be considered an argument *a fortiori:* if the earthly judge, who was not a just man, finally paid attention to the widow, how much more speedily will God render justice to those who have faith in him.[55]

Faith in God

To many students of the New Testament, Jesus' promises that whoever prays to God will be satisfied are quite debatable, for it is unthinkable that God would grant requests which are opposed to what is good. The Roman satirist Persius, they say, more appropriately denounced the tastelessness of the faithful who went to the Temple to beg for beauty, riches, and success.

The point is well made. But Jesus knew nothing of such arguments. He put the question in its simplest terms, making the object of prayer an abstraction and rejecting only the possibility that God, who is good, could refuse to grant a prayer offered in genuine faith, and, above all, in humility.[56] It is easier, another parable of Luke says, for God to grant the prayer of a publican and a sinner who does not dare raise his eyes to heaven than that of a haughty Pharisee who prides himself on his punctilious observance of fasts and tithe-paying.[57]

What is fundamental in this whole section of the teachings of Jesus is the idea of God as a father. I do not mean that this was a wholly new idea. The theologians exaggerate when they seek to persuade us of a sharp contrast between the wrathful, despotic God of the Old Testament and the loving, paternal God of the New. Nor is it true, as has often been said,[58] that in the Old Testament God is never addressed as a father. The appellation occurs in, among other places, Psalm 89:26, and the Kaddish, the Hebrew prayer that is not only the "twin"[59] of the Pater Noster but also the model from which Jesus took his inspiration, for it contains the same declarations of faith. It is equally untrue that the New Testament contains nothing of the concept of God's severity, which appears there at least as an absolute and despotic paternal authority demanding filial submission. And the God of Jesus, too, is capable of feeling remorse, of making plans without imparting them to his subjects, of having enemies and favorites, of making exceptions and performing miracles on his own instance. Besides, this dual nature of God—kind and tyrannical—is common to all theistic religions, especially those of the East.[60]

The attribution of "father" qualities to God is an unconscious gratification of a profoundly atavistic need. These qualities are analogous to the functions and properties of the father in a primitive society. It was he to whom every question was presented for solution; he was the arbiter on whom the lives and deaths of all the members of the family depended absolutely. But he also trained the young men to hunt and initiated them into the life of the adult. And he was the sole defender against external perils and against any usurpation by elder brothers.

Among the Hebrews in particular, the figure of God was shaped into closer and closer resemblance to that of the chieftain of a tribe, terrible in his anger but generous in his protection and leadership of his people. The Jewish scholar Aron offers the interesting hypothesis that Jesus deliberately went back to the Kaddish (which is still recited today by Jewish mourners in intercession for their dead), recalling the mournful day when he himself had intoned it to God at the tomb of the old carpenter Joseph.[61]

If God is *our father,* all men, being his sons, should live as brothers in one great family. This is the basis of Jesus' message, the source of his precepts of humanity, mercy, compassion for those who suffer, for the poor, for the oppressed. In sum, it is the foundation of the conditions that Jesus sets for the real bond between man and God, conditions that are purely religious and moral, in no way dogmatic or ritual.[62]

In any case, Jesus could not have "invented" a God much different from the deity that he had been taught since childhood to know. Side by side with its assurances of faith and confidence in a merciful father, Christianity has retained expressions of fear of a monarch who is the absolute master of existence. The Oriental custom of prostrating oneself at an altar and striking one's forehead three times against the ground has been only somewhat attenuated in the modern practice of kneeling or bowing during the mass.[63]

Jesus, in sum, only emphasized the ultimate stage in the development that the idea of God had undergone among his own people: ever less fearful, ever more merciful.

From 'Elohīm to Yahweh

The earliest names used to indicate the divinity worshiped by the Israelite people (names that continued to be used even later) reveal the polytheistic origin of the Hebrew religion,[64] even though most Catholic students contest it.[65] 'Elohīm is the plural of 'El or 'Elohāh, which means "he who is feared," and 'Adonai is the plural of 'Ādōn, which means "the Lord." As the writings of the Old Testament show, as late as the seventh century B.C. the Hebrew people, although they had already selected a national god, had not yet begun to doubt the existence and power of other gods belonging at the same time to other peoples, such as Hadad, the Canaanite god of the heavens; Chemosh, the Moabites' patron-god; the Ammonites' Moloch; Baal and Astarte of Tyre and Sidon.

The name of Yahweh (Jehovah) is found for the first time in Exodus, where it is given as that of the God of Israel.[66] It is generally related to the root of the verb "to be" (hwh), and hence it is said to mean "I Am That I Am," or, in the monotheistic sense, "I am the only god that exists." In actuality, the term can also mean simply that the God of Israel had been and continued to be the same one— that is, always loyal to his people.[67]

But, according to the philologists, Yahweh has nothing in common with the root verb hwh: it goes back, instead, to a primitive Yāh or Yāhu[68] (surviving, for example, in the word "Hallelujah"), which is similar to the name of the Babylonian divinity Jau,[69] and which may be traceable even to the Greek Ζεύς (Zeus), to the Latin Jov- (Jove), to deus, to the High German Zin, to the Old Irish dīa, to the Persian deivas, etc. All these, in turn, derive from the Sanskrit djv, which means "heaven."

From this interrelation some scholars deduce the existence of a primordial monotheism among all men, or at least among the Indo-European races, with the common concept of a god who dwelt in the sky.[70] It is more probable, however, that all religions possessed an analogous naturalistic origin, dictated by fear and even awe of the sky, which seemed to be the locus of all the forces of nature (the sun, the moon, the rain, the thunder, etc.).[71] Except for Andrew Lang and Wilhelm Schmidt, who maintain the theory of a primordial monotheism, all the other authorities agree in the belief that, on the contrary, monotheism is the highest stage in the development of religion. Some ascribe pure and simple naturalistic origins to religion; others prefer the theory of animatism, that is, worship of the *mana,* or supernatural power, with which certain objects and persons were endowed[72] and which had to be controlled by means of magic;[73] still others contend that the origin of religion was animism, in which vital souls, resembling man's, are attributed to all things in nature.[74]

All agree, however, that the foundation of every religion is a feeling of fear and premonition in the face of unfamiliar phenomena, whether natural or biological (birth, death, illness, etc.): the *timor* we find in Lucretius, a psychologically unhealthy state of mind. The word "religion" itself comes from the Latin verb *religere* ("to respect," "to revere"), the contrary of *negligere* ("to ignore").

In opposition to the theory of primordial monotheism, most scholars believe that primitive religions gradually evolved from pluralistic beginnings. What probably came first was a diminution in the number of the many spirits, genii, powers, etc., through their assimilation into a smaller number of deities with similar qualities (for example, "heaven" represents the concentration of the influences of the stars, atmospheric phenomena, the concepts of light and heat, and so on). Subsequently, the need for something concrete to which sacrifices and prayers could be offered led to the materialization of such divinities in the form of idols and fetishes. In a third stage, they came to be considered beings who manifested human shapes and human behavior (anthropomorphism).

Recently published works,[75] however, reject not only Lang's and Schmidt's ideas of a primitive monotheism but also the evolutionary theories of Edward Tylor and Lewis Farnell. According to Raffaele Pettazzoni, all primitive religions can be traced back to three fundamental concepts of a "supreme being": the earth-mother in cultures of an agricultural nature, the heavenly father in pastoral civilizations, and the lord of the beasts in societies based on hunting.[76] The transition to monotheism was not the result of a gradual evolution but was caused by an unplanned "revolution."[77]

The Hebrew religion shows clear traces of all three of these stages: the survival of agricultural rites, reminiscences of totemic animals, relics of ancient astral cults, etc.[78] As in many religions of the agricultural class that symbolized their deities in a stone (for example, the *ka'aba* of the Arabs, the *beth'el* of the Canaanites, the sacred boulder of Mithras), Yahweh, too, in the language of the Psalmists, is often called "the Rock."[79] One can trace to the same stage of religious development the practice of celebrating religious offices in high places, called *bamōth* (*bāmāh* in the singular),[80] which the septuagint translated as στῆλαι (*stēlai*) or ὑψηλά (*hupsēla*) and which Jerome rendered as *excelsa*, for mountains were believed to be holy, as centers of the earth's powers.[81] The New Testament also shows a certain predilection for heights, which provide the background of all the important events in the life of Jesus (his first preaching, the Miracle of the Loaves, the Transfiguration, the Crucifixion).

The transition to the monotheism of Yahweh was probably aided by historical factors, in particular, the need of the Hebrews to isolate themselves from the surrounding peoples, in order not to corrupt a political-theocratic organization that was already well developed. This does not mean that monotheism represents the perfection of religious form. Classical Greece, for instance, which had an infinitely higher civilization than that of the Hebrews, always remained polytheistic.

At any rate, the fact that the Hebrews arrived rather speedily at a monotheistic form of religion made it possible for the One God, Yahweh, to assemble in himself within a few centuries not only all the properties of an arbitrary governor of natural and biological phenomena but also the qualities of a protective sovereign who was at the same time a demanding legislator and judge of human actions.

When the Old Testament sought to verbalize the ways in which this Semitic god let men know his will, it employed a number of different terms: *shekīnāh*, the place or the presence of God;[82] *bath qōl*, his voice; *ma'amar* or *memrā*, his words; *ruaḥ*, his breath, his efflux. These are the first forms of the materialization of a deity, but they do not yet exactly represent an incarnation: even the *shekīnāh* was interpreted as a reflection of God, such as a ray of light that revealed his presence.[83]

This was the concept of God held by the contemporaries of Jesus and by Jesus himself. But, while the Pharisees, confronted by the social and political decline of the country, felt it necessary to invoke a god more demanding and angry than ever, in order to rouse the people out of their lassitude, Jesus, on the contrary, like the majority of the humble masses, believed that he could put his trust in a tolerant and merciful god. Some authors have compared this faith to the confidence that a young man has in his own father after he has committed some offense: reliance on forgiveness and on a wisdom that will lead him back to the right path.[84]

From Yahweh to God

The molding of the concept of God peculiar to Christianity was strongly influenced, during the first five centuries after the death of Jesus, by the infiltration into the Hebraic idea of monotheism of the philosophies of *Neo-Platonism*, the school of Philo of Alexander, and Gnosticism.

To the Neo-Platonists, the concept of ultimate and absolute perfection was a pure abstraction, undefinable (ἄρρητος, *arrētos*) and unknowable ἀγνωστικός, *agnōstikos*), which could be attained neither by thought (δόξα, *doxa*) nor by scientific learning (γνῶσις, *gnōsis*), but only through emotional revelation (ἔρως, *erōs*).

For the followers of Philo, the idea of God vacillated between the personalized Semitic Yahweh, who did not disdain from communicating with his people (Philo was of Jewish origin), and the pure, sublime, and unattainable concept of the Neo-Platonists.

Gnosticism, however, represented an attempt to make the abstract concept of the Neo-Platonists accessible without recourse to anthropomorphism. According to the Gnostic philosophers, God issued out of his silence (σιγή, *sigē*) and his depth (βάθος, *bathos*) by means of emanations called "aeons" (αἰῶνες, *aiōnes*), through which he established contact with the finite world. Through γνῶσις, therefore, man could attain to the idea of God.

These various conceptions are found, sometimes in turn and sometimes confused together, in the Fathers and Doctors of the Church: God is the *deus absconditus* of the Neo-Platonists, inaccessible, but he is also the God who makes his presence known, as he was for the Jews; he is a transcendent spirit and a luminous emanation, as he was for the Gnostics; and so on. Later philosophical speculations have tried to bring some order into this disarray, and—at least among official theologians of the Church—they have consistently approached closer to the idea of God as an abstract concept of the Highest Good and of absolute perfection that nonetheless remains completely demonstrable. This is indeed the argument of Anselm of Aosta (1033–1109): The being who can be considered the most perfect *must* really exist; otherwise it would be possible to conceive of another more perfect than he, who, in addition to all his other attributes, would also have that of existence. It is a sophistry. The same reasoning can be adduced, for example, on behalf of a miraculous island, a haven of all delights, somewhere in the ocean. The very fact that one can imagine it in all its perfection compels it to exist in reality.

Then the Germanic mind, fused with the Latin, introduced a new contribution to the concept of God. Because of the strong German sense of discipline, of duty, of individual responsibility, it emphasized (until ultimately it broke out into the Protestant Reformation) the contrast between the idea of God as perfection and man's recognition of his own imperfection. "God is a creation of our sensibilities," Luther said in his *Great Catechism,* and Ludwig Feuerbach amplified much later: "The divine being is nothing but man's own essence, freed of the restraints of the individual—that is, of the limitations of corporeality and of his own imperfect reality—and made objective: that is, contemplated and adored as another being distinct from himself."[85] This objectivization is not purely theoretical, but immediately practical, for it makes man aware of his cosmic insignificance, forces him into a state of tension, of discontent with himself, and hence stimulates him to action and emulation, showing him what he *should* be.[86]

More tersely, Kant said: "God, so to speak, is the personification of the moral law itself."[87] In other words, God is the awareness of all our duties, not as imperatives of our own conscience (which in reality they should be), but as commandments imposed from without.[88] The need for God, then, is born of the disparity between what man is and what he aspires to be.

Current thinkers tend to view this human finiteness not, like the Gnostics, as a cosmic necessity linked to the imperfection of the created world but as a moral accident, an existential fact in man's own being.[89] Modern progress troubles man, for it proves to him how temporary and precarious all his convictions are, and it offers the constant possibility of newer discoveries in every field. And this heightens man's sense of his own limitations in the face of the infinite and the unknown that surround him. So a state of anxiety springs up, because man knows that he is conditioned by and thrust into a transitory situation that he can only accept as his, even if he has not chosen it, and he knows that he lives in constant insecurity. According to this "theology of crisis," faith in God, for modern man, is not so much the aspiration of traditional religion toward a perfect ideal as it is a need to detach himself from the world about him, to renounce the search for recognition, to reject belief in this life, in order to entrust himself blindly to the invisible. This negative view of the presence of God has been so exaggerated that in consequence men feel the need of some "faith," for its own sake, in something undefined, since "God is and remains for us the absolutely other, the without, the unknown, the unapproachable."[90]

[12]

TIMES OF TRIBULATION

The Death of John the Baptist

In the spring of A.D. 27, perhaps in the month of Iyar (April–May)—
if it is true that his mission was begun the year before—Jesus encountered a serious crisis. It was then that he heard the news of the
death of John the Baptist, his former teacher who had baptized him.
For a long time imprisoned by Herod Antipas in the fortress at
Machaerus, the Baptist had been executed by decapitation on the
order of the tetrarch.

Possibly, the account of his death contained in the Gospels of
Mark and Matthew[1] is drawn from the popular rumors prevalent
at the time. It was said that Antipas' wife, Herodias, hated John
because he constantly reproached her for her adultery, but that John
had been spared by the tetrarch, who often summoned him for discussions and "was much troubled" by his apocalyptic prophecies.
We should note here that this phrase, "he was much troubled," is
an exact translation of the Greek to be found in Codex Vaticanus
1209 B and other manuscripts, πολλά ἠπόρει (*polla ēporei*), and is also
found in most modern translations, while Jerome's Vulgate says instead "*multa faciebat*" ("he did many things"), which would require
the Greek ἠπόρει to be ἐποίει (*epoiei*), but which would make no sense
in this context.

On his birthday, Antipas (who is identified simply as Herod in
the Gospels) wanted to offer a magnificent feast to the dignitaries of
his court, the local officials and the most prominent citizens of the

place. In the midst of the revelry, when the plenitude of food and drink had excited the senses of the guests, the young daughter of Herodias launched impulsively into a dance as a tribute to her stepfather, and all the guests were pleasantly shocked. Among a people as jealous of its women as the Semites, it was certainly not usual to see a princess dance in public.

The girl (the Gospels do not give her a name, but we know from *The Antiquities of the Jews* of Flavius Josephus that she was called Salome) was barely seventeen years old at the time, having been born in A.D. 10. A few years after this banquet, she was to marry the tetrarch Philip, twenty years her senior, and in A.D. 34, when she was a widow, she was to become the wife of that Aristobulus whom Nero made king of Armenia Minor. Her portrait appears with her husband's on the coins of the time.

The Gospels indulge in no descriptions of the dance. That has been the province of modern artists and their imaginations—Oscar Wilde, who wrote a famous play based on the story; Richard Strauss, who built an opera on it; and various Hollywood directors who have put it on the screen. Even without their assistance, we can easily imagine the voluptuous Oriental dance in which, skillfully casting aside one silken veil after another, the girl was finally half-naked before the men, their eyes alight with desire for her marvelous body. At one end of the room, musicians accompanied her sinuous movements, and one of them broke softly into song, perhaps a passage from the Song of Solomon, which is one of those extremely rare Hebrew flowerings of the love lyric, preserved in the Old Testament by some miracle. Because of their remarkably tasteless insensitivity, the traditional exegetes interpret it as a religious allegory, but nothing could be more langorously sensual or less ascetic. We must limit ourselves, unfortunately, to short excerpts:

> *I am the rose of Sharon, and the lily of the valleys.*
> *As the lily among thorns, so is my love among the*
> *daughters.*
> *As the apple tree among the trees of the wood, so is my*
> *beloved among the sons.*
> *I sat down under his shadow with great delight, and his*
> *fruit was sweet to my taste. . . .*

Behold, thou art fair, my love; behold, thou art fair.
Thou hast doves' eyes within thy locks: thy hair is as a
  flock of goats that appear from Mount Gilead.
Thy teeth are like a flock of sheep that are even shorn,
  which came up from the washing. . . .
Thy lips are like a thread of scarlet. . . .
Thy two breasts are like two young roses that are twins,
  which feed among the lilies. . . .

Herod, in ecstasy at the spectacle, fell into one of those rash errors that are often committed by egotistical tyrants who think they can satisfy every whim: he promised that he would give his step-daughter whatever she asked, even the half of his kingdom. Salome, perhaps overwhelmed by such generosity or perhaps playing a part already taught to her by her mother, showed some hesitation and ran to Herodias for counsel: "What shall I ask?"

Her mother replied: "The head of John the Baptist."

Returning to the banquet hall (it was the custom for the women to eat in another room), Salome voiced her wish. "The king was exceeding sorry," but he could not refuse. A guard was sent at once to the prison to behead John, and he brought back the head on a charger.

His disciples were allowed to bury his body, and then they went to give the news to Jesus.

The Miracle of the Loaves

Jesus was profoundly affected by the tragedy, and he was anxious. To him the execution of John was the beginning of a persecution against those who prophesied the kingdom, and he was afraid for himself and for his disciples. All the Gospels agree here in relating that as soon as he had heard the news, Jesus quickly departed, accompanied by his disciples, and sought refuge "in a desert place."[2] Luke particularizes, saying that he withdrew to the region of Bethsaida, not far from Capernaum but well within the Tetrarchy of Philip, beyond Herod's jurisdiction.

Now, in almost identical words, all four Gospels describe one of the most mystifying of the miracles of Jesus: that of the five loaves and the two fishes, which he broke in his hands and caused to increase until they could feed some five thousand persons—"besides women and children," Matthew says—all sitting "upon the green grass"; afterward, what was not eaten was gathered up and filled twelve baskets.[3] Not satisfied by this marvel, Mark and Matthew report that it was repeated a few days later almost exactly.[4] The number of loaves and of baskets (seven instead of five and twelve) and that of the diners (four thousand instead of five thousand) were changed and Matthew speaks vaguely of "a few little fishes." It is hardly necessary to remark that we are confronted here by one of those extra-natural events that require explanation.

The mystics find a symbolic value in the two multiplications. In the first, the number of loaves (five), to which the number of the faithful (five thousand) corresponds, represents the universe with the points of its cosmogony; the two fish represent the spiritual element; the twelve baskets are the signs of the Zodiac. The symbols of the second miracle, of course, are different, because of the different meanings of the numbers four and seven.[5]

The rationalists deny the miracle altogether (the second being, for them, only a retelling of the first), remarking first of all how grotesque it is to imagine Jesus "materializing" loaves and fishes out of nothing with his hands, like the pigeons and the colored ribbons that a magician draws out of his hat. Then they point out the physical impossibility (even if the multiplication could have occurred) of immediately doling out the food to five thousand persons or more: it would have taken several hours. Finally, they attack the illogical conclusion that there were twelve baskets of leftovers. Why such waste of food? How did all those empty baskets manage to be at hand in the desert place? The rationalists tend to believe that Jesus merely made the symbolic gesture of breaking the bread and distributing it among his Apostles in order to give his audience an example of brotherly sharing.[6]

The mythologists[7] are of the opinion that the whole episode was invented by the Evangelists to attribute to their master, as the new savior, an action similar to the miracle of the manna[8] ascribed to Moses, the Hebrew people's first savior, during the flight from Egypt, and they itemize the parallels: flight, a desert place, the hunger of a large crowd, doubt whether enough food could be found, the decision to satisfy the multitude with a miracle.

That the whole matter is myth rather than fact is the view of all the other commentators (except, of course, the traditional exegetes). It is noteworthy that the Evangelists themselves, although they tell the story as if it were historically true, do not conceal its allegorical meaning, contrasting the material sustenance of the bread and fish with the spiritual nourishment of the words. Even the detail of the baskets filled with leftovers is not overlooked; it symbolizes the eternal fertility of thought, which is never consumed.[9]

A long disquisition in the Gospel of John, which follows the story of the miracle, openly authorizes the episode's interpretation as a specific symbol of the Eucharist: "Moses gave you not that bread from heaven; but my Father giveth you the true bread from heaven. . . . I am the bread of life: he that cometh to me shall never hunger. . . . I am the living bread which came down from heaven; if any man eat of this bread, he shall live forever,"[10] and so forth. And a Catholic author confirms that the early Church was so convinced of this interpretation that for many centuries the Eucharist was represented not by the Last Supper (which appeared only during the Renaissance) but by the Miracle of the Loaves, and the baskets as well as the fish (the symbol of Christ, IXΘYΣ) were set before the Lord's table—always seven of them, as in the second account.[11]

If one wishes, one can find an incidental allusion to the primitive organization of the Church in the numbers that occur in both miracles as well as in other details: the multitude stands for the congregation of the faithful, or the Church itself; the bread is the word of truth; the number twelve is identical with the number of ministers of the Church (the Twelve Apostles); the number seven, in the second miracle, recalls the number of deacons in the Church of Jerusalem.[12]

Jesus Walks on the Water

It is difficult to understand why the Evangelists placed so important and so conspicuous an event as the Miracle of the Loaves in this period, when Jesus, out of fear of Herod, had decided to interrupt his work. Perhaps they wished to fill the long silence into which the master had withdrawn in the desert of Philip's tetrarchy.

The Gospels' uncertainties and contradictions on this period are numerous. Luke, who locates the miracle at Bethsaida, has nothing to say of Jesus' movements immediately thereafter. Mark, who assumes that the miracle was performed in Galilee, has Jesus join his disciples on a ship for Bethsaida, which then, unexpectedly, lands at the Plain of Gennesaret. Matthew follows Mark almost literally. John tells us that after the miracle Jesus set out for Capernaum!

Out of all this confusion, only one note of harmony seems to be discernible: during the exile of Jesus in Bethsaida there must have been some sort of popular demonstration, perhaps instigated by the Apostles themselves, intended to persuade Jesus to clarify his political position and lead a revolution that would set up the expected kingdom. But Jesus lacked the boldness for this—nor was it his mission—and he departed secretly. "When Jesus therefore perceived that they would come and take him by force, to make him a king," the Gospel of John relates, "he departed again into a mountain himself alone."[13] Matthew and Mark add that meanwhile, on his specific orders, the Apostles at once boarded a boat.[14] Following the shore of the Lake of Gennesaret, they steered for Capernaum, making it appear that Jesus was with them. But shortly afterward, having changed his mind, he set out to walk along the small expanse of shore[15] that separated the beach of Bethsaida from that of Capernaum, and he overtook his followers just before they were ready to land. The Apostles and the crowd, which was disappointed that it had been unable to hear him in Bethsaida and which had gone back to the other shore of the lake (John says expressly that many boats had come from as far away as Tiberias[16]), were so astonished to see him that they thought he was a miraculous apparition: "they supposed it had been a spirit," Matthew and Mark say, "and cried out."[17]

It was easy for popular imagination to transform the episode into a full-fledged miracle: Jesus walked on, not alongside, the water. Matthew adds an embellishment that lays more emphasis on a detail that would have been a piece of remarkable ostentation, however pointless, and that underlines Simon Peter's childlike ingenuousness. Seeing Jesus walk on the water, Matthew says, the fisherman wanted to emulate him, but no sooner was he on the lake than he began to sink, and he cried out: "Lord, save me!" Jesus had to reach out his hands and pull him to safety.

It seems to me unnecessary to attribute "occult powers of levitation" to Jesus, as the esoterics do,[18] in order to explain how he managed to walk on the water, and equally useless to view the story in the Gospels as merely an attempt to make a fact out of a hallucination that some Apostle had after the death of Jesus.[19] This myth is another designed to stress the power of faith; and it is not misplaced here (as it would be if it were based on a subsequent "vision"). The miracle serves to counterbalance the negative impression created by the flight of Jesus and to re-establish faith in his powers. His antagonist is made to be Simon Peter, who was to go down in history especially because he denied Jesus after his arrest. In fact, Matthew says, Jesus rebuked him as he drew him to safety: "O thou of little faith, wherefore didst thou doubt?"[20]

It is easy to conceive of the persuasive value of this episode when it was read out and discussed in Christian assemblages.

The Syrophoenician

Jesus went back to Capernaum, but assuredly not to stay. After what had happened at Bethsaida, even this no longer seemed a safe refuge. Ever more alarming news of the apprehensions of Herod Antipas came to him. "It [Jesus] is John," the tetrarch reportedly said, "whom I beheaded: he is risen from the dead."[21] Jesus therefore resolved to go far out of Palestinian territory and to seek a haven abroad for a while.

By heading northwest from Capernaum, in one and a half days of walking, he could reach the city of Tyre, in Phoenicia, after crossing the rugged spurs of the Anti-Lebanon Mountains. There, according to Mark and Matthew, Jesus, accompanied by some of his followers, asked for shelter in the house of a fellow Jew, exhorting him to let no one know of his presence.[22]

But he could not long remain hidden. Even in as big a city as Tyre, the prying gossips observe everything that happens around them, and the presence of the little group of foreigners was not unnoticed by one such. Mark calls her a "Syrophoenician."[23] This was the term used by the Greeks and Romans to designate the residents of this area and to distinguish them from the Phoenicians of the African coast, who were called Libyophoenicians.

However she might have learned of the reputation of Jesus for thaumaturgy, the woman knew it. She presented herself before him and besought him to cure her daughter, who was possessed of an evil spirit. Especially irritated that his presence was already known, Jesus did not even reply to her, and some of the disciples sought at once to get rid of her. She turned spiteful and began to curse. The disciples called on Jesus: "Send her away; for she crieth after us." He told her sharply: "I am not sent but unto the lost sheep of the house of Israel. . . . Let the children first be filled: for it is not meet to take the children's bread, and to cast it unto the dogs."

"Yes, Lord," she retorted, "yet the dogs under the table eat of the children's crumbs."

Jesus was pleased by her cleverness, and he agreed to perform the cure. One writer has observed that Jesus treated the Syrophoenician in the same way in which he had dealt with his mother at the marriage feast in Cana, first brusquely turning his back and then acceding to the request.[24]

The story is generally taken as a parable that reflects the intense arguments (to which we have already referred) that arose after the death of Jesus on the propriety of bringing the good tidings and the work of salvation to the heathen.[25] But, if we compare this incident with the Gospel passage that recounts the cure of the centurion's son, which is also a case of a pagan who asks and receives help from Jesus on behalf of a child, we are struck by the contrast in the Nazarene's behavior. With the centurion, he had been quick to act, and he had even spoken words of praise for the exemplary faith of such a foreigner, regretful at the fact that he had not found its like among his own compatriots. If, then, the story of the Syrophoenician is true, has one not the right to think that the refusal of Jesus and his rude words were no more than the reactions of an uncontrolled impulse of vexation at having been recognized?

Again, Jesus had been able to exploit the faith shown by the centurion as an example for his own people, but here in a foreign land such an example could no longer serve the same purpose.

Both instances alike seem to show, in short, that, even if Jesus did not at all share the prejudices of the Pharisees and the majority of Israelites against the heathen, and even if he could be more or less readily persuaded to help pagans, nonetheless he never entertained the idea of dedicating himself to preaching to them.[26] The universality of Christianity, as we have already pointed out, was to be Paul's concept.

A Sign Is Asked

The Gospels do not specify how long Jesus remained in Phoenicia. Certainly he stayed until he had reliable assurances that Herod Antipas' suspicions had been allayed. On the basis of various indefinite indications in the accounts of his work immediately after his return to his own country, that journey must have been made toward the end of the month of Elul (August–September) or at the beginning of Tishri (September–October), and, since the Miracle of the Loaves occurred in April (the grass was green in the fields), at least five months must have elapsed.

One cannot, however, accept Mark's statement that, "departing from the coasts of Tyre and Sidon," Jesus traveled "through the midst of the coasts of Decapolis,"[27] which was at the southern end of the Tetrarchy of Philip. A journey by way of Sidon, which is in Phoenicia considerably to the north of Tyre, would have subjected him to a long and painful passage over the Lebanon and Anti-Lebanon mountain ranges, through Syria, and across large desert areas. It is obvious that there has been a copyist's error. Mark might have said: "departing from the coast of Tyre by way of [Beth] Saida"; in fact, if the prefix *beth,* which means "house of" and is common to many Palestinian place names (*Beth*-lehem, *Beth*-ania, *Beth*-abara, etc.) is detached, the Hebrew words for Saida and Sidon might easily have been confused.[28] (See Figure V.)

Jesus did not remain long in retirement in Bethsaida. Mark and Matthew say that a few days after his arrival he tried to resume his preaching in Galilee:[29] specifically, in Magdala. Mark says it was in Dalmanutha (a place that did not exist), but in this case, too, it is easy to correct the mistake. "Dalmanutha" was probably a corruption of

Magdalayatha, which means "the village of the Magdalene."[30] Here the ugly disputations with the Pharisees started again.[31]

"Master," one of them declared sarcastically, "we would see a sign from thee."

"Why doth this generation seek after a sign?" Jesus countered, with a deep sigh.[32] "When it is evening, ye say, It will be fair weather; for the sky is red. And in the morning, It will be foul weather to day; for the sky is red and lowering. O ye hypocrites! ye can discern the face of the sky; but can ye not discern the signs of the times? . . . There shall no sign be given . . . but the sign of the prophet Jonas [Jonah]. . . . The men of Nineveh shall rise in judgment with this generation, and shall condemn it; because they repented at the preaching of Jonas; and, behold, a greater than Jonas is here. The queen of the south shall rise up in the judgment with this generation, and shall condemn it: for she came from the uttermost parts of the earth to hear the wisdom of Solomon; and, behold, a greater than Solomon is here."

These Biblical quotations must be explained, for they may well be obscure. The prophet Jonah had predicted: "Yet forty days, and Nineveh shall be overthrown."[33] But the inhabitants had listened to him, done penance, and been saved. Not so the Pharisees, the Gospels say, even though they stand in the presence of a prophet far greater than Jonah. The Queen of Sheba (probably Yemen, in Arabia) had traveled from her distant land to meet Solomon, whose reputation for wisdom had dazzled her. Not so the Pharisees, even though they stood before a man far more just than Solomon.

Such self-praise by Jesus would of course be distasteful if we did not remember that it represents the Evangelists' ideas and certainly does not really report things actually said by the Nazarene. Matthew's insertion at this point of a wholly out-of-place and irrelevant comparison between Jonah, who lived "three days and three nights in a whale's belly," and Jesus, who, after his death, was to remain "three days and three nights in the heart of the earth," is enough by itself to demonstrate that the discourse ascribed to Jesus was fabricated after his death.

On the subject of "signs from heaven," the apocryphal Gospel of Thomas has Jesus say, more concisely: "You examine the appearance of heaven and earth, but He who is in front of you you do not

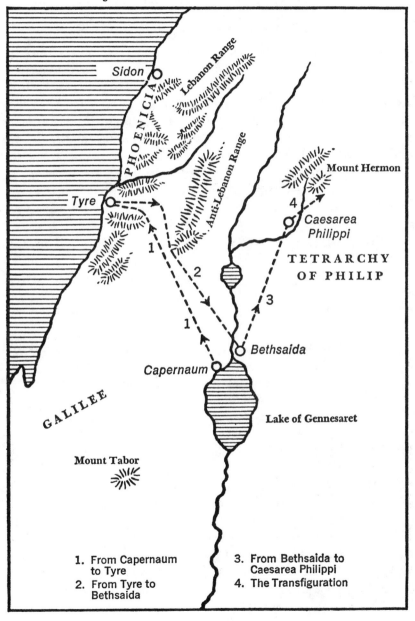

FIGURE V
JESUS WITHDRAWS FROM GALILEE

Sidon

Lebanon Range

PHOENICIA

Anti-Lebanon Range

Mount Hermon

Tyre

1

4

Caesarea
Philippi

2

TETRARCHY
OF PHILIP

3

1

Bethsaida

Capernaum

GALILEE

Lake of Gennesaret

Mount Tabor

1. From Capernaum
   to Tyre
2. From Tyre to
   Bethsaida

3. From Bethsaida to
   Caesarea Philippi
4. The Transfiguration

recognize, and this moment you know not how to examine!"[34] "Moment" (or "conjuncture") is the translation of the Greek καιρός (*kairos*),[35] which appears as such in the Coptic text of Thomas and which signifies the astrological aspect of the skies from which the ancients claimed to be able to foresee the future.

Matthew and Luke add a curious parable as a corollary:[36] "When the unclean spirit is gone out of a man, he walketh through dry places, seeking rest, and findeth none. Then he saith, I will return into my house from whence I came out; and when he is come, he findeth it empty, swept and garnished. Then goeth he, and taketh with himself seven other spirits more wicked than himself, and they enter in and dwell there: and the last state of that man is worse than the first. Even so shall it be also with this wicked generation."

Jesus had barely finished speaking when a woman in the crowd cried out: "Blessed is the womb that bare thee, and the paps which thou hast sucked."

"Yea," Jesus retorted, "rather blessed are they that hear the word of God, and keep it."[37]

The Disciples' Doubts

Jesus and the disciples who had followed him to Magdala boarded a boat to return to Bethsaida, across the Lake of Gennesaret. Jesus was still full of scorn for the petty mockeries of the Pharisees, and he wanted to take advantage of the interlude aboard the boat to instruct his friends to pay no attention to the Pharisees' insinuations.[38] "Take heed," he said, "and beware of the leaven of the Pharisees." But he had to interrupt himself because he became aware that, instead of listening to him, the disciples were talking among themselves and seemed concerned and apprehensive. When he asked them why, they replied: "It is because we have no bread."

"Why reason ye, because ye have no bread?" Jesus scolded angrily. "Have ye your heart yet hardened? Having eyes, see ye not? and having ears, hear ye not? and do ye not remember? When I brake the five loaves among five thousand, how many baskets full of fragments took ye up?"

"Twelve," they replied.

"How is it that ye do not understand that I spake it not to you concerning bread, that ye should beware of the leaven of the Pharisees and of the Sadducees?"

Many of the sayings that the Gospel of John has put in later contexts,[39] though still elaborating on the Miracle of the Loaves, can be adapted to this situation:

"Labor not for the meat which perisheth, but for that meat which endureth unto everlasting life, which the Son of man shall give unto you," Jesus said.

And again he was asked: "What sign shewest thou then, that we may see and believe thee? . . . Our fathers did eat manna in the desert; as it is written, He gave them bread from heaven to eat."

"Moses gave you not that bread from heaven," Jesus countered, "but my father giveth you the true bread from heaven."

Not yet understanding that Jesus was not talking of bread that could be eaten, the sluggish listeners exclaimed: "Lord, evermore give us this bread."

Angrily he replied: "I am the bread of life. . . . Ye also have seen me, and believe not."

More amazed than before, they muttered to one another: "Is not this Jesus, the son of Joseph, whose father and mother we know?"[40]

But Jesus cut them off abruptly: "Murmur not among yourselves. . . . I am the living bread, which came down from heaven; if any man eat of this bread, he shall live forever."

It was not easy for such humble, illiterate fishermen to cut through to the essence of a hermetic utterance of this nature. Accustomed to meeting the practical problem of food day by day, directed by Jesus himself toward the solution of that very problem when he spoke to them of the future kingdom as the cessation of material cares, when he taught them to ask God in their prayers for their daily bread, when he demonstrated that he could easily increase the bread supply itself, they did not understand that Jesus was speaking figuratively and that what he called bread was the spiritual nourishment of his teachings.

But it was not only the most devoted of the disciples who were troubled. Ultimately a certain coldness and aloofness grew among the mass of Galileans who had had the opportunity to hear Jesus preach. More especially, the harsh ordeals of recent months (the fears and anxieties of Jesus and his companions, their sudden flights, his long silence) had already begun to stir second thoughts among many who on the spur of the moment had trustingly embraced his alluring promises. The road that led to the kingdom, they began to think, was less smooth than Jesus would have had them believe. "This is a hard saying," they protested. "Who can hear it?"[41]

Jesus Discouraged

Jesus was not insensitive to the indifference and the hostility that were mounting round him. He had felt called upon to carry a message of love and peace to his brothers. He had believed that this redeeming message, accompanied by efficacious proofs and concrete examples, would be enthusiastically welcomed. Indeed, the way in which it had been received seemed to give substance to his hopes. But now he saw that lack of faith was apparent among those who had been won over by his words, and he had to recognize how far from victory the spirit of the kingdom of God still was.[42]

For the first time, evidences of his bitter disappointment appear in the Gospels: "Doth this offend you?"[43] "But there are some of you that believe not. . . . Therefore said I unto you, that no man can come unto me, except it were given unto him of my Father."[44] Sometimes he even interrupted his prayers[45] to ask his disciples: "Whom say the people that I am?"[46] Those who were closest to him tried vainly to comfort him, declaring: "John the Baptist; but some say, Elias [Elijah]; and others say, that one of the old prophets is risen again"; "Twenty-four prophets have spoken in Israel, and all are summed up in thee."[47] But these consolations did not soothe Jesus, who replied: "Ye have deserted him who stands living before you, and ye speak of the dead."[48]

Even his blood brothers took the liberty of mocking him.[49] The Feast of Tabernacles (in the middle of the month of Tishri, i.e., September–October) was at hand, and they urged him: "Depart hence, and go into Judea, that thy disciples may also see the works that thou doest. For there is no man that doeth any thing in secret, and he himself seeketh to be known openly. If thou do these things, shew thyself to the world."

Jesus did not grasp their sarcasm; he answered sadly: "My time is not yet come; but your time is always ready. The world cannot hate you; but me it hateth, because I testify of it, that the works thereof are evil. Go ye up unto this feast: I go not up yet unto this feast: for my time is not yet full come."

It was truly an anguished time for Jesus. Many of his disciples deserted him out of hand;[50] so many that one day, more discouraged than ever, he asked the Twelve Apostles: "Will ye also go away?"

Simon Peter answered for all of them: "Lord, to whom shall we go? thou hast the words of eternal life. And we believe and are sure that thou art that Christ, the Son of the living God."[51] (This is the King James Version; the Septuagint says that Peter voiced recognition of Jesus as ἅγιος, *hagios*, "a saint," or "holy.")

But this was not enough to restore his courage. His disillusion evoked presentiments of his own death. One day he revealed himself in sorrow:[52] it was inevitable that he must endure severe persecution; that he would be rejected by the elders, by the chief priests, and by the Scribes; that he, too, would probably be executed, like John the Baptist. He said such things frankly, without concealing his own fear.[53] This does not mean he said them in public, as has often been argued.[54] Peter spoke to him privately, in rebuke: "Be it far from thee, Lord; this shall not be unto thee."

Peter's reproach was more than justified;[55] but Jesus turned on him in a terrible burst of anger, and, back in the company of all the Apostles, who were perplexed because they had not heard what Peter had said or understood the earlier remarks of Jesus,[56] the master cried out at Peter: "Get thee behind me, Satan; thou art an offense unto me; for thou savorest not the things that be of God, but those that be of men."

The Primacy of Peter

Yet it was this same rough Simon Peter who gave Jesus the most valuable proof of veneration and love.

Jesus had once more left Galilee. With the few who were still loyal to him, he took refuge near the city of Caesarea Philippi in the extreme north of the Tetrarchy of Philip, near the Syrian border.

This was the ancient Paneas, which Philip had renamed in 3 B.C., in honor of the emperor Tiberius Caesar. "Philippi" had been added by the tetrarch in honor of himself, but it did serve to distinguish the city from Caesarea on the coast of Samaria. Herod the Great had had a temple built there which he dedicated to Rome and Augustus, and the pagan population was large.[57] But, just as Jesus had never gone into the Galilean city of Tiberias, which was also inhabited by pagans, so he avoided Caesarea Philippi too. Near the city, in the foothills of Mount Hermon, there are a number of caves that can provide comfortable shelter, not far from the upper reaches of the river Jordan.

It was here that Jesus, again questioning his companions anxiously, asked: "Whom say ye that I am?" Impulsively, Peter said: "Thou art the Christ, the Son of God."[58] Jesus was stunned, even frightened, by so strange an assertion, and he sternly ordered the Apostles never again to say such a thing of him.[59]

One cannot grasp how traditional theologians can assert that Jesus was *always* conscious of his own character as the Messiah and that he not only wanted but asked his disciples to accept him as such.[60] The Gospel passage just quoted demonstrates the contrary so clearly that one is tempted to insert here, as the Protestant theologian Cullmann does,[61] the angry outburst of Jesus at Peter ("Get thee behind me, Satan"), and to view it not as a resentful retort to the fisherman's gentle rebuke but as a mark of horror at the temptation to proclaim himself the Messiah, a temptation in no way different from that of assuming a throne, which he had already resisted in the wilderness at the beginning of his ministry. This especially, more than any other factor, leads one to believe that at no time did Jesus have any ambition to offer himself as the Messiah.[62]

The problem of the Messiahship of Jesus (over which we shall have to spend more time later), however, is not the only one presented by the above verses. The Gospel of Matthew (but only that Gospel, and the fact is significant) inserts, between Peter's proclamation and the refusal of Jesus to consider himself the Messiah, an extremely interesting and extremely controversial passage, a portent of important developments in the later history of Christianity. After Peter exclaimed: "Thou art the Christ, the Son of the living God," Matthew says, Jesus replied: "Blessed art thou, Simon Bar-jona: for flesh and blood hath not revealed it unto thee, but my Father which is in heaven. And I say also unto thee, That thou art Peter, and upon this rock I will build my church; and the gates of hell shall not prevail against it. And I will give unto thee the keys of the kingdom of heaven: and whatsoever thou shalt bind on earth, shall be bound in heaven; and whatsoever thou shalt loose on earth, shall be loosed in heaven."[63]

Having addressed Simon with the patronymic, "son of Jonah" —unless, as Cullmann believes,[64] Jesus used *barjona* in its metaphorical meaning, "the terrorist"—but having in no case, as others contend,[65] called him "a child of doves" or "a child of frailty," Jesus gave Simon his new name, Peter, thus signifying that Peter was to be the foundation, the rock, of the new structure that Jesus was erecting. Jesus, however, was not resorting to a play on words (the pun, which is inherent in Greek and the Romance languages—for example, *Pierre,* a man's name, and *pierre,* a "stone"—is not reproducible in English). This, of course, would have been most unsuitable to the solemnity of the investiture. In Aramaic, which Jesus and his contemporaries spoke, the word for "rock" is *kēphas,* devoid of gender, and in many New Testament passages Simon is called, not Simon Peter, but Simon Cephas—Simon the Rock.

That Jesus intended to rebuild a religious community with the few disciples who were still loyal to him is not unlikely. This was a necessary measure now that it was clear that the attainment of the kingdom was still distant and that he must therefore alter his own course of conduct. In view of the recent defections, he wanted, in a way, to impose a new covenant of loyalty on those who still intended to follow him. He turned first to prayer:[66] "Now is my soul troubled: and what shall I say? Father, save me from this hour: . . . Father, glorify my name." (This is the reading of the Greek text of John 12:28; in the King James Bible, cf. John 17:1, 5.)

Then, according to John, a voice came out of heaven: "I have both glorified it, and will glorify it again." Some of those who were with Jesus said that they heard a roll of thunder; others said an angel had spoken. Jesus told them: "This voice came not because of me, but for your sakes." Then he adjured them to "walk while ye have the light," meaning that they must have faith and accept without argument the conditions he was about to lay down for the rebuilding of the community. But this does not necessarily imply that he intended also to appoint a leader (while he was still alive) in the person of Simon Peter.

The passage in Matthew dealing with Peter's investiture[67] is obviously an interpolation.[68] This is made clear by a number of considerations:

1. The other canonical Gospels do not mention it, and the omission of so important a historical fact is inexplicable, especially in the Gospel of Mark, which, according to a venerable tradition, reproduces all Peter's teaching. The apocryphal Gospel of Thomas gives the leadership role to James the Just.[69]

2. Matthew himself, in the verses that follow immediately, relates that Jesus called Simon "Satan" and thrust him away, saying that he had no understanding. It is rather remarkable that he should give such shameful treatment to the man whom he had chosen as his successor.

3. A little further on in the Gospels, the Apostles engage in rivalry and struggle over the importance of each of them. This would be incomprehensible if the choice had already been made.

4. Neither the Acts of the Apostles nor Paul's Epistles contain any reference to Peter's primacy. Decisions seem always to have been made unanimously, and the most authoritative among the Apostles seems sometimes to have been, if anyone, James, the brother of Jesus. This has led some authors to believe that there was a kind of family succession of the same type as the dynastic caliphates among the Mohammedans.[70]

5. The word ἐκκλησία (ekklēsia), which appears here, is absolutely foreign to both the vocabulary and the mentality of the authors of the Gospels. It is really astounding that some scholars have the audacity to contend that it might very well have been used by Jesus himself.[71]

6. The idea of a hierarchic organization of his own disciples was contrary to the teachings of Jesus, for he insisted on the complete equality of all the faithful, and further on he explicitly warns the Apostles not to vie for supremacy among themselves.

7. Here the text speaks of a kingdom situated in heaven, which was inconceivable to Jews of that time.

The Papacy

History demonstrates, beyond the possibility of refutation, how slowly and through what a variety of causal factors Christianity over the centuries arrived at the institution of a single head (the pope of Rome). For a long time, the first Christian communities continued to govern themselves democratically. The leadership of each congregation was passed on to the eldest, the πρεσβύτερος (*presbuteros*), from which our word "priest" is derived, and he was assisted by διάκονοι (*diakonoi*), "deacons." The growth of the congregations led later (but certainly not before the end of the second century) to the necessity of vesting permanent authority in one of the eldest residents of the major large cities, under the title of πατριάρχης (*patriarchēs*); this patriarch had the duties, with respect to outlying communities, of an inspector, or ἐπίσκοπος (*episkopos*)—that is, what is now a bishop.

Logically, the bishop living in Rome began to assume a more authoritative character with respect to his colleagues, because of the privileged position that accrued to him by reason of his residence in that capital city. But this supremacy was neither so quickly nor so easily established. Evidence of official recognition cannot be adduced from individual declarations such as that of Irenaeus, bishop of Lyons at the end of the second century, who said that the Roman Church should be considered more important than the rest *propter potiorem principalitatem*,[72] or that of Cyprian, who a half-century later called Rome *ecclesia principalis*,[73] even if the writings ascribed to them and containing such statements are authentic.[74]

It is certain, on the contrary, that the Eastern bishops, and especially the bishop of Byzantium, which Constantine chose as the new capital of the Roman Empire in 323, have never recognized and will never recognize such "sovereignty."[75] Even in the West, as late as the end of the fourth century, many refused to accord to the bishop of Rome the title that he claimed: *princeps sacerdotum*.

The word "pope" itself (a Latinized form of the vernacular Greek πάπας, *papas*, which ordinarily means "father") was used for a long time to designate any priest (it is still so used in Russia: the genitive is *papa*); later it was limited to bishops and patriarchs. Only since the fifth century has the title been restricted in the West to the bishop of Rome.

The first clear evidence of Roman primacy occurred approximately halfway through the fifth century, in the *Decretum Gelasianum*. From then on, reinforcement of the pope's supremacy in matters of doctrine became more frequent and more decisive. But both his attributes and his limitations were always to be subjects of discussion. Meanwhile, the first eight Ecumenical Councils (from the First Nicene, in 325, to the Fourth Constantinople, in 869) were all held in the East, and all were called and presided over by emperors. But even when such councils were convoked by popes (the first such was the Lateran Council of 1123), and especially because so often through the centuries they were dominated by popes whose morality and behavior were unpapal and who were elected and deposed in consonance with the political ends of temporal sovereigns, the other bishops often resolutely resisted the popes' views when decisions were to be made, and this evoked frequent sharp conflicts between "papalism" and "episcopalism," which erupted into resounding schisms.

The Roman pontiff upholds his primacy of jurisdiction by basing it first of all on the tradition that Peter went to Rome with the specific rank of "leader of all Christianity," conferred at his investiture by Jesus. Thus the pope claims an unbroken line of succession from Peter through all his successors, and his doctrinal authority is alleged to be derived from the Biblical statement that "whatsoever thou shalt bind on earth, shall be bound in heaven; and whatsoever thou shalt loose on earth, shall be loosed in heaven." Here the metaphor of binding and loosening has the express connotation of imposing and annulling moral duties, in conformance with a terminology that was used by the rabbis of the time of Jesus.[76] In other words, "to bind" and "to loose" were the technical expressions for "to declare forbidden" and "to declare permissible" any action in its relation to the duties laid down by the Law.[77]

Pontifical primacy of jurisdiction and papal infallibility were finally approved in 1870, by Vatican Council I. The two principles were virtually imposed on the Council by Pius IX, who said: "If any say that the Pontiff of Rome has only the duty of inspection and direction, but not full and final power of jurisdiction over the entire

Church, not only in matters of faith and morals but also in everything that concerns the discipline and government of the Church
throughout the world, or if any say that he has only the major part
but not the whole of this supreme power . . . their names shall be
anathema." (Canon D 1831.)

But this did not still the quarrels between the episcopalists and
the papalists. At the recent Vatican Council II, a heavy majority
demanded the restoration of "those powers that belong to the
bishops by divine right and that in the course of the centuries have
been diminished by the Roman Pontiff." But Pope Paul VI lost no
time in shattering all such hopes, and in the Constitution *De Ecclesia*
that he promulgated on November 21, 1964, he confirmed that "the
Vicar of Christ and pastor of the whole Church has full, supreme,
and universal power, which he can always exercise freely," and that
"the college or body of bishops has authority only in conjunction
with the Pontiff of Rome."

The Church

The Protestants, who have not accepted the authority of the
bishop of Rome since the great Lutheran schism of the sixteenth
century, are strongly opposed to the Catholics on the meaning of the
word "church."

The word itself, derived from the Latin *ecclesia*, which is a
transliteration of the Greek ἐκκλησία, originally applied equally to
either the community of the faithful congregated for the performance of their rites (in Hebrew, *qahāl*) or the building in which they
worshiped (in Hebrew, *'ēdāh*). The Greek noun comes from the
verb ἐκκαλεῖν (*ekkalein*), which means "to summon for," in reference
to the external origin of the members.[78] The interpretation of
ἐκκλησία as a "summons to forsake the world"[79] has only a sentimental
value.

Some time after the middle of the second century, the word
ἐκκλησία began to appear at times with the adjective καθολική (*katho-
likē*). The first to use it was Ignatius Theophorus, but it did not yet
have the connotation of a universal body. The adjective served only
to show the unity of the various communities,[80] each of which, how-

ever, still continued to be known by its locality—the Church of
Ephesus, the Church of Corinth, the Church of Antioch, etc.[81] It
may perhaps be deduced from the letters of Ignatius that at this
period each of these churches was ruled by a bishop, chosen from the
elders (the presbyters) and assisted by other presbyters and deacons,
who were elected by the vote of the entire congregation. But the
bishops were far from having any authority over one another; each
was careful to point out that he had no jurisdiction beyond his own
community.[82] If, later, some were occasionally appointed to their
posts by others—for example, by the bishops of Antioch, Alexandria,
Constantinople, or Rome—it was only because the prelates of such
large cities enjoyed a greater prestige.

The pretensions of the bishop of Rome to primacy over all
Christian churches throughout the world, however, were to lead to a
new interpretation of the word "church" itself. Catholic ecclesiology
has limited its meaning to the hierarchic structure that culminates
in the bishop of Rome: an absolute monarchy that claims universal
dominion (theocracy) and whose sovereign wears the golden triple
crown of the pope-king. All that is asked of the great mass of the
faithful (his subjects) is obedience. Occasionally there is talk—
extremely cautious talk—of a lay apostolate, which would cooperate
with the work of the clergy but which would always be subordinate
to it. This, however, has certainly never been intended to have the
meaning of "a universal priesthood of all who believe," which is a
Reformist concept.[83]

The Protestant Reformation, in actuality, gave the word
"church" a definition that falls between that of the Catholics and the
original meaning: it is "the communion of all those who believe, who
are gathered together in the laws of eternal salvation through Christ
and in Christ come down to earth."[84] Therefore, according to the
evangelical concept, the Church is a phenomenon, not an institution;
it is the contact between each individual believer and God, and it
requires no group of people.[85] Even if the New Testament speaks of
"churches" in the sense of local communities, Protestant theology
holds that it always signifies the various means by which Christ, who
is unique, presents himself in diverse places. Different forms of
organization and liturgy, whether they result from the historical
evolution of Christianity or from its geographical expansion, preju-

dice neither the uniqueness of the apostolic foundation of the Church nor its universality. The "one true Church," according to the Protestants, does not depend on some ecclesiastical organization but comes into being wherever two or more are gathered together in Christ's name, in the certainty of his presence.

The Protestants too recognize the necessity of a priesthood (pastors or ministers, presbyters or elders, deacons, etc.), but only as an auxiliary, not under any pretension to represent God on earth. All the members of the Church, they hold, are equally children of God and directly responsible before him. Christ's redeeming mission includes all who believe, without any need for intermediaries. Therefore, all the faithful together constitute the "universal priesthood." The clergymen charged with leadership differ from the other members of the Church only insofar as they undertake, by their own choice, missions of preaching, evangelizing, directing choirs, or other clerical duties.

[13]

THE NEW BEGINNING

The Transfiguration of Jesus

Jesus had allowed himself to give way to the discouragement that followed the defection of some of his disciples and the refusal of his contemporaries to understand him. Fleeing to Caesarea Philippi, he had begun to contemplate abandoning his ministry. But, even though their number was smaller, a group of followers (probably only the Twelve Apostles) had remained loyal, had tried to comfort him in his exile, had shown their own belief in his Messiahship. He felt hope and zeal beginning to grow again in his heart. Peter's announcement: "Thou art the Christ," which had at first frightened him, seemed less absurd to him now. The intensity of his own religious faith had even led him to see some sign that this was God's will. If he could rely on the loyalty of this little handful of people, if he had succeeded in so exalting them that they believed he was the expected Messiah, why should he not once more attempt the great mission? Why not, indeed, go out of Galilee, which was so resistant to his preaching, and carry the good tidings to the heart of Judea, to Jerusalem itself?

When Jesus announced this decision to his disciples, they too, after so many months of inactivity, were filled with new vigor—the master had not deceived them, he was ready now to launch the final drive for the creation of the kingdom. It was a new beginning!

The Synoptic Gospels chose to mark this new surge of activity with the story of a remarkable event: the Transfiguration of Jesus.[1]

One evening, six days after the new decision (Luke says it was eight days), Jesus called Peter, James, and John to accompany him in the ascent of "a high mountain"—that is, some ledge of Mount Hermon,[2] which looked down eighty-five hundred feet on the city of Caesarea Philippi (and not Mount Tabor, on which tradition locates the story, because Tabor is too far from that city and is not a mountain that could be called *excelsum*, since it is only some eighteen hundred feet high). It was the end of the day, and the sun was sinking behind the ridges of the mountain. One brilliant ray struck through the clouds and dazzled the eyes of the three Apostles. Jesus was walking ahead of them and suddenly they saw him "transfigured": surrounded by the last sunlight, his body seemed to vanish. "His raiment," Mark says, "became shining, exceeding white as snow; so as no fuller on earth can white them." Then all at once it seemed to the three disciples that Jesus stood between two figures who miraculously "appeared in glory": Moses and Elijah.

All three disciples prostrated themselves in awe and Peter stammered: "Master, it is good for us to be here; and let us make three tabernacles: one for thee, and one for Moses, and one for Elias [Elijah]." The Gospel of Mark adds: "For he wist not what to say." But Jesus did not reply to the foolish proposal.

Moses and Elijah had meanwhile disappeared in the shadow of a cloud, and a voice came out of it and said: "This is my beloved Son: hear him."

Mythologists and rationalists alike have labored prodigiously to find some plausible explanation of this amazing vision. Did one of the three Apostles (Luke says that they "were heavy with sleep") have a dream that he later related to the others as a fact?[3] Were the figures of Moses and Elijah perhaps two members of an Essene group who had set a meeting there with Jesus in order to encourage him to resume his preaching?[4] Is the story an adaptation of Biblical passages designed to put Jesus on the same level with Moses (on Mount Sinai) and with Elijah (who was carried up into heaven), or was it a hallucination of all three Apostles, the result of their limitless adoration of their master?[5]

But the story requires neither a mystical nor a realistic explanation. The Transfiguration is a myth that symbolizes the renewal of the ministry of Jesus: "It is a didactic illustration for a religious lesson. Here, in a single picture, is everything that the pupil has to remember: Moses with the Tables of the ancient Law, Elijah on behalf of all the prophets, Jesus bearing the new Law . . . and Peter, the cornerstone of the Church, with John and James. And, above them all, God the Father. The picture also has a mnemonic purpose: it helps one to remember the major points of the Church's doctrine."[6]

This is a milestone in the story of Jesus. The inauguration of his work of salvation, his role as redeemer, which for Paul coincides with his death and the Resurrection, is anticipated here in the Transfiguration (his own recognition of his Messiahship, confirmed by the voice of God out of the cloud). Later, it would be carried back to his baptism (again an investiture, with the voice of God from on high), and then still further to his birth, and finally to the Annunciation to Mary.

"Think Not That I Am Come to Send Peace"

Once more burning with zeal, and having newly consolidated his prestige in the eyes of the Apostles, Jesus left Caesarea Philippi and headed south, intending to stop first at Capernaum, his customary base, before going on toward Judea. But he was not unaware of the difficulties and the dangers inherent in his plan, and he had no intention of concealing them from his disciples. If they still wished to remain with him, they were entitled to know that they must endure hardships and not hesitate at obstacles:[7] "He that taketh not his cross, and followeth after me, is not worthy of me." The metaphor of taking up the cross could not logically have been employed by Jesus himself; it is a later figure of speech born among the Christians after the Nazarene's death.

"For whosoever will save his life," Jesus continued, "shall lose it: and whosoever will lose his life for my sake shall save it. For what is a man profited, if he shall gain the whole world, and lose his own soul? Or what shall a man give in exchange for his soul?" This is a warning of the end, derived from a Biblical psalm,[8] which plays on the double meaning of the word "life" ("soul"): he who is too much concerned with the needs of his physical life shall become so identical with the world, which is doomed, that he shall lose his spiritual life—his soul.[9]

"He that denieth me before men shall be denied before the angels of God."

Jesus wanted particularly to disabuse his disciples of a hope that he himself had overoptimistically aroused in their hearts: that the establishment of the kingdom was near. Jesus had come to recognize his mistake in putting too much faith in the religious maturity of his audiences, and he saw also that the wickedness of the world was still offering too much resistance. He would now have to limit himself to preaching "preparation" for the great final day, a task that might be protracted and arduous. He devoted himself therefore to making certain of at least a small nucleus of followers who could ultimately carry on his work after he was gone.

Almost as if to excuse to his disciples his own and their earlier naïve impatience, Jesus told them a parable: "A certain man had a fig tree planted in his vineyard; and he came and sought fruit thereon, and found none. Then said he unto the dresser of his vineyard, Behold, these three years I come seeking fruit on this fig tree, and find none: cut it down; why cumbereth it the ground? And he answering said unto him, Lord, let it alone this year also, till I shall dig about it, and dung it; and if it bear fruit, well; and if not, then after that thou shalt cut it down."[10]

In short, Jesus was asking the disciples to continue to have faith in him and to wait a little longer. If we contrast the pessimism of these later statements with the serenity and the wealth of confidence with which he had announced the kingdom in the beginning, we can imagine the dreadful days of bitterness through which he lived in the long months of idleness in some cave on Mount Hermon, and the storm that must have raged in his soul.

But now he could not go backward: "I am come to send fire on the earth," he admitted;[11] "and what will I if it be already kindled?" Then, since the Twelve were staring at him in amazement, he added, almost ironically: "Think not that I am come to send peace on earth: I come not to send peace, but a sword. For from henceforth there shall be five in one house divided, three against two, and two against three. The father shall be divided against the son, and the son against the father; the mother against the daughter, and the daughter against the mother; the mother-in-law against her daughter-in-law, and the daughter-in-law against her mother-in-law; and a man's foes shall be they of his own household. . . . If any man come to me, and hate not his father, and mother, and wife, and children, and brethren, and sisters, yea, and his own life also, he cannot be my disciple."[12]

And again: "Which of you, intending to build a tower, sitteth not down first, and counteth the cost, whether he have sufficient to finish it? Lest haply, after he hath laid the foundation, and is not able to finish it, all that behold it begin to mock him? . . . Or what king, going to make war against another king, sitteth not down first, and consulteth whether he be able with ten thousand to meet him that cometh against him with twenty thousand? . . . So likewise, whosoever he be of you that forsaketh not all that he hath, he cannot be my disciple."[13]

The choice that Jesus imposed was quite drastic: either to live for "this world" with its passions, its loyalties, its risks of sin, or to make a clear break in the hope of eternal salvation in the initiation of a revolutionarily altered world. And Jesus wished his disciples to have no further illusions: "Wide is the gate, and broad is the way that leadeth to destruction . . . strait is the gate, and narrow is the way, which leadeth unto life."[14]

This was the problem that, as the ancients remarked, had faced Hercules at the crossroads: the choice between the burdensome, difficult path of virtue and the easy, comfortable path of sin. But here it was no longer a case of the conscious, rational choice open to Hercules, but of an emotional commitment to a wholly unnatural and irrational standard of conduct (the rupture of family ties, the assumption of the cross, the abnegation of personal freedom, etc.), which implied the surrender of one's own will and one's possibilities of free election to a superior being in which one trusted blindly.

Jesus brooked neither discussion nor doubt on the subject: "And why call ye me Lord, Lord, and do not the things which I say? Whosoever cometh to me, and heareth my sayings, and doeth them, I will shew you to whom he is like: He is like a man which built an house, and digged deep, and laid the foundation on a rock: and when the flood arose, the stream beat vehemently upon that house, and could not shake it: for it was founded upon a rock. But he that heareth, and doeth not, is like a man that without a foundation built a house upon the earth; against which the stream did beat vehemently, and immediately it fell."[15]

Luke adds another parable: "When once the master of the house is risen up, and hath shut to the door, and ye begin to stand without, and to knock at the door, saying, Lord, Lord, open unto us; and he shall answer and say unto you, I know you not whence ye are: Then shall ye begin to say, We have eaten and drunk in thy presence, and thou hast taught in our streets. But he shall say, I tell you, I know you not whence ye are; depart from me, all ye workers of iniquity. There shall be weeping and gnashing of teeth, when ye shall see Abraham, and Isaac, and Jacob, and all the prophets, in the kingdom of God, and you yourselves thrust out. And they shall come from the east, and from the west, and from the north, and from the south, and shall sit down in the kingdom of God. And, behold, there are last which shall be first, and there are first which shall be last."[16]

Many of these paradoxical utterances of Jesus, evidently intended to root evil and selfishness out of the hearts of his followers, would if taken literally persuade many Christians into an unnatural denial of life, into a perversion of asceticism and isolation. The Gospel of Thomas says expressly: "Many stand outside at the door, but it is only the solitaries [*monachoi*] who will enter into the bridal chamber."[17] The authority on this Gospel, Jean Doresse, translates the Greek word as "perfect," pointing out, however, that it is to be understood as referring to those who abandon everything, even fathers, mothers, and brothers, in order to achieve perfection.[18]

It is easy to imagine the Apostles' dismay when they heard these instructions, and it seemed to them that the concrete kingdom of peace and happiness for which they had hoped was disappearing into the realm of the unattainable, or at least being indefinitely put off. Jesus was aware of this, and he tried to reassure them with a vague promise, which, however, once more set a finite time, even if in rather broad terms, for the inception of the expected kingdom: "Verily I say unto you, That there be some of them that stand here, which shall not taste of death, till they have seen the kingdom of God come with power."[19]

Later, John the Evangelist pretended that this promise had been made to him personally and confirmed by Jesus in these words, after a jealous objection by Simon Peter: "If I will that he tarry till I come, what is that to thee?"[20]

"Who Among Us Shall Be the Greatest?"

As he was speaking, Jesus closely observed the disciples, who were walking beside him, in order to see how they were receiving his counsels, and now and then he turned to study those who followed behind him. He saw that what he had said was being much debated, and he promised himself that he would question them as soon as he could.

But meanwhile they had reached Capernaum. It was on the very day when all adult Israelites had to pay a special tax, as a contribution to the costs of rebuilding the Temple; it amounted to one half-shekel, the equivalent of the Greek didrachma—$\delta\iota\delta\rho\alpha\chi\mu\text{ο}\nu$. Hence, it must have been the end of the month of Adar, the last in the Hebrew calendar, for we know that this collection was made at that time. In other words, it was March of A.D. 28. The exile of Jesus in Caesarea Philippi had lasted four or five months.

The tax collectors intercepted the group as it entered the town: "Doth not your master pay tribute?"[21]

Peter responded affirmatively, and immediately approached Jesus to report the question. Jesus hesitated a moment, then smiled and said to him: "What thinkest thou, Simon? of whom do the kings of the earth take custom or tribute? of their own children, or of strangers?"

"Of strangers."

"Then are the children [of the kingdom of God] free [of assessment for God's Temple]. Notwithstanding, lest we should offend them, go thou to the sea, and cast a hook, and take up the fish that first cometh up; and when thou hast opened his mouth, thou shalt find a piece of money; that take, and give unto them, for me and thee."

According to the Greek text, the coin was a $\chi\rho\upsilon\sigma\text{ο}\hat{\upsilon}\varsigma$ $\sigma\tau\alpha\tau\acute{\eta}\rho$ (chrusous statēr), about twenty-five drachmas (not four, as many commentators say), enough to pay a didrachma (two drachmas) for Jesus and the same for each of the Apostles, not merely for Jesus and

Peter. The last part of the quotation ("for me and thee"), indeed, is not found in most Greek manuscripts. The incident shows that Jesus intended to resume his ministry without provoking trouble, for a refusal to pay the tax would have seemed an insult to the dignity of the Temple and too overt an affront to the Hebrew law. But this essential significance has often escaped the exegetes, who prefer to concentrate their attention on the "miracle" of the coin found in the fish's mouth, or to take pleasure in yet another proof of the divine powers of Jesus, without taking into account the reasons why the miracle was performed; or else they simply deny its historical accuracy.[22]

It is quite credible that the twenty-five drachmas were in reality the proceeds from Peter's sale of a large quantity of fish after he had done a day's work on the Lake of Gennesaret.[23] Or perhaps the detail of the coin in the fish's mouth arose out of a curious misunderstanding. The lake frequently yields fish on whose bodies there are two circular markings, very similar to coins, and these fish have a remarkable incubation procedure: the male collects all the eggs laid by the female and keeps them in his gills and his mouth until the gestatory period has been completed; then, with a violent effort, he spews out the whole school of baby fish.[24]

As soon as Jesus and all the Apostles had entered the house that sheltered them in Capernaum, Jesus turned to the group, whose discussion had aroused his curiosity during the journey, and he asked: "What was it that ye disputed among yourselves by the way?"[25] But they hesitated to answer, and looked at the floor. Jesus, however, persisted, and finally one of them admitted that they had been debating which of them should be the greatest in the kingdom of God. Jesus sat down, summoned all of them to him, and began: "If any man desire to be first, the same shall be last of all, and servant of all."[26]

He paused a moment, to search his mind for a parable that would serve to fix the thought more firmly in their memories. As he looked about, he noticed a little boy who had left his play and was watching him openmouthed. He embraced the boy affectionately, drew him close, and, surrounded by his ambitious disciples, he began to speak again: "Whosoever therefore shall humble himself as this little child, the same is greatest in the kingdom of heaven." What

Jesus was saying, in other words, was that whoever understood a child would understand his meaning.

The disciples were dumfounded. This was an ordinary little boy like all the others who were, unfortunately, so numerous in those days: ragged, tattered, his eyes already infected, his face marked by skin eruptions and constantly vexed by flies[27]—a child whose parents took special pains not to wash him or keep him clean, not only because water was so scarce but because dirty eyes and a dirty face were supposed to ward off the evil eye.

To emphasize what he had said first (that one must be the last and the least and the servant of all), Jesus chose such a boy as an illustration because of the simplicity of character of these children, their artless faith, their resigned submission to the wishes of their elders. He who sought to be first, to earn admission into the kingdom of heaven, must learn the capacity to abdicate his own rights, his own ambitions, his own privileges: "for we shall all stand before the judgment seat of [God]," Paul says,[28] and so none should presume that his deserts are greater than another's.

Jesus resorted to another parable: "Which of you, having a servant plowing, or feeding cattle, will say unto him by and by, when he is come from the field, Go and sit down to meat? And will not rather say unto him, Make ready, wherewith I may sup, and gird thyself, and serve me, till I have eaten and drunken; and afterward thou shalt eat and drink? Doth he thank that servant because he did the things that were commanded of him? I trow not. So likewise ye, when ye shall have done all those things which are commanded you, say, We are unprofitable servants, we have done that which was our duty to do."[29]

The necessity of being humble in order to earn admission into the kingdom is further explained in another parable in Luke: "When thou art bidden of any man to a wedding, sit not down in the highest room; lest a more honorable man than thou be bidden of him; And he that bade him and thee come and say to thee, Give this man place; and thou begin with shame to take the lowest room. But when thou art bidden, go and sit down in the lowest room; that when he that bade thee cometh, he may say unto thee, Friend, go up higher: then shalt thou have worship in the presence of them that sit at meat with thee. For whosoever exalteth himself shall be abased; and he that humbleth himself shall be exalted."[30]

It seems to me that this parable, the attribution of which to Jesus is certainly erroneous, does not exactly exemplify the pure concept of disinterested humility that was in the Nazarene's mind, but rather is an incitement to a calculating hypocrisy. Jesus particularly counseled his disciples not to be concerned with the opinions of others and to rely only on the recognition that God would accord to their virtues: "The disciple is not above his master, nor the servant above his lord. . . . If they have called the master of the house Beelzebub, how much more shall they call them of his household? Fear them not therefore. . . . And fear not them which kill the body . . . but rather fear him which is able to destroy both soul and body. . . . Are not two sparrows sold for a farthing? and one of them shall not fall on the ground without your Father. But the very hairs of your head are all numbered. Fear ye not therefore; ye are of more value than many sparrows."[31]

Be Not a Stumbling Block

All these lessons were an excellent rebuke to the vanity of the Apostles. But they did not understand, and they inquired again how they should behave in order to be like children. And Jesus explained: "Whosoever shall offend one of these little ones that believe in me [that is, offend a man as simple as a child[32]], it is better for him that a millstone were hanged about his neck, and he were cast into the sea."[33] Paul was to elaborate: "Let us therefore not judge one another any more: but judge this rather, that no man put a stumbling block or an occasion to fall in his brother's way."[34]

The meaning of the word σκάνδαλον (skandalon), used here by the Gospels, is really, as we have had occasion earlier to note, "doubt," "obstacle," "stumbling block," with a broad graduation of connotations—to do evil to another, to cover another with disgrace, to defame, to lend money usuriously, etc.[35] The very different meaning that is given today to the word "scandal" (an action that offends modesty or good taste) has seduced many commentators into the mistake of interpreting the Gospels' words as an exhortation by

Jesus to modesty and to respect for childish innocence. This is a reading that, aside from its etymological error, makes no sense in the specific instance to which it is related. Actually, this scriptural fragment deals with the requirement that the followers of Jesus accept his teaching entirely, adhering to the rigid line of conduct that is imposed on them. They are to be obedient and subservient to God, as children are to their parents. The "scandal," then, as Paul properly saw, is in falling away from the law of loving one's neighbor and in attempting, through bad example, to attack the sureness and purity of another's faith, or in insinuating doubt into his soul.[36]

Jesus, indeed, pointed out how the true Christian should behave to avoid being a stumbling block even to himself: "If thy hand or thy foot offend thee [insofar as they make one sin], cut them off, and cast them from thee: it is better for thee to enter into life [the kingdom] halt or maimed, rather than having two hands or two feet to be cast into everlasting fire. And if thine eye offend thee, pluck it out, and cast it from thee: it is better for thee to enter into life with one eye, rather than having two eyes to be cast into hell fire."[37]

In the Gospel of Mark, these words are immediately followed by a corollary that the other Synoptics insert in different places[38] and that not all commentators, therefore, believe should be read with the passage just quoted: "Salt is good: but if the salt have lost his saltness, wherewith will ye season it? Have salt in yourselves, and have peace one with another."

Taken out of its context, the passage is customarily interpreted as a flattering comparison between the properties of salt and the Apostles' task of "giving savor" to their words when they preached the lessons taught to them by Jesus. But this interpretation is a pure product of imagination, because it is not justified by any of the contexts in which the passage is found in the Gospels. Collated, however, with what Jesus had said earlier, the fragment can be understood as a comparison between tasteless salt and disciples who have lost the sense of their religious obligation.[39] Certainly Jesus was thinking of the "salt of the covenant"[40] prescribed in Leviticus to purify and consecrate sacrificial meat.[41]

The comparison between the eye and the light, too, which occurs in Matthew and Luke,[42] should be related to this concept; in no way does it have the meaning of an exhortation to moral purity that is so often ascribed to it. The form in which it has been handed down by the Synoptic Gospels can in truth give rise to an ambiguity of meaning: "The light of the body is the eye: therefore when thine eye is single, thy whole body also is full of light; but when thine eye is evil, thy body also is full of darkness. Take heed therefore that the light which is in thee be not darkness." Had the exegetes documented themselves better, instead of fantasying, they would not have fallen into absurd commentary in this case, either. One might annotate the excerpt just quoted with a sentence from the Gospel of Thomas, which is quite clear: "If a light exists inside a luminous one, then it gives light to the whole world; but if it does not give light, it means that it is a darkness."[43] In other words, faith should illuminate and guide men, or it is worthless.

All these discussions between Jesus and his Apostles on the necessity for the believer to keep absolute faith with God's law must have suggested much later, when the Church had become a complex organization, the course to be adopted, by analogy, toward any "member" of the "body" of the Church whose evil conduct had made him a "stumbling block." The demands of community life led to the formulation of a system for disciplining those who transgressed the rules. The Gospel of Matthew even includes, as an appendix to the principles laid down by Jesus, a compendium of disciplinary rules that presupposes some ecclesiastical authority endowed with enforcement powers, which obviously cannot have existed in the time of Jesus: "If thy brother [that is, a member of the community] shall trespass against thee, go and tell him his fault between thee and him alone: if he shall hear thee, thou hast gained thy brother. But if he will not hear thee, then take with thee one or two more, that in the mouth of two or three witnesses every word may be established. And if he shall neglect to hear them, tell it unto the church: but if he neglect to hear the church, let him be unto thee as an heathen man and a publican. Verily I say unto you, Whatsoever ye shall bind on earth, shall be bound in heaven; and whatsoever ye shall loose on earth, shall be loosed in heaven."[44]

Has Matthew forgotten here that only a little earlier he had conferred this power on Peter alone, and does he now extend it to all the faithful even when they are gathered together in a congregation, as the Protestants believe?[45] If in this matter too, as in so many other details, the early Church was organized in conformity with Jewish customs, then the Protestant thesis is correct. Much earlier, the Old Testament had stated the requirement that in any litigation the testimony of two or three witnesses be presented to priests and judges in a formal sitting.[46] The highest court had the power to impose three degrees of punishment: *nīddui*, or the temporary banishment of the offender (usually for thirty days), followed by a fine payable in money; *ḥērem*, or permanent banishment of the offender from synagogue ceremonies, from public teaching, and from all business; and *shammāta*, or execution.

In the Catholic Church, these three Jewish penalties roughly correspond to the interdict (exclusion from certain religious functions); excommunication (of two grades: *excommunicatus tolerandus*, a person barred only from the sacraments and from divine service, and *excommunicatus vitandus*, one to whom all civil and social dealings with believers are forbidden); and finally, at least until the seventeenth century, death, preferably at the stake.

The first case of excommunication was probably that decided by Paul against a brother of the community of Corinth, who was living in sin with his father's wife.[47] But the sinner may have repented his offense later, for Paul suggested to the Church of Corinth that it "ought rather to forgive him, and comfort him, lest perhaps such a one should be swallowed up with overmuch sorrow."[48]

The Parables of Forgiveness

If one eliminates the insertion that contains the rules of discipline, the Gospel of Matthew no longer presents any abruptness of transition between its exhortations to follow God's law without presenting "stumbling blocks" to one's fellows and its counsels of toleration and forgiveness.[49] In the latter, undoubtedly, its text is much more appropriate to the true spirit of the teachings of Jesus.

Peter asked him: "Lord, how oft shall my brother sin against me, and I forgive him? till seven times?"

"I say not unto thee, Until seven times; but, Until seventy times seven."

Then Jesus tells a parable. It is that of the "servant without compassion," whose master, out of pity, had forgiven him a debt of ten thousand talents, but who in his turn would not remit a fellow servant's tiny obligation of a hundred pence; his master therefore punished him by revoking his own forgiveness. "So likewise," Jesus observed, "shall my heavenly Father do also unto you, if ye from your hearts forgive not every one his brother their trespasses."

The parable has a double moral. God will withdraw a pardon already granted if the beneficiary is wanting in compassion for his fellows,[50] or he will grant forgiveness only to those who in their turn know how to forgive.[51] It is the same principle stated in the Lord's Prayer: "Forgive us our trespasses, as we forgive those who trespass against us."

Other parables, reported not only by Matthew, are perhaps even more effective in making clear the need to forgive those who do wrong, to be merciful to those who have erred, to be ready to lead them in charity back to the right path, as a reflection of the absolution that God grants to those who offer proof of repentance.

God rejoices over a sinner who repents, one of these parables says, like a shepherd who recovers "a sheep which is gone astray" after he has left ninety-nine others untended while he searches for the lost one.[52] In my opinion, there is nothing paradoxical or absurd in the moral of this parable,[53] even though the Evangelist may have expressed himself rather badly. It does not mean that God (the shepherd) abandons his care of the ninety-nine sheep in order to find the only one that has wandered away; he knows he can safely leave them untended for the time, because they are docile and contented, and they will not wander.

What is quite strange is the Gnostic interpretation of this parable. Doresse summarizes[54] that contained in Valentinus' *Gospel of Truth,* which is quoted by Irenaeus:[55] since the ancients, who counted on their fingers, used the left hand for numbers through ninety-nine and then began with one hundred on the right hand, the "strayed hundredth sheep" was the lost soul that completed the tally and represented the right hand, which was the symbol of perfection!

The joy of God at the return of a sinner to the faith, another parable says, is like that of a woman who loses one of her ten pieces of silver, sweeps and searches her house for it, going into the dark places with a candle, and at last finds it.[56]

But the most revealing is the Parable of the Prodigal Son.[57] Even if it is not a report of a fact, the story is effectively realistic because it has a believable base. In a border area like Galilee, there must have been many instances of young men, whether impelled by a spirit of adventure or compelled by need, who left home in search of work,[58] like the son in the parable, wandering through foreign lands on their anticipated inheritances and running through their resources in a short time. To dramatize the straits to which the young man was reduced, Luke tells us that he had to be satisfied with the leavings of swine—not "acorns," as it is so often translated, but "husks" ($\kappa\epsilon\rho\alpha\tau\iota\omega\nu$, keratiōn) of the pod-like fruit of the carob tree, which abounds in Palestine; the thick, dark leaves provide refreshing shade for man and beast, and the fruit is extremely delicious. But the detail of the swine is inaccurate, because the Jews were forbidden to breed them.

Theologians view the second part of the parable as the paradigm of the sacrament of penitence: the examination of conscience, when the prodigal son "came to himself"; the repentance, when he decided to return to his father; the confession, when he said: "Father, I have sinned"; the satisfaction of his guilt, when he acknowledged: "[I] am no more worthy to be called thy son: make me as one of thy hired servants"; the absolution, when his father kissed him.[59]

Quite apart from this sacramental superstructure, the original purpose of the parable was to illustrate the necessity for indulgence toward those who sin, and the central figure is not the prodigal son but the forgiving father,[60] who is the symbol of God himself.

"He That Is Not with Me . . ."

The New Testament also explores the theme of mercy and tolerance in the relations between the Christian Church and other religious confessions, but with results quite different from before. The Gospel of Mark introduces the problem,[61] supposing that John the Apostle had interrupted Jesus with what was intended to be a proof of his zeal: "Master, we saw one casting out devils in thy name, and he followeth not us: and we forbade him."

But Jesus disappointed the sedulous disciple, who must certainly have expected to be praised: "Forbid him not: for there is no man which shall do a miracle in my name, that can lightly speak evil of me. For he that is not against us, is on our part."

But the Gospel of Matthew, although it does not recount the same story, gives the final sentence in diametrical opposition: "He that is not with me is against me."[62] The Gospel of Luke, with its usual superficial approach, gives both versions, only slightly separated.[63]

Which of the two forms represents the real thought of Jesus? We cannot allow a facile sentimentalism to persuade us to judge Jesus by the mature standards of modern liberalism, which uncompromisingly rejects every kind of intolerance. The harsh reproaches that Jesus directed at the Pharisees because they persisted in their error, his fateful predictions for all those who did not accept his gospel, his specific demand on the Apostles for unconditional obedience—all these clearly reveal a man who was so convinced he was the fount of the sole truth that he would not admit of any other. All his generous insistence on *caritas*, on harmony, on brotherhood, then, applied only within the narrow limits of those who believed in him; the rest of the world was barred. Like all the Jews of his time, his overwhelming belief in the unique nature of the national religion prevented him from even imagining a tolerant relation with other faiths. Nonetheless, he was also so confident of the force of expansion of his own gospel, so certain of the inevitable triumph of the Messianic kingdom, that he could declare that the separation of the "wheat" from the "chaff" would be accomplished only in "the last days," at the harvest itself, and in any case through the judgment of God, not that of men.

After his death, however, the historical Church quickly manifested a tendency not only to consider itself a sect of perfect beings and therefore to scorn any communication with the world around it, but also to arrogate to itself the right to judge that world. The apocalyptic literature of the first centuries, almost entirely anti-Roman, and the apologetic literature from Tertullian to Lactantius are characterized by such a hatred and intolerance for pagan beliefs that one hardly knows whether to justify them as the effect or to view them as the cause of the persecutions suffered by the Christians.

What is more, the obsession with protecting from every taint of error that truth of which the heads of the Church professed to be the sole depositaries, while they crystallized it in dogmas and articles of faith, very quickly led to the harshest condemnations even of those brothers who dared to suggest varying interpretations of it. An unbroken record of intolerance and intransigence is provided by the history of the various Councils, almost all of which were convoked for the purpose of condemning as heresy or apostasy whatever opinion did not perfectly conform to the beliefs of the highest religious authority of the time (a pope or an emperor). One might list also the multitude of victims of the Inquisition, and so on. Blind submission to the authority of the Church is a more important duty for a Catholic than the performance of charitable works or faith in Christ: "*Foris ab ecclesia constitutus,*" St. Augustine wrote, "*aeterno supplicio punieris, etiamsi pro Christi nomine vivus incendiaris*" ("He who puts himself outside the authority of the Church will be damned to eternal torture, even if he allows himself to be burned alive for the sake of Christ").[64]

This authoritarian foundation, over the centuries, has allowed the Church to consolidate its organizational structure while moving ever further from those principles of tolerance and mercy that are at the very basis of the teachings of Jesus.

From the very beginning, the Church has had to do battle against two kinds of "error": doctrinal and disciplinary errors on the part of brothers who questioned dogma or who rebelled at the excessive authority of the bishop of Rome, and moral errors on the part of scientists, philosophers, writers, who propounded scientific principles, theories, and concepts that did not accord with the doctrine of the Church. One effect of its obduracy toward brothers who fell into error has been the erosion of the framework of Christianity and the growth of heretical sects, schismatic churches, and reform movements, so that today, although Christians total approximately eight hundred million, almost half are outside the Catholic Church (the Eastern Orthodox, the Anglicans, the Protestants, the Copts, the Nestorians, the Ethiopians, etc.); and the proliferation of indiscriminate condemnations by means of bulls and encyclicals, even in modern times (*Miraris vos* in 1832, *Syllabus errorum* in 1864, *Pascendi* in 1907, *Divini Redemptoris* in 1937, etc.),[65] against rationalism, modernism, scientism, etc., has been a ponderous but effective brake applied to the advance of culture in Catholic countries.

Today especially, when it must contend with a world that claims as its greatest victory the democratic conception of society, which sees genuine new ideals of civilization and morality in the overthrow of parochialism and racialism, in tolerance for differing political ideologies and divergent opinions of other kinds, which recognizes the high ethical virtue of divorce as a remedy for matrimonial mistakes, of birth control as a form of insuring freedom from hunger, of the renunciation of war, the stubbornness and backwardness of the Church of Rome trouble the minds of Catholics. Indeed, since, unlike Protestants, they are not equipped to know how to comport themselves according to the imperatives of strong personal conscience in the face of unforeseen conditions, they look to the Church as an indispensable bulwark and a guide to morals and customs, and they wait for it to take the initiative.

There is another reason the Church is so reluctant to become contemporary: it is afraid that its subjects, accustomed to following it passively, will not know how to make good use of their own freedom. The Church sees itself as the final bastion in the defense of a particular ethical conception of life, and it cannot alter a line of conduct that has been traditional for twenty centuries lest it stir doubt among the faithful on the worth of everything it has taught in that time.

Hence, the results of Vatican Council II may have been a source of disappointment to all those who, with an ingenuous trust in the Council and in the candor of Pope John XXIII (1959–63), had hoped for a bold break with the past; but they were not surprising to those who coldly and rationally reckoned with the exigencies of the Church.

Carefully read, the final documents of the Council represent not so much a step taken by the Church toward the world as an invitation to the world to come toward the Church. Nor could it have been otherwise. The ecumenical dialogue with the "separated brothers" could have no other meaning for the Church of Rome than the return of those brothers to its bosom, since the Church considers itself the unique repository of truth, and a step by it toward the others would mean that truth and error would be indiscriminately placed on the same level. To exonerate the Jews of Jesus' time of the charge of deicide would not only give the lie to what the sacred texts, however wrongly, present as a historical fact, but also strike directly at the basic points of the Christological conception (the "betrayal" by the Jews was a necessity, predicted earlier by Holy Writ). To accept divorce, birth control, etc., would be an admission of the possibility of modification in that institution of matrimony which the Church for its own reasons, wholly fallacious though they be, as we shall see, considers a sacrament originated by Jesus.

[14]

IN SAMARIA

Jesus Leaves Galilee

Jesus had not gone back to Capernaum with the intention of remaining there long. But we have no means of knowing whether he prepared calmly for his departure for Jerusalem or whether instead it was undertaken impulsively—almost in flight—after new threats by Herod Antipas. The Gospels of Matthew and Mark say only that he left Galilee and went to Judea;[1] Luke leaves the matter open to speculation, because he reports the departure for Jerusalem twice, each time with different details. First he says that one day Jesus decided to start for Jerusalem because the time was come that he should resume his preaching of the good tidings. Actually, when Jerome translated the New Testament into Latin, he gave this passage a false meaning, since it contains the word ἀνάλημψις (*analēmpsis*), which means "renewal," "recommencement," "resumption," and which allows the suggestion that Jesus knew he was to be crucified in Jerusalem and assumed into heaven. The error has been perpetuated in translations into modern languages, in such forms as: "the time of his assumption was at hand." Many modern Bibles, the King James among them, read: "the time was come that he should be received up."[2] But the word *analēmpsis* is used in the active sense ("resumption" or "reassumption," that is, the act of resuming or reassuming) and cannot be read in the passive ("to be assumed," "to be taken up," "to be received up"). The author of the Acts of the Apostles—and so much the better if, as tradition says, it was Luke—

is careful to use the passive of ἀναλαμβάνω (analambanō) to indicate the assumption of Jesus into heaven.[3]

A little later, however, Luke reports that one day—the same day (in ipsa die) on which Jesus had told his disciples the parable of the master of the house who closes his door on those who knock—some Pharisees came to him and said: "Get thee out, and depart hence; for Herod will kill thee."[4] Was this a lie on the part of the Pharisees to get Jesus out of Galilee, as Alfred Loisy wonders,[5] or did Herod really want Jesus to be warned so that the tetrarch would not again have to resort to violence, as he had done with John? In any case, one can be sure the Pharisees were acting in the interest not of Jesus but of Herod Antipas. The warning they gave the Nazarene was anything but a mark of sympathy.

Resigning himself to obeying Herod, but allowing himself the satisfaction of delivering a gratifying insult in the process, Jesus replied: "Go ye, and tell that fox, Behold, I cast out devils, and I do cures to-day and to-morrow, and the third day I shall be perfected. Nevertheless I must walk to-day, and to-morrow, and the day following: for it cannot be that a prophet perish out of Jerusalem."

According to the sacred interpretation, as might easily be guessed, Jesus is speaking here of his own passion. But probably he sought only to request three days of grace, the time he would need to cross the border of Galilee and get outside Herod's jurisdiction. The reference to prophets who die in Jerusalem may have been suggested to him by a tragic occurrence of which he had been told not long before.[6] A group of pilgrims from Galilee (perhaps accompanied by a "prophet") had been slaughtered by the Romans while they were in the midst of offering their sacrifices. It is possible, of course, that the group might have created some sort of trouble in the city and so provoked the reprisal by the occupation forces. The German scholar Heinrich Holtzmann offers the theory that they were members of a seditious group and that among those arrested was the famous Barabbas,[7] who was certainly a patriot and a political "prophet" and who was tried at almost the same time as Jesus.

Jesus had said of the news that the pilgrims' deaths were no proof of their guilt; but their fate should be a warning to everyone.[8] He cited also the eighteen residents of Jerusalem who had been killed when a tower of Siloam fell on them. Had they been punished by divine justice because their sins were greater than those of all the other people of the city? Certainly not. But anyone might die by violence while he was in a state of sin, and that was sufficient evidence of the urgency of adopting a new life.

Now, when the Pharisees were urging him to lose no time in leaving, Jesus permitted himself another sorrowful observation: "O Jerusalem, Jerusalem, which killeth the prophets, and stonest them that are sent unto thee: How often would I have gathered thy children together, as a hen doth gather her brood under her wings!" He turned then to the people with him, grieving that, out of too much love for the Galileans, he had so long deferred this task. "And ye would not! Behold, your house is left unto you desolate: and verily I say unto you, Ye shall not see me, until the time come when ye shall say, Blessed is he that cometh in the name of the Lord."[9]

In Samaria

Jesus was much embittered by the unbelief and the indifference with which he had been received by his countrymen, and, after he had announced his definite departure, he could not hold back a violent curse: "Woe unto thee, Chorazin! woe unto thee, Bethsaida! for if the mighty works which were done in you had been done in Tyre and Sidon, they would have repented long ago. . . . But I say unto you, It shall be more tolerable for Tyre and Sidon at the day of judgment, than for you. And thou, Capernaum, which art exalted unto heaven, shalt be brought down to hell: for if the mighty works, which have been done in thee, had been done in Sodom, it would have remained until this day. But I say unto you, that it shall be more tolerable for the land of Sodom in the day of judgment, than for thee."[10] With these dismal predictions, which have all the qualities of threatening Biblical prophecies, Jesus bade a final farewell to his homeland without any affection for those places where he had spent his childhood and where his fearful mother wept in silence.

What route did Jesus take in order to reach Judea? Matthew and Mark say that he "passed beyond Jordan." But there are two reasons this statement is unacceptable. First of all, Transjordan, or at least that part of it that was then called Perea, was dangerous for Jesus because it was within Herod Antipas' jurisdiction. In the second place, Luke and John say instead that he went down through Samaria, and the wealth of detail offered by them makes it difficult to disregard everything they have to recount. Some, in an effort to bring all four Gospels into harmony, suppose that only Jesus, James, and John (who are specifically mentioned as having been in Samaria) took this route, while Peter and the rest of the Apostles, with some other disciples, crossed the Jordan into Perea and later, with the women who were already in the Nazarene's service, rejoined the smaller group.[11]

The journey through Samaria would in no way contradict the earlier prohibition that Jesus imposed on the Apostles against working in such areas; this was not a matter of preaching now, but simply a means of shortening the distance.[12] Nevertheless, the Gospels do not scant the mutual hostility between Galileans and Samaritans. Luke says that Jesus had barely entered Samaria when he sent his companions into the nearest city to see how the people would react to his presence. The result of the exploration was not encouraging: the Samaritans refused to admit him.

The province of Samaria, which lay between Galilee and Judea, was inhabited by a mixed population of Israelites and descendants of Assyrian colonists who had settled there during the period of Assyrian domination. The Samaritans professed Judaism, but had broken off all religious relations with the two bordering provinces, and they did not adhere to the cult of the Temple of Jerusalem. This explains their aloofness to these pilgrims out of Galilee.

Wounded by such hostility, Jesus exclaimed: "The foxes have holes, and the birds of the air have nests; but the Son of man [I] hath not where to lay his head."[13]

James and John, the two sons of Zebedee, sought to prove their devotion when they saw their master's sorrow: "Lord, wilt thou that we command fire to come down from heaven, and consume them?"[14]

But Jesus rebuked them: "Ye know not what manner of spirit ye are of. For the Son of man [I] is not come to destroy men's lives, but to save them."

It was after this incident that Jesus, when his anger had abated, affectionately teased the two brothers with the nickname of Boanerges ("Sons of Thunder").

Perhaps only to emphasize the haste with which Jesus and his companions were compelled to travel through inhospitable Samaria, Luke tells two more brief stories.[15] A certain man wanted to join them, but first he asked leave to bid farewell to his family. "No man having put his hand to the plow," Jesus replied, "and looking back, is fit for the kingdom of God." In other words, when one has taken so grave a decision as that of following Jesus, one cannot be concerned with anything else. Similarly, another man, who asked permission to bury his father before he became one of the disciples, was told by the Nazarene: "Let the dead bury their dead."

There have been various interpretations of this curious statement. According to Loisy, Bultmann, and others, it alludes to a proverb whose meaning has since been lost; Perles offers the reading: "Leave the dead to the gravediggers," but he does not offer any basis for it; de Grandmaison and most of the Catholic commentators prefer an allegorical meaning: "Let him who is not interested in the kingdom—that is, him who is dead in spirit—bury those who are dead according to the flesh."[16]

It amazes me that it has occurred to none of these scholars that in Aramaic the word for "the dead" is *mēthā* and that it is easily confused with *māthā*, which means "the villagers." Hence, without resorting to intricate hypotheses, I believe the sentence should be corrected to read: "Let the people of your village bury the dead." This does not detract from the exhortation to abandon worldly concerns if one wishes to accept the discipline of Jesus.

Taking advantage of Jesus' journey through Samaria, Luke inserts an incident[17] that is intended to demonstrate how a real will to goodness can sometimes be found in so-called unbelievers, the same purpose served by Luke's earlier parable of Pauline inspiration—the episode of the Good Samaritan, who generously helped a stranger whom he found injured in the road, while a Pharisee and a Levite passed by on the other side. In this instance, too, the unbeliever is a Samaritan, who, cured of leprosy with nine other afflicted Jews, is the only one of them who feels impelled to turn round and thank Jesus.

The Woman of Samaria

In the Gospel of John, however, we find a very beautiful tale,[18] which, though it is not historically true and has only an allegorical and instructive value,[19] fits appropriately into the story of the life of Jesus: his encounter with the woman of Samaria.

They met, according to John, in the outskirts of the city of Sychar, on the exact site of the famous well of Jacob into which, the Bible says, Joseph was cast by his brothers with murderous intent, before they decided to sell him as a slave. For a long time, it was thought that this site should be identified with the modern village of 'Askar, very near the Jordan.[20] But "Sychar" would seem to be a corruption of "Shechem," the modern Balatah, at the foot of Mount Gerizim, which was holy to the Samaritans and on which they had built a temple that was destroyed by John Hyrcanus in 129 B.C.[21]

It was noon, the Evangelist says, and the day was hot; in fact, as we know, it was the end of the month of Adar (the middle of March). At that season in Palestine the grain is already high in the fields, and the first fruits are ripe in the orchards. The rains, which are copious in the preceding month, have almost abated. In a short while, they will have ceased altogether, and until the beginning of October the people must subsist on the rain water that they have collected in tanks. The luckier ones may have natural springs on their land. The fresh water from these, in differentiation from what is stored, is called *aqua viva* ("living water").[22]

Jesus, wearied from his march, sat down by that fountain. Meanwhile, the disciples went into the nearby village of Shechem to buy food. A Samaritan woman approached the well to fetch water. "Give me to drink," Jesus requested.

"How is it," the woman replied rather ironically, "that thou, being a Jew, askest drink of me, which am a woman of Samaria?"

Jesus was vexed. "If thou knewest . . . who it is that saith to thee, Give me to drink, thou wouldest have asked of him, and he would have given thee living water."

"Sir, thou hast nothing to draw with, and the well is deep: from whence then hast thou that living water? Art thou greater than our father Jacob, which gave us the well, and drank thereof himself, and his children, and his cattle?"

"Whosoever drinketh of this water shall thirst again," Jesus said: "but whosoever drinketh of the water that I shall give him shall never thirst."

"Sir," the woman said then, "give me this water, that I thirst not, neither come hither to draw."

"Go, call thy husband, and come hither."

"I have no husband."

"Thou hast well said," Jesus smiled, ". . . for thou hast had five husbands; and he whom thou now hast is not thy husband; in that saidst thou truly."

The woman blushed, for Jesus had recognized that he was dealing with one whose morals were not overrigid. "Sir," she said, "I perceive that thou art a prophet." Now she understood the hidden meaning of the earlier words of Jesus, his reference to "living water," and, setting her pitcher on the ground, she pointed a finger at the peak of Mount Gerizim and said earnestly: "Our fathers worshiped in this mountain: and ye say that in Jerusalem is the place where men ought to worship."

"Woman, believe me," Jesus interrupted gently; "the hour cometh, when ye shall neither in this mountain, nor yet at Jerusalem, worship the Father. Ye worship ye know not what: we know what we worship: for salvation is of the Jews. But the hour cometh, and now is, when the true worshipers shall worship the Father in spirit."

The woman said: "I know that Messias [Messiah] cometh: . . . when he is come, he will tell us all things."

"I that speak unto thee am he."

The woman was astounded. But she had no time in which to answer, for at that very moment the disciples returned from Shechem with their purchases. They were shocked to see their master debating with a woman, but none of them asked him to explain. She, meanwhile, ill at ease before the frank stares of so many strangers, started back to the village, forgetting the pitcher she had set on the ground. Then the disciples drew near, showing Jesus what they had bought, and urged him: "Master, eat."

But the Nazarene was deep in thought: he was speculating on the reaction that his words would evoke if the woman repeated them to the people of Shechem. She would be sure to do so. What he had said was too unbelievable, and simply because she was a woman she would be unable to refrain from discussing it with everyone she knew. So, when the disciples reminded him of food, Jesus replied, almost as if he were talking to himself: "I have meat to eat that ye know not of."

The disciples questioned one another: "Hath any man brought him ought to eat?"

He explained. "My meat is to do the will of him that sent me. . . . Say not ye, There are yet four months, and then cometh harvest? . . . He that reapeth receiveth wages, and gathereth fruit unto life eternal: that both he that soweth and he that reapeth may rejoice together. And herein is that saying true, One soweth, and another reapeth. I sent you to reap that whereon ye bestowed no labor; other men labored, and ye are entered into their labors."

The disciples bowed their heads at their master's reproaches, which in truth they felt were unwarranted.

The Gospel of John ends the long story by saying that some of the people of Shechem, excited by the woman's tales, went to hear Jesus, and for two days he was housed in the town.

The Question of Marriage

Instead of proceeding due south from Shechem in a straight line, Jesus and his companions found it more suitable to take a diagonal course so that they would reach a point near the Jordan on the road that Simon Peter and the other disciples had taken across Perea. Thus the two groups rejoined in order to enter Judea together. But they may first have allowed themselves a few days of rest, because they were still on "the coasts of Judea" when, according to Matthew and Mark,[23] Jesus and the Apostles engaged in a prolonged and interesting discussion on the question of marriage.[24]

In Palestine, the family was ruled entirely by the man. The wife, who was purchased, was an instrument, a chattel of the head of the family, who could even be returned to the seller, or, if she should "find no favor in his [the husband's] eyes,"[25] could be put away by means of a *gēt* (a "bill of divorce"); she, for her part, had no rights and no authority. The Hebrews' racial pride outlawed marriage with foreigners. The purpose of marriage was solely the procreation of young, a survival of the old patriarchal system, justified by the need (common to all agricultural and pastoral societies) to assure an abundance of labor. A woman who was left widowed and childless was supposed to become the wife of one of the husband's surviving brothers, even if he was already married, in order to perpetuate the husband's name and to provide heirs for his property. This was the law of "levirate" (*levir*, in Latin, means "brother-in-law"), established by the Pentateuch.[26] Polygamy was not prohibited; in an instance of levirate, it was actually obligatory.

The Christian concept of marriage was to be formed by crossbreeding the Hebraic institution with the Roman. In Roman society, matrimony was viewed as a relation of legal "guardianship" in which the wife was protected by the husband, who, in a fashion, replaced her father. Marriage was legally valid only when both parties consented to it and actually lived together. The wife was highly respected by reason of her functions as a mother and as the first teacher of the children (the word "matrimony," etymologically, comes from *matris munia,* or "the duties of a mother"); she had equal rights of inheritance, and, if her husband committed adultery, she could sue for divorce and for the partition of their property. Polygamy was absolutely forbidden. The class structure of the society did not permit a citizen to marry a slave or a former slave, but concubinage with either was not considered disgraceful. It had, however, one serious drawback: neither the concubine nor her children had any rights of inheritance.

Christianity modified the "property" concept of marriage that came from Hebraic laws, and espoused the heathen view based on love and fidelity. It embraced Roman monogamy, and extended the rights of the wife to both the present and the former slave, but did not really match the heathen concept by granting equal rights to both parties.

However, there is no sign of any of this in the Gospels. In substance, they reaffirm the Hebraic conception of marriage, citing almost verbatim the provisions laid down in the Old Testament. The sole difference was this: in consonance with his earlier admonitions against being a "stumbling block" to one's fellows, Jesus warned against abusing the right of divorce, since such abuse might put a man into the position of committing adultery by marrying a woman whose husband had put her away. Nevertheless, it is not too clear how far Jesus was disposed to accept divorce and remarriages. The Gospels report two viewpoints that are not readily reconciled:

1. "Whosoever shall put away his wife, saving for the cause of fornication, causeth her to commit adultery: and whosoever shall marry her that is divorced, committeth adultery."[27]

2. "Whosoever shall put away his wife, and marry another, committeth adultery. . . . And if a woman shall put away her husband, and be married to another, she committeth adultery."[28]

The first version does not deny the right of divorce, which was, indeed, compulsory in cases of "fornication" (πορνεία, *porneia*, meaning infidelity on the part of the wife), and the divorced husband did not lose the right, for any reason, to marry a virgin or a widow. The only consequence appears to have been that the repudiation made the disowned wife an adulteress, and hence "unclean."

The second proposition, however, while also not denying the right of divorce, does forbid remarriage. Here it is to be noted that a divorce by the wife is obviously contemplated as well (and in Palestine, as we know, this would have been impossible).

How has the Church comported itself in the matter? Paul vacillates between the two doctrines. He admits divorce if there is incompatibility between the spouses because of religious conflict,[29] and he does not forbid remarriage,[30] but he advises against it.[31] He, personally, was opposed to marriage in general, seeing in it only an expedient, a licit outlet for lust: "It is better to marry than to burn."[32] Clement of Alexandria, Origen, Chrysostom, Tertullian, Jerome, and others accept divorce if the wife is at fault, but not remarriage. Augustine not only allows a man who has put away an unfaithful wife to remarry in order to have children, but even authorizes the repudiation of a faithful wife if she is barren.[33]

The Council of Trent (Session XXIV, c. 7), forgetting what the Gospels said and the varying views of so many learned men of God, resolved to forbid divorce in any circumstances, proclaiming the indissolubility of marriage even when there has been infidelity. Marriage was here strangely exalted and sanctified—it was supposed to "confer some divine grace" (?), even though no passage in the Bible authorizes such an inference[34] or sets forth sacramental forms for matrimony. No doubt it is unnecessary to call the attention of anyone with common sense to the extremely grave consequences that this denaturalization of the marriage bond has produced and continues to produce in society, and yet the Church persists in seeking to maintain by force certain conditions that are extremely painful and are sometimes immoral.[35]

The majority of the Protestant sects, although they do not differ much from the Catholics in their view of marriage, have returned to the authentic Gospel position, allowing divorce for "fornication"; but to the Calvinists and the Anabaptists divorce is possible only, as in Paul's system, when there is a conflict of religious belief.[36] It is only since the French Revolution that real progress has been made by the laic conception, the secular interpretation of marriage as a bond based on love and other personal interests, and hence as a tie that can logically be loosed when the conditions on which it is based cease to obtain.

"It Is Not Good to Marry"

The dangers of divorce cited by Jesus caused the disciples to reply: "If the case of the man be so with his wife, it is not good to marry."[37]

Jesus agreed, but he pointed out more realistically: "All men cannot receive this saying, save they to whom it is given. For there are some eunuchs, which were so born from their mother's womb: and there are some eunuchs, which were made eunuchs of men: and there be eunuchs, which have made themselves eunuchs for the kingdom of heaven's sake. He that is able to receive it, let him receive it."

It is truly astonishing how a mistaken interpretation of the final sentence of this lesson of Jesus has encouraged—if indeed it did not establish it—two characteristic aspects of Christianity: the practice of celibacy and the exaltation of chastity and virginity. The Greek text[38] says: ὁ δυνάμενος χωρεῖν, χωρείτω (ho dunamenos chōrein, chōreitō), and the word chōrein can be read in two ways: "to leave," "to withdraw oneself," "to go away," or "to understand," "to grasp intellectually," and the latter is precisely the meaning intended here, just as the Gospels have employed it in similar sentences ("He who hath ears to hear, let him hear," etc.). Jesus resorted to such favorite personal idioms for a species of dialectic different from that of Socrates but no less effective in stimulating the acquisition of truth through personal effort.[39] Jerome, in the Vulgate, has also translated the sentence ambiguously: "*Qui potest capere, capiat.*" This, too, can be read, to the distortion of the original meaning, as: "Let him who is in a position to do as much do likewise." Hence, Matthew's emphasis on εὐνουχία (*eunouchia*) is viewed by the Church as an order laid down by Jesus for the celibacy and chastity of the clergy. And it is generally argued that abstinence and freedom from the responsibilities of marriage can be quite advantageous when one intends to dedicate oneself entirely to a major undertaking.

But it is not possible that Jesus should have wished to impose such a commandment.[40] In Judaism, marriage was a sacred duty as much for men as for women; in the Old Testament, those who do not marry and produce children are sometimes likened to murderers. Nor did the first Christians impose any rule of celibacy. It is well known, and Paul confirms the fact,[41] that Peter, James (the brother of Jesus), and other Apostles were married, although Tertullian was later to deny it, contending that the women who accompanied the Apostles were not wives but merely "women of the house,"[42] or, in simpler modern usage, priests' housekeepers.

If the discourse on *eunouchia* does represent an actual declaration by Jesus, it can be understood only as an adjuration to a form of penitence and also of abasement (voluntarily reducing oneself to the level of the "barren," who—whether their impotence was congenital or traumatic—were considered unclean and contemptible). Even Paul, when he is most enthusiastic on behalf of celibacy, admits[43] that he is imbued with the fixed idea of the imminence of the end of this world, which requires ascetic preparation for the kingdom.

Certainly, then, it was an extremist interpretation of Matthew's phraseology that in the early centuries of Christianity led directly to the savage custom of castration, perhaps encouraged by the influence of some of the mystery cults of Phrygia, Asia Minor, and Greece, which were dedicated to the cult of the Earth Mother, the Μεγάλη

Μήτηρ (*Megalē Mētēr*), whose priests were obliged to castrate themselves.[44] A most curious case is that of the famous philosopher Origen, who castrated himself in early youth and later decided that he had been mistaken in taking the evangelical passage thus literally! The third-century Eastern sect called the Valesians (from the name of the Arab monk Valesius) was composed exclusively of eunuchs, and the practice became so epidemic that Emperors Constantine, Leo I, and Justinian had to prohibit mutilation.

Without going to such excesses, Christian asceticism, in the third century, produced the practice of monasticism. At first in solitude, later in groups, many persons resorted to self-exile from the temptations of the world, choosing to live in lonely and barren places. They called themselves monks (μοναχοί, *monachoi*), anchorites (from ἀναχωρεῖν, *anachōrein*, which means "to withdraw oneself"), or hermits (from ἔρημος, *erēmos*, "a desert place"). To fortify their own faith and to enhance their merits, these ascetics often engaged in bizarre practices. They dressed in sackcloth (a rough fabric lined with goat's or camel's hair and also with knots and shards of metal wherever it touched the skin); they ate grass (the "grazers" and the "browsers"); they stood erect for whole days on pillars (the "stylites"); they dragged about heavy iron chains (the "chain-bearers"); they had themselves sealed into tiny cells (the "recluses"); they refused ever to lie down (the Acoemeti, "sleepless ones"); and so on.[45]

Anthony (251–336) seems to have been the first to advocate cenobitism (from κοινὸς βίος *koinos bios*, "life in common"), in that he allowed some of his imitators to build their own cells near his. But this was not yet an out-and-out community, with its own rules of discipline. That came somewhat later with Pachomius. Soon the custom spread among all the Eastern Christians and then into the West, and cloisters, for women as well as for men, multiplied rapidly. At first only for laymen, in the fifth century they began to be organized under special laws, and each had to obtain approval for its own rules.

Contrary to general belief, however, celibacy for ecclesiastics is not really of ancient origin. The first indications of a tendency to suggest that priests at least abstain from sexual relations appeared in the fourth century; but these were isolated rules limited to individual communities and had no general application. The oldest may be that applying to certain churches in Spain, which came out of the Synod of Elvira in 306: "*Episcopus vel quilibet alius clericus aut sororem aut filiam virginem tantum secum habeat; [debent] abstinere se a coniugibus suis et non generare filios.*"[46]

In 386, celibacy was prescribed in Africa as well. In the East, however, priests have never been forbidden to marry, even today. In the West, the custom of celibacy is connected in large measure with the feudal system: legitimate inheritance had to be restricted to the first-born son to prevent the breaking up of properties. The strongest pressure on behalf of priestly celibacy in the West arose after the year 1000, especially under the very harsh rule of Pope Gregory VII.

The Council of Trent made celibacy binding on the priests of the entire Occident. This was still not enough to suppress "modernist" movements within the body of the clergy itself, and they openly sought revocation of the order. In this century, such requests have been made to the Holy See by German Catholic groups (1940) and many others (1960), but the response has always been negative[47] despite the Church's awareness that the vow of celibacy may lead the weaker brethren into embarrassing compromises or even foster homosexuality.

Although arising from the same view of abstention as a meritorious sacrifice, and from fanatical imitation of the virginity of the Madonna, the propaganda on behalf of feminine chastity and virginity that the Church has always poured out is of another character. Paul was an early panegyrist of it; then Cyprian took up the subject, cataloguing the advantages of a virgin ("She has not to suffer the agony of giving birth"; "She need not obey a husband"; etc.). He was followed by Ambrose; by the poet-bishop Avitus, who consoled his sister, Fuscina, for her early enclosure in a convent by describing the "horrors" of the married state; by Jerome, who asserted that the young maiden was "more fortunate" than the married woman; and finally by a modern theologian who devoted a hundred and fifty-one pages to the attempt to prove that "the virgin has none of the worries of the wife"![48]

All civilizations, including those furthest from Christianity, have always highly esteemed feminine chastity; the basis for it was the necessity of assuring in women that minimum of virtue without which the patriarchal family could not have existed, since the paternity of the children would always be in doubt.[49] Then, too, in the early centuries the exhortation of the Christian woman to chastity may have been required to counteract the easy customs of her heathen environment. But the cult of feminine virginity in Christianity has degenerated into a species of unhealthy aberration. It goes to the extreme of exalting and even sanctifying a girl who has lost her virginity to an unwanted lover as though she had actually suffered martyrdom "for her faith," and it justifies a woman who commits a crime in order to preserve her physical integrity. What is the origin of so serious a misunderstanding? In my opinion, it is the error of making virginity the focal point of feminine morality, a "virtue," without taking into account the fact that such "virtue" is in essence no more than a peculiar physical conformation that in itself has absolutely nothing to do with any moral values. There is no logical argument that can make one believe that the sexual act (in response to a basic law of nature) should be sinful or immoral.

"Male and Female Shall Be the Same"

The psychoses of asceticism, chastity, and castration in the early centuries were undoubtedly abetted, especially in the East, by the influences of Platonism and Gnosticism. If the world in which we live is the creation of a malign aeon (the Gnostic doctrine), in contrast to which there is the world of light, then the flesh is only sin and suffering, and the redemptory work of the good aeon, Jesus Christ, becomes operative precisely in that it frees us from this world. In the world of perfection, sex will no longer exist: the soul, which has become feminine through its animal passions and has fallen into degeneration and corruption (the Platonic doctrine), will revert, when it rises, to its original masculinity.

Many writings of the Gnostic and Manichean Christians constantly reiterate the necessity for such a "union" or "annihilation" of male and female elements. The most genuinely Gnostic illustration is contained in a passage of a third-century treatise, the *Philosophumena* of Pseudo-Isidore:[50] "If the Mother of the Gods [Cybele] mutilated Attis in the very moment he was her lover, this means that from its own height the blessed nature of the eternal superior beings draws the masculine element of the soul to itself. Attis was mutilated—that is, he was separated from the earthly and lower parts of creation—in order that he might pass over into eternal existence, where there is neither female nor male but a new creature, a new man who is androgynous."[51]

But perhaps the very first formulation of ideas on the subject is to be found in the Gospel of Thomas: "And if you make the male and the female one, so that the male is no longer male and the female no longer female . . . then you will enter the Kingdom";[52] and similarly in other details.[53] But the most characteristic is the following: "Simon Peter says to them: 'Let Mary go out from our midst, for women are not worthy of life!' Jesus says: 'See, I will draw her so as to make her male so that she also may become a living spirit like you males. For every woman who has become male will enter the Kingdom of heaven.' "[54] And again: "When you strip yourselves without being ashamed, when you take off your clothes and lay them at your feet like little children and trample on them! Then you will become children of Him who is living."[55]

Other writings contain more or less accurate quotations of these excerpts from the Gospel of Thomas, or of variations of them. A homily of the second century, known as the Second Epistle of Clement, reproduces Thomas 27 and comments: "The male with the female means that the brother who looks at his sister sees nothing feminine in her, and she in turn sees nothing masculine in him." The Gospel of Philip[56] explains that the separation of the female from the male, which occurred originally when Eve was created from a part of Adam's body, was the beginning of degeneration and that Christ had come to bring the two together again. In another Gnostic treatise, which is called the Codex Brucianus but which is unsigned, it is stated: "All will be made one in Him who is one."

Furthermore, even the canonical Gospel of John is not devoid of like assertions: "That they all may be one; . . . I in them and thou in me, that they may be made perfect in one";[57] and even more explicitly Paul says: "There is neither male nor female: for ye are all one in Christ Jesus."[58]

Knowledge of this doctrine helps us to understand a characteristic ascetic custom in use among the Christians since the second century and perhaps longer, especially in Asia Minor and North

Africa: the "spiritual marriages" of ascetics, in utter chastity, to virgins of the same religious belief, who were called παρθένοι συνείσακτοι (*parthenoi suneisaktoi*), in Latin, *virgines subintroductae*, as if to show the possibility of abolishing the sexes (or at least sexuality) through the virtues of mysticism. An interesting document in this connection is an allegorical work called the Shepherd of Hermas, which dates back to the first half of the second century. Its protagonist tells of having spent an entire night lying in the midst of four young virgins and doing nothing but praying.[59]

Very swiftly this custom fell under suspicion because of quite understandable derelictions, and the word συνεισάγειν (*suneisagein*) acquired a new meaning: "to live together unlawfully." Irenaeus issued a pronouncement against it, recalling the state of innocence in which Adam and Eve had lived until they knew evil;[60] Tertullian denounced the custom under which, after the agape, "*adulescentes cum sororibus dormiunt*";[61] Cyprian pronounced an order to prevent "*virgines cum masculis habitare, non dico simul dormire, sed nec simul vivere.*"[62] So also was it attacked by John Chrysostom, Gregory of Nazianzus, and others.

Perhaps the earliest instance of the "married" virgin's danger of losing the chastity to which she had committed herself was that with which Paul had to concern himself in Corinth: "If any man think that he behaveth himself uncomely toward his virgin, if she pass the flower of her age, and need so require, let him do what he will, he sinneth not: let them marry. Nevertheless he that standeth steadfast in his heart, having no necessity, but hath power over his own will, and hath so decreed in his heart that he will keep his virgin, doeth well."[63] Usually, Paul is said to be speaking here of a father who has tried to keep his daughter a virgin, not allowing her to marry, or of a betrothed young Jew who, following the custom of his people, sets the marriage date in the distant future and fears he will be unable to "respect" his prospective bride during the long engagement period. But the most recent studies indicate that the passage is a reference to cases of "spiritual marriage."

The bizarre aspiration to sexlessness, joined to the conviction that the pleasures of the flesh are immoral and that woman, since she is the object of them, is therefore an instrument of sin (as shown by the failure of the experiment with the *virgines subintroductae*), has given rise to widespread misogyny among Christians. The numerous writings of the Church Fathers and apologists on this subject are fascinating—from Tertullian's *De cultu foeminarum* and *De virginibus velandis,* which insist that woman is "the devil's door," to Augustine's *De nuptiis,* which contends that the delight enjoyed in the sexual act is the result of original sin, and other pleasantries of the same character. Even after the patristic age, this misogyny flourished for centuries. In 1321, for example, a certain Guillaume Belibasta, a Languedocian Catharist, was to teach that women could not enter into the kingdom unless the spirits that inhabited their bodies first became male.

The Gnostic doctrine can find some support in the response that, according to the Synoptic Gospels, Jesus made to an interesting question submitted to him by some Sadducees: given the law of levirate, which prescribed that a widow without children should become the wife of her husband's brother, suppose that such a woman becomes the wife of three, four, or more brothers in turn, having been left a childless widow by each—when the kingdom comes and the just rise again, to which of the men shall she be actually married? Jesus answered categorically: "In the resurrection they neither marry, nor are given in marriage [*neque nubent neque nubentur*], but are as the angels of God in heaven."[64]

Since life will be eternal in the kingdom, there will be no further use for marriage, the purpose of which is the propagation of the species. Shall all then be men, or, as the Gnostics think, sexless? Tertullian, in his *De resurrectione carnis,* suggests the likelihood that all the risen will regain their old bodies, identical and intact, including the genitals, but it will no longer be necessary to perform certain functions.

[15]

IN JUDEA

New Teachings

At last Jesus and his disciples entered Judea, where he intended to resume spreading the good tidings. In contrast to the fertility of Galilee, this province is for the most part arid and poor. Its rather irregular mountains, largely of limestone, extend like chalky-colored folds broken by many crevasses, and they have but a sparse growth of brush and dwarf thistles. The vegetation thickens on the lowest slopes and in the valleys, where there are carob trees, vines, fig trees, and olive trees with their bright silvery leaves, but these trees, too, have a hard life; a moderately strong downpour is enough to wash away the soil and uproot the weaker and younger growths.

Almost as soon as he was within Judea, Jesus had an auspicious encounter with a group of women who held out the babies they carried in their arms, asking him to bless the children and pray for them.[1] The disciples, knowing how weary their master was, wanted to send away the women, but Jesus intervened. "Suffer little children," he said, "and forbid them not, to come unto me; for of such is the kingdom of heaven." Lovingly he laid his hands on their heads.

Once again he was giving the disciples a precept and an example, that they might learn to be as calm, respectful, modest, and innocent as children. The gesture of Jesus in caressing the children, however, was enough to provide the sinuous minds of theologians with the pretext for ascribing evangelical origin to yet another sacrament: that of the chrism (from the Greek χρῖσμα, *chrisma*), or confirmation. But confirmation is really of much later origin: it was instituted to overcome the hazards of administering baptism at too early an age. Through this sacrament, a young person who has reached the age of reason is required to *confirm* his acceptance of the baptism that he received without his knowledge and to "take up knowingly the obligation of following the new life with faith, love, and hope."[2] In actuality, the Catholic sacrament of confirmation (which the Protestants do not accept) is only an imitation of the Jewish *bar mitzvāh,* the ceremony in which Jesus had taken part at the age of twelve and through which boys are admitted as adults into the community of Israel. Like the *bar mitzvāh,* the confirmation is an unconscious re-enactment of the diverse rites of initiation into adult life that are still prevalent today among primitive peoples. But its minutiae (the sign of the cross on the forehead, the slap on the cheek, etc.) are much more reminiscent of the medieval ceremony and oath of loyalty of knighthood.

The first subject that Jesus developed in his preaching in Judea was of major importance: disdain of material possessions and the condemnation of wealth as an instrument of corruption. This theme had already appeared in the teachings of Jesus, but the foundation that he now erected for it was new. And the basis that from now on he was to propose for all his precepts was equally new.

Earlier, the dramatic promulgation of the Beatitudes, the summons to social and economic equality, the call to take no thought for the morrow, etc., were evidences of confidence in the imminence of the kingdom, of which the various "mighty works" had been virtually an anticipation. Now, after the profound crisis of discouragement, which had been intense enough to make him suspend his work, Jesus had freed himself of many of the alluring illusions that he had so enthusiastically cherished in the beginning.

Jesus no longer believed that his own impassioned appeal was enough to make the world immediately adopt the law of love, on the realization of which his kingdom would be inaugurated. He had accepted the fact that the forces of evil were still dominant. It was too soon for the establishment of a new age of collective happiness; first he must teach people how to overcome the causes of evil. He no longer proclaimed the blessedness of those who suffered, who were

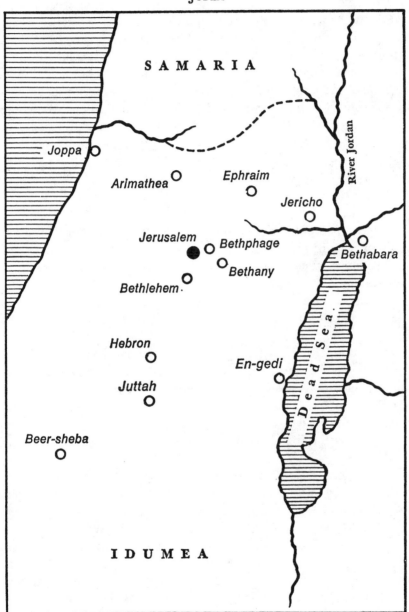

FIGURE VI
JUDEA

hungry and thirsty, who were persecuted, as if divine justice were on the point of springing to their defense; instead, he began to teach men to have compassion for those who suffered, who were hungry and thirsty, who were persecuted, and to go to their assistance. He no longer called for total disregard of daily needs, as if the era of living happily without burdens were about to open; instead, he counseled resigned endurance of daily hardship. It was not that he had given up hope of the kingdom, but he was no longer certain of its immediate advent. Thus he felt the need to set up standards for the choice of a higher spiritual deportment in the long period of waiting for the ultimate event.

The Rich Young Man

The expedient to which the Evangelists resort to open the new phase of teaching is a supposed meeting between Jesus and "a rich young man"[3] who asked: "Good Master [*Rabbi tōbā*[4]], what good thing shall I do, that I may have eternal life?"

Jesus at once gave him an excellent lesson in modesty, which was, among other things, a clear proof that he had never thought of himself as identical with God: "Why callest thou me good? there is none good but one, that is God." Then he specifically replied to the young man's question: "If thou wilt enter into life, keep the commandments. . . . Thou shalt do no murder, Thou shalt not commit adultery, Thou shalt not steal, Thou shalt not bear false witness; Honor thy father and thy mother."

"All these things have I kept from my youth up: what lack I yet?"

Jesus looked at him with a smile and said: "If thou wilt be perfect, go and sell that thou hast, and give to the poor, . . . and come and follow me."

This admonition has been the occasion of much commentary. Luther and, after him, almost all the Protestant sects have arbitrarily separated the two counsels: "Keep the commandments" is an *indispensable* condition to the gaining of salvation, but "Sell that thou hast" is merely an *ancillary* condition. This interpretation, obviously, is useful for soothing the consciences of the rich. Luther approved of wealth and sought to exhort everyone to hard work as the means of eliminating the curse of misery and rooting out the idleness and parasitism of the monasteries.[5] Calvin narrowed the concept, declaring that work was a means of worshiping God, that wealth was a proof of divine protection and generosity toward its possessor, and that it was therefore the duty of man to toil unremittingly and to waste neither time nor money.[6] All this has given rise in Protestant countries to the way of life of the respectable middle class, full of energy, parsimonious and provident, which has, however, degenerated into the greedy and corrupt manifestations of the profit motive.

It seems by no means certain to me that Jesus intended these two directives to be separated. The convenient Protestant interpretation, which is shared by many Catholics,[7] is refuted by the categorical condemnation of wealth that Jesus voiced in the Sermon on the Mount ("Woe unto you that are rich!") and by what he said now in bitter reproof of the rich young man's attitude when, looking away from Jesus, he departed because he lacked the courage to accept the message: "Verily I say unto you, That a rich man shall hardly enter into the kingdom of heaven. And again I say unto you, It is easier for a cord [not 'camel'] to go through the eye of a needle, than for a rich man to enter into the kingdom of God."

The Gospel of Thomas frequently corroborates this belief: to find the kingdom, one must "fast from the world," one must learn to reject it, especially if one is rich.[8] The same concept is repeated in various Agrapha (which means "unwritten things" and which is used to designate sayings attributed to Jesus outside the four canonical Gospels).[9] It thus seems beyond question that the thought is genuinely representative of Jesus, or at least of the Christians of the apostolic age.

More correctly therefore than the Protestants, the Catholics hold that "Keep the commandments" and "Sell that thou hast" are indivisible conditions for salvation. In view of the impracticability of their observance by those who must live in the world as it is, however, the Catholics have in recent times turned to the view that the renunciation of wealth is not indispensable to salvation for *all* the faithful. Canon law, indeed, is a vigorous defender of the private property of the rich against the demands of the disinherited for economic equalization.

"Sell that thou hast, and give to the poor," therefore, is understood to be restricted to those who resolve to "follow" Jesus as disciples—that is, to enter the priesthood. Poverty, in fact, is one of the three vows—the others being chastity and obedience—on which the rules of all religious orders are based.

In actuality, however, practical needs (the essential requirements of the religious community, funds for charity and works of assistance, etc.) and fortuitous occurrences (gifts, legacies, inheritances, etc.) soon prevailed on the regular as well as the secular clergy to pay less and less attention to the precept of poverty.

We have traveled a long way from the counsels that Jerome gave as early as the fourth century: "Others build churches, erect impressive columns, ornament doors with silver and ivory, and embellish altars with precious jewels. I do not condemn any. Let each man follow his own belief. But your task is other than these: to clothe Christ in the poor, to visit him in the sick, to feed him in the hungry, to welcome him in those who have no roof over their heads. Let us live as if we had nothing and possessed everything. Let the wealth of the Christian be what is enough to feed him and clothe him."

God and Mammon

The shocking incongruities of the accumulated riches in the hands of the Church, the destitution of the masses, and the open alliance of the Church itself with the rich have given rise in every epoch to movements of protest, such as the Poor Men of Lyons (the Waldenses), the Patarines, and even the Franciscans. Not only do all these groups go back to the interpretation of Jesus' message given by the Evangelists, they broaden it according to more timely social criteria, advocating not the "renunciation" of worldly goods but an equitable distribution of them that takes into consideration the needs of everyone.

We have already said that such an exemplary Christian communism would not have been possible even in the days of the first apostolic community. Paul very early edited the teachings of Jesus that condemned wealth into a warning not to be too greedy for worldly goods and an exhortation to share them out joyfully among the needy,[10] and he added that "they that will be rich, fall into temptation, and a snare, and into many foolish and hurtful lusts, which drown men in destruction and perdition. For the love of money is the root of all evil."[11] More categorically, the Evangelists declared: "No man can serve two masters: for either he will hate the one, and love the other: or else he will hold to the one, and despise the other. Ye cannot serve God and mammon."[12] *Mammōn* is a word of uncertain Semitic origin meaning "hidden treasure"; here, however, it is used as a kind of idol, a personification of the lust for gold.

Luke adds two parables, though they are inspired by the new Pauline concept, that illustrate the condemnation of wealth as a source of sin and as an offense to suffering, but their tone is much less uncompromising than that of the Sermon on the Mount.

The first of these two parables is rather disconcerting, since we like to picture Jesus as always unselfish and averse to compromise. An unfaithful steward, Luke says, was discharged by his employer, who asked him for an accounting of his stewardship. The steward was concerned at the consequences: "What shall I do? . . . I cannot dig; to beg I am ashamed. I am resolved what to do, that, when I am put out of the stewardship, they may receive me into their houses." Summoning his master's debtors, he instructed each to write out a bill substantially lower than what was really owed. Thus, to win the gratitude of his confederates, he committed a fraud that did great damage to his master's interests. The moral of the parable is stated in these words that are put into the Nazarene's mouth: "Make to yourself friends of the mammon of unrighteousness; that, when ye fail, they may receive you into everlasting habitations."[13]

It is hardly a happy example,[14] even though it is clear that what is held up for emulation is not the dishonesty but only the shrewdness of the steward: one should learn to make use of riches, even if they are dishonestly acquired, in order to gain merit with those who can help in one's time of need (that is, with God).[15]

The other parable, which in a way is a popular legend, is more interesting.[16] Lazarus (a Hellenized form of the Hebrew 'Eleāzār), who had spent his days begging for crumbs of bread at a rich man's door while the rich man's dogs licked his sores, died and was laid to rest "in Abraham's bosom" (a rabbinical term for the peaceful world after death).[17] The rich man, who had daily feasted "sumptuously," was hurled into hell the moment he died. From the verb *epulabatur* ("he feasted") in the Vulgate and by suggestion of the Latin *epulo* ("a crapulent man"), popular imagination has invented a name for the rich man—Epulon—and with only a little more effort it has discovered the very house in Jerusalem in which he lived!

The parable has a strong Ebionite tinge: Lazarus is rewarded solely because of his poverty and the rich man is punished solely because of his wealth.[18] Consideration is given not to the good or the evil that each did, but only to the sufferings of the one and the pleasures of the other.[19] This concept, however, which Jesus would have gladly expounded at the time of the Sermon on the Mount, though not at this later stage, is followed by an appended warning to the rich to repent and pay heed to Moses and the prophets.[20] In the Gospel According to the Hebrews, indeed, Jesus is made to say to the rich young man: "Many of thy brothers, the sons of Abraham, lie covered with filth and dying of hunger, while thy house is full of many things and not anything goes out of it unto them."[21] This may have been the inspiration of the author of the Gospel of Luke when he inserted the parable of Lazarus.

Similarly, Paul says: "Charge them that are rich in this world, that they be not highminded, nor trust in uncertain riches, but in the living God, who giveth us richly all things to enjoy; That they do good, that they be rich in good works, ready to distribute."[22]

The reprobation of wealth so manifest in Jesus and in the earlier stories of the Gospels was somewhat diluted by contact with Roman society. In actuality, private property, even when it is excessive, is not a violation of any civil law; but it does transgress the moral law, and hence it is a sin for the Christian, who should strive for perfect equality with all his brothers and work at least toward the abolition of want with all its frightful consequences.

"Who Then Can Be Saved?"

Perplexed by the words of Jesus, which seemed harshly condemnatory of everyone who showed any attachment to worldly possessions, the disciples asked him: "Who then can be saved?"

Jesus studied them thoughtfully before he replied: "With men this is impossible; but with God all things are possible."

"Behold," Simon Peter said, "we have forsaken all, and followed thee; what shall we have therefore?"

"Every one that hath forsaken houses, or brethren, or sisters, or father, or mother, or wife, or children, or lands, for my name's sake," the master reassured him, repeating a promise made many times before, "shall receive a hundredfold, and shall inherit everlasting life." Then, after a long pause, he repeated his enigmatic refrain, striking a blow that crumbled the Apostles' self-seeking dreams: "But [in Greek there is a δέ (de) that must not be overlooked[23]] many that are first shall be last; and the last shall be first."[24]

In obvious contrast to this lesson in humility, a prophecy is inserted into the Gospel of Matthew,[25] between Peter's question and the answer of Jesus, which is highly flattering to the Apostles and which Luke repeats in part in another connection.[26] Yet it is most difficult to believe that it was really spoken by Jesus: "In the regeneration, when the Son of man shall sit in the throne of his glory, ye also shall sit upon twelve thrones, judging the twelve tribes of Israel." The hypercritical will ask if the promise applied also to Judas, the betrayer.

There is no point in discussing the inappropriateness of this prophecy. More probably, it was precisely the absence of any specific promise by Jesus that disappointed the Apostles, who asked themselves whether they were not wasting their time for nothing. But Jesus confirmed what he had said earlier, telling another parable:

"The kingdom of heaven is like unto a man that is an householder, which went out early in the morning to hire laborers into his vineyard. And when he had agreed with the laborers for a penny a day, he sent them into his vineyard. And he went out about the third hour, and saw others standing idle in the marketplace, And said unto them, Go ye also into the vineyard, and whatsoever is right, I will give you. And they went their way. And again he went out about the sixth and ninth hour, and did likewise. And about the eleventh hour he went, and found others standing idle, and said unto them, Why stand ye here all the day idle? They say unto him, Because no man hath hired us. He saith unto them, Go ye also into the vineyard; and whatsoever is right, that shall ye receive. So when even was come, the lord of the vineyard saith unto his steward, Call the laborers, and give them their hire, beginning from the last unto the first. And when they came that were hired about the eleventh hour, they received every man a penny. But when the first came, they supposed that they should have received more: and they like-wise received every man a penny. And when they had received it, they murmured against the goodman of the house, Saying, These last have wrought but one hour, and thou hast made them equal unto us, which have borne the burden and heat of the day. But he answered one of them, and said, Friend, I do thee no wrong: didst thou not agree with me for a penny? Take that thine is, and go thy way: I will give unto this last even as unto thee. Is it not lawful for me to do what I will with mine own? Is thine eye evil, because I am good? So the last shall be first, and the first last."[27]

The immediate antagonism that the literal significance of the parable evokes in anyone of good sense (the idea of justice distorted by the arbitrary behavior of a powerful master, who, it should be noted, is the symbol of God) has impelled scholars to look for a hidden explanation that would eliminate its absurdity. Loisy thinks he can find it: the last shall be rewarded like the first because divine justice is the same for all men of good will.[28] But this does not alter the awkwardness of a distribution of rewards that disregards a man's deserts, his zeal or dereliction in good works. It is an unfathomably capricious God who rewards those who have obeyed his law only at the end of their lives as highly as he compensates those who have obeyed him throughout their lives.

Unfortunately, this was apparently the concept of God that the Galilean entertained: generous and merciful to those who submitted to him, worshiped him and prayed to him, but always as arbitrary as an absolute monarch—much like an Oriental despot. The same Parable of the Laborers in the Vineyard, and thus the same concept of God's "justice," is found in the ancient rabbinical literature.[29] The idea of a god—as we have already indicated in another chapter —is closely contingent on the conditions and conceptions of life that prevail in the environment in which it is developed, and thus one cannot demand of Jesus a theology that meets the needs of modern life.

What is called the Parable of the Marriage Feast, or of the Great Supper,[30] has a similar value, and it is not without a polemic thrust at those who refuse to believe in the teachings of Jesus. The author of the Gospel of Luke, who did not understand the meaning of the parable (the arbitrariness of God's selection of those who shall live in the kingdom), introduces it with another comment of an Ebionite flavor that accords poorly with the rest in that it predicts certain remuneration for *all* who practice mercy: "When thou makest a dinner or a supper, call not thy friends, nor thy brethren, neither thy kinsmen, nor thy rich neighbors; lest they also bid thee again, and a recompense be made thee. . . . Call the poor, the maimed, the lame, the blind: And thou shalt be blessed: for they cannot recompense thee; for thou shalt be recompensed at the resurrection of the just."[31]

With slight variations among the Gospels of Matthew, Luke, and Thomas, the parable tells of a man (Matthew says he was a king) who prepared a great feast or nuptial banquet, inviting many guests. At the appointed time, he sent his servants to fetch the guests, but they declined the invitation on various pretexts: one had to see to his farm, another to his merchandise, a third was to be married. Then the angry host sent his servants into the streets and market-places to gather together the poor, the blind, the halt, "both bad and good" ($\pi o\nu\eta\rho o\acute{v}s$ $\tau\epsilon$ $\kappa a\grave{\iota}$ $\mathring{a}\gamma a\theta o\acute{v}s$, *ponērous te kai agathous*), and so the hall was filled with guests.

It is understandable how, from such a lesson (the "wicked" too shall share in the kingdom, if God so wishes), Luther could derive his paradoxical maxim: "Sin hard, but believe even harder!"

Matthew also has a pendant, which may originally have been a parable in its own right but which is incorporated here into the Parable of the Marriage Feast.[32] When everyone was at the table, the host entered the room, and, seeing that one of his guests was not wearing the proper garment (the white caftan with sleeves that was customarily given to each guest to wear over his own clothes), he had him seized and thrown into prison. The whole passage ends with these words: "For many are called, but few are chosen."

Rabbi Johanan ben Zakkai, who lived about A.D. 70, was the author of a lesson that had many things in common with Matthew's parable.[33] Johanan too speaks of "wise" men who put on their caftans in good time and stood ready at the king's door, and of "foolish" men who had not prepared themselves and were shut out from the feast. It might be argued that Matthew's parable is derived from Johanan's (the Gospel was certainly written after A.D. 70), but the resemblance can also be attributed to the fact that both parables were conceived by people of the same period and the same mentality. As a matter of fact, the common elements (the kingdom represented by a feast and God by a peevish, capricious prince) also appear frequently in other writings of the time.

This explains why the Apostles, accustomed as they were to the extravagances of the tyrants of their age, having seen the collapse of their hopes for a just reward for the sacrifices they had made, and now hearing Jesus speak no longer of a kingdom "for all" but instead of a limited one, began to speculate on their own chances of gaining access to it and even attaining privileged positions not as a matter of right but through favoritism. On that same evening, Jesus had barely finished confiding once more to his disciples his direly pessimistic apprehensions ("Behold, we go up to Jerusalem, and the Son of man shall be betrayed . . . and they shall condemn him to death"),[34] and they were all deep in thought, when Salome, the mother of James and John, approached the Nazarene unobtrusively, prostrated herself (προσκυνοῦσα, *proskunousa*), and asked to speak to him.[35] Annoyed, he inquired what she wanted.

Salome hesitated a moment. Then her two ambitious sons, who had stood back a little, asked Jesus to promise that he would grant whatever they asked. When he requested clarification, Salome said: "Grant that these my two sons may sit, the one on thy right hand, and the other on the left, in thy kingdom."

Jesus must often have had to suffer patiently under the ignorance and the pettiness of his disciples,[36] but this time his anger burst out full: "Ye know not what ye ask. Are ye able to drink of the cup that I shall drink of?"

"We are able," they answered shamelessly.

Was it perhaps worth trying to explain? Jesus saw that this was not the case. "Ye shall drink indeed of my cup, and be baptized with the baptism that I am baptized with: but to sit on my right hand, and on my left, is not mine to give, but . . . of my Father." In his indignation, Jesus had spoken loudly, and so the ten other Apostles had grasped the insidious maneuver of James and John. They were greatly angered,[37] not by the tastelessness of the request, which Jesus had already properly rejected, but because of their own jealousy.[38]

Jesus called them round him then and calmly rebuked them, repeating ideas which he had often expressed before but which the Twelve had never understood: "Ye know that the princes of the Gentiles exercise dominion over them, and they that are great exercise authority upon them. But it shall not be so among you: but whosoever will be great among you, let him be your minister. . . . Even as the Son of man came not to be ministered unto, but to minister, and to give his life a ransom for many."[39]

In Jericho

By now Jesus and the disciples had reached Jericho. From there it was barely fifteen miles to Jerusalem. Jericho, the enchanting city that Antony had given to Cleopatra as a summer retreat, lay along the last stretch of the Jordan, in the midst of an oasis of leafy palms, and its length was more than a hundred stadia, a five-hour walk. It had been built on the ruins of an ancient Canaanite village that modern archaeological excavations have laid bare. A place of orchards and gardens, in that very moderate climate it bore crops year after year: bananas, pomegranates, almonds, oranges, dates with the savor of honey.

Jesus and his disciples, in animated conversation as they walked through this paradise, breathed in the aroma of balsam. In the orchards, peasants were gashing the branches with sharp stones or fragments (they were said to resist the blade of a knife[40]) and eagerly collecting the sap in bowls, where it quickly thickened into a kind of gum of a golden red color—myrrh.

Along the road, a blind beggar (Mark says his name was Bartimeus and he was the son of Timeus, but this would be redundant, since the Hebrew *bar* means "son of"), hearing their voices, asked for help.[41] The disciples who were walking ahead of Jesus told him to be quiet, but the beggar merely called more loudly. Loisy supposes that he may not actually have been blind, but only cataractous, since the Greek text in all three Synoptic Gospels says that he *"regained his sight"* (ἀνέβλεψε, *aneblepse*).[42]

In any case, the healing of the beggar helped to spread the word of the thaumaturgic powers of Jesus among the people of Jericho. The beneficiary himself told everyone. When the Galilean pilgrims came into the city proper, a large throng was there to greet them. It included the usual cripples, hysterics, deaf-mutes, and victims of eye infections, all of whom wanted to be cured.

At the same time, a rich tax-collection contractor named Zaccheus,[43] who was well known in the city, was passing along the same road. He, too, was curious to see the thaumaturge, but he was a man of short stature and the crowd was too large. So, careless of his professional standing, he hoisted himself onto the branches of a sycamore, the African fig tree with the small leaves, similar to the mulberry but with stronger branches. The people were astonished at what he had done, and they pointed him out to one another where he perched in his tree.

Jesus looked toward him. From the way in which people spoke of Zaccheus, Jesus could guess that he was a person of some consequence, so he walked over to the tree and, looking up at the contractor, said: "Zaccheus, make haste, and come down, for to-day I must abide at thy house."

We already know (compare the story of Levi-Matthew in Capernaum) what it meant to a publican—accustomed to being hated and despised—to be treated cordially for once. Zaccheus was overjoyed to be the host of Jesus and the Apostles at dinner. Naturally, the citizens of Jericho, like those of Capernaum, were outraged, and they muttered among themselves. But Zaccheus was basically a good man. He clung to his business because it paid well and afforded him a luxurious life without cares. He was not greedy, however, and now, indeed, he was so moved at the sight of all those penniless men clustered about Jesus that he wanted to do something generous for them. Giving them a considerable amount of money (Luke says it was the half of his goods) for charitable works, he pledged himself to make fourfold restitution to anyone he might have cheated. This was precisely twice the amount stipulated in the Law for redress by thieves.[44]

The generosity of Zaccheus excited the Apostles. Being now so near Jerusalem, Luke relates,[45] they thought that the kingdom of God was really beginning to take shape. Had they not just seen a manifestation of what Jesus had so enthusiastically foretold: the repentance of the rich, the dispersal of their wealth among the poor, equality for all?

Jesus did not share his companions' optimism. He took advantage of the opportunity, however, to counsel them again on the importance of making good use of the gifts of providence, whether these were material or spiritual.

The nucleus of a new parable[46] had come to his mind a few hours earlier, in the streets of Jericho, when they had walked past the old palace of Herod the Great, which was now the summer residence of his son, the ethnarch Archelaus. During his own childhood, Jesus remembered, immediately after Herod's death, Archelaus had run to Rome to obtain the succession, but he had not succeeded in his purpose because the Jews themselves, weary of the despotic Herodian dynasty, had persuaded Augustus to dissolve the kingdom. Augustus had then divided Palestine into tetrarchies, and Archelaus had received only a part of his father's domain.

Jesus took this historical item as a point of departure that afforded an excellent haggadah for his parable. A nobleman went abroad to obtain investiture as the king of his own land, to which he planned to return. Before his departure, he summoned his servants and entrusted a certain sum to them (Luke says he gave a pound to each of ten servants,[47] while Matthew speaks instead of an unequal distribution of talents among three servants) with instructions to manage it well. His subjects, who hated him, sent a messenger meanwhile to say: "We will not have this man to reign over us." Nonetheless, he received his kingdom, and the nub of the parable is in what followed. On his return home, the new king counted the money that he had left behind: he rewarded the two of his servants who had used it wisely, the amount of each reward being proportioned to the extent of the profit that the servant had made; but the third servant, who from fear of his master's anger had buried his share in the ground, was punished.

Both Matthew and Luke end the story with a saying of Jesus[48] which each of them has already noted in another context,[49] and which Mark and Thomas quote separately:[50] "Unto every one which hath shall be given; and from him that hath not, even that he hath shall be taken away from him."

If, as it is customarily interpreted, the parable means that in the kingdom reward will be proportioned to merit, it is in diametrical opposition to that of the Laborers in the Vineyard. But there is no reason for surprise in the fact that incongruities and contradictions exist in Jesus' teachings in the form in which they have been handed down to us. It is possible, first of all, that the various versions represent the divergent points of view among the compilers and editors of the Gospels. It is also possible, however, that the contradictions actually occurred in Jesus' teachings, which were not fitted into any specific system of philosophy but were suggested spontaneously by fortuitous circumstances and were shaped by irrational, emotional impulses.

And it should hardly be necessary to point out how arbitrary and how contrary to history it would be (because, though it is possible *post eventum*, it could not have been possible at the time when the parable is supposed to have been spoken) to identify the nobleman (Archelaus) with Jesus himself, who ascends from the earth into heaven ("goes into a far country") and then returns (the Parousia), or the subjects, who do not want Archelaus as their king, with the Jews who called for the crucifixion of Jesus, and so on.

Mary of Bethany

Having resumed their journey after a sojourn of a few days in Jericho, Jesus and his disciples made a last halt before Jerusalem at the village of Bethany, whose name means "the house of date trees." The capital was about fifteen stadia away—less than two miles. Here in Bethany, therefore, rather than in the congested Holy City itself, Jesus took up residence. By good luck, he had encountered an extremely hospitable family: a young man called Lazarus and his two sisters, Mary and Martha.

From the moment of his arrival, Jesus had established a warm and close friendship with the two women: Martha, the elder and more sedate, went to great lengths to assure the stranger of a fitting welcome; Mary, in contrast, sat at the feet of Jesus and absorbed every word he said, her eyes fixed on his.[51] The Gospel of John tells us somewhat later that she was the same Mary—the sinner—who had anointed the head of Jesus and bathed his feet with her own tears.[52] But one cannot accept this enormous blunder by the Evangelist.

Mary of Bethany—so we are led to believe by the accounts of Luke and even of John himself—was a chaste and unworldly young girl. She had not yet learned the utility of masking one's impulses. She was fascinated by Jesus and it never occurred to her that the ecstasy that she visibly felt in his presence could be uncharitably interpreted by others. Martha, however, was no longer so unsophisticated in such matters. She tried repeatedly to tell her sister with a glance that her behavior was not fitting. Mary could not grasp the meaning of these warning looks. Finally, Martha found a means to her end, one of those practical solutions in which feminine astuteness is so rich. "Lord," she said to Jesus, "dost thou not care that my sister hath left me to serve alone? bid her therefore that she help me."

But even Jesus did not understand what Martha meant to convey; he, too, was pure and chaste, and he saw nothing improper in the sudden adoration that shone in the girl's face. So he answered: "Martha, Martha, thou art careful and troubled about many things; But one thing is needful: and Mary hath chosen that good part."

If Luke took the trouble to recall this episode in Jesus' life, certainly he did not intend to insert a trivial detail into his Gospel. Martha and Mary are the symbols in the New Testament of what in the Old Testament was represented by Leah and Rachel: one stands for the active life, entirely absorbed with external works; the other for the contemplative life, wholly caught up in mystical communion with God.

It is probable, however, that the two women are also historically authentic. We shall see their names again, and not in subordinate parts in the life of Jesus. Therefore, it is not inappropriate to be satisfied with the literal meaning of Luke's story and to picture Jesus, in the company of these two good women in the quiet intimacy of the house in Bethany, preparing himself for the ordeal of preaching in Jerusalem. He intended to take the occasion of the next major holy day for his entrance into the capital without attracting too much attention, and by mingling with the crowds of pilgrims and sightseers, to find an audience more easily. The best opportunity would be afforded him in the following month, Tishri (September–October), and he waited patiently for its arrival. From sunset of the ninth day to sunset of the tenth was Yom Kippur (the annual Day of Atonement), and it was followed in a few days by Sukkoth (the Feast of Tabernacles, or of Booths).

Yom Kippur was the only day of the year when the high priest entered the Holy of Holies, the innermost room of the Temple, to sprinkle the blood of a sacrificial goat on the site of the Ark of the Covenant and, particularly, on the *kappōreth* (rendered in the Scriptures as ἱλαστήριον, *hilastērion*), a slab of gold that rested over the Ark itself and supported two cherubim; its name means "expiatory," "propitiatory," but is commonly known as the Mercy Seat. The high priest sprinkled blood also on the horns of the golden Altar of Incense and on the ground around it. Then he came out of the sanctuary, and, laying his hands on the head of another goat, which was called the scapegoat (both animals had been chosen by lot early in the morning, the one as the sacrifice, the other as the scapegoat), he intoned a solemn public confession of all the sins of the people of Israel and commanded that the scapegoat be taken into the desert and hurled from a precipice.[53] The death of the scapegoat (the magic significance of which is found also in many other religions) freed the people of their collective guilt, which the priest had taken on himself.

The Feast of Tabernacles, which is celebrated about the middle of Tishri, is in contrast a popular rejoicing that lasts eight days— the relic of an ancient rite to propitiate the protective god of the soil, from the days when the Hebrew religion still had a naturalistic-agricultural basis. The month of Tishri, in fact, marked the end of work in the fields: the last days of the harvest, when the threshing of grain had already been completed, and the time for gathering in the figs, the vegetables, the mint, the thyme. From time immemorial, the peasants had built huts of a sort (the tabernacles) in this season, roofing them with thatch, so that they could sleep in the fields and guard the crops that had not yet been harvested. In a later period (and this was the significance of the festival in the time of Jesus), Sukkoth was linked to the legend of Moses, and the temporary booths built of branches were supposed to commemorate the tents in which the Israelites slept during their forty years in the wilderness after the Exodus from Egypt.

[16]

JERUSALEM!

The Entry into the Holy City

Jesus had given his disciples no specific program for the entrance into Jerusalem, and they were consumed with impatience as they waited in the various houses in Bethany that had taken them in. But at last the great day was at hand.

To give the event a more dramatic symbolic character, Christian tradition prefers to believe that the entrance was made on the Sunday before the Passover. Apart from the fact that in those times Sunday did not even exist, all the circumstances narrated by the Gospels give reason to believe that it occurred instead on the first day of the Feast of Tabernacles.

On that day, Jesus brought his disciples together and started out from Bethany for the capital. They had not far to go, but they were barely within sight of the first houses when Jesus stopped.[1] This was Bethphage—not so much a village as a suburb of Jerusalem itself, lying as it did at the foot of the Mount of Olives, directly facing the height on which the Temple stood. The name *Bēth-phagē*, to be exact, means "the district house"—in other words, the municipal customs post.[2] The etymological research that has led to the meaning "the house of the fig trees" is in error.

"Go your way into the village over against you," Jesus told two of his disciples, "and as soon as ye be entered into it, ye shall find a colt tied, whereon man never sat; loose him, and bring him. And if any man say unto you, Why do ye this? say ye that the Lord hath need of him; and straightway he will send him hither."

The two disciples carried out his orders. As soon as they had returned to Jesus and the ten other Apostles, a kind of saddle was improvised out of their cloaks and Jesus mounted. He meant to make his entrance into Jerusalem fittingly, like a rabbi who rides gravely on his beast at the head of his pupils. But there is also a Biblical prophecy[3]—and Matthew is careful to quote it—that says that the Messiah-King, the liberator of the people of Israel from the dominion of Darius, shall enter Jerusalem mounted on an ass. And so it pleased the Apostles to consider the entrance of Jesus into the Holy City.

Actually, the Biblical quotation caused the author of the Gospel of Matthew to make a curious error. The Hebrew text of Zechariah says: "upon an ass, and upon a colt the foal of an ass." The word "and" here is a conjunction that, according to contemporary usage, could have either an explanatory and emphatic meaning ("better still") or a purely additive one ("and as well").[4] The Evangelist mistakenly read it in this second sense (though the two other Synoptics did not), and so he tells us that Jesus rode on the ass *and* the colt!

Even when this muddle has been clarified (though some fanatical exegetes stupidly insist on taking it literally, arguing that Jesus mounted the she-ass and had the colt tied to the saddle), it is still difficult to explain why Jesus had insisted on an animal "whereon never man sat." Did he perhaps, as Justin Martyr believed,[5] wish to make it clear that here was the founder of a *new* religious society? The symbolism seems rather forced. Perhaps the phrase is only an artless attempt by the authors of the Gospels to show homage to their master.[6]

The circumstances of the Feast of Tabernacles were admirably suited to afford the atmosphere of a genuine "Triumphal Entry." According to the custom laid down by the Mosaic Law,[7] the faithful thronged to the Temple waving green branches of palm trees (or of myrtles or willows), crying: "Hosanna [*Hōsha-nāh*]!" The word means "Save us, we beseech thee."

So it was now along the short stretch of road between Bethphage and Jerusalem and then, once they had passed through the Sheep Gate,[8] in the streets of the city. The pilgrims, who were also on their way to the Temple, waved their branches and shouted their hosannas, turning sometimes to Jesus and his disciples as if to make them partners in their rejoicing. The Apostles interpreted this as a mark of deference and a recognition of the Messiah.[9] The ritual benediction: "Blessed be the kingdom of our father David," becomes, in Matthew: "Hosanna to the Son of David."

The occasion continues to be marked by Christians today, but, as we have pointed out, at the wrong time: Palm Sunday, a week before Easter. Where palms cannot be obtained, substitutes are used: olive branches in Italy, boxwood branches in France, laurel in the Basque country, elm and hazel in Canada, cypress in the Baltic lands . . .

If the entrance had really been a triumphal one, the demonstrations and rejoicings would have had immediate consequences, for they would certainly have alarmed the Roman authorities and the Jewish leaders as well.[10] For the moment, Jesus was satisfied to mingle with the crowds and attend the ceremonies in the Temple.

The high priest wore, over his long white robe, the *me'îl,* a short, seamless vest without sleeves; colored a deep blue, it was ornamented with tassels of various colors and little golden bells. He also wore the *'ēphōd,* a chasuble with two folds, woven of red, purple, and scarlet thread and embroidered in gold, with a rich girdle, "even of gold."[11] In these vestments, he stood before the faithful and opened the feast, which would continue for seven days.

The most impressive aspect of the ceremony came in the evening: the Temple was illuminated by four huge Menorahs (candelabra), which thrust their resinous torches toward heaven, while thousands of worshipers, each also carrying a burning torch, moved in procession beneath them, and the priests, arrayed on the steps of the Temple, chanted sacred songs.

That night, after he had carefully observed everything, Jesus went back to Bethany with the Twelve.[12] He was not yet ready to risk a public proclamation of his message.

The Woman Taken in Adultery

The next day, Jesus set out again from Bethany for Jerusalem. As he trudged along the hot, dusty road, he felt a need for some refreshment, and, seeing a fig tree, he walked directly to it, hoping he might still find some fruit on it. The time, as we have said, was the middle of September, when all the crops had been harvested.

Unfortunately, this tree could no longer offer anything but leaves. Keenly disappointed, Jesus hurled an angry curse at the harmless tree: "No man eat fruit of thee hereafter for ever."[13]

Since they date the occurrence in March or April, about the time of the Passover, the Catholic commentators are at a loss to explain how, logically, Jesus could have expected to find ripe figs at that time of year. So they invent nonsense, like Igino Giordani, who says that the Jews used to eat the buds as well as the fruit of the fig tree![14]

Notwithstanding our more accurate establishment of the date, which makes the incident less implausible, it would be worthless if it did not conceal some allegorical meaning that would justify its having been reported by the Gospels. Ordinarily, the episode is purported to mean that just as the barren tree was accursed, so the Jewish (or some other) nation shall never bear fruit pleasing to God. Not all scholars share this view, however. Even Augustine was shocked, and he questioned: *"Quid arbor fecerat, fructum non afferendo? Quae culpa arboris infaecunditas?"*

Later that day, Jesus had barely arrived at the gates of Jerusalem when he and his companions came upon a tragic sight: an adulterous woman had been taken outside the city to be stoned,[15] as the Law required,[16] after a summary proceeding with at least two or three witnesses, and "the hands of the witnesses shall be first upon him [or her] to put him to death."[17] The story, which is contained only in the Gospel of John, cannot be true. That penalty had been abolished before the time of Jesus; moreover, Palestine was then under Roman jurisdiction, which extended also to penal cases.

The tale is worth repeating, nevertheless, for its instructive character. John says that as Jesus passed by the scene, he was asked to join in the judgment, and he took his place with the others to hear the accusations by the injured husband. When it was time for him to give his own opinion, he was troubled. He had always preached forgiveness and understanding for the sins of others; how could he now associate himself with those who wanted to condemn the wretched woman to death? She stared at him in terror, but Jesus did not even look at her. With his eyes fixed on the ground, he wrote something in the dust with his finger. Was he cataloguing, as Jerome thinks, the sins of the very men who had taken it upon themselves to judge the woman, or was he avoiding her glance, as François

Mauriac believes, in order to conceal his own inner confusion and to avoid adding to the accused woman's feeling of shame?[18]

Finally, when the others insisted that he speak his mind, he rose and said: "He that is without sin among you, let him first cast a stone at her." A staggering mandate!

Long before, the Old Testament had gloomily conceded that "there is no man that sinneth not,"[19] and Paul was to corroborate the thought again;[20] but in this passage of John there is a new concept that until then had been put into words only by the Stoic philosopher Lucius Annaeus Seneca, a contemporary of Jesus who was condemned to death by Nero. From the grim recognition of the universality of human imperfection, Seneca derived a law of fellowship with the duty of forgiveness.

The words of Jesus, the Evangelist says, troubled the thoughts of the priests, the judges, and the witnesses. One by one, they rose and left in silence. In a few minutes, Jesus and the adulteress were completely alone in a vast stillness. "Woman," he said, "where are those thine accusers? hath no man condemned thee?"

"No man, Lord."

"Neither do I condemn thee; go, and sin no more."

This, one of the most exquisite stories in the Gospel of John, has had a strange history. It is totally absent from all the most ancient manuscripts and from the Syriac, Coptic and Armenian versions. It was unknown to Christian writers before Ambrose and Augustine: the latter, furthermore, was critical of what he called the excessive leniency of Jesus. When it finally gained circulation, one group of codices inserted the story in the Gospel of Luke instead of that of John, and with many alterations. Either it was written very late[21] (the style is quite different from that peculiar to John) or for a long time it was suppressed for the same reasons that made it so repugnant to Augustine.[22]

The Purification of the Temple

Instead of the story of the pardon granted to the adulteress, the Synoptic Gospels relate another remarkable action, performed by Jesus during his second visit to Jerusalem, which the Gospel of John expressly places at the start of the religious life of Jesus: the cleansing of the Temple.[23]

As we have said earlier, the Temple was an enormous structure, which Herod the Great had begun in 18 B.C.[24] as a replacement of the very old building which Solomon had erected with a huge expense in money and human life and which Nebuchadnezzar had destroyed in 586 B.C. In the interval, a modest building had served as a temporary substitute.

Herod's new Temple, which was also to be destroyed (by the Roman emperor Titus in A.D. 70), stood, like its predecessors, east of the city on the plateau of a hill now called Mount Moriah; the site is occupied today by the Dome of the Rock (sometimes incorrectly called the Mosque of Omar) and the sacred courtyard (the Haram) that surrounds the mosque itself. The Temple of Herod appeared to the observer as an irregular series of three levels, progressively higher and smaller. At the center of the highest level was the sanctuary (in Hebrew, qōdesh, which etymologically means "reserved," "separated"), a reproduction of that of Solomon; its golden dome dominated the city.

Inside the sanctuary stood the resplendent Altar of Incense, as well as the sacred seven-branched Menorah and the golden table on which the priests laid the showbread; behind a pentagonal door, always covered by a heavy veil, was a small, dark room, the Holy of Holies, which only the high priest was allowed to enter, and only on the Day of Atonement.

The sanctuary was surrounded by a small vestibule reserved for the priests (the Priests' Court), which was separated by a wall from the larger surrounding area (the Men's Court) that was open to all male worshipers. (See Figure VII.) From here a stairway with fifteen steps led down to the lower platform, which was still larger; this area was called the Women's Court (ḥāzarath nashīm), because women too were admitted, separately, to worship. Then a second stairway, with twelve steps, which encircled the Women's Court on all sides but the west, led down to the great trapezoidal courtyard accessible to all comers, even the heathen. Thus it was called the Court of the Gentiles (har ha bayīth). Its two longest sides measured 1,640 feet and 1,050 feet, respectively.[25] It was bounded on the south by the Royal Portico. On the east, it ended at the somewhat off-perpendicu-

FIGURE VII
THE TEMPLE OF JERUSALEM

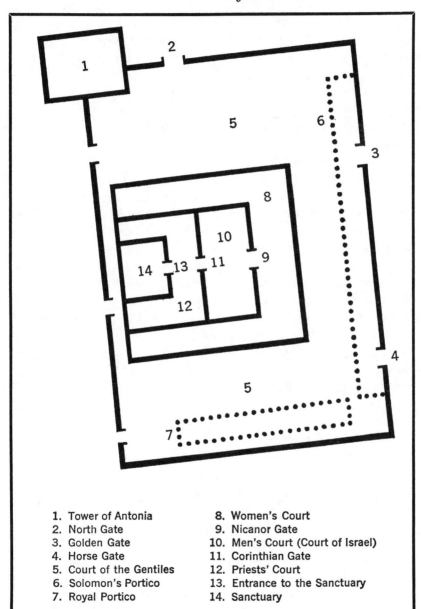

1. Tower of Antonia
2. North Gate
3. Golden Gate
4. Horse Gate
5. Court of the Gentiles
6. Solomon's Portico
7. Royal Portico
8. Women's Court
9. Nicanor Gate
10. Men's Court (Court of Israel)
11. Corinthian Gate
12. Priests' Court
13. Entrance to the Sanctuary
14. Sanctuary

lar line of 162 huge pillars of white marble, with capitals done in the Corinthian style; this section constituted Solomon's Portico.

Solomon's Portico had three colonnades, and here was the so-called merchants' quarter (ḥanūyōth). The vendors were especially busy on days of religious observance, when they were thronged with crowds that commingled Jewish pilgrims, Eastern merchants (especially Phrygians), Roman soldiers, tourists, and curious locals. Here one could buy or sell everything needed for sacrifices: sheep, doves, salt, grain, wine, incense, oil. In addition, there was a thriving trade in secular goods. It was the same impious and revolting business that is today so prosperous a parasite of the Cathedral of Milan, of the shrines of Lourdes and Loreto, and of every other place where there is an especially popular object of adoration.

At the northern end of the Temple stood the high Tower of Antonia, the headquarters of the army of occupation; from its top the eternally watchful and suspicious Roman sentries kept constant vigil over the interior of the Temple, particularly on feast days.[26]

The Gospels testify to the intensity of the horror and contempt that raged in the pure heart of Jesus when he saw the vast and shameful trafficking in Solomon's Portico, and they tell us that he "made a scourge of small cords"[27] and drove out the buyers and the sellers, overturning the money-changers' tables and the merchants' counters and crying: "Take these things hence; make not my Father's house a house of merchandise. . . . Is it not written, My house shall be called of all nations the house of prayer?[28] but ye have made it a den of thieves." His eyes flashed lightning, the Gospel According to the Hebrews says.[29]

"By what authority doest thou these things?" his adversaries raged.

Anger led Jesus into a damaging retort that was to raise serious problems for him later: "Destroy this temple, and in three days I will raise it up."

The immediate reaction was mockery: "Forty and six years was this temple in building, and wilt thou rear it up in three days?"

As he so often did, Jesus had spoken allegorically (what he meant here was the cult of the Temple, not the physical structure), but the people took him literally. The essence of the entire episode is to be found in this controversy, all the rest of the story being choreography, without any historical foundation. It is altogether impossible to believe that Jesus could have been capable of making such a scene, the violence of which would have provoked the Roman troops, if not the priests, to arrest him on the spot, always alert as they were for the faintest sign of trouble.

The real source from which the authors of the Gospels developed the story of the cleansing may have been quite different. Either Jesus did actually, but in private, express his revulsion to the Apostles, and his unreserved denunciation was later transformed into a legend of action, or the story is a distortion of fact that attributes to Jesus an earlier historical event of which there is clear proof:[30] the expulsion of certain Samaritans who had profaned the Temple in A.D. 7 by strewing human bones about its interior. Or it may have been derived from the life of one Jesus of Ananius, who, prophesying in the Temple in A.D. 70, predicted the destruction of Jerusalem and was flogged.[31] It is known that at least some details of the Gospel story were doubted even in antiquity. Origen, for instance,[32] conceded that the scourge of small cords was merely a figure of speech and never really existed.[33]

Nicodemus

One evening, when, as had already become his custom, he had gone back to the house in Bethany, Jesus had a remarkable visitor: a "doctor" of the Temple named Nicodemus, who, out of consideration for what people might say, dared not openly admit his admiration of Jesus and wanted to talk with him in the safety of darkness.[34] Even if this meeting really did occur (the Synoptic Gospels say not a word about it), in the spiritual Gospel of John it seems to be above all a pretext for presenting a doctrinal debate on the regeneration that was required of those embracing the Christian religion, and also an exhortation to the timid crypto-Christians (symbolized by Nicodemus) whose fear of other people's opinions kept them from embarking on the necessary *metanoia*.

"Except a man be born again," Jesus responded to the polite and even laudatory greeting of Nicodemus, "he cannot see the kingdom of God." Once again, there is an exploitation of double meanings. Nicodemus, who was only imperfectly acquainted with the message of Jesus, was completely bewildered by this reply and thought that Jesus was talking of physical rebirth.

"How can a man be born when he is old?" he protested. "Can he enter the second time into his mother's womb, and be born?"

Jesus explained that no one who was not reborn "in the spirit" could enter the kingdom of heaven. "That which is born of the flesh is flesh; and that which is born of the Spirit is spirit. Marvel not that I said unto thee, Ye must be born again. The wind bloweth where it listeth, and thou hearest the sound thereof, but canst not tell whence it cometh, and whither it goeth: so is every one that is born of the Spirit." In other words, it is an inner rebirth and is no more visible than the touch of the wind.

Possibly this saying of Jesus should be read with a passage from the apocryphal Gospel of Thomas: "If the flesh was produced for the sake of the spirit, it is a miracle. But if the spirit was produced for the sake of the body, it is a miracle of a miracle."[35] But here we have a clear Gnostic interpretation, which in the Gospel of John is barely latent.

Nicodemus asked then how the rebirth was to be accomplished. Jesus could not suppress a certain irony: "Art thou a master of Israel, and knowest not these things?"

The theologians' explanations of this passage are extremely diverse. Some, for instance, arrive at this meaning: "He who is not born again from on high [ἄνωθεν, anōthen—that is, through the work of the Holy Spirit] shall not . . .";[36] others prefer: "He who is not truly reborn (denuo) through baptism . . ."[37]

At this point, John goes into a long dogmatic disquisition that almost all scholars, believers or otherwise,[38] consider to be, as indeed it is, the Evangelist's own reflections on the Jews' unbelief and on the necessity of having faith in Jesus.

On the subject of the potentials for the miraculous and of the powers that arise from faith, the Synoptic Gospels, instead, revert here, in a few verses, to the fig tree that Jesus had cursed a day earlier. They finish the story thus: On their way to Jerusalem for the third time, Jesus and the disciples passed the tree and saw that it had completely dried out, down to the root. Simon Peter, remembering the malediction that Jesus had uttered, said to him. "Master, behold,

the fig tree which thou cursedst is withered away!" Jesus answered
that this was proof of the power of faith; he added: "If ye had faith
as a grain of mustard seed, ye might say unto this sycamine tree, Be
thou plucked up by the root, and be thou planted in the sea; and it
should obey you."[39]

This is the third such declaration that we have encountered, at
least in the Gospel of Matthew.[40] The Gospel of Thomas contains
two that seem to have resulted from contamination with that of
Matthew: "If ye become my disciples and hearken unto my words,
even these stones shall do your commands"; and: "If two are at
peace with one another in the same house, they can say to the
mountain, Be moved, and it will be moved."[41]

By What Authority?

During the Feast of Tabernacles, as he had planned, Jesus began
his preaching in Jerusalem, improvising his rostrum squarely in the
porticoes of the Temple, just as the rabbis customarily did. They
were naturally upset by this intrusion, and they did not know how
to assess the Nazarene's strange teachings.[42] "Who is he?" they asked
one another in surprise. Some of the more kindhearted were inclined
to tolerate his presence: "He is a good man." Many others had a
different view: "Nay, he deceiveth the people." And so the chief
priests and the other notables went up to him and demanded:[43] "By
what authority doest thou these things? and who gave thee this
authority to do these things?"

"I will also ask of you one question," Jesus retorted quickly,
"and answer me, and I will tell you by what authority I do these
things. The baptism of John, was it from heaven, or of men?"

The rabbis were thoughtful. If they said that John's authority
to baptize was divine, Jesus might argue: "Why then did ye not
believe in him? And why could I too not have authority from God?"
If they said that John had had no divine authority, they would have
to deal with the mass of the people, many of whom still believed
that John was an authentic prophet. So, to avoid compromising
themselves, they replied: "We cannot tell."

This gave Jesus his opportunity to get adroitly around their questions to him: "Neither do I tell you by what authority I do these things."

For the moment they were silenced, and left him, having no basis for action against him. Jesus exploited the occasion to tell a parable that sought to show the wisdom of blindly obeying an accredited prophet, such as John the Baptist and, by implication, himself, as the interpreter of the voice of God: "What think ye? A certain man had two sons; and he came to the first, and said, Son, go work to-day in my vineyard. He answered and said, I will not; but afterward he repented, and went. And he came to the second, and said likewise. And he answered and said, I go, sir; and went not. Whether of them twain did the will of his father?"

"The first," everyone replied. It should be observed, however, that through a remarkable error the Greek text says: "The last." That is ridiculous. Even Jerome, when he translated the reply into Latin, and after him all the Christian scholars, despite their firm conviction that the Scriptures were infallible, conceded and corrected the error in this instance.

Jesus continued, explaining his parable: "The publicans and the harlots go into the kingdom of God [more easily than] you. For John came unto you in the way of righteousness, and ye believed him not: but the publicans and the harlots believed him: and ye, when ye had seen it, repented not afterward, that ye might believe him."[44]

However readily one accepts the correction of the crowd's reply, one cannot agree with Jerome's translation of the Greek προάγουσι (proagousi) as praecedent, or "precede," "go before," which almost all modern translations have followed, including the King James. For this would mean that all the rest would also be admitted to the kingdom, regardless whether they repented, being merely subordinated to the publicans and the harlots.

The Wicked Husbandmen

Every time Jesus mentioned John the Baptist, the thought of his predecessor's violent death led to the fear that he, too, would be killed by his opponents; this became almost an obsession and

darkened his thinking. It influenced the Parable of the Wicked
Husbandmen, which the Synoptic Gospels set immediately after
what we have just considered. A landowner had a fine vineyard,
surrounded by hedges and equipped with a winepress and everything needful. He rented it out, and when it was time for the grapes
to be gathered, he sent a servant to collect his due. But the husbandmen in the vineyard beat the servant and sent him back empty-
handed. The master sent another servant, who received the same
treatment. Then he decided to send his son; surely the husbandmen
would respect him. But when they saw the master's son arriving,
they decided to kill him and seize the property. "What therefore,"
Jesus asked, "shall the lord of the vineyard do unto them?"

There was a long pause while Jesus looked into the eyes of each
of his hearers in turn; then, in a voice of thunder, as if he were
pronouncing sentence on them, he concluded: "He will miserably
destroy those wicked men, and will let out his vineyard unto other
husbandmen, which shall render him the fruits in their season."[45]

The parable reintroduces themes and characters that have already appeared in other comparable parables in the Gospels, of
which it is a kind of synthesis:[46] the master of the vineyard (God),
the servants (the prophets and the Apostles), the wicked husbandmen
(the unbelieving Jews), the son (the Messiah), etc. Its thesis is obvious, given the social conditions peculiar to the time: the plague of
large landholdings, the absentee owners of which lived in luxury,
far from their estates, and remembered the wretched workers only
when it was time to collect from them, never when they needed
help.[47] To interpret the parable in this light, however, as so many
English scholars do, is to risk defending the rebellious husbandmen
as the champions who restore a reversed social balance. The Evangelists' purpose in putting this parable into the mouth of Jesus was
exactly the opposite: to condemn the evildoers (the husbandmen)
who since the beginning of time had persecuted and murdered the
prophets (the servants and the son) but who would be struck down
by the terrible vengeance of God (the lord of the vineyard).

This, unfortunately (as we have already seen in other parables),
is a concept of God as an absolute and vengeful sovereign which we
should prefer not to find in the teachings of Jesus and which recalls

the Yahweh of the Old Testament. The real source of the parable is a passage in Isaiah.[48]

Furthermore, the story smells rather of anti-Semitism[49] and brings to mind the quarrels that, after the death of Jesus, arose between the Petrinists and the Paulinists over the removal of Christianity from the Jewish to the Greco-Roman world, as well as the old calumny of deicide by the Jews—unless, as Harnack believes,[50] the wicked workmen are supposed to represent not the entire Jewish nation but only the official caste of Israel, those Pharisees and priests whom indeed the Gospels present to us as opponents of the teachings of Jesus. The verses immediately after this parable[51] declare, in fact, that the Pharisees and the priests recognized that Jesus was speaking of them, especially when, likening the rejected prophet to "the stone which the builders rejected, [which] is become the head of the corner" (a comparison drawn from the literature of the Psalms[52]), Jesus added: "Therefore I say unto you, The kingdom of God shall be taken from you, and given to a nation bringing forth the fruits thereof."

The "doctors," rather than becoming angry at the words of Jesus (although the Evangelists have already ascribed hostile emotions to them), were stunned by his audacity. Having heard him quote passages from the Bible and refusing to recognize him as a qualified teacher, the Gospel of John says,[53] they demanded: "How knowest this man letters, having never learned?"

"My doctrine," Jesus answered, "is not mine, but his that sent me. If any man will do his will, he shall know of the doctrine, whether it be of God, or whether I speak of myself."

This same Gospel of John, which breaks down the ministry of Jesus in Jerusalem into three phases, makes use earlier of a similar homily by Jesus,[54] but it is a Christological digression.

The rabbis shook their heads and laughed at the claims of Jesus —which they considered impertinent—to present himself as a true teacher of religion. He misinterpreted their reproachful gestures, and, suddenly seized again by the fear that his life was in danger, he cried out in anguish: "Why go ye about to kill me?"

Even the spectators to the confrontation tried to reassure him: "Thou hast a devil: who goeth about to kill thee?"

"I have done one work," Jesus stammered, trying to explain his terror, "and ye all marvel."

It must be pointed out that his determination to emphasize the Jews' unbelief, which would ultimately bring them to "deicide," has so forced the hand of the author of the Gospel of John that he makes Jesus a rather sorry figure.

"Unto Caesar the Things Which Are Caesar's"

Then the scheming "doctors" tried to trap him in a fault and to compromise him.[55] "We know that thou art true, and teachest the way of God in truth, neither carest thou for any man," they began. "Tell us therefore, What thinkest thou? Is it lawful to give tribute unto Caesar, or not?"

The question was extremely dangerous. The Jews paid their tribute to the Romans grudgingly—it was tangible proof of their political subjugation. Since for them the idea of the Messianic kingdom was identical with that of national independence, they expected that Jesus could not help *denying* the legitimacy of the payment, and this would have provided grounds for denouncing him to Pontius Pilate. If Jesus said instead that the payment was proper, he would have lost prestige among the people.[56]

But the Nazarene saw through their malice and guile, and avoided the ambush. "Why tempt ye me?" he said out of a sudden new despondency. But then, after a few minutes' thought, he stood boldly up to them. "Show me the tribute money."

They handed him a coin. It was a silver denarius. On one side it bore the head of Tiberius, surrounded by the inscription: TI(BERIUS) CAESAR DIVI AUG(USTI) F(ILIUS) AUGUSTUS ("Tiberius Caesar, Son of the Divine Augustus, Augustus"); on the other side was the empress, Julia Livia, symbolizing Pax (Peace), with a scepter and flowers, accompanied by another inscription: PONTIF(EX) MAXIM(US) ("High Priest").[57]

"Whose is this image and superscription?" he asked.

"Caesar's."

"Render therefore unto Caesar the things which are Caesar's; and unto God the things that are God's." So Jesus saved himself with an epigram, ambiguous, oracular, and perhaps ironic as well,[58] which spared him the necessity of a compromising answer, and his questioners were disappointed.

But not posterity. The sentence was to be taken as a sober definition of the political philosophy of Jesus when the inevitable problems arose—the problems of co-existence between the Christian community and society as a whole, between the Church and the state, and in the last analysis between the spiritual and the temporal powers.

Precisely because it is intentionally ambiguous, Jesus' reply is susceptible of any interpretation. At first glance, it would appear to call for a sharp division of the two powers, a precise and peremptory rejection of every connection between religion and politics, which was to be corroborated later by the Gospel of John: "My kingdom is not of this world."[59] But it is absolutely unhistorical to ascribe to Jesus and his contemporaries, as Harnack does,[60] a conception of this kind that puts man's moral and civil duties on a level of equality. This concept of parity is an accomplishment—still much challenged —of modern liberal thought.[61]

In the culture in which Jesus lived, given the traditional theocratic aspirations of the Hebrew people and the expectation of a Messianic kingdom, it is impossible to read the sentence otherwise than as a purely transitory acceptance of the civil power. The state, with its laws and its taxes—all the more so in its then current guise as a dominating foreign power—was something temporary and imperfect, doomed to vanish with the "end of days."[62] Jesus conceded only the expediency—especially in order to avoid violence[63]—of resigning oneself to paying taxes in coins bearing the image of Tiberius, and he did this in the same spirit in which he had advised Peter to pay the tribute of the didrachma in Capernaum.

Such was to be the attitude of the early Christian community, at least in Jerusalem. Under the Roman Empire, however, when even religion was controlled by the state, this saying of Jesus had to be interpreted in the opposite sense, as an admonition to accept without challenge the subordination of religion to the temporal power. Even the authority of heathen civil governments, wherever they existed, accorded with the will of God, Paul said, and "whosoever therefore resisteth the power, resisteth the ordinance of God."[64]

A few lines later, he adds that rulers "are God's ministers [λειτουργοί, *leitourgoi*]." Various other writers of the same era are no less explicit.[65]

Christianity and the Empire

No occasion for conflict arose as long as there were no Roman citizens among the Christians. Christianity, in fact, was long viewed by the pagans as a Hebraic sect, and the Jewish communities in the Roman Empire, inasmuch as they consisted of foreigners, always enjoyed autonomy.[66] The Jews outside Palestine (the Diaspora) preserved the strongest ties within their groups, isolating themselves as much as possible from the life that surrounded them by retreating into their ghettos in order to keep faith with their own religion and their own customs.[67] In Rome itself, they had their synagogues and their catacombs in the Via Appia and the Via Nomentana.[68] Even when they became converts to Christianity, they quite logically held to the same habits, which to the Romans seemed "*sinistra, foeda, prava,*"[69] just as their reticence was put down to misanthropy, "*in odium generis humani.*"[70]

Such behavior, however, while it might be resented among foreigners but could give no cause for persecution, would have been intolerable in Roman citizens. It is otherwise impossible to explain how there could have been so many executions and martyrdoms among Christians in the first two centuries and how in the third century these grew into outright and bloody mass persecutions. There can be no other reason the Romans, who were noted for their uncommon tolerance of all religions and all rituals, would have made a cruel exception of Christianity.

One must study the problem objectively and not persist in looking at it as a struggle between good men and wicked men, between the weak and the strong.[71] But a distinction must be made between the prosecutions of Christians during the first two centuries and the persecutions in the third. Actually, no official measures were taken by the state in the first two centuries. It has long since been proved that no *institutum neronianum* prohibiting the Christian religion ever existed, despite the persistent beliefs of Zeiller, Lortz, and some others, who base their theories on a not too intelligible passage in Tertullian;[72] nor were such ordinances promulgated by the emperors who succeeded Nero.

If, then, the Christians were not persecuted by reason of a special law against their religion, what could have been the reasons for their arrests and executions? According to Le Blant, the authorities always fell back on the laws governing common crimes and alleged *sacrilegium, laesa maiestas,* or *coitus illicitus.*[73] Raffaele Pettazzoni holds a similar view,[74] for he points out that with regard to the Christians the government acted on the basis of the same considerations that, in 186 B.C.,[75] had brought about the prohibition of the Bacchanalia (with the arrest and execution of seven thousand persons) because it was a mystery religion which swore its members to secrecy. These hypotheses are not at all convincing. At least the charge of sacrilege, which in those days meant theft of sacred objects, was inconceivable for the Christians; nor does it seem likely that they were persecuted as members of "unlawful associations," since we know that the Christian communities were organized as perfectly legal *collegia funeraria,* or "burial societies."

Theodor Mommsen's statement that in the first two centuries Christians were punished always and only for criminal offenses, arising out of the *jus coercitionis,* to the extent to which their behavior disturbed the public peace,[76] may explain occasional instances, but it is inadequate to account for the hundreds of victims. Truth may be more nearly approached by Paolo Brezzi's view that the Roman authorities looked on the Christians with suspicion and sought some means of holding them in check, considering them irrational fanatics and therefore dangerous madmen.[77] Indeed, the word *superstitio* appears frequently in pagan writings that deal with Christianity, and it is accompanied by adjectives that demonstrate considerable contempt: *prava et immodica,*[78] *nova et malefica,*[79] *exitiabilis,*[80] *vana et demens.*[81] Nor could the pagans judge them in any other light, when they observed with what lunatic fanaticism the Christians, in their heroic but incomprehensible scorn of life, often deliberately sought the privilege of becoming martyrs (many records of their interrogations testify to the fact).

I believe that the measures taken against the Christians in the first two centuries were the pure and simple reflection of the deep aversion and resentment aroused in the ruling class and most of the middle class of Rome by the sectarians' behavior, which was politically and socially culpable: indifference to national traditions, going to the extreme of renunciation of their earthly country as transient and utterly imperfect; abstention from public life; refusal to bear arms in time of war; alien concepts of family relationships; refusal to worship the emperors.

This last offense in particular was always charged to the Christians, and in a sense it embraced all the others. To pay homage to the divinity of the emperor was not to grant the capricious demand of a megalomaniac tyrant but rather to accept the authority of the empire, personified in the sovereign, and to evidence devotion to the country—quite as Catholics today find it perfectly legitimate to attribute divine honors to the person of the pope as the head of the Church.

Even the real, systematic persecutions, ordered in the third century by Decius (reigned 249–51) and Diocletian (285–305), were intended to maintain the integrity of the empire and the ethical and civil traditions of Rome, which were threatened by the concepts of the Christians,[82] for by this time Christianity had made wide inroads among the poorest classes. Diocletian in particular was convinced that, all things considered, one of the causes of the crisis in the empire was the defeatism and anti-patriotism of the Christians. The idea that one's real country does not exist on earth had already been conceived by the Stoics; but the loyalty that the Stoics simultaneously professed toward their earthly nation as well as to a universal fatherland was equally genuine. This was not the case with the Christians.[83]

Diocletian's endeavor, with its onerous bureaucratic and military reforms, achieved only an illusory readjustment. In effect, it brought on a social and economic crisis that was reflected in a far-reaching spiritual collapse. It was just this collapse that nurtured a sudden resurgence of Christianity. In earlier times, the sect had especially attracted the lower classes with its apocalypticism (the promise of a kingdom of bliss) and its mystical and magical apparatus; now it drew its major support from the middle and upper classes because of its opposition to the imperial authority.

Church and State

In the first and second centuries, Christianity was repellent to the state because of its negative attitude toward civil and political affairs and its nature as an organization independent of governmental laws (its members could not marry outside the sect, it operated its own charitable system, employment was sought and offered only within the group, it had its own peculiar forms for funerals, etc.).[84] Conversely, from the third century on, concern mounted at the influence Christianity might be able to exert on public life and on the administration of government. The complaint of Cyprian, bishop of Carthage from 248 to 258, that the Church had become by worldly ambitions and excessive hunger for riches, even among the bishops, who were not above indulging in financial speculation and lending money at usurious interest,[85] and the enormous confiscations of Christians' property carried out by Emperor Valerian (reigned 254–60), are enough to illustrate the threat represented by the Church at that time, both because of its financial resources and because of the social level of its adherents. Christians were no longer a heroic minority of "saints," whose fanaticism was looked on as an aberration, but a mass of persons ready—and this outraged the upright Cyprian[86]—even to become apostates at the first hint of danger to their economic interests and, the moment the peril had passed, to revert to their defiance of the state's laws on the ground that conscience alone must determine whether they should obey this or that law.[87]

What was now most to be feared, in the view of the highest authorities of the empire, was the Christians' pretension to the right to demand a civil and political system of their own choosing. "Those who maintain that Christ's doctrine is opposed to the state," Augustine was to write, "call for armies, citizens, tax collectors, rulers who meet the requirements of Christian doctrine, and yet they still have the impudence to declare that doctrine opposed to the state!"[88]

But by this time it was impossible to uproot Christianity. In 311, a few years after Diocletian's abdication, his successor, Galerius (reigned 305–11), was compelled to grant freedom of worship to the Christians, hoping thus to mollify their antagonism. Finally, Constantine the Great frankly sought their support in his struggle to seize the thrones of Maxentius and Maximian and subsequently against his former ally, Licinius, offering them not only broad guaranties of freedom but high public offices (Edict of Milan, 313).

Until then, the Christians had given wide circulation to a violently apocalyptic literature that depicted Rome as "the great whore ... with whom the kings of the earth have committed fornication, and the inhabitants of the earth have been made drunk with the wine of her fornication" (the apocalyptic Book of Revelation, ascribed to John the Evangelist); that called Rome "Babylon" (the same text), or "the scourge of mankind" (the Sibylline Oracles), or "the eagle" whose "vain body" was perishing (the Apocalypse in the Second Book of Esdras); that said the emperor was the "beast" that worked the commands of Satan (the Book of Revelation). Now the Christians no longer boggled at collaborating with the "beast."

This moment marked the beginning of the real triumph of the Church as a political organization. It signified also a major change in the problem of Church relations with the temporal power. In its first phase, the problem was solved peacefully, by compromise. Christians were made eligible for government employment, they received title to the pagan basilicas, they were indemnified for losses suffered during the persecutions, they were subsidized, they were authorized to accept contributions, they were exempted from taxes, etc. In exchange, they renounced some of their basic principles: they no longer refused to bear arms, they gave the emperor the power of decision on theological matters in the Councils, as well as that of appointing and removing bishops, and in effect they worshiped him, calling him the Thirteenth Apostle and Pontifex Maximus.

At the same time, the recognition of Christianity as the state religion made it also the mass religion. Through a mere imperial edict its followers were expanded overnight by many millions. Then the Church was organized on the model of the state's bureaucracy, bishoprics being distributed by dioceses—that is, in conformity with the administrative districts of the empire.

However, with its exclusivist character as the *one* true faith and its grandiose theocratic aspiration, inherited from the Jews, to control even politically all the nations of the world "in the Lord's name," Christianity could not long retain this dual aspect (since in fact the emperor was also the head of the Church) or tolerate the practice of other religious confessions. Its first act was to subject the pagans to all the agonies that it had suffered during the period of persecutions and to try to suppress paganism altogether. It took over the major mystery cults (that of the mother-goddess was replaced by that of the Madonna, that of the invincible sun-god by the adoration of Christ slain and risen, in analogy to the setting and rising of the sun, etc.); it destroyed or appropriated to its own use the pagan shrines; it redistributed the prerogatives of the old inferior gods to its own saints; in 416 it obtained the enactment of a law barring pagans from public employment;[89] and so on.

Above all, the Church claimed the right to final determination of the morality and the legality of every act not only of its members but even of the chief of state himself. The maxim of Jesus: "Render unto Caesar the things which are Caesar's and unto God the things that are God's," left Caesar now with very little. The Church had begun to dominate the state.

Whereas in 212 Tertullian had written to Scapula, proconsul of Africa, to pray him to give Christianity at least equality with the other religions, and had declared the complete subordination of the Church to the emperor,[90] in 346 Julius Firmicus Maternus sent a pitiful declaration to the Emperors Constantius II and Constans in which he demanded that heathen beliefs *amputanda sunt penitus atque delenda.*[91] Not much later, Ambrose prevailed on Emperor Gratian to seize the property of the vestal virgins and the pagan priests, to confiscate the lands on which the temples stood, and to remove the altar of the goddess of victory from the Curia, the senate building.

In 494, Pope Gelasius I wrote to Emperor Anastasius I: "The chief powers on which the world is established are two: the sacred authority of the pope and the rule of the king. But the task of the popes is the greater in that, at the final judgment, they will have to give an accounting for the acts of the kings." Therefore the pope urged the king "to bow his head meekly before those who preside over the things of God."

A little earlier, in his *De Civitate Dei,* Augustine had developed the theory—which was to be maintained throughout the Middle Ages—that since the only true fatherland of every Christian was the future kingdom of heaven, earthly life was merely a precondition and preparation for it and must hence be completely governed by the Church. The victory of this concept was celebrated on Christmas night of the year 800, when Charlemagne received his crown from the pope. In order to furnish ostensible authority for this action, a deliberate forgery had been perpetrated: the so-called *Constitutum Constantini*, according to which, in gratitude for a miraculous cure of his leprosy, Constantine the Great had *granted* to Pope Sylvester I and his successors total jurisdiction over and title to *"omnes occidentalium regionum provincias, loca et civitates"* ("all the provinces, lands, and towns of the Western Empire"). From then on, every Western emperor was to be crowned in a papal investiture, and the pope was to have the right of election, removal, and, of course, control of the sovereign. Caesarian-Papalism had been transposed into theocracy.

In the Middle Ages, the interference of the Church in the empire was marked by periods of light and shadow, depending on the docility of the emperors and the forcefulness of the popes, but the theocratic claims of the Church were frequently reconfirmed. These claims, however, were severely set back later, first by the creation of the great European monarchies during the Renaissance and then by the secession of the Protestant world. Blows were subsequently struck by the secular policies of the reformist princes in the eighteenth century, by the French Revolution, and then by the liberal movement of the nineteenth century.

Yet the medieval concept has not been altered even today. The encyclical *Quas primas* of Pius XI (December, 1925), establishing the Feast of Christ the King, expressly asserted that it would be a grave error to seek to eliminate the authority of Christ in matters of public concern, and that earthly rulers should recognize that they govern not on the basis of their own laws but by the will of Christ. Similar ideas, even if tempered by a generalized exhortation to universal brotherhood, are restated in *Pacem in terris* of John XXIII (April 11, 1963).

Ecclesiastical theories on the relation of Church and state have been adapted to the times only in the sense that the Church has abandoned the position taken by Thomas Aquinas that the sole rightful form of government is the empire, which was ordained by God and derives from natural law; today the Church accepts monarchies as well, and even, when it must, republics.

[17]

THE MESSIAH

Is This in Truth the Messiah?

The spirited debates between Jesus and the priests and Scribes, the Gospel of John says,[1] attracted the worshipers who were going daily to the Temple for the Feast of Tabernacles. This was especially true of the exchange in which Jesus had cried out his fear of a death plot against him. Although everyone who had witnessed the incident had tried to calm his apprehensions, the news of the strife between him and the Temple authorities had spread, as incomplete and distorted as such stories always are, and some of those who observed that he continued to teach could not conceal their surprise: "Is not this he, whom they seek to kill? But, lo, he speaketh boldly, and they say nothing unto him."

"Do the rulers know indeed that this is the very Christ?"

"Howbeit we know this man whence he is: but when Christ cometh, no man knoweth whence he is."

Jesus heard these remarks, and he turned on the gossips in fury: "Ye both know me, and ye know whence I am: and I am not come of myself, but he that sent me is true, whom ye know not. But I know him: for I am from him, and he hath sent me."

Read literally, this would seem to mean that Jesus admitted he was only a man, the man whom all could claim to know, but also a man charged with a prophetic mission that allowed him to assume he could understand and interpret God's word better than others.

From the author of the Gospel of John, however, we can expect some Gnostic intention. In other words, for John, Jesus is here professing to be an aeon emanating from God.

By any and all means, John was determined to draw attention to the skepticism and the contempt manifested by the Jews toward the teachings of Jesus. Indeed, at this point, they sharply bade him to be silent. To that the Nazarene replied: "Yet a little while am I with you, and then I go unto him that sent me. Ye shall seek me, and shall not find me: and where I am, thither ye cannot come."

The Evangelist thus imputes to Jesus foreknowledge of his death and Resurrection, inappropriately, we must add, for even if one admits that Jesus had the gift of knowing the future, his adversaries would have been unable to understand his cryptic allusion to it. But John, delighted with his own invention, stupidly persists in carrying on the dialogue between Jesus and the priests as a game of equivocations.

"Whither will he go," they wondered, "that we shall not find him? will he go unto the dispersed [Diaspora] among the Gentiles, and teach the Gentiles?"

Immediately following this episode, John recounts another incident[2] in which again it is infinitely easier to detect the symbolism than the historical accuracy. It is the final day of the Feast of Tabernacles; the ceremonies in the Temple are brought to an end with the solemn "libation of water," the function of which is to thank the deity for this scarce element of nature and to assure further rain.[3] On this occasion, Yahweh is addressed under the name *Anî-wehu,* which is probably derived from the Old Testament expression *Anî-hū.*[4] Long-drawn-out trumpet calls announce that the priest who has gone to draw water from the sacred pool of Siloam has returned and entered the courtyard of the Temple. All the worshipers are hushed as he gravely ascends the stairs, holding his water jar in a hieratic pose until he arrives at the sacrificial altar, where the high priest in his splendid vestments awaits him. Here the water is mingled with wine and poured into two silver cups, which are set beside the altar, while the whole corps of priests recites psalms, circling the altar seven times.[5]

Suddenly the profound religious hush is shattered by a thundering voice: "If any man thirst, let him come to me, and drink. He that believeth on me, as the Scripture hath said, out of his belly shall flow rivers of living water."

It was Jesus. Carried away by the impressive ceremonial of the libation, he sought to attract the attention of the throng by crying aloud these two allusions to the prophecies of Isaiah.[6] Rather childishly, the Evangelist would have us believe they were sufficient to ignite a passionate discussion of Jesus' Messiahship among the congregation. "Of a truth this is the Prophet," many said at once. Others said: "This is the Christ." But the skeptics countered: "Shall Christ come out of Galilee? Hath not the Scripture said, That Christ cometh of the seed of David, and out of the town of Bethlehem, where David was?"

Some of the Temple guards who had seen and heard everything ran to notify "the chief priests and the Pharisees," who now were really alarmed and demanded: "Why have ye not brought him?"

"Never man spake like this man," the guards replied by way of explanation.

"Are ye also deceived? Have any of the rulers or of the Pharisees believed on him? But this people who knoweth not the law are cursed."

The guards stood ready to arrest Jesus if the order was given, but they were prevented by one of the Pharisees, who had stood aside in deep thought. This, the Gospel says, was Nicodemus, the man who had secretly gone to talk with Jesus the night before. Turning to his colleagues, he stood firm against any illegal proceeding: "Doth our law judge any man before it hear him, and know what he doeth?"

"Art thou also of Galilee?" they retorted angrily. Nevertheless, they yielded to his prudent counsel, resolving to attempt another amicable confrontation with Jesus.

Here we have all the ingredients required for a fine Christological structure: the Messiahship of Jesus, the allusion to his power of salvation through baptism ("the water that satisfieth eternally"), the unbelief and the antagonism of the wicked ("the priests and the Pharisees"), the unsureness of the people, the conversion of the just (Nicodemus).

The Messiah Is (Not) the Son of David

In the Synoptic Gospels the discussion of the Messiahship of Jesus is handled quite otherwise than in John.[7]

Let us point out once more, to refresh the reader's recollection, that the word "Messiah"—in Hebrew, *Māshîaḥ;* in Aramaic, *Meshîḥā;* in Greek, Χριστός (*Christos*)—was originally a title of the kings of Israel because they were "anointed" (this is the literal meaning of the Semitic words and of their Greek equivalent), or consecrated with holy oil; later it became, on the basis of certain passages of the Old Testament that were regarded as prophecies, the designation of the unknown descendant of the royal family of David who, it was hoped, would one day appear to reclaim the throne of his ancestors and to restore the independence and prosperity of his country. It does not follow, however, as even some theologians honestly admit,[8] that the expectation of the Messiah was as widespread among the people as the evangelical tradition would have one think. Possibly some hysterical patriots (such as the leaders of the Zealot movement) or some fanatical preachers had occasionally claimed to be the messengers of the future Messiah, or even the Messiah himself, without thereby having aroused any dangerous thoughts in men's minds, as Catholic theology asserts.[9]

In any case, the Evangelists undoubtedly viewed Jesus as one of these reformers (or, rather, as the one of them who was the true and only Messiah), and it is reasonable that they should have devoted at least a portion of their writings to the subject. But the ambiguity (which arose some time after the death of Jesus) between the Hebraic conception of a Messiah-King and that of a religious Messiah, the origin of which was primarily Paulinist, is reflected in the Gospels by frequently contradictory statements.

In the instance that we are about to take up, the Gospels indicate that the rabbis very likely went up to the Nazarene and asked him shrewdly: "Do you think Christ is David's son?" If Jesus replied affirmatively, as was to be expected, they intended to question him on his parentage and ancestry, and thus give the lie to the rumor that he might be the redeemer of Israel foretold by the Prophets.

Jesus' reply was and remains confusing: "How say they that

Christ is David's son? And David himself saith in the Book of Psalms, The Lord said unto my Lord, Sit thou on my right hand. . . . David therefore calleth him Lord; and whence is he *then* his son?"[10]

This answer, reported in almost identical words by all three Synoptics, seems then to deny that the Messiah must descend from David, and furthermore it contains no contention by Jesus that he is the person in question. How is this to be explained, when the Judaic conception of the Messiah was based on precisely this precondition and when the Davidic descent of Jesus is asserted, at least in Matthew and Luke, from the earliest chapters and supported with appropriate genealogies? Traditional exegesis, for the most part, blandly disregards the fact that problems of interpretation exist in this passage; at best, the Galilean's reply is viewed as a "defiance" of his enemies,[11] a kind of "riddle," "not lacking in irony,"[12] intended to confound them. This approach to the solution of the problem is not serious.

Nevertheless, it is quite impossible to accept the literal meaning of the Gospel text and to ascribe to Jesus a clear denial that the Messiah must belong to the house of David, or to contend that the whole Gospel section is worthless because the passage of the Psalm cited by Jesus is not even a Messianic prophecy[13] (the speaker there, indeed, is not David himself but an anonymous poet who seeks to praise: "The Lord said unto my lord [David], Sit thou at my right hand . . .").

Modern Biblical criticism has arrived at these conclusions, but it is absurd to argue that they express the views of Jesus, or, rather, of the Evangelists who attributed these words to him. On the contrary, it is reasonable to believe that both Jesus and the Evangelists, in accord with all the Israelites of the time, were convinced that the Psalm was prophetic in meaning and that the Messiah must indeed be a descendant of David.

Nor is the explanation offered by Loisy[14] any more persuasive: that Jesus did not mean to confound the rabbis with an ironic answer but sought to state a more sublime concept of the Messiah than theirs. In other words, he had no intention of casting doubt on the belief in the necessity of Davidic descent but believed that the Messiah's spiritual quality must come from some much higher source—that is, directly from God. This hypothesis was hinted at in the early evolution of the Messianic idea after the death of Jesus; it presupposes speculation on a Jesus with two identities: the son of David according to the flesh and the Son of God according to the spirit.

It is my belief that only one plausible explanation is possible: as in many other instances (and we have already adduced some of them), the Gospels are reporting *one* interpretation of an idea—in this case, of the Messiah—even though it does not accord with other interpretations reported elsewhere; and what prevails here is precisely that Paulinist Christological doctrine that tends to make the Nazarene a moral and religious Messiah, rather than the more frankly Hebraic and hence Judeo-Christian doctrine of a political Messiah.

The Messenger of God

One must, then, absolutely rule out the theory that Jesus himself and his contemporaries thought of the Messiah (whether political or moral) as a divine being, a heavenly messenger appointed by God to restore justice in the world and to act as the arbiter and judge of human destinies.

Forgetting the voluminous Biblical literature in support of the Messiah's descent from David, Catholic theologians,[15] the modernist Loisy,[16] the Protestant Schweitzer,[17] and numerous others, all of whom seek to prove that precisely this divine element was inherent in the Messianism of Jesus and all the Jews of his time, base their arguments solely on the authority of two apocalyptic texts. One of these is the apocryphal Ecclesiasticus, the work of a certain Jesus, the son of Sirach, who lived about a hundred and fifty years before the Nazarene; the other is the Book of Daniel, which may be of even later origin. Both speak of a supernatural being who shall come down from heaven in human guise (*kebar 'enōsh*) to establish a new era.

These are not, however, very cogent authorities. First of all, they could not have been so influential as the Holy Scriptures, or so widely circulated that they could have overthrown the traditional Biblical concept of the Davidic Messiah; in the second place, the Book of Daniel in particular is of most uncertain date, and there is no lack of suspicions that at least the sections containing the prophecies of the heavenly messenger are apocryphal.[18] And yet it would not be difficult to interpret the "one like the Son of man" of which they speak, not as a divine emissary, but as a collective allegory of the people of Israel.[19]

In any case, the idea of a Messiah who should be a man of flesh and blood, and, more specifically, singled out as a member of the former royal family, was so deeply rooted in the Judaic mentality that it survived in Christianity, side by side with the concept of him as a divine being, even after the new religion, released from the chains of Hebraicism, lost its ethnic character and spread throughout the Greco-Latin world.

The dogma of the dual nature of Jesus, which was to evolve out of centuries of debate, polemic, contradiction, and sensational schisms, and the identification of Jesus with the expected Messiah were barely at the stage of birth in the apostolic age. The literature of the New Testament demonstrates the uncertainty that existed on the matter. Side by side with the denial attributed to Jesus in the scriptural passage examined earlier[20] ("Whence is he *then* his son?"), the Gospels contain no less firm declarations of the opposite viewpoint (particularly the genealogical tables of Matthew and Luke); sometimes both the Davidic Messiah and the heavenly Messiah appear in the same sentence, such as that of Luke in the episode of the Annunciation: "He . . . shall be called the Son of the Highest: and the Lord God shall give him the throne of his father David."[21]

The Apostles, who lived with Jesus through every day, who knew his parents and his brothers, who observed his exultations and his despairs, who rejoiced in the sublime manifestations of his greatness of soul, and who endured his violent outbursts of anger, could not consider him other than a human being. As is obvious from the Gospels, their attitude toward him was that of disciples, not always respectful and not always persuaded, as well as that of fanatical followers of a leader sent by God to rouse the people of Israel from their sloth and to inaugurate a new era.

From very ancient Gospels, later declared apocryphal by the Church, such as the Gospel According to the Hebrews, the Gospel of Ebionites, and the Gospel of the Nazarenes (works, that is, current in the original Jewish Christian communities), it is clear that Jesus was considered a prophetically inspired *man*. The Acts of the

Apostles, approved by the Church as a canonical text, contains a sermon by Peter in which he speaks of Jesus as "a *man* approved of God among you by miracles and wonders and signs, which God did by him."[22] But not even once do the Synoptic Gospels ascribe to Jesus an explicit declaration of his own heavenly origin.[23] And today, at least among certain advanced Protestant theologians, there is a tendency to maintain that the activity of Jesus as an intermediary between God and man does not necessarily imply speculation on a supernatural being.[24]

Perhaps at most one can establish from the Synoptic Gospels that Jesus felt a religious vocation that led him to dedicate himself to preaching and to furnishing an example of absolute obedience to God, to duty, and to justice.[25] This was his "Messianic consciousness," which was not fully understood even by his Apostles, who expected more concrete and immediate deeds of him.[26]

Only the Gospel of John flatly attributes to Jesus the certainty of his own divinity. We already know, however, that the Fourth Gospel is of exceedingly little worth as a historical document and that Christian theologians themselves describe it as the "pneumatic"—that is, "spiritual"—Gospel because it can be accepted only as a philosophical Christological dissertation.

If we accepted as historical certain statements that John puts into the mouth of Jesus—"I am the light of the world"; "The Father himself, which hath sent me, hath borne witness of me"; "I proceeded forth and came from God";[27] etc.—we should be likely to look on Jesus as pathologically abnormal. The Evangelist himself was convinced of that; after attributing a number of such statements to Jesus, he concludes by describing the indignation of the priests: "Then took they up stones to cast at him."[28] But Jesus, the same Gospel adds, "hid himself and went out of the Temple."

The Son of God

The crisis that followed immediately on the death of Jesus, with the bewilderment of the Apostles and their dispersion—as the literature of the New Testament attests—makes it plain that they ascribed a totally earthly character to his Messiahship and that his death left them momentarily paralyzed. A dead Messiah, who could no longer act for the welfare of the people of Israel, was an absurdity.[29]

However, in order to account for the fact that some time later they all came together again in Jerusalem for the purpose of rebuilding the shattered sect, it is not necessary to suppose either the occurrence of something unforeseen or a change in their own Messianic conception. For the Jews (and the superstitition passed over into Christianity), it was not so impossible to imagine that someone who had died might come back to life. Evidence of such a superstition is to be found, among other places, in the Biblical stories of Elijah's reviving of the widow's son in Sarepta and of Elisha's resurrection of the Shunammite's son,[30] as well as in the analogous accounts, following the same pattern, of the raising of the dead by Jesus, to say nothing of the various apparitions of long dead prophets, like that of Moses and Elijah to Jesus on the mountain of the Transfiguration.

In the Apostles' faith there was no bar to a belief in the Second Coming of the promised Messiah (the Parousia), once they had overcome their initial disappointment and despair. The Mandeans, the followers of John the Baptist, also expected their master to be born again, and naturally they took Jesus for an impostor.[31]

In no way, however, did this expectation of the Second Coming imply the deification of Jesus; even less, the need to correlate his Messiahship and his death. The idea of a Messiah who must suffer and die in order to accomplish the redemption of the people of Israel was totally alien to the Jews.[32] Even if traditional theology likes to pretend that the notion already existed in the lifetime of Jesus,[33] everyone knows that it was instead the most startling of the innovations introduced into Christianity by Paul. And its source is also known: in the Hellenistic culture, in which the Apostle of Tarsus had been brought up and in which he performed his missionary work, the salvationist function of Jesus as a mediator between God and man could be understood and accepted only as that of an exceptional being received into immortality (in the manner of so many pagan heroes taken up onto Olympus at the command of Zeus), or better still as that of the many demi-gods, such as Attis and Adonis, whom the mysteriological Greco-Oriental cults adored for just such redemptive deaths.

The "infamy of the cross," which was a stumbling block for the

Apostles, disordering all their thinking and leading them to look for the Second Coming, was precisely what Paul skillfully exploited for the construction of his own Christology. Not having personally known Jesus or shared the Apostles' hopes and dreads, Paul took no account of the master's earthly activity and made his function as a redeemer begin and end with his death. It must be pointed out that on the subject of the personality of Jesus, Paul's thinking is not always consistent. Or, rather, today it is impossible to know exactly what he thought; what the Church calls Pauline Christology, like the Christology that it attributes to the authors of the Gospels, was probably shaped little by little during the first centuries of Christianity.[34] In Paul's Epistles, Jesus is sometimes a man[35] who was "declared [ὁρισθέντος, horisthentos] to be the Son of God . . . according to the Spirit of holiness";[36] at other times he is the "image" (εἰκών, eikōn) of God,[37] having the "form" (μορφή, morphē) of God and being equal (ἴσα, isa) with God;[38] but in every case he is always below God; he is "the firstborn of every creature."[39]

The Apostles found it difficult to follow Paul in this original conception. For them the memory of Jesus as a man was too vivid, and they could not conceive of him transformed into a divine incarnation. Moreover, the concept would have offended their Jewish beliefs. And their nationalist pride rebelled at the thought of admitting the Gentiles to the bliss of the Chosen People; the Jews had endured too much from the harshness and the contempt of the Romans to be genuinely concerned for their conversion. Hence, they remained bound to their traditional Messianism.

The three Synoptic Gospels show signs of the coexistence of both of these Christologies and there is evidence of an attempt to blend them. The old idea of Jesus as a perfect man "adopted" by Yahweh at the moment of his baptism (an idea that persisted in many apocryphal texts as well as in Mark, the first of the Synoptics) is modified in the later Gospels of Matthew and Luke to become that of God's choice of Jesus at his birth, or even that of God's deliberate "creation" of him. The spirit of God, which according to Mark had descended on Jesus during his baptism as a sign of divine approval, becomes for the two other Evangelists the means employed by Yahweh to bring about Mary's motherhood.

The Gospel of John, which is of still later composition, oscillates between these concepts and that of Paul, with a certain tendency toward a Gnostic interpretation. In this Gospel, Jesus is now a marvelous being who communicates to men the truths inspired in him by God,[40] now a creature of God[41] who recognizes that God is greater than he,[42] now indeed a being who is one with God,[43] or, better, an emanation of God. The Gospel of John is much concerned with the philosophical explanation of the ways in which this emanation operates, but one cannot say that it is always clear, because the author strives to adapt his ideas to the Hermetic Greek beliefs rather than to a coherent Gnostic system. The eminent Protestant theologian Charles H. Dodd has pointed out a number of passages in the *Corpus Hermeticum* that are extraordinarily like passages in the Gospel of John.[44]

Perhaps the Gnostic doctrine is explained more felicitously in the writings of Justin Martyr (who died about 166); he was probably a contemporary of the editor of the Fourth Gospel.[45] In any case, to John it was not a matter of Yahweh's having taken on mortal shape, in the style of the pagan gods, because this would have been too awkward for the concept of divinity that was peculiar to the Jews. The Evangelist has to confine himself to calling Jesus the Word, the Logos (Λόγος), of God[46]—that is, his "Voice," his "Message," the expression of divine will and divine power.

The Logos is on the order of the *bath qōl* and the *shekīnāh* of the Old Testament (we discussed these in the section on Yahweh and his attributes), but it is not altogether the same thing. It is not possible to find a Gnostic doctrine in Judaism at this time, as Ferdinand Baur, Karl Adam, and others do.[47] For the Hebrews, the *bath qōl* was purely and simply the voice of God, which, it was believed, could now and then be heard, dreadful and terrible, without any visible sign of its source (like the voice that rebuked Eve after the theft of the apple); the *shekīnāh* was a glorious, resplendent manifestation of the Eternal, in the form of light. The Logos of John, on the other hand, was a complete incarnation in a real and durable physical body (the entire life of Jesus). It is not even a theophany; it is a reproduction or duplication of God, or, rather, the emanation and the physical materialization of one of his qualities (his voice, his will).

The concept does not lend itself too readily to comprehension, and for the most part theologists fell back on the more ingenuous and less refined, though more understandable, idea of Jesus as the Son of God.

This new terminology having been ratified, it was thought desirable to show that it had already existed in the Biblical texts as a denotation of a being chosen by God and that ancient Hebraic thought, too, had thus accepted the idea of divine paternity. Actually, the Old Testament does contain the phrase *ebed Yāhweh,* which, however, means "the servant of God," "the slave of God," "God's liege subject." The Greek text of the Septuagint translates it equivocally as παῖς Θεοῦ (*pais Theou*), inasmuch as *pais,* like the Latin *puer,* can mean either "little boy" or "slave." Subsequently, it was quite simple to replace *pais* in the sense of "boy" with υἱός (*hyos*), which means "son."

Once this change had taken hold, an attempt was made to assign "Son of God" as the meaning of another expression, which Jesus frequently used: "the Son of man"—*ben-ādām* in Hebrew, *bar-nāshā* in Aramaic. As we have already had occasion to explain, this second term, however, has no affinity with the first; if anything, indeed, it represents the exact contrary, because it is simply the equivalent of "man" (the son of mankind), and often, too, it is used as a substitute for the pronoun "I."

Man and God

The doctrine of Jesus as the Son of God was not readily accepted—or, at any rate, understood—in the same way by all of Christendom. For centuries it was the theme of violent quarrels among the Fathers and Doctors of the Church, taking precedence over much more important questions bearing on the teachings of Jesus. Some clerics, such as Theodotus of Byzantium (ca. 190) and his followers, and later Paul of Samosata, bishop of Antioch in 260, maintained the old apostolic concept that the affiliation of Jesus to God was purely symbolic, in the sense that Jesus was really a man adopted by God at the time of his baptism (adoptianism). Others, such as Tertullian (d. ca. 220), were of the opinion that the gestation of Jesus took place at the creation of the world, in the instant in which God spoke the *Fiat lux* ("Let there be light") of Genesis;[48] then, appearing to the Patriarchs and inspiring the Prophets, God's Word-Son became "accustomed" to living among men.[49] Vacillating between this belief, which was still very close to the Hebraic *bath qōl*, and that of the Gnostic Logos, Tertullian said in the same treatise that the Word was a kind of radiation from the Father which, descending into a virgin ("*delapsus in virginem quandam*"), took on a human body.[50] Sabellius, a priest in Ptolemais between about 240 and 260, maintained that Jesus had been no more than a human body assumed by God in order to be able to show himself (Docetism, from δοκέω, *dokeō*). Origen (185–ca. 254), the chief spokesman of Gnosticism, argued instead that Jesus should be understood not exactly as an incarnation of God but as a being distinct from him, even though of divine substance, because he was an emanation of God, and, in any event, always in second place with respect to God and hence subordinated to him (subordinationism).

A synod convoked in Antioch in 264 attempted to resolve the controversy by declaring that Jesus had been begot by God, but *ab aeterno,* and therefore was eternal, like God. The absurdity of this definition (it is impossible to beget *ab aeterno,* because the act necessarily requires a time when the begetter already existed and another when that which is created begins to exist) caused fresh quarrels. In the Eastern Church, Arianism, the doctrine of Arius (280–336), prevailed and received wide dissemination. It reverted to the idea that Jesus had been only a man, refusing to accept either that God could have assumed human shape or that Jesus could be co-eternal with him, inasmuch as all things, including Jesus, had been created. Therefore, Arius concluded, Jesus could be said, because of his perfection, to be *like* God, but not identical with him.

The First Council of Nicaea (325), presided over by Constantine the Great, condemned Arius to exile as a heretic and approved the doctrine of his antagonist, Athanasius, bishop of Alexandria, who upheld the identity between God and Jesus. Thus the Council elevated to the rank of dogma a doctrine which a short time before had been condemned as heresy by the Synod of Antioch. The dogma was embodied in the so-called Nicene Creed: "Jesus Christ, the Son of God, begot, not made, by the Father as his only Son, of the same substance with the Father, God of God, Light of Light."[51]

Even among the Council Fathers there was considerable disagreement: of the three hundred and eighteen bishops in attendance, at first only seventeen refused to subscribe to the Creed; then they were joined by a number of others, who had approved the document only out of deference to the emperor but who now withdrew their signatures.[52] Conflicting views were voiced once more: Basil the Great and an eminent group of Fathers with him stood for the absolute identity of God and Jesus; Acacius and the Acacians, for similarity only; Priscillian, Eunomius, and their followers, for dissimilarity. By this time, the Arians had become so numerous that Constantine was persuaded to recall Arius from exile and to depose Athanasius.

Between Arians and Athanasians, Nicenes and anti-Nicenes, stood the Semi-Arians, who, like Arius, denied the identity of God and Jesus but who differed from him in admitting the divine nature of Jesus. Since the Greek for "identity" is ὁμοουσία (homoousia) and for "similarity" or "resemblance" it is ὁμοιουσία (homoiousia), it was a bitter truth that all these fierce battles were fought over one small i!

The battles went on, constantly growing harsher, during the fourth and fifth centuries. Apollinaris, bishop of Laodicea (d. 390), maintained that Jesus had had a human body but a divine soul; Cyril, bishop of Alexandria (d. 441), contended that Jesus had been a perfect man, physically and spiritually, but that the Logos had increased his perfection by taking up residence in him as in a temple; Nestorius (ca. 430) argued that the two natures—the human and the divine—existed together in him, each with its own independence and personality; Dioscorus and later Eutyches (excommunicated in 451) believed that the two characters had mingled in him and become absorbed together to form one single nature (Monophysitism).

A synod had to be summoned to seek clarity. It was called by Theodosius II for Ephesus, in 431. Cyril, finding that he had arrived ahead of his Nestorian opponents, made haste to open the sessions and impose his own doctrine. Nestorius, arriving immediately afterward, gathered his partisans and deposed Cyril for having acted illegally. Annoyed, Theodosius exiled both of them. Then Eutyches took advantage of the situation to persuade the emperor to convoke the Council of Ephesus (449) and to have the Monophysite doctrine approved. When the Council opened, the debates were so impassioned that a number of the debaters were left dead. and it went into history as t   um).

So it v   iother Council be hel   to condemn Monophysi   y revised to state that t   ntical Christ in two natι   divided and not separat   ot eliminate their differ   operties and been unitec   i single substance ("hyj

Naturɑ   ιew formula of "hyposta   romise. The conclusion   alcedonians, particularly   ιs, patriarch of Constantι   atever one's opinion as t   certain that the Man-Go   ...αο σιιιgιc operative entity and hence that he had only one activity and one will—the divine (Monotheletism).

In the sixth century, controversies arose among the Monophysites themselves: Severus of Antioch believed that Jesus had been a kind of "mixture" and that during his life his body had been as corruptible as that of any other man (phthartolatry); Julian of Hallicarnassus, a contemporary of Severus, maintained, on the other hand, that Jesus had had an incorruptible body until after the Resurrection (aphthartodocetism); Gaianus of Alexandria contended that the body of Jesus was eternal, and had never been created (aktistetism); in opposition, Theodosius declared that Jesus had been created (ctistolatry).

It was not until the Third Council of Constantinople (680) that Monophysitism and Monotheletism were once more condemned and it was reiterated that the two natures, human and divine, existed in Jesus Christ without "division, conversion, separation, or confusion." Nevertheless, Monophysitism continued to exist; today it is embraced by the Coptic Church and the Abyssinian Church (about ten million people), the Armenian Church (four million), and the

Jacobite Church (one million). Twentieth-century theology seeks to avoid not only the discussions so dear to old Greek metaphysics, unhistorically imposed on the relations between the two substances in the person of Christ, but also the modern critical studies on the origin of the dogma; it prefers the view that "the secret of the person of Jesus is impregnable even to reflection based on faith."[53]

Father, Son, and Holy Ghost

Matters became still more complicated when a third character was interposed between the Father and the Son: the Holy Ghost. The authors of the New Testament had mentioned it so explicitly that it was impossible not to take it into consideration. Yet the problem of the Holy Ghost attracted no particular attention virtually until the fourth century, for all the concern of the theologians was concentrated on the Son.[54]

The "Ghost" or "Spirit" is an element of Judaic origin: the Hebrew word *rūaḥ* ("sigh," "breath," etc.) was used to designate the divine influence and inspiration that descended invisibly, as a sign of God's presence. It was manifest, for example, to the Prophets, and aided them in their work. In response to the need, innate in all mankind, to objectivize abstract concepts, the Jews symbolized it in the form of a dove, *rūaḥ* being a noun of feminine gender. Often encountered in the Old Testament, it appears also in the New, especially to attend and approve the baptism of Jesus, and, after his death, to inspire the Apostles when they reassembled in Jerusalem on the day of Pentecost.[55]

But Paul, taking as his point of departure the etymological meaning of the Greek word with which the Septuagint only approximately translated the Hebrew *rūaḥ*—πνεῦμα (*pneuma*), which means "breeze," "breath," "wind," "air," the same as *spiritus* in Latin—somewhat distorted its original meaning and defined it as the divine atmosphere in which the Christian lives, which penetrates and fills all his being; more specifically, he called it sometimes perspicacity, sometimes mystic exultation and ecstasy, certainly influenced by an analogous concept of religious elation that was present in the Greek mystery cults. In a broader interpretation of Paul's theology, it is possible also to conceive of the Spirit as "the moral force that guides the Christian to live according to the faith."[56] Paul frequently uses it with the adjective ἅγιον (*hagion*), which means "holy." Whence the literal Latin translation: *Spiritus Sanctus* ("the Holy Spirit," "the Holy Ghost").

In the Gospels of Matthew and Luke,[57] the Spirit, departing to a lesser degree from its original significance but already assuming a certain artless consistency, is used to denote the genetic "force" or "power" by which the Eternal incarnated himself in Mary, materializing in the form of a shadow. It is worth remarking, as a matter of curiosity, that, since *rūaḥ* is a feminine noun, it is called in some of the apocryphal writings "the mother" of Jesus!

The materialization of the Spirit becomes complete in the Fourth Gospel. For John it is no longer a more or less abstract manifestation of divine power, but, in the same manner as Jesus, a derivation of God. John also calls it παράκλητος (*paraklētos*)—that is, the "intercessor," "messenger," "counselor," that Jesus promises to send to the disciples after his death, by way of consolation (it is translated as "comforter" in the King James Bible).

Given this personification of the Spirit too, Christian theology should at a given time have asked itself what degree of divinity should be ascribed to it and what should be its precise relations with God and Jesus. In actuality, the Christian Olympus no longer consisted only of a dualism (Father and Son), it was now a trinity. The term *Trias* (Τριάς) appeared for the first time in Theophilus of Antioch as early as the end of the second century, and it was later accepted by the Eastern Church, while Latin-speaking areas adopted *Trinitas*, used for the first time, at about the same period, by Tertullian.[58]

It is true that the conjunction: "the Father, the Word, and the Holy Ghost," can be found in the First Epistle of John,[59] but that is the sole instance in the Scriptures, and it is undoubtedly a later addition because the verse does not appear in any manuscript before the fifteenth century and is never cited by any Father of the Church, whether Greek or Roman, even after the third century, when the trinitarian debates intensified.

Naturally, all those who, like Paul of Samosata, Sabellius, and Irenaeus, had refused to accept a duplication of divinity in Father and Son opposed its triplication even more strongly. At the very most, they were willing to concede that Father, Son, and Holy Spirit were three *means* by which God, who was unique, might show himself: three aspects, three attributes, as for example the sun might have the three attributes of its face, its light, and its heat (modalism). Tertullian, while recognizing the three separate persons, resorts[60] to comparisons of the same kind to explain their relations: root, tree, and fruit; source, river, and stream; sun, ray, and beam. For Arius, Eunomius, Macedonius, and others, the Holy Spirit was a "creation" of God, like Jesus. Origen, however, brought the Spirit into his Gnostic hierarchy: Jesus was an emanation of God, and the Spirit, in turn, was an emanation of Jesus.

There was a great confusion of words to define these three persons: they were said to be essences (οὐσίαι, *ousiai*), or natures (φύσεις, *phuseis*), or orders (τάξεις, *taxeis*); they were called *gradus, formae, species, potentiae*, etc.,[61] and when each had to be distinguished from the others, the Father was called the Principle (ἀρχή, *archē*), the Beginning, God in and of himself, the First God, *Deus Princeps*, the Supreme Being, the Father of All, the King of Kings;[62] the Son was called the Word, the Logos, the Message, the Voice, the Judgment, the Will of the Father, the Power of the Father, the Vicar of the Father, the Measure of the Father, the Right Hand of God, the Arm of God, the Gleam, the Virtue, the Wisdom of God, the Counselor of the Father;[63] finally the Holy Spirit received such names as Paraclete, Messenger, Gift of God, Finger of God, Shape of the Father, and Seal of the Son.[64]

The first official definition of the Trinity came only in 381, in the First Council of Constantinople, which established the creed that the divine nature (οὐσία, *ousia*) is identical, but that there are three eternally distinct substances (ὑποστάσεις, *hypostaseis*): the Father was not begot (he exists of himself), the Son was begot, but *ab aeterno*, and the Spirit proceeds from the Father. In a certain sense, the hierarchic distinction established by Origen was accepted, but not subordinationism, because the three persons were defined as co-essential and co-equal, with an iota of priority for the Father.

However, this did not put an end to the disputes.

Augustine (d. 430), dissenting from what had been proclaimed in Constantinople, believed that the Holy Ghost did not proceed directly from the Father (as the Arians maintained—in this they agreed with the Council) or directly from the Son (as the Gnostics believed), but directly from *both at once,* and that the Trinity constituted a kind of common manifestation of divinity, in the same way, for example, in which memory, intellect, and will make up the three components of the human mind[65]—in other words, the three persons were distinguished as *amans,* or "loving" (God), *amatus,* or "loved" (the Son), and *amor,* or "love" (the Holy Spirit). By some means, the Holy Spirit is the bond between the two others.[66] In a council of bishops held in Toledo in 589, the Spanish clergy adopted the Augustinian theory, and the phraseology of the Constantinopolitan Creed was modified accordingly: Father, Son, and Holy Spirit are three substances of the same divine nature and the Spirit proceeds from both the Father *and the Son* (the Filioque clause).

The Filioque opened a tragic chapter in the history of Christianity.[67] In 896 it was declared a heresy by Photius, patriarch of Constantinople, for the East continued to cling to a more strictly monotheistic conception than the West. As a consequence, a definitive separation took place in 1054 on the initiative of the patriarch Michael Cerularius, and the Eastern Orthodox Church (which counts today over a hundred and sixty million adherents) became wholly independent of the Church of Rome.

But Luther, Calvin, and the other leaders of the Reformation adopted the trinitarian concept of the Catholics and even went to the same extremes in punishing those few who attempted to challenge it: the physician Michael Servetus was burned at the stake by the Calvinists of Geneva because he dared to attack this dogma of Christian faith, and in Wittenberg, too, the opponents of the Trinity were condemned.

The Lord

The practical impossibility (which is not limited to Christians of moderate schooling) of *understanding* the dogma of the Trinity led to the average believer's being completely unaware of the existence of a Holy Spirit in his religious devotions and of his confusing the two other persons of the Trinity. Thus he considers Jesus the one true God, and the Supreme Being whom Jesus labored so hard to make his followers understand, love, and worship with faith and devotion has been replaced by Christ in the adoration and liturgy of the Church: the focus of Catholic ritual is the Mass, which repeats allegorically the sacrifice of the death of Jesus, and Communion, which frankly symbolizes his flesh and blood; the religious calendar is based on the commemoration of the most important events in the life of Jesus (Christmas, Epiphany, Easter, Ascension Day); and so on.

The protracted Christological conflicts reveal how fiercely but uselessly men of good sense fought to prevent this deformation, which inevitably has one or the other of two effects: either it actually destroys the rigorous Judaic monotheism practiced by Jesus himself, establishing a second god at the side of the traditional sole deity, or it leads to a humanization and hence a debasement of God himself, which is in considerable conflict with the idea of superiority and absolute abstraction that should be the conception of the Eternal.[68] Furthermore, the belief that Jesus was born "of woman" at a specific moment in history contradicts the idea of his eternal pre-existence,[69] and, conversely, the unimpaired physical virginity of Mary from conception through birth makes Jesus a mere god of passage on earth, so little endowed with human character as to imperil the dogma of redemption.[70]

When Christian theology asserts that *from the very outset* the Apostles were convinced that Jesus was equal and co-eternal with God,[71] it attempts to explain this incredible idea by invoking the Apostles' own certainty that they were imbued with the grace of the Holy Ghost purely and simply through the constant, invisible presence of Jesus among them, even after his death: hence their ability to prophesy, to heal the sick, to drive out devils, to speak in tongues.[72] These would be the major if not the only reasons, it holds, that could have induced devout Israelites, wary and jealous guardians of the faith of their fathers, unreservedly to ascribe pagan methods of apotheosis to Jesus and therefore to offer him the supreme homage of an adoration previously reserved for God alone.

Such an explanation is both puerile and antihistorical. Quite aside from the documentation of the Christological disputes that dragged out through centuries, the theory is sufficiently vitiated by the hesitation and doubt that beset many Church Fathers[73] when they had to choose between those prayers that should be addressed to Christ and those that should be directed to God, between the attributes to be assigned to the Son and the titles reserved to the Father, lest the divine monarchy be severed into a dualism.

Despite such qualms, it ultimately became the custom to speak of Jesus not only with the epithet of Christ (Messiah), which in the early period preceded rather than followed his name, and with the whole range of titles of which only a sample has been given above, but also as the Lord. The equivalent in the Romance languages (*Seigneur, Signore, Señor*) is derived from the Latin *senior,* which means "older," and hence its significance is only that of respectful deference (today *signore* and *señor* are generally used in addressing any man). Such is not the case with *Dominus,* which for the ancient Romans, meant "Lord," "Master," "Sovereign," and so forth, and still less with the Greek equivalent, Κύριος (*Kurios*), which meant "mighty" or "endowed with supreme power." It is well known that in the customary language of that period the epithet *Kurios* was a title of honor applied to the emperors. Its connotations are not limited, however, to secular submission or to the flattery of courtiers; it has also a religious coloration, both because the sovereign was considered the descendant and successor of the gods and because an effort was made to elevate him by apotheosis to the level of the gods.[74] Indeed, it was not uncommon to worship the emperor under the double attribution of Κύριος-Σωτήρ (*Kurios-Sōtēr*), or "Lord-Savior."[75]

Christian theology denies any influence of the cult of the emperor in the application of this appellation to Jesus,[76] pointing out that the word *Kurios* was already familiar in the Septuagint, the Greek translation of the Old Testament. This is true; but there the word is always and exclusively used, either alone or in conjunction with Θεός (*Theos*), to denote the supreme sovereignty of Yahweh. The pure Jews refused utterly to allow the title of Master or Lord for anyone other than God; even their own kings were called only Messiah—anointed of God. However, evidence exists that in the Diaspora the Jews at last resigned themselves to calling the emperor *Kurios.*[77] The practice of invoking Jesus under that title can have been derived only from this custom.

[18]

THE JUDGMENT

"I Am the Good Shepherd"

Still far removed from the theological quarrels over the Trinity, the contemporaries of Jesus were waiting for a physically real Messiah, and it was logical for them to think that, as a pretender to the throne by virtue of his Davidic descent, the Messiah should make his appearance with far different signs of power and quite another following than did this humble prophet with his dozen rough fishermen who spoke a poor Aramaic due to their clumsy Galilean accent. Before him, others had presented themselves in more or less good faith as the expected Messiah, and hence there was nothing surprising in the priests' determination to avert unfortunate incidents by silencing Jesus.

If it is possible to concede any credit for historical accuracy to the author of the Fourth Gospel, Jesus must have stayed out of Jerusalem for at least three months after the threat to stone him, for John relates that the Nazarene risked a public appearance again at another religious festival that fell just three months after the Feast of Tabernacles. This was Hanukkah, the Feast of Dedication, which the Evangelist translates into Greek as Ἐγκαίνια (*Egkainia*). It was celebrated annually on the twenty-fifth day of the month of Kislev (about the middle of December) to commemorate the reconsecration of the Temple sanctuary by the Maccabees in 164 B.C., six and a half years after the destruction of the holy place by Antiochus Epiphanes.[1] For an entire week, the city abandoned itself to wild rejoicing. The faithful went to the Temple every day, and every evening its courtyard and the nearby streets were so alive with spectacular illuminations that the occasion came to be known popularly as the Feast of Lights (τὰ Φῶτα, *ta Phōta*).[2]

Jesus also entered the holy edifice, followed by the little band of his faithful disciples, and that very fact may have inspired the Parable of the Good Shepherd: "He that entereth not by the door into the sheepfold, but climbeth up some other way, the same is a thief and a robber. But he that entereth in by the door is the shepherd of the sheep. . . . He calleth his own sheep by name, and leadeth them out. And when he putteth forth his own sheep, he goeth before them, and the sheep follow him: for they know his voice. And a stranger will they not follow. . . . All that ever came before me are thieves and robbers: but the sheep did not hear them. . . . The thief cometh not, but for to steal, and to kill, and to destroy: I am come that they might have life. . . . I am the good shepherd, . . . and know my sheep, and am known of mine. As the Father knoweth me, even so know I the Father."[3]

There is no need to examine the content of the parable overcritically and to point out, as for example Cullmann does,[4] the bad taste of calling the prophets who had come before Jesus "thieves and robbers." The context of the story reveals that the disrespect is not intentional but simply a maladroit contrast employed by the Evangelist to give greater emphasis to the Nazarene's merits. To explain the origin of the parable, we should do better to remember how completely unoriginal the comparison of the deity with the good shepherd is, since it is found quite often in the literature of the Old Testament. This parable, jointly with that of the Lost Sheep, led to the Christianization of a beautiful Greek sculpture of the Alexandrian period, which portrays a shepherd carrying a lamb on his shoulders. The first Christian copies go back to the second century; they were done in Rome for the crypt of Lucina and the sarcophagus of Gaiola.

The reappearance of Jesus not only in the Temple but in Solomon's Portico itself[5] aroused new alarm among the priests. They told their congregants that he was a madman possessed of a devil and should not be listened to. To Jesus they said: "How long dost thou make us to doubt? If thou be the Christ, tell us plainly."

"I told you, and ye believed not: the works that I do in my Father's name, they bear witness of me. But ye believe not, because ye are not of my sheep. . . . My sheep hear my voice, and I know them, and they follow me; And I give unto them eternal life. . . . My Father, which gave them me, is greater than all."

Then they made again as if to stone him, and Jesus asked: "Many good works have I showed you from my Father; for which of those works do ye stone me?"

"For a good work we stone thee not; but for blasphemy; and because that thou, being a man, makest thyself God."

Once more Jesus tried to save himself with a shrewd Biblical quotation which was intended to show that he considered himself the Son of God by virtue of the right by which all the prophets could make the same claim: "Is it not written in your law, I said, Ye are gods [and all of you are children of the Most High]?[6] If he called them gods, unto whom the word of God came, and the Scripture cannot be broken; Say ye, Thou blasphemest, because I said I am the Son of God? . . . But if I do [the works of my Father], though ye believe not me, believe the works: that ye may know, and believe, that the Father is in me, and I in him."

The priests were not won over by this line of argument, which was really rather sophistic, and Jesus had to flee a second time. Leaving the Temple with considerable bitterness, he halted a moment to watch the worshipers who were placing their offerings in the "treasury" (γαζοφυλάκιον, gazophylakion)—three spout-shaped receptacles whose openings were set in the outer wall of the sacred edifice at the visitors' entrance and each of which bore an inscription designating the purpose of the offering that was put into it.[7]

There Jesus saw a small woman in ragged clothes, whose hands trembled as she put a tiny coin into one of the receptacles: a gerah, almost worthless, which corresponded to two Greek lepta (λεπτά)—what the King James Bible calls "two mites, which make a farthing."[8] Jesus was touched, and he called his disciples' attention to the widow's offering: she had given all that she could, perhaps going without food for that day, and her offering was worth far more than all the rest, even the ostentatious gifts of the rich who did not have to deprive themselves of anything.

"There Shall Not Be Left One Stone Upon Another"

When they had got well out of the Temple, the disciples turned again to contemplate the impressive complex.[9] One of them exclaimed: "Master, see what manner of stones and what buildings are here!"

"Seest thou these great buildings?" Jesus replied. "There shall not be left one stone upon another, that shall not be thrown down." He too stared at the Temple.

These words are obviously intended to allude to the time when the Jewish religion should perish and be succeeded by a new, purer, less formalistic faith, in accordance with the lessons that Jesus had already given to his followers. It was still the Feast of the Dedication of the Temple, and his anger was the greater because the priests had virtually driven him out of it.

This prophecy, which may even have represented what Jesus really thought, has been read instead as an allusion to one of those innumerable apocalyptic upheavals that were to announce the end of this world and the inauguration of the anticipated kingdom of God. Taken literally, the prediction of Jesus, the nature of which was allegorical and spiritual, would appear to have been realized in A.D. 70, when the Temple of Jerusalem was in fact destroyed by the Romans. This historical event gave the Evangelists (who are positively known to have written their Gospels after that date) a point of departure for a bizarre and incoherent disquisition known as the "eschatological discourse" (from ἔσχατον, *eschaton,* which means "ultimate," "extreme"), dealing with the final fate of humanity, which is one of the pillars of the Christian religion. (In the Gospel of Mark, the passage is usually referred to as the Little Apocalypse.)

When Jesus and the Apostles had reached the slopes of the Mount of Olives, which the road to Bethany passes, they stopped to rest, the Synoptic Gospels relate,[10] and four of them—Peter, James, John, and Andrew—asked: "Tell us when shall these things be? and what shall be the sign when all these things shall be fulfilled?"

"Take heed lest any man deceive you," Jesus answered.[11] "For many shall come in my name, saying, I am Christ; and shall deceive many. And when ye shall hear of wars and rumors of wars, be ye not troubled: for such things must needs be;[12] but the end shall not be yet. For nation shall rise against nation, and kingdom against kingdom;[13] and there shall be earthquakes in divers places, and there shall be famines and troubles: these are the beginnings of sorrows. Behold, I send you forth as sheep in the midst of wolves: be ye therefore wise as serpents, and harmless as doves. . . . When they persecute you in this city, flee into another. . . . They shall deliver you up to councils; and in the synagogues ye shall be beaten: and ye shall be brought before rulers and kings for my sake, for a testimony against them. And the gospel must first be published among all nations. . . . And when they bring you unto the synagogues, and unto magistrates, and powers, take ye no thought how or what thing ye shall answer, or what ye shall say: For the Holy Ghost shall teach you in the same hour what ye ought to say. And ye shall be betrayed both by parents, and brethren, and kinsfolks, and friends. . . . And ye shall be hated of all men for my name's sake. . . .

"And when ye shall see Jerusalem compassed by armies . . . when ye shall see the abomination of desolation (let him that readeth understand), then let them that be in Judea flee to the mountains: And let him that is on the housetop not go down into the house . . . to take any thing out. . . . And let him that is in the field not turn back for to take up his garment. But woe to them that are with child, and to them that give suck in those days! And pray ye that your flight be not in the winter, neither on the sabbath day. . . . For in those days shall be affliction, such as was not from the beginning of the creation unto this time, neither shall be.[14] And they shall fall by the edge of the sword, and shall be led away captive into all nations: and Jerusalem shall be trodden down of the Gentiles, until the times of the Gentiles be fulfilled. And except those days should be shortened, there should no flesh be saved: but for the elect's sake those days shall be shortened.

"Then if any man shall say unto you, Lo, here is Christ, or there; believe it not. For there shall arise false Christs, and false prophets, and shall show great signs and wonders, to seduce, if it were possible, even the elect. But take ye heed; behold, I have foretold you all things. . . . For wheresoever the carcass is, there will the eagles be gathered together.

"Immediately after the tribulation of those days shall the sun be darkened, and the moon shall not give her light, and the stars shall fall from heaven.[15] . . . Then shall all the tribes of the earth mourn, and they shall see the Son of man coming in the clouds of heaven, with power and great glory. And he shall send his angels with a great sound of a trumpet: and they shall gather together his elect from the four winds. Now learn a parable of the fig tree: When his branch is yet tender, and putteth forth leaves, ye know that summer is nigh. So likewise ye, when ye shall see all these things, know that it is even at the doors."

"Verily I say unto you, This generation shall not pass, till all these things be fulfilled. Heaven and earth shall pass away, but my words shall not pass away.

"But of that day and hour knoweth no man, no, not the angels of heaven, neither the Son, but my Father only. But as the days of Noe [Noah] were, so shall also the coming of the Son of man be. For as in the days that were before the flood, they were eating and drinking, marrying and giving in marriage, until the day that Noe entered the ark, until the flood came, and took them all away. Likewise also as it was in the days of Lot; they did eat, they drank, they bought, they sold, they planted, they builded; But the same day that Lot went out of Sodom it rained fire and brimstone from heaven, and destroyed them all. . . . Two men shall be in the field; the one shall be taken, and the other left. Two women shall be grinding together; the one shall be taken, and the other shall be left."

This exhaustive catalogue is followed by a few exhortations to constant vigilance while awaiting the end[16] and by various parables elaborating on that requirement because the end may be sudden: the master who returns unexpectedly to his house from a long journey and rewards the servants whom he finds diligently engaged in their tasks but punishes those caught idle; the five foolish virgins, who, appointed to meet the bridegroom, forgot to put sufficient oil in their lamps and had to go back and fill them, and who found, when they returned to the place of the wedding, that they were shut out; the householder who keeps watch because he knows he may be robbed.

Other terror was proffered by Paul, for whom "the day of the

Lord so cometh as a thief in the night . . . [as] sudden destruction, as travail upon a woman with child."[17]

The Abomination of Desolation

The "eschatological discourse" has been the subject of much thought by critics of every period, primarily because of its catastrophic quality, which violates the apostolic spirit that saw the "end of time" and the inauguration of the kingdom as happy events,[18] and also because of the strange mixture of predictions of the siege of Jerusalem with others not only dealing with subsequent disasters but also frankly including the persecutions of the Christians under the empire. Someone has offered the juvenile suggestion that there might have been some misplacing of pages in an original manuscript of the Gospel of Mark and that the other Evangelists copied it mechanically without taking the trouble to restore order in the original text.[19]

The real problem is quite different. One must extract from the harangue a coherent doctrine, which perhaps was even based on an actual statement by Jesus but which has been encrusted with successive layers of revision at different periods. The additions, however, were not affixed wholly at the beginning or at the end of the original passage; individual parts of it have been amplified in accordance with the readings and interpretations of the faithful of various times. One clue is the intrusion, totally incongruous in this long direct quotation, of the parenthetical admonition: "(let him that readeth understand)," which is obviously intended for readers rather than listeners.

Jesus might well have said: "There will be more wars and hatred, conflicts and famine, in the world, and the just will again be persecuted, but nonetheless men must persevere in preparing for the kingdom. In the end, evil will be overcome." After the death of Jesus, his disciples continued to be confident of the imminent end of the world, to some degree because they were still under the spell of their master's frequent promises ("The kingdom of God is at hand"; "There be some of them that stand here, which shall not taste death, till they have seen the kingdom of God come with power"; "This generation shall not pass, till all these things be ful-filled"), and they went about in search of portents.

The same illusion was shared by Paul. His Epistles testify amply to his conviction that the wait would be of the briefest (συνεσταλμένος, *sunestalmenos*)[20] and that the Great Day was imminent (ἐνεστῶσαν ἀνάγκην, *enestōsan anagkēn*),[21] certain to arrive before he and his contemporaries had died.[22] But in his Second Epistle to the Thessalonians (and for this reason some critics believe it to be apocryphal), there is also a reference to ὁ κατέχων (*ho katechōn*) and τὸ κατέχον (*to katechon*)—that is, "he who holds back" or "that which holds back." Even Augustine found this cryptic;[23] it has caused others to think in terms of an Antichrist[24] who would im-pede the realization of the kingdom but who would manifest him-self "with all power and signs and lying wonders, and with all de-ceivableness of unrighteousness,"[25] and thus seem to fulfill the pre-monitory signs for which the Apostles were searching.

Certainly the tragic events witnessed by the first generation of Christians must often have led them to believe that the expected moment was at hand, and these events were studied with fear and hope. Once the illusion of the imminent end of the world had been dissipated, the various comments on these events were retained in the literature of the New Testament to edify and admonish the faithful, and they were enriched with further illustrations drawn from the first persecutions and the early martyrology. If they were no longer valid as signs of the imminence of the Last Judgment, they had merit still as a cogent argument to justify God's wrath and the fact that he continued to withhold his mercy from mankind.

In the first century of Christianity, when the ultimate catastro-phe was still believed to be actually imminent, the portents of the "abomination of desolation"—τὸ βδέλυγμα τῆς ἐρημώσεως (*to bdelugma tēs erēmoseōs*), which corresponds to the Hebrew *shiqqûtz meshō-mēn* to be found in the Book of Daniel[26]—were in plain fact to be seen everywhere. In A.D. 44, there was a widespread and terrible famine, with resultant epidemics, that could well induce thoughts of the triumph of evil. In 53, disastrous earthquakes occurred in Phrygia, and in 61 another earthquake destroyed the famous city of Laodicea. In 64, a tremendous fire broke out in Rome and Nero had several Christians executed, rightly or wrongly, as the criminals responsible. In 66, the Palestinian revolts against the Romans began; Vespasian crushed them savagely, taking thousands of prisoners who were sent into forced labor as diggers on the isthmus of Corinth.

In 70, finally, the Romans terminated the war with the Jews by besieging Jerusalem and destroying the Temple. This was unquestionably the most grievous tragedy of all to the early Christians, and hence it plays so great a part in the "prophecies" of the "eschatological discourse." According to Flavius Josephus, 1.1 million Jews died during the siege.[27] Even if the number is an exaggeration, the battle was undoubtedly a major one for the people of Israel, and they defended themselves fanatically for months. The siege began in April, precisely when the Passover festival filled the city with the greatest swarm of visitors, and lasted into early September. Famine struck early, and soon became so severe that the defenders were compelled to eat the leather of their girdles and shoes; there were even some cases of cannibalism. On July 17, the daily sacrifices in the Temple had to be suspended because of a lack of men qualified to perform them. On August 6, the Temple began to burn, amid the anguished cries of the multitudes whom the attack had squeezed into the higher levels of the city, and the shouts of the heroic soldiers who had taken up positions within the sacred building for a last-ditch defense and who now found themselves caught between the sword and the flame. On September 8, the entire upper city fell into the Romans' hands and Titus ordered it leveled, including even its walls.[28]

Ecclesiastical history relates that when the destruction of Jerusalem was near, the city's Christian community fled across the Jordan to the town of Pella, where it remained until the end of the war. Thus it survived.

Even the reference to "false prophets" in the "eschatological discourse" has a historical foundation. It is an established fact that not long after the death of Jesus, a certain Dositheus in Samaria professed to be the Messiah, to the great irritation of the Nazarene's disciples.[29] It appeared that he had been a follower of John the Baptist, whom he now aspired to succeed in the leadership of the sect that John had founded. Dositheus was soon supplanted by Simon Magus, who is mentioned in the Acts of the Apostles[30] because he tried to persuade Peter and the rest to sell him the power of effecting miraculous cures. Later, one Menandrus of Antioch claimed to be an incarnation of the Power of God, and in Judea a man called Theudas professed himself the Messiah and managed to acquire more than four hundred disciples.

The Millenarians (Chiliasts)

Whether all these disasters were really predicted by Jesus (as traditional exegesis would like to think) or whether the prophecies were composed *post eventum* (as logic would have us think), in any case there is one certainty: since the end of the world, accompanied by the Parousia of Jesus as judge and as inaugurator of a new order, had not occurred in the lifetimes of the first Christians, their successors resigned themselves in disappointment and discouragement to a further postponement of the Day of Judgment. After the fall of Jerusalem, new portents were alleged to be contained in other calamitous events, particularly in the persecutions. In their uncertainty, the believers coupled the earlier prophecy of the Gospels, which could no longer be altered—"This generation shall not pass, till all these things be done"—with its less categorical and more mysterious corollary—"But of that day and that hour knoweth no man."[31]

To explain away the default in the realization of the promise embodied in the first sentence (which might have raised doubts of the prophetic powers of Jesus), the Church Fathers maintained that when Jesus said "this generation," he did not mean his actual contemporaries but rather "the generation of the faithful of all time," or even the entirety of "the human race." As for the admission by Jesus (ascribed to him in the second sentence) that he did not know when this would come to pass, Origen and Athanasius resorted to a quibble: it was not in his divine quality but as a man that he did not know, because he lacked the knowledge born of experience.[32] Augustine, on the other hand, advanced the idea that Jesus did know with certainty, but he did not want to disclose the truth "because that was not required of his teaching."[33]

Modern Catholic critics agree in conceding at least that the prophecies of the future end of the world were superimposed on the immediate predictions concerning Jerusalem,[34] which, they say, may have been made by Jesus at two different times;[35] they add that in the immediate predictions he foresaw the punishment of the Jewish people for their unbelief and in the future prophecies he foretold his Second Coming.[36] In any case, Catholic theology has renounced any attempt to set a date for the Parousia.

None of this alters the fact that ever since the death of Jesus there have been troubled visionary souls with the illusion that they could identify the warning omens of the end of the world. It was not only the Apostles, Paul, and the Evangelists who lived in immediate expectation of it; as late as the end of the second century, many people believed their lives were mere time-serving in a world destined to disappear within a few years. Much of the work of Tertullian, for example, bears witness to this.

Above all, a statement contained in the Book of Revelation has provided the basis for much "precise" eschatological calculation. According to Revelation, the first resurrection would take place when "the thousand years were finished."[37] "The thousand years," obviously, has a figurative meaning in Revelation, as the symbol of an extremely long period, but it was read as an exact chronological stipulation. Here was the source of the various sects of millenarians, or chiliasts—from χιλιάς (chilias), which means "a thousand"—who were convinced that God's judgment would be handed down exactly one thousand years after the birth or after the death of Jesus. The chronicles of the Middle Ages reveal a fantastic surge of religious fanaticism in the year 1000.

When this expectation also went unfulfilled, a new interpretation arose: "the thousand years" was not meant as the date for the end of the world but as the period in which corruption would reach its peak. In other words, the triumph of evil would endure a thousand years, after which God's wrath would break loose inexorably. After the year 1000, therefore, the searchers looked for signs, not of the "end" of the world, but of the "beginning" of the final millennium.

The identification of these signs was naturally a highly subjective matter. In 1130, Joachim of Floris thought he had found proof of humanity's entrance into the last millennium of life in the corruption of the Church of his time; others after him found portents in other phenomena, and so it went until the founding of the Adventists at the beginning of the nineteenth century by the American

William Miller (they number about one million today). Their first calculations flatly predicted the Second Coming for March 22, 1844, and then for October 22 of the same year. They have persisted in setting new dates without any loss of faith. On June 14, 1960, a little band of fanatics in Italy withdrew to Mont Blanc in expectation of a second universal deluge from which they expected to be saved by the height of the mountain.

Between 1868 and 1878, an Italian teamster, Davide Lazzaretti, intoxicated by the utopian socialist ideals of Saint-Simonianism, proclaimed a holy crusade against the monarchy and the Church, announcing the end of the world and claiming to be the Messiah of the new kingdom. He was shot down by the *carabinieri* as he led a march of psalm-singing "apostles" in picturesque garb.[38] His cause was inherited by others: in 1964, the High Priestess of the Law of David (as the group calls itself), one Elvira Giro of Vicenza, and her few followers instituted a lawsuit against the Italian government for the recovery of Davide Lazzaretti's vestments, which are preserved in the Criminal Museum in Turin.

A far more interesting segment of the millenarian camp—partly because of its much more numerous adherents—is the Protestant sect of the Russellites, now known as Jehovah's Witnesses. Founded in the United States in 1872 by Charles T. Russell and subsequently given its final shape under Joseph F. Rutherford, today it has thousands of followers all over the world.[39] For them, the signs of the end began to appear in 1914: World Wars I and II, the Japanese earthquake of 1923, the persecutions of the Jews by the Nazis, the dropping of the atomic bomb on Hiroshima, etc.[40]

And if, as is quite probable, these second thousand years also pass without any ultimate catastrophe, other visionaries will be able to find in other portents the inception of a new final millennium before the judgment of mankind.

The Universal Judgment

The idea of the end of this world and the initiation of a better age after the Day of Judgment is not exclusively Christian. Persian Mazdaism believed in the ultimate victory of Ahura-Mazda, the god of goodness, after three thousand years. The religion of the Mayas, the pre-Colombian people of Central America, spoke of a series of cataclysms that on four occasions had brought about the destruction and re-creation of the world as the result of offenses to the gods.[41] In Judaism, the legends of the universal flood, of the destruction of Sodom and Gomorrah, and of the plagues of Egypt took on the meaning of authentic collective catastrophes from which only the just were saved.

The most interesting innovation offered by Jesus was that he did not insist too much on the negative side of the judgment (the punishment of the wicked). Rather, he sought to open men's hearts to the hope of being spared and received into the new kingdom through faith in the forgiveness and generosity of God. This kingdom, like all those awaited by the other religions, was expected, logically, to have its seat on this earth.

However, the allocation of an extra-terrestrial site to the kingdom—for reasons that are discussed in the appropriate place—and particularly the gloomy forebodings, already stirring in the proto-Christians, as to the possibility of putting the utopian visions of Jesus into practice in this world led to a new ascendancy for the concept of a punitive judgment. In the Gospel of Matthew, it must be admitted in all fairness, an interpolated description of the judgment,[42] even though in part it yields to apocalyptic fantasies and expresses the concept of a kingdom beyond this world, still retains some moderate balance between the rewards promised to the just and the punishments threatened for the wicked. Above all, it emphasizes the necessity of fulfilling the law of love dictated by Jesus. One might say that the idea of the judgment is joined to it secondarily, more as a warning than as an eschatological reality:

"When the Son of man shall come in his glory, and all the holy angels with him, then shall he sit upon the throne of his glory: And before him shall be gathered all nations; and he shall separate them one from another, as a shepherd divideth his sheep from the goats: And he shall set the sheep on his right hand, but the goats on the left. Then shall the King say unto them on his right hand, Come, ye blessed of my Father, inherit the kingdom prepared for you from the foundation of the world: For I was ahungered, and ye gave me meat; I was thirsty, and ye gave me drink: I was a stranger, and ye took me in: Naked, and ye clothed me: I was sick, and ye visited me: I was in prison and ye came unto me. Then shall the righteous answer him, saying, Lord, when saw we thee ahungered, and fed thee? or thirsty, and gave thee drink? When saw we thee a stranger, and took thee in? or naked, and clothed thee? Or when saw we thee sick, or in prison, and came unto thee? And the King shall answer and say unto them, Verily I say unto you, Inasmuch as ye have done it unto one of the least of these my brethren, ye have done it unto me.

"Then shall he say also unto them on the left hand, Depart from me, ye cursed, into everlasting fire, prepared for the devil and his angels: For I was ahungered, and ye gave me no meat: I was thirsty, and ye gave me no drink: I was a stranger, and ye took me not in: naked, and ye clothed me not: sick, and in prison, and ye visited me not. Then shall they also answer him, saying, Lord, when saw we thee ahungered, or athirst, or a stranger, or naked, or sick, or in prison, and did not minister unto thee? Then shall he answer them, saying, Verily I say unto you, Inasmuch as ye did it not to one of the least of these, ye did it not to me. And these shall go away into everlasting punishment: but the righteous into life eternal."

Far different from Matthew's is the grotesque picture of the universal judgment drawn by the author of Revelation, supposedly John the Apostle; according to Christian tradition, it was written during the reign of Domitian, between A.D. 94 and 96, but it is probably even later. Influenced by the tragic events of the time, it takes the form of a strange and monstrous vision to depict the struggle between early Christianity and paganism, illuminating the edifying picture of the final victory of the new religion with the lightning flashes of the destruction of the world of the wicked and the inauguration of the kingdom of the just. "In the Spirit on the Lord's day," the author of Revelation saw, in the midst of seven golden "candlesticks" (lampstands), "one like unto the Son of man," dressed in a garment that hung down to his feet, "girt about the paps with a golden girdle," with hair white as wool and eyes "as a flame of fire." In his right hand he held seven stars.

The lampstands (candles were not used in Biblical times) represent the seven churches (Ephesus, Smyrna, Pergamum, Thyatira, Sardis, Philadelphia, and Laodicea) and the stars are the angels of these churches. The being who appears to the author

350 THE LIFE OF JESUS

gives him specific messages for the churches: expel those who advocate the doctrine of the Nicolaitans; pay no attention to certain false prophetesses; be ever faithful and watchful. And then there is a vision of God on his throne: "like a jasper and a sardine stone," surrounded by a rainbow that shone like an emerald. The throne was surrounded also by twenty-four elders with golden crowns; before it stood seven burning lamps (the seven spirits of God) and four beasts—a lion, a calf, a man, and an eagle—each having six wings and eyes all over its body, and day and night they repeated: "Holy, holy, holy, Lord God Almighty." God handed the sealed book of the future to a Lamb with seven horns and seven eyes and bade him open it amid the hymns of all about him.

As the Lamb broke each of the book's seven seals, fantastic apparitions appeared to symbolize the calamities that should go before the final inauguration of the Messianic kingdom: four armed men, mounted respectively on a white, a black, a red, and a pale horse; an earthquake; angels standing ready to destroy sinful mankind, except for 144,000 people—twelve thousand for each of the twelve tribes of Israel; a storm of hail and fire; oceans changed into blood; eclipses of the sun and the moon; a bottomless pit that sent swarms of locusts upon the earth; thousands of horsemen armed with fire and brimstone, etc. Then a woman appeared in heaven, clothed with the sun, and the moon under her feet, and upon her head a crown of twelve stars, and she cried out in the pains of childbirth. A red dragon with seven heads and ten horns fought the archangel Michael in the sky; a monster, something like a leopard, with the mouth of a lion and the feet of a bear, rose out of the sea; another beast came "up out of the earth"; a harlot clothed in purple and scarlet, drunk with the blood of the saints and the martyrs, sat astride a dragon. Finally there were rejoicing and jubilation in heaven when an angel proclaimed that "Babylon" had fallen: the King of Kings appeared in all his splendor, and an angel chained the dragon "for a thousand years." Then came the universal judgment and the definitive inauguration of the "heavenly Jerusalem."

It would require too much time and space to explain the symbolism behind the characters and events described in Revelation: on the one hand, there are clear allusions to the Roman Empire, to the corruption of the heathen (the harlot), to the persecutions, etc., and, on the other, to Jesus Christ, to the victory of Christianity, and so forth.

John's apocalyptic revelation inspired a number of other no less imaginative fantasies through which the Christian doctrine of the universal judgment was evolved and elaborated over the centuries until it culminated in the proclamation of faith issued in the sixteenth century by the Council of Trent. Although it may seem incredible, that doctrine was based not on serious theological speculation but on this pathological literature of visionaries. On the Day of Judgment, the Church teaches, all the dead will rise in their former bodies, and together with the angels (who will also have to stand before the final judgment) they will appear before God and Jesus. The supreme judge will be the Messiah, seated on a majestic thrown and assisted by the Apostles, the saints, and the martyrs.

This choreographic spectacle of the Great Day of Wrath (the *Dies Irae* of medieval hymnology) will be staged, according to tradition, in the Valley of Jehoshaphat (Josaphat), which the imagination of the religious pretends to be able to identify as the valley of the brook of Kidron (Cedron), east of Jerusalem. It has been the theme of artistic masterpieces of many periods, from the simple, schematic drawings of the paleo-Christians to the works of Giotto, Michelangelo, Dürer, and others.

The Personal Judgment

Aside from being essentially puerile (the resurrection of *all* humanity that has ever existed—billions upon billions of people reassuming their original bodies, disintegrated ages earlier, and crowding into a narrow Judean valley; assessments, centuries and centuries after death, of the rewards and punishments earned in life, etc.), the doctrine of the universal judgment fits poorly with the consistent predictions of Jesus that the advent of the kingdom was *imminent*: concretely, he envisaged it as the inception of a new age of justice and general happiness on earth.

Nor is this all. In direct contradiction of the "eschatological discourse" and of the fantasms of Revelation, other passages of the New Testament seem to uphold without qualification the belief that the kingdom will not come like a meteor, a sudden sign from heaven, but that *it is within men:* ἐντὸς ὑμῶν *(entos humōn)*,[43] a phrase that, however it is translated—"among you," "within you," "in the midst of you"—means always that the kingdom has already begun. In other words—as the Parables of the Kingdom made abundantly clear—it must come into existence as soon as any man has the will to live according to the law of God, and it must grow little by little like the mustard seed, like the grain sown in good earth, like the bread to which leaven has been added. God's judgment is immediately effective, enabling the just to live more happily. The Gospel of John says explicitly: "He that believeth on him is not condemned: but he that believeth not is condemned already. . . . And this is the condemnation, that light is come into the world, and men loved darkness rather than light."[44] This concept of a kingdom already in being probably replaced the expectation of the Parousia in the heart of the Christian community, disappointed as it was that Jesus' promises had not materialized. Thus the conviction was born that the kingdom itself existed properly in the churches and communities of the elect.[45]

Based on this innovation, there has been a strong tendency in modern times among Protestant and independent theologians to deprecate the doctrine of "the four last things"—that is, the predictions bearing on the Last Judgment—as absurd and unacceptable. The partisans of the so-called consistent eschatology, adherents of the liberal school, admit in Jesus only the intention to teach a moral standard for the creation of a better society.[46] Similarly, the greatest theologian of the school of "demythologization," Rudolf Bultmann, asserts: "The judgment was not deferred until the end of time: it takes place in the present; the attitude that men adopt toward Christ is the judgment of the world: it consists in the separation of those who believe in him from those who do not believe but remain in darkness."[47] The kingdom coincides therefore with the congregation of those who believe in Christ, who differentiate themselves from the world of sin by the kingdom's injunction to live according to a new concept of human relations based on Christian justice, brotherhood, peace, and love for one's fellows.

Catholic theology, determined that nothing contained in the Gospels shall be wasted, accepts the idea of a realization of the kingdom in the "Church," but it does not at the same time relinquish its belief in the universal judgment, which is always an efficacious warning to transgressors of Christ's law and a comforting hope for followers of it. Once all millenarian illusions are put aside, however, this hope rests only on a promise without a definite term. But the constant postponement of its fulfillment does not perturb the Church, which indeed profits thereby to chastise those of little faith, since the Church maintains that the kingdom will come only when *all* have been converted to its law.

It is hardly necessary to point out the absurdity of this doctrine. Nothing militates against the possibility that the world may one day be destroyed by some astronomical cataclysm or through other natural causes, but it is presumptuous to believe that such an event would be the consequence of our moral conduct.

This consideration apart, the idea of a universal judgment at some distant date raises the vital questions of the real value of the redemptory work of Jesus in the world as it is and of what becomes of those who have and have not believed in Christ during this protracted wait. In the early centuries of Christianity, it was believed simply that they descended into a subterranean world where they waited for the Day of Judgment, a view that was still held, in the fourth century, by Hilary of Poitiers, by Ambrose, by Chrysostom, by Cyril of Jerusalem. It was Gregory of Nazianzus (d. ca. 390) who first explored the hypothesis that the martyrs, at least, were taken directly to God, immediately after death, in compensation for their extraordinary merits.[48] This privilege was subsequently extended to all who died in the grace of God, even if they had not suffered martyrdom. The rest, however, continued to stay in the underworld and in addition were subjected to punishments and torments. Thus there arose an anticipatory distinction between "the good" and "the wicked," which had not been foreseen in the literature of the New Testament: a "personal" judgment at the moment of the individual's death, in advance of the collective summons before the bar of the Great Judge.

Theology finds it passably difficult to explain the difference between the two judgments, and there is no lack of disputes and doubts on the matter. Even in the fourteenth century, for instance, Pope John XXII maintained that the just, although passing to a better life at the moment of death, were not yet allowed the blessed vision of God, which was to be the reward granted only after the universal judgment. In spite of the opposition of such theologians as William of Ockham and Michael of Cesena, the pontiff insisted on his own point of view and went to the length of imprisoning a Dominican who had contradicted him.

Even today, though they have been calmed down by the dogmatic definition of the Council of Trent, theologians are constrained to admit the existence of an insoluble conflict between the "in this moment" of the personal judgment and the "not yet" of the universal judgment, between final blessedness or damnation and the measures prescribed *ad interim* by the personal judgment. In contrast to what was awaited by Jesus and his contemporaries, these measures, like those of the universal judgment, represent not a divine intervention designed to perfect human life through the triumph of goodness and the utter elimination of evil but rather a posthumous reward or punishment for one's behavior during life.

The popular imagination, cozened by sophisticated ecclesiastical instruction, pictures the blessedness of the invisible kingdom of heaven in such splendid colors, and the agonies of the underworld in such black ones, that the problem of the afterlife becomes at once fascinating and terrifying. Death itself takes on a tremendous significance, not only because, for the Christian, it is the beginning of a *real,* eternal existence of bliss or anguish, but because it is the decisive moment that determines the divine verdict. How one behaved during one's life is not so important as the instant of death, when one is either reconciled with God, even after a life that was not always exemplary, or struck down by his wrath.

It is a fundamental inversion of the pagan world's concept of life and of its real values. Mme. de Staël put it extremely well: "Paganism deified life, Christianity deifies death." The whole of Greek philosophy was a glorification of life, a moral guide to righteous living in this world on the principles of justice and probity. Life was a joy, a divine gift. For the Christian, however, it is a constant risk, fraught with temptations, a short and perilous passage through a vale of tears. "Nothing in life is so dear to our hearts," Tertullian wrote, "as the earliest possible departure from it."[49]

Heaven, Hell, Purgatory, and Limbo

From a sentence found only in the Gospel of Luke (the response of Jesus, dying on the cross, to the good thief crucified beside him, who had repented: "Verily I say unto thee, to-day shalt thou be with me in paradise"[50]) a name has been given to the place of eternal blessedness where the just shall dwell—that kingdom of heaven which the unfulfilled promises of Jesus persuaded theologians to locate at some indefinite point in the air.

The Greek word used by Luke, Παράδεισος (*Paradeisos*), is a transliteration of the Persian *pairidaeza*, which means "a walled garden," "a park," and which particularly applied to the picturesque hanging gardens that the Persian satraps had built in their palaces. A Hebrew equivalent might be *gan be 'ēden*, or "garden of delight," derived from the Sumerian *edin*, which meant simply "plain" or "countryside."[51] The Vulgate employs the phrase "*paradisus voluptatis* and *paradisus deliciae*."

Many religions contain the belief in a place of rest and happiness for the just and the brave after death: Elysium for the Greeks, Valhalla for the Norse, the Isles of the Blessed for the Assyrians and the Babylonians, Jenna (the "garden" par excellence) for the Mohammedans, etc. But the formation of the Christian idea of Paradise was derived almost exclusively from the Biblical record of the first habitation given to man, and lost through the fault of Adam and Eve. The Paradise Lost of Judaism, the kingdom of this world preached by Jesus, and that of heaven taught by the Church, all represent man's unconscious aspiration toward an abstract world of peace, of well-being, and of happiness.

According to the Biblical myth, the earthly Paradise that was the privileged domain of the first human couple lay to the east of Palestine in a fertile area of Mesopotamia, watered by a broad river that branched out in four tributaries. Here the descendants of Adam might have rejoiced in an eternally benign climate, rich in vegetation, and offering every kind of fruit, without ever facing the necessity of work.

The concept of the kingdom preached by Jesus was sublimated to the point that it was identified once more with the Hebraic Paradise. The theologians' legitimate concentration on presenting it as a purely spiritual state of blessedness did not, however, prevent the mass of believers from falling back into the idea of a place of delights and unending joy. Imagination and, even more, the understandable human hunger for a little peace and justice, at least in some distant future, triumphed over the theological abstractions.

Medieval religious literature describes Paradise in terms of an innocent and overwhelmed sensuousness, a world of enchantment for eye and ear, as in, among so many other writings, the *Voyages of St. Brendan,* by an unknown monk of the eleventh century, and *De Jerusalem celesti,* by Giacomino of Verona, in which Paradise is a city of streets and squares paved with gold, of palaces of crystal, of columns of a metal finer than gold, of gardens of lilies, roses, violets. Dante Alighieri distributed the blessed among the various levels of heaven, according to their deserts, amid music, song, and dance, in a dazzling blaze of light.

In contrast with these possibilities of bliss there was the awesome thought of eternal damnation: hell. We have encountered the concept before: in Latin, *inferna* means simply "a subterranean place" and is the equivalent of the Greek ᾅδης (*hades*), the German *Hölle,* etc. Its equivalent in Hebrew was *she'ōl,* which, etymologically, means "a void place," "a hole beneath the earth."

The primitive religions had not developed the idea of the punishment of the wicked after death; only that of a subterranean region where all the dead, without distinction between the good and the evil, went on living[52] in an existence that knew neither joys nor sorrows but was either a kind of escape from the customary conditions of earthly life or a continuation of earthly life. Hence the ordinary tools of existence were buried with the dead, as well as their clothes and weapons, and the bodies were embalmed or anointed in order to preserve them against decay.

Later, a distinction began to be made between two regions of the beyond (probably as a reflection of the division of human society into classes that commanded and made laws and other classes that had always to obey). In Greek mythology, for example, Elysium was for the blessed, while Tartarus, with its punishments and tortures, was for those who had violated the laws of society.

The Old Testament speaks of "eternal darkness" with "weeping and gnashing of teeth" for the "unjust," and the concept of punishment by fire also appears in the writings attributed to the prophet Isaiah. This belief was crystalized in the New Testament with an analogical reference to Gehenna (rendered in the King James Bible as "hell"). This name (Γέεννα, a rather approximate phonetic transcription of Gē-Hinnōm) was given to the valley of the Hinnom, a deep creek southwest of Jerusalem, where the original inhabitants used to burn human victims in honor of the Canaanite god Moloch. In memory of this idolatry, the Jews considered the valley a place accursed, and they used it for the destruction of everything unclean and of other refuse that required to be burned. The Evangelists ascribe the use of the word "Gehenna" to Jesus as an allusion to the fire that was to destroy all of sinful humanity (as Sodom and Gomorrah had been destroyed) in the apocalyptic universal judgment.

But the concept of a punitive function that would last over a long period of time, of fire and a place where there is great suffering, is not once mentioned in the New Testament. The Russian theologian Paul Evdokimov shows how the conception of hell was an opinion of the Scholastics, the fruit of a simplistic theology (of a penitential nature), by comparing it with certain affirmations of the Gospels ("I come not to judge the world but to save the world," etc.). "Is it even thinkable," Evdokimov asks, "that alongside an eternal heaven God would prepare an eternal hell as well, a hell which in a certain sense would be a defeat for the divine plan, and at least a partial victory of evil?"[53]

In due course, the world of the beyond became still more detailed.

In the fourth century, when it was being debated whether the martyrs of the persecutions must wait in their tombs for the Last Judgment or whether it might be granted to them to be assumed at once into God's glory, as Gregory of Nazianzus advocated, Augustine advanced the hypothesis that before they could be accepted into eternal bliss, they had to undergo at least a process of expiation, the term of which was variable, in order to be "purified" of any faults not pardoned or atoned for during their lives. This suggestion, which was endorsed by Gregory of Nazianzus, Gregory of Nyssa, and Basil, had been offered as a mere personal theory, but early in the sixth century it began to be taught as a positive fact.[54]

Caesarius of Arles was the first to distinguish between mortal sins, which sent the sinner directly to the punishments of hell, and venial sins, which were less serious and for which expiation in purgatory was allowed. Then Gregory the Great made this doctrine an article of faith, and the Council of Lyons in 1274 elaborated the dogmatic formula. Ultimately, the existence of purgatory was declared a truth of faith by the Council of Trent (December 3, 1563, Session XIV). However, the difficulties of obtaining unanimity led to fierce debates, and the Council had to recommend that "sermons to the faithful avoid the more difficult and subtle questions that contribute nothing to edification or piety," and that "nothing be revealed of uncertain or improbable matters."

It was in the Middle Ages, too, during the time of the Scholastics, that a fourth territory was added to the world beyond the grave: limbo. Derived from the Latin *limbus* ("border," "limit"), it was imagined as a zone outside hell, not subject to the demons' jurisdiction, which was the residence of those guiltless and just persons who had died unbaptized and hence outside Christianity, though they had no sins to pay for in hell. There were no tortures in limbo, but there were none of the joys of heaven.

Souls or Bodies?

This progressive transformation and complication of the kingdom preached by Jesus, which from a kingdom of the living had been mutated into several kingdoms of the dead, was accompanied by another very serious problem: if the "resurrection of the flesh" would occur only at the day of universal judgment, how in the interim could the dead reach the four regions of the afterworld?

Christian theology supposes that the provisional condition of the dead in those kingdoms is that of "pure spirits," or "souls," waiting to resume the bodies that meanwhile remain provisionally in their tombs.

Such a solution could never have entered the minds of men of Hebraic tradition. To them the idea that the individual was dualistically composed of soul and body was utterly alien. The word *nephesh* (which is most inappropriately translated as "soul") appears seven hundred and forty-five times in the Old Testament, and each time it means the "vital spirit" of the individual, the very life in the physical body. The body is designated by the word *bāsār*, which deprived of the breath of life, is σάρξ (*sarx*), or "flesh": corruptible matter. And in the New Testament, too, the expression "to save one's own soul" means to "to save one's own life."[55]

For Jesus, then, as for the Apostles and for all Christians of Jewish origin, a continuation of existence or a return to it could be understood only as the persistence or the renewal of the breath of life in a *bāsār*. Consider the resurrections performed by Elijah, by Elisha, by Jesus, and the resurrection of Jesus himself in the Gospel stories. According to Jesus, admission into the "kingdom" therefore meant the gift of *physical* eternal life, on this earth, for the just, and, on the other side, the punishment of the wicked was nothing more or less than the denial of life, condemnation to nonexistence.

Only in a Hellenic environment was it possible to conceive of ascribing an autonomous existence to the *nephesh*, which for the Jews was an abstract quality, a condition, not an entity. The Greeks, in fact, considered the human soul a divine and immortal essence, which lived in the body, Plato says, as in a prison, alert to find freedom in the moment of death.

Yet not even Paul, impregnated as he was with Hellenism, who first brought this foreign concept into Christianity, had a clear understanding of the Greek philosophers' distinction between body and soul. Still close to the materialistic concept of his compatriots, he could not help thinking that this "principle" which continued to live after death was something corporeal. In a well-known passage of his First Epistle to the Corinthians, he reasons thus: "All flesh is not the same flesh: but there is one kind of flesh of men, another flesh of beasts, another of fishes, and another of birds. There are also celestial bodies, and bodies terrestrial: but the glory of the celestial is one, and the glory of the terrestrial is another. . . . So also is the resurrection of the dead. It is sown in corruption; it is raised in incorruption. . . . There is a natural body, and there is a spiritual body."[56]

For several centuries the Doctors of the Church could not avoid viewing the soul in this light, as a piece of matter more refined than the body, similar to the matter of which the angels were made. "If the soul is not a body," Tertullian said, "then it is nothing,"[57] and he supposed it to be fragile, brilliant, and blue in color.[58]

It was still not quite clear whether what was meant was the transformation of the physical body into a spiritual body (the Pauline idea) or the resumption of life in a new body, different from that possessed on earth. The explanation was provided later by the cult of the martyrs: the conviction that they must be immediately assumed into the glory of God at death and the awkward fact that their corpses remained quite visibly and tangibly on earth forced the beliefs of Christians concerning the soul to shift markedly toward those of the pagans. So they began to believe in a sharp distinction between the two elements of soul and body, and a separate life for each.

The next subject of debate was whether a soul was created by God and put into a body each time someone was born (creationism) or whether the soul was handed down from father to son (traducianism). Augustine thought he could resolve the problem by the statement that the soul was not a substance but an intellective and moral force common to all men by their very nature. But this doctrine made it extremely embarrassing for the theologians to explain *how* this abstract force could vary from individual to individual and have a life independent of the body. That explanation became possible only when Christian theology began to look to Aristotle rather than to Plato—in other words, with Thomas Aquinas in the thirteenth century.

According to Aristotle, every living being is endowed with a soul, which he calls ψυχή (*psyche*), corresponding to the vitality of the body; man has in addition νοῦς (*nous*), or intellect, the faculty of reasoning. Thomas, accepting the Aristotelian distinction, defined the *psyche* as the "sensitive and vegetative soul" and considered it an active virtue of male blood, which becomes the soul in the newborn body composed of the mother's female blood.[59] As soon as the child acquires the capacity to reason, God creates in him the *nous* as well: the rational soul, which absorbs the vegetable soul and takes its place. This soul is eternal, even when it is separated from the body (*manet in suo esse cum fuerit a corpore separata*).[60]

It was still necessary to determine the substance that makes up this strange part of our being that lives in the body for a few years and then continues to exist on its own account. However, as might be expected, all the theological lucubrations on the subject are extravagant and discordant, even if most of them tend to the belief that it is an incorporeal, invisible, spiritual essence.

Martyrs and Saints

We have pointed out how the veneration of the martyrs became one of the major factors that induced the Christians to imagine immediate bliss for them, in compensation for their merits, and to consider them saints. If, like Jesus, they were ready to sacrifice their very lives for the faith, it was fitting that, also like Jesus, they rise again to new life.

But the words "martyr" and "saint" underwent noteworthy changes before they attained their present meanings. "Martyr" (in Greek, μάρτυρ, *martur,* and μάρτυς, *martus*) means "witness," and indeed in the early days the term was used to designate the Apostles, even during their lifetimes, inasmuch as they could testify as witnesses to the works and the Resurrection of Jesus.[61] Then the word was extended to include all those whose conduct could be said to bear witness to their faith, and finally it was limited to those who had died as a result of the persecutions. The corresponding Latin noun is *confessor.*

The word "saint," whether in Greek (ἁγνός, *hagnos,* and ἅγιος, *hagios*), in Latin (*sanctus*), or in Hebrew (from the root *qdsh*), means "consecrated to the deity," "dedicated to worship,"[62] and therefore the first Christians used it to designate the leaders of their communities. Paul's Epistles are addressed "to the saints which are at Ephesus," "to the saints . . . which are at Colosse," etc.

During the persecutions, as was proper, worshipful respect was paid to the martyrs with pilgrimages to the scenes of their martyrdom, ceremonies at their tombs, the erection of chapels, the jealous care of relics. Hymns and tales of their exemplary conduct were written to perpetuate their memories, "martyrologies" (lists of anniversaries) were compiled, the names of martyrs were taken as baptismal names. There were protests, too, for the worship of the martyrs threatened to overshadow what was due to God and to

Christ,[63] and at times the festivities in their honor provided occasions for debauchery and intemperance.[64]

After the persecutions had ended, it became customary to recognize as "holy," and worthy of veneration, all those who, even if they had not suffered martyrdom, had been outstanding by reason of their goodness and their religious zeal. In every century faith in Christ has produced innumerable authentic paragons of virtue and good works, marvelous exemplars of unselfish abnegation and heroism, whom even the unbeliever is constrained to admire and respect. But many times the imagination of the hagiographers and the blind devotion of the people have gone to excess in ascribing to the saints various gifts and accomplishments that are unbelievable, and there have even been sanctifications of individuals who were not altogether holy.

The Christian pantheon swiftly acquired a remarkable number of saints immediately after the religion had won official recognition from Constantine, because of the obvious necessity of adapting it to the traditions of the heathen. They adored, in fact, a considerable multitude of gods, demigods, heroes, nymphs, etc., who were the patrons of cities, forests, fountains, crossroads; who stood guard over health; who took a hand in marriages, births, business—in every minute, one might say, of ordinary life. Hence a double phenomenon of sanctification is to be observed: the new converts tended to attribute to one or another martyr the powers that they had been accustomed to impute to individual pagan divinities, and the Church itself replaced local heroes with its own saints, or, when these were unavailable, it permitted the heathen deities to be converted to Christianity.

Some instances were in truth astounding. Venus Aphrodisia, for example, continued to be worshiped by the masses, but under the new name of St. Phredisia; Apollo the ephebus became St. Ephebus; Ceres Flava turned into St. Flavia; Bacchus, whom the pagans called Soter (Savior), was revised into St. Soter, and so on. In the pagan calendar, the feast in honor of Dionysus was immediately followed by that of Demetrius: the same dates in the Christian calendar became the days of St. Dionysius and St. Demetrius. The Apollonian games suggested St. Apollinaris. The ides of the months were personified by St. Ida. The habitual Roman phrase of good wishes, *"perpetua felicitas,"* provided two saints, St. Perpetua and St. Felicity. Naturally, false lives had to be invented for all these false saints—exemplary lives filled with edifying details—and tribute was paid to the martyrdoms they were supposed to have undergone.

Only in very recent times has there been a courageous attempt to purge the Christian pantheon, but it did not survive: in fact, the action of Pope John XXIII, who in August of 1962 had the temerity to strike off St. Philomena and St. George, aroused great outrage. And yet the lady was nothing but a copy of mythological Proserpine, and the gentleman duplicated, down to his name, the Egyptian god Horus, the dragon-killer.

The fabrication of saintly legends even drew on other religions. In the Middle Ages, a biography of St. Barlaam and St. Josaphat that circulated among the monasteries was nothing but a transcript of the life of Buddha in Christian terms.[65]

Another set of saints was drawn from persons and things mentioned in the Gospels:[66] St. Amator, according to legend, was Mary's servant; St. Restitutus was the man, blind from birth, whose sight Jesus restored; St. Martial, the protector of Limoges, was the little boy of Capernaum whom Jesus held up as an example to his Apostles; St. Rufus, the patron of Avignon, was the son of the Cyrenian who helped Jesus to carry his cross on Calvary; St. Lazarus, St. Martha, and St. Mary were the brother and sisters who had been the hosts of Jesus in Bethany and who, carried by some miracle to the Provençal coast, were supposed to have founded the Christian community of Marseilles; St. Veronica was the personification (and transposition of the *vera icona* ("authentic image"), the cloth with which Jesus wiped his face along the Via Dolorosa.

Naturally, the "putative" father of Jesus was also sanctified, as St. Joseph, even though there is no evidence that he was ever converted to Christianity.

Just as it was characteristic of the individual pagan deities to have various attributes and special functions and to protect specific classes of persons, the same prerogatives were allotted among the various saints. Thus every city, every art, every trade or profession now has its patron saint; every variety of disease has a saint peculiarly talented, if he is called on, to speed its cure; and so on. But these prerogatives are often assigned in an extremely peremptory fashion, finding a basis in the mere name of the saint or in some approximate relation with the persons or things protected. St. Lucy, because of her name (from the Latin *lux, lucis,* meaning "light"), is the guardian of eyesight; St. Gotthard is invoked by sufferers from gout; St. Latinus presides over those made ill by milk (from *lac, lactis,* meaning "milk"). In 1956, an apostolic brief from the Holy See nominated a patron for radio and mail; St. Gabriel the archangel, inasmuch as he was God's special messenger and had carried the Annunciation to the Madonna; on February 14, 1958, the Catholic Congregation of Rites issued a decree recognizing St. Clara of Assisi as the patron of television because, according to her hagiographic record, on Christmas Eve, 1252, when she was already gravely ill and confined to her bed, she had a miraculous vision: "she began to hear the organ, the responses and the entire holy office of the Brothers of the Church of St. Francis, as if she had been present there, and in addition she saw the Manger of our Lord, Jesus Christ."

[19]

THE LAST SUPPER

Lazarus

Determined to flee from Jerusalem after the second threat of the priests to stone him, Jesus, the Gospel of John tells us, took refuge "beyond Jordan, into the place where John at first baptized"[1]—that is, near Bethabara, not too far from the mouth of the river, but well into the semi-wilderness of Perea.

A few days later, he received a message from Martha and Mary of Bethany (the only persons who knew the secret of his whereabouts): Lazarus, their brother, was ill and wanted his friend with him.[2] When Jesus learned the details of the illness, he diagnosed it with assurance: "This sickness is not unto death." He could not see any necessity for him to go to Lazarus and thus risk arrest. Two days later, however, perhaps after a second message saying that Lazarus had died, he abandoned all procrastination and said to his Apostles: "Let us go into Judea again."

"Master," one of them objected, "the Jews of late sought to stone thee; and goest thou thither again?" Another suggested that he wait at least for the protection of darkness.

"Are there not twelve hours in the day?" Jesus retorted. "If any man walk in the day, he stumbleth not, because he seeth the light of this world. But if a man walk in the night, he stumbleth, because there is no light in him." Then he added: "Our friend, Lazarus, sleepeth," but the Apostles misunderstood, and he had to explain: "Lazarus is dead. And I am glad for your sakes that I was not there, to the intent ye may believe; nevertheless let us go unto him."

Thomas, the solitary, was so selflessly moved that he cried: "Let us also go, that we may die with him."

Lazarus had already been in the grave for four days, but the funeral ceremonies at his home had barely begun when Jesus arrived. Early burial was then, as it still is, a practice made necessary by the climate, which could cause rapid decomposition. Therefore, the entire funeral ritual was postponed until after the interment. It was customary for all who had known the deceased to pay not one but many successive visits of condolence to his survivors. The bereaved sat on stools in the inner entrance of the house to receive the callers, and, as each one entered, their lamentations were renewed.

As soon as Martha heard that Jesus had arrived in Bethany but did not wish to go to her house, lest his presence become known, she ran to find him. But she did not even greet him; her first words were, rather, an affectionate reprobation: "Lord, if thou hadst been here, my brother had not died. . . . I know that whatsoever thou wilt ask of God, God will give it thee."

Jesus tried to comfort her: "Thy brother shall rise again."

Martha was almost angry. "I know that he shall rise again in the resurrection on the last day."

She turned and ran back to her house. Mary looked at her questioningly, as if to inquire why she had been away so long. Martha put her lips close to Mary's ear and whispered: "The Master is come, and calleth for thee." Mary rose from her chair at once and left the room in a state of excitement that went unobserved by none of the visitors.

She too, as soon as she saw Jesus, made him the same tender reproach as her sister, and broke into tears. Jesus flushed, visibly upset, but he had no time to make excuses. Some of Mary's relatives had followed her, and they were observing everything; it was useless now to try to keep his arrival a secret. Somewhat apprehensively, he asked: "Where have ye laid him?"

Jesus wept as they accompanied him to the grave, and they said to one another: "Behold, how he loved him!" Others wondered: "Could not this man, which opened the eyes of the blind, have caused that even this man should not have died?"

Groaning within himself, Jesus arrived at the grave—a cave with a huge stone at its mouth. "Take ye away the stone," he ordered.

"Lord," Martha said, "by this time he stinketh: for he hath been dead four days."

"Said I not unto thee, that, if thou wouldest believe, thou shouldest see the glory of God?"

When the stone had been removed, Jesus looked up to heaven and implored God to assist him in working the miracle; then, stretching out his hand toward the tomb, he cried in a loud voice: "Lazarus, come forth."

His hands and feet still bound with graveclothes and his face covered with a small cloth, the dead man rose and emerged. "Loose him," Jesus said, "and let him go."

It is pointless to renew the debate on the impossibility of this miracle and to ask sarcastically, as Strauss does,[3] why Jesus did not instead resuscitate John the Baptist or someone else more important and useful than Lazarus; or to suppose, with Renan,[4] that it was a preconceived fraud to which Lazarus was a party, intended to help Jesus reinforce his disciples' faith; or to conclude that Lazarus had not really died but was mistakenly believed to be dead—in short, to look for any rational explanation of so inconceivable an occurrence, especially in the case of a corpse already in an advanced stage of organic decomposition.[5]

The story of the resurrection of Lazarus appears only in the Gospel of John, and therefore, notwithstanding certain realistic details supplied with the touch of an artist, we must expect of it only an allegorical meaning, and we must interpret it as a myth transformed into a narrative.[6]

Is Lazarus supposed to be the symbol of a world buried in the tomb of error, which Jesus awakens with his message, as the esoterics hold?[7] Or does the resurrection allude to some mystic procedure of initiation, like that of the Egyptian hierophant who plunged himself into a three-day sleep, as the Theosophists believe?[8] Or is it simply, as it seems to me to be, a prototype of the doctrine of the resurrection of the just, created to illustrate the teachings of the early Christian communities?

The Anointment by Mary

The Gospel of John concludes the account of Lazarus' resurrection by saying that the story of the miracle spread quickly, and once more the priests and the doctors, more alarmed than ever, debated whether they should arrest Jesus.[9] This latter point is confirmed by Mark and Matthew.[10]

So Jesus fled from Bethany again, not into Perea this time. Instead, he chose the city of Ephraim as his hiding place; this was still within Judea, about twenty-five miles north of Jerusalem. He must have remained there for several months, for the Gospels do not put him in Bethany again until the time of Passover, and they tell us that Lazarus, Martha, and Mary prepared a festive dinner to celebrate his return.

According to John, it was six days before Passover;[11] according to Matthew and Mark, it was only two.[12] In any case, it was the first half of the month of Nisan, with which at that time the year began, and according to the Christian calendar the year was exactly A.D. 30, if the chronology we have followed so far is accurate.

Some exegetes, however, paying no attention to the dates given in the Gospels, assume that the feast in Bethany was held about a month earlier, on the fourteenth or fifteenth day of Adar (some time in February), which was then the last month of the year, because these were the dates of Purim, and in Palestine in those days this festival was celebrated with great banquets, accompanied by the exchange of gifts of food among friends.[13] The holiday marked the rescue of the Jews living in Persia in the times of Xerxes I through the efforts of Esther, the beautiful Jewess who was the favorite concubine of this same Xerxes. The feast was called Purim (*pūrīm* means "lots") because Xerxes had earlier set the date for the extermination of the Jews by drawing lots. In this instance, too, in the judgment of scholars, we have a case of the historical-legendary disguise of an astronomical holy day: *pūrū*, imported from Mesopotamia, with which the end of the year was celebrated.

In any case, the exact date of the supper in Bethany is of no great importance: whether it was held on Purim or a few days before Passover, it is of a religious rather than a historical nature.

The Gospel of Luke does not mention this supper, but since the versions in Mark and Matthew resemble Luke's story of the sinner who anointed Jesus,[14] and since the Gospel of John makes a conglomeration of the various versions,[15] many scholars believe that they all deal with the same incident but report it in different ways. The name of the owner of the house is always the same: Simon. However, a complication arises with respect to Simon of Bethany: he is called "the leper." Since it was impossible for a leper to associate with healthy people, various suggestions have been advanced: either he was in fact a former leper, now cured, or the supper was held in his house without him because his infectious disease required that he be segregated or perhaps because he had already died.[16] To me it seems most likely, as Klausner supposes,[17] that there was simply a mistake between two very similar Hebrew words, one of which means "the leper" and the other of which means "the humble one."

The central theme of the story is that at a certain point, Mary, elated by the return of Jesus after so long an absence, wanted to show him the extent of her joy and her devotion, and so she perfumed his hair and beard with the fragrant essence of nard, following the custom at the feasts of the rich. The ointment refreshed and softened skin dried out by sun and dust. Then Mary went to the extreme of breaking the vial, which was of precious alabaster, from which she had taken the essence, perhaps to prove to Jesus that she intended to sacrifice its entire contents to him and would never use the vial again for anything.[18]

When they saw this, the disciples were angry: nard was extremely expensive. Made from a brownish herb native to India, it took about a hundred and fifty pounds of the roots and stems to make less than a quart of the ointment. One of the disciples (John says it was Judas Iscariot) protested: "To what purpose is this waste? Why was not this ointment sold for three hundred pence, and given to the poor?"

But Jesus reproached them: "Why trouble ye the woman? for she hath wrought a good work upon me. For ye have the poor always with you; but me ye have not always. For in that she hath poured this ointment on my body, she did it for my burial."

The meaning of this episode is clear, and the story, in my view, should not be identified with that of Luke's sinner. It seems to me, rather, that the two are almost antithetical: the story in Luke exalts the sinner's *caritas,* the loving act that is capable of redeeming her from sin; the story of Mary of Bethany, on the contrary, seems to state that adoration of Christ and faith in him are greater than works of charity.

Otherwise, if it were taken literally, as a simple factual report, the story would have many ridiculous aspects; above all the pessimistic assumption by Jesus that the poor must always exist, as well as the likening of Mary's loving act to the preparation of a corpse, which would be a jest in very poor taste.

Judas

In bold contrast with the tender devotion of the girl of Bethany, the Gospels turn immediately afterward to the treachery of Judas Iscariot.[19] When and how did the disloyal Apostle establish contact with the priests? The Evangelists had no means of knowing —certainly neither Judas nor the priests enlightened the disciples of Jesus. Therefore, we must also content ourselves with guess work. Perhaps Judas spoke to the priests when Jesus was preaching in the Temple;[20] perhaps he went on an impulse to the high priest's home[21] and urged him to arrest Jesus before the Passover influx of pilgrims into Jerusalem could lead to outbreaks;[22] or Judas might even have suggested the night of the supper itself as the best time, since all the people would be in their own houses for the religious banquet.[23]

Some students, such as Charles Guignebert,[24] put no credence in the betrayal by Judas but consider it an invention designed to make the arrest of Jesus more believable and to justify the tradition that Jews must have betrayed the Nazarene. Hence he believes that the very name Judas was expressly chosen as a synonym for Jew. That this is its etymology is indubitable; but there is also the fact that Judas was a very common name in Palestine.

The whole episode gives rise to graver questions. If Jesus already knew, as the Gospels affirm, that he would be betrayed by Judas, why did he do absolutely nothing to prevent it? Why did he allow Judas to remain among the Apostles? How could Judas himself have been so close to Jesus for so long, even serving as treasurer for the little apostolic community, and then suddenly resolve to perform so base an act? If he was disillusioned with the teaching of Jesus, would it not have been enough for him to secede? Not only was the betrayal the result of discouragement, it implies a hatred that Jesus surely did not deserve. Over the centuries, answers to these questions have been sought, but all the explanations are personal and debatable.

That money should have been the prime motive seems impossible, even if the amount paid to Judas far exceeded the "thirty pieces of silver" to which Matthew refers.[25] The other Synoptic Gospels say only that he received "money" (ἀργύριον, *argurion*), and Peter refers only to a "reward" (μισθός, *misthos*)[26] which was enough to enable him to buy a field. Moreover, Matthew himself reveals the lack of a historical basis for his own version when he says that the amount to be given to Judas was put at thirty pieces of silver in order to fulfill a prophecy by Zechariah.[27] Actually, the Evangelist makes the mistake of crediting the prophecy to Jeremiah, and in this connection one cannot help smiling at the comical ingenuity with which Augustine tries to excuse so glaring a blunder. Matthew, Augustine says,[28] knew very well that the sentence came from Zechariah, but he also knew that he was writing at the dictation of the Holy Ghost, and he dared not taken the liberty of correcting it. And why, Augustine proceeds, did the Holy Ghost dictate an inaccuracy? To show that all the Prophets were equally inspired and that it did not matter whether what was said by one was ascribed to another!

If it was not a desire for money that led Judas to commit treason, what other motive could have impelled him? To have been made one of the Twelve Apostles, he must have sincerely believed, at least in an earlier period. It is possible to speculate that in his disappointment at not seeing the materialization of the kingdom, all his hopes suddenly collapsed and he became convinced that Jesus was a false Messiah.[29] Still, this would hardly justify so loathsome a betrayal.

Others ascribe his act to fear. When Judas saw that Jesus was risking arrest, and when he, ahead of the other Apostles, who were entranced by their own fanaticism, recognized the danger that threatened all of them, he allowed his fright to take control. He was not even aware of the enormity of his own behavior; frightened, he wanted to make an end, he wanted to rid himself of the weight of his fears and of the man by whom perhaps he was still fascinated. Pure terror drove him to the crime.[30]

Simply too ingenious, to me, is the hypothesis of Paulus that Judas, on the contrary, thought that by bringing about the arrest of Jesus he could strike a bold blow: he was counting on a popular rising which would have culminated in the rescue of the Messiah and launched the long awaited final revolution.[31]

In ancient times, too, there was a tendency to thrust the otherwise inconceivable betrayal by Judas into the general framework of divine purposiveness. The Gnostic sect of the Cainites, which justified the fratricide committed by Cain (if the history of humanity was to develop as it has done, Cain's crime was necessary, and therefore foreordained by God), took a similar view of the treachery of Judas. The death of Jesus was essential for the salvation of mankind; therefore, Judas, who made it possible, showed himself capable of rising to the level of the Gnostics and understanding far better than the other Apostles that Jesus *had to* die. For this reason, the Cainites celebrated the *mysterium proditionis:* Judas himself was a victim, who sacrificed himself for our salvation and made himself an instrument of redemption.[32]

It is interesting to observe how this paradoxical thesis has been treated very recently by the novelist Roger Caillois,[33] who makes Pontius Pilate, as well as Judas, a divine instrument. Caillois has Judas say to Pilate: "We are the indispensable artisans of the redemption. We are the instruments of the supreme outrage required to shake the moral conscience of the world. . . . You will be execrated, but console yourself. He knows that he could not have redeemed mankind without my pretended betrayal and your fictitious cowardice."

On the subsequent fate of Judas, the literature of the New Testament provides only curt indications, in Matthew[34] and in the Acts of the Apostles.[35] Overcome with remorse, Judas tried to return the thirty pieces of silver, and when the priests refused the money, he threw the coins into the Temple, then hanged himself. But somehow he fell from the sycamore to which he had tied his rope; "he burst asunder in the midst, and all his bowels gushed out."

The priests used the thirty pieces (which, being blood money, could not be kept for the Temple) to buy a property known as "the potter's field" as a burial ground for strangers (Acts states that it was called "*Akeldama* . . . the field of blood").

It is in this passage that the author of the Gospel of Matthew admits his debt to Jeremiah (Zechariah), but he makes another error in translating from the Hebrew. In that language, the text of Zechariah says: "Cast it [the money] into the Temple, for the treasury,"[36] but Matthew says that the priests "bought with them [the pieces of silver] the potter's field": the Hebrew words for "treasury" and "potter" are written very similarly. Actually, almost all modern translators of the Old Testament, including those of the King James Bible, made the same mistake as Matthew, rendering Zechariah 11:13: "Cast them to the *potter* in the house of the Lord," instead of: "Cast them for the *treasury* . . ."

Preparations for the Passover

When it was almost the eve of Passover, called "the first day of the feast of unleavened bread,"[37] Jesus sent two of the Apostles (Luke says they were Peter and John) from Bethany to Jerusalem with instructions to prepare everything necessary for the ritual evening meal in the house of a friend, who had generously invited Jesus and the Apostles. Actually, it was customary for the families of Jerusalem to welcome strangers to their tables on that solemn occasion. The guests did not pay, but it was a general practice to leave with the host the skin of the lamb that had been sacrificed.[38] A slave or a member of the family was to meet the Apostles, holding a jar of water on his head as a means of identification.[39]

The date of this dinner is an extremely important question, for it is closely linked to the date of the death of Jesus. We know that the Passover meal was supposed to be eaten on the night of the fourteenth and fifteenth of Nisan (the changeover from one day to the next occurred at sunset). The rules governing the celebration were explicit: "And in the fourteenth day of the first month is the passover of the Lord. And in the fifteenth day of this month is the feast";[40] "In the first month, on the fourteenth day of the month at

even, ye shall eat unleavened bread";[41] on the fourteenth of Nisan
the previously selected lamb was to be sacrificed, "and they shall
eat the flesh in that night, roast with fire, and unleavened bread;
and with bitter herbs."[42]

However, like all the other Hebraic holy days, this was a mov-
able feast. The Hebrews, in fact, did not have a fixed calendar. Each
month began with the appearance of the new moon; its arrival was
officially noted and announced from the Temple with a bonfire and
a sound of trumpets. The twelve lunar months, each of which had
twenty-nine or thirty days, constituted the lunar year of three hundred and sixty days. To reconcile it with the solar year, therefore, it
was necessary to add an extra month, according to the seasons,
every three or four years; this month followed Adar and was therefore called Veadar ("and-Adar"). Neither the pattern of twenty-nine-
and thirty-day months nor the insertion of the second Adar was
subject to precise rules; both were determined in purely empirical
fashion by the priests of the Temple. Consequently, even the observance of the fourteenth and fifteenth of Nisan (which, astro-
nomically, should have coincided with the fullness of the moon) was
often approximate.

The Gospels afford no help. In fact, they complicate the question, because there is a divergence between the three Synoptics and
the Gospel of John: the former say that the dinner was held in the
usual manner on the eve of Passover (the fourteenth of Nisan),
but the latter implies that it took place on the night before the
eve (the thirteenth). At first glance it would seem clear that John's
date could be disregarded without further thought, since, in his
usual unreliable fashion, he not only disagrees with the statements
of the three other Evangelists but also, worse, dates the dinner a
day ahead of the ritual time. But the chronology of the Synoptic
Gospels, as we shall see, presents a number of problems in relation
to what follows.

The Church seems to prefer John's date, which is particularly
attractive because it makes possible an impressive symbolism: the
death of Jesus coincides with the moment at which the paschal lamb
is sacrificed in the Temple. However, one must then either strip
the Last Supper of its sacrificial character, since it is no longer the
Passover meal,[43] or else prove that in the time of Jesus it was lawful

also to hold the feast a day ahead of time. The latter is the usual choice, based on the argument that such was the practice of the Pharisees, in contrast with the traditional and official observance.[44] But the argument is fallacious. Only the priests' decision could carry any practical weight,[45] and Passover, like all the other observances, was solemnly proclaimed by them for all the population alike. The Pharisees, even if they had wished to do so, would not have been permitted to make their sacrifices in the Temple a day earlier.

Passover was in truth a subject of controversy between the Pharisees and the Sadducees, but only on a theoretical level and with regard to a single contingency: if the fifteenth of Nisan fell on the day after the Sabbath, the Pharisees contended that the dinner should be advanced by a day in order not to disturb the repose of the Sabbath; but it is not true that they always held it a day before the others.[46]

In any event, and even if one grants the demonstrability of the coincidence of the Sabbath and the eve of Passover in the same year in which Jesus died, and if one concedes further that the priests had followed the Pharisees' view, the day of the Last Supper (the thirteenth of Nisan) would be a Friday, and, as we shall see, this dislocates everything that followed it.

"One of You Shall Betray Me"

According to a legend that Catholic tradition embraces with satisfaction, the Last Supper of Jesus and the Apostles was served in the richly appointed house of a certain Mary, who was the sister of Simon Peter and who had a son, still very young, named Mark, the future Evangelist.[47] Therefore, this same Mark could have been the "man" who waited for Peter (his uncle) and John at the gates of the city, holding a jar of water on his head, and led them to his own house to prepare the banquet hall. From what the Gospels give us to understand, it was a "large upper room." This was the usual term for a kind of trellised bower that the people of Palestine had on the roofs of their houses, which, as we know, were like terraces and could easily be reached by stairs. The poor built primitive shelters, using branches and old cloth to form a kind of tent; the rich built walls and furnished the enclosed space with stools, rugs, and cushions.

Late in the evening, as was proper, Jesus and the Apostles sat down to dinner in a place of this kind. The Law required at least ten persons to be present for any ritual; this group was more than enough.

The Gospel of John does not describe the meal, but it reports one interesting detail[48] about which the Synoptics say nothing. As soon as the supper was ready, Jesus undressed and wrapped himself in a towel, filled a bowl with water, and began to wash the feet of his Apostles, drying them with the same towel that covered him. When he reached Simon Peter, the embarrassed Apostle tried to protest: "Lord, dost thou wash my feet?"

"What I do thou knowest not now; but thou shalt know hereafter."

"Thou shalt never wash my feet," Peter insisted.

"If I wash thee not, thou hast no part with me."

"Lord, not my feet only, but also my hands and my head."

Jesus rebuked him gently for his childish show of zeal: "He that is washed needeth not save to wash his feet . . . and ye are clean, but not all."

At this the Apostles were stunned, and they stared at their master. He silently set down the bowl and the towel with a gesture of weariness, clothed himself again, and took his place at the table, in the seat of honor that had been reserved for him. In those days, one lay on a pallet to eat, supporting the left shoulder with cushions; it was the best position because it was close to the floor, which was cooler. Now, looking fixedly at the Twelve Apostles, who had been watching him in astonishment, Jesus said slowly, in a voice full of sorrow:

"Know ye what I have done to you? Ye call me Master and Lord: and ye say well; for so I am. If I then, your Lord and Master, have washed your feet; ye also ought to wash one another's feet. For I have given you an example. . . . If ye know these things, happy are ye if ye do them. I speak not of you all: I know whom I have chosen. . . . He that eateth bread with me, hath lifted up his heel against me."[49] After a little silence, he spoke again, the words almost bursting out of his anguished heart: "Verily, verily I say unto you, that one of you shall betray me."[50]

The Apostles were shocked into silence. No one spoke. No one moved. At last, with great effort, Simon Peter mustered enough strength to ask the Apostle between himself and Jesus whom the master meant. The neighbor turned to Jesus and whispered: "Lord, who is it?"

"He it is," Jesus answered in a low voice, "to whom I shall give a sop, when I have dipped it." He took a piece of bread, dipped it in a bowl of sauce that was on the table, then rose and carried it to Judas Iscariot, bidding him: "That thou doest, do quickly."

The others, who had not heard the answer Jesus gave his neighbor, could not grasp the meaning of what he said to Judas, and they thought that, since Judas managed the funds for the group, Jesus had told him to go out and purchase something still needed for the evening. Judas took the soaked bread, left the table, and disappeared in the darkness outside.

The Synoptic Gospels, too, though more tersely, report the unmasking of Judas by Jesus,[51] and they add a curse against him that is attributed to Jesus himself: "The Son of man indeed goeth, as it is written of him: but woe to that man by whom the Son of man is betrayed! good were it for that man if he had never been born."

It is logical that the whole episode of the washing of feet and the cursing of Judas should be read not so much for its historical accuracy (which is open to much doubt) as for its hermeneutic significance—the symbology of baptism, of faith in Christ, of religious purification in the washing—as well as for its admonition to be unwavering in faith, to resist temptation, including, as in the case of Judas, the ultimate temptation of abjuring Christ.

The Last Supper

The Synoptic Gospels give only a few verses to the story of the Supper,[52] but one can infer from them that the usual ritual was modified in order to give the ceremony a special character centered on the person of Jesus. As we pointed out earlier in discussing the first Passover meal in which Jesus, as a child, took part, the festival almost certainly derived from a very early totemic cult of a type that students of religion encounter among almost all peoples at an extremely primitive stage: the animal sacrificed is the symbol (totem) and protector of an ethnic group. Later, with the disappearance of the hunting culture, of which totem worship is characteristic, and the development of an agricultural-pastoral civilization, the celebration loses its original function and takes on a new one: at Passover (the vernal equinox) the Hebrews marked the rebirth of the earth with its fruits, especially grapes and grain, and the increase of the herds. It was therefore an agricultural-pastoral feast that could be summarized, essentially, as a ceremony of thanks to Yahweh for these gifts. Still later, the memory of all these archaic origins became blurred; Passover, like almost all the traditional rituals, became invested with a historical-nationalistic import, which linked it to the legend of Moses. The Passover repast came to be considered a commemoration of the hasty meal gulped down by the Hebrews in flight from Egypt.

The etymology of the Hebrew name for the festival, *Pesah*, which was approximately taken over into Greek and Latin and thence into the Romance languages and even, adjectivally, into English (*Pâques*, in French, and *Pasqua*, in Italian, mean both "Easter" and "Passover"—that is, the spring festival—and, in English, the adjective for both is "paschal"), helps in tracing this evolution, even if philologists' opinions do not always converge.[53] On the one hand, *Pesah* can be traced back to the verb root *psh* ("to be festive") and means "the Feast of Feasts": the great pre-Mosaic festival of totemic or agricultural nature. On the other, *Pesah* can be followed back to the verb root *psh* ("to go leaping before") and thus to the legend of the angel who, in the tenth Egyptian plague, spared (passed over) the houses inhabited by Hebrews.

The ceremonial of the Passover dinner (the Seder) followed a precise pattern. The most respected person present, or the eldest, was charged with conducting a thanksgiving ritual at the start. He poured the first cup of sweet wine (*tirōsh*) and pronounced the first prayer of benediction: "Blessed art thou, O Lord, who hast created the fruit of the vine." Everyone then drank in a religious hush, while the women and the servants carried round the roast lamb and great bowls of bitter herbs (lettuce, horseradish, parsley), and a special sauce, *harōseth,* of a reddish color, made with dates, figs, and almonds cooked in wine and cinnamon. The celebrant, followed by the others, took a pinch of the herbs, dipped it in the *harōseth,* and ate it after he had pronounced the second benediction: "Blessed art thou, O Lord, who hast created the fruits of the earth."

Then he poured a second cup of wine, and in a dramatic voice he briefly recalled the significance of the festival and called on everyone to chant the first portion of the Hallel—Psalms 113, which begins: "Praise ye the Lord," and 114, which begins: "When Israel went out of Egypt." When the singing had ended, it was time for the last benediction. Breaking a piece of unleavened bread and putting a bit of sauce on it, the celebrant gave a portion to each person at the table, saying: "Blessed art thou, O Lord, who has caused the earth to bring forth bread." He then took the third cup of wine. That signaled the commencement of the meal itself, which consisted of the lamb and liberal portions of wine. When the entire animal had been eaten—nothing but the bones was supposed to be left—the feast ended with a last cup of wine and the singing of the final portion of the Hallel, Psalms 115 through 118.

If we compare this pattern with the description of the Last Supper given by the Gospels, we find major modifications by which a ceremony of gratitude to God for the gifts of wine, bread, and the fruits of the earth is transformed into a mystery-cult ritual. A critical examination of the Scriptural passages, in the light of Christological doctrine as it was shaped by the thought of the first Christian community and Paul, enables us to see this transformation.

Codex D (or Codex Bezae Cantabrigiensis) gives us the primitive text, chapter 22 in the Gospel of Luke, which should also be that of the other Evangelists:

14. "And when the hour was come, he sat down, and the twelve apostles with him."

15. "And he said unto them, With desire I have desired to eat this passover with you before I suffer;"

16. "For I say unto you, I will not any more eat thereof, until it be fulfilled in the kingdom of God."

17. "And he took the cup, and gave thanks, and said, Take this, and divide it among yourselves:"

18. "For I say unto you, I will not drink of the fruit of the vine, until the kingdom of God shall come."

19. "And he took bread, and brake it, saying: This do in remembrance of me."

Here, Jesus desires only to make of the Passover, in addition to a ceremony of gratitude to Yahweh for the "good things" thus far given according to the Old Covenant, a thanksgiving for the promise of the kingdom (the New Covenant), in which these things would be everlasting and abounding. The meal was intended therefore to be a hope and a token of the harmony and the felicity that would be enjoyed in the kingdom of God.[54] And thus it continued to be understood by the proto-Christians. Indeed, it is related in the Acts of the Apostles[55] that immediately after the death of Jesus, they were in perfect accord (ὁμοθυμαδόν, homothumadon) in maintaining the custom of the breaking of bread (ἡ κλάσις τοῦ ἄρτου, ē klasis tou artou), taking their meals together every day, and especially on the Sabbath, κατ' οἶκον (kat oikon), which can mean either "in their own houses" or "going from one house to another, in turn," and with joyous and simple hearts, exactly according to the Jewish custom of gathering families and friends together in gladness at Passover. The proto-Christians used to give such a gathering the fitting name of agape (ἀγάπη), which means "love," "hearty acceptance," "brotherhood." The exhortation of Jesus: "This do in remembrance of me," was taken as an invitation to preserve their recollections of him and of their life with him during those few years of their experiment.[56]

The word εὐχαριστία (eucharistia) is a relatively late designation for the ceremony, and it is derived from one detail of the ritual: the thanks to Yahweh (that is the meaning of the Greek word) given by Jesus at the beginning of the feast.

The Blood of the New Covenant

The drastic alteration of the Eucharist, which had started as a ceremony commemorating Jesus and thanking Yahweh, into a mystery-cult ritual came as a sequel to the entrenchment of Paul's Christology. The fortuitous death of Jesus, an innocent victim of political fears of both the Romans and the Jewish ruling class, so soon after the Last Supper, at which the flesh of a sacred animal (the lamb) had been consumed after its immolation to Yahweh as a propitiatory and expiatory offering, gave Paul the idea of fusing the two events and thus erecting a parallel between Jesus and the paschal lamb.

On this level of a simple symbolic comparison between two innocent victims, each sacrificed to further the interests of the sacrificers, there was nothing remarkable in Paul's idea. Vicarious sacrifice was no more repugnant to the Jewish religion than to many others. We have already had occasion to note the Hebrew belief in the scapegoat, which, as in analogous Babylonian, Hittite, and Egyptian rites, was a passive victim to which all the sins of the nation were transposed through a magic power by the high priest on the Day of Atonement, and whose death therefore stood for the cancellation of all those guilts. Man has always believed that innocence arouses compassion and evokes mercy, and a deep-rooted concept in the Hebraic religion (as we have also seen earlier) was that of the possibility of ransom, in every instance of purification and expiation, by means of an unblemished victim: a dove, a lamb, a calf, etc. Nor were the Jews strangers to the idea that innocent victims might be chosen from among human beings (Jephtha's daughter, Isaac, etc.), any more than were the Greeks (Iphigenia, Alcestis, etc.).

Paul's Christology, however, did not envision Jesus solely as an expiatory victim. With a very different wealth of imagination, Paul, under the influence of the mystery cults so widespread in the Greco-Oriental environment in which he lived, merged Jesus with the redeemer divinities—Orpheus, Dionysus, Attis, etc.—worshiped by those religions. These divinities too suffered and died in order to give men an opportunity of spiritually attaining divine blessedness. Believers had to be "initiated" into the secret cult (μυστήριον, *mystērion*) through catechesis (understanding of the significance of the ritual), fast, and purification. They were then admitted among the members of the religious community that enjoyed the god's protection and they could perform the act of mystical union, or communion, with the god himself by eating the flesh of a sacred animal that was his symbol.[57] The animal's flesh and blood infused the qualities of the deity into him who consumed them. Paul, too, thought in terms of a magic power inherent in the bread of the Eucharist, as the pagans imagined it in their idolothytes (the animals sacrificed to their gods).[58]

No great effort is required to recognize the affinities between the stages of Orphic initiation (catechesis, fasting, purification) and those of the Christian novitiate: preparation for the "mystery" of the Eucharist, fasting, confession, and absolution of sins. But the replacement of the sacred animal with the very person of Christ makes the ceremony grotesque and horrifying. If Jesus is to be considered a human being, the Lord's Supper assumes the characteristics of a cannibal ritual; if Jesus is to be considered the Son of God, the pure and exalted idea of God held by Jesus degenerates into belief in a ruthless god who demands the savage, perpetually renewed sacrifice of his chosen Son.

Once Paul's innovation had gained acceptance, even the agape of the Apostles lost both its meanings—the eucharistic (gratitude to the deity) and the commemorative (of Jesus)—by becoming part of the "mystery" of Communion. The bread and the wine were made symbols of the person of Jesus: more specifically, of his body and his blood.

The text of the Gospels was then filled out with the additions made by Paul, who, violating historical truth to meet a theological exigency, and declaring with great shamelessness that everything had been *directly* reported to him by Jesus himself, caused Jesus to say, after the breaking of bread: "Take, eat; this is my body, which is broken for you," and, when he makes the libation with the wine: "This cup is the new testament [covenant] in my blood."[59]

As an anticipation of the blessedness promised by Jesus in the kingdom, the apostolic agape had a festive character. Paul shifted the emphasis to the death of Jesus; for him the Last Supper was the proclamation of the Lord's death,[60] and the joyous brotherly feast became a sacrament shrouded in frightening mystery. Indeed, in keeping with the Greco-Oriental soteriological rituals, Paul inserted into the Christian Communion the concept of divine punishment (even by death) for anyone who dared to eat the Host without proper initiation: "Whosoever shall eat this bread, and drink this cup of the Lord, unworthily, shall be guilty of the body and blood of the Lord. . . . For this cause many are weak and sickly among you, and many sleep."[61]

Even today, most of the faithful are convinced that it would be a frightening sacrilege to approach the Communion table without absolute spiritual purity and without having first cleansed their bodies through the appropriate fast.

Following Paul in his fiction that it was Jesus himself who proclaimed the symbolism of the bread and wine as his own body and his own blood, the theologians are concerned by the question whether, during the Last Supper, Jesus ate and drank what he had called his body and his blood. Doubts of this kind are unfounded if one reckons that the Nazarene really said: "I will not drink of the fruit of the vine," and not: ". . . of this my blood," since he had no intention of offering himself as a dinner for his Apostles.[62]

When one remembers that such symbolology was Paul's idea and did not originate with Jesus himself, the ceremony loses that monstrous character that alarms the theologians. The idea of attributing sacramental properties to blood is not really very remarkable. The use of blood is common to many religions, whether to propitiate the gods, to placate the souls of the dead (Homer describes the shades in Hades drinking the blood of two sheep sacrificed by Ulysses), to seal marriages and alliances, to fortify magic love charms, and so on. Blood, whether mixed with wine or represented by it, is often invested with magic powers: an Egyptian papyrus says that Osiris gave Isis and Horus a cup of wine and blood to drink so that after his death they would search for him, sorely lamenting, until he came back to life and could rejoin them.[63]

For the Hebrews, too, blood was sacred: "For the life of the flesh," Leviticus says, "is in the blood: and I have given it to you upon the altar to make an atonement for your souls: for it is the blood that maketh an atonement for the soul."[64] The sacrifices of purification also required invariably that the altar be sprinkled with the blood of the victim. In particular, Hebrew males made a gift of their blood to Yahweh through circumcision: the blood that flowed when the foreskin was cut with the ritual knife was a physical evidence of submission to the deity and a propitiatory offering for the child that was making its entrance into life.

In the idea that Jesus shed his blood to placate Yahweh's wrath there is a strong parallelism with the blood of the bullocks sacrificed by Moses to seal the covenant of protection negotiated with Yahweh on Mount Sinai. The wait preached by the Prophets of the Old Testament, after they had denounced the people of Israel for angering Yahweh with their violations of the Mosaic covenant (the Old Covenant), was indeed offered in terms of the hope that there would be a reconciliation with the deity and the negotiation of a New Covenant with him, which would have to be sealed with a new propitiatory sacrifice. Paul's Christology made it possible to consider Jesus the designated victim, and the expression of Paul and the Gospels: "This cup is the new testament of my blood," had complete verification in the Biblical sentence: "Behold the blood of the covenant, which the Lord hath made with you."[65]

The Bread and the Wine

The parallel between the Passover lamb and Jesus, who were sacrificed at approximately the same time—both innocent victims—was to be confused with and superimposed upon the parallel between the bread and wine of the Last Supper and the flesh and blood that they represented.

Consequently, the apostolic custom of repeating the breaking of bread in memory of Jesus as often as possible became a magic ritual that renewed the sacrifice and the "passion" of a redeeming god. The word for the paschal ceremony was endowed with a new meaning to suit the purpose. We have already discussed the etymology of the Hebrew Pesaḥ. Since it was phonetically transcribed into Greek as Πάσχα (Pascha), there was no difficulty for Irenaeus, and later Tertullian and Cyprian, to introduce into Christianity a false etymology that derived Pascha from "passion," mistakenly linking the Greek noun with the verb πάσχειν (paschein), which means, literally, "to suffer."[66]

Christianity subsequently assimilated many elements of the cult of the sun-god, and some of its symbols passed into the ritual of the Eucharist: the Host and the monstrance, which stood for the sun and its rays; the paschal candle and the flint, which represented the victory of light over darkness; the officiating bishop's miter, which was a Persian head-covering symbolizing the sunrise. Even Easter eggs, as earlier in the worship of Dionysus, represented the sun by their yolks, the air in which it moves by their whites, and the ellipsis of its supposed orbit by their shells.

For many centuries, the Church took the official view that in the bread and wine of the Eucharist the body and blood of Jesus were represented only symbolically. So Augustine reiterated in the fourth century, so Pope Gelasius I a century later, and so various others.[67] Some sects did not hesitate to modify the symbols: the Encratites, the Marcionites, and the Aquarians (of the second and third centuries), being abstainers because they considered wine the work of the god of evil, celebrated the Lord's Supper with water; the Artotyrites, a Galician sect of the third century, with bread (ἄρτος, *artos*) and cheese (τυρός, *tyros*), on the pretext that this had been the diet of the ancient Patriarchs; the Peputians mixed the meal of the paschal bread with a few drops of infant's blood.[68]

Then, about the middle of the ninth century, a monk in Corbie, Pascasius Radbertus, conceived the idea of preaching that, at the moment of the consecration of the Host, the bread and wine were really transformed into the body and blood of Jesus, and his thesis began to take hold despite much opposition. Among his opponents in the eleventh century was Berengarius of Tours, archdeacon of Angers, who argued that it was impossible for any substance to transform itself into another pre-existing substance and for the essences of the bread and wine to depart from the substance in order to leave room for those of flesh and blood. Modern doubters might add that it can be scientifically proved that the bread and wine ingested during Communion produce exactly the same biological effects in our bodies as do bread and wine that have not been consecrated.[69] Nonetheless, the reasoning of Berengarius aroused sharp protests: many Councils were held on the matter, and the Roman Synod of 1079 forced him to recant.

It was only in 1125 that Hildebert, bishop of Tours, dared for the first time to use two terms that have since become canonical: consubstantiation (the co-existence of the bread and wine, without the loss of their characteristics, with the body and blood of Jesus) and transubstantiation (the transformation of the nature of the bread and wine into flesh and blood). In the fifteenth century, the

Council of Constance forbade the faithful to take Communion in both constituents: that is, in practice, the distribution of wine was abolished and the ceremony was reduced to the consumption of the Host alone, on the theory that not only the body but also the blood of Jesus passed into it.

The Protestant Reformation reopened the question, taking its stand for the symbolic presence alone (consubstantiation), while the Council of Trent asserted once more that in the Eucharist are contained truly and substantially the body, the blood, the soul, and the divinity of Jesus Christ (transubstantiation). Among Catholics the doctrine of transubstantiation has taken on some corollaries, with useless disputes of its nature: whether the quantity and the weight of the Host remain the same or are increased by the addition of the body and blood of Jesus; whether the Host contains *all* the body of Jesus or only the flesh without the bones; whether the entire body is in each Host or whether it is divided each time into as many parts as there are Hosts to be consecrated; whether, when the Host is crumbled, the body of Jesus is also crumbled; and so on.

The absurdity of the dogma troubled even the faithful, so from time to time the Church had to reconfirm it. The latest such occasion was in September, 1965, in the encyclical *Mysterium fidei* of Pope Paul VI.

The Mass

The Acts of the Apostles tell us that the breaking of bread always took place at the beginning of a dinner of brotherhood (agape),[70] which always ended, on the other hand, with a prayer of thanks and the elevation of the cup of benediction. Cyprian declares that in those days the bit of bread was offered on the palm of the hand,[71] but the faithful were also permitted to take home larger portions of the consecrated bread.[72]

Later, the breaking of bread and the libation of wine were brought together in such a way that they became a single act, which, however, was separate from the dinner. This change appears to date from the beginning of the second century, for the famous letter in which Pliny the Younger, governor of Bithynia, informs Emperor Trajan that Christians had been denounced to him adds that they gathered for their ceremonies on stated days, before dawn (*stato die ante lucem*), and that under his orders they had ended the practice of taking their evening meals together.[73]

The first description of the morning ceremony is given by Justin (ca. A.D. 150).[74] Basically, the liturgy he describes is already that of the Mass, but it would appear that the officiant was still allowed a certain discretion, at least in his choice of prayers and of readings from the holy texts.

The word "Mass" does not appear until the fifth century. It may have been derived from the formal termination of the ceremony: "*Ite, missa est*" ("Go, the observance is ended"). But, while it originally meant any religious service at all, it was later restricted to the celebration of the Eucharist by a priest.

When Constantine officially recognized Christianity, in 313, its observances were moved into the great basilicas that the emperor himself turned over to the Christians, and from that time onward the ceremonial began to be enriched and to take on both solemnity and pomp: the clerics robed themselves in varicolored vestments and surrounded themselves with a luxuriance of lights, flowers, and incense. As the solemnity grew, so did the physical distance within the church between the officiating priests and the worshiping faithful. Parapets were raised between the altar and the people; in the Eastern Church, these ultimately became painted partitions, or iconostasis, which made the altar almost entirely invisible to the congregation and thus heightened the atmosphere of sacred mystery.[75]

Until the fifth century, it appears to have been customary to restrict the *flentes* ("weepers"), or penitents, who were clothed in rags that unmistakably marked them as sinners, to the atrium, the portico before the entrance of the church. Later, they were admitted to the narthex, or inner vestibule, as *audientes* ("hearers"), together with the catechumens (those who had not yet been baptized). There they were allowed to listen to the readings from the Scriptures and to the sermons, but not to take part in worship; later still, they were permitted, as *consistentes* ("standers"), to join in the liturgy with the rest, but they still could not receive the Eucharist.[76]

In the fifth century, however, the custom of private repentance began to spread, employing auricular confession (confession whispered into the ear of the priest), but this was not made mandatory until 1215, after the Fourth Lateran Council. In the fifteenth century, the first confessionals appeared, shaped like pulpits and open on all sides. In 1565, Charles Borromeo ordered that all the confessionals in his diocese should be closed on two sides, so that the priest would hear the confession through a grill. This became general practice.

The Church was much less concerned, at least until the time of the Council of Trent, with making certain of the religious instruction of its faithful. Baptism was enough to assure acceptance as a true Christian, so that even infants could receive the Eucharist, provided they had been baptized. In such cases, their lips were barely moistened with the consecrated wine.

Since the twelfth century, the Eucharist has been administered only to those who have reached the "age of discretion," but there were long battles over the time at which that age begins. Thomas Aquinas says it begins "when the child is able to reason,"[77] but this is a tautology. The specification laid down by Pope Pius X is also rather vague. In his decree *Quam singulari* of August 8, 1910, he defined the age of reason as that at which the child is capable of distinguishing, at least approximately (*aliqua cognitione*), the bread of the Eucharist from ordinary bread.

Just as it was rigorous in demanding the purification of sins through the practice of confession and penitence, the Church was for many centuries equally harsh in imposing an absolute fast on those who took Communion. Only lately has its obduracy relaxed. The regulations for fasting prescribed in the constitution *Christus dominus* of Pope Pius XII (January 6, 1953) made wide concessions —"any nonalcoholic beverage" and even "some solid food" were permitted to those who would otherwise suffer "serious hardship"— the hardships being such things as "the lateness of the hour" or "a journey of not less than two kilometers." Finally, in 1964, Pope Paul VI reduced the obligation of fasting to barely an hour prior to Communion.

So, little by little, the ceremony for which Jesus sought a social and revolutionary meaning, as a symbol of equality and of the joy of being united in a single faith, has been degraded into a cold and mechanical routine. The loving act of Jesus, who shared out the bread and the wine to everyone at the table, has been denatured into the hurried movements of a priest who rations out tasteless disks that look like cardboard.

[20]

THE TRIAL

"Before the Cock Crow . . ."

When the Passover dinner was finished and they had sung the last hymn of the Hallel, Jesus and the eleven remaining disciples prepared to return to Bethany.[1] But first Jesus had something important to tell them. He feared that he was about to be arrested, and he wanted to prepare the disciples against the event. If, however, he succeeded in avoiding arrest, he planned to set out the next day from Jerusalem, which had become too dangerous, on a new withdrawal into Galilee. He intended to travel alone, to minimize attention; the disciples would rejoin him later.

"All ye shall be offended with me because of this night," he began, "for it is written, I will smite the shepherd, and the sheep of the flock shall be scattered abroad.[2] But after I am risen again [μετὰ τὸ ἐγερθῆναί με, *meta to egerthēnai me*, which was later translated to 'risen from the tomb,' was used by Jesus in its literal sense of 'when I awake tomorrow morning'], I will go before you into Galilee." Simon Peter wanted to accompany him, but Jesus said: "Thou canst not follow me now; but thou shalt follow me afterwards."

"Lord, why cannot I follow thee now? Though all men shall be offended because of thee, yet will I never be offended."

Bitterly Jesus shook his head. "Before the cock crow [in other words, 'before dawn tomorrow'], thou shalt deny me."

Simon Peter was wounded by what he took as a comparison with Judas. "Though I should die with thee, yet will I not deny thee." And the other Apostles echoed him in this pledge of loyalty. But Jesus was sorrowful and disheartened. Paulus, the rationalist, expresses surprise that Jesus should have made no effort to prevent the dispersion of his followers, merely predicting its inevitability.[3] This very much resembles the fatalism of the Greek tragedies.

At this point, the Gospel of John contains a long speech in which Jesus exhorts the disciples to love one another and always to follow his precepts. These, however, are preachments that presume the certitude of Jesus' death; mixed with mystical theological digressions that are most unsuitable in the mouth of Jesus, they are followed by an impassioned plea to God to protect the disciples after the Nazarene's death.[4] Even a cursory study of these long chapters quickly reveals the seams of the various fragments composed for the edification of the faithful and the liturgy of the Church.

More realistically, the Synoptic Gospels convey the impression that at least for the moment Jesus allowed himself to be persuaded by the Apostles' pledges of loyalty. Therefore, he attempted to soften the unpleasant impression that his own pessimism had made on them, and seeking to show his confidence that they would be able to protect him even in great danger, he asked whether any of them was armed.

The response was eager: "Lord, behold, here are two swords!" It is most unlikely that the Apostles had swords (unless they had found them in the room where they had dined), because it was forbidden to carry weapons on the eve of Passover. Perhaps these were two knives that had been used in carving the lamb.[5]

"It is enough," Jesus said; and he and his companions went on their way.

In the Garden of Gethsemane

To reach Bethany they had to pass the Mount of Olives, and, as was his custom, Jesus wanted to stop there a while, even on this night and despite the lateness of the hour.[6] The place where they paused was called Gethsemane (in Hebrew, *gath shemāné*), which meant "the olive press."[7] It was not so much a structure as a natural cave, well protected against the weather, which even in autumn retained the high temperatures best suited to the squeezing of olives.[8]

Jesus accompanied the disciples as far as the press itself, where they took shelter against the night chill, and he went on alone to pray, followed only by Peter, James, and John. He was trembling and miserable, and he finally admitted his fears to them: "My soul is exceeding sorrowful unto death: tarry ye here and watch." With tremendous effort he went on a little farther, his hands seeking something to which to cling; then, exhausted, he fell to the ground.[9] "Abba, Father," he besought God, "all things are possible unto thee; take away this cup from me: nevertheless not what I will, but what thou wilt."[10]

As he prayed, prostrate on the ground, "his sweat was as it were great drops of blood."[11] It was an attack of hematohidrosis—that is, an extreme dilation of the subcutaneous capillary vessels.[12] Binet-Sanglé explains that this phenomenon is the effect of excessively high blood pressure resulting from violent emotion, an outburst of anger, or a great fright.[13] The blood flows into the pores, causing an edema and an ecchymosis if it is arrested by the interstices of the skin, or even making its way out through the pores in the form of drops. Hematohidrosis, observed earlier by Aristotle and Galen, is quite frequent in highly sensitive persons and in hysterics.

Throughout Christian history, this passage of the Gospels has been sharply attacked because it shows a human weakness in Jesus,[14] unworthy not only of the Son of God[15] but even of a philosopher who disciplines himself to disdain death.[16] In many Codices, including that of the Vatican, the whole passage has been eliminated. But it has been justly observed that its very incongruity attests to the authenticity of the Gospels.[17]

How touching is the faith of Arculf, bishop of Gaul in the seventh century, who, during a pilgrimage to the Holy Land, discovered the marks left by the knees of Jesus in the soil of Gethsemane![18]

Jesus had adjured Peter, James, and John not to fall asleep and to wait for him; he needed to feel that his friends were with him, sharing his agony, and that he would be able to talk to them when he went back.[19] But, when the crisis had ebbed and he went to find them, they were sleeping. The very late hour, their physical fatigue, and the heaviness of the meal had got the better of their good intentions. Jesus was irritated by this, and he wakened Peter with a reproach: "What! could ye not watch with me one hour?" The voice of Jesus roused the two others, and he bade all three: "Watch and pray."

He withdrew again, but he was uneasy. Soon he returned to where he had left his disciples on guard to warn him of any untoward occurrence. They had fallen asleep again; when Jesus woke them and bitterly upbraided them, they stood rubbing their eyes in confusion, unable to justify themselves. But now their vigilance would have been too late. Jesus heard the shuffling of feet among the trees of the olive grove, and the voices of people coming near. "It is enough," he said. "The hour is come: behold, the Son of man is betrayed into the hands of sinners. . . . He that betrayeth me is at hand."

At that instant the light of the moon, which was full, fell directly on Judas, who was walking toward Jesus, and on a number of armed men badly hidden by the trees.[20] Judas went up to Jesus and kissed his hand. This was the usual mark of respect that the pupils of the rabbis showed toward their teachers. In this case, the Gospels point out, it was a prearranged signal to enable the soldiers to arrest the right man.

Jesus confronted the soldiers and demanded: "Whom seek ye?"

"Jesus of Nazareth."

"I am he."

At this, the Gospel of John says, they moved backward in awe and fell to the ground. It has also been told of many other great men of antiquity, such as Marius and Mark Antony, that with words and a look they could disarm the assassins sent to murder them,[21] but in the case of Jesus it is more likely that the Evangelist was thinking in terms of a miracle.

In the ensuing confusion, one of the three Apostles who were with Jesus (the Gospel of John says it was Simon Peter) drew his sword (or knife) and striking out at random cut off the ear of a soldier or a "servant of the high priest."[22] But Jesus made him lay aside his weapon, and then he gave himself up.

The detail of the ear is most improbable; the assailant would have been arrested on the spot.[23] The eccentric French poet Baudelaire, pretending to accept the story as fact, was to say with blasphemous intent: "Peter did well to deny Jesus, who forbade him to kill that scum!"

Jesus had barely been taken into custody when, forgetting all their good intentions of a few hours before, all the Apostles, including those who had been roused from their sleep near the olive press by the excitement and had come out, fled in terror. The soldiers could at best seize the edge of the cloak of "a young man,"[24] but even he escaped, stark naked, abandoning the outer garment that he had used as a sheet.

Traditional exegesis gladly accepts the belief that this young man was not one of the disciples but was instead young Mark, in whose house the Last Supper had been served,[25] and who, though he had not been asked to do so, had followed Jesus among the Apostles. Most scholars, however, doubt the whole incident,[26] which they consider an invention for the express purpose of fulfilling a prophecy of Amos: "And he that is courageous among the mighty shall flee away naked in that day."[27]

Before the Sanhedrin

The Gospel passages that deal with the trial of Jesus are among those most debated by students. The first question to settle, however, is whether the men who arrested Jesus were Roman soldiers or law-enforcement officers (shoterim) of the high priest. If they were the former, the statement that he was taken before the Sanhedrin itself would be false; if they were the latter, then it should be established whether the high priest had any authority to make arrests and hold trials. It is most unlikely that the Romans would have left the Jews any judicial competence,[28] even though the highest Jewish tribunal, the Sanhedrin, continued to exist. Before the foreign occupation of the country, it had had this power among many others.

Various scholars, including the historian of the Church Lietzmann, Omodeo, and Salvador, maintain that the whole Synoptic account of the proceedings before the Sanhedrin is untrue, and that Jesus was condemned by the Romans alone.[29] Others, such as Loisy, Cullmann, and Goguel, are inclined to concede that the Sanhedrin tried to hold some informal proceedings, a simple interrogatory intended to furnish enough evidence to enable it to lodge charges against Jesus with the Roman authorities, who alone had the power to condemn him.[30] The traditionalists, however, impute to the hearing before the Sanhedrin all the character of a full and formal trial that required only formal ratification by the Romans.[31]

Even if this were so, the procedure that was followed, to judge by what the Gospels report, was altogether irregular. The Sanhedrin, presided over by the high priest under the title of *nāsī* ("prince")[32] and composed of seventy-one members drawn from priestly families and from those lay families most notable for their wealth and their racial purity,[33] held its sessions in a part of the Temple called Gazith, near the Court of Israel.[34] Its day was limited to the hours between the two ritual sacrifices of the morning (about the ninth hour) and the evening (about the sixteenth hour). An interval of twenty-four hours was required between the conclusion of testimony and the rendering of a verdict.[35] Deliberations could continue into the night only when the judges found it impossible to agree at once on the guilt or innocence of the accused. This was the procedure prior to the Roman occupation, which, however, according to the Gospels, was not observed in the trial of Jesus. Furthermore, the Sanhedrin never sat on the Sabbath or on religious holidays, still less during Passover.[36]

A keen analysis by the eminent scholar Nicola Jaeger emphasizes the trial's many procedural flaws and deviations from the rules of Jewish law: the taking of testimony at night, the immediate pronouncement of sentence in defiance of the prescribed interval of twenty-four hours, the lack of a minimum of two witnesses whose testimony was absolutely identical, the credibility arbitrarily given to statements by the accused that had been elicited by the prosecutor's tricks, etc.[37]

Indeed, the Gospels state that the trial was held *immediately* after the arrest—at the latest, then, at the third or fourth hour of the fifteenth day of Nisan[38] (Luke has it repeated a few hours later) —and, what is more, in the *house* of the high priest rather than in the legal forum. In addition, the Evangelists do not even agree on the name of the high priest: Mark and Luke give no name, Matthew calls him Caiaphas, which seems probable, and John calls him Annas, who had been removed from the post at least fifteen years earlier.[39] The Catholic harmonists try to reconcile these conflicting points and to make the illegality of the trial appear less flagrant by assuming that there was first a short interrogation in the home of Annas, the former high priest, during the night, followed by a proper trial in the morning at which Caiaphas presided over the Sanhedrin.[40] Probably the story of the nocturnal trial was merely a fabrication to fill the gap of the night itself—the few hours between the third and the ninth—which Jesus must have spent under heavy guard.

The description of the interrogation undergone by Jesus before the Sanhedrin conforms to the procedure, which is confirmed by the Talmud, adopted against a political agitator (*mesīth*). The members of the Sanhedrin began by asking the accused for details of his activities and his purposes.[41]

'I spake openly to the world," Jesus answered. "I ever taught in the synagogue, and in the Temple, whither the Jews always resort; and in secret have I said nothing. Why askest thou me? ask them which heard me: . . . behold, they know what I said."

One of the guards who flanked him during the interrogation slapped him, saying: "Answerest thou the high priest so?"

"If I have spoken evil, bear witness of the evil: but if well, why smitest thou me?"[42]

In the Order of Nezikin,[43] the Talmud permits itself a certain irony at this point, noting that, by replying with such irritation to the man who had slapped him, Jesus violated the very maxim that he had taught to his disciples: "Whosoever shall smite thee on thy right cheek, turn to him the other also."[44]

It was now time for the cross-examination of witnesses. The Gospels do not mention the fact, but, according to the Talmud, the procedure required that at least two witnesses be heard and that they be hidden behind a screen, yet still able to see the defendant, who, meanwhile, was made more visible by two extra candelabra. In the trial of Jesus, there were "many" witnesses,[45] or perhaps only "two,"[46] who testified: "This fellow said, I am able to destroy the Temple of God, and to build it in three days."

The Evangelists tell us that this was "false" testimony, but they are again influenced by prophecies, this time in Psalm 35, verse 11: "False witnesses did rise up: they laid to my charge things that I knew not." Far from being false, the testimony was merely a very slight distortion of a sentence that Jesus had uttered: "Destroy this temple, and in three days I will raise it up."[47] If this was not altogether blasphemous, at least in the second clause it voiced a considerable presumptuousness.

"Guilty of Death"

When the witnesses had been heard, the high priest turned to Jesus with the prescribed question: "Answerest thou nothing? What is it which these witness against thee?"[48] Jesus stood silent; Caiaphas, not satisfied, pressed further: "Art thou the Christ?"[49]

According to Mark, the answer of Jesus was affirmative: "I am" ('Εγώ εἰμι, *Egō eimi*).[50] But, if we compare this with the texts of Matthew and Luke,[51] we are not certain that the editor of Mark altogether understood the Aramaic words that might have been used by the accused.[52] Orientalists agree that the Aramaic words translated by these two Evangelists: "Thou hast said" (Σὺ εἶπας, *Su eipas*) and "Ye say that I am" (Ὑμεῖς λέγετε ὅτι ἐγώ εἰμι, *Humeis legete hoti egō eimi*), do not mean a clear "Yes" in that tongue but are rather a way of evading a question and can also be interpreted as "No."[53] The same ambiguity can be achieved in English by shifting the accented word: "*You* say I am," and "You *say* I am."

But it is a vain quibble, because the Evangelists assuredly had no intention of portraying their master as one cleverly playing with words in the hope of escaping judgment. The possibility that the reply of Jesus can be interpreted as a denial is in fact destroyed by what follows immediately in the Gospels: "Hereafter shall ye see the Son of man sitting on the right hand of power, and coming in the clouds of heaven."[54]

"Art thou then the Son of God?" the prosecutor exclaimed, as if not believing his own ears. In anger and sorrow he ripped his robe across his breast. This gesture was no histrionic demonstration; it was the ritual prescribed for anyone who heard a blasphemy uttered.[55] The garment must be torn not along the seam but in the middle of the fabric so that the damage was irreparable, and the breast must remain bared as high as the heart, the shreds of cloth hanging down.[56]

"Ye have heard the blasphemy," Caiaphas cried, turning to his colleagues of the Sanhedrin. "What further need have we of witnesses? What think ye?"[57]

This last sentence was, in effect, the prescribed call for a vote. The Gospels do not linger over the mechanics of it but go directly to the outcome: a *unanimous* verdict that Jesus was "guilty of death."[58] Then the spectators spat in his face and struck him, while others mocked: "Prophesy unto us, thou Christ. Who is he that smote thee?"[59] This detail, too, which was hardly suitable to the dignity of the Sanhedrin, was probably inspired by a Biblical passage: "I gave my back to the smiters, and my cheeks to them that plucked off the hair: I hid not my face from shame and spitting."[60]

Apart from the illegality of the immediate verdict and the other procedural flaws that we have already mentioned, the conclusion of the trial further bolsters the belief that the whole interrogation as described is a falsehood. First of all, it is impossible that Jesus himself would have so announced his own glorification at the right hand of Yahweh and his "coming in the clouds of heaven." In the second place—even if Jesus had actually expressed such grandiose hopes— his conviction for blasphemy and crimes against the Mosaic religion, if it had been decreed by the Sanhedrin, would have entailed a religious penalty (death by stoning or strangulation) and would have required no ratification by the Roman governor.[61]

One thing is certain: during the journey from the house of Caiaphas (or wherever the trial was supposed to have been held) to the Roman headquarters in the Pretorium, where Pilate conducted his business, the charge against Jesus underwent a drastic change. According to the Gospels, the Sanhedrin had decided that Jesus should be executed for having uttered blasphemies; in the Pretorium, however, its members accused him of a political crime.[62]

Pontius Pilate

Before they tell what happened when Jesus was brought before Pilate, all four Gospels make certain of fulfilling the Nazarene's prediction that "before the cock crow," Simon Peter would have three times denied him.

The Apostle, they say,[63] had followed Jesus at a distance and had stealthily wormed his way into the outer hall of the house of Caiaphas, where he sat by the fire with the high priest's servants. First a maid and then others present thought they recognized him as a disciple of Jesus, and their suspicions were strengthened by the fact that he was a Galilean. The Galilean dialect was quite easily identified because of its improper pronunciation of the gutturals.[64] But every time the question was put to Simon Peter, he made a downright denial, going as far as to say that he had never even known Jesus. The third time, the cry of a rooster reminded him of the master's prediction, and he left the house in bitter tears.

The incident has only a purely symbolic import, the more so because it would have been impossible to hear a rooster in Jerusalem: there was a specific prohibition in populated areas against keeping such fowls, which were considered unclean, lest they contaminate holy objects.

Jesus, surrounded by many members of the Sanhedrin, was meanwhile being taken to the Pretorium.[65] It was long believed that the civil arm of the Pretorium, which was not only the garrison but the seat of the occupying power, was in Herod's Palace, in the western part of the city near the Jaffa Gate.[66] But archaeological excavations undertaken between 1927 and 1932, in the vicinity of the Tower of Antonia at the northwest corner of the Temple wall, fortunately led to a major discovery that made it possible to redirect the theories of scholars.[67] The diggers uncovered a courtyard approximately a hundred and fifty by a hundred and sixty feet, thickly paved in hard stone of the color of Veronese marble.[68] This confirmed John's reference to the site of Pilate's court as the Pavement (Λιθόστρωτος, Lithostrōtos), which was on the highest place in the city and which, according to John, the Jews called Gabbatha.[69] The area surrounding the Tower of Antonia, which was known as Bezetha, was in fact the highest of the four hills of Jerusalem. (See Figure VIII.)

As soon as the Jews had entered, Pilate demanded: "What accusation bring ye against this man?"

The members of the Sanhedrin knew quite well that the single charge of blasphemy against the Mosaic Laws would have no interest for the Roman representative, so they described Jesus as a political agitator—that is, a Zealot: "We found this fellow perverting the nation, and forbidding to give tribute to Caesar, saying that he himself is Christ a king."[70]

Pilate ordered Jesus placed directly before him for the customary questioning: "Hearest thou not how many things they witness against thee?" Jesus said nothing, and Pilate continued: "Art thou the King of the Jews?"[71]

Jesus answered: "Sayest thou this thing of thyself, or did others tell it thee of me?"

Pilate replied: "Am I a Jew? Thine own nation and the chief priests have delivered thee unto me: what hast thou done?"

"My kingdom is not of this world; if my kingdom were of this world, then would my servants fight, that I should not be delivered . . . But now is my kingdom not from thence."

"Art thou a king then?"

"Thou sayest that I am a king. To this end was I born, and for this cause came I into the world, that I should bear witness unto the truth. Every one that is of the truth heareth my voice."[72]

Pilate studied Jesus long and thoughtfully. The Roman was a man of culture, keenly interested in philosophical problems, permeated with an intelligent and subtle skepticism. With some irony, but also with a real desire to know what went on in the mind of this unschooled Jew, he asked: "What is truth?"

There was no easy answer. Jesus could have described to Pilate his own emotional certainty of a transcendent truth known only to God, which man must accept obediently without seeking to inquire into its reasons. But Pilate would have found it only too easy to retort with all the objections and all the doubts available to Greek dialectic. Jesus preferred to remain silent.

The procurator had found insufficient evidence to warrant a judgment against him. Turning again to the accusers, Pilate pointed at Jesus, upright between two legionaries, his hands bound behind his back, and declared: "I find no fault in this man."

According to the Gospels, this was Pilate's final decision, but he was made to revise it by the pressures put upon him by the accusers of Jesus.

FIGURE VIII
JERUSALEM

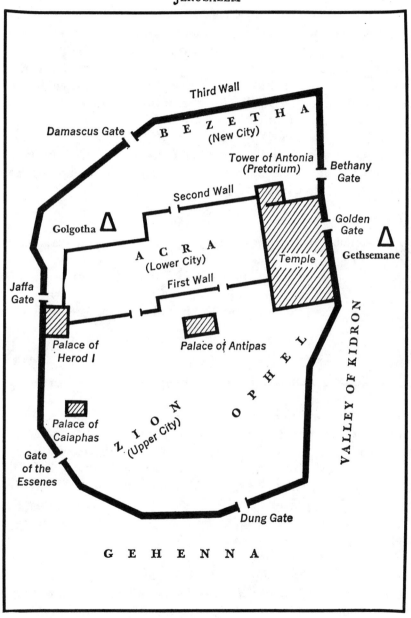

"Behold the Man!"

The indecisiveness ascribed to Pilate, his indulgence of the Jewish leaders, and, at the same time, his good will toward Jesus are all equally without historical foundation. They are the products of an opportunistic distortion of truth perpetrated by the Christians, as their religion spread over the empire, in order to exculpate the Romans of all responsibility for the death of Jesus.[73] This rehabilitation of Pilate (down to the proverbial gesture of washing his hands) has resulted in the imposition of the entire guilt on the Jewish people, who for centuries, consequently, have undeservedly suffered execration by the Christian world under the infamous charge that they are "the nation that murdered God."

This result was also the intention of the statement (which, incidentally, appears only in Luke) that when Pilate learned Jesus was a Galilean, he wanted to remove him at once to the tribunal of Herod Antipas for judgment there.[74] The statement is not only debatable but also undoubtedly false. Juridically, there was no need to extradite the accused from the *forum delicti commissi* to the *forum originis,* because the sole competent judge was the Roman procurator; nor was it in Pilate's character, if for no other reason than the dignity of his office, to show such deference to the petty Jewish tetrarch.[75]

Luke also undertakes Pilate's defense, telling us that when Herod Antipas sent Jesus back, the Roman governor summoned the Jewish priests and magistrates again and reiterated his decision to release the defendant: "Ye have brought this man unto me, as one that perverteth the people; and, behold, I, having examined him before you, have found no fault in this man touching those things whereof ye accuse him: No, nor yet Herod: for I sent you to him: and, lo, nothing worthy of death is done unto him. I will therefore chastise him, and release him."[76] Pilate thereupon gave orders to his legionaries that Jesus was to be flogged.

Under Roman custom, flagellation could be executed with either of two different instruments: the *flagella,* which was an ordinary leather strap, or the *flagra,* a small iron chain with pellets of metal or bone at the tip. The use of the *flagra* was ordinarily restricted to the punishment of slaves who had committed especially serious offenses. In the Basilica of Saint Praxedes in Rome, there is preserved a post, about thirty-two inches high, of which the faithful are told that it is the *identical* one over which Jesus was made to bend, naked, for this punishment.

Zealous to stir their readers to greater horror at the humiliation of a god subjected to the shameful punishment of the lash, the Gospels add the dressing of coarse tricks played by the soldiery in derision of Jesus. According to the Evangelists, the troops removed his clothes and robed him in a cloak of scarlet and purple like that of a king; they thrust a reed into his hand as a scepter, and, weaving a crown of thorns, they placed it on his head as a diadem. Then, laughing, they knelt before him, crying: "Hail, King of the Jews!" They slapped him, they spat in his face, they struck him on the head with clubs.[77]

The episode has been variously discussed. There has been debate, too, whether it was really a crown of thorns that was placed on his head or whether it was only one of shrubs, or of acanthus,[78] or of *akkābīth* (*Gundelia tournefortii*),[79] without any intention of adding to his sufferings.[80] But, when one reflects that the catalogue of these outrages ascribed to the Roman soldiery repeats almost verbatim certain passages of the Old Testament,[81] reputedly prophetic, one begins to suspect that the entire episode is a sheer invention.

Perhaps the account of the Roman soldiers' brutalities was inserted into the New Testament only in order to meet this need of making the life of Jesus conform to the Old Testament's Messianic prophecies, despite the fact that it works against the intention of exonerating the Romans of the charge of deicide. The editors of the Gospels of Matthew and Mark attempted to attribute these acts to the members of the Sanhedrin as well, but the only effect is that of an unnecessary repetition.

The Gospel of John outdoes the others in its zeal to purge Pilate of all responsibility, recounting once more how, in an effort to quell the soldiers' uproar, he led Jesus outside again in all his misery, his body covered with the welts of the whips, the crown of thorns on his head, the purple cloak thrown over him, and showed him to the populace, saying in a tone of pity in order to move the throng to compassion: "Behold the man!"

But the chief priests were wholly unmoved and shouted even more vigorously: "Crucify him! We have a law, and by our law he ought to die, because he made himself the Son of God."

Pilate took Jesus back into the Pretorium and asked him: "Whence art thou?" But Jesus said nothing. Pilate tried again: "Speakest thou not unto me? knowest thou not that I have power to crucify thee, and have power to release thee?"

"Thou couldest have no power at all against me," the Nazarene replied, "except it were given thee from above; therefore he that delivered me unto thee hath the greater sin."[82]

Jesus or Barabbas?

Pilate supposedly wanted to save Jesus at all costs.[83] The Gospels say that it was customary at Passover for the Roman governors to grant the Jews' petition for the release of one of their compatriots, regardless of the charge on which he had been imprisoned,[84] and that Pilate sought to have them choose Jesus in place of another whom he might earlier have intended to set free: a certain Barabbas, who, it appears, was guilty of sedition.

In actuality, there is no proof that such a custom ever existed among the Romans, either in Palestine or in any other country under the empire. Indeed, it is far more credible that such a gesture of generosity would never have been envisaged by the Romans. Legally, the *abolitio*—the suspension of a trial—was possible only when a plaintiff withdrew a civil action (and this was not relevant in the cases of Jesus and Barabbas, both accused of public offenses). As for *indulgentia*—reprieve or amnesty after sentence—that was solely within the emperor's competence, and the procurators had no authority to grant it.[85]

The character of Barabbas himself has been much discussed. In Hebrew, his name meant "son of a father" or "son of a rabbi" (*bar-abbā*), and hence it is not really a proper name. Some minor manuscripts of the Gospels call him Jesus Barabbas.[86] This could suggest the possibility that he actually was named Jesus but concealed the fact out of respect for the Nazarene—or in order to prevent confusion. The opposite view was taken by Origen,[87] who, having seen this form in an old manuscript, observed: "The name 'Jesus' must have been inserted by some heretic, because it is not fitting for a criminal."[88]

None of this prevented the liberal scholar Reinach from offering his own remarkable version of the facts. Jesus, he says, was executed not "instead of" but "as" Barabbas.[89] The French scholar bases his theory on a passage from the Greek-Jewish philosopher Philo of Alexandria, who says that on certain feast days the people of Alexandria in Egypt amused themselves by carrying on their shoulders a mock king called Karabas, who was analogous not only to the Roman Saturn (personified by a soldier chosen by lot at the end of every year, during the Saturnalia) but also to the Babylonian Zoganes.[90] At the Babylonian Sacean festivities, a prisoner condemned to death was chosen to play the part of a king named Zoganes, and throughout the five days of the festival he enjoyed every royal right and privilege; then he was flogged and hanged. Therefore, Reinach concludes, when the Gospels tell us that Jesus was condemned "in the place of" Barabbas, they mean that he was condemned "as" Barabbas. The theory wobbles. The change of name from Karabas to Barabbas is arbitrary, and the custom could apply only to the Sacean feast or the Roman Saturnalia, not to the Jewish Passover.[91]

We might be closer to the truth (unless we presume a complete fiction on the part of the Evangelists) if we suspected that actually, at the time of the trial of Jesus, a patriot nicknamed Barabbas was also on trial in Jerusalem, and that, though his fate is unknown to us, the incident suggested the story told by the Gospels, almost as a distant reflection of the discouragement suffered at the time by the Apostles when they saw an ordinary rebel put on the same level with their master and probably dealt with much less severely.

The Gospels say that Pilate, in a last effort to save Jesus, addressed himself directly to the people of Jerusalem thronging below the windows of the Pretorium: "Ye have a custom, that I should release unto you one at the Passover: will ye therefore that I release unto you the King of the Jews?"[92]

There was some hesitation among the people, but the priests and the elders prodded them to ask for the release of Barabbas. So, when Pilate repeated his question, they all shouted: "Release unto us Barabbas."

"What will ye then," Pilate asked once more, "that I shall do unto him whom ye call the King of the Jews?"

"Crucify him!"

Resigned to his failure, Pilate sent then for a basin of water, and he washed his hands in the sight of the multitude, saying: "I am innocent of the blood of this just person; see ye to it."

This is only further proof of the improbability of the whole account of the trial—it is impossible to imagine the representative of Rome bowing to the caprice of the mob and going to the extent of allowing it to carry out the punishment. The trial, if in truth it was ever held, was conducted by the Roman authorities alone, on the charge that Jesus was a political agitator or, at best, a man who was capable of furnishing the pretext and the occasion of an uprising in the city.[93] Pilate sentenced him on the basis of the *lex Julia maiestatis*, without any need to justify his decision in the eyes of the Jews. The penalty of crucifixion (prescribed by the Roman, not by the Jewish, law) was pronounced in the ritual form: "I sentence thee: thou shalt go upon the cross. Lictor, bind his hands. Let him be flogged!" (*Condemno: ibis in crucem. Lictor, conliga manus. Verberetur!*)[94]

According to the tradition of the Church, the sentence must have been pronounced at least one hour before midday. It is not necessary to point out the absurdity of trying to compress so many events into so short a time—between the fourth and the eleventh hours of the morning: the arrest, the interrogation in Annas' house, the interrogation in the house of Caiaphas, the trial before the Sanhedrin, the three interrogations by Pilate, the session with Herod Antipas, the flagellation, the offer to replace Jesus with Barabbas, the final sentencing. As usual, it was a matter of making a few prophecies "come true"; and for symbolic reasons, too, it was necessary to accelerate the condemnation of Jesus in order to allow his Passion exactly three days' duration.

If the facts set forth in the Gospels are a faithful record, it is more logical to suppose that they covered a greater period of time. If Jesus was arrested on the night of the fourteenth of Nisan, no formal action was taken on the next day, which was Passover, and even the two trials before the Sanhedrin and Pilate could not have been held less than a day apart. But historical accuracy cannot be claimed for the report of a fact to which none of the Apostles was a witness and which the Evangelists could only reconstruct, concerned as they were more for religious symbolism than for veracity.

One writer has pointed out how the progression of the Passion of Jesus might have been drawn from that of Plato's Socrates.[95] A sentence in Plato's *Republic* that comments on the death of Socrates might indeed have been equally applied to Jesus: "It was essential to destroy his good name: if others believed him just, he would have honor and profit thereby, and then there would always be the question whether indeed he had played at goodness for an ulterior motive. . . . Hence he must be stripped of everything, he must be held to be the wickedest of men . . . whipped, tortured, imprisoned, nailed to a cross, or torn to pieces."

The mythologist Paul Louis Couchoud draws up this meager estimate of Jesus and his end: "He was an obscure person who died in Jerusalem, it is not known how, in an ill-planned attempt at insurrection, and who had the incredible luck to be deified."[96]

St. Pilate and St. Procula

One very cogent reason to doubt that the trial before Pilate ever took place is the utter lack of any report of it by him in the imperial archives in Rome, though an event of this kind would have required him to make one, and of any reference to it by later historians. The Christians have tried to fill the gap with a forgery: it was easily proved that the so-called Acts of Pilate (*Acta Pilati*) was an apocryphal document of the fourth century A.D.[97]

As for the judgments made during the first centuries on Pilate, there are great differences, depending on whether the views were framed in periods of indifference toward Rome, or in others when there was fear of offending the lords of the world.

Historically, it is known that Pilate was removed as procurator in 36, after the Samaritans complained to the proconsul of Syria, Vitellius, that Pilate had used excessive cruelty in putting down one of their protest demonstrations. He was exiled to Vienne, in

Gaul. A tradition repeated by the Greek historian Eusebius, at the end of the third century, has it that Pilate, tortured by remorse, committed suicide by throwing himself into the Tiber and that his body was carried out to sea, then to the mouth of the Rhone, and thence, against the current of the river, it finally reached the Swiss lakes. There is a Mount Pilatus near the Lake of Lucerne. Other legends say that he died, also a suicide, in Vienne itself.[98]

The rehabilitation of Pilate, however, is clear in the canonical Gospels and also in many of the apocryphal ones; so much so that in Ethiopia the Coptic Church has forthrightly included in its calendar of saints that vacillating man who, Tertullian says, was "already a Christian in his innermost heart."[99] It is the opinion also of some modern theologians.[100] The presumed conversion of Pilate is described in a fragment from an ancient Egyptian manuscript of the Gospel of John, preserved today in the John Rylands Library in Manchester.[101] It is much more fully discussed in an apocryphal text in Ethiopian called the Gospel of Gamaliel, discovered in recent years by a scholar from the University of Freiburg, Father Van den Oudenrijn. Its text relates that after the death of Jesus, Pilate repented of having allowed himself to be manipulated by Herod Antipas and by the priests Caiaphas and Annas, and in desperation he became a convert to the new religion. The tale ends with these words: "Now Pilate was in his garden, talking of the miracles of Jesus with his wife, Procula, and behold, a voice came out of the clouds and said to them: 'Pilate, knowest thou the souls of those who ascend to Paradise on this cloud? They are the resurrected thief and the centurion. Thou too, in thine own time, shalt be beheaded in Rome. Thy soul and thy wife's soul shall ascend together into the heavenly Jerusalem.' "

Pilate's wife is referred to also in a verse of the Gospel of Matthew, which says that while Pilate was in his tribunal, absorbed in his interrogation of Jesus, his wife sent him a warning: "Have you nothing to do with that just man; for I have suffered many things this day in a dream because of him."[102] Friedrich Klopstock, in his poem *Der Messias,* imagines that in this premonitory dream Socrates appeared to the lady and urged her to intercede on behalf of Jesus.[103]

The name of Pilate's wife, besides being cited by Gamaliel, is given to us in another apocryphal text, the Gospel of Nicodemus, in the second chapter: she is called Claudia Procula, "a pious woman of Jewish tendencies" (θεοσεβὴς καὶ ἰουδαίζουσα, *theosebēs kai ioudaizousa*). Procula is venerated as a saint by the Orthodox Church.

The story of Procula was inserted in these Gospels for the edification of the Roman matrons, many of whom, even before Christianity, had been drawn to the Oriental mystery religions and some of whom had even been converted to Judaism.

$$\left[\,21\,\right]$$

DEATH AND RESURRECTION

Golgotha

Dressed once more in his own clothes instead of the "royal robe," Jesus was taken for his execution to a place called Golgotha.[1] This does not mean "the place of a skull" (in Hebrew, *gulgoleth*), the meaning assigned to it by the Gospels, including that according to Matthew, which tradition pretends was written in Aramaic by a Palestinian! The exact name is *Gol-Goath*, which means simply "the hill of Goath" and which appears earlier in Jeremiah.[2]

Yielding to the influence of the Evangelists' version of the name, Christian piety has tried to identify the site with some height that resembles a skull. Since the time of Emperor Constantine, tradition has fixed on a modest rise a little north of the Palace of Herod, because it has more or less the dome-like appearance of the upper part of a cranium (in Latin, *calvaria*). Here Constantine caused a shrine to be built, the present-day Church of the Holy Sepulcher; his mother, Helena, was privileged to be the first to own a chip of wood which she believed, or persuaded others to believe, had come (after more than three hundred years!) from the cross of Jesus.

The conviction that Jesus must have been crucified on a high place answers a need of a purely religious nature. In all creeds of Uranian origin, certain mountains (because they are closer to heaven) have a sacred character: Olympus for the Greeks, Gerizim for the Samaritans, Sinai for the Jews, Tabor and Golgotha for the Christians.[3] The appearance of the real Calvary, however, is a blow to a widely held image. Painters, writers, and even film directors have preferred to show it as a steep height with a sharp peak on which the cross of Christ stands out starkly against the background of heaven. In reality, it is much lower than one might have believed.

For many centuries, the seeming certainty (dissipated only recently by the discovery of the *Lithostrōtos,* or "Pavement," near the Tower of Antonia) that the trial of Jesus was held in Herod's Palace caused pilgrims to the Holy Land to abandon themselves to devout emotion, reflecting at every step on the martyrdom of Jesus, as they followed a route that in fact he had never taken—the Via Crucis, or Via Dolorosa. There is no validity to the location of the so-called stations of the cross: the places where he first stumbled, where he encountered his mother, where he stumbled again, etc. Of the fourteen stations, only two mark incidents reported in the Gospels: the meetings with Simon the Cyrenian and with the group of pious women.[4]

Simon, a native of Cyrene, which had a very large Jewish community (Strabo says it amounted to a quarter of the entire population), was on his way home from the fields, according to the Gospels, when he was requisitioned by the Roman soldiers and made to carry on his shoulders the two large lengths of wood that would be used to form the cross, since Jesus was physically too exhausted to bear them. For this act of charity (even though it was imposed on him), Christian tradition has sought to thank him, and it has made him the father of Rufus and Alexander, two Christian neophytes who are mentioned in Paul's Epistles.[5] Irenaeus says that the Gnostic Docetae, since they believed that the body of Jesus was only apparent, taught that Simon was transfigured by Jesus into his own resemblance and was therefore crucified in his stead, while Jesus, who had assumed the appearance of Simon, stood near the cross and mocked his executioners.[6] The fact that Simon was "coming out of the country," where he had been at work, precludes the possibility that, as is generally believed, Jesus could have been executed on a religious holiday.

Only the Gospel of Luke tells of the encounter between Jesus and the women, who "bewailed and lamented him" at the sight of the cross. His reply to them was another Biblical reversion: "Daughters of Jerusalem, weep not for me, but weep for yourselves, and for your children. For, behold, the days are coming, in the which they shall say, Blessed are the barren, and the wombs that never bare, and the paps which never gave suck. Then shall they begin to say to the mountains, Fall on us; and to the hills, Cover us. For if they do these things in a green tree, what shall be done in the dry?"[7]

Even if one leaves aside the fact that, in the condition in which he was, and surrounded by soldiers, it would have been impossible for Jesus to stop and address a speech to the women of Jerusalem,[8] there is still the problem of explaining the play of words on "green tree" and "dry." Cullmann interprets it thus: "If the Romans execute me as a Zealot, which I am not (the green tree), what will they do to the real Zealots?"[9] I believe rather that it was Luke's intention to convey a prophecy of the persecutions: "If they do this to me, who am only the beginner, the first green shoot of Christianity, what will they not do when the tree has grown?"

Jesus and the soldiers reached the place chosen for the execution, and while the cross was being put together, a compassionate soldier offered him a cup of wine and myrrh (ἐσμυρνισμένον, esmurnismenon), or perhaps wine and rōsh, an opiate distilled from the poppy.[10] In either case, it was a mild soporific that would dull him somewhat and reduce his sufferings. We may dismiss Matthew's statement that the wine was mixed with gall (χολή, cholē) and vinegar.[11] Once again the insistence on fulfilling a Biblical prophecy[12] produced nonsense.

The Cross

The Romans employed various forms of capital punishment: *decapitatio* or *capitis obtruncatio* ("decapitation"), which was the most merciful and the noblest, inasmuch as it meant instant death; *damnatio ad bestias* ("condemned to [be eaten by] the beasts") which was more painful; *combustio* at the stake; and the *crux*. The last was the most shameful form of execution, reserved for slaves and foreigners. Cicero calls it *"crudelissimum teterrimumque supplicium"*;[13] Tacitus, *"supplicium servile."*[14] Instances of the crucifixion of men who had led social revolts were well known in Roman history.[15]

The penalty of crucifixion was probably derived from the

Persian practice of impalement, which the Romans learned through the Carthaginians. But, whereas in the Orient the stake alone was used, the victim's arms being nailed above his head or tied behind his back,[16] the Romans added a horizontal traverse on which the arms were extended and then nailed. Thus the cross was shaped like a T (*crux commissa* or *patibulata*). The vertical pole that was set in the ground was called the *stipes* and the horizontal beam was the *patibulum*. The tradition that they intersected to form what is now called the Latin cross, so that part of the *stipes* extended above the *patibulum*—that is, the † (*crux immissa*)—was originated by Tertullian[17] or Justin;[18] perhaps it was suggested by the symbol for the sun, which often took the form of a swastika or an X, sometimes enclosed by a wheel, sometimes not.[19] Or perhaps the tradition of the *crux immissa* arose out of the need to explain how the inscription (*titulus*) nailed above the head of Jesus could be seen.

The oldest known graphic representation of the Crucifixion, very remarkably, is a rather blasphemous one that goes back to the third century. It is a crude drawing, discovered on the Palatine in 1856 on a wall of the imperial palace, and it shows Jesus on the cross with the head of an ass, in accord with the revolting slander of onolatry (worship of the ass) that was directed against the early Christians. Of only slightly later origin, two etched stones (a sardonyx in Munich and a cornelian in the British Museum) still depict the cross as a T. The first example of a *crux immissa* dates from the fifth century: a fragment of an ivory casket, also preserved in the British Museum.[20]

According to Roman practice, a stout peg was inserted between the victim's thighs and nailed to the upright so that the body would be supported and its weight would not tear the hands, which were nailed to the cross. In Greek, this support was called πῆγμα (*pēgma*); the Latin word was *sedile;* but Justin calls it *cornu* and likens it to the horn of a rhinoceros,[21] while Tertullian calls it *staticulum*.[22] The *suppedaneum*, the support for the feet that is shown in paintings and sculptures of the Crucifixion, however, did not exist. The cross did not rise very high above the ground, and the condemned man's feet could almost touch it; hence they were often tied with ropes. Once the T-shaped cross[23] had been firmly implanted, the victim was lifted so that he was sitting on the peg,[24] and he was held in position while his hands and finally his feet were nailed down.

Only the rationalist Paulus insists that Jesus' feet were not transfixed by nails—in order to add plausibility to his theory that Jesus did not really die but fled when it was dark.[25] Tradition holds that his feet were nailed, especially because this fulfills yet another prophecy.[26] However, while the Latin Church contends that only three nails were used for the Crucifixion (one for each hand, the third for both feet, one of which was placed over the other), the Eastern Church maintains that four were used, and in its art Jesus is shown with his feet apart.

Many ancient Fathers, Augustine among them, assert that Jesus was nailed completely naked to the cross. The loincloth usually shown in paintings was appended for reasons of decency. The inscription above his head—only two words: REX IUDAEORUM (THE KING OF THE JEWS), as Mark says,[27] and not JESUS OF NAZARETH THE KING OF THE JEWS in three languages—was not a jest but a procedural requirement of Roman law, to show the crime for which he was being executed.

And, too, the sharing out of his clothes among the soldiers on guard (there were supposed to be four for each victim, according to the rules) followed a Roman custom. The *lex de bonis damnatorum* required this division of the *spolia*.[28] The colorful detail that the legionaries drew lots to settle the matter may be only an invention of the Evangelists, for the verse that reports it follows too literally one from the Psalms: "They part my garments among them, and cast lots upon my vesture."[29]

For the same reason—that is, accommodation of a Biblical prophecy[30]—there is considerable doubt of the authenticity of the tradition that Jesus was crucified between two thieves, and all the more so because the Gospels themselves admit that this had to happen in order to fulfill the Scriptures.

The Catholic scholar Léon-Dufour has pointed out the excessive similarities between passages in the Old Testament (more than twenty) and the various stages of the Passion of Jesus.[31] The desire, for both liturgical and didactic purposes, to make historical events accord with prophetic themes is obvious—an understandable enough concern for the Church but a formidable obstacle for any-one intent on objective study of the facts.

'Elohī, 'Elohī, lāmā shebaqtanī?

The Gospels relate that when many of the sight-seers who had gone to watch the execution of Jesus actually saw him on the cross, they began to mock: "Ah, thou that destroyest the temple, and buildest it in three days, Save thyself. . . . If thou be the Son of God, come down from the cross. . . . If he be the King of Israel, let him now come down from the cross, and we will believe him."[32] An orgy of human vileness and stupidity, as Renan justly remarks.[33]

The two thieves who were crucified beside him, Matthew says, also reviled him.[34] Luke, however, conceived an edifying little tale on this subject: though one of the thieves mocked Jesus, the other reproached his colleague and asked Jesus to accept him into the kingdom; Jesus answered: "Verily I say unto thee, To-day shalt thou be with me in paradise."[35] It can be argued that the promise was not kept, because Jesus himself, according to legend, waited three days to ascend into heaven. But it is clear that the good thief's re-pentance is an allegory,[36] suitable to encourage hardened sinners to change their ways, or at least to repent in the hour of their deaths. It is in the nature of the religious homily to treat moral symbols as historical facts.[37]

At the sixth hour, the Synoptic Gospels say—that is, about noon—a great darkness fell upon everything and lasted until the ninth hour; a raging wind, meanwhile, ripped the veil of the Temple, and the graves opened.[38] These were the wretched hours during which the tortured man was in a state of coma.

The whole chronology of the Passion is too mechanical: at the third hour Jesus was nailed to the cross, at the sixth hour the coma set in, at the ninth hour the agony began. In addition to all this, there is no way of explaining the hiding of the sun. Was it an eclipse? There is no evidence that any was reported in Jerusalem in that period, and even Origen admits this.[39] Was it a sudden thicken-ing of the clouds, or the menacing gusts of the southwest wind, the ḥamsīn, that often brought dense clouds of sand out of the Arabian

Desert?[40] Or was it only imagination, born of the Evangelists' sorrow at the thought of the tragedy—with, again, the help of a prophetic passage?[41] It is common knowledge that in pagan legends heavenly phenomena of like nature underline the deaths and the celestial assumptions of famous figures: Romulus was carried up during a storm, and Caesar ascended to become a constellation while Rome was covered with *"obscura ferrugine"* ("dark fog").[42]

As for the rending of the Temple's veil, it is often seen as an analogy with Caiaphas' rending of his own garment—in this instance as a manifestation not of anger but of anguish.

In his agony, Jesus could still find strength enough to murmur: "I thirst." Immediately a soldier stuck a sponge filled with vinegar on the tip of his spear and held it against the dying man's lips. The sponge was used for corking clay jars.[43] In the various attempts at explaining this action, it has been argued that the sponge did not really contain vinegar but a rather sour light wine and that the Roman soldier did not mean to make light of Jesus. But there is no doubt that the Evangelists have deliberately told the story as if his intent had been evil, because it was their aim not to report a probable fact but to fulfill the prophecy of a Psalm: "In my thirst they gave me vinegar to drink."[44]

The author of the Gospel of John falls into a queer error when he says that the legionary offered the sponge to Jesus on the end of a hyssop branch (ὑσσώπῳ, *hussōpō*).[45] Rather a difficult feat, since the hyssop produces only extremely slender and fragile stems. The Greek word used by the Evangelist is a mistake for ὑσσῷ (*hussō*), which means "lance," "spear," "javelin."

Not much later, Jesus spoke his last words. Luke makes him say: "Father, into thy hands I commend my spirit."[46] John's version is simply: "It is finished."[47] But Mark and Matthew report a more anguished outcry, which is also more believable in a moment of supreme human suffering: " *'Elohī, 'Elohī, lāmā shebaqtanī?*"[48] The Aramaic sentence means: "My God, my God, why hast thou forsaken me?" In Hebrew it would be: " *'Elī, 'Elī, lāmā 'azabtānī?*"[49]— an exact quotation from a Psalm,[50] and assuredly not the hybrid mixture of Hebrew and Aramaic ascribed to Jesus in the original texts of the Gospels.

Mark and Matthew add a foolish sequel to their version, supposing that some among the Jewish onlookers heard the dying man's plea and remarked: "Behold, he calleth Elias [Elijah] . . . let us see whether Elias will come to take him down." No spectator would have been allowed near enough to hear the words murmured in a whisper, and in any case it is absurd to imagine that the Jews were incapable of understanding their own language.[51]

Some of the women who had remained loyal to Jesus—Mary of Bethany, Mary Magdalene, and Salome, the mother of the two Zebedees—wept silently at some distance from the cross. Then they saw his head fall forward in death. It is merely a legend that the mother of Jesus was at the foot of the cross with John the Apostle, to whom Jesus is supposed to have entrusted her care. Only the Gospel of John mentions this,[52] for catechetical reasons. Places of execution were closely guarded by Roman legionaries and it was forbidden to go close to them.[53]

The whole story of the death of Jesus is a theological-ritual dramatization. The details (the two thieves, the vinegar, the division of his garments, the spectator's insults, the darkness, the rent veil, the earthquake, the last words of Jesus) are all fulfillments of prophecies or edifying symbols.[54]

The reality was simpler and more tragic. Jesus was tried and executed as a political criminal, he died in agony, forsaken by all, even by God (in the Garden of Gethsemane Jesus had confidently declared that God could have sent a band of angels to rescue him),[55] and his sufferings would have no other witnesses than his executioners.

The Causes of Death

At nightfall, as their law required, the Roman legionaries performed the breaking of the legs (crurifragium), if the condemned men were still alive, lest someone take advantage of the darkness to set them free. To judge by the Gospel of John,[56] this was not done to Jesus, because he was dead. But a legionary thrust a lance into his side, and blood mixed with water came forth. Christian legend has even given this soldier a name: Longinus. Taken in actuality from the Greek λόγχη (longchē), which means "lance," the so-called proper name simply means "the lancer." The lance probably did not strike hard enough to go through the abdomen of Jesus and reach his heart, despite tradition, which questions whether the blow did not hasten his last moments. It was only a small incision in his side, to make certain that the condemned man was really dead and not merely unconscious.[57] The water that came out of the wound with the blood was lung fluid oozing through because of circulatory stagnation.[58]

Death came from other causes. Many students, especially physicians, have tried to isolate them. According to Sergio Marigo,[59] the death of Jesus was brought on by an embolism that closed off an artery. Verut, Le Bec, Giovanni Judica Cordiglia, and others[60] blame instead a traumatic shock and a sudden syncope as a result of the intensification of pain. R. Withaker suggests a rupture of the myocardium caused by a sharp movement, perhaps in an effort to change position.[61]

All these hypotheses, however, envisage an unforeseen death from exceptional causes probably peculiar to cases of this kind. In them is an attempt to justify the debatable version of the facts offered by the Gospels: the three-hour stages of the death, the three-day period of the judgment, death, and Resurrection, etc. Even as long ago as the time of Origen,[62] students of the subject were astounded at the swiftness of the death of Jesus and considered it a miracle, for it was well known that the agony of the crucified never ended in less than two days. Hynek points out that death in such cases occurs through the slow development of tetanic cramps brought on by spasmodic muscular contractions; the cramps start in the striated muscles of the forearm, then extend into the whole arm, the upper body, the abdomen, the legs.[63] At the same time, Franco La Cava and Joseph Hammer say, the position of the body impedes the circulation of the blood and a progressive carboxyhemia is produced, terminating in an asystolic heart block.[64] That death is extremely slow is emphasized by Binet-Sanglé, Kurt Berna, and others.[65] The contraction of the muscles and the enforced immobility impose an enormous burden on the heart; its pulse is inexorably slowed and the blood stagnates in the capillary vessels. Poisoned by the waste matter that the heart can no longer eliminate, the muscles are affected by tonic spasms, which cause unbearable spastic phenomena. As a consequence of the diminution in circulation, the blood carries progressively less oxygen to the lungs but is increasingly contaminated by carbon dioxide, and the victim feels that he is suffocating.

It is inconceivable that in this condition Jesus should have been able, as the Evangelists pretend, to quote verses from the Bible or even to ask for something to drink, which, incidentally, is a need that is never felt in agonies of this sort. Even if Jesus had died because of an embolism or a syncope, physicians assert, at most he might have uttered an inarticulate sound. If he died from asphyxiation or asystolia, he expired little by little, exhausted of strength and breath.

Beginning in the fifteenth century, the graphic arts showed a macabre relish for emphasizing the details of the Passion. In *Ecce Homo,* Dürer's was the first with pierced hands and feet. The Flemish specialized in portraying the wound in the side, the sores, the torrent of blood . . . In the sixteenth century, a horrifying dream by the visionary Marguerite Marie Alacoque gave birth to the cult of the Sacred Heart, but already at the end of the thirteenth century St. Lutgarta in one of her ecstasies had felt Jesus press his own heart against hers, and her sister, the Venerable Ida, since she could do no less, dreamed that she herself had entered so deeply into the "wound of love" that she had touched the heart of Jesus. A few years later, Catherine of Siena had a similar dream.[66]

Another major problem for the Evangelists was that of having Jesus buried before night. This arose from a basic moral consideration. The Jewish religion did not allow any corpse to remain unburied overnight.[67] Deuteronomy was most specific in cases of hanging: "His body shall not remain all night upon the tree, but thou shalt in any wise bury him that day; *(for he that is hanged is accursed of God)*."[68]

How could this dreadful fate be averted in the case of Jesus— that is, that he should be accursed of God—since it was certain that the Roman soldiers would definitely not attend to taking him down for at least another day and would then throw him into a common grave with the other crucified men? The Gospels have to resort to the introduction of a new character, never mentioned before and never to be heard of again: Joseph of Arimathea (Ramathem or Ramathaim, near the border of Samaria), a man of standing, in fact a member of the Sanhedrin, and a crypto-Christian, to whom the Evangelists innocently attribute the courage to call on Pilate and ask permission to remove Jesus from the cross at once in order to bury him. They take no account of the absurdity of their own invention. At the very time when all the most fanatical followers of Jesus are in flight lest they be accused of complicity, this eleventh-hour convert dares to risk expulsion from the Sanhedrin and from his own social circle in order to perform an act of mercy toward the cadaver of a rebel whom everyone else has deserted.[69] Pilate, so remarkably indulgent toward Christians, grants permission. Joseph of Arimathea has the body taken down, buys a winding sheet for it and inters it in a new grave which he has had dug in his own garden and which is closed with a stone so heavy that only twenty men together can move it. In the seventh century, the monk Arculf claimed to have seen the tomb and its limestone floor with reddish streaks as if it were still bathed in living blood.[70]

Only the Gospel of Matthew adds an episode whose incongruousness and naïveté clearly demonstrate its falsity:[71] the Pharisees (but only those of Galilee) asked Pilate to establish a guard of Roman sentinels at the tomb, and of course he agreed at once.[72]

The Date of Death

The Gospels are unanimous in stating that the ritual funeral services could not be held immediately (with the anointing of the body and the wrapping of it in bandages) because by now the Day of Preparation, called in Greek Παρασκευή (*Paraskeuē*), had ended. In other words, the Holy Sabbath was beginning, and such works were forbidden on that day. John specifies indeed that this Sabbath was an important one: it was Passover.

As we have already had occasion to point out, there is a serious chronological discrepancy between the Synoptics and the Gospel of John with respect to the Last Supper and hence to the trial and the death of Jesus. In the Synoptics, the Supper is held in due course on the eve of Passover, the death occurs on the first day of the holiday and the burial comes that same evening, when it is already almost the Sabbath. John dates the Supper on the night before the eve of

Passover, the death on the eve, and the beginning of the holiday coincidentally with the Sabbath. Both sources then agree again in saying that the tomb was discovered to be empty on the day after the Sabbath (the day that subsequently became for Christians the "Sunday" of the Resurrection). Compared on the basis of the names of days now in use, the differences stand out more clearly:

Date	SYNOPTICS	JOHN
13 Nisan	——	Thursday: Last Supper
14 Nisan	Thursday: Last Supper	Friday: death
15 Nisan	Friday (Passover): death	Saturday (Passover):——
16 Nisan	Saturday:——	Sunday: Resurrection
17 Nisan	Sunday: Resurrection	——

As early as the first centuries of Christianity, the discrepancy gave rise to the Easter controversy between East and West, known as that of "the fourteenth day," over the celebration of the anniversary. The Council of Nicaea cut off all argument in 325 by decreeing, whether in deference to the glory of the Resurrection or in reaction against Jewish practices,[73] that thenceforth the Christian Easter would be celebrated on Sunday. However to preserve a certain respect for the ancient determination of the Jewish Passover in coincidence with the full moon of the month of Nisan, it was agreed that each year Easter should fall on the Sunday immediately following the first full moon that appears after the vernal equinox (March 21). Therefore, Easter Sunday can fall in the period between March 22 and April 25. But the historian is not satisfied with so easy a resolution of the question, and he complains with Salomon Reinach: "Not even a hundred years of the Christian Era had elapsed and no one any longer knew the exact date of the death of Jesus!"[74]

Fruitless efforts have been made to reconcile the Synoptics and John, or to demonstrate the veracity of them as against him, or, conversely, of him against them; or even to reject all four,[75] contending once more, as did the Didascalia of the third century, that Jesus would not have followed official Jewish practice but would have conformed to the solar calendar of the Community of the

Covenant, the existence of which in his lifetime would seem to be proved by the Qumran manuscripts.

Actually, the dates given by the Synoptics and John seem equally unacceptable. In the case of the Synoptics, it is inadmissible that the arrest and the judgment could have occurred on holy days and that in the midst of the observance of Passover a peasant (Simon the Cyrenian) would be returning from the fields; in the case of John, there is the major difficulty of the celebration of the Passover supper a day ahead of time.

All these problems vanish, however, when one considers that just as every detail in the Gospels' story of the Passion has a cate-chistical-liturgical function, so too the dates satisfy a symbolic concern rather than a historical interest. The Synoptics, closer to the apostolic tradition, sought to underline the coincidence of the Passover repast with the institution of the Eucharist; John, following instead Paul's identification of Jesus with the sacrificial lamb,[76] set the death on the eve of Passover in the hours when in the Temple the throats of the innocent victims were being cut.

In any event, authoritative modern astronomers have made precise calculations in order to establish in what year between A.D. 26 and 36 (the period of Pilate's tenure in Palestine) Passover—the full moon of Nisan—might have fallen on a Friday (according to the clues in the Synoptics) or on a Saturday (according to John's indications).[77] The results, in which the dates that correspond to either source are italicized, are these:

A.D. 27	*Friday, April 11*	A.D. 32	Tuesday, April 15
A.D. 28	Wednesday, March 31	A.D. 33	*Saturday, April 4*
A.D. 29	Sunday, March 20	A.D. 34	*Friday, April 23*
A.D. 30	*Saturday, April 8*	A.D. 35	Tuesday, April 12
A.D. 31	Wednesday, March 28	A.D. 36	Thursday, March 29

If one imputes the maximum of credibility to the Synoptic Gospels, in which, at least, the memory of the Last Supper is still alive, and if one grants that Jesus was arrested *immediately after* such an observance (but not on that very day, nor still less that he was tried and executed posthaste, within a few hours), the most probable date is A.D. 30. It is accepted almost unanimously by students of whatever school, and also it fits logically into the chronology we have followed, as the most probable, for the whole life of Jesus.

The Empty Tomb

Once the observance of the Sabbath was over (and it might be said that in truth the death of Jesus occurred on any Friday after Passover), the women could gather at the tomb with their spices (myrrh and aloes) to anoint the body. But they found the grave opened and empty. Trembling with fear, they ran to tell the others.

The Gospels are quite inharmonious in their versions of this episode. According to John, the discovery was made by Mary Magdalene; according to Mark, Mary Magdalene, Mary, the mother of James, and Salome were there; according to Matthew, Mary Magdalene and "the other Mary"; according to Luke, it was Mary Magdalene, Joanna, Mary, the mother of James, and "other women."[78] According to Matthew, the tomb was still closed when they arrived and it was then thrown open by an angel, garbed in white, who appeared suddenly; according to Mark, the tomb was already empty, and "a young man in a long white garment" told the women that Jesus was "risen" and had gone away, leaving the tomb open; according to Luke and John, the announcement was made by two angels standing like sentinels at the entrance to the tomb.

The Synoptics agree only in their accounts of the women's dismay and astonishment and of the Apostles' incredulity when they heard the news.[79] The Gospel of John stages a comic race between Peter and John the Apostle to see who should arrive first at the tomb. John, the winner, made certain that the tomb was empty and then courteously allowed Peter to enter.[80]

To calm the fears of the women and of the Apostles, Jesus supposedly appeared soon afterward, first of all to Mary Magdalene, who mistook him for the gardener, according to Mark and John; or to all the women at once, according to Matthew; or to two disciples on the road to Emmaus, according to Luke; or only to Peter, as Paul was to report.[81] Later, Jesus was said to have appeared to all the eleven Apostles at once "as they sat at meat" in Jerusalem,[82] or in Galilee "into a mountain" (perhaps that of the Sermon);[83] Paul, indeed, says that he appeared to the *Twelve* Apostles![84] Both before and after this collective vision, he was supposed to have appeared to other disciples who were alone or in groups.[85] Each time, the presence of Jesus was greeted with great fear and incredulity, even though, in order to put them at their ease, he did not hesitate to eat bread and fried fish with his friends or to let them touch him so that they would recognize that he was real.[86]

Subsequently, the faithful found it embarrassing that Jesus had not appeared to his mother as well. Therefore, certain apocryphal texts (Acts of Thaddeus, Pseudo-Justin, etc.) remedied this serious oversight of the canonical Gospels.[87]

It is obvious that the whole story of the Resurrection and the apparitions belongs to the category of miracle inventions, σημεῖα (sēmeia), "signs," attestations of faith, tantamount to miracles,[88] and even Eusebius and Jerome doubted the authenticity of these Gospel passages.[89] But the zeal of the Evangelists, who in order to heighten the miraculous and supernatural emphasize the consternation and the incredulity of those who receive the visitations, impairs what they themselves have earlier and often asserted: the disciples' confidence in the divinity of Jesus and in his Resurrection. If this was what the disciples really felt, the pious ladies would never have bothered even to prepare the spices for the anointing of the body, nor would they have been surprised at finding the tomb empty.

Ancient and modern students of Christianity agree that the belief in the Resurrection is founded on the hallucinations of a female visionary, Mary Magdalene,[90] or on a collective hallucination,[91] and they believe variously that in actuality the body was removed from the tomb by the gardener of Joseph of Arimathea,[92] or by Joseph himself,[93] or on the orders of Mary of Bethany and her family,[94] or at the command of the Sanhedrin[95] or of the former brethren of Jesus, the Essenes.[96] There are also those who think that when Jesus was taken down from the cross he was not actually dead;[97] he was cared for and healed secretly by Joseph of Arimathea, and when he showed himself to the Apostles again, they believed that he had returned from the dead. Paulus baldly pretends to be able to reconstruct all the circumstances: Jesus dressed himself in clothes lent to him by the gardener, but weakness compelled him to remain close to the tomb, and he forbade Mary Magdalene to touch him because his body was still in too much pain; in the afternoon he had recovered sufficiently to go as far as Emmaus; later he was strong enough to undertake the journey to Galilee.[98] But, Paulus finally asks himself, when did Jesus really die? Not long afterward, he answers himself, from a tetanus infection!

We have already had occasion to point out the arbitrary character of this sort of critical procedure, which tries to find rational explanations for the most unbelievable aspects of the life of Jesus and which is thus constrained to resort to hypotheses that are equally without foundation.

The Evangelists have made no attempt to foist off banal factual episodes as mystic phenomena; they have explained an object of faith in historical terms. Such indeed was the Resurrection of Jesus to the first Christians. To those who were skeptical of it, Paul, for example, replied with this paradoxical syllogism, from which every element of logic is banished because it is based on a postulate of pure faith: "Now if Christ be preached that he rose from the dead, how say some among you that there is no resurrection of the dead? But if there be no resurrection of the dead, then is Christ not risen."[99]

If we wish to understand the Resurrection, we should try to reconstruct the steps in the formation of the dogma.

Faith in Christ Risen

Jesus dead was left to his fate by his disciples,[100] as the Gospels demonstrate to us in their accounts of the flight from Gethsemane, Peter's denials, etc. In all probability, the Nazarene was buried by the Romans in a common grave with the two thieves. The Acts of the Apostles, however, shows us the Apostles gathered again in Jerusalem not long afterward "to wait for the promise of the Father."[101] To await, that is, the inauguration of the kingdom, which Jesus had said was imminent.

How and when the decision was taken to renew their association in spite of the earlier fear of inviting the same end as their master's is not ascertainable. There is a hiatus between the last verses of the Gospels and the first chapter of Acts, and it conceals the whole character of the "crisis of faith." But the study of Acts makes it plain that by the time the Apostles reunited in Jerusalem, the death of Jesus no longer seemed an irreparable calamity to them. It had come to resemble the death of any other prophet of the kingdom, and one or another of the Apostles could have taken his place and, as Jesus had done, kept alive the hope of the imminent apocalypse.[102] It appears that in the beginning Peter and John were rivals for this honor; they tried to imitate the works of Jesus, performing cures[103] and calling for *metanoia* so that God "shall send the Christ, which before was preached unto you,"[104] and of whom they once more awaited the coming. Later, the leadership of the community was assumed by James, the brother of Jesus (we do not know whether only because of the relationship or through his own special qualifications), and Peter and John receded into subordinate places.

Meanwhile, Paul had come into the picture. With his overwhelming personality and his ambition, he lost no time in interjecting himself among the "pillars" of the community, as he himself rather ironically spoke of James and Peter. Quarrels and conflicts between them and Paul soon arose, especially over the new convert's outrageous proposal to carry the religion beyond the borders of Judaism. At the same time, Paul brought into Christological doctrine a new element that even the Apostles accepted, although they differed in its interpretation. Claiming to have heard the voice of Jesus on the road to Damascus in the middle of a dazzling light that had left him blind for several days (but he himself had to admit that none of those with him at the time had heard anything[105]), Paul convinced himself that though Jesus had really died, he must have risen, leaving his earthly body behind in order to take on a "spiritual" one—that is (since the word had not yet acquired a metaphysical meaning for Paul), a body composed of some impalpable element such as light or air. It was thus that he had shown himself on the Damascus road. If this had happened, Paul argued, it was because of a special purpose of God: to reward Jesus for his holiness.[106] Jesus, therefore, was comparable to those heroes who, as Greek mythology narrates, were carried up into the world of the gods because of their virtues: unselfish heroes who had worked and suffered for the benefit of mankind and whom mankind continued to call upon in times of need. The Crucifixion of Jesus was not a "scandal," a horrible crime that had cut short (as the Apostles thought) his endeavor to initiate the kingdom. The death and Resurrection of Jesus were rather the glorious fulfillment of his mission. Blending his own semipagan conception of the assumption of Jesus into a new life as a reward for his virtues with the Jewish doctrine of the necessity of a reconciliation with Yahweh and a "second covenant," Paul taught that exactly this had been the task of Jesus and these had been his merits in the eyes of God: a vicarious sacrifice through himself in his saintliness and innocence that expiated the collective guilts of all. This was the source of the speculations on the Last Supper that compared Jesus with the paschal lamb, the bread and wine of the thanksgiving to Yahweh with the body and blood of Jesus.

The Apostles, with their rigid Judaic attitudes, found it inconceivable that a messiah should have to die in order to save his people; to them, the concept of a human being ascended to the character of a divinity was a sacrilege against the idea of monotheism. The hope of the Resurrection of Jesus could still be accepted, but only in the sense that Jesus—like the ancient Prophets, of whom the Old Testament asserted that this had also been possible—would be able to return into his old body and live again among men. In fact, the expectation of this Parousia tends to become more concrete when the faithful are taught that Jesus had already resumed his physical body just after his death, before corruption could have set in, and that this phenomenon had been personally verified, *oculata fide*,[107] by a number of persons. Paul's vision on the road to Damascus goes back presumably to some time between A.D. 43 and 44; the Synoptic Gospels were not composed until at least thirty years after that, and John's was later still. This time lag made it possible to distribute a number of such apparitions of Jesus in times anterior to Paul's vision. But, whereas Paul had spoken of a new "pneumatic" nature of Jesus and, in allusion to the Parousia, said that he "shall descend from heaven,"[108] Peter and the other Apostles were convinced that "neither did his flesh see corruption"[109] and that he continued to live concretely in a body subject to all normal physical and organic laws.[110] In his appearances in the Gospels, indeed, Jesus walks with his disciples, eats with them, permits doubting Thomas to touch the wound in his side, and so forth. That we are not dealing here with historical accounts is shown also by the fact that the texts do not agree on the duration of these apparitions. Mark compresses all of them into one day, and Luke copies from him; Matthew draws them out over the whole time required to travel from Jerusalem to the mountains of Galilee; John gives no clear indications but seems to consider them prolonged;[111] Acts declares that the apparitions occurred on forty successive days.[112]

After the Resurrection

The dogma of the Resurrection marks the beginning of *real* Christianity: not the revelation preached by Jesus, which, in essence, was nothing but the enlargement and perfection of the traditional Jewish religion, but rather the cult of the person of Jesus, drawing ever closer to the cults of soteriological deities of the type worshiped in the Greco-Oriental mysteries: a god who is incarnated, who suffers for humanity's sake, and who returns to Olympus.[113]

The Resurrection story itself, therefore, has been enriched little by little with new features that represent a further development of this process of adaptation. Such, for instance, is the tradition that Jesus was resurrected on the third day after his burial. Precisely the same interval is claimed for the ritual cycle in the cults of Orpheus, Osiris, Attis, etc. Such too is the belief that Jesus descended into hell in order to carry salvation to the saints and patriarchs of the Old Testament, just as pagan religion imagined that Dionysus had gone down into the lower world to bring back his mother, Semele; that Orpheus had taken the same journey to rescue his lost Eurydice; that Theseus and Pirithoüs had done as much to return Persephone to the living.

The first account of the descent of Jesus into hell did not appear until the fourth century, when a precise doctrine was formulated on the Trinity (using the Nicene symbol). How was the inactivity of the Divine Logos to be explained during the time in which his body remained intact in the grave and before he ascended to the Father's glory? The doctrine of an extra-terrestrial kingdom, which was also affirmed at this period, afforded an appropriate pretext for filling the gap.[114] To give the legend greater credibility, the Church published an apocryphal letter, attributed to Simon Peter, which purported to guarantee the veracity of the story.[115]

The choice of Sunday as the day of Resurrection, on the other hand, came from an adaptation of the cult of the sun-god, which, when Christianity began to spread, was virtually the official religion of the Roman Empire. The deity, whose highest title was Κύριος (*Kurios*), or Dominus, had a special day dedicated to him as "the Lord's day" (*dies dominica*), which the Christians assimilated as the day of their god. They immediately perceived and accepted the analogy between the gloriously resurrected Christ and the rising sun, and its attributes are frequently transferred to Christ in the writings of the early Christians. Even when the author of the Gospel of Mark undertook to depict the Resurrection of Jesus with the detail that the tomb was found opened, he synchronized this discovery with the dawn of the third day after the fatal Friday: that is, with the sunrise on Sunday.[116] The survival of the day's Italian name, *domenica,* is as indicative of its origin in the solar cult as are its names in English (Sunday) and in German (*Sonntag*).

The Ascension of Jesus into heaven at the instant of his Resurrection also has its parallels in the beliefs of other religions, specifically those of Uranian origin. It is logical that when a god is identified with heaven, his acquisition of divinity should become a rite of ascension. In the Middle Ages, this concept was materialized in the image of a ladder that rose out of sight into the infinity of the heavenly vault.[117]

The Church teaches (this time in contrast with Paul) that Jesus ascended into heaven in his physical body. It is useless even to attempt discussion of the impossibility of such a phenomenon. The theologians reply by falling back on the supernatural and miraculous essence of the matter. In any case, it is a ridiculous miracle in the light of the Copernican discoveries that have demonstrated that actually there is no sky *above* an earth that stands in the center of the universe, but that the earth hangs in infinite space among innumerable other heavenly bodies and that any geographical delimitation of the sky itself is impossible.

Obviously, the Ascension of Jesus into heaven can be accepted only as a myth: morally it represents his severence from the human condition and hence symbolizes the purification of the soul that is released from corporeal materiality; theologically it represents the reunion of Jesus the Savior with God in order to intercede for his believers.[118]

The Second Adam

The doctrine of Jesus as an expiatory victim which Paul introduced, even though it attached itself (in a way that satisfied even the Jewish Christians) to the Biblical tradition, endowed the redeeming mission of Jesus with a universal character far superior to the ethnic-social quality given to it by the Apostles. Paul's argument, to the extent that it is possible to reconstruct it from his Epistles, is this: God, as the first chapters of Genesis relate, had made Adam and Eve immortal and blessed, but when they ate of the fruit of the tree of the knowledge of good and evil they allowed themselves to be tempted by sin and thus they angered God. He punished them by abandoning them to sin and sorrow, stripping them and all their descendants of the gift of immortality. "As by one man [Adam] sin entered into the world, and death by sin," Paul wrote, "and so death passed upon all men, for that all have sinned."[119] Later it was to be debated whether the final proposition of this passage, which in Greek reads: ἐφ' ᾧ πάντες ἥμαρτον (eph' hō pantes ēmarton), should not rather be interpreted (as in fact the Vulgate translates it) to mean "in quo omnes peccaverunt," imputing the responsibilty for the fault (original sin) to Adam alone, who despoiled mankind of divine benevolence. This modification in interpretation, however, does not alter Paul's thought of the condemnation to death and sin that has burdened humanity since Adam.

It should hardly be necessary to point out how impossible it is for modern man to look on death as a punishment for his own sins, or, worse, for those committed by his ancestors,[120] since he knows very well that death is a physiological phenomenon common to all living things, including those of the vegetable kingdom, unrelated to guilt. But his aspiration to a state of perfect bliss and innocence (paradise on earth) and his recognition of his own limitations are parts of man's eternal anxiety, caught as he is between his reality as a finite being and his indomitable tendency toward the absolute.[121]

Here, then, is the new solution which—Paul says[122]—has always eluded everyone and which he at last has been able to grasp and to reveal to the world: after an interval of forbearance, during which he allowed man's sins to accumulate, God selected Jesus as the "propitiator" (ἰλαστήριον, *hilastērion*) through whom he could finally give proof of his own justice and his own mercy, forgiving mankind and restoring to it the lost gifts of immortality and bliss.[123] The similarity of the two events (condemnation and salvation alike through the work of one man) is such that Jesus can be called *the second Adam:* as the first plunged humanity into sin and death, so the second has ransomed it. It does then become clear that if the loss of immortality was the punishment inflicted by God on sinful man through Adam, the restitution of that immortality will be the reward of men reconciled with God through the virtue of Jesus— only of these, of course; for those who persist in wickedness there will be "indignation and wrath."[124] In fact, Paul tells us the chronological sequence of this marvelous event: first ("the first fruit") is Jesus; then, with the Parousia, it will be the turn of all the Christians, and immediately afterward the world will end in the destruction of the wicked. Then every hostile force, including death,[125] will be wiped out, our earthly bodies will be dissolved, and we shall "be clothed upon with our house which is from heaven"[126]—in other words, we shall be resurrected in spiritual bodies, incorruptible and eternal.[127]

To define his concept of man's "reconciliation" with God, Paul employs the terminology also used by the mysteriological cults: λύτρον (*lutron*), which in the Greek of the time meant the ransom that had to be paid to "redeem" a prisoner or a slave,[128] and (ἀπο)λύτρωσις (*apolutrōsis*), "release by means of ransom." This latter word was translated into Latin as *redemptio* (whence the English "redemption"), which, etymologically, is the same as "purchase." In analogy to what was taught by the mystery cults, for Paul, too, the death of Jesus the Savior was "the ransom price" paid for the faithful.

The identification of Jesus with God (which, as has been observed, was a development accomplished in the fourth century) was to make only slight alterations in Paul's doctrine of "vicarious

sacrifice." In the Middle Ages, Anselm of Canterbury was to formulate the doctrine of "satisfaction," which the Church approved.
Anselm declared in his *Cur Deus homo?* that man owes God total
obedience. Thus transgressors (and all men since Adam are transgressors) deprive God of a part of what is due to him. To avoid the
inevitable punishment of their faults, they should "satisfy" (*satis-
facere*): restore the losses that they have imposed on God. But how
is this to be done? Since *all* the good that can be done is owed to
God, nothing is gained by undoing a wrong once committed. Only a
perfect being (and hence personally exempted from the penalty of
falling under divine wrath), who agrees to be punished for the sins
of other men, can satisfy God. This perfect being—given the fact
that man is sinful by nature—can be no other than God himself.
Therefore, he has agreed to be incarnated, to offer himself, to suffer,
and to die for others.

Thus we enter the truly staggering vicious circle of a god who
punishes himself in order to be able to forgive the men and women
who have offended him!

Salvation

In the fourth century, while the problems of the Trinity were
beginning to be discussed in the East, the West was occupied with a
vast debate on Christian anthropology and soteriology, and this too
was inspired by Paul's doctrine.

Desiring, as we have already noted, to extend redemption
through Christ to non-Jews as well, Paul had kept up a bitter quarrel with the Apostles, maintaining that observance of the Mosaic
Law (all the ritual practices, fasts, purifications, abstention from
stipulated foods, etc., and especially the duty of circumcision) could
not guarantee salvation. Indeed, it was granted "freely" (δωρεάν,
dōrean) by God after the ransom paid by Jesus through his sacrifice.

Paul arrived at categorical statements of this character: "A man
is not justified by the works of the law, but by the faith of Jesus
Christ";[129] "A man is justified by faith, without the deeds of the
law";[130] "If by grace, then is it no more of works; otherwise grace is
no more grace";[131] Christ has "forgiven you all trespasses, Blotting

out the handwriting of ordinances that was against us";[132] and, baldly: "Christ died for the ungodly. For scarcely for a righteous man will one die."[133]

It would seem that by such teachings Paul belittled the requirement, preached by Jesus, of living a righteous life in order to earn divine forgiveness. Actually, other passages in his Epistles show that he was still convinced of this exigency; but in the excitement of battle, in order to prove God's complete freedom to save whomever he chose, Jew or Gentile, observant or neglectful of the traditional customs, Paul fell into these paradoxical pronouncements. Indeed, he even placed limitations on the extension of the redeeming work of Jesus. From the example of Esau and Jacob, who, though both were sons of Isaac, were so differently treated by God, according to the Old Testament, Paul concluded that God makes his choice according to his own will, regardless of man's works;[134] that salvation "is not of him that willeth, nor of him that runneth, but of God that sheweth mercy";[135] and that, in his inscrutable will, God "foreknows" ($\pi\rho o\acute{\epsilon}\gamma\nu\omega$, proegno) those among the living whom he finds worthy—he has chosen them ab aeterno for filial adoption ($\upsilon\iota o\theta\epsilon\sigma\acute{\iota}\alpha$, hyothesia), and he has justified them without regard to their deserts.[136]

Notwithstanding the clarity with which Paul sought to declare the absolute arbitrariness of God in bestowing the "grace" of salvation, until the fourth century theologians preferred to dilute his doctrine, contending that at least God predestined and justified those who had anticipated their future rewards. But at the end of that century, Augustine published his rigid interpretation of the Pauline doctrine: all mankind being without exception massa perditionis since Adam, because of original sin, it was impossible that God's choice should be determined by our merits; "grace" was freely granted by God, even to those who were unworthy.

Augustine's pessimistic view aroused opposition. Many protested, particularly the British monk Pelagius, who, in a commentary on the Epistles of Paul, maintained that Adam's sin could have worked only against him, not against all his descendants, and that therefore man had not lost the freedom of will to choose between good and evil and thus to attain salvation or damnation through his own natural powers. Grace, he said, serves only to help us not to sin, since through grace it is revealed to us what we ought to seek and what we ought to avoid. The Pelagian doctrine was condemned by the Council of Carthage in 412. By that time, however, the battle between Augustinians, who upheld grace, and Pelagians, who stood for free will, was in full cry.

Toward the end of the Middle Ages, Thomas Aquinas tried afresh to soften the asperities of Augustine's doctrine through a reconciliation between grace and free will, which the Church accepted. In contrast, in the sixteenth century, Martin Luther fell back on Augustine to launch the Reformation. Man, he said, had decayed through original sin and was irremediably corrupt, so that only evil could come from him: all his works were necessarily sinful. Only he who was predestined would have eternal life, and in such cases even he who strives to do so cannot lose his salvation, whatever his sins. Paul's declaration that man is justified only through faith became for Luther, paradoxically, *"Pecca fortiter, sed crede fortius"* ("Sin hard, but believe harder").

In Luther's footsteps, the other great reformer, Calvin, arrived at an even more radical predestination. One is predestined *ab aeterno* to either salvation or damnation, and hence even he who sins does so because it was written that he should. But his descent into sin is proof that God has not chosen him; it is the terrible warrant of his condemnation. Repudiated by the Council of Trent, the doctrines of Luther and Calvin have been given ever greater inner meaning by the Protestants.

In our own time, preceded by the mystical crises of the first reformers and then by such unquiet spirits as Cornelis Jansen, Blaise Pascal, and James Spener, the most advanced Protestant theology, especially in the existentialist sector, has reduced the matter of religion to an obsessive uncertainty of our future destiny. For Sören Kierkegaard, the fear of sin (which would be the sure proof of our *non*-election by God) condemns us to the "paradoxical" path of negation of the world, loneliness, and desperation. Heidegger and his followers consider human life a transience, an awareness of our limitations and of the nullity of our capacities. Martin Heidegger's "being" or "presence"—our existence on earth—is "anxiety, constant anguish, suspense, dissatisfaction, unreal existence." And yet, it is said, it is precisely this "anguish," this feeling of loss, of bewilderment, this knowledge of guilt, that is the positive sign of our need for God, who is experienced as the exact antithesis of this inadequacy in ourselves. Thus this philosophy arrives at the truly stunning conclusion that it is *good* that man sin, for otherwise he would not thirst for God.[137]

And so the "good tidings" preached by Jesus, which held the hope of happiness, of peace, of justice for all men, in this life, have been tortured through the centuries into this perversion of faith that serves no purpose of life because indeed it rejects life, it curses life, it condemns life to an agony of unsureness.

Correlation of the Gospels

	MARK	MATTHEW	LUKE	JOHN	THOMAS
Joseph and Mary		1:18	1:27		
Genealogies of Jesus		1:1-17	3:23-38		
The Annunciation			1:26; 28-38		
Mary's visit to Elisabeth			1:39-56		
Birth of John the Baptist			1:1-25; 57-80		
Joseph's doubts		1:19-24			
Birth of Jesus		1:25	2:1-20		
Circumcision and purification			2:21-38		
Herod, the Magi, the Flight into Egypt		2:1-18			
The unknown years of Jesus		2:19-23	2:39-52		
John the Baptist	1:1-8	3:1-12	3:1-18	1:6-8; 15-28	
Baptism of Jesus	1:9-11	3:13-17	3:21-22	1:29-34	
In the wilderness— the Temptation	1:12-13	4:1-11	4:1-13		
Arrest of John	6:17-18	14:3-5	3:19-20		
Return of Jesus to Nazareth	1:14-15	4:12	4:14-15	4:43	
"No prophet is accepted in his own country"	6:1-6	13:54-58	4:16-30	4:44	
The first disciples	1:16-20	4:18-22	5:1-11	1:35-51	
The demoniac in Capernaum	1:21-28	7:28-29	4:31-37		
Simon's mother-in-law	1:29-31	8:14-15	4:38-39		
Healings by night	1:32-34	4:13-16; 8:16-17	4:40-41		
On the way to Galilee	1:35-39; 3:7-12	4:17; 23-25	4:42-44; 6:17-19		

The daughter of Jairus	5:21-24; 35-43	9:18-19; 23-26	8:40-42; 8:49-56		
The woman who bled	5:25-34	9:20-22	8:43-48		
The deaf-mute	7:32-37	9:32-34			
The blind man	8:22-26	9:27-31		9:1-41	
The leper	1:40-45	8:1-4	5:12-16	4:46-54	
The centurion's son		8:5-13	7:1-10		
The widow's son			7:11-16		
The paralytic	2:1-12	9:1-8	5:17-26		
The tempest calmed	4:35-40	8:18; 23-27	8:22-25		
The man possessed at Gergesa	5:1-20	8:28-34	8:26-39		
The epileptic boy	9:14-29	17:14-20	9:37-44a		
The marriage at Cana				2:1-11	
Levi-Matthew	2:13-17	9:9-17	5:27-32		52b; 108
The fast	2:18-22		5:33-39		51; 82
John's doubts		11:2-11	7:17-35		
The woman who sinned			7:36-50		
The grain and the Sabbath	2:23-28	12:1-8	6:1-5		
The withered hand	3:1-6	12:9-21	6:6-11		
The arthritic woman			13:10-17		
The man with dropsy			14:1-6		
The paralytic at the pool				5:1-6; 7:21-24	15ac; 39; 58
Impurities	7:1-23	15:1-10	(6:39)		
"If I by Beelzebub cast out devils"	3:22-30	12:22-32; 36-37	11:14-22; 12:10		40; 48; 49
Warning against false prophets		7:15-19; 12:33-35	6:43-45		45; 50
"Woe unto you Scribes and Pharisees!"	12:38-40	23:1-39	11:37-54; 20:45-47		44; 93; 106
The Twelve Apostles	3:13-19; 6:7-13; 34	7:6; 9:35-38; 10:1-15	6:12-16; 8:1-3; 9:1-6; 10:1-11; 17-20		47; 77; 78; 97

Correlation of the Gospels (cont.)

	MARK	MATTHEW	LUKE	JOHN	THOMAS
Jesus renounces his family	3:20-21; 31-35	12:46-50	8:19-21		103
The Beatitudes		5:1-12	6:20-26		22; 54; 59; 63; 72; 73
The fulfillment of the Law		5:17-20; 21-28; 33-37	12:57-59; 16:16-17		
The Great Commandment	12:28-34	22:34-40	10:25-37; 20:39-40		
Love for one's neighbor		5:38-48; 6:1-8; 16-18; 7:12	6:27-33		6ab; 66
"Judge not"	4:24	7:1-5	6:37-38; 41-42		30
"My yoke is easy"		11:28-30			94
The sower	4:1-9; 13-20	13:1-9; 18-23	8:4-8; 11-15		9
The tares		13:24-30; 36-43			62
The seed that bears	4:26-29				26
The mustard seed	4:30-32	13:31-32	13:18-19		23
The leaven		13:33	13:20-21		100
The woman who drops grain . .					101
The pearl and the treasure . . .		13:44-46			80; 113
The man who wanted to kill . .					102
The fish		13:47-50			8
The strongbox		13:51-52			
The light	4:21-23	5:14b-16	8:16; 9:33		37; 38
A private discipline?	4:10-12; 33-34	10:26-27; 11:25-27; 13:10-17; 34	8:9-10; 17; 10:21-24	12:37-43	4a; 5; 19
"Take no thought for the morrow"		6:19-21; 25-34	12:13-34		41; 67; 76

The Lord's Prayer	11:24-26	6:9-15; 7:7-11	11:1-13	16:23-24	1; 96; 98
The widow and the judge			18:1-8		
The Pharisee and the publican			18:9-14		
Death of John the Baptist	6:19-29	14:6-12	9:7-9		
Herod's fears	6:14-16	14:1-2			
The Miracle of the Loaves	6:31-44; 8:1-9	14:13-21; 15:32-38	9:10b-17	6:1-4; 27-51	
Jesus walks on the water	6:45-56	14:22-36		6:15-26	
The Syrophoenician	7:24-31	15:21-31; 39			33; 83a; 95
A sign is asked	8:10-13	12:38-45; 16:1-4	11:16; 24-32; 12:54-56		
The disciples' doubts	8:14-21	16:5-12	12:1	6:59-60	57
Jesus discouraged	8:27-28; 31-32; 9:30-32	16:13-14; 21-23; 17:21-22	9:18-19; 22; 44-45	6:61-71; 7:1-9	
The primacy of Peter	8:29-30	16:15-20	9:20-21	(1:42b)	13; 14
The Transfiguration	9:2-13	17:1-13	9:28-36		
Taking the cross	8:34-38	10:38-39; 16:24-27	9:23-26; 14:27	12:25-36	60; 105
Those who will see the kingdom	9:1	16:28	9:27	21:22-24	
"I came not to send peace"		10:34-37	12:49-53; 14:25-33		10; 17
Wait in faith			13:6-9		
It is not enough to say: "Lord"		7:21-27	6:46-49		*Incipit.*; 11; 18
The disciple and the master		10:24-33	6:40; 12:2-9	13:20	79
"Strait is the gate"		7:13-14	13:23-30		
The tribute at Capernaum		17:23-26			
"Who among us shall be the greatest?"	9:33-37	10:40-42; 18:1-5	9:46-48; 10:16		4b; 27a; 6c
"We are unprofitable servants"			17:7-10		
Taking the lowest place			14:7-11		
Avoiding offense	9:42-48	5:19-20; 18:6-10	17:1-2		
The salt of the earth	9:49-50	5:13-14a	14:34-35		

	MARK	MATTHEW	LUKE	JOHN	THOMAS
"The light of the body is the eye"		6:22-23	11:34-36		29
Brotherly forgiveness		18:15-22	17:3-4		35
The merciless servant		18:23-35			
The strayed lamb		18:11-14	15:1-7		111
The lost drachma			15:8-10		
The prodigal son			15:11-32		
"He that is not with me"	9:38-40	12:30	9:49-50; 11:23		
Jesus leaves Galilee	10:1	19:1-2	9:51		
Galileans killed by Pilate			13:1-5		
"Herod will kill thee"			13:31-33		
The imprecation against Jerusalem			13:34-35		
The curse on the cities of Galilee		11:20-24	10:13-15		
Entry into Samaria			9:52-56		
A Scribe wishes to follow Jesus		8:19-22	9:57-62		90
The woman of Samaria				4:3-42	
The ten lepers			17:11-19		
Marriage and divorce	10:2-12	5:31-32; 19:3-9	16:18		
Celibacy "Neque nubent, neque nubentur"		19:10-12		(17:21-23)	27; 42; 110; 118
"Sinite parvulos venire ad me"	12:18-27	22:23-33	20:27-38		
	10:13-16	19:13-15	18:15-17		
The young rich man	10:17-25	19:16-24	18:18-25		32; 61; 84; 85; 114

Passage	Mark	Matthew (6:24)	Luke	John	No.
The unfaithful steward			16:1-15		52a
Lazarus and the rich man			16:19-31		
"Who then can be saved?"	10:26-31	19:25-31	22:30b; 18:26-30		
The wages of the vineyard workers		20:1-16			
The marriage feast		22:1-14	14:12-24		68
The ambition of the Zebedees	10:32-45	20:17-28	18:31-34; 22:24-30a		
The blind beggar in Jericho	10:46-52	20:29-34	18:35-43;		
Zaccheus			19:1-10		
The talents	(4:25)	25:14-30; (13:12)	19:11-27; (8:18)		46
Mary and Martha			10:38-42		
The entry into Jerusalem	11:1-11a	21:1-11	19:28-44	12:12-16	
Return to Bethany	11:11b	21:17			
The curse on the fig tree	11:12-14	21:18-19			
The woman taken in adultery				8:1-11	
Purification of the Temple	11:15-19	21:12-16	19:45-48	2:13-25	
Nicodemus				3:1-12	34
The withered fig tree	11:20-23	21:20-22	(17:56)		21; 53; 110
By what authority?	11:27-33	21:23-27	20:1-8	7:11-13	
The two sons		21:28-32			
The wicked husbandmen	12:1-9	21:33-41	20:9-16		69
The cornerstone	12:10-12	21:42-46	20:17-19		70
"My doctrine is not mine"				7:14-21; (5:17-47)	
The tribute to Caesar	12:13-17	22:15-22	20:20-26		
Is this in truth the Messiah?				7:25-32	
The Diaspora				12:20-24	
The Messiah is (not) the son of David	12:35-37	22:41-46	20:41-44		

Correlation of the Gospels (cont.)

	MARK	MATTHEW	LUKE	JOHN	THOMAS
"I am the light of the world" . . .				8:12-59; 12:44-50	43; 81; 87; 112
The Logos				1:1-5; 9-14	
The good shepherd				10:1-38	
The widow's mite	12:41-44		21:1-4		
"There shall not be left one stone upon another"	13:1-2	24:1-2	21:5-6		28; 65; 117
Eschatological discourse . .	13:3-32	24:3-41; 10:16-25	21:7-33; 10:3; 12:11-12; 17:22-37		
Exhortation to vigilance . .	13:33-37	24:42-47	21:34-38		25; 115
The neglectful servant . . .		24:48-51			
The foolish virgins . . .		25:1-13	12:35-48		
The universal judgment . . .	(9:41)	25:31-46	(10:16)		
"The kingdom of God is within you"			17:20-21	3:13-21	2
The resurrection of Lazarus .				10:39-42; 11:1-45	
Jesus flees to Ephraim . .	14:1-2	26:1-5		11:46-57	
The anointment by Mary . .	14:3-9	26:6-13		12:1-11	
The betrayal by Judas and his fate	14:10-11	26:14-16; 27:3-10	22:1-6		
Preparations for the Passover .	14:12-16	26:17-19	22:7-13		
Jesus washes the Apostles' feet .				13:1	
"One of you shall betray me" .	14:17-21	26:20-25	22:21-23	13:2-17	
The Last Supper	14:22-25	26:26-29	22:14-20	13:18; 21-30 (6:52-58)	
The warning to Peter . . .	14:26-31	26:30-35	22:31-38	13:31-38	

	Matthew	Mark	Luke	John
Exhortations to the disciples . .				14; 15; 16
Jesus prays for his disciples . .				17
In the Garden of Gethsemane . .	26:36-46	14:32-42	22:39-46	18:1
The arrest	26:47-56	14:43-52	22:47-53	18:2-11
Before the Sanhedrin . . .	26:57; 59-68	14:53; 55-65	22:54; 63-71	18:12-14; 19-24
Peter's denial	26:58; 69-75	14:54; 66-72	22:55-62	18:15-18; 25-27
Before Pilate	27:1-2; 11-14	15:1-5	23:1-6; 13-16	18:28-38
Before Herod Antipas . . .			23:7-12	
The flagellation	27:26b-30	15:15b-19		19:1-3
"Behold the man!" . . .				19:4-16a
Jesus or Barabbas? . . .	27:15-26a	15:6-15a	23:17-25	18:39-40
Golgotha	27:31-34	15:20-23	23:26-33a	19:16b-17
Jesus on the cross . . .	27:35-44	15:24-32	23:33b-43	19:18-27
His death	27:45-56	15:33-41	23:44-49	19:28-30
The empty tomb	27:57-66	15:42-47	23:50-55	19:31-42
The Resurrection	28:1-8; 11-15	16:1-8	24:1-12	20:1-18
The appearances	28:9-10; 16-20	16:9-18	24:13-50	20:19-30; 21:1-25
The Ascension		16:19-20	24:51-53	

Notes

CHAPTER 1

JOSEPH AND MARY

1. Gustaf H. Dalman, *Orte und Wege Jesu* (3 vols.; Gütersloh: C. Bertelsmann, 1924), I, 61.
2. Alfred F. Loisy, *Le origini del cristianesimo* (Turin: Einaudi, 1942), p. 62; William B. Smith, *Der Vorchristliche Jesu* (Leipzig: C. G. Röder, 1906), p. 13.
3. Charles Guignebert, *Le problème de Jésus* (Paris: Flammarion, 1914), p. 97.
4. Eduard Meyer, *Ursprung und Anfänge des Christentums* (3 vols.; Stuttgart and Berlin: J. G. Cotta, 1923), II, 423.
5. Matt. 2:23.
6. Isa. 11:1.
7. Mario Puglisi, *Gesù e il mito di Cristo: Saggio di critica metodologica* (Bari: Laterza, 1912), p. 83.
8. William F. Albright, *L'archeologia in Palestina* (Florence: Sansoni, 1957), p. 269.
9. Henry Didon, *Vita di Gesù Cristo* (2 vols.; Florence: Nerbini, 1934), I, 69.
10. Joseph Felten, *Storia dei tempi del Nuovo Testamento* (4 vols.; Turin: S.E.I., 1944), II, 166 ff.
11. Giuseppe Ricciotti, *Vita di Gesù Cristo* (Rome: Tipografia Poliglotta Vaticana, 1948), p. 255.
12. Mark 3:21.
13. John 2:1–12; 19:25–27.
14. Acts 1:14.
15. Cesare Ansaldi, *Nascita e infanzia di Gesù nella leggenda araba* (Rome: Sindacato Italiano Arti Grafiche, 1932), p. 13.
16. Matt. 13:55.
17. Piero Martinetti, *Gesù Cristo e il cristianesimo* (2 vols.; Milan: Denti, 1949), I, 107.
18. Matt. 1:1–17; Luke 3:23–38.
19. Charles Guignebert, *Gesù* (Turin: Einaudi, 1950), p. 135.
20. Albert Reville, *Jésus de Nazareth: Études critiques sur les antécédents de l'histoire évangélique et de la vie de Jésus* (2 vols.; Paris: Fischbacher, 1906), I, 346.
21. Gen. 38
22. Josh. 2:1.
23. Ruth 3.
24. II Kings 11.
25. Reville, *Jésus de Nazareth*, I, 347.
26. Johann A. Rohrbacher, *Storia universale della Chiesa cattolica: Dal principio del mondo fino ai dì nostri* (16 vols.; Turin: Marietti, 1874), II, 465; Giuseppe Ricciotti (ed.), *La Sacra Bibbia* (Florence: Salani, 1940), p. 1383.
27. John of Damascus, *De fide orthodoxa* IV, 14–15.
28. Edmond Bapst, *La vie historique de Notre Seigneur Jésus Christ* (2 vols.; Paris: Imprimerie Générale Lahure, 1924), I, 15.
29. Protevangelium of James 4–5; Pseudo-Matthew 3–4. In the Italian edition of the present

445

work, the apocryphal books of the New Testament are cited from Giuseppe Bonaccorsi (ed.), *Vangeli apocrifi* (Florence: Editrice Libraria Fiorentina, 1948), unless otherwise noted. A standard work in English for these texts is Montague Rhodes James (trans.), *The Apocryphal New Testament* (Oxford: The Clarendon Press, 1924).

30. David F. Strauss, *Vie de Jésus* (2 vols.; Paris: Ladrange, 1839), I, 166.

31. Luigi Asioli, *Vita di Maria* (Milan: Ulrico Hoepli, 1923), p. 57.

32. Otto Hophan, *Maria* (Turin: Marietti, 1953), p. 51.

33. Giovanni B. Alfano, *Vita di Gesù* (Naples: Morano, 1961), p. 13.

34. Ricciotti, *Vita di Gesù*, p. 261.

35. Mark 6:3; Matt. 13:55; Luke 2:27, 33, 41, 48; 4:22; John 1:45; 6:42; Acts 2:22; Rom. 1:3.

36. Alfano, *op. cit.*, p. 18.

37. Luke 1:28.

38. Thomas Aquinas, *Summa Theologica* III, q. 7, a. 9.

39. Charles Spicq, *Théologie morale du Nouveau Testament* (2 vols.; Paris: J. Gabalda, 1965), II, 451–61.

40. Protevangelium of James 11:1; Pseudo-Matthew 9:1.

41. Reville, *Jésus de Nazareth*, I, 147–49.

42. Heb. 1:14 (the authenticity of the Epistle is doubtful, however).

43. Heinrich Klee, *Storia dei dogmi* (2 vols.; Milan: Ufficio della Biblioteca Cattolica, 1854), I, 193.

44. *Ibid.*, I, 185–86.

45. Thomas Aquinas, *Summa Theol.* I, q. 113.

46. Felten, *op. cit.*, II, 167 ff.

47. Giuseppe Roschini, *La vita di Maria* (Rome: Bellardetti, 1946), p. 18.

48. Luke 1:28.

49. Hophan, *Maria*, p. 79.

50. Xavier Léon-Dufour, *Les évangiles et l'histoire de Jésus* (Paris: Editions du Seuil, 1963), pp. 93–94.

51. Francesco Roberti (ed.), *Dizionario di teologia morale* (Rome: Studium, 1954), p. 129.

52. Luke 1:29–38.

53. Luke 1:39–56.

54. Adolfo Omodeo, *Gesù e le origini del cristianesimo* (Messina: Principato, 1913), p. 375.

55. I Sam. 2.

56. Heinrich E. G. Paulus, *Das exegetische Handbuch über die drei ersten Evangelien* (2 vols.; Heidelberg: K. Winter, 1830), I, 74.

57. Walter Bauer, *Das Leben Jesu im Zeitalter der Neutestamentlichen Apokryphen* (Tübingen: J. C. B. Mohr, 1909), p. 18.

58. Protevangelium of James 12:2.

59. Ricciotti, *Vita di Gesù*, p. 258.

60. Franz M. Willam, *La vita di Gesù nel paese e nel popolo d'Israele* (Turin: S.E.I., 1945), p. 21.

61. Num. 5:12–31.

62. Protevangelium of James 13; Pseudo-Matthew 10.

63. Ansaldi, *op. cit.*, p. 20.

64. Matt. 1:18.

65. Matt. 1:19.

66. Matt. 1:25.

67. Iustin Bonaventura Pranaitis, *Cristo e i Cristiani nel Talmud* (Rome: no publisher, 1939), pp. 60–65.

68. Paul Louis Couchoud, *Il mistero di Gesù* (Milan: Bocca, 1945), p. 27 n.

69. Guignebert, *Gesù*, p. 153; Werner Keller, *La Bibbia aveva ragione* (Milan: Garzanti, 1957), pp. 305–6.

70. Maurice Goguel, *La vie de Jésus et l'église primitive* (Paris: Payot, 1932), pp. 52–53.

71. Epiphanius, *Adversus haereses* LXXVIII, 7.
72. John of Damascus, *De fide orthodoxa* IV, 14.
73. Tertullian, *De spectaculis* XXX.
74. Pierre Saintyves, *Le discernement du miracle* (Paris: Émile Nourry, 1909), p. 260.
75. Heinrich E. G. Paulus, *Das Leben Jesu als Grundlage einer reinen Geschichte des Urchristentums* (3 vols.; Heidelberg: K. Winter, 1828), I, 99 ff.
76. Karl H. Venturini, *Natürliche*

Geschichte des grossen Propheten von Nazareth (4 vols.; Copenhagen: Schubothe, 1806), I, 521.
77. Flavius Josephus, *Jewish Antiquities*, XVIII, 3, 4.
78. Aurelio Turcotti, *Vita politica di Gesù* (2 vols.; Turin: Tipografia Borgarelli, 1879–80), I, 38; II, 21.
79. Houston Stewart Chamberlain, *Die Grundlagen des Neunzehnten Jahrhunderts* (Stuttgart, 1900), pp. 210–19; cited in Goguel, *Vie de Jésus*, p. 236.

CHAPTER 2
THE INCARNATION

1. Emilio Bossi, *Cristo nella storia, nella Bibbia, nella mitologia* (Bellinzona: Tipografia Libreria Editrice, 1935), pp. 87 ff.
2. Henri de Lubac, *Buddhismo e Occidente* (Milan: Vita e Pensiero, 1958), p. 88.
3. Raffaele Mariano, *Cristo e Budda e altri Iddii dell'Oriente* (12 vols.; Florence: Barbèra, 1900–1911), I, 117 ff.
4. Goguel, *Vie de Jésus*, pp. 52–53.
5. Ansaldi, *Nascita e infanzia*, p. 14.
6. Frederick Loofs, *What Is the Truth About Jesus Christ?* (New York: Charles Scribner's Sons, 1913), p. 185.
7. Charles Fouard, *Vita di N.S. Gesù Cristo* (2 vols.; Turin: Libraria Editrice Internazionale, 1913 and 1915), I, 88 n.4.
8. Klee, *Storia dei dogmi*, II, 24–26.
9. Ephraem, *Hymn.* XI, 6.
10. Thomas Aquinas, *Summa Theol.* III, 29.
11. Isa. 7:14–16.
12. See notes on this Biblical passage in Giuseppe Ricciotti (ed.), *La Sacra Bibbia* (Florence: Salani, 1940).
13. This is the meaning given by Domenico Bertetto, in *Maria nel Domma cattolico* (Turin: S.E.I., 1955), p. 55, to *hinnēh*, with which the passage begins.
14. Strauss, *Vie de Jésus*, I, 180–81.
15. Salomon Reinach, *Orpheus: Histoire générale des religions* (Paris: Hachette, 1909), p. 267.
16. Bertetto, *op. cit.*, p. 181.
17. Jerome, *Ad Jovin.* I, 26.
18. Ernesto Buonaiuti, *Saggi di storia del cristianesimo*, ed. A. Donini and M. Niccoli (Venice: Pozza, 1957), pp. 178–79.
19. Umberto Fracassini, *Il misticismo greco e il cristianesimo* (Città di Castello: Il Solco, 1922), p. 166.
20. Tertullian, *De carne Christi* 23; Origen, *In Luc. hom.* XIV; etc.
21. Ambrose, *De just. virg.* VIII, 22; Gregory, *In Evang. hom.* XXVI, 1.
22. Joseph Hammer, *Quando Gesù viveva tra di noi* (Turin: S.A.I.E., 1957), p. 47.
23. Francesco Magri, *Gesù Cristo—La vita, la dottrina, le opere, nella storia e nella critica* (Milan: L. Romano, 1945), p. 221.

24. Willam, *La vita di Gesù*, p. 9.
25. Augustine, *De sancta virginitate* 4.
26. Igino Giordani, *Gesù di Nazareth* (2 vols.; Turin: S.E.I., 1945–46), I, 45.
27. Hophan, *Maria*, p. 118.
28. Enrico Meynier, *Storia del cristianesimo* (Torre Pellice: Edizioni Claudiane, 1930), p. 91.
29. Henri Daniel-Rops, *Storia della Chiesa del Cristo* (6 vols.; Turin: Marietti, 1951–58), II, 149.
30. Bertetto, *op. cit.*, p. 167.
31. *Ibid.*, pp. 303 ff.
32. John of Damascus, *Orat. de dormitione virginis* 8.
33. *Ibid.* (from Gen. 8).
34. John of Damascus, *Orat. in Nativ. B. V.* 3 (from Gen. 28:11).
35. Bernard, *Homil. II sup. Missus* 5 (from Exod. 3:3).
36. Bernard, *Sermo in Dom. infra Oct. Assump. B. V.* (from Num. 17:2).
37. *Ibid.* (from Judg. 6:36–40).
38. Arnold of Chartres, *De laudibus virginis* (from I Kings 6).

39. The Vulgate version of this Psalm reads: *"Deus operatus est in medio terrae."* The King James Bible reads: "For God is my King of old, working salvation in the midst of the earth."
40. Augustine, *De natura et gratia* XLII.
41. Henri Daniel-Rops, *Gesù e il suo tempo* (Florence: Sansoni, 1949), p. 118.
42. Walter von Loewenich, *Il cattolicesimo moderno* (Milan: Feltrinelli, 1962), pp. 206–24, gives all the proceedings and arguments.
43. Giovanni Manise, "Maria Santissima," in *Dizionario di Teologia Morale* (Rome: Studium, 1954).
44. Heinrich J. D. Denzinger, *Enchiridion Symbolorum* (Freiburg: Herder Verlag, 1952), n. 1978*a*.
45. René Laurentin, *La Vierge au Concile* (Paris: Lethielleux, 1965).
46. Otto Semmelroth, *Marie archétype de l'église* (Paris: Fleurus, 1965).

CHAPTER 3

THE GOSPEL OF THE NATIVITY

1. Luke 2:1–2.
2. Matt. 2:1.
3. Josephus, *Antiq.*, XVII, 13, 3; XVIII, 1, 1; 2, 1; Giuseppe Ricciotti, *Storia d'Israele* (2 vols.; Turin: S.E.I., 1959), II, 435; Jack Finegan, *Light from the Ancient Past* (Princeton, N.J.: Princeton University Press, 1946), p. 219.
4. Heinrich J. Holtzmann, *Lehrbuch der historisch-kritischen Einleitung in das Neue Testament* (3 vols.; Freiburg: J. C. B. Mohr [P. Siebeck], 1892), I, 324.
5. Marie Joseph Lagrange, *L'évangile de Jésus Christ* (Paris: J. Gabalda, 1928), pp. 30–31.
6. Karl Adam, *Gesù il Cristo* (Brescia: Morcelliana, 1955), p. 85.
7. Domenico Argentieri, *Quando visse Cristo?* (Milan: Bocca, 1945).
8. Bapst, *La vie historique*, I, 42.
9. Marie Joseph Lagrange, *Le judaïsme avant Jésus Christ* (Paris: J. Gabalda, 1931), p. 208.
10. Meyer, *Ursprung und Anfänge*, II, 423 n. 2.
11. Ernest Renan, *Vie de Jésus* (Paris: Michel Lévy Frères, 1928), p. 39.

12. Matt. 2:5–6; cf. Mic. 5:2.
13. Robert Aron, *Gli anni oscuri di Gesù* (Milan: Mondadori, 1963), p. 60; Umberto Grancelli, *Il simbolo nella vita di Gesù* (Verona: Palminteri, 1947), p. 42.
14. Justin, *Dialog. cum Tryphon* LXXVIII.
15. Origen, *Contra Celsum* I, 51.
16. Jerome, *Epist.* 58.
17. Ricciotti, *Vita di Gesù*, p. 276 n.
18. Luke 2:7.
19. Ricciotti, *Vita di Gesù*, p. 274.
20. Hab. 3:2.
21. Marius Lepin, "Storia di Gesù," in *Enciclopedia cristologica*, ed. Gustave Bardy and Alphonse Tricot (Alba: Edizioni Paoline, 1960), p. 268.
22. Protevangelium of James 18:2.
23. Gospel of Thomas, in Bonaccorsi, *Vangeli apocrifi*, p. 247.
24. Luke 2:8–20.
25. Léon-Dufour, *Les évangiles*, p. 92.
26. Oskar Simmel and Rudolf Staehlin, *La religione cristiana* (Milan: Feltrinelli, 1962), p. 24.
27. Soter, *La religione del Cristo* (Turin: Bocca, 1915), pp. 132–34.
28. Franz Altheim, *Il dio invitto: Cristianesimo e culti solari* (Milan: Feltrinelli, 1960), pp. 157 ff.
29. Arthur C. H Drews, *Die Christusmythe* (Jena: E. Diederichs, 1909); Emilio Bossi, *Gesù Cristo non è mai esistito* (MS in the National Library of Turin and Milan, 1924).
30. Domenico Pastorello, *Rivelazione* (Genoa: Edizioni Anteo, 1957).
31. Fracassini, *Il misticismo greco e il cristianesimo*, p. 10.
32. Ricciotti, *Storia d'Israele*, I, 148–49; Henri Daniel-Rops, *Il popolo della Bibbia* (Florence: Sansoni, 1962), p. 25; Karl Barth, *L'epistola ai Romani* (Milan: Feltrinelli, 1962), p. 48.
33. Philo, *De circumcisione* I, 2.

34. Giuseppe Bellino, *Gesù Cristo nelle SS. Scritture e nei SS. Padri e Dottori* (9 vols.; Turin: U.T.E.T., 1914–15), II, 802–3.
35. Petronius, *Fragmenta* 37; Juvenal, *Satirae* XIV, 99; 104; Persius, *Satirae* V, 184; Martial, *Satirae* VII, 82; Tacitus, *Historiae* V, 5; Celsus, *De medic.* VII, 25.
36. Luke 2:21.
37. Bossi, *Gesù non è mai esistito.*
38. Goguel, *Vie de Jésus*, p. 170.
39. Lev. 12:1–8.
40. Exod. 13:1–2, 11–16.
41. Ricciotti, *Vita di Gesù*, p. 282.
42. I Kings 5–6.
43. Felten, *Storia dei tempi*, I, 87.
44. Bernhard Stade, *Storia del popolo d'Israele* (Milan: Bocca, 1896), p. 93.
45. Lev. 1:14–17.
46. Lev. 5:8–9.
47. Luke 2:25.
48. Luke 2:36–38.
49. Luke 2:19.
50. Tacitus, *Hist.* V, 5.
51. Lagrange, *Le judaïsme*, p. 417.
52. Exod. 18.
53. Tacitus, *Hist.* V, 3.
54. Exod. 19:5; Num. 23:9–10; 24:7–8.
55. Gen. 13:14–17.
56. Gen. 22:15–18.
57. Gen. 12:1–3.
58. Gen. 15:18.
59. Exod. 30:22–25.
60. Gustaf H. Dalman, *Die Worte Jesu* (2 vols.; Leipzig: J. C. Hintichs, 1930), I, 237 ff.
61. Flavius Josephus, *The Jewish War*, VI, 5, 4.
62. *Ibid.*, I, 6–10; *Antiq.*, XIV, 3–4; 8; 14–16; Emil Schuerer, *Geschichte des Jüdischen Volkes im Zeitalter Jesu Christi* (3 vols.; Leipzig: J. C. Hinrichs, 1909), I, 216–29.
63. Josephus, *War*, I, 21, 13.
64. Ricciotti, *Storia d'Israele*, II, 377.

65. Josephus, *War*, I, 21, 1–12.
66. Macrobius, *Satur.* II, 4, 11.
67. Matt. 2:16–18.
68. Léon-Dufour, *op. cit.*, pp. 346–47.
69. Matt. 2:2.
70. Justin, *Hist.* XXXVII, 2; Suetonius, *Jul. Caes.* 88.
71. Num. 24:17.
72. Johannes Kepler, *De Jesu Christi Salvatoris nostri vero anno Natalitio* (Prague, 1606).
73. Keller, *La Bibbia aveva ragione*, pp. 311–13.
74. Matt. 2:1–12.
75. Ricciotti, *Vita di Gesù*, p. 287 n.
76. Édouard Schuré, *L'évolution divine du sphinx au Christ* (Paris: Perrin et Cie, 1913), p. 360.
77. Armenian Gospel of the Infancy 11.
78. Giovanni Papini, *Storia di Cristo* (2 vols.; Florence: Vallecchi, 1944), I, 11.

79. Matt. 2:1–18.
80. Bernard Weiss, *Lehrbuch der Einleitung in das Neue Testament* (Berlin: W. Nertz, 1889), p. 22.
81. Tommaso Peyrani, *Il Vecchio e il Nuovo Testamento* (Genoa: Edizioni Anteo, 1961), p. 17.
82. Luke 2:39.
83. Bossi, *Cristo nella storia*, pp. 64–65.
84. Lepin, "Storia di Gesù," p. 271.
85. Strauss, *Vie de Jésus*, I, 287–89.
86. Pseudo-Matthew 16.
87. Hophan, *Maria*, p. 183.
88. Matt. 2:19–23.
89. Ricciotti, *Storia d'Israele*, p. 413.
90. Josephus, *War*, I, 33; *Antiq.*, XVII, 7 ff.
91. Argentieri, *op. cit.*, p. 143, cites the reckoning of P. V. Neugebauer, *Astronomiche Chronologie* (Berlin, 1929).
92. Josephus, *War*, III, 4.

CHAPTER 4

THE UNKNOWN YEARS

1. Bonaccorsi (ed.), *Vangeli apocrifi*, pp. 111 ff., 203 ff.
2. Luke 2:40.
3. Luke 2:52.
4. Ralph Waldo Hynek, *L'aspetto fisico di Gesù* (Turin: L.I.C.E. di R. Berruti e C., 1952), p. 21. (See all Latin codices.)
5. Roberto Vella, *La vita di Gesù messa a confronto con Napoleone I, Garibaldi e col Papato* (Naples: Tipografia di L. Gargiulo, 1863).
6. Matt. 13:55.
7. Origen, *In Matth.* XII, 55; *In Lucam* VII.
8. Eusebius, *Historia Ecclesiastica* IV, 2.
9. Jerome, *Adv. Helvidium; In Matth.* II.

10. Lagrange, *L'évangile de Jésus Christ*, pp. 72–79.
11. Acts 12:17; Gal. 1:19; 2:12.
12. Drews, *Die Christusmythe*, p. 11.
13. Émile Le Camus, *La vie de Notre Seigneur Jésus Christ* (3 vols.; Paris: H. Oudin, 1901), I, 191.
14. Fouard, *Vita di N.S. Gesù Cristo*, I, 125; Albert Bessières, *Vita di Gesù* (Bologna: Cappelli, 1958), p. 73.
15. Ferdinand Prat, *Jésus Christ: Sa vie, sa doctrine, son oeuvre* (2 vols.; Paris: Beauchesne et Fils, 1933), I, 534 ff.
16. Vito Fornari, *Della vita di Gesù Cristo* (2 vols.; Turin: S.E.I., 1949), II, 126.
17. Reville, *Jésus de Nazareth*, I, 96.

18. Fouard, *op. cit.*, I, 243.
19. Aron, *Gli anni oscuri*, p. 77.
20. Adolf Deissmann, *Licht vom Osten* (Tübingen: J. C. B. Mohr, 1923), pp. 49–50; Gustaf Dalman, *Jesus-Jeschua: Die drei Sprachen Jesu* (Leipzig: J. C. Hintichs, 1922), p. 35.
21. Joseph Klausner, *Jésus de Nazareth: Son temps, sa vie, sa doctrine*, trans. from the Hebrew (Paris: Payot, 1933), p. 343.
22. Geremia Bonomelli, *Gesù Cristo Dio-Uomo* (Piacenza: Lorenzo Rinfreschi, 1914), pp. 90 ff., 229.
23. Decree of the Holy Office, June 7, 1918.
24. Leone Tondelli, "Gesù," in *Enciclopedia Treccani*, p. 870.
25. Carlo Falconi, *L'umanità e il Cristo* (Milan: Comunità, 1946), pp. 236–37.
26. Léonce de Grandmaison, *Jésus Christ: Sa personne, son message, ses preuves* (2 vols.; Paris: Bloud & Gay, 1928), II, 206; Loofs, *What Is the Truth About Jesus?*, p. 222.
27. Yogi Ramacharaka, *Cristianesimo mistico* (Turin: Bocca, 1924), pp. 71–72.
28. Luke 2:42.
29. Josephus, *War*, VI, 9, 3.
30. In ancient times, it was common for both the lunar and the solar years to begin in the spring. Since post-Biblical times, however, the Jewish calendar has begun its year in the autumn with the month of Tishri (mid-September to mid-October).
31. Exod. 12:1–40.
32. Wilhelm Schmidt, *Storia comparata delle religioni* (Brescia: Morcelliana, 1949), pp. 79–81.
33. Reinach, *Orpheus*, p. 249.
34. Richard Lewinsohn, *Gli animali nella storia della civiltà* (Turin: Einaudi, 1956), pp. 110–13.
35. Karl T. Keim, *Geschichte Jesu von Nazara* (3 vols.; Zurich: Drell, 1867–73), III, 256.
36. Felten, *Storia dei tempi*, II, 247–49.
37. Exod. 12:16.
38. Luke 2:43.
39. Luke 2:44.
40. Aron, *op. cit.*, p. 90.
41. Paulus, *Das Leben Jesu*, I, 279.
42. Luke 2:47.
43. Ricciotti, *Vita di Gesù*, p. 301.
44. Goguel, *Vie de Jésus*, p. 309.
45. Bernhard Weiss, *Das Leben Jesu* (2 vols.; Stuttgart: J. C. Cotta, 1902), I, 279.
46. Luke 2:48.
47. Luke 2:49.
48. Ricciotti, *Vita di Gesù*, p. 302.
49. Paulus, *Das Leben Jesu*, I, 279.
50. Guignebert, *Gesù*, p. 316.
51. Luke 2:51.
52. Josiah Royce, *Il problema del cristianesimo* (2 vols.; Florence: Vallecchi, 1924), II, 216.
53. Edmond L. Stapfer, *Jésus Christ avant son ministère* (Paris: Fischbacher, 1896), p. 58.
54. Martinetti, *Gesù Cristo e il cristianesimo*, I, 38.
55. Meyer, *Ursprung und Anfänge*, I, 290–91.
56. Grandmaison, *op. cit.*, I, 288.
57. Daniel-Rops, *Gesù e il suo tempo*, p. 166.
58. Finegan, *Light from the Ancient Past*, pp. 217–18.
59. Schuerer, *Geschichte des Jüdischen Volkes*, II, 197.
60. Josephus, *Antiq.*, XVIII, 4.
61. Klausner, *op. cit.*, pp. 205, 226.
62. Keller, *La Bibbia aveva ragione*, pp. 322–23.
63. Josephus, *Antiq.*, XVIII, 23; *War*, VII, 8, 1. The Greek χαναναῖος (cananaios) or χαναανῖτις (cananitis) derives from "Canaan" (Kan'an), the name of the country, and means an inhabitant of that country. But in Greek there

was also καναναῖος, deriving from
the Aramaic qan'ān. This word
had the same significance as the
Greek ζηλωτής (zēlōtēs), meaning
"zealot." Hence, the two meanings have often been carelessly
confused.

64. Oscar Cullmann, *Dio e Cesare: Il
problema dello Stato nella Chiesa
primitiva* (Milan: Comunità,
1957), p. 19.

65. Adolfo Omodeo, *Gesù il Nazoreo*
(Venice: La Nuova Italia, 1927),
p. 31.

66. Cullmann, *Dio e Cesare*, p. 18,
and *passim*.

67. Philo, *De vita contempl.* II, 445–
75; Epiphanius, *Adv. haer.* 120.

68. Pliny, *Naturalis Historia* V, 17, 4.

69. Strauss, *Vie de Jésus*, I, 336; Adolf
von Harnack, *L'essenza del cristianesimo* (Turin: Bocca, 1923), p.
36; Guignebert, *Gesù*, pp. 167–68.

70. Magri, *Gesù Cristo*, p. 168.

71. Klausner, *op. cit.*, pp. 310 ff.

72. Günter Lanczkowski, *Scritture*

Sacre (Florence: Sansoni, 1960),
pp. 51 ff.

73. Millar Burrows, *The Dead Sea
Scrolls* (New York: Viking Press,
1955), p. 52. Jòsef T. Milik, *Dieci
anni di scoperte nel deserto di
Giuda* (Turin: Marietti, 1957),
passim.

74. Edmund Wilson, *The Scrolls from
the Dead Sea* (Cleveland and New
York: Meridian Books, 1964), p.
35. Jean Danielou, *Les manuscrits
de la Mer Morte, et les origines
du Christianisme* (Paris: Editions
de l'Orante, 1957), p. 18.

75. Josephus, *War*, II, 2–13.

76. Philo, *De vita contempl., loc. cit.*

77. Albert Schweitzer, *Das Christentum   und   die   Weltreligionen*
(Munich: C. H. Beck'sche Verlag, 1924), pp. 38–40.

78. Milik, *op. cit.*, p. 76.

79. Burrows, *op. cit.*, pp. 130 ff., 301.

80. John M. Allegro, *The Dead Sea
Scrolls* (Baltimore: Penguin Books,
1956).

CHAPTER 5

THE INITIATION

1. Friedrich Heiler, *Storia delle religioni* (2 vols.; Florence: Sansoni, 1962), II, 101.

2. Danielou, *Les manuscrits de la
Mer Morte*, p. 18.

3. Luke 3:1.

4. Bapst, *La vie historique*, I, 99.

5. Paulus, *Das Leben Jesu*, I, 294.

6. Hammer, *Quando Gesù viveva*,
p. 110.

7. Finegan, *Light from the Ancient
Past*, p. 219.

8. Josephus, *Antiq.*, XVIII, 3, 1;
War, II, 9, 2–3.

9. Drews, *Die Christusmythe*, pp.
83 ff.

10. Josephus, *Antiq.*, XVIII, 5, 2.

11. Zech. 13:4; II Kings 1:8.

12. Dalman, *Orte und Wege Jesu*,
I, 92.

13. Bauer, *Das Leben Jesu*, p. 101.

14. John 1:28.

15. Daniel-Rops, *Gesù e il suo tempo*,
p. 81.

16. Burrows, *The Dead Sea Scrolls*,
p. 300.

17. Matt. 3:10; Luke 3:9.

18. Matt. 3:9*b*; Luke 3:8*b*.

19. Dalman, *Die Worte Jesu*, I, 75.

20. II Esd. 7:50; Jth. 9:12; and other
prophetic passages in apocryphal
books.

21. Mark 1:4; Matt. 3:8, 11; Luke
3:8*a*.

22. Papini, *Storia di Cristo*, I, 87.
23. Ernesto Buonaiuti, *Pietre miliari della storia del cristianesimo* (Modena: Guanda, 1935), p. 226.
24. Mark 1:7; Luke 3:16*a*.
25. Matt. 3:11–12; Luke 3:16*b*–17 (cf. Mal. 3:2).
26. Daniel-Rops, *Storia della Chiesa*, I, 202.
27. Fracassini, *Il misticismo greco*, p. 21.
28. John 4:2.
29. Mark 16:16; Matt. 28:19.
30. Rom. 6:3–11. See also Heinrich Schlier, *Il tempo della Chiesa* (Bologna: Il Mulino, 1965), p. 86.
31. Michael Gough, *The Early Christians* (New York: Frederick A. Praeger, 1961), pp. 30–31.
32. Bellino, *Gesù Cristo nelle SS. Scritture*, III, 212.
33. Tertullian, *De baptismo* I, 4, 9.
34. Meynier, *Storia del christianesimo*, p. 95.
35. Giovanni Luzzi, *Nuovo Testamento: Le Epistole e l'Apocalisse* (Florence: Fides et Amor, 1930), p. 73.
36. Roland H. Bainton, *La riforma protestante* (Turin: Einaudi, 1958), p. 140.
37. Klee, *Storia dei dogmi*, II, 99.
38. Joachim Jeremias, *Unbekannte Jesusworte* (Gütersloh: Gütersloher Verlagshaus, 1963), p. 47.
39. Günther Bornkamm, *Jesus von Nazareth* (Stuttgart: W. Kohlammer, 1957), p. 43.
40. Strauss, *Vie de Jésus*, I, 348–49.
41. Hans J. Schoeps, *I grandi fondatori di religioni* (Florence: Sansoni, 1961), p. 66.
42. Charles H. Dodd, *The Interpretation of the Fourth Gospel* (Cambridge and New York: Cambridge University Press, 1960), pp. 120–22.
43. Stapfer, *Jésus Christ avant son ministère*, p. 195.
44. Alfred F. Loisy, *Les évangiles synoptiques* (2 vols.; Ceffonds: Chez l'Auteur, 1907), I, 206.
45. Klee, *op. cit.*, I, 40.
46. Ps. 2:7.
47. Strauss, *op. cit.*, I, 373.
48. Paulus, *Das Leben Jesu*, I, 373.
49. Reville, *Jésus de Nazareth*, II, 4 n. 2.
50. Mark 1:12–13; Matt. 4:1–2; Luke 4:1–2.
51. Tacitus, *Hist.* V, 6.
52. Keller, *La Bibbia aveva ragione*, pp. 71–72.
53. Mark 1:13 ("*cum bestiis*").
54. Pliny, *Natur. Hist.* VII, 65.
55. Alfano, *Vita di Gesù*, p. 77 n. 1.
56. Lev. 16:29; Num. 29:7.
57. Le Camus, *Vie de Jésus Christ*, I, 505.
58. Matt. 4:3; Luke 4:3.
59. Matt. 4:3–11; Luke 4:3–13.
60. Fouard, *Vita di N. S. Gesù Cristo*, I, 162; Le Camus, *Vie de Jésus Christ*, I, 234; Magri, *Gesù Cristo*, p. 264; and others.
61. Strauss, *op. cit.*, I, 437.
62. Job 1–2; Num. 22:22.
63. Simmel and Staehlin, *La religione cristiana*, p. 20.
64. Schmidt, *Storia comparata delle religioni*, p. 16.
65. Bertrand Russell, *Why I Am Not a Christian* (New York: Simon and Schuster, 1957), pp. 29–30.
66. Guignebert, *Gesù*, p. 210.
67. Venturini, *Natürliche Geschichte*, p. 440.
68. Alexander B. Griswold, Chewon Kim, and Peter N. Pott, *Burma, Korea, Tibet* (Baden-Baden: Holle Verlag, 1963), p. 204.
69. Paulus, *Das Leben Jesu*, I, 377 ff.
70. O. Holtzmann, *War Jesus Ekstatiker?* (Tübingen, 1908), cited in Guignebert, *Gesù*, p. 207.
71. Charles Binet-Sanglé, *La folie de Jésus* (4 vols.; Paris: A. Maloine, 1908, 1910, 1912, 1915), II, 335.

72. B. Weiss, *Das Leben Jesu*, I, 313.
73. Rudolf Bultmann, *Theologie des Neuen Testaments* (3 vols.; Tübingen: J. C. B. Mohr, 1948–54), III, 118.
74. Dalman, *Orte und Wege Jesu*, I, 98 ff.
75. Josephus, *Antiq.*, XVIII, 7, 2.
76. *Ibid.*, XVIII, 109; *War*, I, 28, 2.
77. Mark 6:17–18; Matt. 14:1–4; Luke 3:19–20.
78. Mark 1:14–15; Matt. 4:12, 17; Luke 4:14–15; John 4:43–44.
79. Isa. 52:7.
80. Mark 6:1–6; Matt. 13:54–58; Luke 4:16–30.
81. Aron, *Gli anni oscuri*, pp. 110–15.
82. Isa. 62:1–2.
83. Luke 4:21.
84. Thomas Deman, *Socrate e Gesù* (Florence: Editrice Libraria Fiorentina, 1950), p. 81.
85. Mark 6:3.
86. Jean Doresse, *Vangelo secondo Tommaso* (Milan: Il Saggiatore, 1945), n. 36. (See note 20 to chapter 8, below.)
87. Luke 4:23–27.
88. Loisy, *Les évangiles synoptiques*, I, 836.
89. Luke 4:30.
90. Mark 6:6; Matt. 13:58.

CHAPTER 6
JESUS AS THAUMATURGE

1. John 2:12.
2. Mark 1:16–20; Matt. 4:18–22.
3. Otto Hophan, *Gli Apostoli* (Turin: Marietti, 1950), p. 20.
4. Cullmann, *Dio e Cesare*, p. 25.
5. John 1:25–41.
6. Loisy, *Les évangiles synoptiques*, I, 439–45.
7. Strauss, *Vie de Jésus*, I, 563–64.
8. Mark 1:17; Matt. 4:19.
9. Mark 1:21; Matt. 4:13; Luke 4:31.
10. John 1:44.
11. John 1:43–51.
12. Mark 1:22; Matt. 7:29; Luke 4:32.
13. Klausner, *Jésus de Nazareth*, p. 386.
14. Mark 1:21–28; Luke 4:31–37.
15. Loisy, *Les évangiles synoptiques*, I, 449.
16. Mark 1:25 ("*comminatus est*"); Luke 4:35 ("*increpavit*").
17. Schuerer, *Geschichte des Jüdischen Volkes*, III, 414–20.
18. Mark 1:26; Luke 4:35b.
19. Mark 1:23, 26, 27; Matt. 10:1; Luke 4:33, 36.
20. Mark 1:34, 39; 3:15, 22; Matt. 8:31; Luke 4:33, 35, 41.
21. Rituale Romano, tit. XI, ch. 1–3.
22. Mark 1:32; Matt. 8:16; Luke 4:40.
23. George F. Moore, *Storia delle religioni* (2 vols.; Bari: Laterza, 1922), II, 49.
24. Simmel and Staehlin, *La religione cristiana*, p. 332.
25. Raffaele Pettazzoni, "La confessione dei peccati nell' antichità classica," in *Saggi di storia delle religioni e di mitologia* (Rome: Edizioni Athenaeum, 1946), pp. 125 ff. (The essay dates from 1937.)
26. Ricciotti, *Vita di Gesù*, p. 361.
27. Pliny, *Natur. Hist.* XXVIII, 7.
28. Julian S. Huxley, *Man Stands Alone* (New York: Harper & Bros., 1941).
29. James 5:14–15.
30. Simmel and Staehlin, *op. cit.*, p. 332.
31. Mark 7:36; 8:26; Matt. 9:30.
32. Mark 7:31–37; 8:22–26.

33. John 9:1–38.
34. Mark 1:34.
35. Meyer, *Ursprunge und Anfänge*, II, 270.
36. Luke 4:40*b*.
37. Mark 1:31; Matt. 8:15; 9:25; etc.
38. Bellino, *Gesù Cristo nelle SS. Scritture*, III, 395; IV, 229.
39. Mark 5:25–34; Matt. 9:20–22; Luke 8:43–48.
40. Shabbath 110*a*, cited in Ricciotti, *Vita di Gesù*, p. 414.
41. Luke 8:44.
42. Schuerer, *op. cit.*, II, 484.
43. Mark 5:30.
44. Mark 5:21–24, 35–43; Matt. 9:18–19, 23–26; Luke 8:40–42, 49–56.
45. Felten, *Storia dei tempi*, II, 206.
46. Mark 5:43.
47. Holtzmann, *Lehrbuch*, II, 136.
48. Strauss, *op. cit.*, II, 149.
49. Loisy, *Les évangiles synoptiques*, I, 456.
50. Luke 4:43; Mark 1:38.
51. Mark 3:7–12.
52. Lev. 13–14.
53. Mark 1:40–45; Matt. 8:1–4; Luke 5:12–16.
54. Mark 1:40, 41, 42; Matt. 8:2, 3; Luke 5:12, 13, 14.
55. B. Weiss, *Das Leben Jesu*, II, 177.
56. Paulus, *Das Leben Jesu*, I, 698.
57. Mark 1:43–44; Matt. 8:4; Luke 5:14.
58. Mark 1:45.
59. Mark 2:1–12; Matt. 9:1–8; Luke 5:17–26.

60. Mark 2:5; Matt. 9:4; Luke 5:20.
61. Jean Guitton, *Le problème de Jésus*, Vols. VI and VII of *La pensée moderne et le Catholicisme* (8 vols.; Paris: Editions Montaigne, 1950–55), p. 75.
62. Guignebert, *Gesù*, p. 334.
63. Reinach, *Orpheus*, p. 308; Renan, *Vie de Jésus*, p. 89; Giuseppe Miegge, *Per una fede* (Milan: Comunità, 1956), p. 91; Primo Vannutelli, *Il figlio dell'uomo: Studio sugli Evangeli* (Rome: Bardi, 1928), p. 45.
64. Dalman, *Die Worte Jesu*, I, 191–220, discusses the question thoroughly.
65. Grandmaison, *Jésus Christ*, I, 316; Leone Tondelli, *Gesù Cristo: Studio su le fonti, il pensiero e l'opera* (Turin: S.E.I., 1936), pp. 241–42; L. Algisi, "Il Vangelo di S. Marco," in Luigi Moraldi (ed.), *Introduzione alla Bibbia* (4 vols.; Turin: Marietti, 1959), II, 143.
66. Alphonse Robert and André Feuillet, *Introduction à la Bible* (2 vols.; Paris: Desclée et Cie, 1959), II, 215; Oscar Cullmann, *Cristo e il tempo* (Bologna: Il Mulino, 1965), p. 135.
67. Joseph Bonsirven, *Le judaïsme palestinien au temps de Jésus Christ* (2 vols.; Paris: Beauchesne et ses Fils, 1934–35), II, 212.

CHAPTER 7

THE MIRACLES

1. Matt. 8:5–13; Luke 7:1–10; John 4:46–54.
2. Matt. 8:5; Luke 7:2.
3. John 4:46*b*.
4. Luke 7:11–16.
5. I Kings 17:17–24.
6. Matt. 8:12.

7. Mark 4:35–40; Matt. 8:23–27; Luke 8:22–25.
8. Mark 4:38.
9. Matt. 8:25.
10. Luke 8:24.
11. Martinetti, *Gesù Cristo*, I, 114.
12. Paulus, *Des Leben Jesu*, I, 468.

13. Strauss, *Vie de Jésus*, II, 188.
14. Saintyves, *Le discernement du miracle*, p. 58.
15. *Analecta Bollandiana* (1908), XXVII, 85, cited in Saintyves, *op. cit.*
16. Rudolf Bultmann, *Die Geschichte der synoptischen Tradition* (Göttingen: Wandenhoeck & Ruprecht, 1958), pp. 135–36.
17. Mark 5:1; Luke 8:26 (Revised Standard Version).
18. Matt. 8:28 (Revised Standard Version).
19. Mark 5:1–20; Matt. 8:28–34; Luke 8:26–39.
20. Bossi, *Gesù Cristo*, p. 20 n. 2.
21. Archibald Robertson, *Le origini del cristianesimo* (Florence: Parenti, 1960), p. 144; Klausner, *Jésus de Nazareth*, p. 427 n. 2.
22. Couchoud, *Il mistero di Gesù*, p. 146.
23. Mark 9:14–29; Matt. 17:14–20; Luke 9:37–44a.
24. Mark 9:29; Matt. 17:20.
25. Willam, *La vita di Gesù*, p. 93.
26. John 2:1–11.
27. Irenaeus, *Adversus haereses* III, 16, 7.
28. John Chrysostom, *In Ioann. homil.* 21, 2.
29. Ricciotti, *Vita di Gesù*, p. 329.
30. Strauss, *op. cit.*, II, 237.
31. Oscar Rebaudi, *La vida de Jesús Dictada por el Mismo* (Buenos Aires: J. Roldán y Cia., 1948), p. 105.
32. Hammer, *Quando Gesù viveva*, p. 108.
33. Venturini, *Natürliche Geschichte*, II, 61.
34. Dodd, *Fourth Gospel*, p. 297.
35. Emilio Radius, *Vita di Cristo per gli uomini d'oggi* (Milan: Rizzoli, 1958), p. 63.
36. Louis Bouyer, *Il quarto Vangelo* (Turin: Borla, 1964), p. 88.
37. Exod. 17:1–7; Num. 20:1–11.
38. I Kings 17:10–16; II Kings 4:1–6.
39. Bultmann, *Synoptischen Tradition*, p. 374.
40. Gaetano Negri, *La crisi religiosa* (Milan: Dumolard, 1878), pp. 77–83.
41. Augustine, *De civitate Dei* XXI, 8; see also Albertus Magnus, *Summa* II, 8, 31; Thomas Aquinas, *Summa Theol.* I, q. 4, a. 8.
42. Joachim Jeremias, *Die Gleichnisse Jesu* (Zurich: Zwingli Verlag, 1952), p. 130.
43. Rudolf Bultmann, "Neues Testament und Mythologie," in *Kerygma und Mythos*, ed. Hans W. Bartsch, (Hamburg: Reich & Heidrich, 1951), I, 17.
44. Guitton, *Le problème de Jésus*, VI, 45.
45. Benedetto Croce, *Filosofia della pratica, economia, e estetica* (Bari, 1909), p. 129.
46. George Santayana, *L'idea di Cristo nei Vangeli* (Milan: Comunità, 1949), p. 116.
47. Thomas Aquinas, *Summa Theol.* III, q. 43, a. 1.
48. Tacitus, *Hist.* IV, 81.
49. Adolf von Harnack, *Missione e propagazione del cristianesimo nei primi tre secoli* (Milan: Bocca, 1906), p. 80.
50. Martinetti, *op. cit.*, II, 200.
51. Le Camus, *Vie de Jésus Christ*, I, 327.
52. *Constitutio de fide*, April 24, 1870, c. 4.
53. Saintyves, *op. cit.*, p. 73.
54. Harnack, *L'essenza del cristianesimo*, pp. 24–33.
55. Ludwig A. Feuerbach, *L'essenza del cristianesimo* (Milan: Universale Economica, 1952), p. 115. n. 1.
56. Harnack, *L'essenza del cristianesimo*, p. 32.
57. Adam, *Gesù il Cristo*, p. 156.

58. Bultmann, *Synoptischen Tradition*, pp. 29–38.

59. Léon-Dufour, *Les évangiles*, p. 111.

CHAPTER 8

THE LAW AND THE PHARISEES

1. Tacitus, *Annales* IV, 6; Cicero, *De prov. consular*. VI.
2. Mark 2:13; Matt. 9:9; Luke 5:27–28.
3. Klausner, *Jésus de Nazareth*, pp. 400–401.
4. Willam, *La vita di Gesù*, p. 183.
5. Mark 2:15–16; Matt. 9:10–11; Luke 5:29–30; Thomas 108.
6. Daniel-Rops, *Gesù e il suo tempo*, p. 170.
7. Omodeo, *Gesù e le origini*, p. 95; Grandmaison, *Jésus Christ*, II, 10–11.
8. Hos. 6:6.
9. Adolf Julicher, *Die Gleichnisreden Jesu* (2 vols.; Tübingen: J. C. B. Mohr, 1910), II, 178.
10. Oscar Cullmann, *Christologie du Nouveau Testament* (Neuchâtel: Delachaux et Niestlé, 1958), p. 56.
11. Matt. 9:16–17; Luke 5:36–39; Thomas 52*b*.
12. Matt. 11:4–5; Luke 7:22.
13. Isa. 35:5–6.
14. Matt. 11:7–10; Luke 7:24–27; Thomas 82.
15. Mal. 3:1.
16. Matt. 11:11; Luke 7:28.
17. Stapfer, *Jésus Christ avant son ministère*, p. 156.
18. Giuseppe Petrelli, *Il Figliuolo dell'Uomo* (Torre Pellice: Tipografia Subalpina, 1957), p. 32.
19. Luke 7:29–30.
20. Thomas 51. Direct quotations of the Gospel of Thomas are from Jean Doresse, *The Secret Books of the Egyptian Gnostics*, trans. Philip Mairet (New York: Viking Press, 1960), Appendix II: "The Gospel According to Thomas, or The Secret Words of Jesus," trans. Rev. Leonard Johnston in collaboration with the author. Citations of Doresse's critical study, however, are from the Italian edition of his work: *Vangelo secondo Tommaso* (Milan: Il Saggiatore, 1945).
21. Doresse, *Vangelo secondo Tommaso*, p. 155.
22. Luke 7:31–35.
23. Luke 7:36–50.
24. Le Camus, *Vie de Jésus Christ*, II, 80; Marco Marchesan, *Mentalità e carattere di Gesù* (Milan: Istituto di Indagini Psicologiche, 1957), pp. 8–15.
25. Robert T. Herford, *The Pharisees* (Boston: Beacon Press, 1962).
26. Grandmaison, *op. cit.*, I, 256.
27. Josephus, *War*, II, 12.
28. Grandmaison, *op. cit.*, I, 253.
29. *Ibid.*
30. Joseph Salvador, *Jésus Christ et sa doctrine* (Paris: A. Guyot et Scribe, 1838), p. 356.
31. Aron, *Gli anni oscuri*, p. 151.
32. Marcel Simon, *I primi cristiani* (Milan: Garzanti, 1958), p. 13.
33. Ambrogio Donini, *Lineamenti di storia delle religioni* (Rome: Editori Riuniti, 1959), p. 158.
34. Gen. 2:2–3.
35. Exod. 16:23.
36. Exod. 20:10.
37. This law is also set forth in Exod. 23:12.
38. Exod. 31:15.
39. Num. 15:32–36.
40. Ovid, *Ars. amat.* I, 416; Seneca, *De superst. fragm.* XII, 41; Ju-

venal, *Sat.* XIV, 105; Tacitus, *Hist.* V, 4.

41. Felten, *Storia dei tempi,* II, 94.
42. Daniel-Rops *Storia della Chiesa,* I, 23.
43. Mark 2:23–28; Matt. 12:1–8; Luke 6:1–5.
44. I Sam. 21:1–6.
45. Matt. 12:3; Luke 6:3.
46. Mark 2:25.
47. Bonaccorsi (ed.), *Vangeli apocrifi,* p. 4.
48. Mark 3:1–6; Matt. 12:9–13; Luke 6:6–11.
49. Venturini, *Natürliche Geschichte,* II, 421.
50. Matt. 12:11–12.
51. Holtzmann, *Lehrbuch,* II, 241.
52. Luke 13:10–17.
53. Luke 14:1–6.
54. Luke 14:5.
55. John 5:1–16.
56. Léon-Dufour, *Les évangiles,* p. 111.

57. Gen. 32:24–32.
58. Donini, *op. cit.,* p. 54.
59. Jean H. Janssens, *Hermeneutica sacra in omnes libros Veteris ac Novi Foederis* (Turin: Officina Libraria Marietti, 1892), p. 45.
60. Acts 10:28.
61. Acts 11:8.
62. I Cor. 10:25–31; Gal. 2:11–16.
63. Mark 7:1–23; Matt. 15:1–20.
64. Isa. 29:13.
65. See also Doresse, *op. cit.,* n.40.
66. Manise, "Maria Santissima," p. 983.
67. Matt. 23:1–39.
68. Mark 12:38–40; Luke 11:37–54; 13:34–35; 20:45–47; Thomas 44, 93, 106.
69. Thomas 106.
70. Doresse, *op. cit.,* p. 178.
71. Luke 11:45.
72. Matt. 23:27–35.
73. II Chron. 24:20–22.

Chapter 9
JESUS AND THE APOSTLES

1. Alfred Wikenhauser, *Einleitung in das Neues Testament* (Freiburg: Herder Verlag, 1953), p. 133; Francis C. Burkitt, *Il Vangelo e la sua storia* (Turin: Bocca, 1909), p. 109.
2. Mark 6:34; Matt. 9:35–38.
3. Matt. 9:37; Luke 10:2; Thomas 77.
4. Loisy, *Le origini del christianesimo,* p. 85 n. 15; Meyer, *Ursprung und Anfänge,* I, 278–79.
5. Robert and Feuillet, *Introduction à la Bible,* I, 802.
6. Harnack, *Missione e propagazione,* p. 244.
7. Rom. 1:1; I Cor. 3:5b; 3:9.
8. Friedrich Steudel, *Hat Jesus Gelebt?* (Frankfurt: Neuer Frankfurter Verlag, 1910).

9. John 1:40.
10. Jules Lebreton and Jacques Zeiller, *L'église primitive,* Vol. I of *Histoire de l'église* (24 vols.; Paris: Bloud & Gay, 1948), pp. 228–32.
11. Matt. 16:18–19.
12. Salvatore Garofalo, *Dall' evangelo agli evangeli* (Rome: Studium, 1953), pp. 62–63.
13. Hophan, *Gli Apostoli,* p. 44.
14. *Ibid.,* p. 77.
15. *Ibid.,* p. 89.
16. Acts 4:13.
17. Deissmann, *Licht vom Osten,* p. 211.
18. Karl Adam, "La coscienza del Cristo in S. Giovanni," *Humanitas,* No. 7 (July, 1959), p. 490.
19. Wikenhauser, *op. cit.,* p. 207.

20. Garofalo, *op. cit.*, p. 108.
21. Acts 12:2.
22. Ernest Renan, *Les Apôtres* (Paris: Michel Lévy Frères, 1860), p. 102.
23. John 1:43–44.
24. Robert McL. Wilson, *The Gospel of Philip* (London: Mowbray and Co., 1962), preface.
25. Clement of Alexandria, *Paedol.* I, 1, 11.
26. Hophan, *Gli Apostoli*, p. 144.
27. Algisi, *Il Vangelo di S. Marco*, p. 95.
28. John 11:16.
29. John 20:24–29.
30. Doresse, *Vangelo secondo Tommaso.* (See note 20, chapter 8, above.)
31. Mark 6:3; Matt. 13:55.
32. Josephus, *Antiq.*, XX, 9, 1.
33. Eusebius, *Hist. ecclesiastica* II, 3.
34. Pierre Batiffol, *Il valore storico del Vangelo* (Florence: Editrice Libraria Fiorentina, 1913), p. 58.
35. Cullmann, *Dio e Cesare*, p. 24.
36. Dalman, *Orte und Wege Jesu*, p. 351 n. 3.
37. François Mauriac, *Vita di Gesù* (Milan: Mondadori, 1950), p. 37.
38. Mark 6:7–13; Matt. 10:5–15; Luke 9:1–6.
39. Luke 10:1–11, 17–20.
40. Holtzmann, *Lehrbuch*, II, 358.
41. Matt. 10:15; Luke 10:12.
42. Matt. 10:5–6.
43. Matt. 7:6; Thomas 97.
44. Gustave Bardy, *La conversion au christianisme durant les premiers Siècles* (Paris: Aubier, 1948), p. 9.
45. Acts 6:5.
46. Acts 6:1.
47. Simon, *I primi cristiani*, p. 38.
48. Renan, *Les Apôtres*, p. 109; Lebreton and Zeiller, *op. cit.*, p. 139.
49. Acts 7:1–53 (the Biblical quotation is Isa. 66:1).
50. Acts 11:19.
51. Exod. 25:9.
52. Phil. 3:5.
53. Johannes Weiss, *Das Urchristentum* (Göttingen: Vandenhoeck & Ruprecht, 1917), p. 59.
54. Epiphanius, *Adv. haer.* XXX, 16; 25.
55. J. Weiss, *Das Urchristentum*, pp. 309 ff.
56. Simon, *op. cit.*, p. 49.
57. Renan, *Les Apôtres*, p. 170.
58. Ricciotti, *Paolo Apostolo* (Rome: Tipografia Poliglotta Vaticana, 1946), p. 224.
59. Phil. 3:8.
60. II Cor. 6:1.
61. Acts 9:3 ff., 9; II Cor. 12:1–4.
62. Gal. 1:18.
63. Gal. 1:18–19.
64. Acts 15:1–35.
65. Gal. 2:1–10.
66. Gal. 2:7–8.
67. John G. Machen, *The Origin of Paul's Religion* (New York: The Macmillan Co., 1921), p. 173.
68. II Cor. 10:1, 10; Gal. 2:17–21; 3:1; etc.
69. Acts 21:17–25.
70. André Jean Festugière and Pierre Fabre, *Il mondo greco-romano al tempo di Gesù Cristo* (Turin: S.E.I., 1955), p. 43.
71. Karl Bihlmeyer and Hermann Techle, *Storia della Chiesa* (4 vols.; Brescia: Morcelliana, 1955), I, 151.
72. Mark 6:30; Luke 9:10; 10:17.
73. Luke 10:19–21.
74. Acts 1:21.
75. Luke 8:1–3.
76. R. Wilson, *op. cit.*, p. 43.
77. Acts 9:36–39; 16:14–15; Rom. 15:1*b*; 16:6; I Cor. 16:15; II Tim. 4:19, 21.
78. I Cor. 9:5.
79. I Cor. 14:34–35.
80. I Tim. 2:12.
81. I Tim. 5:11–13.
82. I Cor. 11:6–10.

83. John C. V. Durell, *La Chiesa storica* (Turin: Bocca, 1910), p. 5.
84. Harnack, *Missione e propagazione*, p. 313.
85. Igino Giordani, *Il messaggio sociale degli Apostoli* (Turin: S.E.I., 1937), p. 55.
86. Matt. 12:46–50.
87. Mark 3:20–21, 31–35. Where the King James version of Mark 3:21 reads: "his friends," the original Greek text has: οἱ παρ᾽ αὐτου (*hoi par autou*), meaning "his relatives," "his mother and brothers."
88. Luke 14:26.
89. Isa. 53:2*b*–3.
90. Justin, *Dialog. cum Tryph.* 88.
91. Irenaeus, *Adv. haer.* IV, 33, 12.
92. Clement of Alexandria, *Paedol.* III, 1, 3.
93. Origen, *Contra Celsum* VI, 75.
94. Tertullian, *De carne Chr.* IX.
95. Bauer, *Das Leben Jesu*, pp. 311 ff.
96. Ps. 45:2.
97. Daniel-Rops, *Gesù e il suo tempo*, p. 317.
98. *Ibid.*, p. 318.
99. Giovanni Rosadi, *Il processo di Gesù* (Florence: Sansoni, 1903), p. 99 n.
100. Bardy and Tricot, *Enciclopedia cristologica*, p. 899.
101. *Ibid.*
102. Jean Guitton, *Jésus* (Paris: Bernard Grasset, 1961).
103. Giovanni Judica Cordiglia, *L'uomo della sindone è il Cristo?* (Milan: R. Ghirlando, 1941).
104. Hynek, *L'aspetto fisico di Gesù*, p. 67.
105. Binet-Sanglé, *La folie de Jésus*.
106. *Ibid.*, I, 156–58; IV, 451; *et passim*.
107. *Ibid.*, I, 190 ff; IV, 451.
108. *Ibid.*, II, 124–84.
109. *Ibid.*, I, 267 ff.
110. *Ibid.*, I, 267; III, 266; IV, 451.
111. *Ibid.*, III, 177.
112. *Ibid.*, II, 335.
113. *Ibid.*, I, 290.
114. J. Soury, *Jésus et les évangiles* (Paris, 1878).
115. Binet-Sanglé, *op. cit.*, I, 256 ff.
116. Strauss, *Vie de Jésus*, I, 310, 317.
117. Renan, *Vie de Jésus*, p. 331.
118. Meyer, *op. cit.*, II, 216; Albert Schweitzer, *Geschichte der Leben-Jesu-Forschung* (Tübingen: J. C.-B. Mohr, 1913), p. 331.
119. Marchesan, *Mentalità e Carattere di Gesù*.
120. *Ibid.*, pp. 115–18.

CHAPTER 10

THE GOOD TIDINGS

1. Omodeo, *Gesù e le origini*, p. 133.
2. Matt. 5:1–12; Luke 6:20–31; Thomas 54, 59, 63, 73.
3. Luke 6:24–26.
4. Pss. 9:18; 10:18; 12:5; 22:26; 24:4–5; 35:10; 37:11; 41:1–3; 68:5; 113:7; 116:6; 140:12; 146:7, etc.; Prov. 11:4, 28; 14:21, 31; 15:25; 17:5; 19:17; 28:27; 29:23, etc.
5. Salvador, *Jésus Christ*, pp. 357, 401 ff.; Klausner, *Jésus de Nazareth*, p. 527; Aron, *Gli anni oscuri*, pp. 237–38.
6. Eduard Zeller, *Vorträge und Abhandlungen Geschichtlichen Inhalts das Urchristentum* (Leipzig: Fues Verlag, 1875).
7. Paolo Orano, *Cristo e Quirino* (Turin: Bocca, 1908).
8. Martinetti, *Gesù Cristo*, I, 131; Omodeo, *Gesù il Nazoreo*, p. 370.
9. Thomas n. 22.

10. Ferdinand C. Baur, *Lehrbuch der christlichen Dogmengeschichte* (Leipzig: Fues Verlag, 1867), p. 189.
11. Cullmann, *Cristo e il tempo*, p. 59.
12. I Thess. 4:16–17.
13. Dalman, *Die Worte Jesu*, I, 75 ff.
14. Robert and Feuillet, *Introduction à la Bible*, I, 772.
15. Orano, *op. cit.*, pp. 192–94.
16. Fornari, *Della Vita di Gesù Cristo*, II, 258.
17. Epiphanius, *Adv. haer.* XXX, 17.
18. Grandmaison, *Jésus Christ*, I, 371 ff.
19. Jeremias, *Die Gleichnisse Jesu*, p. 172.
20. Donini, *Lineamenti di storia delle religioni*, p. 206.
21. Acts 5:1–11.
22. Tertullian, *Apologeticum* XXXIX, 20–30.
23. Renan, *Les Apôtres*, p. 352.
24. Georges Sorel, *La ruine du monde antique* (Paris: M. Rivière, 1933), p. 27.
25. Salo Wittmayer Baron, *Histoire d'Israël: Vie sociale et religieuse* (2 vols.; Paris: Presses Universitaires de France, 1956–59), I, 231.
26. Alan C. Bouquet, *Breve storia delle religioni* (Milan: Mondadori, 1963), p. 299.
27. Alfonso M. Di Nola, *Cristo in tuta* (Parma: Guanda, 1955), pp. 56–62.
28. Loewenich, *Il cattolicesimo moderno*, pp. 338–44.
29. Gen. 17:4–8.
30. Exod. 24:10.
31. Ps. 106:40–46.
32. Holtzmann, *Lehrbuch*, I, 66.
33. Bultmann, *Theologie*, II, 9.
34. Eduard Zeller, *Geschichte der christlichen Kirche* (Stuttgart: Franck, 1863), p. 188.
35. Moore, *Storia delle religioni*, II, 128; Heiler, *Storia delle religioni*, II, 104.
36. Royce, *Il problema del cristianesimo*, I, 266.
37. Rom. 2:14–15.
38. I Tim. 1:9–10.
39. Rom. 3:20.
40. Barth, *L'epistola ai Romani*, p. 65.
41. Rom. 1:17.
42. J. Weiss, *Das Urchristentum*, p. 522.
43. Matt. 5:17–20.
44. Luke 16:16 (cf. Matt. 11:12–13).
45. Hans Lietzmann, *Der Prozess Jesu* (Berlin: Akademie der Wissenschaften in Kommission, bei W. de Gruyter und Co., 1931), p. 313.
46. Luke 16:17.
47. Matt. 5:17.
48. Matt. 5:18.
49. Dalman, *Jesus-Jeschua*, p. 53.
50. *Ibid.*, p. 69.
51. Matt. 5:21–28, 33–37.
52. Deut. 5:6–18.
53. Exod. 20:2–17.
54. Bossi, *Cristo nella storia*, p. 124.
55. Matt. 5:21–22.
56. Matt. 5:23–26; Luke 12:57–59.
57. Matt. 5:27–28.
58. Giuseppe Bonaccorsi, *Primi saggi di filologia testamentaria* (2 vols.; Turin: S.E.I., 1933), I, 32.
59. Matt. 5:33–37.
60. Deut. 6:4–5; Lev. 19:18.
61. Julicher, *Die Gleichnisreden Jesu*, II, 596.
62. Renan, *Vie de Jésus*, p. 132.
63. I Cor. 13:3.
64. Thomas Aquinas, *Summa Theol.* II, q. 23.
65. Matt. 5:43–48; Luke 6:27–28, 31–36.
66. Royce, *op. cit.*, I, 220.
67. De Lubac, *Buddismo e occidente*, pp. 247 ff.
68. Deman, *Socrate e Gesù*, p. 256.
69. *Ibid.*, p. 261.

70. Matt. 6:1–8, 16–18; Thomas n. 6.
71. Matt. 5:38–42; Luke 6:29–30.
72. Mark 4:24; Matt. 7:1–5; Luke 6:37–38, 41–42; Thomas n. 30, 31.

73. Rom. 12:9–21.
74. Paul Evdokimov, *L'Ortodossia* (Bologna: Il Mulino, 1965), p. 394.

CHAPTER 11

FAITH IN GOD

1. Bonsirven, *Le Judaïsme*, I, 290–300.
2. Batiffol, *Il valore storico*, p. 202.
3. Matt. 11:28–30 (cf. Thomas n. 94).
4. Julicher, *Die Gleichnisreden Jesu*, I, 219.
5. Prat, *Jésus Christ*, I, 329.
6. Mark 4:3–8; Matt. 13:3–9; Luke 8:4–8; Thomas 9.
7. Mark 4:13–20; Matt. 13:18–23; Luke 8:11–15.
8. Doresse, *Vangelo secondo Tommaso*, p. 125.
9. Ricciotti, *Vita di Gesù*, p. 430.
10. Mark 4:26–29; Thomas 26.
11. Mark 4:30–32; Matt. 13:31–32; Luke 13:18–19; Thomas 23.
12. Julicher, *op. cit.*, II, 575.
13. Matt. 13:33; Luke 13:20–21; Thomas 100.
14. B. Weiss, *Das Leben Jesu*, II, 342.
15. Loisy, *Les évangiles synoptiques*, I, 770–72; Julicher, *op. cit.*, II, 569; Omodeo, *Gesù e le origini*, p. 145.
16. II Cor. 9:6–15.
17. Thomas 101, 102.
18. Matt. 13:44–46; Thomas 80.
19. Matt. 13:47–48; Thomas 8; and see the comments in Jeremias, *Die Gleichnisse Jesu*, pp. 179–99.
20. Matt. 13:24–30; Thomas 62.
21. Matt. 13:36–43.
22. Mark 4:10–12; Matt. 13:10–11.
23. Matt. 13:14–15.
24. John 12:37–41.
25. II Cor. 4:3–4.
26. Ricciotti, *Vita di Gesù*, p. 435.
27. Leopold Fonck, *Die Parabeln des*

Herrn im Evangelium (Innsbruck: F. Rauch, 1904), p. 17.
28. Alfano, *Vita di Gesù*, p. 154.
29. Mark 4:21–23; Matt. 5:15–16; 10:26; Luke 8:4–18; 11:33; Thomas 5, 38.
30. Matt. 5:14*b*; Thomas 37.
31. Yogi Ramacharaka, *Cristianesimo mistico*, p. 202.
32. B. Weiss, *Lehrbuch*, p. 191.
33. Klee, *Storia dei dogmi*, II, 156–57.
34. Mark 4:33–34.
35. Luke 12:13–21; Thomas 67, 76.
36. Matt. 6:19–21, 25–34; Luke 12:22–34; Thomas 41.
37. II Thess. 3:10–12.
38. Matt. 6:9–15; 7:7–11; Luke 11:1–13.
39. J. de Fraine, "Oraison dominicale," in Louis Pirot (ed.), *Dictionnaire de la Bible* (12 vols.; Paris: Letouzey, 1960), Vol. VIII.
40. Alfonso M. Di Nola, *La preghiera dell'uomo* (Parma: Guanda, 1960).
41. Mircea Eliade (ed.), *Trattato di storia delle religioni* (Turin: Einaudi, 1954), p. 54.
42. Cited in L. Salvatorelli, *Storia della letteratura latina cristiana* (Milan, 1936), p. 68.
43. Grandmaison, *Jésus Christ*, II, 640.
44. Franklin Loehr, *The Power of Prayer on Plants* (New York: Doubleday, 1959).
45. Mark 11:24.
46. Matt. 7:7–8; Luke 11:9–10; John 16:23–24.
47. Thomas 1.

48. Clement of Alexandria, *Strom.* II, 9, 45.
49. Doresse, *op. cit.*, p. 113.
50. Thomas 96, 98.
51. Matt. 7:9–11; Luke 11:11–13.
52. Luke 11:5–8.
53. Luke 18:1–8.
54. Omodeo, *Gesù e le origini*, p. 332.
55. Guignebert, *Gesù*, p. 303.
56. Julicher, *op. cit.*, II, 607.
57. Luke 18:9–14.
58. Pierre Batiffol, *L'enseignement de Jésus* (Paris: J. Gabalda, 1910), p. 96.
59. Tondelli, *Gesù Cristo*, p. 264.
60. Schweitzer, *Das Christentum*, p. 59.
61. Aron, *Gli anni oscuri*, pp. 232–33.
62. Albert Reville, *Histoire du dogme de la divinité de Jésus Christ* (Paris: Alcan, 1907), pp. 2–3.
63. Santayana, *L'idea di Cristo*, p. 174.
64. Reinach, *Orpheus*, p. 241.
65. Daniel-Rops, *Il popolo della Bibbia*, p. 60 and others.
66. Exod. 3:14.
67. Baldassare Labanca, *Della religione e della filosofia cristiana* (2 vols.; Turin: Ermano Loescher, 1886 and 1888), II, 435.
68. Bouquet, *Breve storia delle religioni*, pp. 267, 315.
69. Felten, *Storia dei tempi*, III, 47.
70. Andrew Lang, *The Making of Religion* (London: C. A. Watts, 1900); Schmidt, *Storia comparata delle religioni*, especially p. 29.
71. Raffaele Pettazzoni, *Dio: Formazione e sviluppo del monoteismo nella storia delle religioni* (Rome: Edizioni Athenaeum, 1922), p. xvi.
72. Robert R. Marett, *The Threshold of Religion* (London: Methuen, 1914).
73. James G. Frazer, *The Golden Bough: A Study in Comparative Religion* (12 vols.; London and New York: The Macmillan Co., 1891 *et seq.*).
74. Edward B. Tylor, *Primitive Culture: Researches into the Development of Mythology, Philosophy, Religion, Art, and Custom* (London: J. Murray, 1871); Lewis R. Farnell, *Attributes of God* (Oxford: The University Press, 1925).
75. Raffaele Pettazzoni, *L'Essere supremo nelle religioni primitive* (Turin: Einaudi, 1957).
76. *Ibid.*, p. 169.
77. *Ibid.*, p. 241.
78. Exod. 32; Lev. 19:4; Num. 21:8–9; Deut. 17:2; etc.
79. Pss. 18:2, 31; 28:1; 42:9; 62:7; 73:26 (Catholic Bible); 95:1; etc.
80. Moore, *Storia delle religioni*, II, 10–11.
81. Heiler, *Storia delle religioni*, I, 8–9.
82. Bonsirven, *op. cit.*, I, 116–44.
83. Klausner, *Jésus de Nazareth*, pp. 289–90.
84. Edmond Stapfer, *Jésus Christ pendant son ministère* (Paris: Fischbacher, 1897), p. 340.
85. Feuerbach, *L'essenza del cristianesimo*, p. 27.
86. *Ibid.*, p. 51.
87. Immanuel Kant, *Vorlesungen über die philosophische Religionslehre* (Leipzig, 1794), p. 135.
88. Baur, *Lehrbuch*, p. 66.
89. Miegge, *L'evangelo e il mito* (Milan: Comunità, 1956), p. 73.
90. Barth, *L'epistola ai Romani*, p. 349.

CHAPTER 12
TIMES OF TRIBULATION

1. Mark 6:19–29; Matt. 14:6–12.
2. Mark 6:31; Matt. 14:13; Luke 9:10b; John 6:1.
3. Mark 6:35–44; 8:4–9; Matt. 14:15–21; 15:32–38; Luke 9:12–17; John 6:5–14.
4. Mark 8:1–9; Matt. 15:32–39.
5. Grancelli, Il simbolo, pp. 117–18.
6. Paulus, Das Leben Jesu, II, 205 ff.; B. Weiss, Das Leben Jesu, II, 187.
7. Strauss, Vie de Jésus, II, 229–32.
8. Exod. 16:14–18.
9. Loisy, Les évangiles synoptiques, I, 936.
10. John 6:27–65.
11. Fouard, Vita di N.S. Gesù Cristo, I, 376–77.
12. Omodeo, Gesù e le origini, p. 267.
13. John 6:15.
14. Mark 6:45, 53; Matt. 14:22, 34.
15. Paulus, Das Leben Jesu, II, 238.
16. John 6:23.
17. Mark 6:49; Matt. 14:26.
18. Yogi Ramacharaka, Cristianesimo mistico, p. 149.
19. Omodeo, Gesù e le origini, p. 269.
20. Matt. 14:31.
21. Mark 6:14–16; Matt. 14:1–2; Luke 9:7–9.
22. Mark 7:24–31; Matt. 15:21–31.
23. Mark 7:26.
24. Bultmann, Synoptischen Tradition, III, 38.
25. Julicher, Die Gleichnisreden Jesu, II, 258.
26. Schlier, Il tempo della Chiesa, p. 163.
27. Mark 7:31.
28. Burkitt, Il Vangelo e la sua storia, p. 118.
29. Mark 8:10; Matt. 15:39.
30. Dalman, Orte und Wege Jesu, III, 136.
31. Mark 8:11–21; Matt. 12:38–45; 16:1–12; Luke 11:16, 29–32; 12:1.
32. Mark 8:12.
33. Jonah 3:4–10.
34. Thomas 95.
35. Doresse, Vangelo di Tommaso, p. 175.
36. Matt. 12:43–45; Luke 11:24–26.
37. Luke 11:27–28; Thomas 83a.
38. Mark 8:14–21; Matt. 16:5–12.
39. John 6:27–58.
40. John 6:42.
41. John 6:60.
42. Goguel, Vie de Jésus, p. 372.
43. John 6:61.
44. John 6:64–65.
45. Luke 9:18.
46. Mark 8:27; Matt. 16:13; Luke 9:18.
47. Thomas 57.
48. Ibid.
49. John 7:1–9.
50. John 6:66.
51. John 6:68–69.
52. Mark 8:31; Matt. 16:21; Luke 9:22.
53. B. Weiss, Lehrbuch, p. 221.
54. Loisy, Les évangiles synoptiques, II, 19.
55. Meyer, Ursprung und Anfänge, I, 116.
56. Mark 9:31; Matt. 7:22; Luke 9:44–45.
57. Dalman, Orte und Wege Jesu, pp. 219–21.
58. Mark 8:29; Matt. 16:16; Luke 9:20 (cf. Thomas 14).
59. Mark 8:30; Matt. 16:20; Luke 9:21.
60. Leone Tondelli, La psicologia di Cristo (Assisi: Pro Civitate Christiana, 1944), p. 7.
61. Cullmann, Christologie, p. 106.

62. Bornkamm, *Jesus von Nazareth,* p. 163.
63. Matt. 16:17–19.
64. Cullmann, *Dio e Cesare,* p. 25.
65. Fouard, *Vita di N.S. Gesù Cristo,* I, 175.
66. John 12:27–36.
67. Matt. 16:18–19.
68. Reinach, *Orpheus,* p. 330; Guignebert, *Gesù,* p. 383; Martinetti, *Gesù Cristo,* I, 136; Roberto Nisbet, *Il vangelo non dice così* (Torre Pellice: Edizioni Claudiane, 1958), pp. 42–45.
69. Thomas 13.
70. Maurice Goguel, *La naissance du Christianisme* (Paris: Payot, 1946), p. 132.
71. Léon-Dufour, *Les évangiles,* p. 432.
72. Irenaeus, *Adv. haer.* III, 3, 2.
73. Cyprian, *De unitate* 59, 14.

74. Pierre Batiffol, *L'église naissante et le catholicisme* (Paris: J. Gabalda, 1927), p. 440.
75. Evdokimov, *L'Ortodossia,* p. 187.
76. Raniero Sciamannini, *La Chiesa di Cristo* (Florence: Città di Vita, 1960), p. 49.
77. Guignebert, *Gesù,* p. 383 n.
78. Sciamannini, *op. cit.,* p. 4.
79. Erik Peterson, *Il mistero degli Ebrei e dei Gentili nella Chiesa* (Milan: Comunità, 1946), p. 25.
80. Harnack, *Missione e propagazione,* p. 303.
81. Durell, *La Chiesa storica,* p. 30.
82. *Ibid.,* pp. 52–61.
83. Loewenich, *Il cattolicesimo moderno,* pp. 110 ff.
84. Klee, *Storia dei dogmi,* I, 56.
85. Simmel and Staehlin, *La religione cristiana,* p. 74.

CHAPTER 13

THE NEW BEGINNING

1. Mark 9:2–13; Matt. 17:1–13; Luke 9:28–36.
2. Dalman, *Jesus-Jeschua,* pp. 202, 216; Le Camus, *Vie de Jésus Christ,* I, 541.
3. Paulus, *Das Leben Jesu,* II, 442.
4. Strauss, *Vie de Jésus,* II, 275.
5. Meyer, *Ursprung und Anfänge,* II, 154.
6. Radius, *Vita di Cristo,* p. 128.
7. Mark 8:34–38; Matt. 10:32–33, 38–39; 16:24–27; Luke 9:23–27; 12:8–9; 14:27.
8. Ps. 49:16–17.
9. Omodeo, *Gesù e le origini,* p. 276.
10. Luke 13:6–9.
11. Luke 12:49; Thomas 10.
12. Matt. 10:34–37; Luke 12:51–53; 14:25–26; Thomas 17, 60, 105.
13. Luke 14:28–33.
14. Matt. 7:13–14; Luke 13:24.
15. Matt. 7:21–27; Luke 6:46–49.

16. Luke 13:25–30.
17. Thomas 79.
18. Doresse, *Vangelo di Tommaso,* pp. 131–32.
19. Mark 9:1; Matt. 16:28; Luke 9:27.
20. John 21:21–24.
21. Matt. 17:24–27.
22. Wikenhauser, *Einleitung in das Neuen Testament,* p. 144.
23. Paulus, *Das Leben Jesu,* II, 502.
24. Ricciotti, *Vita di Gesù,* p. 482.
25. Mark 9:33–35; Luke 9:46.
26. Mark 9:36–37; Matt. 18:1–5; 10:40–42; Luke 9:47–48; Thomas 4*b,* 27*a,* 6*c.*
27. Willam, *La vita di Gesù,* p. 333.
28. Rom. 14:10*b.*
29. Luke 17:7–12.
30. Luke 14:7–11.
31. Matt. 10:24–33; Luke 12:2–9; 6:40.

32. Holtzmann, *Lehrbuch*, II, 154.
33. Mark 9:42; Matt. 18:6; Luke 17:2.
34. Rom. 14:13.
35. Pierre Vanbergen, *Index des thèmes du Nouveau Testament* (Bruges: Biblica, Publications de Saint-André, 1962), p. 106.
36. Barth, *L'epistola ai Romani*, p. 497.
37. Mark 9:43–48; Matt. 18:8–9; 5:29–30.
38. Mark 9:49–50; Matt. 5:13–14; Luke 14:34–35.
39. Julicher, *Die Gleichnisreden Jesu*, II, 70.
40. Lev. 2:13.
41. Holtzmann, *op. cit.*, II, 156.
42. Matt. 6:22–23; Luke 11:34–36.
43. Thomas 29.
44. Matt. 18:15–20.
45. B. Weiss, *Lehrbuch*, p. 110.
46. Deut. 19:15 ff.

47. I Cor. 5:1–5.
48. II Cor. 2:5–11.
49. Matt. 18:21–35.
50. B. Weiss, *Lehrbuch*, p. 112.
51. Julicher, *op. cit.*, II, 312–13.
52. Matt. 18:11–14; Luke 15:1–7; Thomas 111.
53. Omodeo, *Gesù e le origini*, p. 345.
54. Doresse, *op. cit.*, p. 179.
55. Irenaeus, *Adv. haer.* I, XVI, 2.
56. Luke 15:8–10.
57. Luke 15:11–32.
58. Omodeo, *Gesù e le origini*, p. 392.
59. Alfano, *Vita di Gesù*, p. 292.
60. Jeremias, *Die Gleichnisse Jesu*, pp. 113 ff.
61. Mark 9:38–40.
62. Matt. 12:30.
63. Luke 9:50; 11:23.
64. Augustine, *Ad Donatum*, ep. 173.
65. Carlo Falconi, *Storia delle encicliche* (Milan: Mondadori, 1965).

Chapter 14

IN SAMARIA

1. Mark 10:1; Matt. 19:1.
2. Luke 9:51.
3. Acts 1:2, 11.
4. Luke 13:31–33.
5. Loisy, *Les évangiles synoptiques*, II, 126.
6. Luke 13:1.
7. Holtzmann, *Lehrbuch*, II, 376.
8. Luke 13:2–5.
9. Luke 13:34–35.
10. Matt. 11:20–24; Luke 10:13–15.
11. Burkitt, *Il Vangelo e la sua storia*, p. 124 n.
12. Bouyer, *Il quarto Vangelo*, p. 103 n.
13. Matt. 8:19–20; Luke 9:57–58; Thomas 90.
14. Luke 9:54–56.
15. Luke 9:59–62.
16. Grandmaison, *Jésus Christ*, II, 113 n.2.

17. Luke 17:11–19.
18. John 4:5–42.
19. Reville, *Jésus de Nazareth*, I, 317.
20. Dalman, *Orte und Wege Jesu*, II, 98 ff.
21. Albright, *L'archeologia in Palestina*, pp. 310–11.
22. Hammer, *Quando Gesù viveva*, p. 123.
23. Mark 10:1; Matt. 19:1.
24. Mark 10:1–12; Matt. 19:1–9; 5:31–32; Luke 16:18.
25. Deut. 24:1.
26. On the purpose of marriage, see Bertrand Russell, *Marriage and Morals* (New York: Bantam Books, 1966), pp. 116–17; on "levirate," see Deut. 25:5–6.
27. Matt. 5:32; 19:9.
28. Mark 10:11–12; Luke 16:18.
29. I Cor. 7:15–16.

30. I Cor. 7:28; Rom. 7:2–3.
31. I Cor. 7:11; I Tim. 3:2, 12.
32. I Cor. 7:1–9.
33. Augustine, *De adult. coniug.* II, 11; XI, 4.
34. Simmel and Staehlin, *La religione cristiana,* p. 235.
35. Russell, *Marriage and Morals,* pp. 41–42.
36. Bainton, *La riforma protestante,* pp. 352–54.
37. Matt. 19:10–12.
38. Matt. 19:12.
39. Reville, *Jésus de Nazareth,* II, 110.
40. Holtzmann, *op. cit.,* I, 184.
41. I Cor. 9:5.
42. Tertullian, *De exhortatione castitatis.*
43. I Cor. 7:7–8, 26, 32–33.
44. Fracassini, *Il misticismo greco,* p. 119.
45. Daniel-Rops, *Storia della Chiesa,* II, 131.
46. Denzinger, *Enchiridion Symbolorum,* p. 44.
47. See the Allocution of Pope John
XXIII in the Second Day's Proceedings of the Roman Synod (January 26, 1960).
48. Bellino, *Gesù Cristo nelle SS. Scritture,* VIII, 880–1031.
49. Russell, *Marriage and Morals,* pp. 10–11.
50. Doresse, *Vangelo secondo Tommaso,* p. 143.
51. Pseudo-Isidore, *Philosophumena* V, 7, 13–15.
52. Thomas 27.
53. Thomas 110.
54. Thomas 118.
55. Thomas 42.
56. R. Wilson, *The Gospel of Philip,* p. 46.
57. John 17:21–23.
58. Gal. 3:28.
59. Hermas, The Shepherd 9:11–17.
60. Irenaeus, *Demonstr. Praed. Evang.* 12–16.
61. Tertullian, *De ieiunio* XIII, 3.
62. Cyprian, *Epist.* IV, 2.
63. I Cor. 7:36–37.
64. Mark 12:18–27; Matt. 22:23–33; Luke 20:27–38.

CHAPTER 15

IN JUDEA

1. Mark 10:13–16; Matt. 19:13–15; Luke 18:15–17.
2. Simmel and Staehlin, *La religione cristiana,* p. 121.
3. Mark 10:17–25; Matt. 19:16–19; Luke 18:18–25.
4. Dalman, *Die Worte Jesu,* I, 277.
5. Bainton, *La riforma protestante,* pp. 335–36.
6. *Ibid.,* pp. 340 ff.
7. Giordani, *Il messaggio sociale,* pp. 124–26 and others.
8. Thomas 32, 61, 84, 85, 114.
9. Jeremias, *Unbekannte Jesusworte,* pp. 65–68.
10. II Cor. 8:1–15; 9:12–15.
11. I Tim. 6:9–10.
12. Matt. 6:24; Luke 16:13; Thomas 52a.
13. Luke 16:1–15.
14. Jeremias, *Die Gleichnisse Jesu,* p. 39.
15. Strauss, *Vie de Jésus,* I, 631.
16. Luke 16:19–26.
17. Omodeo, *Gesù e le origini,* p. 394.
18. Loisy, *Les évangiles synoptiques,* II, 174.
19. Strauss, *op. cit.,* I, 636.
20. Luke 16:27–31.
21. Origen, *In Matth.* XV, 14.
22. I Tim. 6:17–19.
23. Omodeo, *Gesù e le origini,* pp. 236, 281.

24. Mark 10:26–31; Matt. 19:25–31; Luke 18:26–30.
25. Matt. 19:28.
26. Luke 22:30b.
27. Matt. 20:1–16.
28. Loisy, *Les évangiles synoptiques,* II, 228.
29. Jeremias, *Die Gleichnisse Jesu,* pp. 112 ff.
30. Matt. 22:1–14; Luke 14:15–24; Thomas 68.
31. Luke 14:12–14.
32. Jeremias, *Die Gleichnisse Jesu,* pp. 34–36.
33. Batiffol, *Il valore storico,* p. 205.
34. Mark 10:32–34; Matt. 20:17–19; Luke 18:31–34.
35. Matt. 20:20 ff.
36. Bauer, *Das Leben Jesu,* p. 431.
37. Mark 10:41; Matt. 20:24.
38. Hophan, *Gli Apostoli,* p. 92.
39. Mark 10:42–45; Matt. 20:25–28; Luke 22:24–30a.
40. Pliny, *Natur. Hist.* XII, 25; Tacitus, *Hist.* V, 6.
41. Mark 10:46–52; Matt. 20:29–34; Luke 18:35–44.
42. Loisy, *Les évangiles synoptiques,* II, 251.
43. Luke 19:1–10.
44. Exod. 22:7, 9.
45. Luke 19:11.
46. Matt. 25:14–30; Luke 19:11–27.
47. Felten, *Storia dei tempi,* II, 214.
48. Matt. 25:29; Luke 19:26.
49. Matt. 13:12; Luke 8:18.
50. Mark 4:25; Thomas 46.
51. Luke 10:38–42.
52. John 11:2.
53. Felten, *op. cit.,* II, 257.

CHAPTER 16

JERUSALEM!

1. Mark 11:1–7; Matt. 21:1–7; Luke 19:28–35.
2. Dalman, *Orte und Wege,* p. 267.
3. Zech. 9:9.
4. Strauss, *Vie de Jésus,* II, 302.
5. Justin, *Dialog. cum Tryph.* 53.
6. Strauss, *op. cit.,* II, 306.
7. Lev. 23:40.
8. Bapst, *La vie historique,* II, 169.
9. Mark 11:8–11a; Matt. 21:8–11; Luke 19:36–44; John 12:12–16.
10. Goguel, *Vie de Jésus,* p. 395.
11. Exod. 28:1 ff.
12. Mark 11:11b.
13. Mark 11:12–14; Matt. 21:18–19.
14. Giordani, *Gesù di Nazareth,* p. 644.
15. John 8:1–11.
16. Lev. 20:10; Deut. 22:22–24.
17. Deut. 17:6–7.
18. Mauriac, *Vita di Gesù,* p. 86.
19. I Kings 8:46.
20. Rom. 3:10–12.
21. Bultmann, *Synoptischen Tradition,* II, 146.
22. Le Camus, *Vie de Jésus Christ,* II, 29.
23. Mark 11:15–19; Matt. 21:12–16; Luke 19:45–48; John 2:13–25.
24. Josephus, *Antiq.,* XV, 15; *War,* I, 21, 1.
25. Otto Hophan, *Il lieto messaggio* (Turin: Marietti, 1953), p. 81.
26. Josephus, *War,* V, 5, 8.
27. John 2:15.
28. Isa. 61:10; Jer. 7:10.
29. Bonaccorsi (ed.), *Vangeli apocrifi,* p. 8 n.
30. Marco Turone, *Gesù e Paolo identificati nella storia profana* (Parma: Guanda, 1959), p. 127.
31. Josephus, *War,* VI, 5, 3.
32. Origen, *In Johann.* X, 16.
33. Keim, *Geschichte Jesu,* III, 99.
34. John 3:1–12.
35. Thomas 34.

36. Ricciotti, *Vita di Gesù*, pp. 335–39.
37. Dodd, *Fourth Gospel*, pp. 304 ff.
38. Ricciotti, *Vita di Gesù*, p. 338 n.; Strauss, *op. cit.*, I, 673.
39. Mark 11:20–23; Matt. 21:20–22; Luke 17:5–6 (in part).
40. Matt. 17:20; 18:19; 21:21.
41. Thomas 21, 53, 110.
42. John 7:11–13.
43. Mark 11:27–33; Matt. 21:23–27; Luke 20:1–8.
44. Matt. 21:28–32.
45. Mark 12:1–9; Matt. 21:33–41; Luke 20:9–16; Thomas 69.
46. Omodeo, *Gesù e le origini*, p. 251.
47. Eugenio Zolli, *Guida all' Antico e Nuovo Testamento* (Milan: Garzanti, 1956), p. 78.
48. Isa. 5:1–7.
49. Buonaiuti, *Pietre miliari*, p. 38.
50. Harnack, *Missione e propagazione*, p. 27 n. 1.
51. Mark 12:10–12; Matt. 21:42–46; Luke 20:17–19; Thomas 70.
52. Ps. 118:22–23.
53. John 7:14–21.
54. John 5:17–47.
55. Mark 12:13–17; Matt. 22:15–22; Luke 20:20–26; Thomas 104.
56. Keim, *op. cit.*, III, 133.
57. Felten, *Storia dei tempi*, II, 219.
58. B. Weiss, *Das Leben Jesu*, II, 420.
59. John 18:36.
60. Harnack, *Missione e propagazione*, p. 109.
61. Joseph Lortz, *Storia della Chiesa nello sviluppo delle sue idee* (Alba: Edizioni Paoline, 1952), p. 27.
62. Cullmann, *Dio e Cesare*, p. 59.
63. Holtzmann, *Lehrbuch*, I, 226.
64. Rom. 13:1–2.
65. Rinaldo Orecchia, "Lo Stato nel pensiero cattolico," *Studium* (Rome), Nos. 7–8 (August, 1959), pp. 557–64.
66. Schuerer, *Geschichte des Jüdischen Volkes*, III, 71 ff.
67. Bardy, *La conversion*, pp. 90–105.
68. Festugière and Fabre, *Il mondo greco-romano*, p. 99.
69. Tacitus, *Hist.* V, 5.
70. Tacitus, *Annales* XV, 44.
71. Paolo Brezzi, *Dalle persecuzioni alla pace di Constantino* (Rome: Studium, 1960), p. 23.
72. Lebreton and Zeiller, *L'église primitive*, p. 294; Lortz, *op. cit.*, p. 38; Tertullian, *Ad nationes* I, 7, 14.
73. Edmond F. Le Blant, "Sur les bases juridiques des poursuites dirigées contre les martyrs," in *Comptes-rendus de l'Académie des Inscriptions* (Paris, 1866), Vol. II.
74. Pettazzoni, *Saggi di storia delle religioni*, pp. 161–65.
75. Livy, *Annales* XXXIX, 8–19.
76. Theodor Mommsen, "Die Religionsfrevel nach römischen Recht," *Historiche Zeitschrift* (Berlin), LXIV (1890), 389–429.
77. Brezzi, *Dalle persecuzioni*, p. 40.
78. Pliny the Younger, *Epist.* X, 96, 97.
79. Suetonius, *Nero* XVI.
80. Tacitus, *Annales* XV, 44.
81. Felix Minucius, *Octavius* XIX.
82. Auguste Bouché-Leclerq, *L'intolérance religieuse et la politique* (Paris: Flammarion, 1911).
83. Giuseppe Barbero, *Il pensiero politico cristiano dai Vangeli a Pelagio* (Turin: U.T.E.T., 1962), p. 11.
84. Paul Allard, *Histoire des persécutions* (5 vols.: Paris: Victor Lecoffre, 1884–90), II, 98 ff.
85. Cyprian, *De lapsis* V–VI.
86. *Ibid.*, VIII, 11.
87. Paolo Brezzi, "Il senso comunitario nel cristianesimo delle origini," *Comunità* (Milan), No. 71 (1959), pp. xi–xvi.
88. Augustine, *Epist.* CXXXVIII, 15.
89. Codex Theod. XVI, 10, 11.

90. Tertullian, *Ad Scapulam* 2.
91. Julius Firmicus Maternus, *De er-* | *rore profanarum religionum* XXIX, 1.

CHAPTER 17

THE MESSIAH

1. John 7:25–36.
2. John 7:37–53.
3. Moore, *Storia delle religioni*, II, 43.
4. Dodd, *Fourth Gospel*, pp. 349–50.
5. Felten, *Storia dei tempi*, II, 255.
6. Isa. 55:1; 12:3.
7. Mark 12:35–37; Matt. 22:41–46; Luke 20:41–44.
8. Dodd, *op. cit.*, p. 87.
9. Tondelli, *Gesù Cristo*, p. 209.
10. Ps. 110:1.
11. Grandmaison, *Jésus Christ*, II, 223.
12. Bapst, *La vie historique*, II, 35.
13. Meyer, *Ursprung und Anfänge*, II, 446.
14. Loisy, *Les évangiles synoptiques*, II, 360–63.
15. Grandmaison, *op. cit.*, II, 240; Guitton, *Jésus*, p. 225; and others.
16. Loisy, *Les évangiles synoptiques*, II, 212.
17. Schweitzer, *Geschichte der Leben-Jesu-Forschung*, p. 370.
18. Zolli, *Guida all'Antico e Nuovo Testamento*, p. 118.
19. Reville, *Jésus de Nazareth*, I, 169.
20. Mark 12:37; Matt. 22:45; Luke 20:44.
21. Luke 1:32.
22. Acts 2:22.
23. Reville, *Histoire du dogme*, p. 14.
24. Bultmann, *Theologie*, I, 44.
25. *Ibid.*, p. 433.
26. Loofs, *What Is the Truth About Jesus?*, p. 241.
27. John 8:12, 16, 29, 42, 46; 9:5; 10:30; 14:11; etc.
28. John 8:59.
29. Wilhelm Bousset, *Kyrios Christos*

(2 vols.; Göttingen: E. A. Huth, 1921), II, 22–23.
30. I Kings 17:22–24; II Kings 4:32–37.
31. Bihlmeyer and Techle, *Storia della Chiesa*, I, 152.
32. Bousset, *loc. cit.*; Dalman, *Jesu-Jeschua*, p. 157; J. Weiss, *Das Urchristentum*, p. 75.
33. Hilarin Felder, *Gesù di Nazareth* (Turin: S.E.I., 1945), p. 32; Guitton, *Jésus*, p. 310.
34. Alfred F. Loisy, *Les origines du Nouveau Testament* (Paris: É. Nourry, 1936), pp. 306 ff.
35. Rom. 5:15; I Cor. 15:21; I Tim. 2:5.
36. Rom. 1:3–4.
37. II Cor. 4:4.
38. Phil. 2:6.
39. Col. 1:15.
40. John 3:34; 5:31, 32, 37; 7:28–29; 8:16, 18, 28, 40; 12:44–50; 15:5.
41. John 1:34; 5:19; 8:54; 9:35–37; 11:41–42; 12:27–28; 15:10, 23; 17:1.
42. John 14:28.
43. John 10:30, 38; 14:10, 11, 13; 17:21.
44. Dodd, *op. cit.*, pp. 34 ff.
45. Reville, *Histoire du dogme*, pp. 43–44.
46. John 1:1, 14.
47. Baur, *Lehrbuch*, p. 67; Adam, "La coscienza," p. 495.
48. Tertullian, *Adv. Prax.* VII.
49. *Ibid.*, VI.
50. *Ibid.*, IX.
51. Denzinger, *Enchiridion Symbolorum*, para. 54, p. 29.

52. Meynier, *Storia del cristianesimo*, pp. 69–70.
53. Simmel and Staehlin, *La religione cristiana*, p. 200.
54. Bihlmeyer and Techle, *op. cit.*, I, 264.
55. Acts 2:2–4.
56. Bultmann, "Neues Testament und Mythologie," pp. 30–31.
57. Matt. 1:18; Luke 1:35.
58. Tertullian, *Adv. Valent.* XVII.
59. I John 5:7.
60. Tertullian, *Adv. Prax.* VIII.
61. Klee, *Storia dei dogmi*, I, 127.
62. *Ibid.*, I, 143–44.
63. *Ibid.*, I, 145–47.
64. *Ibid.*, I, 159–60.
65. Augustine, *De Trinit.* IX, 18.
66. *Ibid.*, VIII, 10.
67. Simmel and Staehlin, *op. cit.*, p. 373.

68. Bonomelli, *Gesù-Cristo Dio-Uomo*, p. 54.
69. Bultmann, "Neues Testament und Mythologie," p. 23.
70. Loewenich, *Il cattolicesimo moderno*, p. 196.
71. Guitton, *Jésus*, p. 218.
72. Grandmaison, *op. cit.*, II, 571–76.
73. Jules Lebreton, *Histoire du dogme de la Trinité* (2 vols.; Paris: G. Beauchesne, 1928), II, 174–247.
74. Deissmann, *Licht vom Osten*, pp. 243–76.
75. Bihlmeyer and Techle, *op. cit.*, II, 49.
76. Grandmaison, *op. cit.*, II, 563–64.
77. Dalman, *Die Worte Jesu*, II, 112.

CHAPTER 18

THE JUDGMENT

1. Fouard, *Vita di N.S. Gesù Cristo*, II, 100.
2. Josephus, *Antiq.*, XII, 7, 7.
3. John 10:1–30.
4. Cullmann, *Dio e Cesare*, pp. 30–31.
5. John 10:23.
6. Ps. 82:6.
7. Alexandre Westphal, *Jésus de Nazareth* (Lausanne: Editions La Concorde, 1915), p. 120.
8. Mark 12:41–44; Luke 21:1–4.
9. Mark 13:1–2; Matt. 24:1–2; Luke 21:5–6.
10. Mark 13:3–4; Matt. 24:3; Luke 21:5–7.
11. Mark 13:5–32; Matt. 24:4–41; 10:16–25; Luke 21:8–33; 10:3; 12:11–12; 17:22–36.
12. Dan. 2:28.
13. Isa. 19:2.
14. Dan. 12:1.
15. Isa. 13:10.

16. Mark 13:33–37; Matt. 24:42–44; 25:1–13; Luke 12:35–48; 21:34–35; Thomas 25, 115.
17. I Thess. 5:2–3.
18. Julicher, *Die Gleichnisreden Jesu*, pp. 142–43.
19. Alfano, *Vita di Gesù*, p. 347 n. 3.
20. I Cor. 7:29.
21. I Cor. 16:22 (*Māranathā* means: "The Lord is coming"); I Cor. 7:26 (the original Greek text speaks of: ενεστῶσαν ἀναγκην, "imminent distress"); Rom. 13:11; 16:20.
22. I Thess. 3:13; 4:15.
23. Augustine, *De civitate Dei* XX, 19, 2.
24. Ricciotti, *Paolo Apostolo*, p. 382.
25. II Thess. 2:9–10.
26. Dan. 12:11.
27. Josephus, *War*, VI, 9, 3.
28. Felten, *Storia dei tempi*, I, 307–12.

29. Clement of Alexandria, *Omel.* II, 23; Origen, *Contra Cels.* I, 57; VI, 15.
30. Acts 8:9, 18–24.
31. Mark 13:30, 32; Matt. 24:34, 36; Luke 21:32.
32. Origen, *In Matth.* XXX; Athanasius, *Contra Arium* III, 43–46.
33. Augustine, *Enarratio in Psalm.* XXXVI, Sermon I, 1.
34. Batiffol, *L'enseignement*, p. 278 and others.
35. Lagrange, *L'évangile de Jésus Christ*, pp. 473–86.
36. Giordani, *Gesù di Nazareth*, I, 666–68.
37. Rev. 20, 21.
38. Donini, *Lineamenti di storia delle religioni*, p. 261.
39. *Let God Be True* (New York: Watchtower Bible and Tract Society, 1952), p. 253.
40. *Ibid.*, pp. 245–50.
41. Donini, *op. cit.*, p. 114.
42. Matt. 25:31–46.
43. Luke 17:20–21.
44. John 3:18.
45. Donini, *op. cit.*, p. 259.
46. Schweitzer, *Geschichte der Leben-Jesu-Forschung*, chap. xxv.
47. Bultmann, *Theologie*, II, 386.
48. Meynier, *Storia del cristianesimo*, p. 82.
49. Tertullian, *Apologet.* XLI.
50. Luke 23:43.
51. Pirot (ed.), *Dictionnaire de la Bible*, see under "Paradise."
52. Moore, *Storia delle religioni*, II, 61.
53. Evdokimov, *L'Ortodossia*, p. 482.
54. Meynier, *op. cit.*, p. 82.
55. Dalman, *Die Worte Jesu*, I, 127; Evdokimov, *op. cit.*, p. 87.
56. I Cor. 15:39–44.
57. Tertullian, *Apologet.* VII.
58. Tertullian, *De anima* IX.
59. Thomas Aquinas, *Summa Theolog.* I, q. 118, a. 1.
60. *Ibid.*, I, q. 77, a. 8.
61. Acts 1:8, 22; I Cor. 15:1 ff.
62. Bardy, *La conversion*, pp. 31–33.
63. Basil, *In Psalm.* CXIV, 1; Theodoret, *Gr. affect. curat. disp.* VIII; Augustine, *De vera religione* LV; *Ad Faust.* XX, 21.
64. Gregory of Nazianzus, *Carm.* CCXVIII; Augustine, *Confess.* VI, 2; *Civ. Dei* VIII, 27.
65. De Lubac, *Buddismo e Occidente*, p. 28.
66. Daniel-Rops, *Storia della Chiesa*, II, 173.

CHAPTER 19

THE LAST SUPPER

1. John 10:39–42.
2. John 11:1–44.
3. Strauss, *Vie de Jésus*, II, 168.
4. Renan, *Vie de Jésus*, p. 185.
5. Dimitrii Merezhkovski, *Morte e Resurrezione* (Florence: Marzocco, 1948), p. 274.
6. Couchoud, *Il mistero di Gesù*, p. 149.
7. Soter, *La religione del Cristo*, p. 221.
8. Schuré, *L'évolution divine*, pp. 392–93.
9. John 11:47–57.
10. Mark 14:1–2; Matt. 26:1–5.
11. John 12:1.
12. Mark 14:1; Matt. 26:2.
13. Felten, *Storia dei tempi*, II, 259–60.
14. Mark 14:3–9; Matt. 26:6–13; Luke 7:36–50.
15. John 12:1–11.
16. Paulus, *Das Leben Jesu*, III, 582.
17. Klausner, *Jésus de Nazareth*, p. 466.
18. Holtzmann, *Lehrbuch*, III, 172.

19. Mark 14:10–11; Matt. 26:14–16; Luke 22:1–6.
20. Loisy, *Les évangiles synoptiques*, II, 502.
21. Keim, *Geschichte Jesu*, III, 462.
22. B. Weiss, *Das Leben Jesu*, II, 162.
23. Merezhkovski, *Morte e Resurrezione*, p. 109.
24. Guignebert, *Gesù*, pp. 539–46.
25. Matt. 26:15.
26. Acts 1:18.
27. Zech. 11:12; Matt. 27:9.
28. Augustine, *De consensu Evang.* III, 7.
29. Klausner, *op. cit.*, pp. 417–77.
30. Loisy, *Les évangiles synoptiques*, II, 502.
31. Paulus, *Das Leben Jesu*, III, 451.
32. Irenaeus, *Adv. haer.* I, 35.
33. Roger Caillois, *Ponzio Pilato* (Turin: Einaudi, 1963).
34. Matt. 27:3–10.
35. Acts 1:18.
36. Zech. 11:13.
37. Mark 14:12; Matt. 26:17; Luke 22:7; John 13:1.
38. Willam, *La vita di Gesù*, p. 387.
39. Mauriac, *Vita di Gesù*, p. 127.
40. Num. 28:16.
41. Exod. 12:18.
42. Exod. 12:6–8.
43. Martinetti, *Gesù Cristo*, I, 163–66.
44. Ricciotti, *Vita di Gesù*, pp. 657–58; Giordani, *Gesù di Nazareth*, p. 688; Bapst, *La vie historique*, II, 207.
45. Goguel, *Vie de Jésus*, p. 418.
46. Klausner, *op. cit.*, pp. 474, 477.
47. Hophan, *Gli Apostoli*, pp. 315–16.
48. John 13:2–20.
49. Ps. 41:9.
50. John 13:21–30.
51. Mark 14:17–21; Matt. 26:20–25; Luke 22:21–23.
52. Mark 14:22–25; Matt. 26:26–29; Luke 22:14–20.
53. H. Haag, "Pâques," in Pirot (ed.), *Dictionnaire de la Bible*, Vol. VI.
54. Reinach, *Orpheus*, p. 330.
55. Acts 2:42, 46; 20:7, 11.
56. Paulus, *Das Leben Jesu*, III, 527.
57. Festugière and Fabre, *Il mondo greco-romano*, pp. 316–19.
58. I Cor. 10:16, 19–33.
59. I Cor. 11:23–25.
60. I Cor. 11:26.
61. I Cor. 11:27, 30.
62. Meyer, *Ursprung und Anfänge*, III, 179.
63. Tondelli, *Gesù Cristo*, p. 457.
64. Lev. 17:11.
65. Exod. 24:8.
66. Moore, *Storia delle religioni*, II, 8 n.
67. Augustine, *Enarr. in Psalm.* XCVIII, 9; Gelasius, *De duabus naturis in Christo.*
68. Klee, *Storia dei dogmi*, II, 145–46.
69. Antonio Franzé, *Gesù* (Polistena: R. Pascale, 1941), p. 148.
70. Acts 2:46.
71. Cyprian, *De lapsis* XXVI.
72. Bihlmeyer and Techle, *Storia della Chiesa*, I, 132.
73. Pliny, *Epist.* X, 97.
74. Justin, *Apolog.* 65–67.
75. Igino Pagnini, "La messa nei primi secoli," *La Rocca* (Assisi), March, 1954, pp. 12–13; Evdokimov, *L'Ortodossia*, p. 503.
76. Falconi, *L'umanità e il Cristo*, p. 356 n.
77. Thomas Aquinas, *Summa Theol.* III, q. 80.

CHAPTER 20

THE TRIAL

1. Mark 14:26–31; Matt. 26:30–35; Luke 22:31–38; John 13:31–38.
2. Zech. 13:7.
3. Paulus, *Das Leben Jesu*, III, 588.
4. John 14–17.
5. Holtzmann, *Lehrbuch*, III, 413.
6. Mark 14:32–42; Matt. 26:36–46; Luke 22:39–45; John 18:1.
7. Dalman, *Die Worte Jesu*, II, 340.
8. Keim, *Geschichte Jesu*, III, 300.
9. Ricciotti, *Vita di Gesù*, p. 681.
10. Mark 14:33.
11. Luke 22:44.
12. Pierre Barbet, *La passione di Nostro Signore Gesù Cristo* (Turin: L.I.C.E. di R. Berruti e C., 1950).
13. Binet-Sanglé, *La folie de Jésus*, I, 198.
14. Origen, *Cont. Cels.* II, 24; Calvin, *Inst. christ. relig.* XI, 16, 12.
15. Bauer, *Das Leben Jesu*, p. 171.
16. Strauss, *Vie de Jésus*, II, 472.
17. Batiffol, *Il valore storico*, p. 223.
18. Dalman, *Die Worte Jesu*, II, 344.
19. Loisy, *Les évangiles synoptiques*, II, 561.
20. Mark 14:43–45; Matt. 26:47–50; Luke 22:47–48; John 28:2–5.
21. Ricciotti, *Vita di Gesù*, p. 687.
22. Mark 14:47.
23. Rosadi, *Il processo di Gesù*, p. 170.
24. Mark 14:51–52.
25. Hophan, *Gli Apostoli*, p. 318.
26. Loisy, *Les évangiles synoptiques*, II, 589.
27. Amos 2:16.
28. Rosadi, *op. cit.*, p. 194.
29. Lietzmann, *Der Prozess Jesu*, pp. 313 ff.; Omodeo, *Gesù e le origini*, p. 295; Salvador, *Jésus Christ*, pp. 520–70.
30. Loisy, *Le origini del cristianesimo*, p. 75; Cullmann, *Christolo-gie*, p. 50; Goguel, *Vie de Jésus*, p. 459.
31. Ricciotti, *Vita di Gesù*, pp. 725 ff.; Tondelli, *Gesù Cristo*, p. 490; Fouard, *Vita di N.S. Gesù Cristo*, II, 263 ff.; Edmond L. Stapfer, *La mort et la résurrection de Jésus Christ* (Paris: Fischbacher, 1898), p. 103.
32. Didon, *Vita di Gesù Cristo*, II, 81.
33. Felten, *Storia dei tempi*, II, 21.
34. Fouard, *op. cit.*, II, 272.
35. Keim, *op. cit.*, III, 474, which cites the Mishnah (Sanhedrin 4:1).
36. Klausner, *Jésus de Nazareth*, pp. 484 ff.
37. Nicola Jaeger, *Il processo di Gesù* (Turin: S.P.E., 1962), p. 31.
38. Tondelli, *Gesù Cristo*, p. 491 n.2.
39. Schuerer, *Geschichte des Jüdischen Volkes*, II, 197.
40. Léon-Dufour, "Passion," in Pirot (ed.), *Dictionnaire de la Bible*.
41. John 18:19.
42. John 18:20–22.
43. Pranaitis, *Cristo e i Cristiani nel Talmud*, pp. 88–91.
44. Matt. 5:39.
45. Mark 14:56–57.
46. Matt. 26:60–61.
47. John 2:19.
48. Mark 14:60; Matt. 26:62.
49. Mark 14:61; Matt. 26:63; Luke 22:67.
50. Mark 14:62.
51. Matt. 26:64; Luke 22:70.
52. Cullmann, *Christologie*, p. 103.
53. Cullmann, *Dio e Cesare*, p. 37.
54. Mark 14:62; Matt. 26:64; Luke 22:69.
55. Loisy, *Les évangiles synoptiques*, II, 609.
56. Keim, *op. cit.*, III, 336.

57. Mark 14:63–64a; Matt. 26:65–66a; Luke 22:71.
58. Mark 14:64b; Matt. 26:66b.
59. Matt. 26:67–68.
60. Isa. 50:6.
61. Guignebert, Gesù, p. 555.
62. Jaeger, op. cit., pp. 31–42.
63. Mark 14:54; Matt. 26:58, 69; Luke 22:54b–55; John 18:15, 18.
64. Schoeps, I grandi fondatori di religioni, p. 58.
65. Mark 15:1; Matt. 27:1–2; Luke 23:1; John 18:28.
66. Guignebert, Gesù, p. 558.
67. Albright, L'archeologia in Palestina, p. 198.
68. Tondelli, Gesù Cristo, p. 135.
69. John 19:13.
70. Luke 23:2.
71. Mark 15:2; Matt. 27:11; Luke 23:3; John 18:33.
72. John 18:34–37.
73. Bauer, op. cit., p. 129.
74. Luke 23:8–12.
75. Tondelli, Gesù Cristo, pp. 507–8.
76. Luke 23:13–16.
77. Mark 15:15b–19; Matt. 27:26b–30; Luke 23:11; John 19:1–3.
78. Dalman, Jesus-Jeschua, p. 263.
79. Klausner, op. cit., p. 492.
80. Paulus, Das exegetische Handbuch, III, 649.
81. Isa. 50:6; Mic. 5:1.
82. John 19:4–11.
83. John 19:12a.
84. Mark 15:6; Matt. 27:15; Luke 23:17.
85. Guignebert, Gesù, p. 562.
86. Loisy, Les évangiles synoptiques, II, 646.
87. Origen, In Matth., Sermon 121.
88. Bauer, op. cit., pp. 527–28.
89. Reinach, Orpheus, pp. 316–38.
90. Philo, Ad Flaccum VI.
91. Guignebert, Gesù, pp. 568–69.
92. Mark 15:8–15; Matt. 27:17–26; Luke 23:17–25; John 18:39–40.
93. Goguel, Vie de Jésus, p. 465.
94. Keim, op. cit., III, 390.
95. Deman, Socrate e Gesù, p. 19.
96. Couchoud, Il mistero di Gesù, p. 95.
97. Adolf von Harnack, Sokrates und die alte Kirche (Berlin: J. Ricker, 1900), p. 21.
98. Fouard, op. cit., II, 301.
99. Tertullian, Apologet. XXI.
100. Schlier, Il tempo della Chiesa, p. 109.
101. Gough, The Early Christians, p. 39.
102. Matt. 27:19.
103. Friedrich Klopstock, Der Messias, canto VII, ll. 399–449.

CHAPTER 21

DEATH AND RESURRECTION

1. Mark 15:22; Matt. 27:33; Luke 23:33; John 19:17.
2. Dalman, Jesus-Jeschua, p. 336.
3. Eliade, Trattato di storia delle religioni, p. 112.
4. Mark 15:21; Matt. 27:32; Luke 23:26–31.
5. Rom. 16:13; I Tim. 1:20.
6. Irenaeus, Adv. haer. I, 24, 4.
7. Isa. 3:16–24; Hos. 10:8; Rev. 6:16.
8. Loisy, Les évangiles synoptiques, II, 661.
9. Cullmann, Dio e Cesare, pp. 55–56.
10. Keim, Geschichte Jesu, III, 417 n.5.
11. Matt. 27:34.
12. Ps. 69:21.
13. Cicero, In Verrem V, 64.
14. Tacitus, Annales IV, 3, 11.
15. Baron, Histoire d'Israël, p. 250.
16. Keim, op. cit., III, 415.
17. Tertullian, Adv. Marcion III, 22.
18. Justin, Apolog. I, 55.

19. Merezhkovski, *Morte e Resurrezione*, p. 236.
20. Bardy and Tricot, *Enciclopedia cristologica*, p. 994.
21. Justin, *Dialog. cum Tryph.* 91.
22. Tertullian, *Adv. nationes* I, 12.
23. Cicero, *In Verrem* V, 66.
24. Irenaeus, *Adv. haer.* II, 24.
25. Paulus, *Das Leben Jesu*, III, 669, 754.
26. Ps. 22:16*b*.
27. Mark 15:26.
28. B. Weiss, *Das Leben Jesu*, II, 540.
29. Ps. 22:18.
30. Isa. 53:12.
31. Léon-Dufour, "Passion," in Pirot (ed.), *Dictionnaire de la Bible.*
32. Mark 15:29–32; Matt. 27:39–44; Luke 23:35–39.
33. Renan, *Vie de Jésus*, p. 212.
34. Matt. 27:44.
35. Luke 23:39–43.
36. Loisy, *Les évangiles synoptiques*, II, 677.
37. Santayana, *L'idea di Cristo*, p. 188.
38. Mark 15:33; Matt. 27:45, 52; Luke 23:44–45.
39. Origen, *In Matth.*, *Sermon* 134.
40. Merezhkovski, *Morte e Resurrezione*, pp. 192–93.
41. Amos 8:9–10.
42. Virgil, *Georgics* I, 465–67; Ovid, *Metamorphoses* XV, 782–802.
43. Stapfer, *La mort*, p. 219.
44. Ps. 69:21.
45. John 19:29.
46. Luke 23:46.
47. John 19:30.
48. Mark 15:34; Matt. 27:46.
49. Dalman, *Jesus-Jeschua*, p. 184.
50. Ps. 22:1 (Ps. 22:2 in Catholic versions).
51. Omodeo, *Gesù e le origini*, p. 297.
52. John 19:25–27.
53. B. Weiss, *Das Leben Jesu*, II, 540.
54. Loisy, *Le origini del cristianesimo*, II, 105.
55. Heiler, *Storia delle religioni*, II, 105.
56. John 19:31–39.
57. Strauss, *Vie de Jésus*, II, 590; Renan, *Vie de Jésus*, p. 214.
58. Franco La Cava, "Il reperto necroscopico di Longino sul costato di Gesù Cristo," *Medicus* (Milan), No. 1 (January, 1946), pp. 61 ff.
59. Sergio Marigo, "Le cause di morte in Cristo," *Studium* (Rome), Nos. 7–8 (August, 1950), pp. 356–65.
60. Giovanni Judica Cordiglia, *Un colpo di lancia al cuore di Cristo* (Milan: R. Ghirlando, 1937), p. 265.
61. R. Whitaker, "The Physical Causes of the Death of Our Lord," *Catholic Medical Guardian* (London), 1935, pp. 85 ff.
62. Origen, *In Matth.*, Sermon 140.
63. Hynek, *L'aspetto fisico di Gesù*, p. 75.
64. La Cava, *op. cit.*, p. 62; Hammer, *Quando Gesù viveva*, pp. 554–55.
65. Binet-Sanglé, *La folie de Jésus*, I, 228 ff.
66. Bardy and Tricot, *op. cit.*, pp. 725–39.
67. Felten, *Storia dei tempi*, II, 204.
68. Deut. 21:23.
69. Goguel, *La naissance*, p. 44.
70. Dalman, *Die Worte Jesu*, II, 381.
71. Matt. 27:62–66.
72. Loisy, *Les évangiles synoptiques*, II, 709; Paulus, *Das exegetische Handbuch*, III, 837.
73. Loisy, *Le origini del cristianesimo*, p. 244.
74. Reinach, *Orpheus*, p. 315.
75. Albertine Jaubert, *La date de la Cène: Calendrier biblique et liturgie chrétienne* (Paris: J. Gabalda, 1957).
76. I Cor. 5:7.
77. Ricciotti, *Vita di Gesù*, p. 191;

Argentieri, *Quando visse Cristo?,* pp. 56–57, citing names and texts.

78. John 20:1; Mark 16:1; Matt. 28:1; Luke 24:10.
79. Mark 16:8, 13; Matt. 28:8; Luke 24:5, 11.
80. John 20:4–5.
81. Mark 16:9; John 20:14–17; Matt. 28:9; Luke 24:13 ff.; I Cor. 15:5.
82. Mark 16:14; Luke 24:36 ff.
83. Matt. 28:16; Lebreton, *Histoire du dogme de la Trinité,* II, 610.
84. I Cor. 15:5.
85. Mark 16:12; John 21:1–2; I Cor. 15:6–8.
86. Luke 24:13–32, 36–49; John 21:9–14.
87. Bauer, *Das Leben Jesu,* p. 263.
88. Bultmann, *Theologie,* III, 404.
89. Joseph Sickenberger, *Introduzione al Nuovo Testamento* (Turin: Marietti, 1942), p. 64.
90. Origen, *Cont. Cels.* II, 55; Renan, *Vie de Jésus,* pp. 449–50.
91. Guignebert, *Gesù,* pp. 643 ff.
92. Tertullian, *De spectaculis* XXX.
93. Holtzmann, *Lehrbuch,* III, 105; Klausner, *Jésus de Nazareth,* p. 517.
94. Renan, *Les Apôtres,* p. 34.
95. Reville, *Jésus de Nazareth,* I, 162.
96. Strauss, *op. cit.,* II, 671.
97. Samuel Butler, *The Fair Haven* (London: A. C. Fifield, 1913), p. 215.
98. Paulus, *Das Leben Jesu,* III, 829–30, 832.
99. I Cor. 15:12–23.
100. Loisy, *Le origini del cristianesimo,* p. 92.
101. Acts 1:4.
102. Felder, *Gesù di Nazareth,* p. 173.
103. Acts 3:1–10.
104. Acts 3:20.
105. Acts 22:9.
106. Rom. 1:4.
107. Thomas Aquinas, *Summa Theol.* III, q. 55, a. 2 *ad* 1.
108. I Thess. 4:15–17.
109. Acts 2:31.
110. J. Weiss, *Das Urchristentum,* p. 347.
111. Renan, *Les Apôtres,* p. 36.
112. Acts 1:3.
113. Bousset, *Kyrios Christos,* p. 197; Robertson, *Le origini del cristianesimo,* p. 97.
114. Goguel, *Vie de Jésus,* pp. 79–80.
115. I Pet. 3:19–20.
116. Loisy, *Le origini del cristianesimo,* p. 243.
117. Eliade, *op. cit.,* pp. 115–17.
118. Thomas A. Lacey, *Il Cristo storico* (Turin: Bocca, 1907), p. 139.
119. Rom. 5:12.
120. Bultmann, "Neues Testaments und Mythologie," p. 20.
121. Nicola Taccone-Callucci, *L'uomo-Dio* (Milan: L. Romano, 1881), pp. 169–71.
122. Col. 1:26; Eph. 3:8–9.
123. Rom. 3:25–26; 5:14 ff.
124. Rom. 2:7–8.
125. Rom. 5:12–21.
126. II Cor. 5:2.
127. I Cor. 15:51–54.
128. Deissmann, *Licht vom Osten,* p. 278.
129. Gal. 2:16; 3:11.
130. Rom. 3:28.
131. Rom. 11:6.
132. Col. 2:13–14.
133. Rom. 5:6.
134. Rom. 9:11.
135. Rom. 9:16.
136. Rom. 8:28–30; Eph. 1:5; Gal. 4:5.
137. Barth, *L'epistola ai Romani,* p. 160.

Bibliography

Since the literature on the subject is virtually endless, the Bibliography has been limited to those works actually cited in this book.

I. Sources

a) Christian Sources

The critical apparatus of the Italian editions of the Bible listed below are relevant to the author's documentation and have therefore been included in the present edition. However, direct quotations from books of the Bible (including the Apocrypha) are from the King James Version unless otherwise noted.

1. *Antico e Nuovo Testamento.* Edited by GIOVANNI LUZZI. Florence: Fides et Amor, 1930.
2. *La Sacra Bibbia.* Edited by GIUSEPPE RICCIOTTI. Florence: Salani, 1940.
3. *La Sacra Bibbia.* Edited by "CASA DELLA BIBBIA." Geneva: Wyss S.A., 1961.
4. *Nuovo Testamento.* Edited by PIERO ROSSANO. Turin: Marietti, 1963.
5. *Novum Testamentum Graece et Latine.* Edited by SISTO COLOMBO. Turin: S.E.I., 1931.
6. *Paolo. Lettere.* Edited by GIUSEPPE RICCIOTTI. Rome: Tipografia Poliglotta Vaticana, 1949.
7. *Vangeli apocrifi.* Edited by GIUSEPPE BONACCORSI. Florence: Editrice Libraria Fiorentina, 1948.—An English edition containing descriptions and texts of the apocryphal works is: *The Apocryphal New Testament.* Translated by MONTAGUE RHODES JAMES. Oxford: The Clarendon Press, 1924.
8. *The Gospel of Philip.* Translated from the Coptic text with an Introduction and commentary by ROBERT MCLACHLAN WILSON. London: Mowbray, 1962.

9. *Vangelo secondo Tommaso.* The translation and critical study by JEAN DORESSE. Milan: Il Saggiatore, 1945.—Orig. title: *Les livres secrets des Gnostiques d'Égypte.* Vol. II: *L'évangile selon Thomas ou les Paroles secrètes de Jésus.* Paris: Libraire Plon, 1939.—Eng. trans.: *The Secret Books of the Egyptian Gnostics.* Translated by PHILIP MAIRET. Appendix II: "The Gospel According to Thomas, or The Secret Words of Jesus," translated by THE REV. LEONARD JOHNSTON in collaboration with the author. New York: Viking Press, 1960.

10. AURELI, ALESSANDRO. *Letteratura cristiano-latina nel Medioevo.* Milan: Vallardi, 1945.

11. JEREMIAS, JOACHIM. *Unbekannte Jesusworte.* Gütersloh: Gütersloher Verlagshaus, Gerd Mohn, 1963; 1st ed., 1948.—Eng. trans.: *Unknown Sayings of Jesus.* Translated by REGINALD H. FULLER. London: Society for Promoting Christian Knowledge, 1957.

12. MIGNE, JACQUES PAUL. *Patrologiae cursus completus accurante J. P. Migne.* Paris: Frères Garnier, 1844 *et seq.*

13. SALVATORELLI, LUIGI. *Storia della letteratura latina cristiana.* Milan: Vallardi, 1936.

b) Jewish and Pagan Sources

14. JOSEPHUS, FLAVIUS. *Jewish Antiquities.* Translated by H. ST. J. THACKERAY *et al.* (The Loeb Classical Library.) 6 vols. London and Cambridge, Mass.: William Heinemann and Harvard University Press.

15. ———. *The Jewish War.* Translated by H. ST. J. THACKERAY *et al.* (The Loeb Classical Library.) 2 vols. London and Cambridge, Mass.: William Heinemann and Harvard University Press.

16. PLINY THE YOUNGER. *Epistulae* (X, 96).—Eng. trans.: *Letters.* Translated by WILLIAM MELMOTH, revised by W. M. L. HUTCHINSON. (The Loeb Classical Library.) 2 vols. London and Cambridge, Mass.: William Heinemann and Harvard University Press.

17. PRANAITIS, IUSTIN BONAVENTURA. *Cristo e i Cristiani nel Talmud.* Italian-Hebrew bilingual edition. Rome: no publisher, 1939; 1st ed., St. Petersburg, 1892.—Eng. trans.: *The Talmud Unmasked: The Secret Rabbinical Teachings Concerning Christians.* With an Editor's Note signed by E. N. (EUGENE NELSON) SANCTUARY. New York, 1939.

18. SUETONIUS TRANQUILLUS. *Nero* (XVI); *Claudius* (XXV, 4).—
Eng. trans.: *Lives of the Caesars.* Translated by J. C. ROLFE.
(The Loeb Classical Library.) 2 vols. London and Cambridge,
Mass.: William Heinemann and Harvard University Press.

19. TACITUS. *Annales* (XV, 44–45).—Eng. trans.: *The Histories.
The Annals.* Translated by CLIFFORD H. MOORE and JOHN
JACKSON. (The Loeb Classical Library.) 4 vols. London and
Cambridge, Mass.: William Heinemann and Harvard Univer-
sity Press.

II. LIVES OF JESUS AND STUDIES OF THE NEW TESTAMENT

a) Catholic Works

Starting with the postulate that the Gospels are infallible because they
were written "under divine inspiration," the Catholic biographers deliberately
refrain from critical research, taking their impetus instead from the Gospel
story for reasons both apologistic and moralistic. They prefer to follow John,
notoriously the least reliable of the Evangelists from a historical point of view
but rich in mystical themes. Or else they "harmonize" the Synoptic Gospels
one with the other and then with John, but without serving notice that there
are repetitions and interpolations.

20. ADAM, KARL. *Gesù il Cristo.* Brescia: Morcelliana, 1955.—
Orig. title: *Jesus Christus.* Augsburg: Haas & Grabherr, 1931.
—Eng. trans.: *The Son of God.* Translated by PHILIP HERE-
FORD. New York: Sheed & Ward, 1934.

21. ALFANO, GIOVANNI BATTISTA. *Vita di Gesù.* Naples: Morano,
1961.

22. ANSALDI, CESARE. *Nascita e infanzia di Gesù nella leggenda
araba.* Rome: Sindacato Italiano Arti Grafiche, 1932.

23. BATIFFOL, PIERRE. *L'enseignement de Jésus.* Paris: J. Gabalda,
1910; 1st ed., 1905.

24. ———. *Il valore storico del Vangelo.* Florence: Editrice Libraria Fiorentina, 1913.—Orig. title: *Orpheus et l'évangile.*
Paris: J. Gabalda, 1910.—Eng. trans.: *The Credibility of the
Gospel.* Translated by THE REV. G. C. H. POLLEN S.J. London
and New York: Longmans, Green, 1912.

25. BESSIÈRES, ALBERT. *Vita di Gesù.* Bologna: Cappelli, 1958.—
Orig. title: *Vie de Jésus.* Paris: Spes, 1951.

26. BONACCORSI, GIUSEPPE. *Primi saggi di filologia testamentaria.*
2 vols. Turin: S.E.I., 1933.

27. BONOMELLI, GEREMIA. *Gesù Cristo Dio-Uomo*. Piacenza: Lorenzo Rinfreschi, 1914.
28. BRAUN, FRANÇOIS MARIE. *Gesù: Storia e critica*. Florence: Editrice Libraria Fiorentina, 1950.—Orig. title: *Où en est le problème de Jésus?* Paris: J. Gabalda, 1932.
29. CAPECELATRO, ALFONSO. *La vita di Gesù Cristo*. 2 vols. Rome: Desclée, 1888; 1st ed., Naples: Morano, 1868.
30. "DANIEL-ROPS, HENRI" (HENRY PETIOT). *Gesù e il suo tempo*. Florence: Sansoni, 1949.—Orig. title: *Jésus et son temps*. Paris: A. Fayard, 1945.—Eng. trans.: *Jesus and His Times*. New rev. Catholic ed. Translated from the French by RUBY MILLAR. New York: E. P. Dutton, 1954; London: Eyre and Spottiswoode, 1955.
31. DEMAN, THOMAS. *Socrate e Gesù*. Florence: Editrice Libraria Fiorentina, 1950.—Orig. title: *Socrate et Jésus*. Paris, n.d.
32. DIDON, HENRY. *Vita di Gesù Cristo*. 2 vols. Florence: Nerbini, 1934.—Orig. title: *Jésus Christ*. Paris: Libraire Plon, Nourrit, 1891.—Eng. trans.: *Jesus Christ Our Saviour's Person, Mission and Spirit*. New York: Appleton and Company, 1891; *The Life of Jesus Christ*. London: Kegan Paul, Trench, Trubner, 1928.
33. FELDER, HILARIN. *Gesù di Nazareth*. Turin: S.E.I., 1945.—Orig. title: *Jesus von Nazareth: Ein Christusbuch*. Paderbon: F. Schöningh, 1937.—Eng. trans.: *Jesus of Nazareth*. Authorized translation by BERCHWANS BITTLE. London: G. E. J. Coldwell, 1938.
34. FONCK, LEOPOLD. *Die Parabeln des Herrn im Evangelium: Exegetisch und Praktisch Erläutert*. Innsbruck: F. Rauch, 1904. —Eng. trans.: *The Parables of the Gospel: An Exegetical and Practical Explanation*. Translated from the 3d German ed. by E. LEAHY, edited by GEORGE O'NEILL. New York: F. Pustet, 1915.
35. FORNARI, VITO. *Della vita di Gesù Cristo*. 2 vols. Turin: S.E.I., 1949; 1st ed., 3 vols., Florence: Barbera, 1869, 1877, 1893.
36. FOUARD, CHARLES. *Vita di N.S. Gesù Cristo*. Turin: Libraria Editrice Internazionale, 1913, 1915.—Orig. title: *La vie de Notre Seigneur Jésus Christ*. Paris: Victor Lecoffre, 1880.— Eng. trans.: *The Christ, the Son of God: A Life of Our Lord and Saviour Jesus Christ*. Translated from the 5th French ed. with the author's sanction by GEORGE F. X. GRIFFITH. London and New York: Longmans, Green, 1946.

37. GIORDANI, IGINO. *Gesù di Nazareth.* 2 vols. Turin: S.E.I., 1945–46.
38. GRANDMAISON, LÉONCE DE. *Jésus Christ: Sa personne, son message, ses preuves.* 2 vols. Paris: Bloud & Gay, 1928.—Eng. trans.: *Jesus Christ: His Person, His Message, His Credentials.* Translated by DOM BASIL VHELAN, ADA LANE, and DOUGLAS CARTER. London: Sheed & Ward, 1930; New York: Sheed & Ward, 1961.
39. GUARDINI, ROMANO. *La figura di Gesù Cristo nel Nuovo Testamento.* Brescia: Morcelliana, 1960.—Orig. title: *Das Bild von Jesus dem Christus im Neuen Test.* Würzburg: Werkbund Verlag, 1936.
40. GUITTON, JEAN. *Le problème de Jésus.* 2 vols. Vols. VI and VII of *La pensée moderne et le Catholicisme.* 8 vols. Paris: Aubier, Editions Montaigne, 1950–55.—Eng. trans.: *The Problem of Jesus.* Translated by A. GORDON SMITH. New York: P. J. Kenedy & Sons, 1955.
41. ———. *Jésus.* Paris: Bernard Grasset, 1961; 1st ed., 1956.
42. HAMMER, JOSEPH. *Quando Gesù viveva tra di noi.* Turin: S.A.I.E., 1957.—Orig. title: *Die Erdenjahre Unseres Herrn Jesus Christus.* Freiburg: Herder Verlag, 1943.
43. HOPHAN, OTTO. *Il lieto messaggio.* Turin: Marietti, 1953; 1st ed., 1945.—Orig. title: *Die Frohe Botschaft: Leben und Lehren unseres Herrn.* Schwyz: Drittordenszentrale, 1941.
44. JAEGER, NICOLA. *Il processo di Gesù.* Turin: S.P.E., 1962.
45. LAGRANGE, MARIE JOSEPH. *L'évangile de Jésus Christ.* Paris: J. Gabalda, 1928.—Eng. trans.: *The Gospel of Jesus Christ.* Translated by members of the English Dominican Province. London: Burns, Oates & Washbourne Ltd., 1938; Westminster, Md.: Newman Press, 1943.
46. LEBRETON, JULES. *La vie et l'enseignement de Jésus Christ Notre Seigneur.* 2 vols. Paris: Beauchesne, 1931; 1st ed., 1923. —Eng. trans.: *The Life and Teaching of Jesus Christ Our Lord.* Translated by FRANCIS DAY. London: Burns, Oates & Washbourne, 1935; 2d ed., 1950.
47. LE CAMUS, ÉMILE. *La vie de Notre Seigneur Jésus Christ.* 3 vols. Paris: Oudin, 1901; 1st ed., 1883.—Eng. trans.: *The Life of Christ.* Translated by WILLIAM A. HICKEY. New York: The Cathedral Library Association, 1906–8.
48. LÉON-DUFOUR, XAVIER. *Les évangiles et l'histoire de Jésus.* Paris: Editions du Seuil, 1963.

49. LEPIN, MARIUS. *Jésus Messie et Fils de Dieu.* Paris: Letouzey, 1923; 1st ed., 1900.—Eng. trans.: *Christ and the Gospel; or Jesus the Messiah and Son of God.* Authorized English version. Philadelphia: J. J. McVey, 1910.

50. MAGRI, FRANCESCO. *Gesù Cristo—La vita, la dottrina, le opere, nella storia e nella critica.* Milan: L. Romano, 1945.

51. MARCHESAN, MARCO. *Mentalità e carattere di Gesù.* Milan: Istituto di Indagini Psicologiche, 1957; 1st ed., 1956.

52. MAURIAC, FRANÇOIS. *Vita di Gesù.* Milan: Mondadori, 1950.—Orig. title: *La vie de Jésus.* Paris: Flammarion, 1936.—Eng. trans.: *Life of Jesus.* Translated by JULIE KERNAN, illustrated by GEORGE BUDAY. New York and Toronto: Longmans, Green, 1937; New York: David McKay Co., 1951.

53. PAPINI, GIOVANNI. *Storia di Cristo.* 2 vols. Florence: Vallecchi, 1944; 1st ed., 1921.—Eng. trans.: *Life of Christ.* Freely translated from the Italian by DOROTHY CANFIELD FISHER. New York: Harcourt, Brace, 1923; *The Story of Christ.* Translated by MARY PRICHARD AGNETTI. London: Hodder & Stoughton, 1923.

54. PETRELLI, GIUSEPPE. *Il figliuolo dell'Uomo.* Torre Pellice: Tipografia Subalpina, 1957.

55. PINARD DE LA BOULLAYE, HENRY. *Jésus et l'histoire. Conférences de Notre Dame de Paris (année 1929).* Paris: Spes, 1929.

56. PRAT, FERDINAND. *Jésus Christ: Sa vie, sa doctrine, son oeuvre.* 2 vols. Paris: Beauchesne, 1933.—Eng. trans.: *Jesus Christ: His Life, His Teaching and His Work.* Translated from the sixteenth French edition by JOHN J. HEEHAN. Milwaukee: Bruce Publishing Co., 1950.

57. RADIUS, EMILIO. *Vita di Cristo per gli uomini d'oggi.* Milan: Rizzoli, 1958.

58. RICCIOTTI, GIUSEPPE. *Vita di Gesù Cristo.* Rome: Tipografia Poliglotta Vaticana, 1948; 1st ed., Milan: Rizzoli, 1941.—Eng. trans.: *Life of Christ.* Translated by ALBA I. ZIZZAMIA. Abridged and edited by ALOYSIUS CROFT. Popular ed. Milwaukee: Bruce Publishing Co., 1952.

59. TONDELLI, LEONE. *Gesù Cristo: Studio su le fonti, il pensiero e l'opera.* Turin: S.E.I., 1936.

60. ———. *La psicologia di Cristo.* Assisi: Pro Civitate Christiana, 1944.

61. VANNUTELLI, PRIMO. *Il figlio dell'uomo: Studio sugli Evangeli.* Rome: Bardi, 1928; 1st ed., 1923.

62. ———. *Sinossi degli Evangelisti.* Rome: Marietti, 1942; 1st ed., 1931.

63. VILLA FAUSTO. *Il processo di Gesù.* Turin: S. Lattes, 1925.

64. WESTPHAL, ALEXANDRE. *Jésus de Nazareth.* Lausanne: Editions La Concorde, 1915; 1st ed., 1914.

65. WIKENHAUSER, ALFRED. *Einleitung in das Neue Testament.* Freiburg: Herder Verlag, 1953.—Eng. trans.: *New Testament Introduction.* Translated by JOSEPH CUNNIGHAN. New York: Herder and Herder, 1954.

66. WILLAM, FRANZ MICHEL. *La vita di Gesù nel paese e nel popolo d'Israele.* Turin: S.E.I., 1945.—Orig. title: *Das Leben Jesu im Lande und Volke Israel.* Freiburg: Herder Verlag, 1934.

b) Protestant and Modernist Catholic Works

In Germany particularly, the Protestant Reformation, with its principle of unrestricted research, encouraged the flowering of diverse schools of New Testament studies concentrated on separating the historical reality of Jesus and his real teachings from the subsequent amplifications.

The liberal, or historical, school (Harnack, Holtzmann, Sabatier, B. Weiss, etc.) endeavors to extract the message of Jesus from the Gospels and to strip it of dogma, of Messianic interpretation, and of the influences of Gnosticism.

The *Formgeschichte,* or "form-criticism," school (Dibelius, Bultmann, Cullmann, etc.) seeks through critical literary examination of the texts of the Gospels to reconstruct the extent to which the New Testament was elaborated after the oral traditions of the first Christians.

The Tübingen school (headed by Ferdinand C. Baur) considers the Gospels an adulterated blending (dating from the first century A.D.) of Petristic Judaic sectarianism, to which Christianity was only an evolution of Hebraic conceptions, and of Pauline Hellenistic universalism, which tended to modify the Jewish religion under the influence of Greek Stoicism.

The comparative school (Bousset, Burkitt, etc.) engages in very profound research into the relations between Christianity and the other Near Eastern religions or the Greek mystery cults.

The eschatological school (J. Weiss, Goguel, Schweitzer, Wrede, etc.) concentrates particularly on the eschatological element—the anticipation of the kingdom—in the Gospels.

Critical work analogous to that of all these schools is considered necessary by a minority of Catholic scholars, the so-called modernists (Buonaiuti, Loisy, etc.), excommunicated by the Church of Rome.

67. BAPST, EDMOND. *La vie historique de Notre Seigneur Jésus Christ.* 2 vols. Paris: Imprimerie Générale Lahure, 1924.

68. BAUER, WALTER. *Das Leben Jesu im Zeitalter der Neutesta-mentlichen Apokryphen.* Tübingen: J. C. B. Mohr, 1909; 1st ed., 1840.

69. BORNKAMM, GÜNTHER. *Jesus von Nazareth.* Stuttgart: W. Kohlammer, 1957; 1st ed., 1951.—Eng. trans.: *Jesus of Nazareth.* Translated by IRENE and FRASER McLUSKEY, with JAMES N. ROBINSON. New York: Harper & Row, 1960.

70. BOUSSET, WILHELM. *Kyrios Christos.* 2 vols. Göttingen: E. A. Huth, 1921; 1st ed., 1913.

71. BULTMANN, RUDOLF. *Die Geschichte der synoptischen Tra-dition.* Göttingen: Wandenhoeck & Ruprecht, 1958; 1st ed., 1921.—Eng. trans.: *History of the Synoptic Tradition.* New York: Harper & Row, 1963.

72. BUONAIUTI, ERNESTO. *Gesù il Cristo.* Rome: Formiggini, 1926.

73. BURKITT, FRANCIS CRAWFORD. *Il Vangelo e la sua storia.* Tu-rin: Bocca, 1909.—Orig. title: *The Gospel History and Its Transmission.* Edinburgh: T. & T. Clark, 1906.

74. BUSHNELL, HORACE. *Il carattere di Gesù.* Bologna: Zanichelli, 1925.—Orig. title: *The Character of Jesus, Forbidden His Possible Classification with Men.* New York: Charles Scrib-ner's Sons, 1910; first published as Chapter 10 of *Nature and the Supernatural* (New York: Charles Scribner's Sons, 1851).

75. DALMAN, GUSTAF HERMANN. *Die Worte Jesu.* 2 vols. Leipzig: J. C. Hintichs, 1930; 1st ed., 1898.—Eng. trans.: *The Words of Jesus.* Edinburgh: no publisher, 1902.

76. ———. *Jesus-Jeschua: Die drei Sprachen Jesu.* Leipzig: J. C. Hintichs, 1922; 1st ed., 1889.—Eng. trans.: *Jesus-Jeschua: Stud-ies in the Gospels.* Authorized translation by THE REV. PAUL P. LEVERTOFF. New York: The Macmillan Co., 1929.

77. ———. *Orte und Wege Jesu.* 3 vols. Gütersloh: C. Bertels-mann, 1924; 1st ed., 1886.—Eng. trans.: *Sacred Sites and Ways.* Translated by THE REV. PAUL P. LEVERTOFF. New York: The Macmillan Co., 1935.

78. GLOVER, TERROT REAVELEY. *The Jesus of History.* New York: Association Press, 1917.

79. GOGUEL, MAURICE. *La vie de Jésus et l'église primitive.* Paris: Payot, 1932; 1st ed., 1925.—Eng. trans.: *The Life of Jesus.* Translated by OLIVE WYON. New York: The Macmillan Co., 1933.

80. JEREMIAS, JOACHIM. *Die Gleichnisse Jesu.* Zurich: Zwingli Verlag, 1952; 1st ed., 1947.—Eng. trans.: *The Parables of Jesus.*

Rev. ed. translated by S. H. HOOKE. New York: Charles Scribner's Sons, 1955.

81. KEIM, KARL THEODOR. *Geschichte Jesu von Nazara.* 3 vols. Zurich: Drell, 1873; 1st ed., Ebend, 1867.—Eng. trans.: *The History of Jesus of Nazara: Considered in Its Connection with the National Life of Israel, and Related in Detail.* 6 vols. Translated by ARTHUR RANSOM. London and Edinburgh: Williams & Norgate, 1873–83.

82. LACEY, THOMAS ALEXANDER. *Il Cristo storico.* Turin: Bocca, 1907; 1st ed., 1906.—Orig. title: *The Historic Christ.* London: Longmans, 1905.

83. LIETZMANN, HANS. *Der Prozess Jesu.* Berlin: Akademie der Wissenschaften in Kommission, bei W. de Bruyter und Co., 1931.

84. LOISY, ALFRED FIRMIN. *Les évangiles synoptiques.* 2 vols. Ceffonds: Chez l'Auteur, 1907.

85. LUDWIG, EMIL. *Le fils de l'homme.* Paris, 1930.—Orig. title: *Der Menschensohn: Geschichte eines Propheten.* Berlin: Ernst Rowohlt Verlag, 1927.—Eng. trans.: *The Son of Man: The Story of Jesus.* Translated from the German by EDEN and CEDAR PAUL. New York: Boni & Liveright, 1928; rev. ed., New York: Fawcett Publications, 1957.

86. MEREZHKOVSKI, DIMITRII SERGIEEVICH. *Gesù sconosciuto.* Florence: Marzocco, 1948.—Eng. trans.: *Jesus the Unknown.* Translated from the Russian by H. CHROUSCHOFF MATHESON, with a Preface by THE VERY REV. W. R. INGE. London: Jonathan Cape, 1933; New York: Charles Scribner's Sons, 1934.

87. ————. *La missione di Gesù.* Florence: Marzocco, 1948.— Eng. trans.: *Jesus Manifest.* Translated by EDWARD GELLIBRAND. New York: Charles Scribner's, Sons, 1936.

88. ————. *Morte e Resurrezione.* Florence: Marzocco, 1948.

89. NISBET, ROBERTO. *Il vangelo non dice così.* Torre Pellice: Edizioni Claudiane, 1958.

90. OMODEO, ADOLFO. *Gesù il Nazoreo.* Venice: La Nuova Italia, 1927.

91. REVILLE, ALBERT. *Jésus de Nazareth: Études critiques sur les antécédents de l'histoire évangélique et de la vie de Jésus.* 2 vols. Paris: Fischbacher, 1906; 1st ed., 1897.

92. ROSADI, GIOVANNI. *Il processo di Gesù.* Florence: Sansoni, 1903.—Eng. trans.: *The Trial of Jesus.* Edited, with a Preface, by EMIL REICH. New York: Dodd, Mead, 1905.

93. SCHWEITZER, ALBERT. *Geschichte der Leben-Jesu-Forschung.* Tübingen: J. C. B. Mohr, 1913; 1st ed., 1906.—Eng. trans.: *The Quest of the Historical Jesus: A Critical Study of Its Progress from Reimarus to Wrede.* Translated by W. MONTGOMERY. London: A. C. Black, 1910; New York: The Macmillan Co., 1948.

94. SMITH, WILLIAM BENJAMIN. *Der Vorchristliche Jesu.* Leipzig: C. G. Röder, 1906.

95. STAPFER, EDMOND LOUIS. *Jésus Christ avant son ministère.* Paris: Fischbacher, 1896.—Eng. trans.: *Jesus Christ Before His Ministry.* Translated by LOUISE SEYMOUR HOUGHTON. New York: Charles Scribner's Sons, 1896.

96. ———. *Jésus Christ pendant son ministère.* Paris: Fischbacher, 1897.—Eng. trans.: *Jesus Christ During His Ministry.* Translated by LOUISE SEYMOUR HOUGHTON. New York: Charles Scribner's Sons, 1897.

97. ———. *La mort et la résurrection de Jésus Christ.* Paris: Fischbacher, 1898.—Eng. trans.: *The Death and Resurrection of Jesus Christ.* Translated by LOUISE SEYMOUR HOUGHTON. New York: Charles Scribner's Sons, 1898.

98. TACCONE-GALLUCCI, NICOLA. *L'uomo-Dio.* Milan: Romano, 1881.

99. WEISS, JOHANNES. *Die Predigt Jesu vom Reiche Gottes.* 2 vols. Göttingen: Vandenhoech & Ruprecht, 1900; 1st ed., 1892.

c) Esoteric Works

The esoterics give the parables and miracles narrated in the Gospels a mystical-symbolic interpretation based on the principles of Theosophy. They see in Christianity one of the many aspects of universal religion and in Jesus one of the innumerable incarnations of the one God.

100. BESANT, ANNIE. *Esoteric Christianity; or The Lesser Mysteries.* New York: J. Lane, 1902; New York: Theosophical Press, 1957.

101. GRANCELLI, UMBERTO. *Il simbolo nella vita di Gesù.* Verona: Palminteri, 1947.

102. "RAMACHARAKA, YOGI" (WILLIAM WALKER ATKINSON). *Cristianesimo mistico.* Turin: Bocca, 1924.—Orig. title: *Mystic Christianity, or The Inner Teachings of the Master.* Chicago: Yogi Publishing Society, 1908.

103. REBAUDI, OSCAR. *La vida de Jesús dictada por él mismo.* Buenos Aires: J. Roldán, 1948.

104. Schuré, Édouard. *L'évolution divine du sphinx au Christ.* Paris: Perrin, 1913.—Eng. trans.: *From Sphinx to Christ.* Translated by Eva Martin. London: Rider, 1928; Philadelphia: David McKay Co., 1928.

105. ———. *I grandi iniziati.* Bari: Laterza, 1932.—Orig. title: *Les grands initiés: Esquisse de l'histoire secrète des religions.* Paris: Perrin, 1889.—Eng. trans.: *The Great Initiates: Sketch of the Secret History of Religions.* Translated by Fred Rothwell. Philadelphia: David McKay Co., 1922.

106. "Soter" (F. S. Attal). *La religione del Cristo.* Turin: Bocca, 1915.

d) Rationalist, Mythologist, and Radical Works

The Rationalists (Reimarus, Paulus, Venturini, etc.), obedient to the Illuminist principle that no truth can be accepted alone, that a "rational" explanation of it is always to be sought, have dedicated themselves to the naturalistic explanation of the miracles contained in the Gospels, which they view as a fantastic transformation of actual fact as a result of superstition and of the fanaticism of the Apostles. The rationalists' conclusions have led an ever greater number of scholars, even the eclectics (Renan, Schenkel, Seeley, etc.), to separate what is historical in the life of Jesus from what is the artifact of faith.

The mythologists (Strauss, Couchoud, Bossi, etc.) maintain that the historical element in the New Testament is almost imperceptible; all the rest is legend embroidered by the early Christians and is to be explained by the theory of myth inspired by Hegel. The latest of the mythologists (Bossi, Puglisi, etc.) have cast doubt even on the existence of Jesus, whom they believe to be an adaptation of the solar myth.

The radical historians (Martinetti, Orano, etc.) do not as a rule deny the existence of Jesus, but they ascribe a primarily political and revolutionary intent to his activity.

107. Alfaric, Prosper. *Pour comprendre la vie de Jésus.* Paris: F. Rieder, 1929.

108. Argentieri, Domenico. *Quando visse Cristo?* Milan: Bocca, 1945.

109. Binet-Sanglé, Charles. *La folie de Jésus.* 4 vols. Paris: A. Maloine, 1908, 1910, 1912, 1915.

110. Bossi, Emilio ("Milesbo"). *Gesù Cristo non è mai esistito.* MS in the National Library of Turin and Milan, 1924.

111. ———. *Cristo nella storia, nella Bibbia, nella mitologia.* Bellinzona: Tipografia Libraria Editrice, 1935.

112. Couchoud, Paul Louis. *Il mistero di Gesù.* Milan: Bocca, 1945.—Orig. title: *Le mystère de Jésus.* Paris: F. Rieder, 1924. —Eng. trans.: *The Enigma of Jesus.* Translated by "Winifred

WHALE" (WINIFRED STEPHENS), with an Introduction by SIR JAMES FRAZER. London: Watts, 1924.

113. DREWS, ARTHUR CHRISTIAN HEINRICH. *Die Christusmythe.* Jena: E. Diederichs, 1909.—Eng. trans.: *The Christ Myth.* Translated by C. D. BURNS. London: T. F. Unwin, 1910; Chicago: The Open Court Publishing Co., 1911.

114. FRANZÉ, ANTONIO. *Gesù.* Polistena: R. Pascale, 1941.

115. GUIGNEBERT, CHARLES. *Gesù.* Turin: Einaudi, 1950.—Orig. title: *Jésus.* Paris: La Renaissance du Livre, 1933.—Eng. trans.: *Jesus.* Translated by S. H. HOOKE. New York: Alfred A. Knopf, 1935; New York: University Books, 1956.

116. JULICHER, ADOLF. *Die Gleichnisreden Jesu.* 2 vols. Tübingen: J. C. B. Mohr, 1910; 1st ed., Freiburg: J. C. B. Mohr, 1888 and 1899.

117. KLAUSNER, JOSEPH. *Jésus de Nazareth: Son temps, sa vie, sa doctrine.* Translated from the Hebrew. Paris: Payot, 1933.—Orig. title: *Jĕshuha-Notzri.* Jerusalem: Jewish Publishing House, 1922.—Eng. trans.: *Jesus of Nazareth: His Life, Times, and Teaching.* Translated from the original Hebrew by HERBERT DANBY. New York: The Macmillan Co., 1925.

118. LABANCA, BALDASSARE. *Gesù di Nazareth.* Turin: Bocca, 1910.

119. LOOFS, FREDERICK. *What Is the Truth About Jesus Christ?* New York: Charles Scribner's Sons, 1913.

120. MARTINETTI, PIERO. *Gesù Cristo e il cristianesimo.* 2 vols. Milan: Denti, 1949; 1st ed., 1933.

121. ORANO, PAOLO. *Cristo e Quirino.* Turin: Bocca, 1908.

122. PASTORELLO, DOMENICO. *Rivelazione.* Genoa: Edizioni Anteo, 1957.

123. PAULUS, HEINRICH E. G. *Das Leben Jesu als Grundlage einer reinen Geschichte des Urchristentums.* 3 vols. Heidelberg: K. Winter, 1828.

124. ———. *Das exegetische Handbuch über die drei ersten Evangelien.* 2 vols. Heidelberg: K. Winter, 1830; 1st ed., 1804.

125. PUGLISI, MARIO. *Gesù e il mito di Cristo: Saggio di critica metodologica.* Bari: Laterza, 1912.

126. REIMARUS, HERMANN SAMUEL. *Geschichte der Leben-Jesu-Forschung.* Tübingen: J. C. B. Mohr, 1906; 1st ed., Hamburg: Campe, 1774.

127. RENAN, ERNEST. *Vie de Jésus.* Paris: Michel Lévy Frères, 1928; 1st ed., Paris: Michel Lévy, 1863; the definitive edition is the

thirteenth, 1867.—Eng. trans.: *The Life of Jesus.* Complete ed. London and New York: Brentano's, 1863; translated by CHARLES EDWIN WILBOUR, New York: Carleton, 1864; trans. newly rev. from the 13th and final ed., London and Toronto: J. M. Dent and Sons; New York: Modern Library, 1927.

128. SALVADOR, JOSEPH. *Jésus Christ et sa doctrine.* Paris: A. Guyot et Scribe, 1838.

129. SCHLEIERMACHER, FRIEDRICH ERNST DANIEL. *Das Leben Jesu.* Vol. VI of Schleiermacher's *Sammtliche Werke.* Berlin: G. Reimer, 1864.

130. SEELEY, JOHN ROBERT. *Ecce homo.* Turin: Bocca, 1910.—Orig. title: *Ecce Homo: A Survey of the Life and Works of Jesus Christ.* London: J. M. Dent, 1866; New York: E. P. Dutton, 1907; reprinted, 1932.

131. STEINER, RUDOLF. *Das Christentum als mystiche Tatsache und die Mysterien des Alentums.* Leipzig: M. Altmann, 1910.—Eng. trans.: *Christianity as Mystical Fact and the Mysteries of Antiquity.* Translated from the German and with notes by E. A. FROMMER, GABRIELLE HESS, and PETER KAENDLER, and with an Introduction by ALFRED HEIDENREICH. West Nyack, N.Y.: Rudolf Steiner Publications, 1961.

132. STEUDEL, FRIEDRICH. *Hat Jesus Gelebt?* Frankfurt: Neuer Frankfurter Verlag, 1910.

133. STRAUSS, DAVID FRIEDRICH. *Vie de Jésus.* 2 vols. Paris: Ladrange, 1839.—Orig. title: *Das Leben Jesu, Kritisch Bearbeitet.* Tübingen: C. F. Osiander, 1835–36.—Eng. trans.: *The Life of Jesus, Critically Examined.* Translated from the fourth German edition by MARIAN EVANS. New York: C. Blanchard, 1855.

134. TURCOTTI, AURELIO. *Vita politica di Gesù.* 2 vols. Turin: Tipografia Borgarelli, 1879–80.

135. TURONE, MARCO. *Gesù e Paolo identificati nella storia profana.* Parma: Guanda, 1959.

136. VELLA, ROBERTO. *La vita di Gesù messa a confronto con Napoleone I, Garibaldi e col Papato.* Naples: Tipografia di L. Gargiulo, 1863.

137. VENTURINI, KARL H. *Natürliche Geschichte des grossen Propheten von Nazareth.* 4 vols. Copenhagen: Schubothe, 1806.

138. WEISS, BERNHARD. *Das Leben Jesu.* 2 vols. Stuttgart: J. C. Cotta, 1902; 1st ed., 1882.—Eng. trans.: *The Life of Christ.* Translated by JOHN WALTER HOPE and M. G. HOPE. 3 vols. Edinburgh: T. & T. Clark, 1883–84.

139. ———. *Lehrbuch der Einleitung in das Neue Testament.* Berlin: W. Nertz, 1889.—Eng. trans.: *A Manual of Introduction to the New Testament.* Translated from the German by A. J. K. DAVIDSON. 2 vols. New York: Funk & Wagnalls, 1889.

III. MARIOLOGY

a) Catholic Works

140. ASIOLI, LUIGI. *Vita di Maria.* Milan: Ulrico Hoepli, 1923; 1st ed., 1916.
141. BERTETTO, DOMENICO. *Maria nel domma cattolico: Trattato di Mariologia.* Turin: S.E.I., 1955; 1st ed., 1949.
142. HOPHAN, OTTO. *Maria.* Turin: Marietti, 1953.—Orig. title: *Maria: Unsere Hohe liebe Frau.* Lucerne: Räber, 1947.
143. LAURENTIN, RENÉ. *Court traité de théologie mariale.* Paris: Lethielleux, 1959.
144. ———. *La Vierge au Concile.* Paris: Lethielleux, 1965.
145. MANISE, GIOVANNI. "Maria Santissima," in *Dizionario di Teologia Morale.* Rome: Studium, 1954.
146. ROSCHINI, GIUSEPPE. *La vita di Maria.* Roma: Bellardetti, 1946.
147. SEMMELROTH, OTTO. *Marie archétype de l'église.* Paris: Fleurus, 1965.

b) Protestant Works

148. LOEWENICH, WALTER VON. *Il cattolicesimo moderno* (Chapter 6). Milan: Feltrinelli, 1962.—Orig. title: *Der moderne Katholizismus.* Witten/Ruhr: Luther Verlag, 1956.

IV. APOSTLES, HISTORY OF THE CHURCH

a) Catholic Works

149. ALLARD, PAUL. *Histoire des persécutions.* 5 vols. Paris: Victor Lecoffre, 1884–90.
150. BARDY, GUSTAVE. *La conversion au christianisme durant les premiers siècles.* Paris: Aubier, 1948.
151. BATIFFOL, PIERRE. *L'église naissante et le catholicisme.* Paris: J. Gabalda, 1927; 1st ed., 1909.—Eng. trans.: *Primitive Ca-*

tholicism. Translated by H. L. BRIANÇEAU, from the 5th French ed., revised by the author. London: Longmans, Green, 1911.

152. BIHLMEYER, KARL, and TECHLE, HERMANN. *Storia della Chiesa*. 4 vols. Brescia: Morcelliana, 1955.—Orig. title: *Kirchengeschichte*. Paderbon: F. Schöning, 1911.

153. BREZZI, PAOLO. *Dalle persecuzioni alla pace di Costantino*. Rome: Studium, 1960.

154. "DANIEL-ROPS, HENRI" (HENRY PETIOT). *Storia della Chiesa del Cristo*. 6 vols. Turin: Marietti, 1951–58.—Orig. title: *Histoire de l'église du Christ*. Paris: Fayard, 1950–55.

155. FESTUGIÈRE, ANDRÉ JEAN, and FABRE, PIERRE. *Il mondo greco-romano al tempo di Gesù Cristo*. Turin: S.E.I., 1955.—Orig. title: *Le monde greco-romain au temps de Notre Seigneur*. Paris: Bloud & Gay, 1935.

156. GIORDANI, IGINO. *Il messaggio sociale degli Apostoli*. Turin: S.E.I., 1937.

157. HOPHAN, OTTO. *Gli Apostoli*. Turin: Marietti, 1950.—Orig. title: *Die Aposteln*. Lucerne: Räber, 1946.—Eng. trans.: *The Apostles*. Westminster, Md.: Newman Press, 1962.

158. LE BLANT, EDMOND FRÉDÉRIC. "Sur les bases juridiques des poursuites dirigées contre les martyrs," in *Comptes-rendus de l'Académie des Inscriptions* (Paris, 1866), Vol. II.

159. LEBRETON, JULES, and ZEILLER, JACQUES. *L'église primitive*. Vol. I of *Histoire de l'église*. 24 vols. Paris: Bloud & Gay, 1948; 1st ed., 1934.—Eng. trans.: *The History of the Primitive Church*. Translated from the French by ERNEST C. MESSENGER, with a Foreword by AUGUSTIN FLICHE and VICTOR MARTIN. 4 vols. London: Burnes, Oates & Washbourne, 1949; New York: The Macmillan Co., 1949.

160. LE CAMUS, ÉMILE. *L'oeuvre des Apôtres: Fondation de l'église chrétienne*. 3 vols. Paris: Oudin, 1891, 1905, 1906.

161. LORTZ, JOSEPH. *Storia della Chiesa nello sviluppo delle sue idee*. Alba: Edizioni Paoline, 1952.—Orig. title: *Geschichte der Kirche in ideengeschichtlicher Betrachtung*. Münster: Aschendorffsche Verlagsbuchhandlung, 1932.—Eng. trans.: *History of the Church*. Adapted from the 5th and 6th German eds. by EDWIN KAISER. Milwaukee: Bruce Publishing Co., 1939.

162. MARTINI, CARLO M. *Il problema storico della resurrezione negli studi recenti*. Rome: Tipografia P.U.G., 1959.

163. PAGNINI, IGINO. "La messa nei primi secoli," *La Rocca* (Assisi), March, 1954, pp. 12–13.

164. RICCIOTTI, GIUSEPPE. *Paolo Apostolo*. Rome: Tipografia Poli-glotta Vaticana, 1946.—Eng. trans.: *Paul the Apostle*. Trans-lated by ALBA I. ZIZZAMIA. Milwaukee: Bruce Publishing Co., 1953.

165. ROHRBACHER, JOHANN ANTON. *Storia universale della Chiesa cattolica: Dal principio del mondo fino ai dì nostri*. 16 vols. Turin: Marietti, 1874.—Orig. title: *Universalgeschichte der Katholischen Kirche*. Münster: Thässing, 1864.

166. SCIAMANNINI, RANIERO. *La Chiesa di Cristo*. Florence: Città di Vita, 1960.

b) Protestant and Modernist Catholic Works

167. BAINTON, ROLAND HERBERT. *La riforma protestante*. Turin: Einaudi, 1958.—Orig. title: *The Reformation of the Sixteenth Century*. Boston: Beacon Press, 1951.

168. BAUR, FERDINAND CHRISTIAN. *Das Christentum der drei ersten Jahrhunderte*. Tübingen: Fues Verlag, 1863.—Eng. trans.: *The Church History of the First Three Centuries*. 3d ed. Translated from the German by A. MENZIES. 2 vols. Edin-burgh: T. & T. Clark, 1878–79.

169. BUONAIUTI, ERNESTO. *Saggi di storia del cristianesimo*. Edited by A. DONINI and M. NICCOLI. Venice: Pozza, 1957.

170. ————. *Pietre miliari della storia del cristianesimo*. Modena: Guanda, 1935.

171. DEISSMANN, ADOLF. *Licht vom Osten*. Tübingen: J. C. B. Mohr, 1923; 1st ed., 1909.—Eng. trans.: *Light from the An-cient East: The New Testament Illustrated by Recently Dis-covered Texts of the Graeco-Roman World*. Translated by LIONEL R. M. STRACHAN. London: Hodder & Stoughton, 1911; New York: George H. Doran Co., 1927.

172. DURELL, JOHN CARLYON VAVASOR. *La Chiesa storica*. Turin: Bocca, 1910.—Orig. title: *The Historic Church: An Essay on the Conception of the Christian Church and Its Ministry in the Sub-Apostolic Age*. Cambridge: The University Press, 1906.

173. GOGUEL, MAURICE. *La naissance du Christianisme*. Paris: Payot, 1946; 1st ed., 1933.—Eng. trans.: *The Birth of Chris-tianity*. Translated by H. C. SNAPE. London: Allen & Unwin, 1953.

174. GOUGH, MICHAEL. *The Early Christians*. London: Thames and Hudson, 1961; New York: Frederick A. Praeger, 1961.

175. HARNACK, ADOLF VON. *Missione e propagazione del cristiane-simo nei primi tre secoli.* Milan: Bocca, 1906.—Orig. title: *Die Mission und Aufbreitung des Christentums in den ersten drei Jahrhunderten.* Leipzig: J. C. Hinrichs, 1902.—Eng. trans.: *The Expansion of Christianity in the First Three Centuries.* Translated and edited by JAMES MOFFATT. London: Williams and Norgate; New York: G. P. Putnam's Sons, 1904–5.

176. ———. *Sokrates und die alte Kirche.* Berlin: J. Ricker, 1900.

177. LOISY, ALFRED FIRMIN. *Le origini del cristianesimo.* Turin: Einaudi, 1942.—Orig. title: *La naissance du christianisme.* Paris: Émile Nourry, 1933.—Eng. trans.: *The Birth of the Christian Religion and The Origins of the New Testament.* Authorized translation from the French by L. P. JACKS. New Hyde Park, N.Y.: University Books, 1962.

178. MEYER, EDUARD. *Ursprung und Anfänge des Christentums.* 3 vols. Stuttgart and Berlin: J. G. Cotta, 1921–23.

179. MEYNIER, ENRICO. *Storia del cristianesimo.* Torre Pellice: Edizioni Claudiane, 1930; 1st ed., Florence: Pubblicazioni Evangeliche, 1924.

180. OMODEO, ADOLFO. *Gesù e le origini del cristianesimo.* Messina: Principato, 1913.

181. ROBERTSON, ARCHIBALD. *Le origini del cristianesimo.* Florence: Parenti, 1960.—Orig. title: *The Origins of Christianity.* London: Lawrence & Wishart, 1953; New York: International Publishers, 1954.

182. WEISS, JOHANNES. *Das Urchristentum.* Göttingen: Vandenhoeck & Ruprecht, 1917.—Eng. trans.: *The History of Primitive Christianity.* Completed by RUDOLF KNOPF. Translated by four friends and edited by FREDERICK C. GRANT. 2 vols. New York: Wilson-Erickson, 1937.

c) Rationalist and Radical Works

183. MOMMSEN, THEODOR. "Die Religionsfrevel nach römischen Recht," *Historiche Zeitschrift* (Berlin), LXIV (1890), 389–429.

184. RENAN, ERNEST. *Les Apôtres.* Paris: Michel Lévy Frères, 1866. —Eng. trans.: *The Apostles.* London: Mathieson, 1890.

185. SALVADOR, JOSEPH. *Histoire de la naissance de l'église, de son organisation et de ses progrès pendant le l^{er} siècle.* Paris: Guyot et Scribe, 1838.

186. SIMON, MARCEL. *I primi cristiani.* Milan: Garzanti, 1958.— Orig. title: *Les premiers chrétiens.* Paris: Edition P.U.F., 1933.
187. SOREL, GEORGES. *La ruine du monde antique.* Paris: M. Rivière, 1933; 1st ed., 1901.
188. ZELLER, EDUARD. *Geschichte der christlichen Kirche.* Stuttgart: Franck, 1863; 1st ed., 1848.
189. ———. *Vorträge und Abhandlungen Geschichtlichen Inhalts des Urchristentum.* Leipzig: Fues Verlag, 1875.

V. THEOLOGY, DOGMA, POLITICAL AND SOCIAL QUESTIONS

a) Catholic Works

190. ADAM, KARL. "La coscienza del Cristo in S. Giovanni," *Humanitas,* No. 7 (July, 1959), pp. 489–99.
191. BARBERO, GIUSEPPE. *Il pensiero politico cristiano dai Vangeli a Pelagio.* Turin: U.T.E.T., 1962.
192. BARDY, GUSTAVE, and TRICOT, ALPHONSE. *Enciclopedia cristologica.* Alba: Edizioni Paoline, 1960.—Orig. title: *Encyclopédie populaire des connaissances christologiques.* Paris: Librairie Bloud & Gay, 1946.
193. BELLINO, GIUSEPPE. *Gesù Cristo nelle SS. Scritture e nei SS. Padri e Dottori.* 9 vols. Turin: U.T.E.T., 1914–15.
194. BOUYER, LOUIS. *Il quarto Vangelo.* Turin: Borla, 1964.— Orig. title: *Le Quatrième Evangile: Introduction à l'Evangile de Jean.* Tournai: Casterman, 1960.
195. BREZZI, PAOLO. "Il senso comunitario nel cristianesimo delle origini," *Comunità* (Milan), No. 71 (1959), pp. xi–xvi.
196. DENZINGER, HEINRICH JOSEPH DOMINIK. *Enchiridion Symbolorum.* Freiburg: Herder Verlag, 1952; 1st ed., Wirceburg: Staelin, 1854.
197. GAROFALO, SALVATORE. *Dall'evangelo agli evangeli.* Rome: Studium, 1953.
198. JANSSENS, JEAN HÉRALD. *Hermeneutica sacra in omnes libros Veteris ac Novi Foederis.* Turin: Officina Libraria Marietti, 1892.
199. JANSSE, LUCIEN. *La proprieté, le régime des biens dans les civilisations occidentales.* Paris: Les Editions Ouvrières, 1953.
200. LABANCA, BALDASSARE. *Della religione e della filosofia cristiana.* 2 vols. Turin: Ermanno Loescher, 1886 and 1888.

201. LEBRETON, JULES. *Histoire du dogme de la Trinité*. Vol. I: *Des origines à Saint Augustin*. Vol. II: *Au Concile de Nicée*. Paris: G. Beauchesne, 1928; 1st ed., 1910.—Eng. trans.: *History of the Dogma of the Trinity: From Its Origins to the Council of Nicaea*. Translated by ALGAR THOROLD from the eighth edition. London: Burns, Oates & Washbourne, 1939.

202. MORALDI, LUIGI (ed.). *Introduzione alla Bibbia*. 4 vols. Turin: Marietti, 1959.

203. NEGRI, GAETANO. *Crisi religiosa*. Milan: Dumolard, 1878.

204. ORECCHIA, RINALDO. "Lo Stato nel pensiero cattolico," *Studium* (Rome), Nos. 7–8 (August, 1959), pp. 557–64.

205. PARENTE, PIETRO, PIOLANTI, ANTONIO, and GAROFALO, SALVATORE. *Dizionario di teologia dommatica*. Rome: Studium, 1952; 1st ed., 1943.

206. PETERSON, ERIK. *Il mistero degli Ebrei e dei Gentili nella Chiesa*. Milan: Comunità, 1946.—Orig. title: *Le mystère des Juifs et des Gentils dans l'église*. Paris: Desclée, de Brouwer, 1935.

207. PIROT, LOUIS (ed.). *Dictionnaire de la Bible*. 12 vols. Paris: Letouzey, 1960; 1st ed., 5 vols., 1895–1912.

208. ROBERT, ALPHONSE, and FEUILLET, ANDRÉ. *Introduction à la Bible*. 2 vols. Vol. I: *Introduction générale. Ancien Testament*. Vol. II: *Nouveau Testament*. Paris: Desclée, 1959.

209. ROBERTI, FRANCESCO (ed.). *Dizionario di Teologia morale*. Rome: Studium, 1954.

210. SAINTYVES, PIERRE. *Le discernement du miracle*. Paris: Émile Nourry, 1909.

211. SANTAYANA, GEORGE. *L'idea di Cristo nei Vangeli, o Dio nell'uomo*. Milan: Comunità, 1949.—Orig. title: *The Idea of Christ in the Gospels; or God in Man: A Critical Essay*. New York: Charles Scribner's Sons, 1946.

212. SCHLIER, HEINRICH. *Il tempo della Chiesa*. Bologna: Il Mulino, 1965.—Orig. title: *Die Zeit der Kirche*. Freiburg: Herder Verlag, 1955.

213. SICKENBERGER, JOSEPH. *Introduzione al Nuovo Testamento*. Turin: Marietti, 1942.—Orig. title: *Die Geschichte des Neuen Testaments*. Bonn, 1910.

214. SIMMEL, OSKAR, and STAEHLIN, RUDOLF. *La religione cristiana*. A Catholic and Protestant collaboration. Milan: Feltrinelli, 1962.—Orig. title: *Christiche Religion*. Frankfurt: Fischer Bücherei, 1957.

215. SOLERI, GIACOMO. *Economia e morale.* Turin: Borla, 1960.
216. SPICQ, CHARLES. *Théologie morale du Nouveau Testament.* 2 vols. Paris: J. Gabalda, 1965.
217. THOMAS AQUINAS. *Summa Theologica.* Translated by FATHERS OF THE ENGLISH DOMINICAN PROVINCE. 3 vols. New York: Benziger Bros., 1947–48.
218. VANBERGEN, PIERRE. *Index des thèmes du Nouveau Testament.* Bruges: Biblica, Publications de Saint-André, 1962.
219. ZOLLI, EUGENIO. *Guida all'Antico e Nuovo Testamento.* Milan: Garzanti, 1956.

b) Protestant, Modernist, Catholic, and Orthodox Works

220. BARTH, KARL. *L'epistola ai Romani.* Edited by GIUSEPPE MIEGGE. Milan: Feltrinelli, 1962.—Orig. title: *Der Römerbrief.* Zurich: Evangelischer Verlag Zollikon, 1919.—Eng. trans.: *The Epistle to the Romans.* Translated from the 6th ed. by EDWYN C. HOSKYNS, with a new Preface by the author. London: Oxford University Press, H. Milford, 1933.
221. BAUR, FERDINAND CHRISTIAN. *Lehrbuch der christichen Dogmengeschichte.* Leipzig: Fues Verlag, 1867.
222. BULTMANN, RUDOLF. "Neues Testaments und Mythologie," in *Kerygma und Mythos.* Edited by HANS W. BARTSCH. Hamburg: Reich & Heidrich, 1951; 1st ed., 1948.—Eng. trans.: *Kerygma and Myth: A Theological Debate.* London: Society for Promoting Christian Knowledge, 1953; New York: Harper & Row, 1961.
223. ———. *Theologie des Neuen Testaments.* 3 vols. Tübingen: J. C. B. Mohr, 1948–54.—Eng. trans.: *Theology of the New Testament.* Translated by KENDRICK GROBEL. New York: Charles Scribner's Sons, 1951.
224. CULLMANN, OSCAR. *Dio e Cesare: Il problema dello Stato nella Chiesa primitiva.* Milan: Comunità, 1957.—Orig. title: *Der Staat im Neuen Testaments.* Basel, 1956.
225. ———. *Christologie du Nouveau Testament.* Neuchâtel: Delachaux et Niestlé, 1958.—Orig. title: *Die Christologie des Neuen Testaments.* Tübingen: J. C. B. Mohr, 1957.—Eng. trans.: *The Christology of the New Testament.* Translated by SHIRLEY C. GUTHRIE and CHARLES A. M. HALL. Philadelphia: Westminster Press, 1959.
226. ———. *Cristo e il tempo.* Bologna: Il Mulino, 1965.—Orig. title: *Christus und die Zeit.* Zurich: Evangelischer Verlag Zol-

likon, 1946.—Eng. trans.: *Christ and Time: The Primitive Christian Conception of Time and History.* Translated from the German by FLOYD V. FILSON. Philadelphia: Westminster Press, 1950.

227. DODD, CHARLES HAROLD. *The Interpretation of the Fourth Gospel.* Cambridge and New York: Cambridge University Press, 1960; 1st ed., 1953.

228. EVDOKIMOV, PAUL. *L'Ortodossia.* Bologna: Il Mulino, 1965.—Orig. title: *L'Orthodoxie.* Paris: Delachaux & Niestlé, 1959.

229. FALCONI, CARLO. *L'umanità e il Cristo.* Milan: Comunità, 1946.

230. ———. *Storia delle encicliche.* Milan: Mondadori, 1965.

231. HARNACK, ADOLF VON. *L'essenza del cristianesimo.* Turin: Bocca, 1923.—Orig. title: *Das Wesen des Christentums.* Leipzig: J. C. Hinrichs, 1900.—Eng. trans.: *What Is Christianity?* New York: G. P. Putnam's Sons, 1901; London: Williams & Norgate, 1901; translated by THOMAS BAILEY SAUNDERS, with an Introduction by RUDOLF BULTMANN, New York: Harper & Bros., 1957.

232. HOLTZMANN, HEINRICH JULIUS. *Lehrbuch der historisch-kritischen Einleitung in das Neue Testament.* 3 vols. Freiburg: J. C. B. Mohr (P. Siebeck), 1892; 1st ed., 1884.

233. KLEE, HEINRICH. *Storia dei dogmi.* 2 vols. Milan: Ufficio della Biblioteca Cattolica, 1854.—Orig. title: *Lehrbuch der Dogmengeschichte.* Bonn: Mainz, 1837.

234. *Let God Be True.* New York: Watchtower Bible and Tract Society, 1952; 1st ed., 1946.

235. LOEWENICH, WALTER VON. *Il cattolicesimo moderno.* Milan: Feltrinelli, 1962.—Orig. title: *Der moderne Katholizismus.* Witten/Ruhr: Luther Verlag, 1956.

236. LOISY, ALFRED FIRMIN. *Les origines du Nouveau Testament.* Paris: Émile Nourry, 1936.—Eng. trans.: *The Birth of the Christian Religion and The Origins of the New Testament.* Authorized translation by L. P. JACKS. New Hyde Park, N.Y.: University Books, 1962.

237. MACHEN, JOHN GRESHAM. *The Origin of Paul's Religion.* New York: The Macmillan Co., 1921.

238. MIEGGE, GIUSEPPE. *Per una fede.* Milan: Comunità, 1956.

239. ———. *L'evangelo e il mito.* Milan: Comunità, 1956.

240. REVILLE, ALBERT. *Histoire du dogme de la divinité de Jésus Christ.* Paris: Alcan, 1907; 1st ed., Paris: Baillière, 1869.

241. SCHWEITZER, ALBERT. *Das Christentum und die Weltreligionen.* Munich: C. H. Beck'sche Verlag, 1924.—Eng. trans.: *Christianity and the Religions of the World.* Translated by JOHANNA POWERS. London: Allen & Unwin, 1923; New York: Henry Holt, 1939.

242. TROELTSCH, ERNST. *Le dottrine sociali delle Chiese e dei gruppi cristiani.* 2 vols. Florence: La Nuova Italia, 1949.— Orig. title: *Die Soziallehren der christlichen Kirchen und Gruppen.* Stuttgart: J. C. Cotta, 1912.—Eng. trans.: *The Social Teaching of the Christian Churches.* Translated by OLIVE WYON. New York: The Macmillan Co., 1931.

c) Rationalist and Radical Works

243. BOUCHÉ-LECLERQ, AUGUSTE. *L'intolérance religieuse et la politique.* Paris: Flammarion, 1911.

244. BUTLER, SAMUEL. *The Fair Haven.* London: A. C. Fifield, 1913; New York: M. Kennerley, 1914.

245. DI NOLA, ALFONSO M. *Cristo in tuta.* Parma: Guanda, 1955.

246. FEUERBACH, LUDWIG ANDREWS. *L'essenza del cristianesimo.* Milan: Universale Economica, 1952.—Orig. title: *Das Wesen des Christentums.* Leipzig: O. Wigand, 1841.—Eng. trans.: *The Essence of Christianity.* Translated by MARIAN EVANS, New York: C. Blanchard, 1855; translated by GEORGE ELIOT, New York: Harper & Bros., 1957.

247. HUXLEY, JULIAN SORELL. *Man Stands Alone.* New York: Harper & Bros., 1941; *The Uniqueness of Man.* London: Chatto & Windus, 1941.

248. ROYCE, JOSIAH. *Il problema del cristianesimo.* 2 vols. Florence: Vallecchi, 1924.—Orig. title: *The Problem of Christianity.* New York: The Macmillan Co., 1913.

249. RUSSELL, BERTRAND. *Marriage and Morals.* London: G. Allen, 1929; New York: Bantam Books, 1966.

250. ———. *Why I Am Not a Christian, and Other Essays on Religion and Related Subjects.* London: G. Allen, 1927; New York: Simon and Schuster, 1957.

VI. HISTORIES OF RELIGIONS

251. ALTHEIM, FRANZ. *Il dio invitto: Cristianesimo e culti solari.* Milan: Feltrinelli, 1960.—Orig. title: *Der unbesiegte Gott:*

Heidentum und Christentum. Hamburg: Ernest Rowoht Verlag, 1957.

252. BOUQUET, ALAN COATES. *Breve storia delle religioni.* Milan: Mondadori, 1963.—Orig. title: *Comparative Religion.* London and New York: Penguin Books, 1941.

253. DE LUBAC, HENRI. *Buddismo e Occidente.* Milan: Vita e Pensiero, 1958.—Orig. title: *Le rencontre du Bouddhisme et de l'Occident.* Paris: Aubier, Editions Montaigne, 1952.

254. DI NOLA, AFONSO M. *La preghiera dell'uomo.* Parma: Guanda, 1960.—Eng. trans.: *The Prayers of Man.* New York: Ivan Obolensky, 1960.

255. DONINI, AMBROGIO. *Lineamenti di storia delle religioni.* Rome: Editori Riuniti, 1959.

256. ELIADE, MIRCEA (ed.). *Trattato di storia delle religioni.* Turin: Einaudi, 1954.—Orig. title: *Traité d'histoire des religions.* Paris: Payot, 1948.—Eng. trans.: *The History of Religions: Essays in Methodology.* Edited by MIRCEA ELIADE and JOSEPH M. KITAGAWA. Chicago: University of Chicago Press, 1959.

257. FARNELL, LEWIS RICHARD. *Attributes of God.* Oxford: The University Press, 1925.

258. FRACASSINI, UMBERTO. *Il misticismo greco e il cristianesimo.* Città di Castello: Il Solco, 1922.

259. FRAZER, JAMES GEORGE. *The Golden Bough: A Study in Comparative Religion.* 12 vols. London and New York: The Macmillan Co., 1891 *et seq.;* abridged ed., *The Golden Bough: A Study in Magic and Religion.* New York: The Macmillan Co., 1922.

260. GRISWOLD, ALEXANDER, KIM, CHEWON and POTT, PETER H. *Burma, Korea, Tibet.* Baden-Baden: Holle Verlag, 1963.—Eng. trans.: *The Art of Burma, Korea, and Tibet.* London: Methuen, 1964; New York: Crown Publishers, 1965.

261. HEILER, FRIEDRICH. *Storia delle religioni.* 2 vols. Florence: Sansoni, 1962.—Orig. title: *Die Religionen der Menschhelt in Vergangenheit und Gegenwart.* Stuttgart: Reclam Verlag, 1959.

262. LANG, ANDREW. *The Making of Religion.* London: Watts, 1900.

263. LEWINSOHN, RICHARD ("MORUS"). *Gli animali nella storia della civiltà.* Turin: Einaudi, 1956.—Orig. title: *Eine Geschichte der Tiere: Ihr Einfluss auf Zivilisation und Kultur.* Hamburg: Ernest Rowohlt Verlag, n.d.—Eng. trans.: *Animals, Men, and Myths.* New York: Fawcett Publications, 1964.

264. LOEHR, FRANKLIN. *The Power of Prayer on Plants.* New York: Doubleday, 1959.

265. MARETT, ROBERT R. *The Threshold of Religion.* London: Methuen, 1914; New York: The Macmillan Co., 1914.

266. MARIANO, RAFFAELE. *Cristo e Budda e altri Iddii dell'Oriente.* 12 vols. Florence: Barbèra, 1900–1911.

267. MILL, JOHN STUART. *Essays on Religion.* London: Longmans, Green, 1873.

268. MOORE, GEORGE FOOT. *Storia delle religioni.* 2 vols. Bari: Laterza, 1922.—Orig. title: *History of Religions.* New York: Charles Scribner's Sons, 1913, 1919; reprinted, 1937.

269. PETTAZZONI, RAFFAELE. *Dio: Formazione e sviluppo del monoteismo nella storia delle religioni.* Rome: Edizioni Athenaeum, 1922.

270. ———. *Saggi di storia delle religioni e di mitologia.* Rome: Edizioni Athenaeum, 1946.—Eng. trans.: *Essays on the History of Religions.* Translated by H. J. ROSE. Leiden: Brill, 1954.

271. ———. *L'Essere supremo nelle religioni primitive.* Turin: Einaudi, 1957.

272. PEYRANI, TOMMASO. *Il Vecchio e il Nuovo Testamento.* Genoa: Edizioni Anteo, 1961.

273. REINACH, SALOMON. *Orpheus: Histoire générale des religions.* Paris: Hachette, 1909.—Eng. trans.: *Orpheus: A History of Religions.* Translated by FLORENCE SIMMONDS, revised and partly rewritten by the author. New York: M. Liveright, 1930.

274. SCHMIDT, WILHELM. *Storia comparata delle religioni.* Brescia: Morcelliana, 1949.—Orig. title: *Ursprung und Werden der Religion.* 12 vols. Münster: Aschendorff, 1912–35.—Eng. trans.: *The Origin and Growth of Religion: Fact and Theories.* Translated from the original German by H. J. ROSE, based on the author's larger work *Ursprung und Werden der Religion.* London: Methuen, 1931.

275. SCHOEPS, HANS JOACHIM. *I grandi fondatori di religioni.* Florence: Sansoni, 1961.—Orig. title: *Die Grossen Religionsstifter.* Erlangen: Holle Verlag, 1950.

276. TYLOR, EDWARD BURNETT. *Primitive Culture: Researches into the Development of Mythology, Philosophy, Religion, Art, and Custom.* London: J. Murray, 1871; Boston: Estes & Lauriat, 1874; New York: Harper & Row, 1958.

277. VANEL, ANTOINE. *L'iconographie du dieu l'orage, dans le*

proche-Orient ancien jusq'au VIIe siècle avant Jésus Christ. Paris: J. Gabalda, 1965.

VII. History and Geography of Palestine

278. Albright, William Foxwell. *L'archeologia in Palestina.* Florence: Sansoni, 1957.—Orig. title: *The Archaeology of Palestine.* New York and Chicago: Fleming H. Revell Co., 1932; rev. ed., Harmondsworth and Baltimore: Penguin Books, 1960.

279. Allegro, John Marco. *The Dead Sea Scrolls.* Harmondsworth and Baltimore: Penguin Books, 1956.

280. Aron, Robert. *Gli anni oscuri di Gesù.* Milan: Mondadori, 1963.—Orig. title: *Les années obscures de Jésus.* Paris: Bernard Grasset, 1961.—Eng. trans.: *Jesus of Nazareth: The Hidden Years.* Translated from the French by Frances Frenaye. New York: William Morrow, 1962.

281. Baron, Salo Wittmayer. *Histoire d'Israël: Vie sociale et religieuse.* 2 vols. Paris: Presses Universitaires de France, 1956 and 1959.—Orig. title: *Historiyah hevrutit vedatit shel 'am Yisrael.* Tel Aviv, 1954, 1955.—Eng. trans.: *A Social and Religious History of the Jews.* 3 vols. New York: Columbia University Press, 1937, 1955, 1957.

282. Bonsirven, Joseph. *Le judaïsme palestinien au temps de Jésus Christ.* 2 vols. Paris: Beauchesne, 1934, 1935.—Eng. trans.: *Palestinian Judaism in the Time of Christ.* Translated by William Wolf. New York: Holt, Rinehart & Winston, 1964.

283. Burrows, Millar. *The Dead Sea Scrolls.* New York: Viking Press, 1955.

284. Danielou, Jean. *Les manuscrits de la Mer Morte, et les origines du Christianisme.* Paris: Editions de l'Orante, 1957.—Eng. trans.: *The Dead Sea Scrolls and the Origins of Christianity.* New York: Criterion Books, 1957.

285. "Daniel-Rops, Henri" (Henry Petiot). *Il popolo della Bibbia.* Florence: Sansoni, 1962.—Orig. title: *Le peuple de la Bible.* Paris: A. Fayard, 1953.

286. Felten, Joseph. *Storia dei tempi del Nuovo Testamento.* 4 vols. Turin: S.E.I., 1944.—Orig. title: *Neutestamentlische Zeitgeschichte, oder Judentum und Heidentum zur Zeit Christi und der Apostel.* 2 vols. Regensburg: G. J. Manz, 1910.

287. FINEGAN, JACK. *Light from the Ancient Past.* 1st ed. Princeton, N.J.: Princeton University Press, 1946.

288. HERFORD, ROBERT TRAVERS. *The Pharisees.* London: Allen & Unwin, 1924; Boston: Beacon Press, 1962.

289. KELLER, WERNER. *La Bibbia aveva ragione.* Milan: Garzanti, 1957.—Orig. title: *Und die Bebel hat doch Recht.* Hamburg, 1955.—Eng. trans.: *The Bible as History: A Confirmation of the Book of Books.* Translated by WILLIAM NELL. New York: William Morrow, 1958.

290. LAGRANGE, MARIE JOSEPH. *Le judaïsme avant Jésus Christ.* Paris: J. Gabalda, 1931.

291. LANCZKOWSKI, GÜNTER. *Scritture Sacre.* Florence: Sansoni, 1960.—Orig. title: *Heilige Schriften.* Stuttgart: Kohlhammer Verlag, 1956.

292. MILIK, JÒZEF TADEUSZ. *Dieci anni di scoperte nel deserto di Giuda.* Turin: Marietti, 1957.—Orig. title: *Dix ans de découvertes dans le désert de Juda.* Paris: Editions du Cerf, 1957.— Eng. trans.: *Ten Years of Discovery in the Wilderness of Judaea.* Translated by J. STRUGNELL. Naperville, Ill.: Alec R. Allenson, 1959.

293. MOORE, GEORGE FOOT. *Judaism in the First Centuries of the Christian Era: The Age of the Tannaim.* 3 vols. Cambridge, Mass.: Harvard University Press, 1927–30.

294. RICCIOTTI, GIUSEPPE. *Storia d'Israele.* 2 vols. Turin: S.E.I., 1959; 1st ed., 1932.—Eng. trans.: *History of Israel.* Milwaukee: Bruce Publishing Co., 1955.

295. ROLLA, ARMANDO. *La Bibbia di fronte alle ultime scoperte.* Rome: Edizioni Paoline, 1959.

296. SCHUERER, EMIL. *Geschichte des Jüdischen Volkes im Zeitalter Jesu Christi.* 3 vols. Leipzig: J. C. Hinrichs, 1909; 1st ed., 1886.—Eng. trans.: *A History of the Jewish People in the Time of Jesus Christ.* 5 vols. Edinburgh: T. & T. Clark, 1886–90.

297. STADE, BERNHARD. *Storia del popolo d'Israele.* Milan: Bocca, 1896.—Orig. title: *Geschichte des Volkes Israel.* Berlin: G. Grote, 1884; reprinted, 1887–88.

298. WILSON, EDMUND. *The Scrolls from the Dead Sea.* London: Oxford University Press, 1955; Cleveland and New York: Meridian Books, 1964.

VIII. MISCELLANEOUS SUBJECTS

299. BARBET, PIERRE. *La passione di Nostro Signore Gesù Cristo, secondo il chirurgo.* Turin: L.I.C.E. di R. Berruti e C., 1950. —Orig. title: *La passion de N.S. Jésus Christ selon le chirurgien.* Issoudun, Indre: Dillen, 1950.—Eng. trans.: *A Doctor at Calvary: The Passion of Our Lord Jesus Christ as Described by a Surgeon.* Translated by the EARL OF WICKLOW. New York: P. J. Kenedy, n.d.

300. BREZA, TEODOR. *La porta di bronzo.* Milan: Feltrinelli, 1962. —Orig. title: *Spiżowa brama.* Warsaw: Czytelnik, 1960.

301. CAILLOIS, ROGER. *Ponzio Pilato.* Turin: Einaudi, 1963.—Orig. title: *Ponce Pilate.* Paris: Gallimard, 1961.—Eng. trans.: *Pontius Pilate.* New York: The Macmillan Co., 1963.

302. "HYNEK, RALPH WALDO" (RUDOLF MARIA HYNEK). *L'aspetto fisico di Gesù.* Translated from the original Bohemian. Turin: L.I.C.E. di R. Berruti, 1952.

303. JAUBERT, ALBERTINE. *La date de la Cène: Calendrier biblique et liturgie chrétienne.* Paris: J. Gabalda, 1957.

304. JUDICA CORDIGLIA, GIOVANNI. *Un colpo di lancia al cuore di Cristo.* Milan: R. Ghirlando, 1937.

305. ———. *L'uomo della Sindone è il Cristo?* Milan: R. Ghirlando, 1941.

306. LA CAVA, FRANCO. "Il reperto necroscopico di Longino sul costato di Gesù Cristo," *Medicus* (Milan), No. 1 (January, 1946), pp. 61 ff.

307. MARIGO, SERGIO. "Le cause di morte in Cristo," *Studium* (Rome), Nos. 7–8 (August, 1950), pp. 356–65.

308. WHITAKER, R. "The Physical Causes of the Death of Our Lord," *Catholic Medical Guardian* (London), 1935, pp. 85 ff.

Index

A

Aaron, 134
Abraham, 7, 63, 82, 179, 241
Abyssinian Church, 329
Acacius, 328
Achilles, 22
Acts of the Apostles, vi, 6, 58, 77, 140, 148, 153, 154, 155, 156, 157, 158, 160, 255–56, 321–22, 344, 372, 386, 425–26
Acts of Paul and Thecla, 155
Acts of Pilate, 407
Acts of Thaddeus, 424
Adam, 7, 30, 270, 271, 355, 430
Adam, Karl, 325
Adonis, worship of, 35–36, 323
Adventists, 346–47
Aeneas, 22
Agape, 380, 382, 386
Agnoetism, 60–61
Agrapha, 277
Aktistetism, 329
Albertus Magnus (d. 1280), 12
Alcmene, mother of Hercules, 22
Alexander the Great (356–323 B.C.), 22, 45, 46
Alfano, G. B., 197
amē hā-'erets ("men of the soil" = rabble), 123, 124, 133, 170
Ambrose, 268, 295, 312, 353
Amphitryon, 22
Anabaptists, 79
Ananias, head of Christian center in Damascus, 156, 174; see also Sapphira
Andrew (brother of Simon), the Apostle, 90–92, 147–48
Angels, 11–12, 18, 19, 20, 21, 23, 28, 37, 84, 138, 196, 239, 341, 350, 417, 423
Anna, holy woman of the Temple, 42–43
Anna, mother of Mary, 9, 31
Annas, High Priest (A.D. 6–15), 69, 395–96, 408
Annunciation, the, 11–14, 19, 24

Anselm of Aosta (1033–1109), 211
Antichrist, the, 343
Antioch, 154, 157, 160, 234, 327
Antipater (d. 43 B.C.), father of Herod the Great, 47; see Herod the Great, sons of
Antonia, Tower of, 298, 399, 411
Antony, Mark (83?–30 B.C.), 47
Aphrodite, 22
Aphthartocetism, 329
Apis, the bull, 23
Apollinaris, bishop of Laodicea, 328
Apollonius of Tyana (1st cent. A.D.), Greek philosopher and miracle worker, 119
Apostles, the Twelve, 152–59, 230, 236–38, 241–47, 262–66, 280–85, 323–24, 330–31, 334, 336–37, 339–45, 351, 370–71, 373–80, 386–87, 390, 392–93, 425; and Jesus, 80, 151–52, 227, 242–43, 258–62, 273, 290–93, 321–22, 324, 377, 391, 393, 423–24, 427–28; meaning of "apostle," 146; names of, 146–47; and Paul, 156–57, 324, 426, 432; selection of, 145–47
Aquinas, Thomas (1225?–1274), 12, 24–25, 118, 187, 314, 360, 388, 434
Arculf, bishop of Gaul, 392, 420
Arians, 327, 328, 332, 333
Aristobulus II, 46–47
Aristobulus III, brother-in-law of Herod the Great, 47; see Herod the Great, sons of
Aristotle, 22, 360, 392
Ark of the Covenant, 290
Armenian Church, 329
Armenian Gospel of the Infancy, 50
Aron, Robert, 59, 87, 206
Art, religious, 10, 11, 12, 42, 78, 161–62, 163, 337, 351, 411, 413, 419, 429
Ascension, the, 429–30
Asclepius (Aesculapius), 119
Assumption of Mary, 31
Assyrians, 12
Astarte (mother-goddess), 27, 38

172; as dualistic, 84–85; and the first-born of the Hebrews, 41; from *'Elohīm* to Yahweh, 207–10; from Yahweh to God, 210; the Logos, 325, 327, 428; modern man's need for, 434–35; as the One God, 84, 209; and Satan, 84–85, 141, 142; the spirit of, 14, 22, 80–81, 88, 142, 324, 330–33

Goguel, Maurice, 65–66
Golgotha, 410, 412
Gomorrah, 71, 82, 357
Good Samaritan, the, 187
Good tidings, the, 87, 145, 169–71, 435
"Gospel," etymology of, 87
Gospels; *see under individual names*
Gōyīm ("pagans"), 133
Grace, 433–34
Gratian (A.D. 359–383), Roman emperor, 312
Great Commandment, the, 186–87
Gregory I (the Great), Pope, 13, 129, 358
Gregory of Nazianzus, 271, 353, 357
Gregory of Nyssa, 357
Gregory VII, Pope, 268
Guignebert, Charles, 370

H

Habakkuk, Book of, 36
Haggadah, 192, 287
Halakah, 191
Hallel, the, 379, 390
Halley, Edmund, 49
Hammer, Joseph, 418
Hannibal (247–183 B.C.), Carthaginian general, 27
Hanukkah, 336–37, 339
Harnack, Adolf von, 120, 304, 306
Hasideans (*Hassīdim*), the, 68, 70; *see also* Pharisees, the
Hasmonean dynasty, 7, 46, 47, 48
"Heaven," "heavens," 76, 173; phenomena of, 49, 53, 80–81, 355–58
Hebrews, ancient: and adultery, 17–18, 19–21, 86; and allegory, 193; and angels, 11, 12; and artistic achievement, 42; Babylonian captivity, 41, 45, 46; and betrothal, 17; blessings (*berākā*) 60, 378–79; burial customs, 366, 419; calendar of, 61–62, 374; chosen by God, 44; and circumcision, 39–40; coins of, 41, 305, 338; and the Covenant, 44–45; under David, 7, 45; and death, 96, 109, 280, 366, 419; and demons, 94–95; and

the Egyptians, 43–44, 46; and fasting, 83; first-born of, 41; under foreign domination, 45–46; under Herod, 47–48, 52–54; history of, 43–46; and "impurity," 139–40; under the Judges, 44; and the Kingdom concept, 7, 45, 46, 305–6; under the Kings, 44–45; and the Law (*see* Law, the); and leprosy, 102–3; marriage and divorce, 17–18, 262–64, 266, 271; origins of, 43; and pagan symbols, 53, 74; and pork, 139, 140; pride of race, 43, 263; and the priestly caste, 44–45, 68 (*see also* Sadducees, the); priests (*see* Priests, Hebrew); and the Promised Land, 44, 64; and the publicans, 122–23; and punishment, 248; and purification, 40, 96–97, 98, 102–3, 139; rabbis (*see* Rabbis); rebellion of 4 B.C., 54; rebellion against Herod, 52–54; rebellion against Pilate, 74; rebellion under Zealot leadership, 68–70; under Rehoboam, 45; religion of (*see* God); religious training of, 60; under the Romans (*see* Rome, the Romans); rulers of, 43–46; schooling, 59; the siege of Jerusalem, 344; under Solomon, 45; and the soul, 358–59; and tithes, 122–23; and virginity, 9; and women, 10–11, 40, 42, 87

Hebrews, Gospel according to the, 137, 280, 298, 321
Hebron, 14
Hegesippus; *see* Eusebius
Heidegger, Martin, 434–35
Helena, mother of Constantine I, 35, 410
Heliogabalus, emperor, 38
Hell, hell fire, 11, 109, 196, 355–58, 428; *see also* She'ōl
"Hellenists," the, 154–55, 174
Hercules, 22, 240
Hermon, Mount, 237
Herod the Great (73?–4 B.C.), king of Judea, 33, 34, 41–42, 47, 48, 50, 52–54, 68, 69, 228, 287, 296
Herod the Great, sons of: Alexander (d. 6 B.C.), 48, 53; (Herod) Antipas (d. ca. A.D. 40), tetrarch under Augustus, 52, 53, 54, 86, 126, 213–15, 217, 219, 221, 255, 258, 402, 406, 408; Antipater (d. 4 B.C.), 47, 48, 52, 53–54; (Herod) Archelaus (d. ca. A.D. 18), ethnarch under Augustus, 52, 53, 54, 68–69, 287, 288; Aristobulus (d. 6 B.C.), 48, 53; Herod (d. A.D. 34), 52, 53; (Herod) Philip (d. A.D.